Landmark Cases of the EU Courts and the

Europa Law Publishing, Groningen 2010

The EU Competition Rules

Landmark Cases of the EU Courts and the European Commission

F.O.W. Vogelaar

Europa Law Publishing is a publishing company
specializing in European Union Law.
For further information please contact Europa Law
Publishing via email: info@europalawpublishing.com
or visit our website at: www.europalawpublishing.com.

Typeset in Scala and Scala Sans, Graphic design by
G2K Designers, Groningen/Amsterdam

NUR 828; ISBN-13: 978-90-8952-091-3

Recommended citation: F.O.W. Vogelaar, *Landmark Cases EU Competition Law*

Preface to the first edition

Before you lies an entirely new case book covering the landmark EC Courts' cases and Commission decisions in the field of EC competition law. The book is the result of a cases reader developed over the twelve years that I have been teaching EC competition law in the postgraduate European Business Law (EBL) programme of the Amsterdam Law School (ALS) at the *Universiteit van Amsterdam*. Turning this internal reader into a 'real book' and putting it on the market makes it possible for me to share the experiences accumulated during many years of teaching, with a much broader audience than just my own ALS/EBL students.

The book aims to provide Legal Masters students throughout Europe with a selection of case law that will be of direct help when studying the subject for the first time. The primary criterion for selection was whether a particular case contributed to the development of one of the doctrines or notions so important to the understanding of EC competition law. Obviously, the selection is necessarily a subjective one, for which only I am responsible. In this selection process, I have concentrated on those cases which are likely to survive all *'modernization'* and *'economization'* of EC competition law. For that reason, the reader will find a good number of the older 'iron' cases rather than the very recent ones simply because the latter, more often than not, add nothing significantly new. Also, the emphasis is mainly on notions of general import and on infringement cases pursuant to the Articles 81(1) and (2) or 82 of the EC Treaty rather than on the very diverse Article 81(3) assessment cases which one might expect to develop further in the future as a direct result of the introduction of the 'directly applicable exception system' by Council Regulation 1/2003 per May 1st, 2004 and the 2004 Guidelines on the application of Article 81(3) directly relating thereto.

My intention has not been to cover all aspects of this complicated though fascinating area of the law, merely to limit the choice of materials to what might be deemed absolutely essential in obtaining a thorough basic knowledge of the law within the format of an introductory course. More content than necessary might have potentially discouraged students from taking an introductory course on EC competition law as an elective course, wherever in Europe. Needless to say, the materials provided in this case book should always be backed up by solid tuition on the subject.

All cases and decisions have been incorporated with their key recitals and texts only, so as to make the amount of text digestible in the context of an introductory course in EC competition law. In doing so, I have chosen to use the texts of the Courts and the Commission as officially published, and therefore sometimes included possible typing errors, inconsistent numbering and blurred lay-outs that may have occurred. Also, most of the footnotes as mentioned in the original texts have been omitted in order to keep the quoted texts as readable as possible. Furthermore, for each case there is the mention of its relevance within the legal system and each case is accompanied by a short summary of its facts and circumstances. For some cases, I have simply chosen to incorporate the Court's own published summary since the point of law to be demonstrated has been clearly made therein. This also applies with reference to certain Commission decisions where either the narrative text taken from one of the Commission's Annual Competition Reports or even from one of the Commission's press releases adequately demonstrates the point at issue.

The chapters and the sequence of cases dealt with therein follow the order in which I normally prefer to lecture the introductory course in EC competition law. Wherever practical, cross-references are made which refer to relevant sources in Community legislation and Commission Notices, to a selection of further cases on the same issue, to leading scholarly articles on the subject and to interesting annotations adding to the understanding of any particular case. In this way, the book also offers the possibility for further reading to those who would find this useful without burdening students with extra extensive obligatory reading material, which would go beyond the necessarily limited scope of their course format. As such the book also provides invaluable and time-saving background information for legal practitioners or corporate in-house counsel in this increasingly important field of the law.

At this point, I wish to express my sincere gratitude in the first place to Ms Marietta Schuerman who very ably helped me to get the texts together, select the relevant additional materials and mould the texts into their present form. Without her help as well as the last-phase help of Ms Titia Bohlken, this would not have happened, or at least, not within the relatively short period of production that we chose to comply with. Furthermore, I wish to thank Ms Janet Major – an alumna of the ALS – and Ms Elizabeth Hunt for their valuable advice on language issues which are indispensable to a non-native speaker in preparing a book like this. I am also indebted to the two groups of students in two consecutive 'user committees' working and studying from 'zero-editions' of this book, one group in the ALS/EBL postgraduate programme and the other in my regular Masters programme at the Amsterdam Law Faculty. With their much valued and constructive comments they contributed to the increased user friendly nature of this book. Also, I should mention my learned friends Wouter Wils, Erik Pijnacker Hordijk, Rein Wesseling and Hans Vedder for their critical comments and suggestions regarding the selection of cases and relating materials for this book. Their 'sneak preview' of the table of contents of the book confirmed to me that the cases selection wasn't far off-course, which was a comforting thought in the final stages of preparation. However, and in spite of all the kind expert help received from all those mentioned above, for any errors that may have remained, I alone am fully responsible. And last, I am very grateful indeed to Ms Jacqueline Lensink of Europa Law Publishing who kindly set the deadline for handing in my manuscript in such a flexible way that this book could be made available to students in time for the start of the lecturing season 2004-2005.

In 2005, I will hopefully supplement this case book with an introductory study book on EC competition law which will be entirely based on all relevant aspects of the now modernized law resulting from Regulations 1/2003 (implementing the Articles 81 and 82 of the EC Treaty) and 139/2004 (the EC Merger Control Regulation) and the many ancillary legislative and explanatory documents/guidelines in relation thereto. In that study book, direct reference will be made to the landmark cases and decisions dealt with in this present issue in an attempt to make the combined use of both books remain as user friendly as possible.

Prof. Floris O. W. Vogelaar
Of the Europa Instituut and the Amsterdam Law School
Faculty of Law of the Universiteit van Amsterdam
July 2004

Preface to the second edition

As it appeared, the first edition of my Landmark Cases book has found a great many users both in The Netherlands and abroad. The book has found its way to many students but at the same time to the libraries of Universities, law firms and business enterprises all over Europe and even in the USA. I have appreciated very much the positive first edition reviews which appeared in various international legal magazines, and I am also very grateful for the many constructive comments received on the first edition. These have made life easier when preparing the second edition which now lies before you. Moreover, it has convinced me of the need by the market of a case study book in this format.

This second edition has updated and expanded the reference to the case law of the European Courts and the decision practice of the European Commission now that the modernization of EC Competition Law is well established in our day-to-day practice after its initial coming into force in May 2004. Updates and further fine-tuning of the cases already featuring in the first edition may be found in the sections on the economic unit doctrine, concerted practices, article 82 and intellectual property rights, the position of third parties in article 86(3), the application practice of the leniency policy of the European Commission, developments concerning 'commitments' in merger control cases, parallel enforcement issues and further developments in the case law of the European Court in the important field of the so-called 'private enforcement'. New features in this second edition are the inclusion of a section on (the review of) the sanctioning practice of the Commission (Ch. IX.E), of materials concerning the ever-increasing importance of the sound reasoning of the Commission's decisions (in fact, law and economics) in a chapter on Judicial Review of Administrative Enforcement (Ch. IX.F) and the dedication of a separate section to the first 'commitments' decisions of the Commission based on article 9 of Regulation 1/2003 (Ch. I.S).

Furthermore, the cross-references have been expanded and where necessary brought up-to-date. However, with the steep increase in learned articles on competition issues in an increasing number of legal magazines, these cross-references remain my personal selection and my responsibility. Consequently, I do hope that no author of a no doubt interesting article feels hard done by for not being included in these cross-references.

Without the expert help and most pleasant assistance of Francesco Russo LL.M. this second edition could not have been finalized with the degree of precision and within the relatively short period within which we had decided to work. The cut-off date of our work on this second edition is September 1st 2006 (and for the cross-references even a little before that date). However and as before, any errors or flaws that could still be spotted in the choice of cases or in the legal extracts chosen, remain entirely my personal responsibility. I do hope that this second edition finds its way to a new generation of Legal Masters students and to young competition law practitioners, but also to those who used the first edition already. I would like to add, though, that this book is a study aid only and that studying the complicated topic of EC Competition Law needs a solid back-up by expert academic tuition and study of one of the text books on the subject currently available on the market. It has been my dream to supplement this book with an introductory study book of my own hand, but this dream unfortunately has not come true so far as the day-to-day dealing with an ever-increasing number of Legal Masters students has prevented me from finalizing this Introduction. But believe me, I have not given up as yet!

Prof. Floris O.W. Vogelaar
Of the Amsterdam Center for Law & Economics, ACLE
Faculty of Law of the Universiteit van Amsterdam
November 2006

Preface to the third edition

A major overhaul of the Landmark Cases book was called for as a result of recent developments in the Union's competition law, if not in the Union as a whole. Since the second edition was published in 2006, public competition law enforcement has been stricter than ever. Increase in fines has triggered an increase in the number of appeals, some successful some not. Settlements and commitment decisions have become a regular method of remedying certain the lesser hard core infringements. New Guidelines on the setting of fines and on Leniency raised all sorts of questions which are now slowly finding their way to the European Courts.

Ever since the modernisation of competition law, it was to be expected that the Commission's emphasis in public enforcement would be on leniency applications rather than on *ex officio* investigations. Cases on the abuse of dominance continued to arise in spite of the Commission's publication of the Guidelines on exclusionary behaviour. Moreover, concentration control cases enriched the case law of the courts with a number of fine cases in which the Courts made it clear that the paradigm of analysis in merger control in essence is not different from antitrust enforcement. These cases are concerned with evidence, factual and economic assessment and the observance of due process by the Commission predominantly.

The economisation of competition law gave rise to a somewhat different approach by the Courts as far as the assessment of economic facts and circumstances are concerned. Competition law enforcement has grown to be more effects based and less clause driven, and the Courts have used their best endeavours to clarify to the public what their role in all of this may be.

For this third edition, many of these developments have been taken on board. Twenty new cases found their way into the book. Those who have worked with the previous editions can be assured that the same principles of case selection and the same reporting format have been applied in accordance with the objectives explained already in the preface to the first edition of this book. In the first chapter, a number of cases have been added in which the basic notions of competition law have been clarified further. In the other chapters, here and there, a new landmark case has been added. However, most of the changes are to be found in Chapter IX (Enforcement and Procedure: Capita) because it is in that field that many of the interesting new landmark cases had to be reported. Across the board, I have updated the 'cross-references' with many interesting new publications. This shows that there is a lively interest amongst academics and practitioners to analyse and comment on many of the fascinating developments mentioned above.

The entry into force of the Treaty of Lisbon on 1st December 2009 prompted an overhaul of a completely different nature. The new *Treaty on the European Union* and the *Treaty on the Functioning of the European Union* required renumbering of all references to the well-known EC Treaty. As a result, in this third edition, even the title of the book had to be adapted to these new Treaties! All Chapter headings, all commentary and all facts descriptions of the cases take into account the new terminology as well as the new numbering. What is more, now that Article 3 has disappeared from the Treaty texts but continues to live in exile in Protocol no. 27, some major changes in the set-up of the

Chapters were required. The former Chapter I-L had to be replaced by a new heading (and content) and Chapter III not only has been renamed 'The *"useful effect"* doctrine", but the reader will also find a short introduction at the beginning of that chapter to help him finding his way in the maze of the TEU and the TFEU. However, be assured that the quoted parts of court cases that date from before Lisbon have remained unaltered.

The preparation of this third edition took take place in solitary confinement after my retirement from active service in the Law Faculty in June 2009. As a guest professor in the Faculty and as a research fellow in the Amsterdam Centre for Law and Economics (ACLE), I am grateful that I have the continuous opportunity to remain in contact with my former colleagues, my former associate professor Dr. Katalin Cseres and my able successor, Professor Rein Wesseling. I am indebted to my former student Karolina Dziemianczyk, who in my last year of active service with much creativity and energy helped me in updating the first two years of case law up to October 2008. However, for this third edition, it is for me alone to assume all responsibility for any errors or omissions. The cut-off date for this third edition has been the 1st of July 2010. Readers are cordially invited to let me know about any suggestions or wishes they may have, as this may benefit a future fourth edition, whenever such edition will be due.

Finally, I would like to thank my personal language editor and wife Elizabeth for her invaluable linguistic comments and corrections. Without her help, this edition would not have been the same.

Floris O.W. Vogelaar
Em. Professor of Competition & Regulation
Of the Law Faculty University of Amsterdam
Research Fellow of the ACLE
July 2010

CHAPTER II

Article 102 TFEU – Dominance & Abuse – Basic Concepts and Notions

Treaty Articles Conversion Table

The EC Treaty article numbering as used in many of the 'older' cases may be confusing. To a certain extent renumbering took place already when the EEC Treaty was amended on the 1st of May 1999 by the Treaty of Amsterdam. That new numbering is now thoroughly amended once again as a result of the entry into force of the Treaty of Lisbon on the 1st of December 2009. The table below shows how over the years the numbering has been in these various Treaties.

EEC Treaty	**Treaty of Amsterdam**	**Treaty of Lisbon**
Competition Rules :		
Art. 3(f), later also art. 3(g) EEC	Art. 3 (1) g EC	Protocol No. 27 on the Internal Market and Competition
Art. 5 EEC	Art. 10 EC	Art. 4(3) TEU
Art. 85 EEC	Art. 81 EC	Art. 101 TFEU
Art. 86 EEC	Art. 82 EC	Art. 102 TFEU
Art. 90 EEC	Art. 86 EC	Art. 106 TFEU
State Aid Rules :		
Artt. 92-94 EEC	Artt. 87-89 EC	Artt. 107-109 TFEU

EEC	=	The European Economic Community Treaty
EC	=	Treaty of the European Community
TEU	=	Treaty on the European Union
TFEU	=	Treaty on the Functioning of the European Union

The TEU, the Protocols attached to it and the TFEU together form the Treaty of Lisbon.

The Court of First Instance was formed in 1989. In the Treaty of Lisbon it has been renamed 'the General Court' ('GC' in abbreviation in this edition). On the contrary, the Court of Justice kept its name. Hence, for the purposes of this edition, the abbreviated reference will continue to be 'ECJ'.

CHAPTER I

Article 101 TFEU – Basic Notions

A. Notion of 'relevant market'

Cross-references for this part:

- ► Notice on the definition of the relevant market, [1997] OJ C 372/3.
- ► T.E. Kauper,'The Problem of Market Definition under EC Competition Law', (1996) *Fordham Corp. L. Inst.* (B. Hawk, ed. 1997), 239.
- ► OECD Report on 'Competition Law and Policy in the European Union', (2006).
- ► O. Odudu, *The boundaries of EC competition law: the scope of Article 81*, Oxford, Oxford University Press, 2006.

Geographical market

1) Case 27/76 *UBC (United Brands Company, Chiquita)* [1978] ECR 207

The Commission had accused United Brands (UBC), a company that brought bananas under the trademark 'Chiquita' on the European market, of infringing Article 102 TFEU EC, amongst others, by charging excessive prices and different prices to similar transactions. UBC challenged the Commission's decision before the ECJ and submitted, inter alia, that the Commission had erred in its analysis of the relevant (geographical) market.

Relevance: notion of 'relevant geographical market' and checklist of 'sufficiently homogeneous conditions of competition'.

[.....]

10 In order to determine whether UBC has a dominant position on the banana market it is necessary to define this market both from the standpoint of the product and from the geographic point of view.
11 The opportunities for competition under Article 86 of the Treaty must be considered having regard to the particular features of the product in question and with reference to a clearly defined geographic area in which it is marketed and where the conditions of competition are sufficiently homogeneous for the effect of the economic power of the undertaking concerned to be able to be evaluated.

[.....]

Paragraph 2. The geographic market

36 The Commission has taken the Federal Republic of Germany, Denmark, Ireland, the Netherlands and the BLEU as the geographic market and it is in respect of this market that it is necessary to consider whether UBC has the power to hinder effective competition.
37 It takes the view that the economic conditions in this part of the Community allow importer/distributors of bananas to market their products there in the ordinary course without there being any significant economic barriers for UBC to overcome compared with other importer/distributors.
38 The other Member States of the Community (France, Italy, the United Kingdom) must however be excluded from this geographic definition of the market notwithstanding the significant presence of UBC in these states, because of the special circumstances relating to import arrangements and trading conditions and the fact that bananas of various types and origin are sold there.
39 The applicant points out that the geographic market where an undertaking's economic and commercial power is taken

into consideration should only comprise areas where the conditions of competition are homogeneous.

40 Although the Commission had good reason to exclude France, Italy and the United Kingdom from the said market it failed to take account of the differences in the conditions of competition in the other Member States which should have led it to come to the same conclusions with regard to the latter as it came to in the case of the three countries referred to above.

41 In fact three substantially different systems of customs duty apply in the Member States concerned: a zero tariff in Germany covering a banana quota which meets most of this country's requirements, a transitional tariff in Ireland and Denmark and the common customs tariff of 20% for imports into Benelux.

42 The Commission has not either taken account of the consumer habits of the Member States concerned (the annual consumption of fresh fruits per capita in Germany is equal to 2.5 times that of Ireland and twice that of Denmark), differing commercial patterns, concentrations and monetary points of view.

43 The applicant draws the conclusion from all these findings that the geographic market taken by the Commission includes areas in which the conditions of competition are so different that they cannot be considered as constituting a single market.

44 The conditions for the application of Article 86 to an undertaking in a dominant position presuppose the clear delimitation of the substantial part of the Common Market in which it may be able to engage in abuses which hinder effective competition and this is an area where the objective conditions of competition applying to the product in question must be the same for all traders.

45 The Community has not established a common organization of the agricultural market in bananas.

46 Consequently import arrangements vary considerably from one Member State to another and reflect a specific commercial policy peculiar to the states concerned.

47 This explains why for example the French market owing to its national organization is restricted upstream by a particular import arrangement and obstructed downstream by a retail price monitored by the administration.

48 This market, in addition to adopting certain measures relating to a "target price" ("prix objectif") fixed each year and to packaging and grading standards and the minimum qualities required, reserves about two thirds of the market for the production of the overseas departments and one third to that of certain countries enjoying preferential relations with France (Ivory Coast, Madagascar, Cameroon) the bananas whereof are imported duty-free, and it includes a system the running of which is entrusted to the "Comité Interprofessionnel Bananier" ("C.I.B.").

49 The United Kingdom market enjoys "Commonwealth preferences", a system of which the main feature is the maintenance of a level of production favouring the developing countries of the Commonwealth and of a price paid to the associations of producers directly linked to the selling price of the green banana charged in the United Kingdom.

50 On the Italian market, since the abolition in 1965 of the State Monopoly responsible for marketing bananas, a national system of quota restrictions has been introduced, the Ministry for Shipping and the exchange control office supervising the imports and the charterparties relating to the foreign ships which carry the bananas.

51 The effect of the national organization of these three markets is that the applicant's bananas do not compete on equal terms with the other bananas sold in these states which benefit from a preferential system and the Commission was right to exclude these three national markets from the geographic market under consideration.
52 On the other hand the six other states are markets which are completely free, although the applicable tariff provisions and transport costs are of necessity different but not discriminatory, and in which the conditions of competition are the same for all.
53 From the standpoint of being able to engage in free competition these six states form an area which is sufficiently homogeneous to be considered in its entirety.
54 UBC has arranged for its subsidiary in Rotterdam - UBCBV - to market its products. UBCBV is for this purpose a single centre for the whole of this part of the Community.
55 Transport costs do not in fact stand in the way of the distribution policy chosen by UBC which consists in selling f.o.r. Rotterdam and Bremerhaven, the two ports where the bananas are unloaded.
56 These are factors which go to make relevant market a single market.
57 It follows from all these considerations that the geographic market as determined by the Commission which constitutes a substantial part of the Common Market must be regarded as the relevant market for the purpose of determining whether the applicant may be in a dominant position.

[.....]

Product market

2) Case 85/76 *Hoffmann-La Roche (Vitamins)* [1979] ECR 461

Hoffmann-La Roche (HLR, Roche), the largest manufacturer of bulk vitamins within the Common Market, stood accused of abusing its dominant position. The company had bound its purchasers by means of exclusive purchasing agreements and fidelity rebates (it had concluded about 26 agreements of that nature with industrial purchasers of its products). Before the ECJ, HLR claimed that the Commission had mistakenly identified two separate (relevant product) markets for the E and C groups of vitamins. In its view, the vitamins formed part of a larger market, which was consequential for the calculation of its market share. The ECJ, however, concurred with the delimitation of the relevant product markets as made by the Commission.

Relevance: notion of 'relevant product market'.

[.....]

28 If a product could be used for different purposes and if these different uses are in accordance with economic needs, which are themselves also different, there are good grounds for accepting that this product may, according to the circumstances, belong to separate markets which may present specific features which differ from the standpoint both of the structure and of the conditions of competition.
However this finding does not justify the conclusion that such a product together with

all the other products which can replace it as far as concerns the various uses to which it may be put and with which it may compete, forms one single market.
The concept of the relevant market in fact implies that there can be effective competition between the products which form part of it and this presupposes that there is a sufficient degree of interchangeability between all the products forming part of the same market in so far as a specific use of such products is concerned.

[.....]

Future market

3) Joined Cases T-374, 375, 384 & 388/94 *European Night Services v. Commission* [1998] ECR II-3141

In this dispute, the CFI annulled a Commission decision concerning an exemption under conditions for the creation of European Night Services (ENS), a cooperative joint venture, which was to provide overnight passenger services on the railway route between Britain and the Continent. The paragraphs quoted below show that the Commission, when assessing the restrictive effects of the ENS agreements on competition, did not only take account of the market as it stood but also considered the market as it might develop over time. In doing so, 'intermodal' transport services were also taken into account, i.e., services provided by train, bus, aeroplane and ships, and these were also compared with the (cost of) transport by private car.

Relevance: notion of 'market as it develops over time'; substitutable 'intermodal' services.

[.....]

First part: definition of the relevant market and absence of any appreciable effect of the ENS agreements on trade between Member States

[.....]

Findings of the Court

90 First of all, it must be noted that, in order to assess the effects of the ENS agreements on competition and on trade between Member States, the Commission defined two relevant service markets in the decision: the market for the transport of business travellers, for whom scheduled air travel and high-speed rail travel are interchangeable modes of transport (the 'intermodal' market for business travel), and the market for the transport of leisure travellers, for whom substitute services may include economy-class air travel, train, coach and possibly private motor car (the 'intermodal' market for leisure travel) (see points 26 and 27 of the decision).
91 The Commission went on to consider, referring to Case 66/86 Ahmed Saeed Flugreisen and Silver Line Reisebüro v Zentrale zur Bekämpfung unlauteren Wettbewerbs [1989] ECR 803, that the relevant geographical market should be confined to the routes actually to be served by ENS (points 28 and 29 of the decision), namely: - London-Amsterdam, - London-Frankfurt/Dortmund, - Paris-Glasgow/Swansea and - Brussels-Glasgow/Plymouth.

92 As that definition of the geographical market has not been challenged by the applicants, it follows that the ENS agreements fell to be assessed solely on the basis of the four separate geographical markets listed above and solely in the context of an intermodal market comprising various modes of transport such as rail, air, coach and motor car. On that basis, therefore, it is necessary to examine whether the Commission correctly evaluated ENS's market shares in order to arrive at the conclusion that the ENS agreements would have an appreciable effect on trade between Member States, bearing in mind that, according to the applicants' notification, those market shares would not exceed the critical threshold of 5% and would, in any event, be insignificant.

93 It is to be noted here that the contested decision makes no reference to the market shares of ENS or of any other operators competing with ENS and also present on the various intermodal markets taken by the Commission as the relevant markets for the purposes of applying Article 85(1) of the Treaty. Consequently, even if - contrary to the applicants' submission - the ENS agreements were to restrict competition, the Court is not in a position, in the absence of any such data concerning the analysis of the relevant market in the contested decision, to make any finding as to whether the supposed restrictions on competition have an appreciable effect on trade between Member States and are thus caught by Article 85(1) of the Treaty, having regard, in particular, to the intermodal competition which is, according to the decision itself, a feature of the two service markets in question.

[.....]

Second part: assessment of the restrictive effect of the ENS agreement on competition

[.....]

-Restrictions on competition among the parent undertakings

139 It is clear from the documents before the Court that, prior to the adoption of Directive 91/440, the railway undertakings in the Member States were neither actually nor potentially in competition with each other because most Member States provided for exclusive rights precluding, de jure or de facto, both the provision of international passenger services and access to the infrastructure (the national rail networks). Prior to the adoption of that Directive, as the parties have stressed, the only basis on which such services were provided in the Community was that of the traditional cooperation agreements between the railway undertakings operating on the various networks concerned. However, following the adoption of Directive 91/440, conditions of competition on the market for rail transport changed and the railway undertakings operating on their national networks became to a certain extent potential competitors for international passenger services, provided that they formed 'international groupings' with other railway undertakings established in other Member States for the purpose of providing international transport services between those Member States (Articles 3 and 10 of the Directive).

140 It would appear from the Commission's arguments that the possibility of providing international services via international groupings is open not only to existing railway undertakings but also to new railway undertakings, including subsidiaries of existing railway undertakings, and that it was on the basis of that premiss that the Commission considered that the ENS agreements restricted competition among the parent

undertakings inasmuch as (a) each of the parties to those agreements could form an international grouping either with an undertaking established in the United Kingdom or with its own subsidiary there and thus compete with ENS, (b) each of those parties could set up a subsidiary specialising as a 'transport operator' and buy from those parties the same necessary rail services as they sold to ENS and (c) each railway undertaking could itself take on the role of transport operator and provide international night passenger services by buying the necessary rail services from the railway undertakings concerned.

[.....]

Relevant market analysis on a case-by-case basis

4) Joined Cases T-125 & 127/97 *Coca-Cola* [2000] ECR II-1733

The following paragraphs make clear that the Commission and national courts alike need to define the relevant market on a case-by-case basis. This issue was raised by The Coca-Cola Company (TCCC), which feared that once the Commission had found that a certain undertaking (here CCSB) was dominant, that undertaking's position on the market would not be investigated anew in other (pending or future) cases before either the Commission or national courts.

Relevance: analysis of relevant market required in each new case.

[.....]

81 Second, a finding of a dominant position by the Commission, even if likely in practice to influence the policy and future commercial strategy of the undertaking concerned, does not have binding legal effects as referred to in the IBM judgment. Such a finding is the outcome of an analysis of the structure of the market and of competition prevailing at the time the Commission adopts each decision. The conduct which the undertaking held to be in a dominant position subsequently comes to adopt in order to prevent a possible infringement of Article 86 of the Treaty is thus shaped by the parameters which reflect the conditions of competition on the market at a given time.
82 Moreover, in the course of any decision applying Article 86 of the Treaty, the Commission must define the relevant market again and make a fresh analysis of the conditions of competition which will not necessarily be based on the same considerations as those underlying the previous finding of a dominant position.

[.....]

85 Nor, in any event, does the possibility that a national court applying Article 86 of the Treaty directly in the light of the decision-making practice of the Commission might reach the same finding that CCSB holds a dominant position mean that the contested finding has binding legal effects. A national court which has to assess action taken by CCSB after the contested decision in the context of a dispute between CCSB and a third party is not bound by previous findings of the Commission. There is nothing to prevent it from concluding that CCSB is no

longer in a dominant position, contrary to the Commission's finding at the time when the contested decision was adopted.

[.....]

B. Notion of 'undertaking'

Cross-references for this part:

- V. Louri, 'Case note on the Fenin Judgment', (2004) 31-4 *LIEI*.
- V. Louri, 'Undertaking as a Jurisdictional Element in EC Competition Rules', (2002) 29 *LIEI*, 143.
- A. Riesenkampff and S. Lehr, 'Membership of Professional Associations and Article 85 of the EC Treaty', (1995/96) 19 *World Competition*, 57.
- W.P.J. Wils, 'The undertaking as subject of EC competition law and the imputation of infringements to natural or legal persons', (2000) 25 *ELR*, 99.

1) Case C-41/90 *Höfner & Elser v. Macrotron* [1991] ECR I-1979

In Germany, an institution called the Bundesansalt had, by virtue of the Arbeidsförderungsgesetz (Law on the Promotion of Employment, AFG), the exclusive right of employment procurement, i.e., headhunting. Some forms of private procurement, however, were tolerated. Höfner and Elsner, recruitment consultants, contracted with Macrotron to find the latter a sales director. When the candidate was not approved of and Macrotron refused to pay, Höfner and Elser started proceedings. The question was whether the contract was void since it breached the Arbeidsförderungsgesetz. The German court turned to the ECJ to obtain a preliminary ruling on the European aspects of the dispute at issue.

Relevance: notion of 'undertaking'.

[.....]

The interpretation of Articles 86 and 90 of the EEC Treaty

[.....]

20 (...) it is necessary to establish whether a public employment agency such as the Bundesanstalt may be regarded as an undertaking within the meaning of Articles 85 and 86 of the Treaty.

21 It must be observed, in the context of competition law, first that the concept of an undertaking encompasses every entity engaged in an economic activity, regardless of the legal status of the entity and the way in which it is financed and, secondly, that employment procurement is an economic activity.

22 The fact that employment procurement activities are normally entrusted to public agencies cannot affect the economic nature of such activities. Employment procurement has not always been, and is not necessarily, carried out by public entities. That finding applies in particular to executive recruitment.

23 It follows that an entity such as a public employment agency engaged in the business of employment procurement may be clas-

sified as an undertaking for the purpose of applying the Community competition rules.

[.....]

2) Case C-35/96 *Commission v. Italy* [1998] ECR I-3851

Here, the ECJ refined the definition of 'undertaking' as given in paragraph 21 of the Höfner case by explaining 'economic activity'.

Relevance: notion of 'economic activity'.

[.....]

36 It must first be noted that, according to settled case-law, the concept of an undertaking covers any entity engaged in an economic activity, regardless of its legal status and the way in which it is financed (Case C-41/90 Höfner and Elser [1991] ECR I-1979, paragraph 21; Case C-244/94 Fédération Française des Sociétés d'Assurances and Others v Ministère de l'Agriculture et de la Pêche [1995] ECR I-4013, paragraph 14; and Case C-55/96 Job Centre [1997] ECR I-7119, paragraph 21), and that any activity consisting in offering goods and services on a given market is an economic activity (Case 118/85 Commission v Italy [1987] ECR 2599, paragraph 7).

[.....]

3) Joined Cases C-159 & 160/91 *Poucet & Pistre v. Cancava* [1993] ECR I-637

In the following two cases, the ECJ further defined the notion of undertaking. In the first dispute, the ECJ was asked whether a French agency charged with managing a social security scheme was an undertaking within the scope of Article 101 TFEU.

Relevance: delineation of 'undertaking' and 'economic activity'.

[.....]

13 It follows that the social security schemes, as described, are based on a system of compulsory contribution, which is indispensable for application of the principle of solidarity and the financial equilibrium of those schemes.
14 It is apparent from the documents that the management of the schemes at issue in the main proceedings was entrusted by statute to social security funds whose activities are subject to control by the State, acting through, in particular, the Minister for Social Security, the Minister for the Budget and public bodies such as the Inspectorate General of Finance and the Inspectorate General for Social Security.
15 In the discharge of their duties, the funds apply the law and thus cannot influence the amount of the contributions, the use of assets and the fixing of the level of benefits. For management of the sickness and maternity scheme, the regional sickness funds may entrust to certain organizations, such as those that are governed in France by the Code de la Mutualité (Code governing mutual societies) or the Code des Assurances (Insurance

Code), the task of collecting contributions and paying out benefits. However, it does not appear that those organizations, which, in the performance of that task, act only as agents of the sickness funds, are referred to by the judgments of the national court.
16 The foregoing considerations must be taken into account in examining whether the term "undertaking", within the meaning of Articles 85 and 86 of the Treaty, includes organizations charged with managing a social security scheme of the kind referred to by the national court.
17 The Court has held (in particular in Case C-41/90 Höfner v Elser [1991] ECR I-1979, paragraph 21) that in the context of competition law the concept of an undertaking encompasses every entity engaged in an economic activity, regardless of the legal status of the entity and the way in which it is financed.
18 Sickness funds, and the organizations involved in the management of the public social security system, fulfil an exclusively social function. That activity is based on the principle of national solidarity and is entirely non-profit-making. The benefits paid are statutory benefits bearing no relation to the amount of the contributions.
19 Accordingly, that activity is not an economic activity and, therefore, the organizations to which it is entrusted are not undertakings within the meaning of Articles 85 and 96 of the Treaty.
20 The answer to be given to the national court must therefore be that the concept of an undertaking within the meaning of Articles 85 and 86 of the Treaty does not encompass organizations charged with the management of social security schemes of the kind referred to in the judgments of the national court.

[.....]

Case cross-reference:
▸ Case C-115-117/97 *Brentjens* [1999] ECR I-6025 (see I-J-3).

4) Case C-343/95 *Diego Calì & Figli v. Servizi Ecologici del Porto di Genova* [1997] ECR I-1547

In this case, the question was whether the notion of 'undertaking' in Article 101 TFEU encompasses a private organisation (namely SEPG) charged by the Consorzio Autonome del Porto (CAP), a public body, with detecting environmental offences in the port of Genoa, especially as far as crude oil and oil products were concerned.

Relevance: delineation of 'undertaking' and 'economic activity'.

[.....]

14 In order to answer the first question, concerning the existence of a dominant position, it must be established whether an activity of the kind carried on by SEPG in this case falls within the scope of Article 86 of the Treaty.
15 Such activities are carried on under an exclusive concession granted to SEPG by a public body.
16 As regards the possible application of the competition rules of the Treaty, a distinction must be drawn between a situation where the State acts in the exercise of official authority and that where it carries on economic activi-

ties of an industrial or commercial nature by offering goods or services on the market (Case 118/85 Commission v Italy [1987] ECR 2599, paragraph 7).
17 In that connection, it is of no importance that the State is acting directly through a body forming part of the State administration or by way of a body on which it has conferred special or exclusive rights (Case 118/85 Commission v Italy, cited above, paragraph 8).
18 In order to make the distinction between the two situations referred to in paragraph 16 above, it is necessary to consider the nature of the activities carried on by the public undertaking or body on which the State has conferred special or exclusive rights (Case 118/85 Commission v Italy, cited above, paragraph 7).
19 On this point, it is clear from the order for reference and the wording of the first question that the main proceedings concern the payment to be made by Calì for anti-pollution surveillance exercised by SEPG in relation to the loading and unloading of acetone products transported by Calì in the oil port of Genoa.
20 Furthermore, it is common ground that the dispute in the main proceedings does not concern the invoicing of any action by SEPG necessitated by pollution actually produced during loading or unloading operations.
21 Article 1 of Order No 32 of the President of CAP referred to above expressly distinguishes, moreover, between surveillance intended to prevent pollution and intervention in a case where pollution has occurred and it provides (Article 1(b)(2)) that those responsible for the pollution are to bear the costs arising from any action deemed necessary or advisable.
22 The anti-pollution surveillance for which SEPG was responsible in the oil port of Genoa is a task in the public interest which forms part of the essential functions of the State as regards protection of the environment in maritime areas.
23 Such surveillance is connected by its nature, its aim and the rules to which it is subject with the exercise of powers relating to the protection of the environment which are typically those of a public authority. It is not of an economic nature justifying the application of the Treaty rules on competition (Case C-364/92 SAT Fluggesellschaft v Eurocontrol [1994] ECR I-43, paragraph 30).
24 The levying of a charge by SEPG for preventive anti-pollution surveillance is an integral part of its surveillance activity in the maritime area of the port and cannot affect the legal status of that activity (Case C-364/92 SAT Fluggesellschaft v Eurocontrol, cited above, paragraph 28). Moreover, as stated in paragraph 8 of this judgment, the tariffs applied by SEPG have been approved by the public authorities.
25 In the light of the foregoing considerations, the answer to Question 1 must be that Article 86 of the EC Treaty is to be interpreted as not being applicable to anti-pollution surveillance with which a body governed by private law has been entrusted by the public authorities in an oil port of a Member State, even where port users must pay dues to finance that activity.

[.....]

Case cross-references:

- Case C-364/92 *SAT Fluggesellschaft v. Eurocontrol* [1994] ECR I-43.
- Case C-224/94 *FFSA* [1995] ECR I-4013.
- Case C-22/98 *Bécu* [1999] ECR I-5665.
- Case T-319/99 *Fenin* [2003] ECR II-357; Case C-205/03 P *Fenin* [2006] ECR I-6295.
- *Reuter/BASF* Commission decision 76/743/EEC [1976] OJ L 254/40.
- *RAI/Unitel* Commission decision 78/516/EEC [1978] OJ L 157/39.

5) Case T-99/04 *AC-Treuhand AG v. Commission* [2008] ECR II-1501

On the basis of an agency agreement with the three main protagonists in the Organic Peroxides cartel (Case COMP/E-2/37.857, OJ 2005 L 110/44), the Zurich (Switzerland) based trust company AC-Treuhand AG had been entrusted with storing certain secret documents, collecting and communicating market data relating to the organic peroxides market activities of the cartel members, and completing logistical and clerical-administrative tasks associated with the organization of cartel meetings in Zurich. The Commission imposed a nominal fine of EUR 1,000 on AC-Treuhand for its role in the operating of the cartel upon which this trust company appealed the Commission's decision on arguments of principle.

Relevance: Could a trust company which itself is not an active player on the relevant market of a cartel be accused of infringing Article 101 TFEU?

[.....]

d) The applicant's classification as a co-perpetrator of the cartel

151 [...], it must be determined whether, in the present case, the objective and subjective conditions for establishing that the applicant shares liability, in that the anti-competitive conduct of the other participating undertakings can be attributed to it, are satisfied. In that regard, it should be pointed out, first of all, that in order to be able to attribute the whole of an infringement to an undertaking, that undertaking must have contributed, even in a subordinate manner, to the restriction of competition at issue, and the subjective condition relating to the manifestation of that undertaking's intention in that regard must be met.

152 Independently of the question whether the applicant was a 'contracting' party to the 1971 and 1975 agreements and whether the agency agreements concluded with the three organic peroxide producers were an integral part of the cartel in the wider sense, the Court notes that it has become apparent that the applicant actively contributed to the implementation of that cartel between 1993 and 1999.

153 First, it is common ground that the applicant stored and concealed on its premises the originals of the 1971 and 1975 agreements of Atochem/Atofina and PC/Degussa, and in the latter case, until as late as 2001 or 2002 (recitals 63 and 83 of the contested decision). Second, the applicant admits to having calculated and communicated to the members of the cartel the deviations of the respective market shares from the agreed quotas, until 1995 or 1996 at the very least, an activity which was expressly provided for in the 1971 and 1975 agreements, and to having stored secret documents on its premises, pursuant thereto. Third, as regards the meetings between the organic peroxide producers which had some anti-competitive content, the applicant admitted to having organised and partly attended five of those meetings, as well as the meeting held in Amersfoort on 19 October 1998 to prepare a proposal regarding the allocation of quotas among the producers. Fourth, it is common ground that the applicant regularly reimbursed the travel expenses which the representatives of the organic peroxide producers incurred in attending meetings with an anti-competitive purpose, and it did so with the manifest intention of covering up any traces of the implementation of the cartel in the books of

those producers, or of not leaving any such traces (see paragraphs 63 and 102 above).

154 Without there being any need to assess in detail the points of dispute between the parties regarding the actual extent of the applicant's participation in the cartel, the Court concludes from the information set out in paragraph 153 above that the applicant actively contributed to the implementation of the cartel and that, contrary to its submissions, there was a sufficiently definite and decisive causal link between that activity and the restriction of competition on the organic peroxide market. At the hearing, the applicant did not dispute the existence of that causal link but merely challenged the legal classification of its contribution as an act of a perpetrator of the infringement, maintaining that its contribution could be classed only as an act of complicity which could have been carried out by any consultancy firm.

155 Accordingly, it is not relevant that the applicant was not formally and directly a contracting party to the 1971 and 1975 agreements. First, for the purposes of applying Article 81(1) EC, the question whether or not there is an agreement which is in writing, or otherwise explicit, between the participating undertakings is not decisive so long as they act in collusion (see paragraphs 115 to 123 above). Second, the applicant itself acknowledges that, by tacit agreement with the organic peroxide producers, it undertook – in its own name and on its own account – some of Fides' activities as specifically provided for under those agreements, such as the calculation and communication of the deviations from the agreed quotas. It should be added that, given that the Commission merely imposed on the applicant a fine of a minimal amount of EUR 1 000 and that that amount as such has not been called into question by the applicant, the Court is not required to give a ruling on the exact extent of the applicant's participation for the purposes of its effect on the lawfulness of the level of the fine imposed.

156 Moreover, in the light of all the objective circumstances characterising the applicant's participation, the Court finds that the applicant acted in full knowledge of the facts and intentionally when it made its professional expertise and infrastructure available to the cartel, in order to benefit from it, at least indirectly, in the course of implementing the individual agency agreements which linked it to the three organic peroxide producers. Quite apart from the question whether the applicant thus also knowingly infringed the rules of professional ethics by which it is bound as a commercial consultant, it clearly could not have been unaware, or indeed it knew, that the objective of the cartel to which it contributed was anti-competitive and unlawful, that objective having become apparent, inter alia, in the context of the 1971 and 1975 agreements which the applicant stored on its premises, from the meetings which were held with an anti-competitive aim and from the exchange of sensitive information in which the applicant actively participated, at least until 1995 or 1996.

157 In the light of all of the above considerations, the Court finds that, in so far as the contested decision establishes that the applicant shares liability for the infringement committed primarily by AKZO, Atochem/Atofina and PC/Degussa, that decision does not exceed the limits of the prohibition laid down in Article 81(1) EC and that, consequently, by imposing on the applicant a fine of EUR 1 000, the Commission did not exceed the powers conferred on it under Article 15(2) of Regulation No 17.

[....]

6) Case C-49/07 *Motosykletistiki Omospondia Ellados NPID (MOTOE)* [2008] ECR I-4863

The non-profit organization MOTOE applied for an authorization to organize motor-cycling events in Greece. The competent ministry turned down the request on formal grounds, inter alia because the Greek representative of the International Motorcycling Federation (FIM) had not given its consent to MOTOE's plans. Litigation ensued in the context whereof the Greek court asked the ECJ to interpret Articles 106 and 102 TFEU in relation to the Greek representative of the FIM .

Relevance: Competition law status of national representatives of international sports federations

[.....]

The Court (Grand Chamber) hereby rules (in the operative part of the judgment):

A legal person whose activities consist not only in taking part in administrative decisions authorising the organisation of motorcycling events, but also in organising such events itself and in entering, in that connection, into sponsorship, advertising and insurance contracts, falls within the scope of Articles 82 EC and 86 EC. Those articles preclude a national rule which confers on a legal person, which organises motorcycling competitions and enters, in that connection, into sponsorship, advertising and insurance contracts, the power to give consent to applications for authorisation to organise such competitions, without that power being made subject to restrictions, obligations and review.

Case cross-reference:

▸ A. Vermeersch, Case note on C-49/97 MOTOE in *C.M.L.Rev.* 2009, 1327-1341.

C. Association of undertakings

1) *FENEX* Commission decision 96/438/EC [1996] OJ L 181/28

According to the Commission, FENEX, a Dutch association of undertakings that represented the interests of forwarding companies, had engaged in anti-competitive behaviour. It annually circulated recommended tariffs or charges to its members for the various logistical services (i.e. the arrangement of transports) they provided. These tariffs were generally adhered to; the resulting increases in price ranged from 3% to 25%, depending on the type of service offered.

Relevance: indication as to when a decision of an association of undertakings infringes Article 101 TFEU (borderline between 'innocent' advice and anti-competitive behaviour).

[.....]

II. Legal Assessment

[.....]

C. The concept of decision by an association of undertakings

(32) During the proceeding, Fenex's representatives argued that the tariffs had merely the force of a recommendation which did not restrict the freedom of forwarding agents to set their tariffs. According to Fenex, such a recommendation does not constitute a decision by an association of undertakings within the meaning of Article 85 of the Treaty.

(33) It should be noted firstly that the drawing up and circulation of tariffs by Fenex is not an occasional activity, but one which on the contrary has been carried out since the beginning of the century.

(34) The tariffs are drawn up and updated annually by the specialized Fenex body, the tariffs committee, which presents an opinion to the board of directors, comprising representatives of the forwarding firms affiliated to Fenex.

(35) The tariffs are then adopted by the board of directors and were, until 22 June 1991, sent to the firms through the intermediary of the affiliated associations, and have, since that date, been sent to them direct.

(36) Account should also be taken of the fact that, although they are presented as non-compulsory recommendations, the tariffs are accompanied by circulars drafted in more mandatory terms.

(37) The Fenex circular of 24 November 1989 setting out the new scale of charges applying as from 1 January 1990 stipulates in this respect:

'The Board of Directors of the Federation of Dutch Forwarding Agents (Fenex), acting in accordance with the opinion of the Fenex Tariffs Committee, has decided as follows:

. . .

The tariff increases for the year [. . .] will be . . . %. This is the result of the trend of costs with which the branch of industry is confronted.'

This formula is used each year by Fenex in its circulars.

(38) In the circular sent by Fenex to its members at the end of 1990 and stipulating the tariff increase for 1991, it is stated:

'In view of the result arrived at, members are urgently recommended to pass on the above-mentioned tariff increase [5 %] in full to consignors.'

(39) Similarly, in a circular sent at the end of 1991 and relating to the increases to be applied at land frontiers in 1992, it is stated:

'Fenex recommends that an additional tariff increase of 5 % be applied for the carrying-out of customs formalities at land frontiers.'

(40) Lastly, it is common ground that it was in the forwarding agents' common interest to coordinate their conduct within Fenex by setting the tariffs for the services in question, which constitute elements of competition between the forwarding agents.

(41) On the basis of the above, the drawing-up and circulation of the tariffs recommended by Fenex must be interpreted as the faithful reflection of the association's resolve to coordinate the conduct of its members on the relevant market.

(42) In accordance with the case-law of the Court of Justice (5), these recommended tariffs constitute decisions by an association of undertakings within the meaning of Article 85 (1).

[.....]

E. Restriction of competition

[.....]

(59) During the proceeding, Fenex's representatives stated that the association's intention was not to affect the proper functioning of the market, but to provide assistance to its members. Such assistance was necessary because of the limited size of some undertakings, which did not have sufficient resources for drawing up their selling prices.
(60) While it is normal practice for a trade organization to provide management assistance to its members, it must not exercise any direct or indirect influence on competition, notably in the form of tariffs applicable to all undertakings regardless of their own cost price structure.
(61) The circulation of recommended tariffs by a trade organization is liable to prompt the relevant undertakings to align their tariffs, irrespective of their cost prices. Such a method dissuades undertakings whose cost prices are lower from lowering their prices and thus creates an artificial advantage for undertakings which have the least control over their production costs (8).
(62) Such a risk is not, however, inherent in the circulation of information that would help the firms to calculate their own cost price structures so as to enable them to establish their selling prices independently.
(63) In the case in point, it is common ground that Fenex did not circulate to its members information that would enable them to determine their selling prices on the basis of their own costs, but that the documents circulated relate to selling prices.
(64) Furthermore, account must be taken of the fact that, in the case of certain services, Fenex's recommended prices are explicitly represented as minimum prices.
(65) During the proceeding, Fenex's representatives stressed that the association had only a limited number of members and that consequently the impact of the relevant practice was very limited.
(66) It should be pointed out in this respect that, according to the case-law of the Court of Justice, 'an agreement may escape the prohibition in Article 85 (1) when it affects the market only to an insignificant extent, having regard to the weak position which those concerned have in the market in the products in question' (9).
(67) Although Fenex comprises a large number of small firms, its membership also includes large firms that provide services worldwide and may act as market leaders.
(68) Similarly, some firms which are members of Fenex are subsidiaries of firms established in other Member States, or themselves have subsidiaries in other Member States, which provide the same services on the same tariff terms.
(69) Account should also be taken of the fact that some Fenex members are active in sea, air or land transport and that in those sectors some of them are market leaders. The circulation of tariff recommendations to undertakings of such size inevitably has a knock-on effect on other undertakings in the sector.
(70) Consequently, having regard to the case-law of the Court of Justice, the Commission considers that the object of the horizontal practice in question is to affect the market significantly and that it falls within the scope of Article 85 (1).
(71) As regards the anti-competitive effects, it should be pointed out that, as the Court of Justice has consistently held, it is unnecessary to consider the actual effects of an agreement or decision by an association of undertakings if it is apparent that it has the object of preventing, restricting or distorting competition (10).

[.....]

D. Economic unit doctrine

1) Case 15/74 *Centrafarm v. Sterling Drug* [1974] ECR 1147

Sterling Drug, a New York based company, owned a patent relating to the mode of preparation of a medical drug. In Europe, only its subsidiaries could legally market the medicinal preparations manufactured according to the patented method. They were not allowed to export the said product (restriction of competition). The ECJ was to decide whether these vertical relations between a parent company and its subsidiaries fell within the scope of Article 101 TFEU .

Relevance: notion of 'economic unit' (basic rule vertical relations: parent company and subsidiaries).

[.....]

38 These questions require the Court to state whether Article 85 of the Treaty is applicable to agreements and concerted practices between the proprietor of parallel patents in various Member States and his licencees, if the objective of those agreements and concerted practices is to regulate differently for the different countries the conditions on the market in respect of the goods protected by the patents.
39 Although the existence of rights recognized under the industrial property legislation of a Member State is not affected by Article 85 of the Treaty, the conditions under which those rights may be exercised may nevertheless fall within the prohibitions contained in that Article.
40 This may be the case whenever the exercise of such a right appears to be the object, the means or the consequence of an agreement.
41 Article 85, however, is not concerned with agreements or concerted practices between undertakings belonging to the same concern and having the status of parent company and subsidiary, if the undertakings form an economic unit within which the subsidiary has no real freedom to determine its course of action on the market, and if the agreements or practices are concerned merely with the internal allocation of tasks as between the undertakings.

[.....]

Case cross-reference:

▸ In similar vein: Case 16/74 *Centrafarm v. Winthrop* [1974] ECR 1183.

2) Case 15/74 *Centrafarm v. Sterling Drug* [1974] ECR 1147

Opinion of Mr. Advocate-General Trabucchi, delivered on 18 September 1974.

Relevance: in his opinion, the Advocate-General looked at the applicability of Article 101 to economic units from a slightly different angle than the ECJ. He also took into account the effect of the alleged unlawful behaviour on third parties. As can be seen in the above judgment, the Court did not (yet) follow his line of reasoning.

[.....]

The question then arises whether these considerations regarding the application of Article 85 also hold good when the aforementioned agreements are concluded exclusively between undertakings forming part of the same group of companies under the control of one parent company. Or, in such circumstances, which include the subsidiaries' lack of independence as regards decisions on marketing policy, should the application of Article 85 be excluded altogether, the only method available to exercise control over the behaviour of the group acting as a body in concert on the market being Article 86, which prohibits abuse of a dominant position?
Declaring that the prohibition in Article 85 did not apply to agreements which regulate the relationships between the members of a group, the Commission had from the outset emphasized the fact that, quite apart from any agreement, there can be no competition between undertakings of this kind. It was on the basis of this elementary principle that the Commission justified its line of reasoning, ushered in by the decision of 18 June 1969 giving negative clearance in Christiani and Nielsen (OJ L 165 of 5.7.1969, p. 12). Under this decision, agreements concluded between undertakings in a group effectively subject to the control of a parent company and who confine themselves to playing their allotted roles in the framework of the same economic entity, escape the prohibition under Article 85, precisely because, under such conditions, neither the subject-matter nor the effect of these instruments restricts competition; this is because competition does not, by definition, exist within the group.

Against this background, consideration can reasonably be given to the applicability of the prohibition laid down under Article 85 when, instead of being confined to regulating internal relationships, the agreements between the undertakings in a group are designed to raise barriers against third parties, and to block the avenues open to them for trade and competition.

The precedents established by this Court might be the source of some difficulty because, in holding that, in the case of groups of concerns under the control of a parent company, the prohibition in Article 85 did not apply to contracts subsisting between such concerns, the Court stressed instead their lack of economic independence and the unity of a group forming an economic whole (Case 22/71, Béguelin, Rec. 1971, p. 958, paragraph 8 of the Grounds; Cases 48/69, 52/69 and 53/69, ICI and Geigy-Sandoz, Rec. 1972, p. 665, paragraphs 132-140, p. 837, paragraphs 43-45; Joined Cases 6-7/73, Istituto Chemioterapico Italiano and Commercial Solvents Company, [1974] ECR 253-254, paragraphs 36-41).

In my view, however, these precedents do not in principle preclude the applicability of Article 85 to agreements or practices in which the component companies of a group alone participate. Béguelin was concerned with a grant by a parent company of exclusive sales rights to one of its subsidiaries, which was established in another Member State, in respect of its products of an undertaking in a third State. It did not matter to competitors or consumers in the Community whether the parent company had the exclusive right of sale in the two States or whether, in one of these States, a subsidiary took its place.

Having regard to the subject-matter of the agreement, the Court decided that the prerequisite of a restriction on competition was lacking.

The other cases cited were concerned with establishing whether anti-competitive conduct on the part of a company established in the Common Market could be laid at the door of the parent company which controlled it and which was established in a third country. One can thus appreciate the peculiar significance, in such a context, of the concept of the economic whole represented by a group. And this enables us to rule out the possibility that these precedents, which were designed to meet clearly defined situations, can militate against application of Article 85 in the case of agreements and practices operating between the members of the same group where such instruments and practices have the object or effect of restraining competition from third parties.

[.....]

Case cross-reference:

▸ *Kodak* Commission decision 70/322/EEG OJ [1970] L 147/24.

3) Case T-102/92 *Viho v. Commission* [1995] ECR II-17

Parker, an English company, made use of subsidiaries to market its products. According to Viho, Parker restricted distribution since the subsidiaries were not allowed to do business outside their allocated territories. Implicitly, the ECJ also responded to the issues raised by AG Trabucchi in the 1974 Centrafarm case.

Relevance: notion of 'economic unit' (basic rule horizontal relations: between subsidiaries).

[.....]

47 As regards the appraisal under Article 85(1) of the Treaty of agreements concluded within a group of companies, the Court of Justice has held that "where a subsidiary does not enjoy real autonomy in determining its course of action in the market, the prohibitions set out in Article 85(1) may be considered inapplicable in the relationship between it and the parent company with which it forms one economic unit" (judgment in Case 48/69 ICI v Commission [1972] ECR 619, paragraph 134). Similarly, in its judgment in Ahmed Saeed Flugreisen and Others, cited above, paragraph 35, the Court of Justice held that "Article 85 does not apply where the concerted practice in question is between undertakings belonging to a single group as parent company and subsidiary if those undertakings form an economic unit within which the subsidiary has no real freedom to determine its course of action on the market" and added that "[h]owever, the conduct of such a unit on the market is liable to come within the ambit of Article 86". It also follows from the case-law of the Court of First Instance that Article 85(1) of the Treaty refers only to relations between economic entities which are capable of competing with one another and does not cover agreements or concerted practices between undertakings belonging to the same group if the undertakings form an economic unit (judgment in Joined Cases T-68/89, T-77/89 and T-78/89 SIV and Others v Commission [1992] ECR II-1403, paragraph 357).

48 It is not disputed in this case that Parker owns 100% of the capital of its subsidiaries established in Germany, France, Belgium and the Netherlands. It is also apparent from the description given by Parker of the operation of its subsidiary companies, which the applicant has not disputed, that the sales and marketing activities of the subsidiaries are directed by an area team which is appointed by the parent company and which controls, in particular, sales targets, gross margins, sales costs, cash flow and stocks. That area team also lays down the range of products to be sold, monitors advertising and issues directives concerning prices and discounts.
49 Consequently, the Court concludes that, in point 2 of its decision, the Commission correctly classifies the Parker group as "one economic unit within which the subsidiaries do not enjoy real autonomy in determining their course of action in the market".
50 The Court of Justice has also held that "in competition law, the term 'undertaking' must be understood as designating an economic unit for the purpose of the subject-matter of the agreement in question even if in law that economic unit consists of several persons, natural or legal" (judgment in Case 170/83 Hydrotherm v Compact [1984] ECR 2999, paragraph 11). Similarly, the Court of First Instance has held that "Article 85(1) of the EEC Treaty is aimed at economic units which consist of a unitary organization of personal, tangible and intangible elements which pursues a specific economic aim on a long-term basis and can contribute to the commission of an infringement of the kind referred to in that provision" (judgment in Case T-11/89 Shell v Commission [1992] ECR II-757, paragraph 311). Therefore, for the purposes of the application of the competition rules, the unified conduct on the market of the parent company and its subsidiaries takes precedence over the formal separation between those companies as a result of their separate legal personalities.
51 It follows that, where there is no agreement between economically independent entities, relations within an economic unit cannot amount to an agreement or concerted practice between undertakings which restricts competition within the meaning of Article 85(1) of the Treaty. Where, as in this case, the subsidiary, although having a separate legal personality, does not freely determine its conduct on the market but carries out the instructions given to it directly or indirectly by the parent company by which it is wholly controlled, Article 85(1) does not apply to the relationship between the subsidiary and the parent company with which it forms an economic unit.
52 While, admittedly, it cannot be excluded that the distribution policy applied by Parker, which consists of prohibiting its subsidiaries from supplying Parker products to customers established in Member States other than that of the subsidiary, may contribute to preserving and partitioning the various national markets and, in so doing, thwart one of the fundamental objectives to be achieved by the Common Market, it nevertheless follows from the abovementioned case-law that such a policy, followed by an economic unit such as the Parker group within which the subsidiaries do not enjoy any freedom to determine their conduct in the market, does not fall within the scope of Article 85(1) of the Treaty.
53 The Court therefore concludes that the Commission was correct in deciding that "the subsidiaries' conduct is therefore to be imputed to the parent company" and that "the integrated distribution system which ensures the sale of Parker products in Spain, France, Germany, Belgium and the Netherlands via the wholly-owned subsidiaries located there fulfils the conditions established by the European Court of Justice with regard to the non-applicability of Article 85".

54 It does not therefore avail the applicant to argue that the agreements at issue infringe Article 85(1) on the ground that they exceed an internal allocation of tasks within the group. It is apparent from its very terms that Article 85(1) does not apply to conduct which is in reality performed by an economic unit. It is not for the Court, on the pretext that certain conduct, such as that to which the applicant objects, may fall outside the competition rules, to apply Article 85 to circumstances for which it is not intended in order to fill a gap which may exist in the system of regulation laid down by the Treaty.

55 It follows that the first part of the plea alleging infringement of Article 85(1) of the Treaty is not well founded.

[.....]

Case cross-reference:

▸ Case C-73/95 P *Viho Europe BV v. Commission* [1996] ECR I-5457, appeal dismissed.

4) Joined Cases T-236/01, T-239/01, T-244/01 to T-246/01, T-251/01 and T-252/01 *Graphite electrodes cartel* [2004] ECR II-1181

Following investigations carried out on its own initiative, the Commission found that various undertakings had participated in a series of agreements and concerted practices in the graphite electrodes sector.
The cartel followed technological improvements which had led to a substantial decline in the consumption of electrodes per ton of steel produced and major restructuring undergone by the steel industry leading to the shutdown of a number of factories.
The Commission found several companies to have been involved, on a worldwide scale, in price fixing and in sharing the national and regional market according to the so-called "home producer" principle.
The same behaviour had been detected and fined by the American and the Canadian Competition Authorities.

Relevance: Possibility to impose fines on a subsidiary company rather than on its parent(s).

[.....]

278 As regards the complaint relating to the initial period of the cartel (1992 to 1995), when UCAR was under the control of Mitsubishi and Union Carbide, it is common ground that UCAR participated in the cartel between May 1992 and March 1998, as 'UCAR International Inc.'. It is on that company, UCAR International Inc., that the Commission imposed a fine for that infringement, and not on the natural or legal persons who allegedly influenced it. Consequently, it was not required to take into consideration any changes which might have taken place during the infringement period in the composition of the legal or economic owners of the company.

279 The fact that UCAR may have formed an economic unit with Mitsubishi and/or Union Carbide, so that it was unable to take autonomous decisions, which the Commission disputes, plays no role in that context. That fact would have been relevant only if the Commission had used its power to impose a sanction on UCAR's parent company for UCAR's conduct, as, moreover, it did in the

case of VAW (recitals 117 to 123 of the Decision), with reference to Case C 286/98 P Stora Kopparbergs Bergslags v Commission (cited at paragraph 113 above, paragraphs 26 to 29). In the present case, on the other hand, the point of whether UCAR's conduct could be attributed to another undertaking did not arise (Joined Cases T-45/98 and T-47/98 Krupp Thyssen Stainless and Acciai speciali Terni v Commission [2001] ECR II-3757, hereinafter 'Krupp', paragraph 189), since the Commission decided to address itself only to UCAR.

280 Nor does the present case concern the questions which may arise as a result of an economic succession in the control of an undertaking, where it is necessary to determine who is accountable for the undertaking's actions, namely the transferor or the transferee (judgment of the Court of First Instance, following appeal and referral back to the Court of First Instance, in Case T 354/94 Stora Kopparbergs Bergslags v Commission, cited at paragraph 113 above, paragraphs 60 and 70; judgment in Case T-9/99 HFB and Others v Commission [2002] ECR II-1487, paragraphs 101 to 108). While it is true that the application of the rule laid down in the case-law that '[i]t falls, in principle, to the natural or legal person managing the undertaking in question when the infringement was committed to answer for that infringement, even if, when the Decision finding the infringement was adopted, another person had assumed responsibility for operating the undertaking' (HFB and Others v Commission, paragraph 101) may prove difficult in certain circumstances, in the present case the Commission imposed a penalty only on UCAR and was therefore not required to examine the questions of the operation and control of UCAR.

281 In any event, the judicially determined rule just referred to must be interpreted as meaning that an undertaking – that is to say, an economic unit consisting of personal, tangible and intangible elements (Case 19/61 Mannesmann v High Authority [1962] ECR 357, 371) – is directed by the organs provided for in its articles of association and that any decision imposing a fine on it may be addressed to the management as provided for in the undertaking's articles of association (management board, management committee, chairman, manager, etc.), even though the financial consequences of the fine are ultimately borne by its owners. That rule would not be observed if the Commission, faced with unlawful conduct on the part of an undertaking, were always required to ascertain who is the owner exercising a decisive influence on the undertaking and were allowed to impose a sanction only on that owner.

282 If UCAR claims to have been 'plundered' by its former owners Mitsubishi and Union Carbide, who, it alleges, encouraged it to set up the cartel in respect of which it is now subject to a sanction, the Commission has rightly stated that the solution to that dispute must be sought in the relations between Mitsubishi and Union Carbide, on the one hand, and UCAR and its present owner on the other, and not at the level of the application of competition law by the Commission. Thus, even if Mitsubishi and Union Carbide had in fact used UCAR as an instrument intended to realise the profits derived from the actions of the cartel, the Commission was entitled to impose a fine only on that 'instrument', while UCAR and/or its owners are free to bring proceedings for damages against Mitsubishi and Union Carbide. Furthermore, UCAR took action against Mitsubishi and Union Carbide in the United

States in order to recover money allegedly extracted from it (recital 42 of the Decision).

283 In so far as UCAR further claims that the Commission should have examined the role played by Mitsubishi and Union Carbide in setting up the cartel, it is sufficient to recall that, according to a consistent line of decisions, even on the assumption that the situation of another economic operator to which the Decision was not addressed was comparable to that of UCAR, that could not in any event constitute a ground for setting aside the finding of an infringement by UCAR, provided that that infringement was properly established on the basis of documentary evidence. Owing to the fact that it infringed Article 81 EC, UCAR cannot escape any penalty on the ground that no fine was imposed on other economic operators such as Mitsubishi and Union Carbide when, as in the present case, those other undertakings' circumstances are not even the subject of proceedings before the Court (Joined Cases C-89/85, C-104/85, C-114/85, C 116/85, C-117/85 and C-125/85 to C-129/85 Ahlström Osakeyhtiö and Others v Commission [1993] ECR I-1307, paragraphs 146 and 197; Acerinox v Commission, cited at paragraph 239 above, paragraphs 156 and 157; and Case T 17/99 KE KELIT v Commission [2002] ECR II-1647, paragraph 101).

284 In those circumstances, the fact that Mitsubishi was convicted in the United States in February 2001 of aiding and abetting a conspiracy among graphite electrode producers and was fined USD 134 million (recital 42 of the Decision) is of no relevance for the purpose of examining the calculation of the fine imposed on UCAR. Nor is there any need to examine whether the Commission had been duly informed of Mitsubishi's or Union Carbide's involvement in the cartel or whether UCAR was actually controlled by Mitsubishi or Union Carbide.

285 Last, as the Commission was entitled to impose a sanction on the undertaking that participated directly in the infringement, i.e. UCAR, it was not required to justify that choice by setting out its reasons for not imposing sanctions on Mitsubishi and Union Carbide. The Commission did not therefore breach its obligation to state reasons under Article 253 EC.

[.....]

Case cross-reference:

► Joined Cases T-31/03, T-74/03, T-87/03 and T-91/03, *Special graphite cartel* [2005] OJ C 205/18.

E. Notion of 'inter-State' trade (effect on trade between Member States)

Cross-references for this part:

► Guidelines on the effect on trade concept contained in Articles 81 and 82 of the Treaty, [2004] OJ C 101/81.

► Case 56/65 *Société La Technique Minière v. Maschinenbau Ulm* [1966] ECR 337 (see I-I-1).

1) Joined Cases 56 & 58/64 *Consten & Grundig* [1966, English special edition] ECR 299

Consten was the sole distributor for Grundig (a German company) for the metropolitan territory of France, the Saar and Corsica. The former agreed not to market products that could compete with those of Grundig, and the latter gave Consten exclusive distribution rights. Consten was also granted the exclusive right to use Grundig's trade-mark GINT (Grundig International) in France. According to the Commission, this contract infringed Article 101 TFEU (partitioning of the market). Consten, of course, was not pleased with the Commission's decision and went to court. The ECJ confirmed the substantive law views of the Commission and held certain aspects of the distribution contract to infringe Article 101. However, the Court concurred with Consten that not the entire contract restricted competition and, therefore, only partially annulled the contested decision.

Relevance: clarification of effect on 'inter-State' trade.

[.....]

The complaints relating to the concept of 'agreements...which may affect trade between Member States'

The applicants and the German Government maintain that the Commission has relied on a mistaken interpretation of the concept of an agreement which may affect trade between Member States and has not shown that such trade would have been greater without the agreement in dispute.

The defendant replies that this requirement in Article 85(1) is fulfilled once trade between Member States develops, as a result of the agreement, differently from the way in which it would have done without the restriction resulting from the agreement, and once the influence of the agreement on market conditions reaches a certain degree. Such is the case here, according to the defendant, particularly in view of the impediments resulting within the Common Market from the disputed agreement as regards the exporting and importing of Grundig products to and from France.

The concept of an agreement 'which may affect trade between Member States' is intended to define, in the law governing cartels, the boundary between the areas respectively covered by Community law and national law. It is only to the extent to which the agreement may affect trade between Member States that the deterioration in competition caused by the agreement falls under the prohibition of Community law contained in Article 85; otherwise it escapes the prohibition.

In this connexion, what is particularly important is whether the agreement is capable of constituting a threat, either direct or indirect, actual or potential, to freedom of trade between Member States in a manner which might harm the attainment of the objectives of a single market between states.

Thus the fact that an agreement encourages an increase, even a large one, in the volume of trade between states is not sufficient to exclude the possibility that the agreement may 'affect' such trade in the abovementioned manner. In the present case, the contract between Grundig and Consten, on the one hand by preventing undertakings other than Consten from importing Grundig products into France, and on the other hand by prohibiting Consten from reexporting those products to other countries of the Common Market, indisputably affects trade between Member States. These limitations on the freedom of trade, as well as those which might ensue for third parties from the registration in France by Consten of the GINT trade mark, which Grundig places on all its products, are enough to satisfy the requirement in question.

Consequently, the complaints raised in this respect must be dismissed.

[.....]

2) Case 8/72 *VCH* [1972] ECR 977

The Commission had refused to grant an exemption to the General and Price Conditions and the General Conditions of Purchase and Sale which had been notified by VCH (Vereniging van Cementhandelaren, Association of Cement Traders), a Dutch association active on the Netherlands cement market. The dispute in issue concerned VCH's 'target prices', advisory resale prices which were in practice generally adhered to by all members and non-members of the Association.

Relevance: effect on inter-State trade when the alleged unlawful behaviour was confined to only one Member State (compartmentalization).

[.....]

(b) Influence on trade between Member States

26 According to the applicant association, the Community nonetheless has no jurisdiction to appraise the cartel to which the contested decision relates because it is a purely national cartel, limited to the territory of the Netherlands, which does not apply in any way to imports or exports and which consequently has no influence over the patterns of trade between Member States.
27 In this respect, it emphasizes more especially the fact that the total production of cement in the Netherlands far from satisfies the needs of the Netherlands economy and leaves a substantial need for imports, that furthermore there is, apart from its members, a large number of cement sellers not affiliated to it and that therefore there is no danger of intra-Community trade being affected.
28 According to Article 85 (1) all agreements which have as their object or effect the prevention, restriction or distortion of competition are incompatible with the Treaty once they may affect trade between Member States.
29 An agreement extending over the whole of the territory of a Member State by its very nature has the effect of reinforcing the compartmentalization of markets on a national basis, thereby holding up the economic interpenetration which the Treaty is designed to bring about and protecting domestic production.

[.....]

3) Joined Cases C-215 & 216/96 *Bagnasco* [1999] ECR I-135

In this case, the ECJ deviates from its view on the notion of effect on inter-State trade as expressed in Grundig and VCH. The effect on trade should be realistic and appreciable. The dispute was whether the (Italian) standard bank conditions (NBU, Norme Bancaria Uniforme), as formulated by the Italian Banking Association (ABI, Associazone Bancaria Italiana), did or did not impede trade. The NBU itself related to the provision of general guarantees that were needed to obtain current-account credit facilities.

Relevance: refinement of *Grundig* and *VCH* (realistic effect). To be seen as '*Delimitis* for trade' (appreciable effect, see I-H-2, p. 44).

[.....]

46 [...] it is appropriate first to consider what effects clauses such as those contained in the general guarantee contracts at issue in the main proceedings might possibly have on trade between Member States.
47 In that regard, the Court has consistently held that, in order that an agreement between undertakings may affect trade between Member States, it must be possible to foresee with a sufficient degree of probability on the basis of a set of objective factors of law or fact that it may have an influence, direct or indirect, actual or potential, on the pattern of trade between Member States, such as might prejudice the realisation of the aim of a single market in all the Member States (Case 42/84 Remia and Others v Commission [1985] ECR 2545, paragraph 22). Accordingly, the effect on intra-Community trade is normally the result of a combination of several factors which, taken separately, are not necessarily decisive (Case C-250/92 Gottrup-Klim v Dansk Landbrugs Grovvareselskab [1994] ECR I-5641, paragraph 54).
48 It is also settled case-law that, whilst Article 85(1) of the Treaty does not require that agreements referred to in that provision have actually affected trade between Member States, it does require that it be established that the agreements are capable of having that effect (Case C-219/95 P Ferriere Nord v Commission [1997] ECR I-4411, paragraph 19).

[.....]

50 It is true that, in principle, the answer to the question whether or not the conditions for the application of Article 85(1) of the Treaty are fulfilled depends on complex economic assessments which it is for the national court to undertake, if appropriate, in accordance with the criteria laid down by the case-law of the Court of Justice. However, in certain circumstances, and having regard to the indications given by the Court, no such analysis appears necessary (see Case C-250/92 Gottrup-Klim v Dansk Landbrugs Grovvareselskab, cited above, paragraph 55). Such is the position in the present case.
51 It must be borne in mind that the Commission, when approached by the ABI concerning the compatibility of the clauses governing the provision of general guarantees in relation to Article 85 of the Treaty, found that the banking service in question involved economic activities which have a very limited impact on trade between Member States and that the participation of the subsidiaries or branches of non-Italian financial establishments was limited (see paragraph 15 of this judgment). Moreover, the Commission has made clear, in reply to a question put to it by the Court, that potential recourse to contracts for credit facilities and contracts for the provision of general guarantees by the main customers of foreign banks, that is to say large undertakings and foreign economic operators, is not great and, in any event, is not a factor of decisive importance in the choice made by foreign banks as to whether or not to establish themselves in Italy, in so far as contracts of the kind at issue in the main proceedings are only rarely used by customers of that kind. The Commission's findings to that effect have not been called in question in the present proceedings.

[.....]

Case cross-references:

▸ Case C-238/05 *Asnef-Equifax v. Ausbanc* [2006] ECR I-11125.

▸ Case C-234/89 *Stergios Delimitis v. Henninger Bräu AG* {1991] ECR I-935.

F. Object or effect

Cross-reference for this part:

▸ Jeffrey L. Harrison and Jules Theeuwes, *Law and Economics*, W.W. Norton, New York – London 2008.

In the following three judgments, both the ECJ and the CFI emphasized that Article 101 TFEU is applicable when competition is restricted either intentionally (object) or by default (effect).

1) Joined Cases 56 & 58/64 *Consten & Grundig* [1966, English special edition] ECR 299

See above for facts of the case (I-E-1, p. 23). Grundig also showed that each case must be assessed in its own economic and legal context.

Relevance: explanation of concept 'restriction of competition' and 'object or effect'.

[.....]

The complaints concerning the criterion of restriction on competition

The applicants and the German Government maintain that since the Commission restricted its examination solely to Grundig products the decision was based upon a false concept of competition and of the rules on prohibition contained in Article 85(1), since this concept applies particularly to competition between similar products of different makes; the Commission, before declaring Article 85(1) to be applicable, should, by basing itself upon the 'rule of reason', have considered the economic effects of the disputed contrast upon competition between the different makes. There is a presumption that vertical sole distributorship agreements are not harmful to competition and in the present case there is nothing to invalidate that presumption. On the contrary, the contract in question has increased the competition between similar products of different makes.

The principle of freedom of competition concerns the various stages and manifestations of competition. Although competition between producers is generally more noticeable than that between distributors of products of the same make, it does not thereby follow that an agreement tending to restrict the latter kind of competition should escape the prohibition of Article 85(1) merely because it might increase the former.

Besides, for the purpose of applying Article 85(1), there is no need to take account of the concrete effects of an agreement once it appears that it has as its object the prevention, restriction or distortion of competition. Therefore the absence in the contested decision of any analysis of the effects of the agreement on competition between similar products of different makes does not, of itself, constitute a defect in the decision.

It thus remains to consider whether the contested decision was right in founding the prohibition of the disputed agreement under Article 85(1) on the restriction on competition created by Grundig products alone. The infringement which was found to exist by the contested decision results from the absolute territorial protection created the said contract in favour of Consten on the basis of French law. The applicants thus wished to eliminate any possibility of competition at the wholesale level in Grundig products in the terri-

tory specified in the contrast essentially by two methods.
First, Grundig undertook not to deliver even indirectly to third parties products intended for the area covered by the contract. The restrictive nature of that undertaking is obvious if it is considered in the light of the prohibition on exporting which was imposed not only on Consten but also on all the other sole concessionnaires of Grundig, as well as the German wholesalers. Secondly, the registration in France by Consten of the GINT trade mark, which Grundig affixes to all its products, is intended to increase the protection inherent in the disputed agreement, against the risk of parallel imports into France of Grundig products, by adding the protection deriving from the law on industrial property rights. Thus no third party could import Grundig products from other Member States of the Community for resale in France without running serious risks.
The defendant properly took into account the whole distribution system thus set up by Grundig. In order to arrive at a true representation of the contractual position the contract must be placed in the economic and legal context in the light of which it was concluded by the parties. Such a procedure is not to be regarded as an unwarrantable interference in legal transactions or circumstances which were not the subject of the proceedings before the Commission.
The situation as ascertained above results in the isolation of the French market and makes it possible to charge for the products in question prices which are sheltered from all effective competition. In addition, the more producers succeed in their efforts to render their own makes of product individually distinct in the eyes of the consumer, the more the effectiveness of competition between producers tends to diminish. Because of the considerable impact of distribution costs on the aggregate cost price, it seems important that competition between dealers should also be stimulated. The efforts of the dealer are stimulated by competition between distributors of products of the same make. Since the agreement thus aims at isolating the French market for Grundig products and maintaining artificially, for products of a very well-known brand, separate national markets within the Community, it is therefore such as to distort competition in the Common Market.
It was therefore proper for the contested decision to hold that the agreement constitutes an infringement of Article 85(1). No further considerations, whether of economic data (price differences between France and Germany, representative character of the type of appliance considered, level of overheads borne by Consten) or of the corrections of the criteria upon which the Commission relied in its comparisons between the situations of the French and German markets, and no possible favourable effects of the agreement in other respects, can in any way lead, in the face of the abovementioned restrictions, to a different solution under Article 85(1).

[.....]

2) Case C-49/92 P *Commission v. Anic* [1999] ECR I-4125

This case concerned a cartel that had been active on the polypropylene market. Anic was one of the undertakings that had been fined by the Commission for participation in the cartel. After an appeal, however, the Court of First Instance partially annulled the

Commission's decision since Anic had shown that the Commission did not have adequate proof for its participation in the cartel. The Commission subsequently brought an action before the ECJ.

Relevance: 'object or effect' to be read disjunctively.

[.....]

121 For one thing, subject to proof to the contrary, which it is for the economic operators concerned to adduce, there must be a presumption that the undertakings participating in concerting arrangements and remaining active on the market take account of the information exchanged with their competitors when determining their conduct on that market, particularly when they concert together on a regular basis over a long period, as was the case here, according to the findings of the Court of First Instance.
122 For another, a concerted practice, as defined above, falls under Article 85(1) of the Treaty even in the absence of anti-competitive effects on the market.
123 First, it follows from the actual text of Article 85(1) that, as in the case of agreements between undertakings and decisions by associations of undertakings, concerted practices are prohibited, regardless of their effect, when they have an anti-competitive object.
124 Next, although the concept of a concerted practice presupposes conduct of the participating undertakings on the market, it does not necessarily imply that that conduct should produce the concrete effect of restricting, preventing or distorting competition.
125 Lastly, that interpretation is not incompatible with the restrictive nature of the prohibition laid down in Article 85(1) of the Treaty (see Case 24/67 Parke Davis v Centrafarm [1968] ECR 55, p. 71) since, far from extending its scope, it corresponds to the literal meaning of the terms used in that provision.
126 The Court of First Instance therefore rightly held, despite faulty legal reasoning, that, since the Commission had established to the requisite legal standard that Anic had participated in collusion for the purpose of restricting competition, it did not have to adduce evidence that the collusion had manifested itself in conduct on the market. The question whether Anic has refuted the presumption set out in paragraph 121 of this judgment must therefore be examined.

[.....]

3) Case C-8/08 *T-Mobile Netherlands BV and others v. NMa (Dutch Competition Authority)*

The Dutch market for mobile telephony is oligopolistic by nature and is characterised by a high degree of concentration. Its five mobile telephony operators met in 2001 and discussed the lowering of their standard dealer compensation for consumer subscriptions as per September 1st, 2001. Furthermore, information was exchanged on the modalities of the dealer compensation system of each of the five operators. When a consumer subscribes to the mobile telephony services of one or the other operator, the dealer acts as an intermediary between the operator and that consumer, and provides the latter with a new telephone

together with his SIM-card. Dealers receive a standard compensation for the performance of their services.
The five operators were found out and the Dutch NCA imposed a fine based on both Article 101 TFEU and the corresponding article in the Dutch Competition Act. On appeal. the administrative Court of Appeal for the Industry (CBB, the highest administrative court in competition matters in the Netherlands) was in doubt whether the exchange of information could be seen as to object or restrict competition since the exchange did not affect the subscription price to be paid by the consumer, but rather the dealers' compensation for their services only. The CBB referred the matter to the ECJ under Article 267 TFEU (then Article 234 EC). Questions were asked as to the required degree of likelihood with which the alleged behaviour would effectively lead to restrictions of competition in the market.

Relevance: interpretation of the notion of 'object to restrict'; likelihood of restrictive effect; causal link; should there be a recurring pattern of anti-competitive behaviour or would a one-off meeting suffice to satisfy the criteria of Article 101?

Findings of the Court

On the first question (actual effect on the market required for behaviour with anti-competitive object):

[.....]

27 With regard to the assessment as to whether a concerted practice is anti-competitive, close regard must be paid in particular to the objectives which it is intended to attain and to its economic and legal context (see, to that effect, Joined Cases 96/82 to 102/82, 104/82, 105/82, 108/82 and 110/82 *IAZ International Belgium and Others* v *Commission* [1983] ECR 3369, paragraph 25, and Case C-209/07 *Beef Industry Development Society and Barry Brothers* [2008] ECR I-0000, paragraphs 16 and 21). Moreover, while the intention of the parties is not an essential factor in determining whether a concerted practice is restrictive, there is nothing to prevent the Commission of the European Communities or the competent Community judicature from taking it into account (see, to that effect, *IAZ International Belgium and Others* v *Commission*, paragraphs 23 to 25).

28 As regards the distinction to be drawn between concerted practices having an anti-competitive object and those with anti-competitive effects, it must be borne in mind that an anti-competitive object and anti-competitive effects constitute not cumulative but alternative conditions in determining whether a practice falls within the prohibition in Article 81(1) EC. It has, since the judgment in Case 56/65 *LTM* [1966] ECR 235, 249, been settled case-law that the alternative nature of that requirement, indicated by the conjunction 'or', means that it is necessary, first, to consider the precise purpose of the concerted practice, in the economic context in which it is to be pursued. Where, however, an analysis of the terms of the concerted practice does not reveal the effect on competition to be sufficiently deleterious, its consequences should then be considered and, for it to be caught by the prohibition, it is necessary to find that those factors are present which establish that competition has in fact been prevented or restricted or distorted to an appreciable extent (see, to that effect, *Beef Industry Development Society and Barry Brothers*, paragraph 15).

29Moreover, in deciding whether a concerted practice is prohibited by Article 81(1) EC, there is no need to take account of its actual effects once it is apparent that its object is to prevent, restrict or distort competition within the common market (see, to that effect, Joined Cases 56/64 and 58/64 *Consten and Grundig* v *Commission* [1966] ECR 299, 342; Case C-105/04 P *Nederlandse Federatieve Vereniging voor de Groothandel op Elektrotechnisch Gebied* v *Commission* [2006] ECR I-8725, paragraph 125; and *Beef Industry Development Society and Barry Brothers*, paragraph 16). The distinction between 'infringements by object' and 'infringements by effect' arises from the fact that certain forms of collusion between undertakings can be regarded, by their very nature, as being injurious to the proper functioning of normal competition (*Beef Industry Development Society and Barry Brothers*, paragraph 17).

[.....]

On the **second question** (causal link required between anti-competitive behaviour and consumer prices):

[.....]

32 Second, with regard to the exchange of information between competitors, it should be recalled that the criteria of coordination and cooperation necessary for determining the existence of a concerted practice are to be understood in the light of the notion inherent in the Treaty provisions on competition, according to which each economic operator must determine independently the policy which he intends to adopt on the common market (see Suiker Unie and Others v Commission, paragraph 173; Case 172/80 Züchner [1981] ECR 2021, paragraph 13; Ahlström Osakeyhtiö and Others v Commission, paragraph 63; and Case C-7/95 P Deere v Commission [1998] ECR I-3111, paragraph 86).

33 While it is correct to say that this requirement of independence does not deprive economic operators of the right to adapt themselves intelligently to the existing or anticipated conduct of their competitors, it does, none the less, strictly preclude any direct or indirect contact between such operators by which an undertaking may influence the conduct on the market of its actual or potential competitors or disclose to them its decisions or intentions concerning its own conduct on the market where the object or effect of such contact is to create conditions of competition which do not correspond to the normal conditions of the market in question, regard being had to the nature of the products or services offered, the size and number of the undertakings involved and the volume of that market (see, to that effect, *Suiker Unie and Others* v *Commission*, paragraph 174; *Züchner*, paragraph 14; and *Deere* v *Commission*, paragraph 87).

34 At paragraphs 88 et seq. of *Deere* v *Commission*, the Court therefore held that on a highly concentrated oligopolistic market, such as the market in the main proceedings, the exchange of information was such as to enable traders to know the market positions and strategies of their competitors and thus to impair appreciably the competition which exists between traders.

35 It follows that the exchange of information between competitors is liable to be incompatible with the competition rules if it reduces or removes the degree of uncertainty as to the operation of the market in question, with the result that competition between undertakings is restricted (see *Deere* v *Commission*, paragraph 90, and Case C-194/99 P *Thyssen Stahl* v *Commission* [2003] ECR I-10821, paragraph 81).

36 Third, as to whether a concerted practice may be regarded as having an anti-com-

petitive object even though there is no direct connection between that practice and consumer prices, it is not possible on the basis of the wording of Article 81(1) EC to conclude that only concerted practices which have a direct effect on the prices paid by end users are prohibited.

37 On the contrary, it is apparent from Article 81(1)(a) EC that concerted practices may have an anti-competitive object if they 'directly or indirectly fix purchase or selling prices or any other trading conditions'. In the present case, as the Netherlands Government submitted in its written observations, as far as concerns postpaid subscriptions, the remuneration paid to dealers is evidently a decisive factor in fixing the price to be paid by the end user.

38 In any event, as the Advocate General pointed out at point 58 of her Opinion, Article 81 EC, like the other competition rules of the Treaty, is designed to protect not only the immediate interests of individual competitors or consumers but also to protect the structure of the market and thus competition as such.

39 Therefore, contrary to what the referring court would appear to believe, in order to find that a concerted practice has an anti-competitive object, there does not need to be a direct link between that practice and consumer prices.

[.....]

49 It should be borne in mind at the outset that Article 81 EC, first, produces direct effects in relations between individuals, creating rights for the persons concerned which the national courts must safeguard and, second, is a matter of public policy, essential for the accomplishment of the tasks entrusted to the Community, which must be automatically applied by national courts (see, to that effect, Case C-126/97 *Eco Swiss* [1999] ECR I-3055, paragraphs 36 and 39, and Joined Cases C-295/04 to C-298/04 *Manfredi and Others* [2006] ECR I-6619, paragraphs 31 and 39).

50 In applying Article 81 EC, any interpretation that is provided by the Court is therefore binding on all the national courts and tribunals of the Member States.

51 As regards the presumption of a causal connection formulated by the Court in connection with the interpretation of Article 81(1) EC, it should be pointed out, first, that the Court has held that the concept of a concerted practice, as it derives from the actual terms of that provision, implies, in addition to the participating undertakings concerting with each other, subsequent conduct on the market and a relationship of cause and effect between the two. However, the Court went on to consider that, subject to proof to the contrary, which the economic operators concerned must adduce, it must be presumed that the undertakings taking part in the concerted action and remaining active on the market take account of the information exchanged with their competitors in determining their conduct on that market. That is all the more the case where the undertakings concert together on a regular basis over a long period. Lastly, the Court concluded that such a concerted practice is caught by Article 81(1) EC, even in the absence of anti-competitive effects on the market (see *Hüls*, paragraphs 161 to 163).

52 In those circumstances, it must be held that the presumption of a causal connection stems from Article 81(1) EC, as interpreted by the Court, and it consequently forms an integral part of applicable Community law.

[.....]

On the **third question** (should the concerted practice show a regular pattern or would a one-off meeting suffice – binding character of interpretation by the Court):

[.....]

58 It is evident from paragraph 162 of Hüls and paragraph 121 of Commission v Anic Partecipazioni that the Court found that that presumption applied only where there was concerted action and where the undertaking concerned remained active on the market. The addition of the words 'particularly when they concert together on a regular basis over a long period', far from supporting the argument that there is a presumption of a causal connection only if the undertakings meet regularly, must necessarily be interpreted as meaning that that presumption is more compelling where undertakings have concerted their actions on a regular basis over a long period.
59 Any other interpretation would be tantamount to a claim that an isolated exchange of information between competitors could not in any case lead to concerted action that is in breach of the competition rules laid down in the Treaty. Depending on the structure of the market, the possibility cannot be ruled out that a meeting on a single occasion between competitors, such as that in question in the main proceedings, may, in principle, constitute a sufficient basis for the participating undertakings to concert their market conduct and thus successfully substitute practical cooperation between them for competition and the risks that that entails.
60 As the Netherlands Government correctly pointed out, together with the Advocate General at points 104 and 105 of her Opinion, the number, frequency, and form of meetings between competitors needed to concert their market conduct depend on both the subject-matter of that concerted action and the particular market conditions. If the undertakings concerned establish a cartel with a complex system of concerted actions in relation to a multiplicity of aspects of their market conduct, regular meetings over a long period may be necessary. If, on the other hand, as in the main proceedings, the objective of the exercise is only to concert action on a selective basis in relation to a one-off alteration in market conduct with reference simply to one parameter of competition, a single meeting between competitors may constitute a sufficient basis on which to implement the anti-competitive object which the participating undertakings aim to achieve.
61 In those circumstances, what matters is not so much the number of meetings held between the participating undertakings as whether the meeting or meetings which took place afforded them the opportunity to take account of the information exchanged with their competitors in order to determine their conduct on the market in question and knowingly substitute practical cooperation between them for the risks of competition. Where it can be established that such undertakings successfully concerted with one another and remained active on the market, they may justifiably be called upon to adduce evidence that that concerted action did not have any effect on their conduct on the market in question.

[.....]

Cross-references for this case:

► E. Loozen, 'The application of a more economic approach to restrictions by object: no revolution after all (Case 8/08 *T-Mobile Netherlands*)' in 2010 *ECLR* 4: 146-150.

► M.J. Frese, 'Tightening the Grip on the Application of Article 81 EC Treaty: The European Court of Justice Guards its Province (case note on case 8/08 *T-Mobile*), in *Legal Issues on Economic Integration* 37, no. 1 (2010): 87-104.

G. Notion of agreement and/or concerted practice

Cross-reference for this part:

▸ O. Black, 'Concerted Practices, Joint Action and Reliance', (2003) 24 *ECLR*, 219.

1) Case C-49/92 *Commission v. Anic* [1999] ECR I-4125

See above for facts of the case (I-F-2, p. 28)

Relevance: Undertaking's responsibility as active participant in a large series of infringements committed by several market actors over a long period of time. Standards of proof.

[.....]

79 Secondly, the agreements and concerted practices referred to in Article 85(1) of the Treaty necessarily result from collaboration by several undertakings, who are all co-perpetrators of the infringement but whose participation can take different forms according, in particular, to the characteristics of the market concerned and the position of each undertaking on that market, the aims pursued and the means of implementation chosen or envisaged.

80 However, the mere fact that each undertaking takes part in the infringement in ways particular to it does not suffice to exclude its responsibility for the entire infringement, including conduct put into effect by other participating undertakings but sharing the same anti-competitive object or effect.

81 Thirdly, it must be remembered that Article 85 of the Treaty prohibits agreements between undertakings and decisions by associations of undertakings, including conduct which constitutes the implementation of those agreements or decisions, and concerted practices when they may affect intra-Community trade and have an anti-competitive object or effect. It follows that infringement of that article may result not only from an isolated act but also from a series of acts or from continuous conduct. That interpretation cannot be challenged on the ground that one or several elements of that series of acts or continuous conduct could also constitute in themselves an infringement of Article 85 of the Treaty.

82 In the present case the Court of First Instance held, at paragraph 204 of the judgment, that, because of their identical object, the agreements and concerted practices found to exist, formed part of systems of regular meetings, target-price fixing and quota-fixing, and that those schemes were part of a series of efforts made by the undertakings in question in pursuit of a single economic aim, namely to distort the normal movement of prices. It considered that it would be artificial to split up such continuous conduct, characterized by a single purpose, by treating it as consisting of several separate infringements, when what was involved was a single infringement which progressively manifested itself in both agreements and concerted practices.

83 In such circumstances, the Court of First Instance was entitled to consider that an undertaking that had taken part in such an infringement through conduct of its own which formed an agreement or concerted practice having an anti-competitive object for the purposes of Article 85(1) of the Treaty and which was intended to help bring about the infringement as a whole was also responsible, throughout the entire period of its participation in that infringement, for conduct put into effect by other undertakings in the context of the same infringement. That is the

case where it is established that the undertaking in question was aware of the offending conduct of the other participants or that it could reasonably have foreseen it and that it was prepared to take the risk.

84 Contrary to Anic's submission, such a conclusion is not contrary to the principle that responsibility for such infringements is personal in nature. It fits in with widespread conception in the legal orders of the Member State concerning the attribution of responsibility for infringements committed by several perpetrators according to their participation in the infringement as a whole, which is not regarded in those legal systems as contrary to the personal nature of responsibility.

85 Nor does such an interpretation neglect individual analysis of the evidence adduced against an undertaking, in disregard of the applicable rules of evidence, or infringe the rights of defence of the undertakings involved.

86 Where there is a dispute as to the existence of an infringement of the competition rules, it is incumbent on the Commission to prove the infringements which it has found and to adduce evidence capable of demonstrating to the requisite legal standard the existence of circumstances constituting an infringement (Case C-185/95 P Baustahlgewebe v Commission [1998] ECR I-8417, paragraph 58). In doing this, the Commission must establish in particular all the facts enabling the conclusion to be drawn that an undertaking participated in such an infringement and that it was responsible for the various aspects of it.

87 When, as in the present case, the infringement involves anti-competitive agreements and concerted practices, the Commission must, in particular, show that the undertaking intended to contribute by its own conduct to the common objectives pursued by all the participants and that it was aware of the actual conduct planned or put into effect by other undertakings in pursuit of the same objectives or that it could reasonably have foreseen it and that it was prepared to take the risk.

[.....]

89 Secondly, the undertakings concerned are able to exercise their rights of defence both in regard to the charge that they actually participated in the infringement and in regard to the actual conduct of which other undertakings are accused but which relates to the same infringement. In the case of agreements or concerted practices having anticompetitive object, they will also be able to exercise those rights in respect of the existence of a common objective, their intention to contribute to the infringement as a whole by their own conduct and their knowledge of the conduct of other participants or its foreseeability and the acceptance of the related risk.

90 The fact that an undertaking has not taken part in all aspects of an anti-competitive scheme or that it played only a minor role in the aspects in which it did participate must be taken into consideration when the gravity of the infringement is assessed and if and when it comes to determining the fine.

[...]

Case cross-reference:

Case T-36/05 *Coats Holdings and Coats v. Commission* [2007] ECR II-110 (summary); appeal pending C-468/07.

2) Case 48/69 *ICI v. Commission (Dyestuffs)* [1972] ECR 619

ICI and others had participated in a price cartel as a result of which the prices of dyestuffs had almost simultaneously increased by uniform percentages throughout the Community. The undertakings that were party to this cartel regularly met in Geneva (i.e., outside the

EC) and had agreed that each member would take its turn in leading a new cycle of price increases. The Commission found that this behaviour amounted to a concerted practice which infringed Article 101 TFEU. ICI challenged the Commission's decision before the ECJ.

Relevance: explanation of notion of 'concerted practice' (parallel conduct).

[.....]

The concept of a concerted practice

64 Article 85 draws a distinction between the concept of "concerted practices" and that of "agreements between undertakings" or of "decisions by associations of undertakings"; the object is to bring within the prohibition of that Article a form of coordination between undertakings which, without having reached the stage where an agreement properly so-called has been concluded, knowingly substitutes practical cooperation between them for the risks of competition.
65 By its very nature, then, a concerted practice does not have all the elements of a contract but may inter alia arise out of coordination which becomes apparent from the behaviour of the participants.
66 Although parallel behaviour may not by itself be identified with a concerted practice, it may however amount to strong evidence of such a practice if it leads to conditions of competition which do not correspond to the normal conditions of the market, having regard to the nature of the products, the size and number of the undertakings, and the volume of the said market.
67 This is especially the case if the parallel conduct is such as to enable those concerned to attempt to stabilize prices at a level different from that to which competition would have led, and to consolidate established positions to the detriment of effective freedom of movement of the products in the Common Market and of the freedom of consumers to choose their suppliers.
68 Therefore the question whether there was a concerted action in this case can only be correctly determined if the evidence upon which the contested decision is based is considered, not in isolation, but as a whole, account being taken of the specific features of the market in the products in question.

[.....]

3) Joined Cases 40-48, 50, 54-56, 111, 113 & 114/73 *European Sugar Industry* [1975] ECR 1663

The Commission had found that various principal sugar producing undertakings had infringed either Article 101 or Article 102 or both Articles. The infringements ranged from concerted practices to unlawful economic pressure on other companies to restrict either the export or import of sugar. The undertakings concerned tried to annul the Commission decision. Their appeal was partly successful.

Relevance: explanation of notion of 'concerted practice'.

[.....]

173 The criteria of coordination and cooperation laid down by the case-law of the Court, which in no way require the working out of

an actual plan, must be understood in the light of the concept inherent in the provisions of the Treaty relating to competition that each economic operator must determine independently the policy which he intends to adopt on the Common Market including the choice of the persons and undertakings to which he makes offers or sells.
174 Although it is correct to say that this requirement of independence does not deprive economic operators of the right to adapt themselves intelligently to the existing and anticipated conduct of their competitors, it does however strictly preclude any direct or indirect contact between such operators, the object or effect whereof is either to influence the conduct on the market of an actual or potential competitor or to disclose to such a competitor the course of conduct which they themselves have decided to adopt or contemplate adopting on the market.

[.....]

4) Case T-8/89 *DSM v. Commission (Polypropylene)* [1991] ECR II-1833

The case was brought before the CFI by DSM, a Dutch undertaking that was active on the polypropylene market. Together with 14 other undertakings, it had been fined by the Commission for infringement of Article 101 TFEU. The polypropylene producers had secretly held meetings in which they discussed, and when necessary adjusted, their commercial policies (mainly the setting of target prices). Moreover, they had tried to compartmentalize the market in question; each undertaking had been allotted a certain sales quota or sales target.

Relevance: example of a concerted practice.

[.....]

2. Application of Article 85(1) of the EEC Treaty
A. Legal characterization

(a) The contested decision

201 According to the Decision (point 81, first paragraph), the whole complex of schemes and arrangements decided on in the context of a system of regular and institutionalized meetings constituted a single continuing "agreement" within the meaning of Article 85(1).
202 In the present case, the producers, by subscribing to a common plan to regulate prices and supply on the polypropylene market, participated in an overall framework agreement which was manifested in a series of more detailed sub-agreements worked out from time to time (Decision, point 81, third paragraph).
203 The Decision (point 82, first paragraph) goes on to state that in the detailed working out of the overall plan express agreement was reached in many areas, such as individual price initiatives and annual quota schemes. In some cases the producers may not have reached a consensus on a definitive scheme, such as quotas for 1981 and 1982. However, their adoption of stopgap measures including exchange of information and the monitoring of actual monthly sales against achievements in some previous reference period not only involved an express agreement to set up and operate such measures but also indicated an implied agreement to maintain as far as possible the respective positions of the producers.

[.....]

(c) Assessment by the Court

225 Contrary to the applicant's assertions, the Commission characterized each factual element found against the applicant as either an agreement or a concerted practice for the purposes of Article 85(1) of the EEC Treaty. It is apparent from the second paragraph of point 80, the third paragraph of point 81 and the first paragraph of point 82 of the Decision, read together, that the Commission characterized each of those different elements primarily as an "agreement".
226 It is likewise apparent from the second and third paragraphs of point 86, the third paragraph of point 87 and point 88 of the Decision, read together, that the Commission in the alternative characterized the elements of the infringement as "concerted practices" where those elements either did not enable the conclusion to be drawn that the parties had reached agreement in advance on a common plan defining their action on the market but had adopted or adhered to collusive devices which facilitated the coordination of their commercial behaviour, or did not, owing to the complexity of the cartel, make it possible to establish that some producers had
expressed their definite assent to a particular course of action agreed by the
others, although they had indicated their general support for the scheme in question and conducted themselves accordingly.
The Decision thus concludes that in certain respects the continuing cooperation and collusion of the producers in the implementation of an overall agreement may display the characteristics of a concerted practice.
227 Since it is clear from the case-law of the Court of Justice that in order for there to be an agreement within the meaning of Article 85(1) of the EEC Treaty it is sufficient that the undertakings in question should have expressed their joint intention to conduct themselves on the market in a specific way (see the judgment in Case 41/69 ACF Chemiefarma v Commission [1970] ECR 661, paragraph 112, and the judgment in Joined Cases 209 to 215 and 218/78 Van Landewyck v Commission [1980] ECR 3125, paragraph 86), this Court holds that the Commission was entitled to treat the common intentions existing between the applicant and the other polypropylene producers, which the Commission has proved to the requisite legal standard and which related to floor prices in 1977, price initiatives, measures designed to facilitate the implementation of the price initiatives, sales volume targets for the years 1979 and 1980 and the first half of 1983 and measures for restricting monthly sales by reference to a previous period for 1981 and 1982, as agreements within the meaning of Article 85(1) of the EEC Treaty.

[.....]

229 For a definition of the concept of concerted practice, reference must be made to the case-law of the Court of Justice, which shows that the criteria of coordination and cooperation previously laid down by that Court must be understood in the light of the concept inherent in the competition provisions of the EEC Treaty according to which each economic operator must determine independently the policy which he intends to adopt on the Common Market. Although this requirement of independence does not deprive economic operators of the right to adapt themselves intelligently to the existing and anticipated conduct of their competitors, it does, however, strictly preclude any direct or indirect contact between such operators the object or effect whereof is either to influence the conduct on the market of an actual or potential competitor or to disclose to such a competitor the course of conduct which they themselves have decided to adopt or contemplate adopting on the market (judgment in Joined Cases 40 to 48, 50, 54 to 56,

111, 113 and 114/73 Suiker Unie and Others v Commission, cited above, paragraphs 173 and 174).

230 In the present case, the applicant participated in meetings concerning the fixing of price and sales volume targets during which information was exchanged between competitors about the prices they wished to see charged on the market, the prices they intended to charge, their profitability thresholds, the sales volume restrictions they judged to be necessary, their sales figures or the identity of their customers. Through its participation in those meetings, it took part, together with its competitors, in concerted action the purpose of which was to influence their conduct on the market and to disclose to each other the course of conduct which each of the producers itself contemplated adopting on the market.

231 Accordingly, not only did the applicant pursue the aim of eliminating in advance uncertainty about the future conduct of its competitors but also, in determining the policy which it intended to follow on the market, it could not fail to take account, directly or indirectly, of the information obtained during the course of those meetings. Similarly, in determining the policy which they intended to follow, its competitors were bound to take into account, directly or indirectly, the information disclosed to them by the applicant about the course of conduct which the applicant itself had decided upon or which it contemplated adopting on the market.

232 The Commission was therefore justified, in the alternative, having regard to their purpose, in categorizing the regular meetings of polypropylene producers in which the applicant participated between December 1977 and September 1983 as concerted practices within the meaning of Article 85(1) of the EEC Treaty.

[.....]

Case cross-reference:

▸ C-5/93 P *DSM NV v. Commission* [1999] ECR I-4695, appeal dismissed.

5) Case T-25/95 *Cimenteries CBR v. Commission* [2002] ECR II-491 (summary of judgment)

In the following judgment, the CFI gave some guidance as to when a certain behaviour does or does not amount to a concerted practice in the sense of Article 101 TFEU. The dispute concerned various (white and grey) cement producers that had concerted to compartmentalize the European cement market, even though Article 101 clearly prohibits market sharing.

Relevance: example of a concerted practice.

[.....]

15. Where an undertaking or association of undertakings has participated, even without playing an active role, in one or more meetings at which a concurrence of wills emerged or was confirmed on the principle of anti-competitive conduct and by virtue of its presence has subscribed to or at least given the impression to the other participants that it was subscribing to the subject-matter of the anti-competitive agreement concluded and subsequently confirmed at those meetings, it must be considered to have participated in

that agreement, unless it proves that it openly distanced itself from the unlawful collusion or informed the other participants that it intended to take part in those meetings with different objects in mind.
In the absence of such proof that it distanced itself, the fact that the undertaking or association of undertakings does not abide by the outcome of those meetings is not such as to relieve it of full responsibility for the fact that it participated in the agreement or concerted practice.

[.....]

17. There is no principle of Community law which precludes the Commission from relying on a single document in order to conclude that Article 85(1) of the Treaty (now Article 81(1) EC) has been infringed, provided that its evidential value is undoubted and that the document by itself definitely attests to the existence of the infringement in question. In order to assess the evidential value of a document, regard should be had first and foremost to the credibility of the account it contains. Regard should be had in particular to the person from whom the document originates, the circumstances in which it came into being, the person to whom it was addressed and whether, on its face, the document appears sound and reliable.
18. The concept of concerted practice implies the existence of reciprocal contacts. That condition of reciprocity is satisfied where the disclosure by one competitor to another of future intentions or conduct on the market has been sought or, at the very least, accepted by the other competitor. It is the same where a meeting in the course of which a party has been informed by its competitor of its intentions or future conduct was initiated by that party and it is apparent from its record of that meeting that no reservations or objections were expressed when the competitor informed it of its intentions. In those circumstances, the attitude of that party at the meeting cannot be reduced to the purely passive role of a recipient of the information which its competitor unilaterally decided to pass on to it, without any request by it.
19. Any direct or indirect contact between economic operators of such a nature as to disclose to a competitor the course of conduct which they themselves have decided to adopt or contemplate adopting on the market constitutes a concerted practice prohibited by Article 85(1) of the Treaty (now Article 81(1) EC) where the object or effect of such contact is to create conditions of competition which do not correspond to the normal conditions of the market in question. In order to prove that there has been a concerted practice, it is not therefore necessary to show that a trader has formally undertaken, in respect of one or several others, to adopt a particular course of conduct or that the competitors have colluded over their future conduct on the market. It is sufficient that, by its statement of intention, the trader eliminated or, at the very least, substantially reduced uncertainty as to the conduct to expect of it on the market.
20. As is clear from the very terms of Article 85(1) of the Treaty (now Article 81(1) EC), a concerted practice implies, besides undertakings concerting together, conduct on the market pursuant to those collusive practices, and a relationship of cause and effect between the two. Subject to proof to the contrary, which the parties concerned must adduce, it must be presumed that the concerted action by which those parties sought to share the market influenced their conduct on that market.
21. Undertakings cannot justify infringement of the rules on competition by claiming that they were forced into it by the conduct of other traders. Nor can the fact that the latter have received public aid justify the adoption

of private anti-competitive initiatives, even if the aid in question was unlawful. While undertakings have the right not only to notify the competent authorities (including the Commission itself) of any infringements of national or Community provisions, but also to make a joint approach for this purpose, which necessarily presupposes the ability to hold preparatory discussions amongst themselves, they are not entitled to take the law into their own hands by substituting themselves for the authorities with competence to penalise any infringements of national and/or Community law and by preventing, through measures adopted on their own initiative, the movement of products within the internal market.

The fact that the Commission may have been lax in connection with the file on the above public aid and might thus have failed to fulfil certain of its obligations under Article 155 of the EC Treaty (now Article 211 EC) cannot justify any infringements of Community law.

22. The concept of a concerted practice refers to a form of coordination between undertakings which, without having been taken to the stage where an agreement properly so-called has been concluded, knowingly substitutes practical cooperation between them for the risks of competition. The criteria of coordination and cooperation used to define that term must be understood in the light of the concept inherent in the provisions of the Treaty relating to competition, according to which each economic operator must determine independently the policy which it intends to adopt on the Common Market. This requirement of independence strictly precludes any direct or indirect contact between traders, the object or effect of which is to create conditions of competition which do not correspond to the normal conditions of the market in question.

23. The mere fact that a producer in a Member State knew that the purpose of the purchases made from it by other European producers was to halt or, at least, reduce its direct sales on Western European markets does not allow the conclusion that it was party to an agreement or concerted practice contrary to Article 85(1) of the Treaty (now Article 81(1) EC). Such knowledge can be deemed to reveal unlawful conduct only if it is established that it was accompanied by the adherence of that producer to the object pursued by the above European producers through the purchases concerned. In as much as the object in question was clearly against the interests of the producer concerned, only evidence of a commitment by that producer that, in return for the purchases under consideration, it would halt or reduce its direct sales on the European markets could be deemed to constitute its adherence to that object.

[.....]

Case cross-reference:

- ▸ Joined Cases C-204, 205, 211, 213, 217 & 219/00 *Cement* [2004] ECR I-123, the ECJ set aside part of the CFI judgment and changed the fine.
- ▸ Case T-120/04 *Peróxidos Orgánicos SA v. Commission* [2006] ECR II-4441.
- ▸ Case T-99/04 *AC-Treuhand AG v. Commission* [2008] ECR II-1501.

6) Case T-168/01 *GlaxoSmithKline v. Commission* [2006] ECR II-2969

This is the case in the first instance before the GC. See for the facts and the final outcome on appeal of this case before the ECJ in the Joined Cases C-501/06 P, C-513/06 P, C-515/06 P and C-519/06 P: I-L-1, p. 59.

Relevance: the notion of agreement, difference between an independent will and a concurrent will.

[.....]

Findings of the Court

65 GSK's arguments lead the Court to examine, in the first place, whether GW and the Spanish wholesalers did manifest an independent will by reference to the Spanish regulations on the wholesale price of medicines reimbursed by the Spanish sickness insurance scheme and therefore whether the conduct with which the Commission was faced was indeed conduct on the part of undertakings and not conduct on the part of the State. Its arguments also lead the Court to examine, in the second place, should it prove necessary to do so, whether GW and those wholesalers manifested a concurrent will, and therefore whether the Commission was indeed faced with bilateral conduct and not with unilateral conduct.

Independence of wills

66 Article 81(1) EC applies only to anti-competitive conduct engaged in by undertakings on their own initiative (Case 267/86 Van Eycke [1988] ECR 4769, paragraph 16; Joined Cases C-359/95 P and C-379/95 P Commission and France v Ladbroke Racing [1997] ECR I-6265, paragraph 33; and Case C-198/01 CIF [2003] ECR I-8055, paragraph 45).
67 Where, in order to decide whether that provision is applicable, it is necessary first to evaluate the possible impact of national regulations, it must be determined whether those regulations leave any scope for competition that might be prevented, restricted or distorted by autonomous conduct on the part of undertakings (Commission and France v Ladbroke Racing, paragraph 66 above, paragraphs 32 and 35, and CIF, paragraph 66 above, paragraph 66).
68 Where it is clear, following that evaluation, that the regulations in question require that undertakings engage in anti-competitive conduct, or eliminate any possibility of competitive activity on their part, Article 81(1) EC does not apply (Commission and France v Ladbroke Racing, paragraph 66 above, paragraph 33, and CIF, paragraph 66 above, paragraph 67).
69 Where, on the other hand, it is clear that those regulations do leave scope for competition that might be prevented, restricted or distorted by autonomous conduct on the part of undertakings, Article 81(1) EC does apply (Commission and France v Ladbroke Racing, paragraph 66 above, paragraph 34, and CIF, paragraph 66 above, paragraph 56).
70 The possibility of excluding particular anti-competitive conduct from the scope of that provision on the ground that it is required by national regulations has been applied restrictively by the Community Courts (CIF, paragraph 66 above, paragraph 67, and Case T-513/93 Consiglio Nazionale degli Spedizionieri Doganali v Commission [2000] ECR II-1807, paragraph 60).

[...]

Concurrence of wills

75 Article 81(1) EC applies only to bilateral or multilateral conduct on the part of undertakings (Case C-49/92 P Commission v Anic Partecipazioni [1999] ECR I-4125, paragraphs 79 and 112) and such conduct may take the

form of agreements, concerted practices or decisions of associations.

76 In order for there to be an agreement, it is sufficient that at least two undertakings have expressed their joint intention to conduct themselves on the market in a specific way (Case 41/69 ACF Chemiefarma v Commission [1970] ECR 661, paragraph 112; Case C-277/87 Sandoz Prodotti Farmaceutici v Commission [1990] ECR I-45, summary publication, paragraph 13; and Bayer v Commission, paragraph 47 above, paragraphs 67 and 173).

77 While it is therefore essential that the decisions in which the Commission applies Article 81(1) EC show the existence of a joint intention to act on the market in a specific way, those decisions, contrary to GSK's contention, are not required to establish the existence of a joint intention to pursue an anti-competitive aim.

[...]

79 Clearly, that conclusion is confirmed by the case-file, which shows, first of all, that GW adopted General Sales Conditions providing for a system of differentiated prices. Then, GW sent those General Sales Conditions to 89 wholesalers with whom it had commercial relations in Spain. On that occasion, it requested them, emphasising the importance which it ascribed to that request, to return a signed copy '[a]s proof of [their] acceptance', within a mandatory period. Those factual elements reveal the intention expressed by GW to seek the Spanish wholesalers' agreement to its General Sales Conditions and, therefore, to make them an offer concerning those conditions. Last, 75 of the 89 wholesalers to whom that offer was made did as requested by GW, signing the General Sales Conditions and returning them to GW within the prescribed period. Those factual elements reveal the intention expressed by those wholesalers to accept GW's offer and thus to form an agreement with GW, as GSK acknowledged at the hearing.

[.....]

Case cross-reference:

▸ Case T-41/96 *Bayer AG v. Commission (Adalat)*, [2002] ECR II-3383, VI-F-1 (page 255) on unilateral behaviour.

▸ O. Black, 'Agreement: concurrence of wills, or offer and acceptance?', (2008) 4 *European Competition Journal* 103-125.

H. Appreciable effect

Cross-references for this part:

▸ Notice on 'agreements of minor importance', [2001] OJ C 368/13.

▸ M. Laurila, 'De Minimis Doctrine in EEC Competition Law: Agreements of Minor Importance', (1993) 14 *ECLR*, 97.

1) Case 5/69 *Völk v. Vervaecke* [1969] ECR 295

Völk, producer of washing-machines, and Vervaecke, distributor, had concluded an exclusive distribution contract in which Vervaecke was given an exclusive sales sector in Belgium and Luxembourg. According to Völk, the latter did not perform his side of the contract, and he started proceedings in Germany. The dispute centred around the ques-

tion of whether this particular distribution contract infringed Article 101, when it turned out that the exclusive sales sector of Vervaecke was, in the words of Völk, extremely small. The ECJ answered the question of whether the proportion of the market acquired by Völk should also be taken into consideration.

Relevance: notion of 'appreciable effect'.

[.....]

2/4 Although the Court is not entitled within the framework of sub-paragraph (a) of the first paragraph of Article 177 to apply the Treaty to a particular case, it may nevertheless derive from the wording of the decision referring the matter the questions which relate exclusively to the interpretation of the Treaty. The question raised relates to agreements which are characterized by the fact that a producer who has granted a distributor the exclusive right of sale of his products for certain countries in the Common Market has undertaken to protect the distributor against deliveries which might be made in those countries by third parties and has obtained from the distributor an undertaking not to sell competing products. The question is thus reduced to whether, in deciding whether such agreements fall within the prohibition set out in Article 85(1) of the Treaty, regard must be had to the proportion of the market which the grantor controls or endeavours to obtain in the territory ceded.

5/7 If an agreement is to be capable of affecting trade between Member States it must be possible to foresee with a sufficient degree of probability on the basis of a set of objective factors of law or of fact that the agreement in question may have an influence, direct or indirect, actual or potential, on the pattern of trade between Member States in such a way that it might hinder the attainment of the objectives of a single market between states. Moreover the prohibition in Article 85(1) is applicable only if the agreement in question also has as its object or effect the prevention, restriction or distortion of competition within the Common Market. Those conditions must be understood by reference to the actual circumstances of the agreement. Consequently an agreement falls outside the prohibition in Article 85 when it has only an insignificant effect on the markets, taking into account the weak position which the persons concerned have on the market of the product in question. Thus an exclusive dealing agreement, even with absolute territorial protection, may, having regard to the weak position of the persons concerned on the market in the products in question in the area covered by the absolute protection, escape the prohibition laid down in Article 85(1).

[.....]

2) Case C-234/89 *Delimitis* [1991] ECR I-935

Delimitis, a publican, had rented a pub from Henninger Bräu, a German brewery. According to the contract, Delimitis was to purchase a certain minimum quantity of beer from the brewery, but he could also obtain beer and soft drinks elsewhere. When the contract was terminated, Delimitis still owed Henninger a sum of money, which included a penalty because he had failed to purchase the agreed amount of beer. Henninger deducted the debt from the deposit paid by Delimitis. Delimitis did not agree with this and went to court, arguing that the agreement was void on the basis of Article 101 anyway.

Relevance: notion of 'appreciable effect'.

[.....]

The compatibility with Article 85(1) of a beer supply agreement containing an access clause

28 A beer supply agreement containing an access clause differs from the other beer supply agreements normally entered into inasmuch as it authorizes the reseller to purchase beer from other Member States. Such access mitigates, in favour of the beers of other Member States, the scope of the prohibition on competition which in a classic beer supply agreement is coupled with the exclusive purchasing obligation. The scope of the access clause must be assessed in the light of its wording and its economic and legal context.
29 As far as its wording is concerned, it should be noted that the clause affords only very limited access if it is regarded as solely authorizing the reseller himself to purchase competing beers in other Member States. However, the degree of access is greater if it also permits the reseller to sell beers imported from other Member States by other undertakings.
30 As far as its economic and legal context is concerned, it should be pointed out that where, as in this case, one of the other clauses stipulates that a minimum quantity of the beers envisaged in the agreement must be purchased, it is necessary to examine what that quantity represents in relation to the sales of beer normally achieved in the public house in question. If it appears that the stipulated quantity is relatively large, the access clause ceases to have any economic significance and the prohibition on selling competing beers regains its full force, particularly when under the agreement the obligation to purchase minimum quantities is backed by penalties.
31 If the interpretation of the wording of the access clause or an examination of the specific effect of the contractual clauses as a whole in their economic and legal context shows that the limitation on the scope of the prohibition on competition is merely hypothetical or without economic significance, the agreement in question must be treated in the same way as a classic beer supply agreement. Accordingly, it must be assessed under Article 85(1) of the Treaty in the same way as beer supply agreements in general.
32 The position is different where the access clause gives a national or foreign supplier of beers from other Member States a real possibility of supplying the sales outlet in question. An agreement containing such a clause is not in principle capable of affecting trade between Member States within the meaning of Article 85(1), with the result that it escapes the prohibition laid down in that provision.
33 The reply to the Oberlandesgericht's fourth question should therefore be that a beer supply agreement which permits the reseller to buy beer from other Member States is not such as to affect trade between States provided that the permission corresponds to a real possibility for a national or foreign supplier to supply the reseller with beers from other Member States.

[.....]

Case cross-reference:

▸ Case C-215-216/96 *Bagnasco* [1999] ECR I-161 (see I-E-3).

I. No *per se* rule/no rule of reason

Cross-references for this part:

► Joined Cases T-374, 375, 384 & 388/94 *European Night Services v. Commission* [1998] ECR II-3141 (see I-A-3).

► P. Manzini. 'The European Rule of Reason – Crossing the Sea of Doubt', (2002) 23 *ECLR*, 392.

► R. Wesseling, 'The Rule of Reason and Competition Law: Various rules, Various reasons' in 'The Rule of Reason – rethinking another Classic of EC Legal Doctrine' (Dr. Annette Schrauwen ed.), Europa Law Publishing Groningen 2005.

In the following two judgments, the Courts make clear that under Article 101(1) there is no question of infringements per se. Each alleged infringement should be analyzed on its own merits.

1) Case 56/65 *Société La Technique Minière v. Maschinenbau Ulm* [1966, English special edition] ECR 235

The first dispute arose when a contract concluded between Société La Technique Minière (LTM), a French undertaking, and Maschinenbau Ulm (MBU), a German company, was not fully executed. The terms of the contract made clear that MBU gave LTM the exclusive right of sale for graders in France. The French company was, however, not content with the quality of the graders. Still, the Tribunal de Commerce de la Seine ordered LTM to fulfil its contractual obligations. LTM appealed, claiming that the agreement was void because it infringed Article 101.

Relevance: no proof of existence *per se* rule.

[.....]

In order to be prohibited as being incompatible with the Common Market under Article 85(1) of the Treaty, an agreement between undertakings must fulfil certain conditions depending less on the legal nature of the agreement than on its effects on 'trade between Member States' and its effects on 'competition'.
Thus as Article 85(1) is based on an assessment of the effects of an agreement from two angles of economic evaluation, it cannot be interpreted as introducing any kind of advance judgment with regard to a category of agreements determined by their legal nature. Therefore an agreement whereby a producer entrusts the sale of his products in a given area to a sole distributor cannot automatically fall under the prohibition in Article 85 (1). But such an agreement may contain the elements set out in that provision, by reason of a particular factual situation or of the severity of the clauses protecting the exclusive dealership.

[.....]

2) Case T-112/99 *Métropole Télévision II* [2001] ECR II-2459

In the judgment below, the CFI emphasized that European competition law does not provide for a rule of reason. The dispute concerned a number of clauses in the agreements that set up TPS (Télévision par satellite). TPS, which was created by six major French (television, telecommunications and/or cable distribution) companies, including Métropole Télévision (M6), was to provide, by satellite and against payment, television programmes and services for French-speaking Europeans. The clauses at issue were a non-competition clause (the parties to the agreement should not compete with TPS), a clause relating to special-interest channels (to obtain the programmes it required TPS was given priority and refusal rights with regard to special-interest channels) and an exclusivity clause (only TPS could broadcast general-interest channels). Pursuant to Article 101 (3) TFEU, the Commission decided to exempt the last two clauses for a period of three years; for the non-competition clause, it issued a negative clearance also for three years. TPS' shareholders did not agree with these limitations and appealed.

Relevance: Article 101 (1) does not imply a rule of reason *"American style"*.

[.....]

-Misapplication of Article 85(1) of the Treaty (failure to apply rule of reason)

[.....]

Findings of the Court

72 According to the applicants, as a consequence of the existence of a rule of reason in Community competition law, when Article 85(1) of the Treaty is applied it is necessary to weigh the pro and anti-competitive effects of an agreement in order to determine whether it is caught by the prohibition laid down in that Article. It should, however, be observed, first of all, that contrary to the applicants' assertions the existence of such a rule has not, as such, been confirmed by the Community Courts. Quite to the contrary, in various judgments the Court of Justice and the Court of First Instance have been at pains to indicate that the existence of a rule of reason in Community competition law is doubtful (see Case C-235/92 P Montecatini v Commission [1999] ECR I-4539, paragraph 133 ('... even if the rule of reason did have a place in the context of Article 85(1) of the Treaty'), and Case T-14/89 Montedipe v Commission [1992] ECR II-1155, paragraph 265, and in Case T-148/89 Tréfilunion v Commission [1995] ECR II-1063, paragraph 109).

73 Next, it must be observed that an interpretation of Article 85(1) of the Treaty, in the form suggested by the applicants, is difficult to reconcile with the rules prescribed by that provision.

74 Article 85 of the Treaty expressly provides, in its third paragraph, for the possibility of exempting agreements that restrict competition where they satisfy a number of conditions, in particular where they are indispensable to the attainment of certain objectives and do not afford undertakings the possibility of eliminating competition in respect of a substantial part of the products in question. It is only in the precise framework of that provision that the pro and anti-competi-

tive aspects of a restriction may be weighed (see, to that effect, Case 161/84 Pronuptia [1986] ECR 353, paragraph 24, and Case T-17/93 Matra Hachette v Commission [1994] ECR II-595, paragraph 48, and European Night Services and Others v Commission, cited in paragraph 34 above, paragraph 136). Article 85(3) of the Treaty would lose much of its effectiveness if such an examination had to be carried out already under Article 85(1) of the Treaty.

75 It is true that in a number of judgments the Court of Justice and the Court of First Instance have favoured a more flexible interpretation of the prohibition laid down in Article 85(1) of the Treaty (see, in particular, Société Technique Minière and Oude Luttikhuis and Others, cited in paragraph 70 above, Nungesser and Eisele v Commission and Coditel and Others, cited in paragraph 68 above, Pronuptia, cited in paragraph 74 above, and European Night Services and Others v Commission, cited in paragraph 34 above, as well as the judgment in Case C-250/92 DLG [1994] ECR I-5641, paragraphs 31 to 35).

76 Those judgments cannot, however, be interpreted as establishing the existence of a rule of reason in Community competition law. They are, rather, part of a broader trend in the case-law according to which it is not necessary to hold, wholly abstractly and without drawing any distinction, that any agreement restricting the freedom of action of one or more of the parties is necessarily caught by the prohibition laid down in Article 85(1) of the Treaty. In assessing the applicability of Article 85(1) to an agreement, account should be taken of the actual conditions in which it functions, in particular the economic context in which the undertakings operate, the products or services covered by the agreement and the actual structure of the market concerned (see, in particular, European Night Services and Others v Commission, cited in paragraph 34 above, paragraph 136, Oude Luttikhuis, cited in paragraph 70 above, paragraph 10, and VGB and Others v Commission, cited in paragraph 70 above, paragraph 140, as well as the judgment in Case C-234/89 Delimitis [1991] ECR I-935, paragraph 31).

77 That interpretation, while observing the substantive scheme of Article 85 of the Treaty and, in particular, preserving the effectiveness of Article 85(3), makes it possible to prevent the prohibition in Article 85(1) from extending wholly abstractly and without distinction to all agreements whose effect is to restrict the freedom of action of one or more of the parties. It must, however, be emphasised that such an approach does not mean that it is necessary to weigh the pro and anti-competitive effects of an agreement when determining whether the prohibition laid down in Article 85(1) of the Treaty applies.

[.....]

Case cross-references:

► Case 5/69 *Völk v. Vervaecke* [1969] ECR 295 (see I-H-1).

► P. Nicolaides, 'An Essay on Economics and Competition Law of the European Community', (2000) 27 *LIEI*, 7.

J. Inherent restrictions

Cross-reference for this part:

▸ Commission Communication - Services of general interest in Europe [2001] OJ C 17/4.

Out of the aforementioned cases relating to the per se rule developed the so-called doctrine of the inherent restrictions. The following three cases give an idea of how this doctrine works.

1) Case 258/78 *Nungesser v. Commission (Maize Seed)* [1982] ECR 2015

This dispute concerned an exclusive licence of breeders' rights. The French research institute INRA had developed a new variety of hybrid maize seeds. Nungesser, a German undertaking, had been given the exclusive right to market INRA's seeds in Germany which meant that Nungesser was protected against competition from both INRA and other undertakings. The issue was whether this protection ran afoul of the prohibition of Article 101 (1).

Relevance: example of an inherent restriction.

[.....]

56 The exclusive licence which forms the subject-matter of the contested decision concerns the cultivation and marketing of hybrid maize seeds which were developed by INRA after years of research and experimentation and were unknown to German farmers at the time when the cooperation between INRA and the applicants was taking shape. For that reason the concern shown by the interveners as regards the protection of new technology is justified.
57 In fact, in the case of a licence of breeders' rights over hybrid maize seeds newly developed in one Member State, an undertaking established in another Member State which was not certain that it would not encounter competition from other licensees for the territory granted to it, or from the owner of the right himself, might be deterred from accepting the risk of cultivating and marketing that product; such a result would be damaging to the dissemination of a new technology and would prejudice competition in the Community between the new product and similar existing products.
58 Having regard to the specific nature of the products in question, the Court concludes that, in a case such as the present, the grant of an open exclusive licence, that is to say a licence which does not affect the position of third parties such as parallel importers and licensees for other territories, is not in itself incompatible with article 85 (1) of the Treaty.

[.....]

2) Case C-250/92 *Gøttrup-Klim v. DLG* [1994] ECR I-5641

The Danish co-operative association distributing farm supplies, a co-operative purchasing association, had amended its statute in such a way that so-called B-members (local farmers' associations), who also participated in competing co-operatives, were expelled. Gøttrup Klim and 36 other B-members were, by reason of these new restrictive provisions, excluded from the Cooperative. They tried to annul the new restrictive provisions in court, arguing that these were prohibited by Article 101 (1).

Relevance: example of an inherent restriction.

[.....]

Restriction of competition

30 A cooperative purchasing association is a voluntary association of persons established in order to pursue common commercial objectives.
31 The compatibility of the statutes of such an association with the Community rules on competition cannot be assessed in the abstract. It will depend on the particular clauses in the statutes and the economic conditions prevailing on the markets concerned.
32 In a market where product prices vary according to the volume of orders, the activities of cooperative purchasing associations may, depending on the size of their membership, constitute a significant counterweight to the contractual power of large producers and make way for more effective competition.
33 Where some members of two competing cooperative purchasing associations belong to both at the same time, the result is to make each association less capable of pursuing its objectives for the benefit of the rest of its members, especially where the members concerned, as in the case in point, are themselves cooperative associations with a large number of individual members.
34 It follows that such dual membership would jeopardize both the proper functioning of the cooperative and its contractual power in relation to producers. Prohibition of dual membership does not, therefore, necessarily constitute a restriction of competition within the meaning of Article 85(1) of the Treaty and may even have beneficial effects on competition.
35 Nevertheless, a provision in the statutes of a cooperative purchasing association, restricting the opportunity for members to join other types of competing cooperatives and thus discouraging them from obtaining supplies elsewhere, may have adverse effects on competition. So, in order to escape the prohibition laid down in Article 85(1) of the Treaty, the restrictions imposed on members by the statutes of cooperative purchasing associations must be limited to what is necessary to ensure that the cooperative functions properly and maintains its contractual power in relation to producers.

[.....]

3) Joined Cases C-115-117/97 *Brentjens* [1999] ECR I-6025

In this dispute, pension arrangements were at issue. Here, supplementary pensions were in the hands of the Building Materials Trade Fund (referred to as 'the Fund' in the judgment), affiliation to which had been made obligatory by Dutch law. Brentjens wanted to be exempted from this affiliation (and the accompanying financial contributions thereto) since he preferred the, in his eyes superior, pension arrangements he himself had made for his employees. When the exemption was not granted, Brentjens started proceedings, claiming that the compulsory affiliation infringed the Treaty.

Relevance: example of an inherent restriction.

[.....]

51 Next, it is important to bear in mind that, under Article 3(g) and (i) of the EC Treaty (now, after amendment, Article 3(1)(g) and (j) EC), the activities of the Community are to include not only a 'system ensuring that competition in the internal market is not distorted' but also 'a policy in the social sphere'. Article 2 of the EC Treaty (now, after amendment, Article 2 EC) provides that a particular task of the Community is 'to promote throughout the Community a harmonious and balanced development of economic activities' and 'a high level of employment and of social protection'.
52 In that connection, Article 118 of the EC Treaty (Articles 117 to 120 of the EC Treaty have been replaced by Articles 136 EC to 143 EC) provides that the Commission is to promote close cooperation between Member States in the social field, particularly in matters relating to the right of association and collective bargaining between employers and workers.
53 Article 118b of the EC Treaty (Articles 117 to 120 of the EC Treaty having been replaced by Articles 136 EC to 143 EC) adds that the Commission is to endeavour to develop the dialogue between management and labour at European level which could, if the two sides consider it desirable, lead to relations based on agreement.
54 Moreover, Article 1 of the Agreement on social policy (OJ 1992 C 191, p. 91) states that the objectives to be pursued by the Community and the Member States include improved living and working conditions, proper social protection, dialogue between management and labour, the development of human resources with a view to lasting high employment and the combatting of exclusion.
55 Under Article 4(1) and (2) of the Agreement, the dialogue between management and labour at Community level may lead, if they so desire, to contractual relations, including agreements, which will be implemented either in accordance with the procedures and practices specific to management and labour and the Member States, or, at the joint request of the signatory parties, by a Council decision on a proposal from the Commission.
56 It is beyond question that certain restrictions of competition are inherent in collective agreements between organisations representing employers and workers. However, the social policy objectives pursued by such agreements would be seriously undermined if management and labour were subject to Article 85(1) of the Treaty when seeking jointly to adopt measures to improve conditions of work and employment.

57 It therefore follows from an interpretation of the provisions of the Treaty as a whole which is both effective and consistent that agreements concluded in the context of collective negotiations between management and labour in pursuit of such objectives must, by virtue of their nature and purpose, be regarded as falling outside the scope of Article 85(1) of the Treaty.
58 The next question is therefore whether the nature and purpose of the agreement at issue in the main proceedings justify its exclusion from the scope of Article 85(1) of the Treaty.
59 First, like the category of agreements referred to above which derive from social dialogue, the agreement at issue in the main proceedings was concluded in the form of a collective agreement and is the outcome of collective negotiations between organisations representing employers and workers.
60 Second, as far as its purpose is concerned, that agreement establishes, in a given sector, a supplementary pension scheme managed by a pension fund to which affiliation may be made compulsory. Such a scheme seeks generally to guarantee a certain level of pension for all workers in that sector and therefore contributes directly to improving one of their working conditions, namely their remuneration.
61 Consequently, the agreement at issue in the main proceedings does not, by reason of its nature and purpose, fall within the scope of Article 85(1) of the Treaty.

[.....]

Case cross-references:
- ▸ Case C-67/96 *Albany* [1999] ECR I-5751.
- ▸ Case C-219/97 *Drijvende bokken* [1999] ECR I-6121.
- ▸ Joined Cases C-148 & 180/98 *Pavlov* [2000] ECR I-6541.
- ▸ Case C-222/98 *Van der Woude* [2000] ECR I-7111.
- ▸ Case C-35/99 *Arduino* [2002] ECR I-1529 (see III-B-4).
- ▸ Case C-309/99 *Wouters* [2002] ECR I-1577.
- ▸ L. Gyselen, 'Annonation Case C-67/96, Albany; Joined Cases C-115-117/97, Brentjens; and C-212/97, Drijvende Bokken)', (2000) 37 *CMLRev*, 425.

4) Case 161/84 *Pronuptia* [1986] ECR 353

This dispute concerned a franchise agreement between Pronuptia de Paris (franchisor), subsidiary of the French Pronuptia de Paris, an undertaking that marketed wedding dresses, and the German Mrs. Schillgalis (franchisee). The agreement contained clauses that gave Mrs. Schillgalis the exclusive right to use the Pronuptia trademark and trade name in a designated region (here, Hamburg, Oldenburg and Hanover). The franchisee, however, refused to pay the arrears of royalties on her turnover. Before the Oberlandesgericht, she claimed that the franchise agreement itself was void since it was contrary to Article 101 TFEU.

Relevance: example of an inherent restriction.

[.....]

The first question

[.....]

12 The Commission emphasizes that the scope of Article 85 (1) is not restricted to particular types of contracts, and infers that in appropriate circumstances Article 85 (1) applies also to contracts for the assignment of business names and trade-marks, registered or not, and the provision of services, as well as the supply of goods.
13 It should be pointed out first of all that franchise agreements, the legality of which has not previously been put in issue before the Court, are very diverse in nature. It appears from what was said in argument before the Court that a distinction must be drawn between different varieties of franchise agreements. In particular, it is necessary to distinguish between (i) service franchises, under which the franchisee offers a service under the business name or symbol and sometimes the trade-mark of the franchisor, in accordance with the franchisor's instructions, (ii) production franchises, under which the franchisee manufactures products according to the instructions of the franchisor and sells them under the franchisor's trade-mark, and (iii) distribution franchises, under which the franchisee simply sells certain products in a shop which bears the franchisor's business name or symbol. In this judgment the Court is concerned only with this third type of contract, to which the questions asked by the national Court expressly refer.
14 The compatibility of franchise agreements for the distribution of goods with Article 85 (1) cannot be assessed in abstracto but depends on the provisions contained in such agreements. In order to make its reply as useful as possible to the Bundesgerichtshof the Court will concern itself with contracts such as that described above.
15 In a system of distribution franchises of that kind an undertaking which has established itself as a distributor on a given market and thus developed certain business methods grants independent traders, for a fee, the right to establish themselves in other markets using its business name and the business methods which have made it successful. Rather than a method of distribution, it is a way for an undertaking to derive financial benefit from its expertise without investing its own capital. Moreover, the system gives traders who do not have the necessary experience access to methods which they could not have learned without considerable effort and allows them to benefit from the reputation of the franchisor's business name. Franchise agreements for the distribution of goods differ in that regard from dealerships or contracts which incorporate approved retailers into a selective distribution system, which do not involve the use of a single business name, the application of uniform business methods or the payment of royalties in return for the benefits granted. Such a system, which allows the franchisor to profit from his success, does not in itself interfere with competition. In order for the system to work two conditions must be met.
16 First, the franchisor must be able to communicate his know-how to the franchisees and provide them with the necessary assistance in order to enable them to apply his methods, without running the risk that that know-how and assistance might benefit competitors, even indirectly. It follows that provisions which are essential in order to avoid that risk do not constitute restrictions on competition for the purposes of Article 85 (1). That is also true of a clause prohibiting the franchisee, during the period of valid-

ity of the contract and for a reasonable period after its expiry, from opening a shop of the same or a similar nature in an area where he may compete with a member of the network. The same may be said of the franchisee's obligation not to transfer his shop to another party without the prior approval of the franchisor; that provision is intended to prevent competitors from indirectly benefiting from the know-how and assistance provided.

17 Secondly, the franchisor must be able to take the measures necessary for maintaining the identity and reputation of the network bearing his business name or symbol. It follows that provisions which establish the means of control necessary for that purpose do not constitute restrictions on competition for the purposes of Article 85 (1).

18 The same is true of the franchisee's obligation to apply the business methods developed by the franchisor and to use the know-how provided.

19 That is also the case with regard to the franchisee's obligation to sell the goods covered by the contract only in premises laid out and decorated according to the franchisor's instructions, which is intended to ensure uniform presentation in conformity with certain requirements. The same requirements apply to the location of the shop, the choice of which is also likely to affect the network's reputation. It is thus understandable that the franchisee cannot transfer his shop to another location without the franchisor's approval.

20 The prohibition of the assignment by the franchisee of his rights and obligations under the contract without the franchisor's approval protects the latter's right freely to choose the franchisees, on whose business qualifications the establishment and maintenance of the network's reputation depend.

21 By means of the control exerted by the franchisor on the selection of goods offered by the franchisee, the public is able to obtain goods of the same quality from each franchisee. It may in certain cases - for instance, the distribution of fashion Articles - be impractical to lay down objective quality specifications. Because of the large number of franchisees it may also be too expensive to ensure that such specifications are observed. In such circumstances a provision requiring the franchisee to sell only products supplied by the franchisor or by suppliers selected by him may be considered necessary for the protection of the network's reputation. Such a provision may not however have the effect of preventing the franchisee from obtaining those products from other franchisees.

22 Finally, since advertising helps to define the image of the network's name or symbol in the eyes of the public, a provision requiring the franchisee to obtain the franchisor's approval for all advertising is also essential for the maintenance of the network's identity, so long as that provision concerns only the nature of the advertising.

23 It must be emphasized on the other hand that, far from being necessary for the protection of the know-how provided or the maintenance of the network's identity and reputation, certain provisions restrict competition between the members of the network. That is true of provisions which share markets between the franchisor and franchisees or between franchisees or prevent franchisees from engaging in price competition with each other.

24 In that regard, the attention of the national Court should be drawn to the provision which obliges the franchisee to sell goods covered by the contract only in the premises specified therein. That provision prohibits the franchisee from opening a second shop. Its real effect becomes clear if it is examined in conjunction with the franchisor's undertaking to ensure that the franchisee has the exclusive use of his business name or symbol in a given territory. In order

to comply with that undertaking the franchisor must not only refrain from establishing himself within that territory but also require other franchisees to give an undertaking not to open a second shop outside their own territory. A combination of provisions of that kind results in a sharing of markets between the franchisor and the franchisees or between franchisees and thus restricts competition within the network. As is clear from the judgment of 13 July 1966 (Joined Cases 56 and 58/64 Consten and Grundig v Commission (1966) ECR 299), a restriction of that kind constitutes a limitation of competition for the purposes of Article 85 (1) if it concerns a business name or symbol which is already well-known. It is of course possible that a prospective franchisee would not take the risk of becoming part of the chain, investing his own money, paying a relatively high entry fee and undertaking to pay a substantial annual royalty, unless he could hope, thanks to a degree of protection against competition on the part of the franchisor and other franchisees, that his business would be profitable. That consideration, however, is relevant only to an examination of the agreement in the light of the conditions laid down in Article 85 (3).

25 Although provisions which impair the franchisee's freedom to determine his own prices are restrictive of competition, that is not the case where the franchisor simply provides franchisees with price guidelines, so long as there is no concerted practice between the franchisor and the franchisees or between the franchisees themselves for the actual application of such prices. It is for the national Court to determine whether that is indeed the case.

26 Finally, it must be added that franchise agreements for the distribution of goods which contain provisions sharing markets between the franchisor and the franchisees or between the franchisees themselves are in any event liable to affect trade between Member States, even if they are entered into by undertakings established in the same Member State, in so far as they prevent franchisees from establishing themselves in another Member State.

27 In view of the foregoing, the answer to the first question must be that:

(1) The compatibility of franchise agreements for the distribution of goods with Article 85 (1) depends on the provisions contained therein and on their economic context.

(2) Provisions which are strictly necessary in order to ensure that the know-how and assistance provided by the franchisor do not benefit competitors do not constitute restrictions of competition for the purposes of Article 85 (1).

(3) Provisions which establish the control strictly necessary for maintaining the identity and reputation of the network identified by the common name or symbol do not constitute restrictions of competition for the purposes of Article 85 (1).

(4) Provisions which share markets between the franchisor and the franchisees or between franchisees constitute restrictions of competition for the purposes of Article 85 (1).

(5) The fact that the franchisor makes price recommendations to the franchisee does not constitute a restriction of competition, so long as there is no concerted practice between the franchisor and the franchisees or between the franchisees themselves for the actual application of such prices.

(6) Franchise agreements for the distribution of goods which contain provisions sharing markets between the franchisor and the franchisees or between franchisees are capable of affecting trade between Member States.

[.....]

K. Ancillary restraints

Cross-reference for this part:

▸ Notice on restrictions directly related and necessary to concentrations (ancillary restraints), [2005] OJ C 56/24.

Just as its counterpart, the inherent restriction, the notion of 'ancillary restraint' has been created in the absence of a prohibition per se. The next two cases give examples of ancillary restraints.

1) Case 42/84 *Remia v. Commission* [1985] ECR 2545

This dispute concerned the contract for the transfer of Remia. Nutricia, the vendor, had included a non-competition clause for the benefit of the purchaser in which it agreed not to produce or sell sauces for a period of ten years on the Netherlands market. The Commission, however, thought that this period was excessively long and has held the clause to be too restrictive.

Relevance: example of an ancillary restraint.

[.....]

The application of Article 85 (1) of the EEC Treaty

17 It should be stated at the outset that the Commission has rightly submitted - and the applicants have not contradicted it on that point - that the fact that non-competition clauses are included in an agreement for the sale of an undertaking is not of itself sufficient to remove such clauses from the scope of Article 85 (1) of the Treaty.

18 In order to determine whether or not such clauses come within the prohibition in Article 85 (1), it is necessary to examine what would be the state of competition if those clauses did not exist.

19 If that were the case, and should the vendor and the purchaser remain competitors after the transfer, it is clear that the agreement for the transfer of the undertaking could not be given effect. The vendor, with his particularly detailed knowledge of the transferred undertaking, would still be in a position to win back his former customers immediately after the transfer and thereby drive the undertaking out of business. Against that background non-competition clauses incorporated in an agreement for the transfer of an undertaking in principle have the merit of ensuring that the transfer has the effect intended. By virtue of that very fact they contribute to the promotion of competition because they lead to an increase in the number of undertakings in the market in question.

20 Nevertheless, in order to have that beneficial effect on competition, such clauses must be necessary to the transfer of the undertaking concerned and their duration and scope must be strictly limited to that purpose. The Commission was therefore right in holding that where those conditions are satisfied such clauses are free of the prohibition laid down in Article 85 (1).

[.....]

2) Case T-112/99 *Métropole Télévision II* [2001] ECR II-2459

See above for facts of the case (I-I-2, p. 47).

Relevance: The GC explains the concept of 'ancillary restraint'.

[.....]

(2) The alternative claim, alleging that the exclusivity clause and the clause relating to the special-interest channels are ancillary restrictions

[.....]

- Findings of the Court

103 It is necessary, first of all, to define what constitutes an 'ancillary restriction' in Community competition law and point out the consequences which follow from classification of a restriction as 'ancillary'. It is then necessary to apply the principles thereby established to the exclusivity clause and to the clause relating to the special-interest channels in order to determine whether, as the applicants assert, the Commission committed an error of appraisal in not classifying those commitments as ancillary restrictions.

The concept of 'ancillary restriction'

104 In Community competition law the concept of an 'ancillary restriction' covers any restriction which is directly related and necessary to the implementation of a main operation (see, to that effect, the Commission Notice of 14 August 1990 regarding restrictions ancillary to concentrations (OJ 1990 C 203, p. 5, hereinafter 'the Notice on ancillary restrictions', point I.1), the Notice on cooperative joint ventures (point 65), and Articles 6(1)(b) and 8(2), second paragraph, of Regulation No 4064/89).

105 In its Notice on ancillary restrictions the Commission rightly stated that a restriction 'directly related' to implementation of a main operation must be understood to be any restriction which is subordinate to the implementation of that operation and which has an evident link with it (point II.4).

106 The condition that a restriction be necessary implies a two-fold examination. It is necessary to establish, first, whether the restriction is objectively necessary for the implementation of the main operation and, second, whether it is proportionate to it (see, to that effect, Remia v Commission, cited in paragraph 87 above, paragraph 20; see also points II.5 and II.6 of the Notice regarding ancillary restrictions).

107 As regards the objective necessity of a restriction, it must be observed that inasmuch as, as has been shown in paragraph 72 et seq. above, the existence of a rule of reason in Community competition law cannot be upheld, it would be wrong, when classifying ancillary restrictions, to interpret the requirement for objective necessity as implying a need to weigh the pro and anti-competitive effects of an agreement. Such an analysis can take place only in the specific framework of Article 85(3) of the Treaty.

108 That approach is justified not merely so as to preserve the effectiveness of Article 85(3) of the Treaty, but also on grounds of consistency. As Article 85(1) of the Treaty does not require an analysis of the positive and negative effects on competition of a principal restriction, the same finding is necessary with regard to the analysis of accompanying restrictions.

109 Consequently, as the Commission has correctly asserted, examination of the objective necessity of a restriction in relation to the main operation cannot but be relatively abstract. It is not a question of analysing whether, in the light of the competitive situation on the relevant market, the restriction is indispensable to the commercial success of the main operation but of determining whether, in the specific context of the main operation, the restriction is necessary to implement that operation. If, without the restriction, the main operation is difficult or even impossible to implement, the restriction may be regarded as objectively necessary for its implementation.
110 Thus, in the judgment in Remia v Commission, cited in paragraph 87 above (paragraph 19), the Court of Justice held that a non-competition clause was objectively necessary for a successful transfer of undertakings, inasmuch as, without such a clause, 'and should the vendor and the purchaser remain competitors after the transfer, it is clear that the agreement for the transfer of the undertaking could not be given effect. The vendor, with his particularly detailed knowledge of the transferred undertaking, would still be in a position to win back his former customers immediately after the transfer and thereby drive the undertaking out of business.'
111 Similarly, in its decisions, the Commission has found that a number of restrictions were objectively necessary to implementing certain operations. Failing such restrictions, the operation in question 'could not be implemented or could only be implemented under more uncertain conditions, at substantially higher cost, over an appreciably longer period or with considerably less probability of success' (point II.5 of the Notice regarding ancillary restrictions; see also, for example, Decision 90/410, point 22 et seq.)
112 Contrary to the applicants' claim, none of the various decisions to which they refer show that the Commission carried out an analysis of competition in classifying the relevant clauses as ancillary restrictions. On the contrary, those decisions show that the Commission's analysis was relatively abstract. Thus point 77 of Decision 1999/329 states as follows:
'Actually, a claim-sharing arrangement cannot function properly without at least one level of cover to be offered being agreed by all its members. The reason is that no member would be willing to share claims brought to the pool by other clubs of a higher amount than the ones it can bring to the pool.'
113 Where a restriction is objectively necessary to implement a main operation, it is still necessary to verify whether its duration and its material and geographic scope do not exceed what is necessary to implement that operation. If the duration or the scope of the restriction exceed what is necessary in order to implement the operation, it must be assessed separately under Article 85(3) of the Treaty (see, to that effect, Case T-61/89 Dansk Pelsdyravlerforening v Commission [1992] ECR II-1931, paragraph 78).
114 Lastly, it must be observed that, inasmuch as the assessment of the ancillary nature of a particular agreement in relation to a main operation entails complex economic assessments by the Commission, judicial review of that assessment is limited to verifying whether the relevant procedural rules have been complied with, whether the statement of the reasons for the decision is adequate, whether the facts have been accurately stated and whether there has been a manifest error of appraisal or misuse of powers (see, to that effect, with regard to assessing the permissible duration of a non-competition clause, Remia v Commission, cited in paragraph 87 above, paragraph 34).

Consequences of classification as an ancillary restriction

115 If it is established that a restriction is directly related and necessary to achieving a main operation, the compatibility of that restriction with the competition rules must be examined with that of the main operation. 116 Thus, if the main operation does not fall within the scope of the prohibition laid down in Article 85(1) of the Treaty, the same holds for the restrictions directly related and necessary for that operation (see, to that effect, Remia v Commission, cited in paragraph 87 above, paragraph 20). If, on the other hand, the main operation is a restriction within the meaning of Article 85(1) but benefits from an exemption under Article 85(3) of the Treaty, that exemption also covers those ancillary restrictions.
117 Moreover, where the restrictions are directly related and necessary to a concentration within the meaning of Regulation No 4064/89, it follows from both Article 6(1)(b) and Article 8(2), second subparagraph, of that regulation that those restrictions are covered by the Commission's decision declaring the operation compatible with the Common Market.

[.....]

L. The overall purpose of the competition rules

Cross-reference for this part:

- ▸ O. Odudu, *The Boundaries of EC Competition Law. The Scope of Article 81*, Oxford Studies in European Law, 2006.
- ▸ N. Dhondt, *Integration of Environmental protection into other EC Policies*, Europa Law Publishing Groningen 2003.
- ▸ K.J. Cseres, *Competition Law and Consumer protection*, European Monographs no. 49, Kluwer Law International 2005.
- ▸ H. Vedder, 'Of Jurisdiction and Justification: Why Competition is good for "Non-Economic" Goals, but may need to be restricted' in *CompLRev* 2009, Vol. 6 no. 1, pp. 5-29.

1) Joined Cases C-501/06 P, C-513/06 P, C-515/06 P and C-519/06 P *GlaxoSmithKline Services Unlimited v. Commission* [2008] ECR I-0000

Glaxo Wellcome ('GW'), the applicant, is one of the subsidiaries of GlaxoSmithKline Services United operating on the Spanish market. Glaxo Wellcome notified to the Commission a document titled "the General Sales Conditions". Moreover, GW sent these General Sales Conditions to wholesalers established in Spain. The Commission adopted the decision providing that GW 'has infringed Article 81 (1) EC by entering into an agreement with Spanish wholesalers operating the distinction between prices charged to wholesalers in the case of domestic resale of reimbursable drugs to pharmacies or hospitals and higher prices charged in the case of exports to any other Member State'. The applicant, GW, sought the annulment of the Commission's decision before the GC and lost its case. Then, a further appeal was filed with the ECJ on legal grounds. The ECJ upheld the judgment of the GC.

Relevance: Would the general purpose of the competition rules be confined to the protection of the welfare of final consumers only?

Findings of the Court

[.....]

58 According to settled case-law, in order to assess the anti-competitive nature of an agreement, regard must be had inter alia to the content of its provisions, the objectives it seeks to attain and the economic and legal context of which it forms a part (see, to that effect, Joined Cases 96/82 to 102/82, 104/82, 105/82, 108/82 and 110/82 IAZ International Belgium and Others v Commission [1983] ECR 3369, paragraph 25, and Case C-209/07 Beef Industry Development Society and Barry Brothers [2008] ECR I-0000, paragraphs 16 and 21). In addition, although the parties' intention is not a necessary factor in determining whether an agreement is restrictive, there is nothing prohibiting the Commission or the Community judicature from taking that aspect into account (see, to that effect, IAZ International Belgium and Others v Commission, cited above, paragraphs 23 to 25).
59 With respect to parallel trade, the Court has already held that, in principle, agreements aimed at prohibiting or limiting parallel trade have as their object the prevention of competition (see, to that effect, Case 19/77 Miller International Schallplatten v Commission [1978] ECR 131, paragraphs 7 and 18, and Joined Cases 32/78, 36/78 to 82/78 BMW Belgium and Others v Commission [1979] ECR 2435, paragraphs 20 to 28 and 31).
60 As observed by the Advocate General in point 155 of her Opinion, that principle, according to which an agreement aimed at limiting parallel trade is a 'restriction of competition by object', applies to the pharmaceuticals sector.
61 The Court has, moreover, held in that regard, in relation to the application of Article 81 EC and in a case involving the pharmaceuticals sector, that an agreement between producer and distributor which might tend to restore the national divisions in trade between Member States might be such as to frustrate the Treaty's objective of achieving the integration of national markets through the establishment of a single market. Thus on a number of occasions the Court has held agreements aimed at partitioning national markets according to national borders or making the interpenetration of national markets more difficult, in particular those aimed at preventing or restricting parallel exports, to be agreements whose object is to restrict competition within the meaning of that article of the Treaty (Joined Cases C-468/06 to C-478/06 Sot.Lélos kai Sia and Others [2008] ECR I-7139, paragraph 65 and case-law cited).
62 With respect to the Court of First Instance's statement that, while it is accepted that an agreement intended to limit parallel trade must in principle be considered to have as its object the restriction of competition, that applies in so far as it may be presumed to deprive final consumers of the advantages of effective competition in terms of supply or price, the Court notes that neither the wording of Article 81(1) EC nor the case-law lend support to such a position.
63 First of all, there is nothing in that provision to indicate that only those agreements which deprive consumers of certain advantages may have an anti-competitive object. Secondly, it must be borne in mind that the Court has held that, like other competition rules laid down in the Treaty, Article 81 EC aims to protect not only the interests of competitors or of consumers, but also the structure of the market and, in so doing, competition as such. Consequently, for a finding that an agreement has an anti-competitive object, it is not necessary that final consumers be deprived of the advan-

tages of effective competition in terms of supply or price (see, by analogy, T-Mobile Netherlands and Others, cited above, paragraphs 38 and 39).

[.....]

Case cross-reference:
E. Loozen, 'The workings of Article 101 TFEU in case of an agreement that aims to limit parallel trade - GlaxoSmithKline Services (C-501/06 P, C-513/06 P, C-515/06 P and C-519/06 P) in 2010 *ECLR* 9: 349-353.

2) Case T-201/04 *Microsoft v. Commission* [2007] ECR II-3601

The Commission established that Microsoft's Windows had become the 'de facto' standard for computer operating systems. Microsoft was accused of monopolizing its technology and in doing so, of causing problems to competitors in the field of interoperability and compatibility of their products with the Microsoft standard. The case was based on Article 102 TFEU. Microsoft appealed the Commission's decision that it had abused its dominance by not granting access to its technology (embedded in secret know-how) so that competitors were deprived from introducing products that might be compatible and interoperable with Windows.
Apart from many other interesting legal and factual issues, the purpose of the competition rules was defined by the GC in the same way as has been done by the ECJ in the previous case.

Relevance: would the general purpose of the competition rules be the protection of consumers only?

[.....]

664 [.....], it must be borne in mind that it is settled case-law that Article 82 EC covers not only practices which may prejudice consumers directly but also those which indirectly prejudice them by impairing an effective competitive structure (Case 85/76 Hoffmann-La Roche v Commission [1979] ECR 461, paragraph 125, and Irish Sugar v Commission, paragraph 229 above, paragraph 232). In this case, Microsoft impaired the effective competitive structure on the work group server operating systems market by acquiring a significant market share on that market.

[.....]

M. Extraterritorial application

1) Case 48/69 *ICI v. Commission (Dyestuffs)* [1972] ECR 619

As said above, ICI tried to annul a Commission decision concerning its participation in a price cartel (I-G-2, p. 35). A complicating factor in this case was that Great Britain, where ICI had its registered offices, was at the time not yet a Member State, which triggered the issue of extraterritoriality.

Relevance: extraterritorial application of EU competition law.

[.....]

The jurisdiction of the Commission

125 The applicant, whose registered office is outside the Community, argues that the Commission is not empowered to impose fines on it by reason merely of the effects produced in the Common Market by actions which it is alleged to have taken outside the Community.
126 Since a concerted practice is involved, it is first necessary to ascertain whether the conduct of the applicant has had effects within the Common Market.
127 It appears from what has already been said that the increases at issue were put into effect within the Common Market and concerned competition between producers operating within it.
128 Therefore the actions for which the fine at issue has been imposed constitute practices carried on directly within the Common Market.
129 It follows from what has been said in considering the submission relating to the existence of concerted practices, that the applicant company decided on increases in the selling prices of its products to users in the Common Market, and that these increases were of a uniform nature in line with increases decided upon by the other producers involved.
130 By making use of its power to control its subsidiaries established in the Community, the applicant was able to ensure that its decision was implemented on that market.
131 The applicant objects that this conduct is to be imputed to its subsidiaries and not to itself.
132 The fact that a subsidiary has separate legal personality is not sufficient to exclude the possibility of imputing its conduct to the parent company.
133 Such may be the case in particular where the subsidiary, although having separate legal personality, does not decide independently upon its own conduct on the market, but carries out, in all material respects, the instructions given to it by the parent company.
134 Where a subsidiary does not enjoy real autonomy in determining its course of action in the market, the prohibitions set out in Article 85 (1) may be considered inapplicable in the relationship between it and the parent company with which it forms one economic unit.
135 In view of the unity of the group thus formed, the actions of the subsidiaries may in certain circumstances be attributed to the parent company.
136 It is well-known that at the time the applicant held all or at any rate the majority of the shares in those subsidiaries.

137 The applicant was able to exercise decisive influence over the policy of the subsidiaries as regards selling prices in the Common Market and in fact used this power upon the occasion of the three price increases in question.
138 In effect the telex messages relating to the 1964 increase, which the applicant sent to its subsidiaries in the Common Market, gave the addressees orders as to the prices which they were to charge and the other conditions of sale which they were to apply in dealing with their customers.
139 In the absence of evidence to the contrary, it must be assumed that on the occasion of the increases of 1965 and 1967 the applicant acted in a similar fashion in its relations with its subsidiaries established in the Common Market.
140 In the circumstances the formal separation between these companies, resulting from their separate legal personality, cannot outweigh the unity of their conduct on the market for the purposes of applying the rules on competition.
140 It was in fact the applicant undertaking which brought the concerted practice into being within the Community.
142 The submission as to lack of jurisdiction raised by the applicant must therefore be declared to unfounded.
143 The applicant complains that insufficient reasons were given in the decision, in that it does not mention the relationship existing between the parent company and its subsidiaries by way of justification of the Commission's jurisdiction.
144 The fact that no statement is included showing why the Commission has jurisdiction does not stand in the way of a review of the legality of the decision.
145 Furthermore, the Commission is not bound to included in its decisions all the arguments which it might later use in response to submissions of illegality which might be raised against its measures.
146 Therefore this objection is unfounded.

[.....]

2) Joined Cases 89, 104, 114, 116, 117 & 125-129/85 *Ahlström (Wood pulp)* [1988] ECR 5193

In this case, the producers and associations concerned, which were all active on the wood pulp market, had allegedly infringed Article 101 by making price agreements. They all had their offices outside the Union. Here, the ECJ further elaborated on the issue of extraterritorial application of EU competition law.

Relevance: extraterritorial application of competition law and effect doctrine.

[.....]

12 It should be noted that the main sources of supply of wood pulp are outside the Community, in Canada, the United States, Sweden and Finland and that the market therefore has global dimensions. Where wood pulp producers established in those countries sell directly to purchasers established in the Community and engage in price competition in order to win orders from those customers, that constitutes competition within the Common Market.
13 It follows that where those producers concert on the prices to be charged to their customers in the Community and put that concertation into effect by selling at prices which are actually coordinated, they are

taking part in concertation which has the object and effect of restricting competition within the Common Market within the meaning of Article 85 of the Treaty.

14 Accordingly, it must be concluded that by applying the competition rules in the Treaty in the circumstances of this case to undertakings whose registered offices are situated outside the Community, the Commission has not made an incorrect assessment of the territorial scope of Article 85.

15 The applicants have submitted that the decision is incompatible with public international law on the grounds that the application of the competition rules in this case was founded exclusively on the economic repercussions within the Common Market of conduct restricting competition which was adopted outside the Community.

16 It should be observed that an infringement of Article 85, such as the conclusion of an agreement which has had the effect of restricting competition within the Common Market, consists of conduct made up of two elements, the formation of the agreement, decision or concerted practice and the implementation thereof. If the applicability of prohibitions laid down under competition law were made to depend on the place where the agreement, decision or concerted practice was formed, the result would obviously be to give undertakings an easy means of evading those prohibitions. The decisive factor is therefore the place where it is implemented.

17 The producers in this case implemented their pricing agreement within the Common Market. It is immaterial in that respect whether or not they had recourse to subsidiaries, agents, sub-agents, or branches within the Community in order to make their contacts with purchasers within the Community.

18 Accordingly the Community's jurisdiction to apply its competition rules to such conduct is covered by the territoriality principle as universally recognized in public international law.

19 As regards the argument based on the infringement of the principle of non-interference, it should be pointed out that the applicants who are members of KEA have referred to a rule according to which where two States have jurisdiction to lay down and enforce rules and the effect of those rules is that a person finds himself subject to contradictory orders as to the conduct he must adopt, each State is obliged to exercise its jurisdiction with moderation. The applicants have concluded that by disregarding that rule in applying its competition rules the Community has infringed the principle of non-interference.

20 There is no need to enquire into the existence in international law of such a rule since it suffices to observe that the conditions for its application are in any event not satisfied. There is not, in this case, any contradiction between the conduct required by the United States and that required by the Community since the Webb Pomerene Act merely exempts the conclusion of export cartels from the application of United States anti-trust laws but does not require such cartels to be concluded.

21 It should further be pointed out that the United States authorities raised no objections regarding any conflict of jurisdiction when consulted by the Commission pursuant to the OECD Council Recommendation of 25 October 1979 concerning Cooperation between Member Countries on Restrictive Business Practices affecting International Trade (Acts of the Organization, Vol. 19, p. 376).

22 As regards the argument relating to disregard of international comity, it suffices to observe that it amounts to calling in question the Community's jurisdiction to apply its competition rules to conduct such as that found to exist in this case and that, as such, that argument has already been rejected.

[.....]

Case cross-references:

▸ *ANSAC* Commission decision 91/301/EEC [1991] OJ L 152/54 (see V-F-2).

▸ I. Rubli, 'Advocate-General's Opinion in Wood-Pulp: Another setback for the Commission's Competition Policy', (1993) 14 *ECRL*, 26.

N. Article 101 (2) TFEU: nullity – task of national courts

Cross-reference for this part:

▸ Notice on the co-operation between the Commission and the Courts of the EU Member States in the application of Articles 81 and 82 EC, [2004] OJ C 101/54.

1) Case C-234/89 *Delimitis* [1991] ECR I-935

Although the task of national courts has considerably changed when Article 101(3) was given direct effect (Regulation 1/2003), the following two paragraphs from "Delimitis" still hold. A national court cannot single-handedly adjust or extend the scope of block exemption regulations.
See above for facts of the case (I-H-2, p. 44).

Relevance: national courts and block exemption regulations.

[.....]

45 On the other hand, the Commission does not have exclusive competence to apply Articles 85(1) and 86. It shares that competence with the national courts. As the Court stated in its judgment in Case 127/73 (BRT v SABAM [1974] ECR 51), Articles 85(1) and 86 produce direct effect in relations between individuals and create rights directly in respect of the individuals concerned which the national courts must safeguard.
46 The same is true of the provisions of the exemption regulation (judgment in Case 63/75, Fonderies Roubaix [1976] ECR 111). The direct applicability of those provisions may not, however, lead the national courts to modify the scope of the exemption regulations by extending their sphere of application to agreements not covered by them. Any such extension, whatever its scope, would affect the manner in which the Commission exercises its legislative competence.

[.....]

O. Article 101 (2) TFEU: scope of nullity

Cross-references for this part:

▸ Case C-234/89 *Delimitis* [1991] ECR I-935 (see I-H-2).

▸ Cases on enforcement in chapters IX & X.

1) Joined Cases 56 & 58/64 *Consten & Grundig* [1966, English special edition] ECR 299

In the following two cases the ECJ addressed the scope nullity of an agreement that infringed Article 101. The facts of the first case are given above (I-E-1, p. 23).

Relevance: scope of nullity (partial nullity).

[.....]

The complaints relating to the extent of the prohibition

The applicant Grundig and the German Government complain that the Commission did not exclude from the prohibition, in the operative part of the contested decision, those clauses of the contract in respect of which there was found no effect capable of restricting competition, and that it thereby failed to define the infringement.

It is apparent from the statement of the reasons for the contested decision, as well as from Article 3 thereof, that the infringement declared to exist by Article 1 of the operative part is not to be found in the undertaking by Grundig not to make direct deliveries in France except to Consten. That infringement arises from the clauses which, added to this grant of exclusive rights, are intended to impede, relying upon national law, parallel imports of Grundig products into France by establishing absolute territorial protection in favour of the sole concessionnaire.

The provision in Article 85(2) that agreements prohibited pursuant to Article 85 shall be automatically void applies only to those parts of the agreement which are subject to the prohibition, or to the agreement as a whole if those parts do not appear to be severable from the agreement itself. The Commission should, therefore, either have confined itself in the operative part of the contested decision to declaring that an infringement lay in those parts only of the agreement which came within the prohibition, or else it should have set out in the preamble to the decision the reasons why those parts did not appear to it to be severable from the whole agreement.

It follows, however, from Article 1 of the decision that the infringement was found to lie in the agreement as a whole, although the Commission did not adequately state the reasons why it was necessary to render the whole of the agreement void when it is not established that all the clauses infringed the provisions of Article 85(1). The state of affairs found to be incompatible with Article 85(1) stems from certain specific clauses of the contract of 1 April 1957 concerning absolute territorial protection and from the additional agreement on the GINT trade mark rather than from the combined operation of all clauses of the agreement, that is to say, from the aggregate of its effects.

Article 1 of the contested decision must therefore be annulled in so far as it renders void, without any valid reason, all the clauses of the agreement by virtue of Article 85(2).

[.....]

2) Case 56/65 *Société La Technique Minière v. Maschinenbau Ulm* [1966] ECR 235

See above for facts of case (I-I-1, p. 46).

Relevance: scope of nullity (partial nullity)

[.....]

The second question relating to the interpretation of article 85(2)

Article 85(2) provides that 'any agreements or decisions prohibited pursuant to this Article shall be automatically void'.
This provision, which is intended to ensure compliance with the Treaty, can only be interpreted with reference to its purpose in Community law, and it must be limited to this context. The automatic nullity in question only applies to those parts of the agreement affected by the prohibition, or to the agreement as a whole if it appears that those parts are not severable from the agreement itself. Consequently any other contractual provisions which are not affected by the prohibition, and which therefore do not involve the application of the Treaty, fall outside Community law.

[.....]

P. Article 101 (3) TFEU

Cross-references for this part:

- ▸ Guidelines on the application of Article 81(3) of the Treaty, [2004] OJ C 101/97.
- ▸ I. Forrester, 'The Reform of the Implementation of Articles 81 and 82 Following Publication of the Draft Regulation', (2001) 28 *LIEI*, 173.
- ▸ Kris Dekeijzer, J. Bourgeois, J. Venit and 5 others, 'Modernization Issue', (2005) 32-1 *LIEI*.
- ▸ E. Psychogiopoulou. 'EC competition law and cultural diversity: the case of the cinema, music and book publishing industries', (2005) 6 *European Law Review*, 838.

The following two examples give some insight in how the criteria of Article 101 (3) are applied, in particular with regard to so-called 'non-economic' criteria that are not explicitly mentioned in Article 101 (3). They show that non-economic interests, such as employment and environment, may sway the balance in favour of an exemption.

1) Case 26/76 *Metro v. Commission (SABA I)* [1977] ECR 1875

The facts of the first dispute are as follows. SABA operated a selective distribution system that had been approved of by the Commission (some provisions were granted a negative clearance; some were exempted). Metro, a self-service wholesale trading company with approximately 30 establishments, was not appointed as a SABA wholesaler since it did not agree with several of SABA's conditions, notably those on the obligation to employ trained sales repair personnel. It claimed that the approved system infringed Article 101 TFEU and sought to annul the Commission's decision.

Relevance: example of an exemption (nowadays: exception) pursuant to Article 101 (3) (employment).

[.....]

42 Article 85 (3) renders exemption from the prohibition pursuant to Article 85 (1) subject to the following conditions: (i) the agreement must contribute to improving the production or distribution of goods or to promoting technical or economic progress, (ii) it must allow consumers a fair share of the resulting benefit, (iii) it must not impose restrictions which are not indispensable to the attainment of these objectives and (iv) it must not afford the undertakings concerned the possibility of eliminating competition in respect of a substantial part of the products in question.
43 With regard to the first condition set out above, the conclusion of supply contracts for six months taking account of the probable growth of the market should make it possible to ensure both a certain stability in the supply of the relevant products, which should allow the requirements of persons obtaining supplies from the wholesaler to be more fully satisfied, and, since such supply contracts are of relatively short duration, a certain flexibility, enabling production to be adapted to the changing requirements of the market.
Thus a more regular distribution is ensured, to the benefit both of the producer, who takes his share of the planned expansion of the market in the relevant product, of the wholesaler, whose supplies are secured, and, finally, of the undertakings which obtain supplies from the wholesaler, in that the variety of available products is increased.
Another improvement in distribution is provided under the clause in the cooperation agreement obliging SABA to compensate wholesalers for service performed under guarantee and to supply spare parts necessary for repairs under guarantee.
Furthermore, the establishment of supply forecasts for a reasonable period constitutes a stabilizing factor with regard to the provision of employment which, since it improves the general conditions of production, especially when market conditions are unfavourable, comes within the framework of the objectives to which reference may be had pursuant to Article 85 (3).
44 Secondly, it must be considered whether the restrictions imposed on wholesalers under the cooperation agreement are indispensable to the attainment of the objectives in view.
45 If there were no undertakings covering a period of a given duration the relationship between the producer and appointed wholesalers could only take the form of occasional contact which would not make it possible to achieve the stability necessary to enable specialist wholesalers and producers to undertake the other obligations which guarantee improved supplies.
In considering that the cooperation agreement, by restricting the period covered by the supply contract to six months, remained within the limits of what is necessary the Commission clearly did not exceed the margin of discretion which it possesses in this sphere.
46 According to Article 85 (3) agreements restricting competition must, in order to qualify for exemption, not only improve the distribution of goods but also allow consumers a fair share of the resulting benefit.

47 According to the contested decision the conditions of supply for wholesalers under the cooperation agreement are such as to provide direct benefit for consumers in that they ensure continued supplies and the provision of a wider range of goods by retailers for private customers.
Furthermore, the lively competition existing on the market in electronic equipment for leisure purposes exercises sufficient pressure to induce SABA and the wholesalers to pass on to consumers the benefits arising from the rationalization of production and the distribution system based on the cooperation agreement.
48 In the circumstances of the present case regular supplies represent a sufficient advantage to consumers for them to be considered to constitute a fair share of the benefit resulting from the improvement brought about by the restriction on competition permitted by the Commission.
Even if it is doubtful whether the requirement in this connexion of article 85 (3) can be said to be satisfied by the assumption that the pressure of competition will be sufficient to induce SABA and the wholesalers to pass on to consumers a part of the benefit derived from the rationalization of the distribution network, the grant of exemption may, however, in the present case be considered as sufficiently justified by the advantage which consumers obtain from an improvement in supplies.
49 Finally, it must be considered whether the obligations contained in the cooperation agreement do not afford the undertakings concerned the possibility of eliminating competition in respect of a substantial part of the products in question.
50 It is clear from the foregoing considerations that the conditions laid down by SABA for appointment as a wholesaler may largely be fulfilled without inconvenience by self-service wholesale undertakings.
Nevertheless, although the supply estimates which wholesalers are obliged to sign under the cooperation agreements in all probability constitute an element foreign to the methods appropriate to that distribution channel, it does not appear that, in weighing up, in the context of the electronic leisure equipment sector, the relative importance of the need for cooperation agreements, giving sufficient coherence to SABA's marketing network, especially with regard to specialist wholesalers, on the one hand, and the surmountable difficulties which that involves for self-service wholesale traders, on the other, and deciding in favour of the former, the commission exceeded its discretionary power in this sphere.
The outcome could be different if, in particular as the result of an increase in selective distribution networks of a nature similar to SABA's, self-service wholesale traders were in fact eliminated as distributors on the market in electronic equipment for leisure purposes.
Nevertheless, it is clear from the foregoing considerations that this was not so when the contested decision was adopted.

[.....]

2) *CECED* Commission decision 2000/476/EC [2000] OJ L 187/47

In this decision, the Commission exempted an agreement on washing machines notified by CECED (Conseil Européen de la Construction d'Appareils Domestiques), an association of undertakings. The aim of the agreement was to stop the production and sale of washing machines with low levels of energy efficiency. As can be seen from the following parts of the decision, environmental concerns were of importance to the Commission.

Relevance: example of an exemption (nowadays: exception) pursuant to Article 101 (3) (environment).

[.....]

B. Article 81(3) of the EC Treaty and Article 53(3) of the EEA Agreement

1. Contribution to economic or technical progress and conferment of benefits on the consumer

(47) The agreement is designed to reduce the potential energy consumption of new washing machines by at least 15 to 20 % (relative to 1994 data on models of washing machines). According to CECED, were models of phased-out machines to be replaced by an equivalent number of machines in categories A, B and C, currently available on the market, 7,5 TWh would be saved in 2015 out of the estimated 38 TWh consumed by the operation of washing machines in the Community in 1995.
(48) Washing machines which, other factors being constant, consume less electricity are objectively more technically efficient. Reduced electricity consumption indirectly leads to reduced pollution from electricity generation. The future operation of the total of installed machines providing the same service with less indirect pollution is more economically efficient than without the agreement.
(49) Such potential improvement in four years of implementation of the agreement is remarkable, compared to improvements in the past. Were energy efficiency to improve at the same rate as it did between 1978 and 1994 without any agreement, the attainment of a 20 % improvement would require eight years, instead of four. In addition to faster and more certain results, there is no evidence that changes in behaviour may nullify the improvement of the efficiency ratio(8).
(50) The agreement is also likely to focus future research and development on furthering energy efficiency beyond the current technological limits of category A, thereby allowing for increased product differentiation amongst producers in the long run(9).
(51) CECED estimates the pollution avoided at 3,5 million tons of carbon dioxide, 17000 tons of sulphur dioxide and 6000 tons of nitrous oxide per year in 2010, working on the basis of average emission values. Although such emissions are more efficiently tackled at the stage of electricity generation, the agreement is likely to deliver both individual and collective benefits for users and consumers.

(a) Individual economic benefits

(52) The level at which the minimum performance standard is set provides a fair return within reasonable pay-back periods to a typical consumer for higher initial purchase costs derived from the more stringent standard in fact set out by CECED. Savings on electricity bills allow recouping of increased costs of upgraded, more expensive machines within nine to 40 months, depending mainly on frequency of use and electricity prices.
(53) While the agreement will eliminate certain models which are in category D and below, it is not possible to determine in advance its effect on the average selling price of those models of washing machines which are not directly affected. Indeed, the restriction in one product-dimension, energy consumption, may increase competition on other product characteristics, including price. Therefore, while the minimum price

of washing machines is likely to increase, it cannot be ruled out that products in categories A and B may become available at a lower price. In a market characterised by strong competition amongst manufacturers and bargaining power from distributors, these benefits are likely to accrue to consumers.
(54) Were these competition-enhancing effects to take place, the narrowing of the price range and the increase in average selling prices would be less pronounced than would otherwise be foreseeable.

(b) Collective environmental benefits

(55) According to Article 174 of the EC Treaty, environmental damage should be rectified at source. The Community pursues the objective of a rational utilisation of natural resources, taking into account the potential benefits and costs of action. Agreements like CECED's must yield economic benefits outweighing their costs and be compatible with competition rules(10). Although electricity is not a scarce resource and consumption reductions do not tackle emissions at source, account can also be taken of the costs of pollution.
(56) The Commission reasonably estimates the saving in marginal damage from (avoided) carbon dioxide emissions (the so-called "external costs") at EUR 41 to 61 per ton of carbon dioxide. On a European scale, avoided damage from sulphur dioxide amounts to EUR 4000 to 7000 per ton and EUR 3000 to 5000 per ton of nitrous oxide(11). On the basis of reasonable assumptions, the benefits to society brought about by the CECED agreement appear to be more than seven times greater than the increased purchase costs of more energy-efficient washing machines. Such environmental results for society would adequately allow consumers a fair share of the benefits even if no benefits accrued to individual purchasers of machines.
(57) The expected contribution to furthering energy efficiency both within the current technological limits of categories A to C and beyond the limits of category A, the cost-benefit ratio of the standard and the return on investment for individual users point to the conclusion that the agreement is likely to contribute significantly to technical and economic progress whilst allowing users a fair share of the benefits.

2. Indispensability of the restrictions

(58) The agreement does not impose on the parties restrictions that are unrelated or unnecessary to the fulfilment of its objective benefits. The outright prohibition of some energy categories does not prescribe any specific technical means for the achievement of the minimum standard, to the exclusion of others, nor does it impose other limitations on any other aspect of the proper or commercial behaviour of the parties.
(59) Regarding the reduction of total electricity consumption through the operation of washing machines, the agreement opts for an approach based on individual product characteristics. The Commission has examined whether it would be possible to devise less restrictive alternatives that would be capable of delivering similar reductions based on other approaches. For instance, the parties could theoretically limit the agreement to the undertaking to contribute to an industry-wide target, information campaigns and a greater focus on fulfilling EU eco-label criteria.

(a) Industry-wide target

(60) The setting of a more stringent industry-wide target could in theory lead to more

indirect pollution abatement whilst allowing manufacturers or importers more flexibility than the application of a mandatory minimum standard. Provided that each party complied with the common target, it would be free to decide on the share of different energy categories within its total product range, by compensating a minor proportion of machines below category C through a predominant proportion of top categories A and B.

(61) However, such a system would face difficulties that would jeopardise the attainment of the expected results. In the specific market context, purchasers that have bargaining power could focus their orders on machines below category C. Whilst the unilateral decision to cease production of such machines could remedy this, it would, in practice, be tantamount to applying the minimum standard. Only a joint agreement with distributors and retailers would help to overcome this problem. If at all workable, such an agreement would have higher transaction and monitoring costs and could be even more restrictive.

(b) Information campaigns

(62) Mere information campaigns, which are a separate part of the agreements, are also plainly less effective than a standard. As previously stated, the existing Community energy label already provides consumers with the necessary information on energy efficiency. However, evidence shows that, as external costs are not fully reflected in consumer's calculations when contemplating a purchase, the provision of information is not sufficient to realise the agreement's environmental benefits to their fullest possible extent. Moreover, the information stressed in the agreement relates to the conditions on the use of the machine, which allow for further reduction of electricity consumption besides the technical efficiency ratio of the machine. Such campaigns are therefore complementary to the standard, rather than being a substitute for it.

(c) Eco label

(63) Commission Decision 96/461/EC(12) of 11 July 1996 establishing ecological criteria for the award of the Community eco label to washing machines covers energy consumption (categories A and B being eligible), water and detergent use as well as consumer information. Some manufacturers have been awarded the eco label. However, it should be remembered that the eco label has as one of its main features its selective character. The label is only awarded to those products with the lowest environmental impact in a product range. It is an instrument that rewards the top environmental class. On the other hand, the CECED agreement aims at phasing out the least energy-efficient products (categories D to G). The eco label is therefore not intended to apply to products such as the ones envisaged in the agreement. The agreement and the eco label are complementary and reinforce each other. The parties to the agreement will always have the possibility, in addition to the agreement, of applying for the award of an eco label, as a supplementary way of enhancing the environmental benefits achieved by their washing machines.

3. No elimination of competition

(64) Major distributors agree that other factors like price, brand image, and technical performance may have more weight in purchase decisions than energy efficiency. Meanwhile, three energy categories, from A to C, and part of D, will still remain available

to manufacturers, once the agreement is fully implemented.

(65) Moreover, whilst not imposing unnecessary restrictions de jure, the agreement does not de facto impose any particular means of improving energy efficiency. The technology needed to produce machines under categories A to C is available to all manufacturers. The parties have therefore a wide variety of technical choices, on which they can effectively compete, to meet the minimum energy efficiency standard.

(66) Though machines pertaining to categories D to F account for a significant volume of final sales, about 90 % of the market (1996) will fall outside the scope of the agreements. Since third parties remain free to produce and to import machines below such categories, the agreement does not appreciably raise barriers to entry into the EEA market.

(67) Therefore, it can be concluded that the cumulative conditions of Articles 81(3) of the EC Treaty and 53(3) of the EEA Agreement are fulfilled.

[.....]

[Footnotes in the original text of the case have not been included]

Case cross-references:

- ▸ Article 11 TFEU.
- ▸ J.A.H. Maks. 'The "New" Horizontal Agreements Approach in the EU: An Economic Assessment', (2002) 37-1 *Intereconomics*, 28.
- ▸ See also Commission's Guidelines on Horizontal co-operation agreements, [2001] OJ C 3/2: the example dealt with in paragraph 198.
- ▸ H.H.B. Vedder, *'Competition Law and Environmental Protection in Europe; Towards Sustainability?'*, Groningen: Europa Law Publishing, 2003.
- ▸ F.O.W. Vogelaar, 'Towards an Improved Integration of EC Environmental Policy and EC Competition Policy: an Interim Report', (1994) *Fordham Corporate L. Inst* (B. Hawk, ed. 1995), 529.

3) Case C-238/05 *Asnef-Equifax v. Ausbanc* [2006] ECR I-11125

The case was brought before the ECJ as a request for preliminary ruling in proceedings between 'Asnef-Equifax' and 'Ausbanc' concerning a register of information between financial institutions on the solvency of customers.

Relevance: could such exchange of information be seen to benefit consumers?

[...]

67 [...] registers such as the one at issue in the main proceedings are capable of helping to prevent situations of overindebtedness for consumers of credit as well as, in principle, of leading to a greater overall availability of credit. In the event that the register restricted competition within the meaning of Article 81(1) EC, those objective economic advantages might be such as to offset the disadvantages of such a possible restriction. It would be for the national court, if necessary, to verify that.

[...]

72 [...] In order for the condition that consumers be allowed a fair share of the benefit to be satisfied, it is not necessary, in principle, for each consumer individually to derive a benefit from an agreement, a decision or a concerted practice. However, the overall

effect on consumers in the relevant markets must be favourable

[.....]

Q. Articles 101 (3) and 107-108 TFEU (i.e. EU State Aid rules)

1) Case C-225/91 *Matra v. Commission* [1993] ECR I-3203

The Portuguese Government had granted aid to Newco, a joint venture for the production of ATVs created by Ford and Volkswagen. Matra, active on the same market, raised objections to this aid. The Commission, however, approved the aid and later wrote to Matra that the joint venture fulfilled all the necessary conditions for exemption under Article 101 (3) as well. Matra appealed these decisions.

Relevance: interrelation between Article 101 (3) and Article 107 TFEU.

[.....]

40 Matra further criticizes the Commission for deciding not to object to the aid in question, without awaiting the outcome of the procedure under Regulation No 17, cited above, with respect to the agreement between Ford and VW, thereby disregarding the link between Articles 85 and 92 of the Treaty.
41 It must be noted in this respect that while the procedure provided for in Articles 92 and 93 leaves a wide discretion to the Commission, and under certain conditions to the Council, in coming to a decision on the compatibility of a system of State aid with the requirements of the Common Market, it is clear from the general scheme of the Treaty that that procedure must never produce a result which is contrary to the specific provisions of the Treaty (judgment in Case 73/79 Commission v Italy [1980] ECR 1533, paragraph 11). The Court has also held that those aspects of aid which contravene specific provisions of the Treaty other than Articles 92 and 93 may be so indissolubly linked to the object of the aid that it is impossible to evaluate them separately (judgment in Case 74/76 Iannelli v Meroni [1977] ECR 557).
42 That obligation on the part of the Commission to ensure that Articles 92 and 93 are applied consistently with other provisions of the Treaty is all the more necessary where those other provisions also pursue, as in the present case, the objective of undistorted competition in the Common Market.
43 When adopting a decision on the compatibility of aid with the Common Market, the Commission must be aware of the risk of individual traders undermining competition in the Common Market.
44 Nevertheless, the procedure under Article 85 et seq. and that under Article 92 et seq. of the Treaty are independent procedures governed by specific rules.
45 Consequently, when taking a decision on the compatibility of State aid with the Common Market, the Commission is not obliged to await the outcome of a parallel procedure initiated under Regulation No 17, once it has reached the conclusion, based on an economic analysis of the situation and without any manifest error in the assessment of the facts, that the recipient of the aid is not in breach of Articles 85 and 86 of the Treaty.

[.....]

Case cross-reference:

▸ Case T-289/03 *British United Provident Association Ltd (BUPA) and others v. Commission* [2008] ECR II-741 (see IV-A-3).

R. Interim measures

Cross-references for this part:

▸ Article 8 of Regulation 1/2003 [2003] OJ L 1/1.

▸ E. Navarro Varona and H. González Durántez, 'Interim Measures in Competition Cases Before the European Commission and Courts', (2002) 23 *ECLR*, 512.

1) Case 792/79R *Camera Care* [1980] ECR 119

Camera Care, an Irish undertaking that repaired, hired and sold photographic equipment, had complained to the Commission about Hasselblad A/B, a Swedish manufacturer of cameras and photographic equipment, and its subsidiary Hasselblad (GB). Allegedly, Hasselblad had terminated its supply agreement with Camera Care and, in the view of the latter, wrongfully refused to continue supplying Camera Care with the equipment and spare parts it needed for the proper continuation of its business. Next to its complaint, Camera Care's application contained a request for interim measures.

Relevance: Conditions for honouring requests to impose interim measures.

[.....]

Power of the Commission to adopt interim measures

[.....]

17 As regards the right to take decisions conferred upon the Commission by Article 3 (1), it is essential that it should be exercised in the most efficacious manner best suited to the circumstances of each given situation. To this end the possibility cannot be excluded that the exercise of the right to take decisions conferred upon the Commission should comprise successive stages so that a decision finding that there is an infringement may be preceded by any preliminary measures which may appear necessary at any given moment.

18 From this point of view the Commission must also be able, within the bounds of its supervisory task conferred upon it in competition matters by the Treaty and Regulation No 17, to take protective measures to the extent to which they might appear indispensable in order to avoid the exercise of the power to make decisions given by Article 3 from becoming ineffectual or even illusory because of the action of certain undertakings. The powers which the Commission holds under Article 3 (1) of Regulation No 17 therefore include the power to take interim measures which are indispensable for the effective exercise of its functions and, in particular, for ensuring the effectiveness of any decisions requiring undertakings to bring to an end infringements which it has found to exist.

19 However, the Commission could not take such measures without having regard to the legitimate interests of the undertaking concerned by them. For this reason it is essential that interim measures be taken

only in cases proved to be urgent in order to avoid a situation likely to cause serious and irreparable damage to the party seeking their adoption, or which is intolerable for the public interest. A further requirement is that these measures be of a temporary and conservatory nature and restricted to what is required in the given situation. When adopting them the Commission is bound to maintain the essential safeguards guaranteed to the parties concerned by Regulation No 17, in particular by Article 19. Finally, the decisions must be made in such a form that an action may be brought upon them before the Court of Justice by any party who considers he has been injured.

[.....]

21 It follows from these considerations that the Commission possesses the powers needed to meet the request of the applicant if it thinks this request is justified in the circumstances. The applicant must therefore be referred back to the Commission so that it may, without prejudice to the rights and interests of the party concerned by the complaint, take a decision upon the request for interim measures upon the conditions set out above.

[.....]

2) Joined Cases 228 & 229/82 *Ford v. Commission* [1984] ECR 1129

Ford AG, a German undertaking, manufactured both left-hand and right-hand drive cars. The latter were sold to Ford Britain, but Ford AG also accepted orders for right-hand drive cars from German Ford dealers. Because of a substantial price difference for right-hand drive cars between British and German dealers, a fair number of British customers preferred to buy their cars on the German market. This prompted Ford AG to change its marketing system. It informed its appointed German dealers that it would no longer supply them with right-hand drive cars. The Commission received a complaint on this new strategy and decided to issue an interim decision in which it ordered Ford AG to resume the sale of right-hand drive cars to its German distributors. At the same time, Ford appealed the Commission's decision criticising the selective distribution system as operated by Ford AG and the main dealer agreement it had concluded with its distributors.

Relevance: limitation of Commission's powers with regard to the ordering of interim measures.

Substance of the case

[.....]

17 With regard to the parties' arguments, as set out above, it is appropriate first to examine whether, in adopting the contested interim measure, the Commission kept within the limits of its powers as established by the provisions of Community law and by the interpretation placed on those provisions by the Court in its order of 17 January 1980.
18 In that order the Court did not examine in detail the form and nature of the interim measures which the Commission may adopt. As the order makes clear, the power to adopt such measures is based on Article 3 (1) of Regulation No 17, which the Commis-

sion also mentioned in the references in the preamble to the contested decision.
19 That provision states that "where the Commission, upon application or upon its own initiative, finds that there is infringement of Article 85 or Article 86 of the Treaty, it may by decision require the undertakings... concerned to bring such infringement to an end." As the Court stated in the aforementioned order the protective measures which the Commission may adopt as interim measures are those which appear indispensable in order to prevent the exercise of the power to make decisions given by Article 3 from becoming ineffectual or even illusory because of the action of certain undertakings. It follows that the interim measures must come within the framework of the final decision which may be adopted by virtue of Article 3.
20 In this case the main proceedings relate to the dealer agreement. It is solely in relation to that agreement that the Commission is in a position to make a finding that there is an infringement of Article 85 (1) and the final decision which the Commission may adopt under Article 3 (1) is that which requires Ford AG to bring the operation of that agreement to an end.
21 The contested interim decision does not relate to that agreement but solely to Ford AG's refusal to supply right-hand drive cars to German dealers and that refusal, according to the Commission, does not infringe either Article 85 or Article 86 of the Treaty. The measure ordered by that decision therefore does not come within the framework of a final decision which may be adopted. In view of its unequivocal wording and in particular of its express order to Ford AG to refrain from taking any measures having the same effect as the circular, the decision ordering interim measures cannot be interpreted in the manner in which the Commission submitted, in the course of the proceedings before the Court, that it should be interpreted, namely as allowing the company to maintain its refusal to supply on condition that it ceases to operate the dealer agreement.
22 Even on the assumption that the Commission, when adopting in pursuance of Article 6 and 8 of Regulation No 17 a decision in application of Article 85 (3) of the Treaty, may regard the refusal to supply as a circumstance which prevents an exemption from being granted in respect of the dealer agreement or may subject the grant or continuation of such an exemption to the requirement that supplies be resumed, it would still have no authority to convert that requirement, by means of a decision ordering interim measures, into a separate, enforceable order which leaves no choice to the undertaking concerned.
23 It must be pointed out that although, by adopting the contested decision, the Commission exceeded the limits of its powers, it was nevertheless not deprived of all possibility of reacting, immediately and in such a way as to influence Ford AG's conduct, to the circular which that company sent to its dealers.

[.....]

S. Commitments under Article 9 Regulation 1/2003

Cross-references for this part:

The following two documents provide an alternative for undertakings in their attempts to reach commitments decisions.

► Commission Regulation (EC) No 622/2008 amending Regulation (EC) No 773/2004 as regards the conduct of settlement procedures in cartel cases, OJ 2008 L 171/3.

► Notice on the conduct of settlement procedures in view of the adoption of Decisions pursuant to Article 7 and Article 23 of Council Regulation (EC) No 1/2003 in cartel cases, [2008] OJ C 167/1.

1) *De Beers*, Comm. Press Release (IP/06/204), summary of decision published in [2006] OJ L 205/24

Relevance: example of commitments offered pursuant to Article 9 of Reg. 1/2003.

IP/06/204, Brussels, 22nd February 2006

Competition: De Beers' commitment to phase out rough diamond purchases from ALROSA made legally binding by Commission decision

Commitments entered into by De Beers to end purchases of rough diamonds as of 2009 from ALROSA, the world's second largest producer, have been rendered legally binding by a formal decision adopted by the European Commission. Following a phasing out from 2006 to 2008, De Beers undertakes to refrain from all purchases of rough diamonds from ALROSA. This will result in more rough diamonds being available on the open market, paving the way for genuine competition in the supply of rough diamonds. The Commission had been concerned that the practices of De Beers may have violated EC Treaty rules on abuse of dominant market positions (Article 82) but has now closed the case in the light of the commitments submitted by De Beers.

Competition Commissioner Neelie Kroes commented: "For the first time in the history of the diamond market there is an opportunity for genuine competition. De Beers' long-running primacy can now effectively be challenged by its biggest competitor, ALROSA. The Commission's decision frees up a viable alternative source for supply of rough diamonds, which will ultimately benefit consumers."

De Beers, based in South Africa, whose registered office is in Luxembourg, is a global operator primarily active in the production and supply of rough diamonds.

ALROSA is a Russian company mainly specialising in the production of rough diamonds.

For much of the 20th century De Beers held an unrivalled position in the diamond market. Its grip over alternative sources of supply will now be broken. This creates a new opportunity for competition in the worldwide rough diamond market.

The commitments offered by De Beers relate to its purchases of rough diamonds from ALROSA and provide for the termination of purchases from ALROSA as of 2009 after a phasing out period from 2006 to 2008. During this period, De Beers' purchases of rough diamonds from ALROSA will decrease from US$ 600m in 2006 to US$ 500m in 2007 and US$ 400m in 2008. This is approximately equivalent to a decrease from

€500m in 2006 to €420m in 2007 and €340m in 2008.
A monitoring Trustee will supervise compliance with these commitments. The text of the commitments, the Trustee Mandate and the Trustee's contact details will be published on the Commission's and De Beers' websites.
The Commission decision, based on Article 9 of the procedural Regulation (1/2003) for the implementation, in the present case of Article 82 (abuse of dominant position) of the Treaty, takes into account the result of consultations on the commitments offered by De Beers (see IP/05/664). This decision brings the proceedings concerning the Trade Agreement to an end. However, if De Beers were to break its commitments, the Commission could impose a fine amounting to 10% of De Beers' total worldwide turnover.
The Commission has received a number of complaints against De Beers' Supplier of Choice distribution system for rough diamonds (see IP/03/64). The Commission is currently assessing these complaints in the light of the market changes resulting from De Beers' commitments.
See also MEMO/06/90.

Case cross-references:
- ▸ Case COMP/A.39.116/B2 – *Coca-Cola.*
- ▸ Case COMP/B-1/38.348 – *Repsol CPP.*
- ▸ Case COMP/C-2/38.173 – *Joint Selling of the media rights by the FA Premier League.*

2) Case T-170/06 *Alrosa Company Ltd v. Commission* [2007] ECR II-2601

See I-S-1 for the facts
The present action was brought by Alrosa seeking the annulment of the Commission's decision addressed to De Beers (see I-S-1).

Relevance: the commitments for an indefinite duration, the principle of proportionality.

[...]

88 By making a particular type of conduct of an operator in relation to third parties binding, a decision adopted under Article 9 of Regulation No 1/2003 may indirectly have legal effects *erga omnes*, which the undertaking concerned would not have been in a position to create on its own; the Commission is thus their sole author from the time at which it makes binding the commitments offered by the undertaking concerned and accordingly assumes sole responsibility for them. It is not obliged in any way to take into account and, *a fortiori*, to take into account on a take-it-or-leave-it basis, the offers of commitment which the undertakings concerned submit to it.

89 Although Regulation No 1/2003 does not define the concept of 'undertaking concerned', it is clear from its wording that that expression relates to undertakings which are responsible for the conduct in question and which are liable to be penalised because of it.
Proceedings under Article 82 EC therefore involve, as a rule, the undertaking which is in a dominant position and the conduct of which is liable to constitute an abuse. If the correct interpretation were to be that all undertakings liable to be affected by behavioural commitments intended to put an end to an established or contemplated abuse must be associated with the offer of commitments in their capacity as undertakings concerned, that would result in the use of Article 9 of

Regulation No 1/2003 being impossible in practice in most of the situations to which Article 82 EC applies.

91 As regards the period in which the decision making commitments binding may remain in force, it should be noted that while Article 9(1) of Regulation No 1/2003 provides that such a decision may be adopted for a specified period, it does not, however, require this. The definitive wording of Article 9 of Regulation No 1/2003 falls to be distinguished in that regard, as the Commission rightly points out, from the wording which had been used at the stage of the Commission proposal for a Council Regulation on the implementation of the rules on competition laid down in Articles 81 [EC] and 82 [EC] (COM(2000) 582 final), which provided that such a decision was 'to be adopted for a specified period'. There is, accordingly, no reason of principle which prohibits the Commission from making commitments for an indefinite period binding.

[...]

131 However, compliance with the principle of proportionality requires that, when measures that are less onerous than those it proposes to make binding exist, and are known by it, the Commission should examine whether those measures are capable of addressing the concerns which justify its action before it adopts, in the event of their proving unsuitable, the more onerous approach.

[...]

139 It is true that the Commission cannot substitute itself for the parties so as to amend the commitments they offer under Article 9 of Regulation No 1/2003 in order that those commitments may address the concerns set out in its preliminary assessment. However, there is nothing to prevent it from making proposed commitments binding only in part or to a particular extent. Moreover, it appears that in the present case, at the meeting of 27 October 2005, the Commission had proposed to the parties that the joint commitments be amended. On that occasion, it announced its intention to take a decision, based on Article 7 of Regulation No 1/2003, which would prohibit them from having any trading relations with effect from 2009 if they did not offer commitments to that effect before the end of November 2005.

140 None the less, the Commission cannot lawfully propose to the parties that they should offer it commitments which go further than a decision which it could have adopted under Article 7(1) of Regulation No 1/2003. In the present case, a decision adopted under that provision which required De Beers to bring to an end with effect from 2009, for an indefinite period, all direct or indirect trading relations with Alrosa would manifestly go beyond what the Commission could have required if it were to comply with the principle of proportionality, having regard to the objective pursued.

141 Only exceptional circumstances, which have not been identified in the Decision and which are not apparent from the file, can justify a decision adopted under Article 9(1) prohibiting undertakings completely and indefinitely from contracting amongst each other. It is true that, where the undertakings concerned have a collective dominant position, it is possible that nothing less than a complete prohibition of any dealings between them may be the only way of preventing abuses. But, while the Commission gave it to be understood in the statement of objections notified to the parties under Article 81 EC that an oligopoly might have existed between Alrosa and De Beers, the analysis

set out in the Decision is based solely on the dominant position of De Beers and not on a possible collective dominant position of the two undertakings. Both in its defence and at the hearing, the Commission confirmed that the Decision should indeed be understood in that way.

Consequently, the CFI annulled the Commission's decision addressed to De Beers.

CHAPTER II

Article 102 TFEU – Dominance & Abuse – Basic Concepts and Notions

General chapter cross-references:

▸ Communication from the Commission — Guidance on the Commission's enforcement priorities in applying Article 82 of the EC Treaty to abusive exclusionary conduct by dominant undertakings, OJ 2009 C 45/7.

▸ Anne C. Witt, 'The Commission's Guidance Paper on Abusive Exclusionary conduct – More radical than it appears?, (2010) 35 *E.L.Rev.* 214-235.

▸ C. Hampton, 'The role of economics under Article 82', (2005) 4 (5) *Competition Law Insight*, 1.

▸ R.E. Bloch, H.G. Kamann, J.S. Brown, J.P. Schmidt, 'A comparative analysis of Art. 82 of EC Treaty and Sec. 2 of the Sherman Act', (2005) 4 *ZweR*, 325.

A. General Issues

Notion of 'dominance'

1) Case 85/76 *Hoffmann-La Roche (Vitamins)* [1979] ECR 461

See above for facts of the case (I-A-2, p. 4).

Relevance: definition of 'dominance' and indications of existence dominance (e.g. market shares, technological advantages, access to finance).

[.....]

38 Article 86 is an application of the general objective of the activities of the Community laid down by Article 3 (f) of the Treaty namely, the institution of a system ensuring that competition in the Common Market is not distorted.
Article 86 prohibits any abuse by an undertaking of a dominant position in a substantial part of the Common Market in so far as it may affect trade between Member States.
The dominant position thus referred to relates to a position of economic strength enjoyed by an undertaking which enables it to prevent effective competition being maintained on the relevant market by affording it the power to behave to an appreciable extent independently of its competitors, its customers and ultimately of the consumers.
39 Such a position does not preclude some competition, which it does where there is a monopoly or a quasi-monopoly, but enables the undertaking which profits by it, if not to determine, at least to have an appreciable influence on the conditions under which that competition will develop, and in any case to act largely in disregard of it so long as such conduct does not operate to its detriment.
A dominant position must also be distinguished from parallel courses of conduct which are peculiar to oligopolies in that in an oligopoly the courses of conduct interact, while in the case of an undertaking occupying a dominant position the conduct of the undertaking which derives profits from that position is to a great extent determined unilaterally.
The existence of a dominant position may derive from several factors which, taken separately, are not necessarily determinative but among these factors a highly important one is the existence of very large market shares.
40 A substantial market share as evidence of the existence of a dominant position is not a constant factor and its importance varies from market to market according to the structure of these markets, especially as

far as production, supply and demand are concerned.
Even though each group of vitamins constitutes a separate market, these different markets, as has emerged from the examination of their structure, nevertheless have a sufficient number of features in common to make it possible for the same criteria to be applied to them as far as concerns the importance of the market shares for the purpose of determining whether there is a dominant position or not.
41 Furthermore although the importance of the market shares may vary from one market to another the view may legitimately be taken that very large shares are in themselves, and save in exceptional circumstances, evidence of the existence of a dominant position.
An undertaking which has a very large market share and holds it for some time, by means of the volume of production and the scale of the supply which it stands for - without those having much smaller market shares being able to meet rapidly the demand from those who would like to break away from the undertaking which has the largest market share - is by virtue of that share in a position of strength which makes it an unavoidable trading partner and which, already because of this secures for it, at the very least during relatively long periods, that freedom of action which is the special feature of a dominant position.
42 The contested decision has mentioned besides the market shares a number of other factors which together with Roche's market shares would secure for it in certain circumstances, a dominant position.
These factors which the decision classifies as additional criteria are as follows:
(a) Roche's market shares are not only large but there is also a big disparity between its shares and those of its next largest competitors (recitals 5 and 21 to the decision);
(b) Roche produces a far wider range of vitamins than its competitors (recital 21 to the decision);
(c) Roche is the world's largest vitamin manufacturer whose turnover exceeds that of all the other producers and is at the head of a multinational group which in terms of sales is the world's leading pharmaceuticals producer (recitals 5, 6 and 21 to the decision);
(d) Although Roche's patents for the manufacture of vitamins have expired Roche, since it has played a leading role in this field, still enjoys technological advantages over its competitors of which the highly developed customer information and assistance service which it has is evidence (recitals 7 and 8 to the decision);
(e) Roche has a very extensive and highly specialized sales network (recital 21 to the decision);
(f) There is no potential competition (recital 21 to the decision).
Furthermore during the proceedings before the Court the Commission adduced as a factor establishing Roche's dominant position the latter's ability, notwithstanding lively competition, to maintain its market shares substantially intact.
43 Before considering whether the factors taken into account by the Commission can in fact be confirmed in Roche's case it is necessary to ascertain, since the applicant challenges their relevance, whether these factors, in the light of the special features of the relevant markets and of the market shares, are of such a kind as to disclose the existence of a dominant position.
44 In this connexion it is necessary to reject the criterion based on retention of market shares, since this may just as well result from effective competitive behaviour as from a position which ensures that Roche can behave independently of competitors, and the Commission, while admitting that there is competition, has not mentioned the factors

which may account for the stability of market shares where it has been found to exist. However if there is a dominant position then retention of the market shares may be a factor disclosing that this position is being maintained, and, on the other hand, the methods adopted to maintain a dominant position may be an abuse within the meaning of Article 86 of the Treaty.

45 The fact that Roche produces a far wider range of vitamins than its competitors must similarly be rejected as being immaterial. The Commission regards this as a factor establishing a dominant position and asserts that "since the requirements of many users extend to several groups of vitamins, Roche is able to employ a sales and pricing strategy which is far less dependent than that of the other manufacturers on the conditions of competition in each market".

46 However the Commission has itself found that each group of vitamins constitutes a specific market and is not, or at least not to any significant extent, interchangeable with any other group or with any other products (recital 20 to the decision) so that the vitamins belonging to the various groups are as between themselves products just as different as the vitamins compared with other products of the pharmaceutical and food sector.

Moreover it is not disputed that Roche's competitors, in particular those in the chemical industry, market besides the vitamins which they manufacture themselves, other products which purchasers of vitamins also want, so that the fact that Roche is in a position to offer several groups of vitamins does not in itself give it any advantage over its competitors, who can offer, in addition a less or much less wide range of vitamins, other products which are also required by the purchasers of these vitamins.

47 Similar considerations lead also to the rejection as a relevant factor of the circumstance that Roche is the world's largest vitamin manufacturer, that its turnover exceeds that of all the other manufacturers and that it is at the head of the largest pharmaceuticals group in the world.

In the view of the Commission these three considerations together are a factor showing that there is a dominant position, because "it follows that the applicant occupies a preponderant position not only within the Common Market but also on the world market; it therefore enjoys very considerable freedom of action, since its position enables it to adapt itself easily to the developments of the different regional markets. An undertaking operating throughout the markets of the world and having a market share which leaves all its competitors far behind it does not have to concern itself unduly about any competitors within the Common Market".

Such reasoning based on the benefits reaped from economics of scale and on the possibility of adopting a strategy which varies according to the different regional markets is not conclusive, seeing that it is accepted that each group of vitamins constitutes a group of separate products which require their own particular plant and form a separate market, in that the volume of the overall production of products which are different as between themselves does not give Roche a competitive advantage over its competitors, especially over those in the chemical industry, who manufacture on a world scale other products as well as vitamins and have in principle the same opportunities to set off one market against the other as are offered by a large overall production of products which differ from each other as much as the various groups of vitamins do.

48 On the other hand the relationship between the market shares of the undertaking concerned and of its competitors, especially those of the next largest, the technological lead of an undertaking over its competitors, the existence of a highly developed sales network and the absence of poten-

tial competition are relevant factors, the first because it enables the competitive strength of the undertaking in question to be assessed, the second and third because they represent in themselves technical and commercial advantages and the fourth because it is the consequence of the existence of obstacles preventing new competitors from having access to the market.
As far as the existence or non-existence of potential competition is concerned it must however be observed that, although it is true - and this applies to all the groups of vitamins in question - that because of the amount of capital investment required the capacity of the factories is determined according to the anticipated growth over a long period so that access to the market by new producers is not easy, account must also be taken of the fact that the existence of considerable unused manufacturing capacity creates potential competition between established manufacturers.
Nevertheless Roche is in this respect in a privileged position because, as it admits itself, its own manufacturing capacity was, during the period covered by the contested decision, in itself sufficient to meet world demand without this surplus manufacturing capacity placing it in a difficult economic or financial situation.
49 It is in the light of the preceding considerations that Roche's shares of each of the relevant markets, complemented by those factors which in conjunction with the market shares make it possible to show that there may be a dominant position, must be evaluated.

[.....]

Case cross-reference:

▸ Case T-155/04 *Selex Sistemi Integrati* [2006] ECR II-4797.

2) Case 27/76 *UBC (United Brands Company, Chiquita)* [1978] ECR 207

See above for facts of the case (I-A-1, p. 2).

Relevance: indications of existence dominance (e.g. market shares).

[.....]

105 In the second place the Commission states that it estimates UBC's market share at 45%.
106 However UBC points out that this share dropped to 41% in 1975.
107 A trader can only be in a dominant position on the market for a product if he has succeeded in winning a large part of this market.
108 Without going into a discussion about percentages, which when fixed are bound to be to some extent approximations, it can be considered to be an established fact that UBC's share of the relevant market is always more than 40% and nearly 45%.
109 This percentage does not however permit the conclusion that UBC automatically controls the market.
110 It must be determined having regard to the strength and number of the competitors.
111 It is necessary first of all to establish that on the whole of the relevant market the said percentage represents grosso modo a share several times greater than that of its competitor Castle and Cooke which is the best placed of all the competitors, the others coming far behind.

112 This fact together with the others to which attention has already been drawn may be regarded as a factor which affords evidence of UBC's preponderant strength.
113 However an undertaking does not have to have eliminated all opportunity for competition in order to be in a dominant position.

[.....]

119 Even if the local attacks of some competitors can be described as "fierce" it can only be placed on record that UBC held out against them successfully either by adapting its prices for the time being (in the Netherlands in answer to the challenge from Velleman et Tas) or by bringing indirect pressure to bear on the intermediaries.
120 Furthermore if UBC's position on each of the national markets concerned is considered it emerges that, except in Ireland, it sells direct and also, as far as concerns Germany, indirectly through Scipio, almost twice as many bananas as the best placed competitor and that there is no appreciable fall in its sales figures even when new competitors appear on these markets.
121 UBC's economic strength has thus enabled it to adopt a flexible overall strategy directed against new competitors establishing themselves on the whole of the relevant market.
122 The particular barriers to competitors entering the market are the exceptionally large capital investments required for the creation and running of banana plantations, the need to increase sources of supply in order to avoid the effects of fruit diseases and bad weather (hurricanes, floods), the introduction of an essential system of logistics which the distribution of a very perishable product makes necessary, economies of scale from which newcomers to the market cannot derive any immediate benefit and the actual cost of entry made up inter alia of all the general expenses incurred in penetrating the market such as the setting up of an adequate commercial network, the mounting of very large-scale advertising campaigns, all those financial risks, the costs of which are irrecoverable if the attempt fails.
123 Thus, although, as UBC has pointed out, it is true that competitors are able to use the same methods of production and distribution as the applicant, they come up against almost insuperable practical and financial obstacles.
124 That is another factor peculiar to a dominant position.

[.....]

126 An undertaking's economic strength is not measured by its profitability; a reduced profit margin or even losses for a time are not incompatible with a dominant position, just as large profits may be compatible with a situation where there is effective competition.
127 The fact that UBC's profitability is for a time moderate or non-existent must be considered in the light of the whole of its operations.
128 The finding that, whatever losses UBC may make, the customers continue to buy more goods from UBC which is the dearest vendor, is more significant and this fact is a particular feature of the dominant position and its verification is determinative in this case.
129 The cumulative effect of all the advantages enjoyed by UBC thus ensures that is has a dominant position on the relevant market.

[.....]

3) Case 322/81 *Michelin* [1983] ECR 3461

NV Nederlandsche Banden-Industrie Michelin was accused of abusing its dominant position on the Netherlands tyre market. Michelin had tried to bind dealers by running a system of discounts and end-of-year bonuses that was rather discriminating and selective.

Relevance: dominance means special responsibilities to 'the market'.

[.....]

55 [...] it should first be observed that in order to assess the relative economic strength of Michelin NV and its competitors on the Netherlands market the advantages which those undertakings may derive from belonging to groups of undertakings operating throughout Europe or even the world must be taken into consideration. Amongst those advantages, the lead which the Michelin group has over its competitors in the matters of investment and research and the special extent of its range of products, to which the Commission referred in its decision, have not been denied. In fact in the case of certain types of tyre the Michelin group is the only supplier on the market to offer them in its range.

56 That situation ensures that on the Netherlands market a large number of users of heavy-vehicle tyres have a strong preference for Michelin tyres. As the purchase of tyres represents a considerable investment for a transport undertaking and since much time is required in order to ascertain in practice the cost-effectiveness of a type or brand of tyre, Michelin NV therefore enjoys a position which renders it largely immune to competition. As a result, a dealer established in the Netherlands normally cannot afford not to sell Michelin tyres.

57 It is not possible to uphold the objections made against those arguments by Michelin NV, supported on this point by the French government, that Michelin NV is thus penalized for the quality of its products and services. A finding that an undertaking has a dominant position is not in itself a recrimination but simply means that, irrespective of the reasons for which it has such a dominant position, the undertaking concerned has a special responsibility not to allow its conduct to impair genuine undistorted competition on the Common Market.

[.....]

Case cross-reference:

▸ R. Subiotto, 'The Special Responsibility of Dominant Undertakings Not to Impair Genuine Undistorted Competition', (1994/95) 18 *World Competition*, 5.

Notion of 'collective dominance'

Cross-references for this part:

▸ Guidelines on the assessment of horizontal mergers under the Council Regulation on the control of concentration between undertakings, [2004] OJ C 31/5.

▸ Case T-88/94 *Kali und Salz* [1995] ECR II-221 (see VII-F-1).

▸ Cases on collective dominance in the context of merger control: Case T-102/96 *Gencor/Lonrho v. Commission* [1999] ECR II-753 and Case T-342/99 *Airtours v. Commission* [2002] ECR II-2585 (see VII-H-1 and VII-H-2).

▸ R. Whish, 'Collective dominance', in: D. O'Keefe, M. Andenas, *Liber Amicorum for Lord Slynn*, Volume 1 (Kluwer, 2000).

4) Joined Cases T-68, 77 & 78/89 *Italian Flat Glass* [1992] ECR II-1403

The Commission had found that three, in theory independent, Italian flat-glass producers had in fact formed a single entity as far as their conduct in the market was concerned. For example, the three undertakings, FP, SIV and VP, had charged identical prices and had given identical discounts. Since the producers operated in an oligopolistic market, the above behaviour amounted to an abuse of a dominant collective position.

Relevance: example of collective dominance.

[.....]

(b) Assessment by the Court

357 The Court notes that the very words of the first paragraph of Article 86 provide that "one or more undertakings" may abuse a dominant position. It has consistently been held, as indeed all the parties acknowledge, that the concept of agreement or concerted practice between undertakings does not cover agreements or concerted practices among undertakings belonging to the same group if the undertakings form an economic unit (see, for example, the judgment in Case 15/74 Centrafarm, cited above, paragraph 41). It follows that when Article 85 refers to agreements or concerted practices between "undertakings", it is referring to relations between two or more economic entities which are capable of competing with one another.

358 The Court considers that there is no legal or economic reason to suppose that the term "undertaking" in Article 86 has a different meaning from the one given to it in the context of Article 85. There is nothing, in principle, to prevent two or more independent economic entities from being, on a specific market, united by such economic links that, by virtue of that fact, together they hold a dominant position vis-à-vis the other operators on the same market. This could be the case, for example, where two or more independent undertakings jointly have, through agreements or licences, a technological lead affording them the power to behave to an appreciable extent independently of their competitors, their customers and ultimately of their consumers (judgment of the Court in Hoffmann-La Roche, cited above, paragraphs 38 and 48).

359 The Court finds support for that interpretation in the wording of Article 8 of Council Regulation (EEC) No 4056/86 of 22 December 1986 laying down detailed rules for the application of Articles 85 and 86 of the Treaty to maritime transport (Official Journal L 378, p. 4). Article 8(2) provides that the conduct of a liner conference benefiting from an exemption from a prohibition laid down by Article 85(1) of the Treaty may have effects which are incompatible with Article 86 of the Treaty. A request by a conference to be exempted from the prohibition laid down by Article 85(1) necessarily presupposes an agreement between two or more independent economic undertakings.

360 However, it should be pointed out that for the purposes of establishing an infringement of Article 86 of the Treaty, it is not sufficient, as the Commission's agent claimed at the hearing, to "recycle" the facts constituting an infringement of Article 85, deducing from them the finding that the parties to an agreement or to an unlawful practice jointly hold a substantial share of the market, that by virtue of that fact alone they hold a collective dominant position, and that their unlawful behaviour constitutes an abuse of that collective dominant position.

[.....]

5) Joined Cases T-24-26 & 28/93 *CEWAL* [1996] ECR II-1201

This case concerned a group of undertakings that sought to distort the competition regime. Here the members of CEWAL, a shipping conference that operated maritime transport routes from and to Africa, were accused of collectively eliminating their main competitor.

Relevance: example of collective dominance.

[.....]

62 It should be stressed that the Court of Justice has held that, in order for such a collective dominant position to exist, the undertakings in question must be linked in such a way that they adopt the same conduct on the market (DIP and Others, paragraph 26).

63 In the Decision under review, the Commission expressly referred to Regulation No 4056/86. Article 1(3)(b) of that regulation defines a 'liner conference' as 'a group of two or more vessel-operating carriers which provides international liner services for the carriage of cargo on a particular route or routes within specified geographical limits and which has an agreement or arrangement, whatever its nature, within the framework of which they operate under uniform or common freight rates and any other agreed conditions with respect to the provision of liner services'. The Court considers that the applicants, which rely on several occasions on Regulation No 4056/86, do not deny that Cewal is a liner conference within the meaning of that provision.

64 The Court further points out that Article 8 of Regulation No 4056/86 states that Article 86 of the Treaty is still potentially applicable. As a result of the close relations which shipping companies maintain with each other within a liner conference, they are capable together of implementing in common on the relevant market practices such as to constitute unilateral conduct. Such conduct may involve infringement of Article 86 if the other requirements for the application of that provision are also met.

65 In this case, the Court finds, in view of the evidence set out in the contested decision, that the shipping companies formed a common entity, the Cewal shipping conference. It appears from the Decision that that structure formed a framework for a number of committees to which conference members belonged, such as the Zaïre Pool Committee and the Special Fighting Committee mentioned on many occasions in the Decision, in particular in points 26, 29, 31 and 32, and the Zaïre Action Committee referred to in point 74. In addition, as emerges from Article 1 of Regulation No 4056/86, by virtue of its nature that common structure is intended to define and apply uniform freight rates and other common conditions of carriage, which the Commission expressly finds to exist in point 61. Consequently, Cewal presents itself on the market as one and the same entity. Lastly, the Court observes, without its being necessary to consider at this stage how to categorize them, that the practices described in the Decision of which Cewal members stand accused reveal an intention to adopt together the same conduct on the market in order to react unilaterally to a change, deemed to be a threat, in the competitive situation on the market on which they operate. Those practices, which are described in precise terms in the Decision, constituted aspects of an over-

all strategy which Cewal members pooled their forces in order to implement.
66 Consequently, the Court considers, in the light of the Decision taken as a whole, that the Commission has sufficiently shown that it was necessary to assess the position of Cewal members on the relevant market collectively.
67 Lastly, it should be stressed that in the judgment in Società Italiana Vetro the Court held, at paragraph 360, that, for the purposes of establishing an infringement of Article 86 of the Treaty, it is not sufficient to 'recycle' the facts constituting an infringement of Article 85, deducing from them the finding that the parties to an agreement or to an unlawful practice jointly hold a substantial share of the market; that by virtue of that fact alone they hold a collective dominant position, and that their unlawful behaviour constitutes an abuse of that collective dominant position. In this case, contrary to what the applicants maintain, this cannot apply. The Commission has sufficiently proved that, quite apart from the agreements concluded between the shipping companies creating the Cewal conference, which are not contested, there were links between the companies such that they adopted uniform conduct on the market. In those circumstances, the Commission was fully entitled to consider that Article 86 could apply, subject only to the other requirements laid down by that provision being met.

[.....]

Case cross-reference:
▸Joined Cases C-395 & 396/96 P *Compagnie Maritime Belge Transports (and Dafra Lines) v. Commission* [2000] ECR I-1365, the ECJ set part of the GC judgment aside (the part upholding the fines for the applicants) and partly annulled Commission decision 93/82/EEC (in so far as it concerned applicants).

Notion of 'abuse'

6) Case 6/72 *Continental Can* [1973] ECR 215

Continental Can, an American producer of (metal) packaging materials, had virtually eliminated all competition in its market sector when it acquired over 80% of shares in two rival companies, the German SLW and the Dutch TDV. The second take-over bid was made by the Europemballage Corporation, which was 100% controlled by Continental Can, and to which the latter had also transferred its interests in SLW. The Commission found that these acquisitions infringed Article 102 as they allegedly strengthened Continental Can's already existing dominant position. The ECJ, when asked by Continental Can to annul the decision, needed to decide whether Article 102 did indeed extend to cases of concentration through acquisition as in the case at hand.

Relevance: notion of 'abuse' explained.

[.....]

C – on Article 86 of the Treaty and abuse of a dominant position

18 In Articles 1 and 2 of the Commission's decision of 9 December 1971 Continental Can is blamed for having infringed Article 86 of the EEC Treaty by abusing the dominant position which it allegedly held through Schmalbach-Lubeca-Werke AG of Brunswick (hereinafter called SLW) in a substantial part of the Common Market in the market for light metal containers for meat, meat products, fish and crustacea as well as in the market for metal closures for glass jars. According to Article 1 the abuse consists in continental having acquired in April 1970, through its subsidiary Europemballage, about 80 per cent of the shares and debentures of TDV. By this acquisition competition in the containers mentioned was practically eliminated in a substantial part of the Common Market.

19 The applicants maintain that the Commission by its decision, based on an erroneous interpretation of Article 86 of the EEC Treaty, is trying to introduce a control of mergers of undertakings, thus exceeding its powers. Such an attempt runs contrary to the intention of the authors of the Treaty, which is clearly seen not only from a literal interpretation of Article 86, but also from a comparison of the EEC Treaty and the national legal provisions of the Member States. The examples given in Article 86 of abuse of a dominant position confirm this conclusion, for they show that the Treaty refers only to practices which have effects on the market and are to the detriment of consumers or trade partners. Further, Article 86 reveals that the use of economic power linked with a dominant position can be regarded as an abuse of this position only if it constitutes the means through which the abuse is effected. But structural measures of undertakings – such as strengthening a dominant position by way of merger – do not amount to abuse of this position within the meaning of Article 86 of the Treaty. The decision contested is, therefore, said to be void as lacking the required legal basis.

20 Article 86 (1) of the Treaty says "any abuse by one or more undertakings of a dominant position within the Common Market or in a substantial part of it shall be prohibited as incompatible with the Common Market in so far as it may affect trade between Member States". The question is whether the word "abuse" in Article 86 refers only to practices of undertakings which may directly affect the market and are detrimental to production or sales, to purchasers or consumers, or whether this word refers also to changes in the structure of an undertaking, which lead to competition being seriously disturbed in a substantial part of the Common Market.

21 The distinction between measures which concern the structure of the undertaking and practices which affect the market cannot be decisive, for any structural measure may influence market conditions, if it increases the size and the economic power of the undertaking.

22 In order to answer this question, one has to go back to the spirit, general scheme and wording of Article 86, as well as to the system and objectives of the Treaty. These problems thus cannot be solved by comparing this Article with certain provisions of the ECSC Treaty.

23 Article 86 is part of the chapter devoted to the common rules on the Community's policy in the field of competition. This policy is based on Article 3 (f) of the Treaty according to which the Community's activity shall include the institution of a system ensuring that competition in the Common Market

is not distorted. The applicants' argument that this provision merely contains a general programme devoid of legal effect, ignores the fact that Article 3 considers the pursuit of the objectives which it lays down to be indispensable for the achievement of the Community's tasks. As regards in particular the aim mentioned in (f), the Treaty in several provisions contains more detailed regulations for the interpretation of which this aim is decisive.

24 But if Article 3 (f) provides for the institution of a system ensuring that competition in the Common Market is not distorted, then it requires a fortiori that competition must not be eliminated. This requirement is so essential that without it numerous provisions of the Treaty would be pointless. Moreover, it corresponds to the precept of Article 2 of the Treaty according to which one of the tasks of the Community is "to promote throughout the Community a harmonious development of economic activities". Thus the restraints on competition which the Treaty allows under certain conditions because of the need to harmonize the various objectives of the Treaty, are limited by the requirements of Articles 2 and 3. Going beyond this limit involves the risk that the weakening of competition would conflict with the aims of the Common Market.

25 With a view to safeguarding the principles and attaining the objectives set out in Articles 2 and 3 of the Treaty, Articles 85 and 90 have laid down general rules applicable to undertakings. Article 85 concerns agreements between undertakings, decisions of associations of undertakings and concerted practices, while Article 86 concerns unilateral activity of one or more undertakings. Articles 85 and 86 seek to achieve the same aim on different levels, viz. the maintenance of effective competition within the Common Market. The restraint of competition which is prohibited if it is the result of behaviour falling under Article 85, cannot become permissible by the fact that such behaviour succeeds under the influence of a dominant undertaking and results in the merger of the undertakings concerned. In the absence of explicit provisions one cannot assume that the Treaty, which prohibits in Article 85 certain decisions of ordinary associations of undertakings restricting competition without eliminating it, permits in Article 86 that undertakings, after merging into an organic unity, should reach such a dominant position that any serious chance of competition is practically rendered impossible. Such a diverse legal treatment would make a breach in the entire competition law which could jeopardize the proper functioning of the Common Market. If, in order to avoid the prohibitions in Article 85, it sufficed to establish such close connections between the undertakings that they escaped the prohibition of Article 85 without coming within the scope of that of Article 86, then, in contradiction to the basic principles of the Common Market, the partitioning of a substantial part of this market would be allowed. The endeavour of the authors of the Treaty to maintain in the market real or potential competition even in cases in which restraints on competition are permitted, was explicitly laid down in Article 85 (3) (b) of the Treaty. Article 86 does not contain the same explicit provisions, but this can be explained by the fact that the system fixed there for dominant positions, unlike Article 85 (3), does not recognize any exemption from the prohibition. With such a system the obligation to observe the basic objectives of the Treaty, in particular that of Article 3 (f), results from the obligatory force of these objectives. In any case Articles 85 and 86 cannot be interpreted in such a way that they contradict each other, because they serve to achieve the same aim.

26 It is in the light of these considerations that the condition imposed by Article 86 is to be interpreted whereby in order to come within the prohibition a dominant position must have been abused. The provision states a certain number of abusive practices which it prohibits. The list merely gives examples, not an exhaustive enumeration of the sort of abuses of a dominant position prohibited by the Treaty. As may further be seen from letters (c) and (d) of Article 86 (2), the provision is not only aimed at practices which may cause damage to consumers directly, but also at those which are detrimental to them through their impact on an effective competition structure, such as is mentioned in Article 3 (f) of the Treaty. Abuse may therefore occur if an undertaking in a dominant position strengthens such position in such a way that the degree of dominance reached substantially fetters competition, i.e. that only undertakings remain in the market whose behaviour depends on the dominant one.

27 Such being the meaning and the scope of Article 86 of the EEC Treaty, the question of the link of causality raised by the applicants which in their opinion has to question exist between the dominant position and its abuse, is of no consequence, for the strengthening of the position of an undertaking may be an abuse and prohibited under Article 86 of the Treaty, regardless of the means and procedure by which it is achieved, if it has the effects mentioned above.

[.....]

Case cross-reference:

▸ H. James, 'Tetra Pak: Exemption and Abuse of Dominant Position', (1990) 11 *ECLR*, 268.

7) Case 27/76 *UBC (United Brands Company, Chiquita)* [1978] ECR 207

See above for facts of the case (I-A-1, p. 2).

Relevance: definition of anti-exploitative abuse.

[.....]

249 It is advisable therefore to ascertain whether the dominant undertaking has made use of the opportunities arising out of its dominant position in such a way as to reap trading benefits which it would not have reaped if there had been normal and sufficiently effective competition.

[.....]

8) Case 85/76 *Hoffmann-La Roche (Vitamins)* [1979] ECR 461

See above for facts of the case (I-A-2, p. 4).

Relevance: definition of anti-competitive abuse.

[.....]

91 For the purpose of rejecting the finding that there has been an abuse of a dominant position the interpretation suggested by the applicant that an abuse implies that the use of the economic power bestowed by a dominant position is the means whereby the abuse has been brought about cannot be accepted. The concept of abuse is an objective concept relating to the behaviour of an undertaking in a dominant position which is such as to influence the structure of a market where, as a result of the very presence of the undertaking in question, the degree of competition is weakened and which, through recourse to methods different from those which condition normal competition in products or services on the basis of the transactions of commercial operators, has the effect of hindering the maintenance of the degree of competition still existing in the market or the growth of that competition.

[.....]

9) Case C-333/94 P *Tetra Pak II* [1996] ECR I-5951

The Tetra Pak group was active on the market for both aseptic and non-aseptic packages. It manufactured cartons for the packaging of fluids (such as milk) and semi-fluids and sold or leased carton-filling machines. The dispute arose out of the rather restrictive agreements it had concluded with its purchasers and/or leaseholders. For example, the machines were only to be used for Tetra Pak cartons; leaseholders had to pay a penalty when they breached their contractual obligations, and Tetra Pak had stipulated the exclusive right to maintain and repair the machines.

Relevance: example of abuse on an ancillary (associated or secondary) market.

[.....]

The second plea

21 In its second plea, Tetra Pak principally casts doubt on the reasoning followed by the Court of First Instance in paragraph 122 of the judgment under appeal, which reads: "It follows from all the above considerations that, in the circumstances of this case, Tetra Pak's practices on the non-aseptic markets are liable to be caught by Article 86 of the Treaty without its being necessary to establish the existence of a dominant position on those markets taken in isolation, since that undertaking's leading position on the non-aseptic markets, combined with the close associative links between those markets and the aseptic markets, gave Tetra Pak freedom of conduct compared with the other economic operators on the non-aseptic markets, such as to impose on it a special responsibility under Article 86 to maintain genuine undistorted competition on those markets."

22 In Tetra Pak's submission, the case-law cited by the Court of First Instance at paragraphs 114 and 115 of its judgment does not justify the conclusion that conduct on a market other than the dominated market, which is not intended to reinforce the position on the dominated market, is covered by Article 86. Tetra Pak maintains that such a conclusion cannot even be justified by the associative links between the various markets

found by the Commission and the Court of First Instance.

23 In developing its argument, Tetra Pak refers particularly to the fact that in its previous case-law the Court of Justice has always examined either abuses which took place on the dominated market and whose effects were felt on another market or abuses which were committed on a market on which the undertaking did not hold a dominant position but which strengthened its position on the dominated market.

24 It must first be stressed that there can be no question of challenging the Court of First Instance's assessment, at paragraph 113 of its judgment, that Article 86 gives no explicit guidance as to the requirements relating to where on the product market the abuse took place. That Court was therefore correct in stating, at paragraph 115, that the actual scope of the special responsibility imposed on a dominant undertaking must be considered in the light of the specific circumstances of each case which show a weakened competitive situation.

25 In that regard, the case-law cited by the Court of First Instance is relevant. Joined Cases 6/73 and 7/73 Commercial Solvents v Commission [1974] ECR 223 and Case 311/84 CBEM v CLT and IPB [1985] ECR 3261 provide examples of abuses having effects on markets other than the dominated markets. In Case C-62/86 AKZO v Commission [1991] ECR I-3359 and Case T-65/89 BPB Industries and British Gypsum v Commission [1993] ECR II-389, the Community judicature found certain conduct on markets other than the dominated markets and having effects on the dominated markets to be abusive. The Court of First Instance was therefore right in concluding from that case-law, at paragraph 116 of the judgment under appeal, that it must reject the applicant's arguments to the effect that the Community judicature had ruled out any possibility of Article 86 applying to an act committed by an undertaking in a dominant position on a market distinct from the dominated market.

26 Nor, for the reasons set out by the Advocate General at point 61 of his Opinion, can Tetra Pak derive any support from the judgments in Case 85/76 Hoffmann-La Roche v Commission [1979] ECR 461 or Michelin v Commission, cited above.

27 It is true that application of Article 86 presupposes a link between the dominant position and the alleged abusive conduct, which is normally not present where conduct on a market distinct from the dominated market produces effects on that distinct market. In the case of distinct, but associated, markets, as in the present case, application of Article 86 to conduct found on the associated, non-dominated, market and having effects on that associated market can only be justified by special circumstances.

28 In that regard, the Court of First Instance first considered, at paragraph 118 of its judgment, that it was relevant that Tetra Pak held 78% of the overall market in packaging in both aseptic and non-aseptic cartons, that is to say seven times more than its closest competitor. At paragraph 119, it stressed Tetra Pak's leading position in the non-aseptic sector. Then, in paragraph 121, it found that Tetra Pak's position on the aseptic markets, of which it held nearly a 90% share, was quasi-monopolistic. It noted that that position also made Tetra Pak a favoured supplier of non-aseptic systems. Finally, at paragraph 122, it concluded that, in the circumstances of the case, application of Article 86 was justified by the situation on the different markets and the close associative links between them.

29 The relevance of the associative links which the Court of First Instance thus took

into account cannot be denied. The fact that the various materials involved are used for packaging the same basic liquid products shows that Tetra Pak's customers in one sector are also potential customers in the other. That possibility is borne out by statistics showing that in 1987 approximately 35% of Tetra Pak's customers bought both aseptic and non-aseptic systems. It is also relevant to note that Tetra Pak and its most important competitor, PKL, were present on all four markets. Given its almost complete domination of the aseptic markets, Tetra Pak could also count on a favoured status on the non-aseptic markets. Thanks to its position on the former markets, it could concentrate its efforts on the latter by acting independently of the other economic operators.

30 The circumstances thus described, taken together and not separately, justified the Court of First Instance, without any need to show that the undertaking was dominant on the non-aseptic markets, in finding that Tetra Pak enjoyed freedom of conduct compared with the other economic operators on those markets.

31 Accordingly, the Court of First Instance was right to accept the application of Article 86 of the Treaty in this case, given that the quasi-monopoly enjoyed by Tetra Pak on the aseptic markets and its leading position on the distinct, though closely associated, non-aseptic markets placed it in a situation comparable to that of holding a dominant position on the markets in question as a whole.

32 An undertaking in such a situation must necessarily be able to foresee that its conduct may be caught by Article 86 of the Treaty. Thus, contrary to the appellant's argument, the requirements of legal certainty are observed.

33 It follows from the foregoing considerations that the second plea in law must be dismissed.

[.....]

Case cross-reference:

► N. Levy, 'Tetra Pak II: Stretching the Limits of Article 86?', (1995) 16 *ECLR*, 104.

10) Case T-228/97 *Irish Sugar* [1999] ECR II-2969

Irish Sugar was held to be dominant on both the (Irish) industrial and retail sugar market. It had, inter alia, been accused by the Commission of hindering competition by means of discriminatory pricing policies.

Relevance: reasonable protection of commercial interests allowed.

[.....]

112 Therefore, whilst the finding that a dominant position exists does not in itself imply any reproach to the undertaking concerned, it has a special responsibility, irrespective of the causes of that position, not to allow its conduct to impair genuine undistorted competition on the Common Market (Michelin, paragraph 57). Similarly, whilst the fact that an undertaking is in a dominant position cannot deprive it of its entitlement to protect its own commercial interests when they are attacked, and whilst such an undertaking must be allowed the right to take such reasonable steps as it deems appropriate to protect those interests, such behaviour cannot be allowed if its purpose is to

strengthen that dominant position and thereby abuse it (United Brands, paragraph 189; BPB Industries and British Gypsum, paragraph 69; Tetra Pak, paragraph 147; Compagnie Maritime Belge des Transports, paragraph 107).

189 Thus, even if the existence of a dominant position does not deprive an undertaking placed in that position of the right to protect its own commercial interests when they are threatened (see paragraph 112 above), the protection of the commercial position of an undertaking in a dominant position with the characteristics of that of the applicant at the time in question must, at the very least, in order to be lawful, be based on criteria of economic efficiency and consistent with the interests of consumers. In this case, the applicant has not shown that those conditions were fulfilled.

[.....]

Case cross-reference:

▸ C-497/99 P *Irish Sugar plc v. Commission* [2001] ECR I-5333, appeal dismissed.

11) Case T-271/03 *Deutsche Telekom AG v. Commission* [2008] ECR II-477

The applicant, Deutsche Telekom AG, operates the German fixed telephone network. According to the Commission, Deutsche Telekom holds a dominant position on the relevant product and service market and infringes Article 101 TFEU by operating abusive pricing in the form of a 'margin squeeze' by charging its competitors for wholesale access prices higher than its prices for retail access to the local network (the Commission's Decision 2003/707/EC). The Commission imposed a fine of € 12.6 million. Deutsche Telekom brought an action, which was dismissed by the GC. Appeal was filed by Deutsche Telekom against the judgment of the GC (Case C-280/08 P, pending).

Relevance: the objective character of Art. 102 TFEU.

[...]

327 The fact that the applicant knew only from 1999 that it was being accused of abuse of its dominant position is irrelevant to the fact that its conduct constituted an infringement from 1 January 1998. An 'abuse' within the meaning of Article 82 EC is an objective concept (*Hoffmann-La Roche* v *Commission*, cited in paragraph 226 above, paragraph 91; *AKZO* v *Commission*, cited in paragraph 189 above, paragraph 69; order in *Piau* v *Commission*, cited in paragraph 233 above, paragraph 37; *Irish Sugar* v *Commission*, cited in paragraph 122 above, paragraph 111). The dominant undertaking's own knowledge of the abusive nature of its conduct is not, therefore, a prerequisite for the application of Article 82 EC.

[...]

Notion of 'substantial part of the Internal Market'

12) Joined Cases 40-48, 50, 54-56, 111, 113 & 114/73 *European Sugar Industry* [1975] 1663

See above for facts of the case (I-G-3, p. 36).

Relevance: substantial part can be a single Member State.

[.....]

I- The question whether the 'southern part of Germany' is a substantial part of the Common Market

441 It is clear from the statement of the reasons upon which the decision is based (p. 20 to 21, paragraph 9, p. 28 under paragraph 16) that when the Commission refers to 'the southern part of Germany' it means the area which it regards as SZV's sales territory as opposed, on the one hand, to the sales territories which it considers belong to NZV and WZW, two companies, of which the sugar producers of the southern and western regions of the Federal Republic of Germany are members and, on the other hand, to the laender of Berlin and the Saar, which it states are for the most part supplied by sugar coming respectively from the Federal Republic of Germany and the French Republic.

[.....]

446 According to the Commission's statistics (cf. annex I to the rejoinder in case 55/73, table v, column 29) consumption 'in SZAG's sales territory less the Saar' increased during each of the four marketing years under consideration to 790 000, 792 000, 872 000 and 826 000 metric tons respectively, and these figures could even increase to the extent to which it would have to be conceded that SZV's sales territory exceeds that of SZAG.

447 According to the available statistics the average number of consumers in the region in question for the years which have to be taken into account can be estimated at 22 million at least.

448 If these figures are compared with the corresponding figures relating to the whole of the Community set out in chapter 5, the 'southern part of Germany', within the meaning which this expression is given in the decision, is found to be sufficiently large, so far as sugar is concerned, to be considered having regard to the other criteria mentioned in chapter 5 as a substantial part of the Common Market in this product.

[.....]

13) Case C-179/90 *Porto di Genova* [1991] ECR I-5889

According to Italian law, dock work is to be performed by dock-work companies whose dockers must have the Italian nationality. These companies were also allowed to organize dock work on behalf of third parties. In the port of Genova, Merci Commerciali had the exclusive right to load and unload ships. It did not, however, render the service as efficient as it should; yet no other company was allowed to compete with Merci by setting up a simi-

lar service in the Port of Genova or to take its place. Siderurgica suffered losses because of this ill performance and started proceedings.

Relevance: a maritime port may qualify as a 'substantial part of the common market'.

[.....]

15 As regards the definition of the market in question, it may be seen from the order for reference that it is that of the organization on behalf of third persons of dock work relating to ordinary freight in the Port of Genoa and the performance of such work. Regard being had in particular to the volume of traffic in that port and its importance in relation to maritime import and export operations as a whole in the Member State concerned, that market may be regarded as constituting a substantial part of the Common Market.

[.....]

Case cross-reference:

▸ L. Gyselen, 'Case C-192/90, Porto di Genova; Case C-18/88, Régie des Télégraphes', (1992) 29 *CMLRev*, 1229.

B. Anti-competitive behaviour (as mentioned in Article 102, litt. a-d EC)

Cross-reference for this part:

▸ D.R. Price, 'Abuse of a Dominant Position – The Tale of Nails, Milk Cartons and TV Guides', (1990) 11 *ECLR*, 80.

Article 102 (a)

1) Case 27/76 *UBC (United Brands Company, Chiquita)* [1978] ECR 207

See above for facts of the case (I-A-1, p. 2).

Relevance: example of excessive (i.e. high) pricing.

[.....]

248 The imposition by an undertaking in a dominant position directly or indirectly of unfair purchase or selling prices is an abuse to which exception can be taken under Article 86 of the Treaty.
249 It is advisable therefore to ascertain whether the dominant undertaking has made use of the opportunities arising out of its dominant position in such a way as to reap trading benefits which it would not have reaped if there had been normal and sufficiently effective competition.
250 In this case charging a price which is excessive because it has no reasonable relation to the economic value of the product supplied would be such an abuse.
251 This excess could, inter alia, be determined objectively if it were possible for it to be calculated by making a comparison between the selling price of the product in question and its cost of production, which would disclose the amount of the profit margin; however the Commission has not

done this since it has not analysed UBC's costs structure.
252 The questions therefore to be determined are whether the difference between the costs actually incurred and the price actually charged is excessive, and, it the answer to this question is in the affirmative, whether a price has been imposed which is either unfair in itself or when compared to competing products.
253 Other ways may be devised - and economic theorists have not failed to think up several - of selecting the rules for determining whether the price of a product is unfair.
254 While appreciating the considerable and at times very great difficulties in working out production costs which may sometimes include a discretionary apportionment of indirect costs and general expenditure and which may vary significantly according to the size of the undertaking, its object, the complex nature of its set up, its territorial area of operations, whether it manufactures one or several products, the number of its subsidiaries and their relationship with each other, the production costs of the banana do not seem to present any insuperable problems.
255 In this case it emerges from a study by the united nations conference on trade and development of 10 February 1975 that the pattern of the production, packaging, transportation, marketing and distribution of bananas could have made it possible to compute the approximate production cost of this fruit and accordingly to calculate whether its selling price to ripener/distributors was excessive.
256 The Commission was at least under a duty to require UBC to produce particulars of all the constituent elements of its production costs.
257 The accuracy of the contents of the documents produced by UBC could have been challenged but that would have been a question of proof.
258 The Commission bases its view that prices are excessive on an analysis of the differences - in its view excessive - between the prices charged in the different Member States and on the policy of discriminatory prices which has been considered above.
259 The foundation of its argument has been the applicant's letter of 10 December 1974 which acknowledged that the margin allowed by the sale of bananas to Irish ripeners was much smaller than in some other Member States and it concluded from this that the amount by which the actual prices f.o.r. Bremerhaven and Rotterdam exceed the delivered Rotterdam prices for bananas to be sold to Irish customers c.i.f. Dublin must represent a profit of the same order of magnitude.
260 Having found that the prices charged to ripeners of the other Member States were considerably higher, sometimes by as much as 100%, than the prices charged to customers in Ireland it concluded that UBC was making a very substantial profit.
261 Nevertheless the Commission has not taken into account in its reasoning several of UBC's letters in which were enclosed a confidential document retracting what is said in its letter of 10 December 1974 and pointing out that the prices charged in Ireland had produced a loss.
262 The applicant also states that the prices charged on the relevant market did not allow it to make any profits during the last five years, except in 1975.
263 These assertions by the applicant are not supported by any accounting documents which prove the consolidated accounts of the UBC group or even by the consolidated accounts for the relevant market.

264 However unreliable the particulars supplied by UBC may be (and in particular the document mentioned previously which works out the "losses" on the Irish market in 1974 without any supporting evidence), the fact remains that it is for the Commission to prove that the applicant charged unfair prices.
265 UBC's retractation, which the Commission has not effectively refuted, establishes beyond doubt that the basis for the calculation adopted by the latter to prove that UBC's prices are excessive is open to criticism and on this particular point there is doubt which must benefit the applicant, especially as for nearly 20 years banana prices, in real terms, have not risen on the relevant market.
266 Although it is also true that the price of Chiquita bananas and those of its principal competitors is different, that difference is about 7%, a percentage which has not been challenged and which cannot automatically be regarded as excessive and consequently unfair.
267 In these circumstances it appears that the Commission has not adduced adequate legal proof of the facts and evaluations which formed the foundation of its finding that UBC had infringed Article 86 of the treaty by directly and indirectly imposing unfair selling prices for bananas.
268 Article 1 (c) of the Decision must therefore be annulled.

[.....]

2) Case 395/87 *Tournier (SACEM III)* [1989] ECR 2521

The director of the Société des auteurs, compositeurs et éditeurs de musique (SACEM), a French copyright-management institution that, inter alia, collected fees whenever a musical work from one of its members was played, was accused of charging excessive royalties in comparison with similar institutions in other Member States.

Relevance: example of excessive pricing for services.

[.....]

38 When an undertaking holding a dominant position imposes scales of fees for its services which are appreciably higher than those charged in other Member States and where a comparison of the fee levels has been made on a consistent basis, that difference must be regarded as indicative of an abuse of a dominant position. In such a case it is for the undertaking in question to justify the difference by reference to objective dissimilarities between the situation in the Member State concerned and the situation prevailing in all the other Member States.

[.....]

3) Case C-62/86 *Akzo* [1991] ECR I-3359

According to the Commission, Akzo, which was dominant on the organic peroxides market, had tried to neutralize ECS, one of its competitors, by charging cut-prices in the flour additives sector. Moreover, the Commission found that Akzo had openly threatened ECS with 'retaliations' (viz. price reductions and selective cuts aimed at ECS's customers) to secure the latter's withdrawal from the market.

Relevance: example of predatory pricing policy. Definition of the notion of 'predatory pricing'.

[.....]

B - The existence of an abuse of a dominant position

1. Preliminary considerations - Criterion of legality of conduct of a dominant undertaking in relation to prices

63 According to the contested decision (point 75) AKZO had abusively exploited its dominant position by endeavouring to eliminate ECS from the organic peroxides market mainly by massive and prolonged price-cutting in the flour additives sector.

64 According to the Commission, Article 86 does not make costs the decisive criterion for determining whether price reductions by a dominant undertaking are abusive (point 77). Such a criterion does not take any account of the general objectives of the EEC competition rules as defined in Article 3(f) of the Treaty and in particular the need to prevent the impairment of an effective structure of competition in the common market. A mechanical criterion would not give adequate weight to the strategic aspect of price-cutting behaviour. There can be an anti-competitive object in price-cutting whether or not the aggressor sets its prices above or below its own costs, whatever the manner in which those costs are understood (point 79).

65 A detailed analysis of the costs of the dominant undertaking might, however, according to the Commission, be of considerable importance in establishing the reasonableness or otherwise of its pricing conduct. The exclusionary consequences of a price-cutting campaign by a dominant producer might be so self-evident that no evidence of intention to eliminate a competitor is necessary. On the other hand, where the low pricing could be susceptible of several explanations, evidence of an intention to eliminate a competitor or restrict competition might also be required to prove an infringement (point 80).

66 AKZO disputes the relevance of the criterion of lawfulness adopted by the Commission, which it regards as nebulous or at least inapplicable. It maintains that the Commission should have adopted an objective criterion based on its costs.

67 In that respect, it states that the question of the lawfulness of a particular level of prices cannot be separated from the specific market situation in which the prices were fixed. There is no abuse if the dominant undertaking endeavours to obtain an optimum selling-price and a positive coverage margin. A price is optimum if the undertaking may reasonably expect that the offer of another price or the absence of a price would produce a less favourable operating profit in the short term. Furthermore, a coverage margin is positive if the value of the order exceeds the sum of the variable costs.

68 According to AKZO, a criterion based on an endeavour to obtain an optimal price

in the short term cannot be rejected on the grounds that it would jeopardize the viability of the undertaking in the long term. It is only after a certain time that the undertaking in question could take measures to eliminate the losses or withdraw from a loss-making branch of business. In the meantime the undertaking would have to accept "optimum orders" in order to reduce its deficit and to ensure continuity of operation.
69 It should be observed that, as the Court held in its judgment in Case 85/76 Hoffman-La Roche v Commission [1979] ECR 461, paragraph 91, the concept of abuse is an objective concept relating to the behaviour of an undertaking in a dominant position which is such as to influence the structure of a market where, as a result of the very presence of the undertaking in question, the degree of competition is weakened and through recourse to methods which, different from those which condition normal competition in products or services on the basis of the transactions of commercial operators, has the effect of hindering the maintenance of the degree of competition still existing in the market or the growth of that competition.
70 It follows that Article 86 prohibits a dominant undertaking from eliminating a competitor and thereby strengthening its position by using methods other than those which come within the scope of competition on the basis of quality. From that point of view, however, not all competition by means of price can be regarded as legitimate.
71 Prices below average variable costs (that is to say, those which vary depending on the quantities produced) by means of which a dominant undertaking seeks to eliminate a competitor must be regarded as abusive. A dominant undertaking has no interest in applying such prices except that of eliminating competitors so as to enable it subsequently to raise its prices by taking advantage of its monopolistic position, since each sale generates a loss, namely the total amount of the fixed costs (that is to say, those which remain constant regardless of the quantities produced) and, at least, part of the variable costs relating to the unit produced.
72 Moreover, prices below average total costs, that is to say, fixed costs plus variable costs, but above average variable costs, must be regarded as abusive if they are determined as part of a plan for eliminating a competitor. Such prices can drive from the market undertakings which are perhaps as efficient as the dominant undertaking but which, because of their smaller financial resources, are incapable of withstanding the competition waged against them.
73 These are the criteria that must be applied to the situation in the present case.

[.....]

Case cross-reference:
▸ N. Levy, 'Case C-62/86, AKZO', (1992) 29 *CMLRev*, 415.

4) Case C-333/94 P *Tetra Pak II* [1996] ECR I-5951

See above for facts of the case (II-A-9, p. 96).

Relevance: example of predatory (i.e. excessively low) pricing policy.

[.....]

The fourth plea

39 In its fourth plea, Tetra Pak submits that the Court of First Instance erred in law when, at paragraph 150 of the judgment under appeal, it characterized Tetra Pak's prices in the non-aseptic sector as predatory without accepting that it was necessary for that purpose to establish that it had a reasonable prospect of recouping the losses so incurred.
40 Tetra Pak considers that the possibility of recouping the losses incurred as a result of predatory sales is a constitutive element in the notion of predatory pricing. That is clear, it claims, from paragraph 71 of the AKZO judgment, cited above. Since, however, both the Commission and the Court of First Instance accept that sales below cost took place only on the non-aseptic markets, on which Tetra Pak was not found to hold a dominant position, it had no realistic chance of recouping its losses later.
41 In AKZO this Court did indeed sanction the existence of two different methods of analysis for determining whether an undertaking has practised predatory pricing. First, prices below average variable costs must always be considered abusive. In such a case, there is no conceivable economic purpose other than the elimination of a competitor, since each item produced and sold entails a loss for the undertaking. Secondly, prices below average total costs but above average variable costs are only to be considered abusive if an intention to eliminate can be shown.
42 At paragraph 150 of the judgment under appeal, the Court of First Instance carried out the same examination as did this Court in AKZO. For sales of non-aseptic cartons in Italy between 1976 and 1981, it found that prices were considerably lower than average variable costs. Proof of intention to eliminate competitors was therefore not necessary. In 1982, prices for those cartons lay between average variable costs and average total costs. For that reason, in paragraph 151 of its judgment, the Court of First Instance was at pains to establish and the appellant has not criticized it in that regard that Tetra Pak intended to eliminate a competitor.
43 The Court of First Instance was also right, at paragraphs 189 to 191 of the judgment under appeal, to apply exactly the same reasoning to sales of non-aseptic machines in the United Kingdom between 1981 and 1984.
44 Furthermore, it would not be appropriate, in the circumstances of the present case, to require in addition proof that Tetra Pak had a realistic chance of recouping its losses. It must be possible to penalize predatory pricing whenever there is a risk that competitors will be eliminated. The Court of First Instance found, at paragraphs 151 and 191 of its judgment, that there was such a risk in this case. The aim pursued, which is to maintain undistorted competition, rules out waiting until such a strategy leads to the actual elimination of competitors.

[.....]

Article 102 (b)

Cross-references for this part:

▸ 'Selective Price Cuts in Fidelity Rebates'. Economic discussion paper (prepared by RBB Economics), (2005) – www.oft.gov.uk.

▸ H.G. Kamann, E. Bergmann, 'The granting of rebates by market dominant undertakings under Art.82 of the EC Treaty', (2005) 2 *ECLR*, 83.

5) Joined Cases 40-48, 50, 54-56, 111, 113 & 114/73 *European Sugar Industry* [1975] 1663

See above for facts of the case (I-G-3, p. 36).

Relevance: artificial seperation of geographical markets.

[.....]

B - The evaluation of the evidence

396 It appears to be quite clear from the documents mentioned, if they are evaluated together with the factors set out in chapters 2 and 3, that RT either expressly or impliedly told the dealers, or deliberately created in their minds the impression, that it would not supply them with sugar or would not supply them with all the quantities for which they applied, unless they complied with its restrictive export policy as applied to the Netherlands or West German markets or deliveries to third countries.

397 The words used in some of its statements are indeed so peremptory that they call to mind instructions to a trade representative rather than negotiations on a footing of equality between a producer and an independent dealer.

398 By compelling dealers to channel their exports to specific consignees or destinations and to impose these restrictions on their own customers RT has restricted the outlets of the dealers and indirectly of their purchasers, which is a practice expressly mentioned by Article 86 (b).

399 Although the incorporation of a denaturing clause in a contract for the sale of sugar does not necessarily amount to an abuse, the extremely hard hearted way in which RT refused to make allowance for the unforeseeable difficulties encountered by Hottlet and the latter's German customer at a later date in despatching sugar to the destination laid down by RT proves in the context of this case to be an integral part of the policy carried out by RT of bringing economic pressure to bear on dealers.

400 There are therefore grounds for finding that RT abused its dominant position on the Belgo-Luxembourg market.

[.....]

6) Case 27/76 *UBC (United Brands Company, Chiquita)* [1978] ECR 207

See above for facts of the case (I-A-1, p. 2).

Relevance: example of a prohibition of resale.

[.....]

151 The Court's examination must be limited to the clause relating to the prohibition of the resale of green bananas in the form in which it was notified to the Commission on 15 November 1968 without it being necessary to consider the clause as drawn up by UBC on 31 January 1976, that is to say at a date subsequent to the Commission's decision.
152 The clause applied in Belgium, Denmark and the Netherlands, in so far as it has been drawn up in writing, prohibited the resale of bananas while still green whether branded or unbranded and even between ripeners of Chiquita bananas.
153 Since UBC thought it should state in the circular letter of 31 January 1976, which it sent to all ripener/distributors including those established in Germany, that the clause had not been put in writing for Germany, it thereby impliedly acknowledges that the said clause was in force on the German market, since it had clearly been implied or mentioned orally.
154 Under the terms of the clause UBC "required their customers to ensure forthwith that the bananas in their possession are not resold to foreign dealers; it had imposed the same requirement on its foreign customers as far as the Netherlands are concerned. It would not hesitate to take such steps as it deems to be necessary if the foregoing is not complied with in some way or other".
155 This wording implies that UBC, far from rejecting the idea of imposing sanctions on duly appointed ripener/distributors which do not comply with its directions, held out this possibility as a threat.
156 Moreover Olesen unquestionably experienced the harsh effects of this clause after UBC refused to supply it and it wanted to obtain supplies of Chiquita bananas from Scipio and the duly appointed Danish distributors.
157 To impose on the ripener the obligation not to resell bananas so long as he has not had them ripened and to cut down the operations of such a ripener to contacts only with retailers is a restriction of competition.
158 Although it is commendable and lawful to pursue a policy of quality, especially by choosing sellers according to objective criteria relating to the qualifications of the seller, his staff and his facilities, such a practice can only be justified if it does not raise obstacles, the effect of which goes beyond the objective to be attained.
159 In this case, although these conditions for selection have been laid down in a way which is objective and not discriminatory, the prohibition on resale imposed upon duly appointed Chiquita ripeners and the prohibition of the resale of unbranded bananas - even if the perishable nature of the banana in practice restricted the opportunities of reselling to the duration of a specific period of time - when without any doubt an abuse of the dominant position since they limit markets to the prejudice of consumers and affects trade between Member States, in particular by partitioning national markets.
160 Thus UBC's organization of the market confined the ripeners to the role of suppliers of the local market and prevented them from

developing their capacity to trade vis-a-vis UBC, which moreover tightened its economic hold on them by supplying less goods than they ordered.
161 It follows from all these considerations that the clause at issue forbidding the sale of green bananas infringes Article 86 of the Treaty.

[.....]

7) Case 85/76 *Hoffmann-La Roche (Vitamins)* [1979] ECR 461

See above for facts of the case (I-A-2, p. 4).

Relevance: example of a loyalty rebate, 'English' clause and exclusive purchase agreement.

[.....]

Section 3: the determination, in the light of Article 86 of the Treaty, of the legal nature of the undertakings to obtain supplies exclusively from Roche and of the system of rebates

89 An undertaking which is in a dominant position on a market and ties purchasers - even if it does so at their request - by an obligation or promise on their part to obtain all or most of their requirements exclusively from the said undertaking abuses its dominant position within the meaning of Article 86 of the Treaty, whether the obligation in question is stipulated without further qualification or whether it is undertaken in consideration of the grant of a rebate.
The same applies if the said undertaking, without tying the purchasers by a formal obligation, applies, either under the terms of agreements concluded with these purchasers or unilaterally, a system of fidelity rebates, that is to say discounts conditional on the customer's obtaining all or most of its requirements - whether the quantity of its purchases be large or small - from the undertaking in a dominant position.
90 Obligations of this kind to obtain supplies exclusively from a particular undertaking, whether or not they are in consideration of rebates or of the granting of fidelity rebates intended to give the purchaser an incentive to obtain his supplies exclusively from the undertaking in a dominant position, are incompatible with the objective of undistorted competition within the Common Market, because - unless there are exceptional circumstances which may make an agreement between undertakings in the context of Article 85 and in particular of paragraph (3) of that Article, permissible - they are not based on an economic transaction which justifies this burden or benefit but are designed to deprive the purchaser of or restrict his possible choices of sources of supply and to deny other producers access to the market.
The fidelity rebate, unlike quantity rebates exclusively linked with the volume of purchases from the producer concerned, is designed through the grant of a financial advantage to prevent customers from obtaining their supplies from competing producers.
Furthermore the effect of fidelity rebates is to apply dissimilar conditions to equivalent transactions with other trading parties in that two purchasers pay a different price for the same quantity of the same product depending on whether they obtain their supplies exclusively from the undertaking in

a dominant position or have several sources of supply.
Finally these practices by an undertaking in a dominant position and especially on an expanding market tend to consolidate this position by means of a form of competition which is not based on the transactions effected and is therefore distorted.
91 For the purpose of rejecting the finding that there has been an abuse of a dominant position the interpretation suggested by the applicant that an abuse implies that the use of the economic power bestowed by a dominant position is the means whereby the abuse has been brought about cannot be accepted. The concept of abuse is an objective concept relating to the behaviour of an undertaking in a dominant position which is such as to influence the structure of a market where, as a result of the very presence of the undertaking in question, the degree of competition is weakened and which, through recourse to methods different from those which condition normal competition in products or services on the basis of the transactions of commercial operators, has the effect of hindering the maintenance of the degree of competition still existing in the market or the growth of that competition.

[.....]

Section 5: the English clause

102 All the contracts in question except five (the Animedica international, Guyomarc'h, Merck B6, Protector and Upjohn contracts) contain a clause, called the English clause, under which the customer, if he obtains from competitors offers at prices which are more favourable than those under the contracts at issue may ask Roche to adjust its prices to the said offers; if Roche does not comply with this request, the customer, in derogation from his undertaking to obtain his requirements exclusively from Roche, is entitled to get his supplies from the said competitor without for that reason losing the benefit of the fidelity rebates provided for in the contracts in respect of the other purchases already effected or still to be effected by him from Roche.
103 In the applicant's view this clause destroys the restrictive effect on competition both of the exclusivity agreements and of the fidelity rebates.
In particular in the case of those contracts which do not contain an express undertaking by the purchaser to obtain his requirements exclusively from Roche the English clause eliminates "the attractive effect" of the rebates at issue since the customer does not have to choose between acceptance of Roche's less attractive offers or losing the benefit of the fidelity rebates on all purchases which he has already effected from Roche.
104 There is no doubt whatever that this clause makes it possible to remedy some of the unfair consequences which undertakings by purchasers to obtain their requirements exclusively from Roche or the provision for fidelity rebates on all purchases accepted for relatively long periods, might have in so far as those purchasers are concerned.
Nevertheless it is necessary to point out that the purchaser's opportunities for exploiting competition for his own benefit are more restricted than appears at first sight.
105 Apart from the fact that the English clause is not in the Guyomarc'h, Merck B6, Animedica International, Protector and Upjohn contracts it is subject to conditions which limit its scope and in fact leave Roche with a wide discretion as to the possibility of the customer's invoking it.
A number of contracts stipulate not only that the offer must come from important competitors but also from large competi-

tors operating on the same scale as Roche or again provide that the offers must not only be comparable as to the quality of the product but also as to their continuity and such a condition, by eliminating a more favourable but occasional method of obtaining supplies, strengthens the exclusivity.
Other contracts stipulate that the offer must come from producers to the exclusion of brokers or commercial agents and such a condition in fact eliminates non-European competitors who operate on the market through commercial firms as was found when the parties at the request of the Court separately undertook an investigation of the market shares.
In some contracts the English clause is linked directly with Roche's pledge to guarantee the best prices "on the local market" and it only operates within these limits, and this not only restricts its scope but brings about a partitioning of the markets which is incompatible with the Common Market.
106 Furthermore the English clause does not remove the discrimination resulting from the fidelity rebates between purchasers in similar circumstances depending on whether or not they reserve their freedom to choose their suppliers.
107 It is particularly necessary to stress that, even in the most favourable circumstances, the English clause does not in fact remedy to a great extent the distortion of competition caused by the clauses obliging purchasers to obtain their requirements exclusively from Roche and by the fidelity rebates on a market where an undertaking in a dominant position is operating and where for this reason the structure of competition has already been weakened.
In fact the English clause under which Roche's customers are obliged to inform it of more favourable offers made by competitors together with the particulars above mentioned - so that it will be easy for Roche to identify the competitor - owing to its very nature, places at the disposal of the applicant information about market conditions and also about the alternatives open to, and the actions of, its competitors which is of great value for the carrying out of its market strategy.
The fact that an undertaking in a dominant position requires its customers or obtains their agreement under contract to notify it of its competitor's offers, whilst the said customers may have an obvious commercial interest in not disclosing them, is of such a kind as to aggravate the exploitation of the dominant position in an abusive way.
Finally by virtue of the machinery of the English clause it is for Roche itself to decide whether, by adjusting its prices or not, it will permit competition.
108 It is able in this way, owing to the information which its own customers supply, to vary its market strategy in so far as it affects them and its competitors.
It follows from all these factors that the Commission's view that the English clauses incorporated in the contracts at issue were not of such a kind as to take them out of the category of abuse of a dominant position has been arrived at by means of a proper construction and application of Article 86 of the Treaty.

[.....]

8) *Soda Ash-Solvay* Commission decision 91/299 [1991] OJ L 152/21

Solvay, the world's largest producer of soda-ash, had taken recourse to a system of rebates to bind its customers and to hinder competition at the same time. This exclusionary behaviour, existing of customers being given significant 'special' discounts, infringed Article 102 TFEU.

Relevance: example of a loyalty or quantity rebate.

[.....]

3. Abuse of dominant position

(a) Exclusionary practices and fidelity rebates

(50) As the Court of Justice has observed in several cases, conduct by a dominant undertaking which undermines the objectives of Article 3 (f) of the EEC Treaty by endangering the structure of competition may constitute an infringement of Article 86. Exclusionary behaviour which hinders existing competition or the development of new competition has been condemned by the Court. Practices designed to block the access of competitors to customers by tying the latter to the dominant supplier have been particularly identified as abusive in leading cases: Case 40/73, Suiker Unie v. Commission (1); Case 85/76, Hoffmann-La Roche v. Commission; Case 322/81, Nederlandsche Banden Industrie - Michelin v. Commission (2). (See also Commission Decision 89/22/EEC British Gypsum/BPB Industries (3).) The present case primarily concerns the tying of customers to Solvay by means of a number of devices which all serve the same exclusionary purpose.

(i) Rebates on marginal tonnage

(51) The assessment under this heading relates to the following:
- the 20 % 'Spitzenrabatt' system in Germany,
- the giving of 'fidelity' cheques in Germany,
- rebates on marginal tonnage in France (BSN, Durand, Perrier, etc.).

In contrast to a quantity discount, which is linked solely to the volume of purchases from the manufacturer concerned, a fidelity rebate involves offering customers financial advantages in order to prevent them from obtaining their supplies from competing producers and when practised by a dominant undertaking may fall under Article 86.

There is no need, in order for fidelity rebates to fall under Article 86, for a contractual obligation or express stipulation that the customer obtain its supplies exclusively from the dominant undertaking. What is important is that the terms of sale of the dominant supplier make it financially attractive for the customer to take its supplies exclusively or mainly from it. The precise means by which this result is achieved are immaterial.

(52) Solvay has since 1982 adopted a system of progressive rebates which according to its own internal documentation is specifically intended to ensure the loyalty of the customer and exclude or limit competition:
- granting customers substantial financial inducements to obtain from Solvay all or the major part of the marginal tonnage which might otherwise have been obtained from a competitor,
- making it difficult or impossible for an existing or potential supplier to enter as second supplier for the marginal tonnage, since in order to match the substantial pecu-

niary advantages offered by Solvay and obtain the order for the top 'tranche' of business, they would have to sell at unprofitable or at 'dumping' prices,
- tying the customer to Solvay for an indefinite period and thereby contributing to the rigidity of the market,
- removing any interest on the part of the customer to canvass Solvay's competitors for some of its requirements.
(53) As an example, any supplier attempting to obtain a share of the business of Vegla in Germany would have had to match an effective 'ex-works' price/tonne for the top [...] Kt of DM 245 per tonne, compared with a 'list price' of DM 403 per tonne and an 'average' price in Germany of DM 360 per tonne.
The price of DM 245 is far below any economic price which the other Community producers could have offered. Any natural-ash producer selling at that price would have been in breach of the anti-dumping minimum price undertakings.
The ability of a second supplier to displace Solvay for a part of the business of a major customer is rendered even more difficult by the obligation of secrecy with regard to the percentage rebate and the cheque payment.
(54) The Commission's objections to the rebate system apply not only to cases where Solvay has complete exclusivity but also to those where it is the principal, but not the sole, supplier. In such cases the progressive rebates contribute to the maintenance of Solvay's overall dominant position by securing its share of the customer's business. The rigidity of the market is preserved since it is extremely difficult for any second supplier to break into Solvay's 'core' business.
Solvay claimed in its written observations in reply to the statement of objections that the rebates were not intended as an inducement to loyalty but simply represented a form of volume rebate which depended upon the customers reaching an objective and predetermined tonnage threshold. Such an argument wholly ignores the character attributed to the rebates in Solvay's own documents.
It is also clear that the various rebates and financial advantages which they confer are not related to any cost savings associated with the quantities delivered. There are substantial differences from country to country in the amount of the rebates, and inside each Member State the 'trigger' tonnage at which the top-slice rebate is activated varies from customer to customer according to its total offtake. For instance, in Germany the 20 % rebate was activated for PLM at [...] tonnes and for Vegla at [...] tonnes.

[.....]

Case cross-reference:

► T-31/91 *Solvay SA v. Commission* [1995] ECR II-1821 (in 91/298/EEC) and T-32/91 *Solvay SA v. Commission* ECR 1995 II-1821 (in 91/299/EEC), Commission decision annulled; Joined Cases C-287 & 288/95 P *Commission v. Solvay SA* [2000] ECR I-2391, appeal dismissed.

9) Case C-333/94 P *Tetra Pak II* [1996] ECR I-5951

See above for facts of the case (II-A-9, p. 96). According to the Commission, the following clauses infringed Article 102. Its decision was upheld by both the GC and the ECJ.

Relevance: example of contract clauses that result in market foreclosure.

[.....]

2.1.2. Operation and maintenance of equipment

(26) There are five clauses concerning the operation and maintenance of equipment, which are intended to give Tetra Pak an exclusivity and a right of inspection in this area:
(iv) it has an exclusive right to maintain and repair equipment (all countries except Spain);
(v) it has an exclusive right to supply spare parts (all countries except Spain);
(vi) it has the right to provide, free of charge, assistance, training, maintenance and updating services not requested by the client (Italy);
(vii) there is a sliding scale for part of the charges made for assistance, maintenance and technical updating (with a possible discount of up to 40% of the basic monthly charge) depending on the number of cartons used on all Tetra Pak machines of the same type (Italy);
(viii) the purchaser is required to inform Tetra Pak of any improvements or modifications to the equipment and to grant Tetra Pak ownership of any resulting intellectual property right (Italy).

[.....]

2.2.3. Cartons

(34) Contracts also contain clauses [...] [such as] clause (xii) giving Tetra Pak the right to inspect the wording or brand names which the client wishes to use on the cartons (Germany, Spain, Greece, Italy, the Netherlands, Portugal, United Kingdom).

[.....]

2.3.4. Wording

(45) Contracts again include Tetra Pak' s right to inspect the wording or brand names which the client wishes to use on cartons (clause (xii))."

[.....]

2.2.7. Fixing of rental and conditions of payment

(38) The rental is made up of the following components (all countries):
(a) (xxi) A 'base rental' payable at the time the machine is placed at the leaseholder' s disposal. Its amount is not necessarily any lower than the selling price of the machines concerned and in fact makes up almost the total sum of present and future rental payments (more than 98% in some cases);
(b) an annual rent, payable quarterly in advance;
(c) (xxii) a monthly production rental, the amount of which decreases according to the number of cartons used on all Tetra Pak machines of the same type. This component replaces the sliding scale of charges ° set at a similar level ° for part of the maintenance costs payable in the case of sale (see clause (vii));

In some countries (Germany, France, Portugal), there is a specific penalty if this fee is not paid within the prescribed period.

[.....]

2.2.8. Term of the lease

(39) The term of the lease and the conditions for its termination vary from one Member State to another:
(xxiii) The minimum term of the lease ranges from three years (Denmark, Ireland, Portugal, United Kingdom) to nine years (Italy).

[.....]

2.3.2. Contract term

(43) (xxvi) The contract is signed for an initial period of nine years, renewable for a further period of five years (Italy) or for the period during which the purchaser remains in possession of the machine (Greece, Ireland, Spain, United Kingdom).

[.....]

10) *British Midland (Zaventem)* Commission decision 95/364/EC [1995] OJ L 216/8

The airport charges for landing and take-off services for carriers that landed at Brussels National Airport had been established by Royal Decree. The same Decree also made mention of a rebate system which became operational after a certain amount of fees had been paid. In practice, this meant that only Brussels-based air companies (such as Sabena) could benefit from the rebate; whereas other companies (such as British Midland) could not possibly pass the established threshold in view of the number of flights they operated from their home airport to Brussels.

Relevance: example of a loyalty or quantity rebate system.

[.....]

Abuse of a dominant position

[.....]

(12) The system of discounts on landing fees established by the Royal Decree of 22 December 1989 has the effect of applying dissimilar conditions to airlines for equivalent transactions linked to landing and take-off services, thereby placing some of them at a competitive disadvantage.
(13) The system of discounts, which operates by reference to the monthly amount of fees due, is based on the number of movements in a month and on the weight of the aircraft. Taking account of these two parameters, the table below indicates the number of daily frequencies (one landing and one take-off) necessary to qualify for the first step (7,5 %), the third step (20 %) and the final step (30 %) of discounts, calculated on the basis of the monthly amount exceeding Bfrs 5 million, for four different types of aircraft.
The threshold of Bfrs 5 million in monthly fees to be attained in order to qualify for a discount is so high that only a carrier based at the airport can benefit, to the detriment of other Community carriers. This is because

the minimum number of daily frequencies required is very high. In the case of Community routes, for example, the airlines use small or medium-sized aircraft (with between 50 and 200 seats, i.e. the DC9, A320, 757 or similar). This means that, in order to reach the level of Bfrs 5 million in fees, which triggers a 7,5 % discount, an average carrier must offer more than seven frequencies per day (example of a DC9 with 110 seats). On Saturdays and Sundays, the number of frequencies is lower, and this therefore increases the number of frequencies necessary during the week to eight or nine. On average, a route on which there is heavy traffic carries four frequencies per day, whereas a regional service will have only two. To obtain a reduction of 7,5 % on the amount of fees exceeding Bfrs 5 million, a carrier providing regional services must offer more than three daily routes to and from Brussels with medium-sized or large aircraft. For example, although Lufhansa flies direct from Brussels to six German cities and accounted in 1992 for more than 2 % of movements at the airport and for 3,3 % of arriving or departing passengers, it does not achieve the amounts of fees necessary to obtain a reduction. Likewise, airlines using large aircraft such as the Boeing 747 must operate more than one flight a day (principally an intercontinental flight) to obtain a discount.

This system, with its high threshold and progressive steps, in non-linear. The reductions offered increase more than proportionally to the number of landings/take-offs, a fact which merely accentuates the differences between heavy-traffic carriers and the rest. Moreover, it is disadvantageous to regional carriers, which, although carrying out a large number of movements per month, use small aircraft and generally fly to Brussels via one route only.

In 1992 Sabena received final-step discounts (30 %) equivalent to an overall reduction of 18 % on its fees, whereas the other qualifying airlines (Sobelair and BA) were eligible for only a first-step discount (7,5 %). No other airline operating at Brussels Airport qualifies for a reduction in its landing fees.

On a route such as Brussels-London, on which Sabena, BM and other carriers compete using the same type of aircraft, Sabena receives a discount of some 18 % on its take-off and landing fees for an equivalent service from the Airways Authority, and this places BM at a competitive disadvantage.

For the above reasons, the fact that the Airways Authority, given its position, applies dissimilar conditions to commercial partners for equivalent transactions, thereby placing some of them at a competitive disadvantage, constitutes an abuse of a dominant position within the meaning of point (c) of Article 86. Since, in the case at issue, a Member State has established this system by way of an administrative act, a State measure of this nature constitutes an infringement of Article 90, read in conjunction with point (c) of Article 86 of the Treaty.

(14) Although the Airways Authority is responsible for proving the take-off and landing services for which the fees are payable, it does not determine the amount of those fees or of any discounts that might be applicable. The Court has held that a Member State infringes Articles 90 and 86 of the Treaty when it requires the undertaking to exploit its dominant position in an abusive fashion by applying to its commercial partners dissimilar conditions for equivalent transactions within the meaning of point (c) of the second subparagraph of Article 86 of the Treaty (judgment of 17 May 1994 in Case C-18/93).

[.....]

(17) While most of the abuses committed by undertakings in a dominant position are designed to maximize their profits or strengthen their dominance, Article 86 also applies to cases in which an undertaking in a dominant position discriminates against its partners for reasons other than its own interest. This may involve, for example, giving preference to another undertaking from the same State or to an undertaking which is pursuing the same general policy. One example of an abuse committed by an undertaking in a dominant position for reasons other than its own interest is afforded by the pilots in the Port of Genoa, who applied preferential tariffs approved by the State to maritime-transport undertakings operating between ports situated on the national territory (see Case C-18/93).
Thus, in the case at issue, unlike in the case of the systems of so-called loyalty rebates examined by the Court (judgment of 13 February 1979 in Case 85/76, Hoffman La Roche, v. Commission (1), and judgment of 9 November 1983 in Case 322/81, Michelin v. Commission (2)), the airways authority is not attempting to obtain the loyalty of its customers or to attract new ones, as has been demonstrated in recitals 13, 14 and 15, but rather the State, acting through its intermediary, is giving preferential treatment to a specific undertaking, i.e. the national airline Sabena.

[.....]

11) Case T-203/01 *Michelin II* [2003] ECR II-4071

According to the Commission, Michelin, a manufacturer of tyres, had pursued a commercial and pricing policy that infringed Article 102. It had abused its dominant position on both the market for new replacement tyres and the market for 'retreaded' tyres (used tyres that have been given a new tread) by means of a complicated system of loyalty-inducing rebates. On appeal, the GC dismissed Michelin's application.

Relevance: far-reaching example of a loyalty rebate system. Emphasis on economic justification.

[.....]

Principles employed in determining whether a rebate system applied by an undertaking in a dominant position constitutes an abuse

[.....]

59 It follows that a rebate system in which the rate of the discount increases according to the volume purchased will not infringe Article 82 EC unless the criteria and rules for granting the rebate reveal that the system is not based on an economically justified countervailing advantage but tends, following the example of a loyalty and target rebate, to prevent customers from obtaining their supplies from competitors (see Hoffmann-La Roche v Commission, cited at paragraph 54 above, paragraph 90; Michelin v Commission, cited at paragraph 54 above, paragraph 85; Irish Sugar v Commission, cited at paragraph 54 above, paragraph 114; and Portugal v Commission, cited at paragraph 58 above, paragraph 52).
60 In determining whether a quantity rebate system is abusive, it will therefore be necessary to consider all the circumstances,

particularly the criteria and rules governing the grant of the rebate, and to investigate whether, in providing an advantage not based on any economic service justifying it, the rebates tend to remove or restrict the buyer's freedom to choose his sources of supply, to bar competitors from access to the market, to apply dissimilar conditions to equivalent transactions with other trading parties or to strengthen the dominant position by distorting competition (see Hoffmann-La Roche v Commission, cited at paragraph 54 above, paragraph 90; Michelin v Commission, cited at paragraph 54 above, paragraph 73; and Irish Sugar v Commission, cited at paragraph 54 above, paragraph 114).

The abusive nature of the quantity rebate system applied by the applicant
- Introduction

[.....]

64 It is apparent from the contested decision that the Commission considers that the quantity rebate system applied by the applicant constitutes an infringement of Article 82 EC because it is unfair, it is loyalty-inducing and it has a partitioning effect (see paragraphs 48 to 52 above).
65 However, it may be inferred generally from the case-law that any loyalty-inducing rebate system applied by an undertaking in a dominant position has foreclosure effects prohibited by Article 82 EC (see paragraphs 56 to 60 above), irrespective of whether or not the rebate system is discriminatory. In Michelin v Commission (cited at paragraph 54 above), the Court, when considering the lawfulness of Commission Decision 81/969/EEC of 7 October 1981 relating to a proceeding under Article [82] of the Treaty (IV/29.491 - Bandengroothandel Frieschebrug BV/NV Nederlandsche Banden-Industrie Michelin) (OJ 1981 L 353, p. 33, 'the NBIM Decision'), did not uphold the Commission's claim that the rebate system applied by Michelin was discriminatory but nevertheless held that it infringed Article 82 EC because it placed dealers in a position of dependence in relation to Michelin.
66 This Court considers that it is necessary, first, to consider whether the Commission had good reason to conclude, in the contested decision, that the quantity rebate system was loyalty-inducing or, in other words, that it sought to tie dealers to the applicant and to prevent them from obtaining supplies from the applicant's competitors. As the Commission acknowledges in its defence, moreover, the alleged unfairness of the system was closely linked to its loyalty-inducing effect. Furthermore, it must be held that a loyalty-inducing rebate system is, by its very nature, also partitioning, since it is designed to prevent the customer from obtaining supplies from other manufacturers.

- The loyalty-inducing nature of the quantity rebates

67 The applicant submits that to equate quantity rebates with target discounts, or even loyalty discounts, is to disregard the fundamental characteristics of the impugned system, namely a system composed of a graduated scale of discounts, based on a large number of very close thresholds, which require only small volumes of purchases to reach the next threshold. The discounts were calculated according to the volumes actually purchased and were on a sliding scale, since the discount granted for each threshold attained decreased as the purchaser moved up the curve. The system was therefore completely transparent to the purchaser. According to the applicant, it was a standard quantity discount system which did not constitute an abuse. The Court of Justice and the Court of First Instance have never imposed a limit on the reference period for quantity discounts. In support of its argu-

ments, the applicant refers in particular to the judgment in Portugal v Commission (cited at paragraph 58 above).

68 The Court notes that there was a scale of quantity rebates for all types of tyres combined, except for 'heavy plant' tyres and retreads, and two different scales for the latter two categories. The contested decision refers only to the rebates in so far as they apply to new replacement truck tyres and to retreaded truck tyres.

69 The scale of quantity rebates (all types combined) comprised, for the period 1990 to 1996, between 47 and 54 steps. The scale of the quantity rebates which formed part of the 1995 general conditions, which is representative of the other years, was as follows: [omitted]

[.....]

70 A similar table, contained in the 1995 general conditions and comprising 18 steps, existed for retreaded tyres during the period 1990 to 1996. For 1995, the table was as follows: [omitted]

[.....]

71 It is clear from the tables reproduced above that the quantity discount rate increased, as the applicant states, according to the turnover achieved with the applicant. The rate shows a rapid increase over the first steps while the increase is much less rapid for the higher steps.

72 In Portugal v Commission (cited at paragraph 58 above, paragraph 51), the Court of Justice held that 'it is of the very essence of a system of quantity discounts that larger purchasers of a product or users of a service enjoy lower average unit prices or - which amounts to the same - higher average reductions than those offered to smaller purchasers of that product or users of that service. It should also be noted that even where there is a linear progression in quantity discounts up to a maximum discount, initially the average discount rises (or the average price falls) mathematically in a proportion greater than the increase in purchases and subsequently in a proportion smaller than the increase in purchases, before tending to stabilise at or near the maximum discount rate. The mere fact that the result of quantity discounts is that some customers enjoy in respect of specific quantities a proportionally higher average reduction than others in relation to the difference in their respective volumes of purchase is inherent in this type of system, but it cannot be inferred from that alone that the system is discriminatory'.

73 However, it cannot be inferred from that paragraph of the judgment in Portugal v Commission (cited at paragraph 58 above) that the quantity rebate system applied by the applicant must automatically be regarded as compatible with Article 82 EC solely because the discount rate per tyre increases according to the quantities purchased. In that judgment, the Court of Justice examined the lawfulness of Commission Decision 1999/199/EC of 10 February 1999 relating to a proceeding pursuant to Article [86] of the Treaty (Case No IV/35.703 - Portuguese Airports) (OJ 1999 L 69, p. 31) in which a discount system had been considered discriminatory. However, the Court emphasised, at paragraph 51 of that judgment, that the application of a quantity rebate system leads to a situation in which 'larger purchasers' enjoy higher average reductions than 'smaller purchasers' and that it cannot be inferred from that alone that the system is discriminatory.

74 However, according to settled case-law (see paragraphs 56 to 60 above), a discount system which seeks to tie dealers to an undertaking in a dominant position by granting advantages which are not based on a countervailing economic advantage and to prevent those dealers from obtaining their

supplies from the undertaking's competitors infringes Article 82 EC.

[.....]

95 It follows from all of the foregoing that a quantity rebate system in which there is a significant variation in the discount rates between the lower and higher steps, which has a reference period of one year and in which the discount is fixed on the basis of total turnover achieved during the reference period, has the characteristics of a loyalty-inducing discount system.
96 Admittedly, as the applicant points out, the aim of any competition on price and any discount system is to encourage the customer to purchase more from the same supplier.
97 However, an undertaking in a dominant position has a special responsibility not to allow its conduct to impair genuine undistorted competition on the common market (Michelin v Commission, cited at paragraph 54 above, paragraph 57). Not all competition on price can be regarded as legitimate (AKZO v Commission, cited at paragraph 54 above, paragraph 70, and Irish Sugar v Commission, cited at paragraph 54 above, paragraph 111). An undertaking in a dominant position cannot have recourse to means other than those within the scope of competition on the merits (Irish Sugar v Commission, cited at paragraph 54 above, paragraph 111).
98 In those circumstances, it is necessary to consider whether, in spite of appearances, the quantity rebate system applied by the applicant is based on a countervailing advantage which may be economically justified (see, in that regard, Michelin v Commission, cited at paragraph 54 above, paragraph 73; Irish Sugar v Commission, cited at paragraph 54 above, paragraph 114; and Portugal v Commission, cited at paragraph 58 above, paragraph 52) or, in other words, if it rewards an economy of scale made by the applicant because of orders for large quantities. If increasing the quantity supplied results in lower costs for the supplier, the latter is entitled to pass on that reduction to the customer in the form of a more favourable tariff (Opinion of Advocate General Mischo in Portugal v Commission, cited at paragraph 58 above, point 106).
99 In that regard, the applicant criticises, first, the fact that the Commission first raised in its defence (points 60 and 100) the objection that in the present case the quantity rebates are not justified by economies of scale. Since that objection was not stated in the statement of objections or in the contested decision, the applicant maintains that all the Commission's arguments relating to it must be rejected as inadmissible.
100 It must be borne in mind that, according to settled case-law, discounts granted by an undertaking in a dominant position must be based on a countervailing advantage which may be economically justified (Michelin v Commission, cited at paragraph 54 above, paragraph 85; Irish Sugar v Commission, cited at paragraph 54 above, paragraph 114; and Portugal v Commission, cited at paragraph 58 above, paragraph 52). A quantity rebate system is therefore compatible with Article 82 EC if the advantage conferred on dealers is 'justified by the volume of business they bring or by any economies of scale they allow the supplier to make' (Portugal v Commission, cited at paragraph 58 above, paragraph 52).

[.....]

Fifth plea: the Commission should have carried out a detailed analysis of the effects of the practices called in question

[.....]

239 The effect referred to in the case-law cited in the preceding paragraph does not necessarily relate to the actual effect of the abusive conduct complained of. For the purposes of establishing an infringement of Article 82 EC, it is sufficient to show that the abusive conduct of the undertaking in a dominant position tends to restrict competition or, in other words, that the conduct is capable of having that effect.

[.....]

241 It follows that, for the purposes of applying Article 82 EC, establishing the anti-competitive object and the anti-competitive effect are one and the same thing (see, in that regard, Irish Sugar v Commission, cited at paragraph 54 above, paragraph 170). If it is shown that the object pursued by the conduct of an undertaking in a dominant position is to limit competition, that conduct will also be liable to have such an effect.
242 Thus, with regard to the practices concerning prices, the Court held in AKZO v Commission (cited at paragraph 54 above) that prices below average variable costs applied by an undertaking in a dominant position are regarded as abusive in themselves because the only interest which the undertaking may have in applying such prices is that of eliminating competitors (paragraph 71) and that prices below average total costs but above average variable costs are abusive if they are determined as part of a plan for eliminating a competitor (paragraph 72). In that case, the Court did not require any demonstration of the actual effects of the practices in question.
243 In the same sense, the Community judicature has held that whilst the fact that an undertaking is in a dominant position cannot deprive it of its entitlement to protect its own commercial interests when they are attacked, and whilst such an undertaking must be allowed the right to take such reasonable steps as it deems appropriate to protect those interests, such behaviour cannot be allowed if its purpose is to strengthen that dominant position and thereby abuse it (United Brands v Commission, cited at paragraph 55 above, paragraph 189; Case T-65/89 BPB Industries and British Gypsum v Commission, cited at paragraph 55 above, paragraph 69; Joined Cases T-24/93 to T-26/93 and T-28/93 Compagnie maritime belge transports and Others v Commission, cited at paragraph 55 above, paragraph 107; and Irish Sugar v Commission, cited at paragraph 54 above, paragraph 112; emphasis added).

[.....]

Case cross-references:

- ▸ Case 322/81 *Michelin* [1983] ECR 3461 (see II-A-3).
- ▸ J. Kallaugher and B. Sher, 'Rebates Revisited: Anti-Competitive Effects and Exclusionary Abuse under Article 82', (2004), 25 *ECLR*, 263.
- ▸ D. Waelbroeck, 'Michelin II: a per se rule against rebates of incentive compatibility', (2005) 1 (1) *Oxford Journal of Competition Law and Economics.*
- ▸ G. Faella, 'The Antitrust Assessment of Loyalty Discounts and Rebates', *Jnl of Competition Law and Economics*, Volume 4, Number 2, June 2008.

Article 102 (c)

12) Case 27/76 *UBC (United Brands Company, Chiquita)* [1978] ECR 461

See above for facts of the case (I-A-1, p. 2).

Relevance: example of discrimination based on destination.

[.....]

182 In view of these conflicting arguments it is advisable to assert positively from the outset that an undertaking in a dominant position for the purpose of marketing a product – which cashes in on the reputation of a brand name known to and valued by the consumers – cannot stop supplying a long standing customer who abides by regular commercial practice, if the orders placed by that customer are in no way out of the ordinary.
183 Such conduct is inconsistent with the objectives laid down in Article 3 (f) of the Treaty, which are set out in detail in Article 86, especially in paragraphs (b) and (c), since the refusal to sell would limit markets to the prejudice of consumers and would amount to discrimination which might in the end eliminate a trading party from the relevant market.
184 It is therefore necessary to ascertain whether the discontinuance of supplies by UBC in October 1973 was justified.
185 The reason given is in the applicant's letter of 11 October 1973 in which it upbraided Olesen in no uncertain manner for having participated in an advertising campaign for one of its competitors.
186 Later on UBC added to this reason a number of complaints, for example, that Olesen was the exclusive representative of its main competitor on the Danish market.
187 This was not a new situation since it goes back to 1969 and was not in any case inconsistent with fair trade practices.
188 Finally UBC has not put forward any relevant argument to justify the refusal of supplies.
189 Although it is true, as the applicant points out, that the fact that an undertaking is in a dominant position cannot disentitle it from protecting its own commercial interests if they are attacked, and that such an undertaking must be conceded the right to take such reasonable steps as it deems appropriate to protect its said interests, such behaviour cannot be countenanced if its actual purpose is to strengthen this dominant position and abuse it.
190 Even if the possibility of a counter-attack is acceptable that attack must still be proportionate to the threat taking into account the economic strength of the undertakings confronting each other.
191 The sanction consisting of a refusal to supply by an undertaking in a dominant position was in excess of what might, if such a situation were to arise, reasonably be contemplated as a sanction for conduct similar to that for which UBC blamed Olesen.
192 In fact UBC could not be unaware of that fact that by acting in this way it would discourage its other ripener/distributors from supporting the advertising of other brand names and that the deterrent effect of the sanction imposed upon one of them would make its position of strength on the relevant market that much more effective.
193 Such a course of conduct amounts therefore to a serious interference with the independence of small and medium sized firms in their commercial relations with the under-

taking in a dominant position and this independence implies the right to give preference to competitors' goods.
194 In this case the adoption of such a course of conduct is designed to have a serious adverse effect on competition on the relevant banana market by only allowing firms dependant upon the dominant undertaking to stay in business.
195 The applicant's argument that in its view the 40% fall in the price of bananas on the Danish market shows that competition has not been affected by the refusal to supply Olesen cannot be upheld.
196 In fact this fall in prices was only due to the very lively competition – called at the time the "banana war" – in which the two transnational companies UBC and Castle and Cooke engaged.
197 The applicant submits that the refusal to supply Olesen could not have any effect on intra-Community trade because in its view all those bananas coming from third countries (Latin America) and merely transiting the Common Market countries before they reach the Member State where they are consumed are not part of intra-Community trade.
198 If this argument was valid the whole of UBC's European trade in goods of third countries would not be governed by Community law.
199 In fact when Olesen's supplies were cut off it was unable to buy Chiquita bananas at Bremerhaven and therefore had to import into Denmark the same quantities of bananas as it did before this step was taken.
200 It was forced to buy bananas bearing other brand names outside Denmark and to import them into Denmark.
201 Furthermore, if the occupier of a dominant position, established in the Common Market, aims at eliminating a competitor who is also established in the Common Market, it is immaterial whether this behaviour relates to trade between Member States once it has been shown that such elimination will have repercussions on the patterns of competition in the Common Market.
202 Consequently the refusal to supply a long standing regular customer who buys with a view to reselling in another Member State has an influence on the normal movement of trade and an appreciable effect on trade between Member States.
203 The finding in the decision that UBC has infringed Article 86 of the Treaty by refusing to supply Olesen is therefore justified.

[.....]

13) Case C-333/94 P *Tetra Pak II* [1996] ECR I-5951

See above for facts of the case (II-A-9, p. 96). The contracts, which Tetra Pak concluded with its customers, varied depending upon the Member State in which the client was doing its business. Especially in Italy, Tetra Pak tried to eliminate competition.

Relevance: example of discrimination based on destination.

[.....]

2.1.1. Equipment configuration

(25) In Italy, Tetra Pak reserves an absolute right of control over the equipment configuration by prohibiting the buyer:
(i) from adding accessories to the machine (Italy);
(ii) from making modifications to the machine, and adding or removing anything to or from it (Italy);
(iii) from moving the machine (Italy).

[.....]

2.2.3. Cartons

(34) Contracts also contain clauses (ix) (all countries) and (x) (Italy) concerning the exclusive use of Tetra Pak cartons, clause (xi) conferring on Tetra Pak ownership of the rights to any improvements (Denmark, Italy) or, at the very least, requiring leaseholders to grant an operating licence to Tetra Pak (France, Ireland, Portugal, United Kingdom) [...]

[.....]

2.1.5. Transfer of ownership or use of equipment

(29) Two clauses in the contract limit the purchaser's right to resell or transfer the equipment to third parties:
(xv) the purchaser is required to obtain Tetra Pak's agreement before selling or transferring the use of the equipment (Italy), resale is subject to conditions (Spain), and Tetra Pak reserves the right to repurchase the equipment at a pre-arranged fixed price (all countries); failure to comply with this clause may give rise to a specific penalty (Greece, Ireland, United Kingdom);
(xvi) the purchaser must ensure that any third party to whom he resells the equipment assumes all his obligations (Italy, Spain).

[.....]

14) Case 27/76 *UBC (United Brands Company, Chiquita)* [1978] ECR 461

See above for facts of the case (I-A-1, p. 2).

Relevance: example of discrimination based on price.

[.....]

224 These price differences can reach 30 to 50% in some weeks, even though products supplied under the transactions are equivalent (with the exception of the Scipio group, subject to this observation that the bananas from Scipio's ripening installations are sold at the same price as those sold by independent ripeners)

225 In fact the bananas sold by UBC are all freighted in the same ships, are unloaded at the same cost in Rotterdam or Bremerhaven and the price differences relate to substantially similar quantities of bananas of the same variety, which have been brought to the same degree of ripening, are of similar quality and sold under the same "Chiquita" brand name under the same conditions of sale and payment for loading on to the purchaser's

own means of transport and the latter have to pay customs duties, taxes and transport costs from these ports.

226 This policy of discriminatory prices has been applied by UBC since 1971 to customers of Germany, the Netherlands and the BLEU and was extended at the beginning of 1973 to customers in Denmark and in November 1973 to customers in Ireland.

227 Although the responsibility for establishing the single banana market does not lie with the applicant, it can only endeavour to take "what the market can bear" provided that it complies with the rules for the regulation and coordination of the market laid down by the Treaty.

228 Once it can be grasped that differences in transport costs, taxation, customs duties, the wages of the labour force, the conditions of marketing, the differences in the parity of currencies, the density of competition may eventually culminate in different retail selling price levels according to the Member States, then it follows those differences are factors which UBC only has to take into account to a limited extent since it sells a product which is always the same and at the same place to ripener/distributors who – alone – bear the risks of the consumers' market.

229 The interplay of supply and demand should, owing to its nature, only be applied to each stage where it is really manifest.

230 The mechanisms of the market are adversely affected if the price is calculated by leaving out one stage of the market and taking into account the law of supply and demand as between the vendor and the ultimate consumer and not as between the vendor (UBC) and the purchaser (the ripener/distributors).

231 Thus, by reason of its dominant position UBC, fed with information by its local representatives, was in fact able to impose its selling price on the intermediate purchaser. This price and also the "weekly quota allocated" is only fixed and notified to the customer four days before the vessel carrying the bananas berths.

232 These discriminatory prices, which varied according to the circumstances of the Member States, were just so many obstacles to the free movement of goods and their effect was intensified by the clause forbidding the resale of bananas while still green and by reducing the deliveries of the quantities ordered.

233 A rigid partitioning of national markets was thus created at price levels, which were artificially different, placing certain distributor/ripeners at a competitive disadvantage, since compared with what it should have been competition had thereby been distorted.

234 Consequently the policy of differing prices enabling UBC to apply dissimilar conditions to equivalent transactions with other trading parties, thereby placing them at a competitive disadvantage, was an abuse of a dominant position.

[.....]

Case cross-reference:

▸ D. Gerardin, 'Price discrimination under EC Law: the need for a case-by-case approach'. Global Competition Law Center, second annual conference, (2005), 1.

▸ L. Peeperkorn, 'Price Discrimination and Exploitation', 2008 *Fordham Corp.L.Inst.* 611-663 (B. Hawk ed. 2009).

15) *GVL* Commission decision 81/1030/EEC [1981] OJ L370/49

GVL was the only German undertaking that managed performers' rights and claims. This so-called collecting society collected, amongst other things, the royalties for the broadcasting or reproducing of its members' (musical) works. Only artists who resided in Germany or had the German nationality could be represented. Even though this practice had already changed, the Commission still thought it necessary to adopt a decision in which it specifically stated that Article 102 had been infringed, especially since GVL persisted in its view that it was not legally bound to manage foreigners.

Relevance: example of discrimination based on nationality.

[.....]

3. Abuse of a dominant position on the market within the meaning of the first paragraph of Article 86

46. The prohibition of abuses contained in the first paragraph of Article 86 must, as the judgments of the Court of Justice show, be viewed in the light of, and having due regard to, the general principles laid down in the EEC Treaty. One of these principles is embodied in Article 7 of the EEC Treaty, which provides that any discrimination on grounds of nationality shall be prohibited. As a rule, therefore, discriminatory treatment by a dominant undertaking on grounds of nationality must be regarded automatically as an infringement of Article 86 (cf. also judgment of the Court of Justice of 30 April 1974, Case 155/73, Sacchi/1974/ECR 409).
47. The refusal by GVL as a de facto monopoly undertaking to conclude management agreements with foreign artists having no residence in Germany constitutes discrimination on grounds of nationality and hence an abuse within the meaning of Article 86. This applies a fortiori since such foreign artists were entirely dependent on the services of GVL, being denied access to other collecting societies, and since this refusal meant that they were placed at a financial disadvantage compared with German and domestic artists and led to their being unable to assert their rights.

4. Discrimination within the meaning of Article 86 (c)

48. GVL's conduct also falls under the special prohibition of discrimination contained in Article 86 (c), since GVL has discriminated against certain trading partners on grounds unrelated to the transaction involved.

(a) Foreign artists as trading partners

49. Artists generally take part in German economic life by having their performances transferred onto sound recordings, broadcast or otherwise presented in public in Germany and by receiving fees and royalties therefor. The transaction ("trade") within the meaning of Article 86 (c) between artists and GVL consists in the fact that GVL's service, namely affording management of rights is provided only in return for valuable consideration, i.e. GVL's administrative share of the royalties collected. The sole decisive factor is the fact that GVL's activity, namely the provision of services, corresponds to a material consideration moving from the artist. Artists are thus the "natural" trading partners of GVL.
50. Conversely, GVL is the "natural" trading partner of artists, since claims by artists for the payment of royalties can be met in practice by GVL alone. Both GVL and artists are

entirely dependent on each other. The business aim of GVL is to safeguard the rights of artists to the payment of royalties and, without GVL, artists are unable to assert their secondary exploitation rights.

The argument that foreign artists were not trading partners of GVL because the latter had not concluded management agreements with them cannot be accepted.

51. A dominant undertaking cannot counter the accusation of discrimination by maintaining that the "trading partner" criterion is lacking, when it prevents some of its natural trading partners from becoming actual trading partners by imposing an additional requirement.

Foreign artists could, by their conduct, namely by taking up residence in Germany, have made themselves actual trading partners of GVL. This shows that foreign artists were also "trading parties" within the meaning of Article 86 (c) and that they were prevented from becoming actual trading partners of GVL only by the additional requirement of residence in Germany imposed by GVL on this category in general.

(b) The discriminatory treatment

52. Prior to 21 November 1980, GVL also discriminated against foreign artists as compared with German artists in that it imposed on foreign artists seeking management services an additional requirement, namely residence in Germany, which it did not impose on German nationals. GVL's conduct therefore consisted, not in a specific refusal to act on behalf of individual foreign artists, but in the imposition of an additional, general requirement on foreign artists. If foreign artists fulfilled this requirement, GVL was prepared to conclude management agreements with them. To this extent, GVL applied generally dissimilar conditions to its trading partners.

(c) Equivalent transaction

53. The prohibition of discrimination contained in Article 86 (c) presupposes, moreover, the existence of equivalent transactions with the trading partners concerned. Foreign artists, like German and domestic artists, transfer their performers' rights in Germany to GVL for exploitation. The transaction effected by the foreign artists, namely assignment of their performers' rights in Germany to GVL, is the same as that effected by German and domestic artists. It may, of course, be that it is more difficult for foreign artists to furnish proof of their rights in Germany than it is for German and domestic artists. But this does not alter the substantive transaction effected by foreign artists, which, where the existence of performers' rights in Germany is proved, does not differ in any respect from that effected by German and domestic artists.

The transaction proposed by foreign artists to GVL is therefore "equivalent" within the meaning of Article 86 (c).

[.....]

16) Case 322/81 *Michelin* [1983] ECR 3461

See above for facts of the case (II-A-3, p. 89).

Relevance: example of applying a rebate system that was not discriminatory.

[.....]

(D) discrimination against certain dealers

87 In a second submission, concerning the discount system in general, the applicant challenges the Commission's finding that its discount system involved the application of dissimilar conditions to equivalent transactions with dealers within the meaning of Article 86 I inasmuch as different discounts were granted to dealers in comparable situations. Michelin NV maintains that the discounts are not discriminatory and that the differences between the rates of discount received by different dealers are due to the application of a discount scale based on the dealer's total purchases from Michelin NV in the previous year.
88 To justify its finding, the Commission in the procedure before the Court relied upon a comparison of the discounts received by various dealers with the annual quantities of heavy-vehicle tyres purchased by them and upon a table showing the number of tyres sold in the various tyre categories in respect of which different rates of discount were granted in 1976 and pointed out a number of inconsistencies and anomalies which in its view emerged from them and demonstrated the existence of discrimination.
89 However, it is clear from what has been stated regarding the operation of the discount system that the amount of the annual variable discount depended primarily on the dealer's turnover in Michelin tyres without distinction of category and not on the number of heavy-vehicle tyres purchased by the dealer.

[.....]

90 Although a system based on individual sales targets fixed or agreed every year for each dealer necessarily involves certain differences between the rates of discount granted to different dealers for the same number of purchases [...] it has not been established that such differences in treatment between different dealers are due to the application of unequal criteria and that there are no legitimate commercial reasons capable of justifying them. It is not therefore possible to infer from such differences that Michelin NV discriminated against dealers.

[.....]

17) *Napier Brown* Commission decision 88/518/EEC [1988] OJ L284/41

Napier Brown (NB), a large sugar merchant, had lodged a complaint with the Commission in which it accused British Sugar (BS), a major producer of sugar and sugar derived products, of abusing its dominant position. British Sugar allegedly tried to remove Napier Brown from the retail sugar market, which the latter had just entered onto, by, amongst others, refusing to supply Napier Brown and by a price-cutting policy. In its decision, the Commission concurred with Napier Brown.

Relevance: example of discrimination by introducing a price squeeze of trading margins.

[.....]

(65) The pricing information indicated above shows that BS has engaged in a price cutting campaign leaving an insufficient margin for a packager and seller of retail sugar, as efficient as BS itself in its packaging and selling operations, to survive in the long term.
(66) The maintaining, by a dominant company, which is dominant in the markets for both a raw material and a corresponding derived product, of a margin between the price which it charges for a raw material to the companies which compete with the dominant company in the production of the derived product and the price which it charges for the derived product, which is insufficient to reflect that dominant company's own costs of transformation (in this case the margin maintained by BS between its industrial and retail sugar prices compared to its own repackaging costs) with the result that competition in the derived product is restricted, is an abuse of dominant position (2).
In the present case, BS's action of reducing the margin between its industrial and retail sugar prices such that it sold retail sugar at a price which no longer reflected its own transformation costs resulted in an abuse of a dominant position and a restriction of competition within the meaning of Article 86. It is clear from the facts as set out above that should BS have maintained this margin in the long term, NB, or any company equally efficient in repackaging as BS without a self-produced source of industrial sugar, would have been obliged to leave the United Kingdom retail sugar market. Thus, taken in the context of the other abuses as outlined above, and of the fact that the intention or natural and foreseeable consequence of the maintenance of this pricing policy by BS would be the removal of NB from the British retail sugar market, the Commission considers that BS's pricing policy constitutes an abuse of a dominant position within the meaning of Article 86.

[.....]

Article 102 (d)

18) Case 311/84 *Telemarketing* [1985] ECR 3261

Centre Belge had set up a telemarketing service that was broadcasted by RTL. RTL was run by the Compagnie Luxembourgeoise, which had a legal monopoly on the television advertising market. At first, Centre Belge could make use of its own telephone lines, but later RTL forbade this. Telesales were only allowed if and when the television viewers were to call the telephone number made available by RTL. In other words, the Compagnie Luxembourgeoise tried to 'export' its dominance on the television advertising market to the telemarketing market. Centre Belge thought that this constituted an abuse of dominance.

Relevance: example of tying.

[.....]

23 The Commission infers from the judgment of the court of 6 March 1974 in Joined Cases 6 and 7/73 (Commercial Solvents and Others v Commission (1974) ECR 223) that there is an abuse of a dominant position for the purposes of Article 86 where an undertaking which occupies a dominant position on a market and which is thus able to control the activities of other undertakings on a neighbouring market decides to establish itself on the second market and for no good reason refuses to supply the product or service in question on the market where it already occupies a dominant position to the undertakings whose activities are centred on the market which it is penetrating.
24 Even if the conduct in issue in the main proceedings were to be regarded not as a refusal to supply but as the imposition of a contractual condition, it would, in the commission's view, be contrary to Article 86. First, Information publicité, as a seller of television time, imposes on all other undertakings for telemarketing operations a condition which it does not impose on itself for the same operations, namely the condition that it must not use its own telephone number; that is an unfair trading condition within the meaning of Article 86 (a). Secondly, Information publicité subjects the conclusion of contracts to the acceptance of supplementary obligations which have no connection with the subject of the contracts, and that is contrary to Article 86 (d).
25 In order to answer the national court's second question, reference must first be made to the aforesaid Judgment of 6 March 1974 (Commercial Solvents), in which the Court held that an undertaking which holds a dominant position on a market in raw materials and which, with the object of reserving those materials for its own production of derivatives, refuses to supply a customer who also produces those derivatives, with the possibility of eliminating all competition from that customer, is abusing its dominant position within the meaning of Article 86.
26 That ruling also applies to the case of an undertaking holding a dominant position on the market in a service which is indispensable for the activities of another undertaking on another market. If, as the national court has already held in its order for reference, telemarketing activities constitute a separate market from that of the chosen advertising medium, although closely associated with it, and if those activities mainly consist in making available to advertisers the telephone lines and team of telephonists of the telemarketing undertaking, to subject the sale of broadcasting time to the condition that the telephone lines of an advertising agent belonging to the same group as the television station should be used amounts in practice to a refusal to supply the services of that station to any other telemarketing undertaking. If, further, that refusal is not justified by technical or commercial requirements relating to the nature of the television, but is intended to reserve to the agent any telemarketing operation broadcast by the said station, with the possibility of eliminating all competition from another undertaking, such conduct amounts to an abuse prohibited by Article 86, provided that the other conditions of that Article are satisfied.
27 It must therefore be held in answer to the second question that an abuse within the meaning of Article 86 is committed where, without any objective necessity, an undertaking holding a dominant position on a particular market reserves to itself or to an undertaking belonging to the same group an ancillary activity which might be carried out by another undertaking as part of its activities on a neighbouring but separate market, with the possibility of eliminating all competition from such undertaking.

[.....]

19) *Hilti* Commission decision 88/138/EEC [1988] OJ L65/19

Hilti, a manufacturer of power-actuated fastening systems (PAF systems) for the building industry, held a dominant position on the market for nail guns. In addition, Hilti was also dominant on the market for Hilti-compatible nails and cartridge strips (viz. the nails and cartridges used in Hilti guns), and this while there were cheaper strips and nails of similar quality available. Following a complaint, the Commission started an investigation and found that Hilti had made the sale of cartridges conditional upon a complement purchase of nails (tying of cartridge strips and nails). Hilti appealed this decision, but both the GC and the ECJ dismissed its application. One of the major questions in this case was whether the relevant product market comprised three separate markets, namely, one for nail guns, one for cartridges and one for nails, or whether there was just one single market.

Relevance: example of tying.

[.....]

IV. Hilti's commercial behaviour

(g) Tying of cartridge strips and nails

(30) The Commission enquiries reveal that Hilti carried out a policy of supplying cartridge strips to certain end-users or distributors (such as plant-hire companies) only when such cartridge strips were purchased with the necessary complement of nails. In reply to a request for information pursuant to Article 11 of Regulation No 17, Hilti originally denied that any such tying took place. 'The salesmen of Hilti GB offer a full Hilti fastening system but there is no doubt that each item of the system can be obtained separately and independently from the other . . . and there is no doubt that there are independent markets for firing tools, which are sold only once to a particular end user, and for the consumable accessories, such as cartridges and fasteners (nails and studs) which have to be replaced currently' . . . 'The customers of Hilti tools are free to place their orders for nails and cartridges, wherever they want' (point 1.2 of the letter of Hilti of 23 March 1983) (2).

(31) During the course of the investigation, however, the following facts emerged.

31.1. In their complaints both Eurofix and Bauco reported that their customers had experienced difficulties when ordering cartridge strips without nails from Hilti. For Eurofix this difficulty goes back as far as 1981. Bauco customers have had difficulties since 1984 when Bauco started selling Hilti compatible nails.

31.2. In reply to letters about the market situation, sent pursuant to Article 11 of Regulation No 17, a Danish and a German independent nail maker each alleged that Hilti had a practice of tying nails and cartridge strips making it difficult for them to sell their nails.

31.3. Internal Hilti GB documentation made available to the Commission's inspectors shows that such tying took place with regard to certain customers. The letter from Hilti GB to Hilti AG of 17 May 1983 concerning a Eurofix customer states: 'The customer has now been advised that an embargo has been placed on cartridge-only sales (only a verbal restriction has been passed to the customer with nothing in writing)'. The internal memo of 24 June 1983 to Midland Region Sales Force from Hilti GB concerning another Eurofix customer states that this customer '.

. . wanted a large quantity of Hilti cartridges. These would appear to be required in connection with Profix (Eurofix) nails and should in no circumstances be supplied to a customer. If any of you have similar requests, will you please inform your area manager immediately'.
31.4. In general, if Hilti considers that the cartridges are for use with nails which Hilti may unilaterally consider as unsafe, such orders are refused. Apparently Hilti considers that any use of Bauco or Eurofix nails in Hilti nail guns is unsafe (1).
(32) In its reply to the statement of objections Hilti acknowledges that in individual cases there was a refusal to supply customers with cartridge strips without nails. Following the undertaking by Hilti, both complainants report that it is now easier to sell their nails, as cartridge strips are generally being made available by Hilti without a complementary supply of nails.

[.....]

(e) Abuse of this dominant position
(74) Hilti has abused its dominant position in the EEC in the relevant market for nail guns and most importantly the markets for Hilti-compatible cartridge strips and nails. It has done this principally through its attempts to prevent or limit the entry of independent producers of Hilti-compatible consumables into these markets. Hilti's attempts to block or limit such entry went beyond the means legitimately available to a dominant company. The different aspects of Hilti's commercial behaviour were designed to this effect and were aimed at preventing Hilti-compatible cartridge strips from being freely available. Without such availability of Hilti-compatible cartridge strips, for which in the EEC Hilti until recently enjoyed protection afforded by patents, independent producers of Hilti-compatible nails have been severely restricted in their penetration of the market. Furthermore, customers have been obliged to rely on Hilti for both cartridges and nails for their Hilti nail guns. By limiting the effective competition from new entrants Hilti has been able to preserve its dominant position. The ability to carry out its illegal policies stems from its power on the markets for Hilti-compatible cartridge strips and nail guns (where its market position is strongest and the barriers to entry are highest) and aims at reinforcing its dominance on the Hilti-compatible nail market (where it is potentially more vulnerable to new competition). The individual aspects of this overall policy of hindering new entrants in the market for Hilti-compatible nails by preventing the free availability of cartridge strips are set out below.
Most of the abuses took place in or were centred on the UK which constitutes a substantial part of the common market. However, at least one of these abuses had direct effects in another Member State and in addition the strategy of Hilti was aimed indirectly at the whole EEC in its attempt both to stop new entrants into the market (who might start exporting) and to prevent otherwise profitable arbitrage.
(i) Tying, reduced discounts and other discriminatory policies on cartridge-only orders
(75) Making the sale of patented cartridge strips conditional upon taking a corresponding complement of nails constitutes an abuse of a dominant position, as do reduced discounts and other discriminatory policies described above on cartridge-only orders. These policies leave the consumer with no choice over the source of his nails and as such abusively exploit him. In addition, these policies all have the object or effect of excluding independent nail makers who may threaten the dominant position Hilti holds. The tying and reduction of discounts were

not isolated incidents but a generally applied policy.

[.....]

Case cross-references:

► T-30/89 *Hilti AG v. Commission (Hilti II)* [1990] ECR II-63 (order); C-53/92 *Hilti AG v. Commission* [1994] ECR I-667, appeal dismissed.

► J.D. Veltrop, 'Tying and exclusive purchasing arrangements under EC competition law', (1994) 31 *CMLRev*, 549.

20) Case C-333/94 P *Tetra Pak II* [1996] ECR I-5951

See above for facts of the case (II-A-9, p. 96).

Relevance: example of tying.

[.....]

The third plea

34 In its third plea, Tetra Pak submits that the Court of First Instance erred in law in holding that the tied sales of cartons and filling machines were contrary to Article 86 in circumstances where there was a natural link between the two and tied sales were in accordance with commercial usage.

35 Tetra Pak interprets Article 86(d) of the Treaty as prohibiting only the practice of making the conclusion of contracts dependent on acceptance of additional services which, by nature or according to commercial usage, have no link with the subject-matter of the contracts.

36 It must be noted, first, that the Court of First Instance explicitly rejected the argument put forward by Tetra Pak to show the existence of a natural link between the machines and the cartons. In paragraph 82 of the judgment under appeal, it found: "consideration of commercial usage does not support the conclusion that the machinery for packaging a product is indivisible from the cartons. For a considerable time there have been independent manufacturers who specialize in the manufacture of non-aseptic cartons designed for use in machines manufactured by other concerns and who do not manufacture machinery themselves". That assessment, itself based on commercial usage, rules out the existence of the natural link claimed by Tetra Pak by stating that other manufacturers can produce cartons for use in Tetra Pak's machines. With regard to aseptic cartons, the Court of First Instance found, at paragraph 83 of its judgment, that "any independent producer is quite free, as far as Community competition law is concerned, to manufacture consumables intended for use in equipment manufactured by others, unless in doing so it infringes a competitor's intellectual property right". It also noted, at paragraph 138, rejecting the argument based on the alleged natural link, that it was not for Tetra Pak to impose certain measures on its own initiative on the basis of technical considerations or considerations relating to product liability, protection of public health and protection of its reputation. Those factors, taken as a whole, show that the Court of First Instance considered that Tetra Pak was not alone in being able to manufacture cartons for use in its machines.

37 It must, moreover, be stressed that the list of abusive practices set out in the second paragraph of Article 86 of the Treaty is not

exhaustive. Consequently, even where tied sales of two products are in accordance with commercial usage or there is a natural link between the two products in question, such sales may still constitute abuse within the meaning of Article 86 unless they are objectively justified. The reasoning of the Court of First Instance in paragraph 137 of its judgment is not therefore in any way defective.

[.....]

C. Abuses against the market structure

Predatory pricing

Cross-references for this part:

- Commission Study of Predatory Pricing, XVth Report on Competition Policy (1986), points 334-336.
- P. Andrews, 'Is Meeting Competition a Defence to Predatory Pricing? – The Irish Sugar Decision Suggests a New Approach', (1998) 19 *ECLR*, 49.

1) Case C-62/86 *Akzo* [1991] ECR I-3359

See above for facts of the case and the relevant paragraphs (II-B-3, p. 104).

Relevance: example of predatory pricing.

2) Case C-333/94 P *Tetra Pak II* [1996] ECR I-5951

See above for facts of the case and the relevant paragraphs (II-A-9, p. 96).

Relevance: example of predatory pricing.

Refusal to supply

3) Case 6/73 *Commercial Solvents* [1974] ECR 223

After several years of regular business, Zoja was informed by its long-lasting supplier, Commercial Solvents, that this undertaking could no longer supply it with aminobutanol. Zoja, which needed large quantities of aminobutanol as a raw material for the production of ethambutol (a product needed for tuberculosis treatment), could not purchase it elsewhere. It claimed that this refusal to sell infringed Article 102, especially since Commercial Solvents itself had started to manufacture and trade ethambutol and had, by doing so successfully, eliminated all possible competition, including that of Zoja.

Relevance: example of a refusal to supply (refusal to sell must be placed in context and does not automatically mean abuse of dominance).

[.....]

(c) Abuse of the dominant position

[.....]

24 It appears from the documents and from the hearing that the suppliers of raw material are limited, as regards the EEC, to Istituto, which, as stated in the claim by CSC, started in 1968 to develop its own specialities based on ethambutol, and in November 1969 obtained the approval of the Italian government necessary for the manufacture and in 1970 started manufacturing its own specialities. When Zoja sought to obtain further supplies of aminobutanol, it received a negative reply. CSC had decided to limit, if not completely to cease, the supply of nitropropane and aminobutanol to certain parties in order to facilitate its own access to the market for the derivatives.
25 However, an undertaking being in a dominant position as regards the production of raw material and therefore able to control the supply to manufacturers of derivatives, cannot, just because it decides to start manufacturing these derivatives (in competition with its former customers) act in such a way as to eliminate their competition which in the case in question, would amount to eliminating one of the principal manufacturers of ethambutol in the Common Market. Since such conduct is contrary to the objectives expressed in Article 3 (f) of the Treaty and set out in greater detail in Articles 85 and 86, it follows that an undertaking which has a dominant position in the market in raw materials and which, with the object of reserving such raw material for manufacturing its own derivatives, refuses to supply a customer, which is itself a manufacturer of these derivatives, and therefore risks eliminating all competition on the part of this customer, is abusing its dominant position within the meaning of Article 86. In this context it does not matter that the undertaking ceased to supply in the spring of 1970 because of the cancellation of the purchases by Zoja, because it appears from the applicants' own statement that, when the supplies provided for in the contract had been completed, the sale of aminobutanol would have stopped in any case.
26 It is also unnecessary to examine, as the applicants have asked, whether Zoja had an urgent need for aminobutanol in 1970 and 1971 or whether this company still had large quantities of this product which would enable it to reorganize its production in good time, since that question is not relevant to the consideration of the conduct of the applicants.

[.....]

4) Case 27/76 *UBC (United Brands Company, Chiquita)* [1978] ECR 207

See above for facts of the case (I-A-1, p. 2).

Relevance: example of a refusal to sell.

[.....]

189 Although it is true, as the applicant points out, that the fact that an undertaking is in a dominant position cannot disentitle it from protecting its own commercial interests if they are attacked, and that such an undertaking must be conceded the right to take such reasonable steps as it deems appropriate to protect its said interests, such behaviour cannot be countenanced if its actual purpose is to strengthen this dominant position and abuse it.
190 Even if the possibility of a counter-attack is acceptable that attack must still be proportionate to the threat taking into account the economic strength of the undertakings confronting each other.
191 The sanction consisting of a refusal to supply by an undertaking in a dominant position was in excess of what might, if such a situation were to arise, reasonably be contemplated as a sanction for conduct similar to that for which UBC blamed Olesen.
192 In fact UBC could not be unaware of that fact that by acting in this way it would discourage its other ripener/distributors from supporting the advertising of other brand names and that the deterrent effect of the sanction imposed upon one of them would make its position of strength on the relevant market that much more effective.
193 Such a course of conduct amounts therefore to a serious interference with the independence of small and medium sized firms in their commercial relations with the undertaking in a dominant position and this independence implies the right to give preference to competitors' goods.
194 In this case the adoption of such a course of conduct is designed to have a serious adverse effect on competition on the relevant banana market by only allowing firms dependant upon the dominant undertaking to stay in business.
195 The applicant's argument that in its view the 40% fall in the price of bananas on the Danish market shows that competition has not been affected by the refusal to supply Olesen cannot be upheld.
196 In fact this fall in prices was only due to the very lively competition - called at the time the "banana war" - in which the two transnational companies UBC and Castle and Cooke engaged.
197 The applicant submits that the refusal to supply Olesen could not have any effect on intra-Community trade because in its view all those bananas coming from third countries (Latin America) and merely transiting the common market countries before they reach the member state where they are consumed are not part of intra-community trade.
198 If this argument was valid the whole of UBC's European trade in goods of third countries would not be governed by community law.
199 In fact when Olesen's supplies were cut off it was unable to buy Chiquita bananas at Bremerhaven and therefore had to import into Denmark the same quantities of bananas as it did before this step was taken.
200 It was forced to buy bananas bearing other brand names outside Denmark and to import them into Denmark.
201Furthermore, if the occupier of a dominant position, established in the Common Market, aims at eliminating a competitor who is also established in the Common Market, it is immaterial whether this behaviour relates to trade between Member States once it has been shown that such elimination will have repercussions on the patterns of competition in the Common Market.
202 Consequently the refusal to supply a long standing regular customer who buys

with a view to reselling in another member state has an influence on the normal movement of trade and an appreciable effect on trade between member states.

Case cross-reference:

▸ Case 22/78 *Hugin* [1979] ECR 1869.

[.....]

5) Case 77/77 *BP v. Commission* [1978] ECR 1513

Due to the oil crisis of the 1970s, BP, producer and distributor of petrol, was forced to reduce its (regular) supplies to the market. ABG, one of its regular customers, albeit occasional, complained that it had received less petrol in comparison with BP's other customers. The Commission found that this behaviour infringed Article 102 TFEU but, taking into account the special circumstances, did not fine BP. BP, however, still wanted to have the decision annulled.

Relevance: example of a refusal to sell in times of acute scarcity of production (i.e. during the first oil crisis).

[.....]

29 It therefore follows that at the time of the crisis and even from November 1972, ABG's position in relation to BP was no longer, as regards the supply of motor spirit, that of a contractual customer but that of an occasional customer.

30 The principle laid down by the contested decision that reductions in supplies ought to have been carried out on the basis of a reference period fixed in the year before the crisis, although it may be explicable in cases in which a continued supply relationship has been maintained, during that period, between seller and purchaser, cannot be applied when the supplier ceased during the course of that same period to carry on such relations with its customer, regard being had in particular to the fact that the plans of any undertaking are normally based on reasonable forecasts.

31 Moreover, the advances in petrol against crude oil agreed to by BP in pursuance of the processing agreement, as they occur within the context of an agreement whose purpose was solely the refining of crude oil supplied by ABG and not the supplying of ABG with motor spirit, cannot serve as a valid argument to compare ABG's position in this case in relation to BP with that of a traditional customer of BP during the above-mentioned reference period.

32 For all these reasons, since ABG's position in relation to BP had been, for several months before the crisis occurred, that of an occasional customer, BP cannot be accused of having applied to it during the crisis less favourable treatment than that which it reserved for its traditional customers.

33 Having regard to the general shortage of petroleum products during the period under review and the difficult position in which the whole of the Netherlands market was placed, the application to ABG by BP of a rate of reduction identical or very close to that applied to its traditional customers would have resulted in a considerable diminution of the deliveries which those customers expected.

34 A duty on the part of the supplier to apply a similar rate of reduction in deliveries to all its customers in a period of shortage without having regard to obligations contracted towards its traditional customers could only flow from measures adopted within the framework of the Treaty, in particular Article 103, or, in default of that, by the national authorities.

[.....]

6) Joined Cases C-468/06 to C-478/06 *Sot. Lélos kai Sia and others v. GlaxoSmithKline AEVE* [2008] ECR I-7139

GSK AEVE is the Greek subsidiary of GlaxoSmithKline plc. established in the UK. GSK AEVE imports, warehouses and distributes pharmaceutical products of the GSK group in Greece. In 2000, GSK AEVE stopped meeting the orders of the wholesalers and began distributing pharmaceutical products to Greek hospitals and pharmacies itself through the company Farmacenter AE. Some of the pharmaceutical wholesalers brought an action before a Greek court claiming that the conduct of GSK AEVE was interrupting supplies of medicinal products which had been ordered and distributing them through Farmacenter constituted unfair and anticompetitive acts and an abuse of the dominant position occupied by GSK AEVE.
The Administrative Appeal Court of Athens referred the case to Luxemburg for a preliminary ruling concerning the interpretation of Article 102 TFEU. The referring court asked whether there may be an abuse of a dominant position contrary to Article 102 TFEU in case a pharmaceuticals company refuses to supply wholesalers who were involved in parallel exports to other Member States. Moreover, the referring court inquired about the relevance of factors such as the degree of regulation to which the pharmaceuticals sector is subjected in certain Member States, the impact of parallel trade on the pharmaceuticals companies' revenues and whether parallel trade is capable of generating financial benefits for the ultimate consumers of medicinal products.

Relevance: An undertaking in a dominant position refuses to supply wholesalers engaged in parallel exports of medicinal products subject to governmental price regulation

[...]

The Court (Grand Chamber) hereby rules *(in the operative part of the judgment)*:

Article 82 EC must be interpreted as meaning that an undertaking occupying a dominant position on the relevant market for medicinal products which, in order to put a stop to parallel exports carried out by certain wholesalers from one Member State to other Member States, refuses to meet ordinary orders from those wholesalers, is abusing its dominant position. It is for the national court to ascertain whether the orders are ordinary in the light of both the size of those orders in relation to the requirements of the market in the first Member State and the previous business relations between that undertaking and the wholesalers concerned.

Case cross-reference:

▸ S. Kingston, Case note on C-468/06 in *C.M.L.Rev.* 2009, 683-701.

D. Acquisition exclusive licence/minority interest/contractual links

1) Case T-51/89 *Tetra Pak I* [1990] ECR II-309

Tetra Pak, the world's major producer and distributor of cartons (and filling machines) for liquids, had acquired an exclusive licence for the sterilization of the said cartons. The Commission claimed that this acquisition considerably restricted competition. It ordered Tetra Pak to bring an end to the exclusivity.

Relevance: example of an abusive acquiring of exclusive licence by dominant competitor.

[.....]

23 Turning to the specific nature of the conduct whose compatibility with Article 86 is considered in the Decision, this Court holds that the mere fact that an undertaking in a dominant position acquires an exclusive licence does not per se constitute abuse within the meaning of Article 86. For the purpose of applying Article 86, the circumstances surrounding the acquisition, and in particular its effects on the structure of competition in the relevant market, must be taken into account. This interpretation is borne out by the case-law of the Court of Justice, in which the concept of abuse is defined as "an objective concept relating to the behaviour of an undertaking in a dominant position which is such as to influence the structure of a market where, as a result of the very presence of the undertaking in question, the degree of competition is weakened and which, through recourse to methods different from those which condition normal competition in products or services on the basis of the transactions of commercial operators, has the effect of hindering the maintenance of the degree of competition still existing in the market or the growth of that competition" (judgment in Case 85/76 Hoffmann-La Roche, cited above, paragraph 91). So, here, the Commission was right not to put in issue the exclusive licence as such, but rather to object specifically under Article 86 to the anti-competitive effect of its being acquired by the applicant. It is plain from the reasoning and conclusions of the Decision that the infringement of Article 86 found by the Commission stemmed precisely from Tetra Pak's acquisition of the exclusive licence "in the specific circumstances of this case". The specific context to which the Commission refers is expressly characterized as being the fact that acquisition of the exclusivity of the licence not only "strengthened Tetra's very considerable dominance but also had the effect of preventing, or at the very least considerably delaying, the entry of a new competitor into a market where very little if any competition is found" (point 45 of the Decision; see also point 60). The decisive factor in the finding that acquisition of the exclusive licence constituted an abuse therefore lay quite specifically in the applicant's position in the relevant market and in particular, as appears from the Decision (point 27), in the fact that at the material time the right to use the process protected by the BTG licence was alone capable of giving an undertaking the means of competing effectively with the applicant in the field of the aseptic packaging of milk. The takeover of Liquipak was no more than the means - to which the Commission has attached no particular significance in applying Article 86 - by which the applicant acquired the exclusivity of the BTG licence, the effect of which was to

deprive other undertakings of the means of competing with the applicant.

[.....]

Case cross-reference:

▸ H. James, 'Tetra Pak: Exemption and Abuse of Dominant Position', (1990) 11 *ECLR*, 268.

2) *Gillette (Wilkinson Sword)* Commission decision 93/252/EEC [1993] OJ 116/21

Stora, a Swedish undertaking, had split and sold the Wilkinson Sword wet-shaving business to Eemland (a Dutch-based company that was to be active in the USA and the Community) and Gillette (which was to be active in the rest of the world). Eemland had been largely financed by Gillette.

Relevance: example of an acquisition of a minority interest by a dominant competitor leading to 'abuse'.

[.....]

(23) An undertaking in a dominant position has a special responsibility not to allow its conduct to impair genuine undistorted competition on the Common Market. By participating in the buy-out of the Wilkinson Sword business, Gillette has failed to discharge that special responsibility and has abused its dominant position. Gillette was instrumental in arranging the buy-out and notwithstanding the care with which the agreements were drafted, the structure of the wet-shaving market in the Community has been changed by the creation of a link between Gillette and its leading competitor. The Court of Justice has referred to an abuse of a dominant position 'relating to the behaviour of an undertaking in a dominant position which is such as to influence the structure of a market where, as a result of the very presence of the undertaking in question, the degree of competition is weakened and... has the affect of hindering the maintenance of the degree of competition still existing in the market or the growth of that competition'. The change in the structure of the wet-shaving market brought about by Gillette's participation in the overall arrangement will have an adverse effect on competition in that market in the Community and therefore Gillette's involvement constitutes an abuse of its dominant position.

(24) In the Joined Cases BAT and Reynolds (hereinafter called the Philip Morris Case), the Court of Justice considered the situation in which a company acquires a minority shareholding in a competitor. The Court indicated that an abuse of a dominant position can arise only where a shareholding in another company results in at least some influence on that company's commercial policy. Gillette has not only become a major shareholder in Eemland but has also become its largest creditor and has acquired important pre-emption and conversion rights and options in Eemland. The position of Gillette is a matter which the management of Eemland will be obliged to take into account and consequently it is a factor which will influence the commercial conduct of Eemland. It follows that Gillette will have at least some influence on Eemland's commercial policy. Although the Court did not strike down the agreements in the Philip Morris Case it is important to note that in that case

the Court was considering a situation in which the shareholding was acquired in and not by the undertaking which was said to occupy a dominant position. In the present Case it is a dominant undertaking, Gillette, which has acquired a substantial shareholding in its principal competitor. Despite the similarities between the form of the agreements in the present Case and the form of the agreements in the Philip Morris Case, Gillette is taking a minority interest in a competitor in circumstances which are fundamentally different from those underlying the Philip Morris Case, and in particular the market is dominated by Gillette which makes the existing competition more vulnerable to structural changes.

(25) Gillette has acquired 22 % of the equity of Eemland, which cannot be disregarded simply because of the absence of voting rights and other usual shareholders' rights or because of Gillette's covenant not to exert or attempt to exert any influence over the Board or any member of the Board of Eemland. Gillette is also a major creditor of Eemland, having contributed US$ 69 million of mezzanine debt (representing 11,6 % of the debt of Eemland) and almost US$ 14 million in equity loan stock, has agreed to make payments to Stora of up to US$ 11 million and has accepted a loan note from Eemland for the sum of US$ 6,4 million in respect of the American business. The level of Gillette's investment in Eemland compares with Eemland's estimated worldwide turnover in 1989 of US$ 123 million. Eemland cannot reasonably be expected to ignore this financial dependence on Gillette. For example, the continuing availability of the interest-free loan from Stora, which Eemland currently enjoys, is dependent upon Gillette's willingness to make the payments of up to US$ 11 million to Stora.

(26) In addition, Gillette has important pre-emption and conversion rights and options in Eemland. These rights ensure that no other competitor on the market such as Warner-Lambert or BIC can improve its competitive position through the acquisition of Eemland. It also ensures that no other company hostile to Gillette can take over Wilkinson and effectively prevents the management of Eemland from entering into a merger or joint venture with someone of whom Gillette does not approve. Consequently the medium and long-term commercial fate of Eemland is to some extent in the hands of Gillette. This is emphasized by the fact that Eemland, having sold the matches and lighters division as originally planned, will be entirely dependent upon its shaving products business, thereby making it more vulnerable to Gillette. The pre-emption rights can be considered as a new barrier to entry in this market, given that they are held by a dominant undertaking (unlike in the Philip Morris Case). Other competitors on the market are adversely affected because they are deprived of one of the most obvious ways of challenging Gillette's market dominance, namely by taking over Eemland. Gillette, which is by far the strongest operator on this market, has entered into a relationship with its strongest competitor and although it has not acquired any direct control over Eemland, this relationship enables Gillette to exercise some influence over Eemland's commercial conduct.

[.....]

E. Dominance and Intellectual Property Rights (IPRs)

Cross-references for this part:

- ▸ Case C-241 & 242/91 P *RTE (Magill TV Guides)* [1995] ECR I-743 (see II-F-4).
- ▸ J.M. Ammann, 'Intellectual Property Rights and Parallel Imports', (1999) 26 *LIEI*, 91.

1) Case 24/67 *Parke & Davis v. Probel* [English special edition 1968] ECR 55

The dispute here concerned a patent for chloramphenicol (medical drug). Parke, holder of the patent on the Netherlands market, prevented import of chloramphenicol from Italy where the medical drug could not be patented. He accused the defendant of infringing his exclusive right by non-authorised import of the drug.

Relevance: the proprietor of an IPR (here: a patent) has a dominant position by law, but the exclusive enjoyment of such a right does not automatically infringe Article 102.

[.....]

Under Article 86 of the Treaty: "any abuse by one or more undertakings of a dominant position within the Common Market or in a substantial part of it shall be prohibited as incompatible with the Common Market in so far as it may affect trade between Member States". For this prohibition to apply it is thus necessary that three elements shall be present together: the existence of a dominant position, the abuse of this position and the possibility that trade between Member States may be affected thereby. Although a patent confers on its holder a special protection at national level, it does not follow that the exercise of the rights thus conferred implies the presence together of all three elements in question. It could only do so if the use of the patent were to degenerate into an abuse of the abovementioned protection.

[.....]

2) Case 40/70 *Sirena v. Eda* [1971] ECR 69

This dispute concerned a contract of assignment of a trademark (namely Prep and Prep Good Morning). Sirena had the exclusive enjoyment of the trademark in Italy; the defendant in Germany. When Eda started to export its products to Italy, Sirena accused it of infringing its trademarks. Eda claimed that Sirena's contract was void since it prevented import.

Relevance: the proprietor of an IPR (here: trademark) has a dominant position, but the exclusive enjoyment of such a right does not automatically infringe Article 102.

[.....]

14 Finally, the request for interpretation seeks to establish in what circumstances the exercise of trade-mark rights is incompatible with the Common Market, and prohibited under Article 86 of the Treaty.

15 It is clear from the wording of this provision that what it prohibits is a combination of three elements: the existence of a dominant

position, its abuse, and the possibility that trade between Member States may thereby be affected.

16 It should first be observed that the proprietor of a trade-mark does not enjoy a "dominant position" within the meaning of Article 86 merely because he is in a position to prevent third parties from putting into circulation, on the territory of a Member State, products bearing the same trade-mark. Since the Article requires that the position in question should extend to at least a "substantial part" of the Common Market, it is also necessary that the proprietor should have power to impede the maintenance of effective competition over a considerable part of the relevant market, having regard in particular to the existence and position of any producers or distributors who may be marketing similar goods or goods which may be substituted for them.

17 As regards the abuse of a dominant position, although the price level of the product may not of itself necessarily suffice to disclose such an abuse, it may, however, if unjustified by any objective criteria, and if it is particularly high, be a determining factor.

[.....]

3) Case 238/87 *Volvo v. Veng* [1988] ECR 6211

Volvo accused Veng of infringing its registered design (body panels). The latter had imported the body panels without Volvo's permission. Veng, in its turn, claimed that Volvo had infringed Article 102 TFEU by refusing to give him the needed licence.

Relevance: the proprietor of an IPR (here: registered design) has a dominant position, but the exclusive enjoyment of such a right does not automatically infringe Article 102. (Compulsory licensing under Article 102?)

[.....]

7 It must first be observed, as the Court held in its judgment of 14 September 1982 in Case 144/81 Keurkoop v Nancy Kean Gifts ((1982)) ECR 2853 with respect to the protection of designs and models, that, as Community law stands at present and in the absence of Community standardization or harmonization of laws, the determination of the conditions and procedures under which protection of designs and models is granted is a matter for national rules. It is thus for the national legislature to determine which products are to benefit from protection, even where they form part of a unit which is already protected as such.

8 It must also be emphasized that the right of the proprietor of a protected design to prevent third parties from manufacturing and selling or importing, without its consent, products incorporating the design constitutes the very subject-matter of his exclusive right. It follows that an obligation imposed upon the proprietor of a protected design to grant to third parties, even in return for a reasonable royalty, a licence for the supply of products incorporating the design would lead to the proprietor thereof being deprived of the substance of his exclusive right, and that a refusal to grant such a licence cannot in itself constitute an abuse of a dominant position.

9 It must however be noted that the exercise of an exclusive right by the proprie-

tor of a registered design in respect of car body panels may be prohibited by Article 86 if it involves, on the part of an undertaking holding a dominant position, certain abusive conduct such as the arbitrary refusal to supply spare parts to independent repairers, the fixing of prices for spare parts at an unfair level or a decision no longer to produce spare parts for a particular model even though many cars of that model are still in circulation, provided that such conduct is liable to affect trade between Member States.

[.....]

Case cross-reference:

▸ Case 53/87 *Maxicar v. Renault* [1988] ECR 6039.

4) *Lederle-Praxis Biologicals*, XXIVth Report on Competition Policy (1994), p. 353.

Lederle-Praxis Biologicals had filed a complaint concerning the refusal of several undertakings to supply it with the registration documents of the Hep B vaccine. Without a licence, Lederle was unable to produce certain multivalents.

Relevance: no obligation to share IPRs.

[.....]

The Commission concluded that, at the current stage of EC competition law, it is highly doubtful whether one could impose an obligation upon a dominant firm (in an eventual EC bulk intermediate Hep B market), as a remedy to ensure the maintenance of effective competition in the national Hep B markets, to share its intellectual property rights with third parties to allow them to develop, produce and market the same products (i.e. multivalents containing the Hep B antigen) which the alleged dominant firm was also seeking to develop, produce and market. This was judged to be all the more precarious in sectors such as the vaccine sector where R&D required high levels of investment. Even a simple refusal to supply could not be considered as an abuse as Lederle was not an existing customer that had found itself in a situation of factual dependence for the supply of Hep B. The companies did not break off an ongoing relationship with Lederle.

5) *IMS Health* Commission decision 2002/165/EC [2002] OJ L 59/18

IMS Health and NDC, two competing US companies, both offered sales data services for the pharmaceutical industry and the healthcare products sector. NDC lodged a complaint against IMS Health accusing it of abusing its dominant position. Apparently, IMS Health had refused to grant NDC a licence to use the so-called "1860 brick structure", a segmentation of Germany into 1860 geographical areas used to report sales information. Without this licence, NDC claimed that it could not provide regional sales reports. The Commission concurred with NDC.

Relevance: compulsory licensing of IPRs in exceptional circumstances.

[.....]

7.3. Abuse of a dominant position

(63) In its complaint, NDC, referring to what is known as the "essential facilities" doctrine, considers that IMS is obliged to license the 1860-brick structure since it is a prerequisite for effective competition on the regional sales data services market. According to that doctrine a company which has a dominant position in the provision of facilities which are essential for the supply of goods or services abuses its dominant position where, without objective justification, it refuses access to those facilities. As stated by the Advocate General in his opinion on the Bronner case: thus in certain cases a dominant undertaking must not merely refrain from anti-competitive action but must actively promote competition by allowing potential competitors access to the facilities which it has developed.

(64) Neither the European Court of Justice nor the Court of First Instance has as yet explicitly referred in its case-law to the essential facilities doctrine. Nevertheless it has ruled in a number of cases concerning refusal from an undertaking in a dominant position to supply goods or services. In two early cases the Court stated that the cutting off of supplies to an existing customer could constitute an abuse. In the Commercial Solvents(26) judgment (paragraph 25), it held that an undertaking in a dominant position as regards production of a raw material could not cease supplying an existing customer who manufactured derivatives of the raw material simply because it had decided to start manufacturing the derivative itself and wished to eliminate its former customer from the market.

(65) Similarly, in the United Brands(27) judgment (paragraph 182), the Court held that an undertaking in a dominant position for the purpose of marketing a product - which cashes in on the reputation of a brand name known to and valued by customers - cannot stop supplying a long standing customer who abides by regular commercial practice, if the orders placed by that customer are in no way out of the ordinary.

(66) In two further cases involving goods or services covered by intellectual property rights, the Court considered whether refusal to supply constituted an abuse. In the Volvo(28) judgment (paragraphs 8 and 9), the Court held that "it was not an abuse of a dominant position for a car manufacturer holding the registered designs for body panels for its cars to refuse to license others to supply replacement panels necessary for the repair of the cars. [...] It must however be noted that the exercise of an exclusive right by the proprietor of a registered design in respect of car body panels may be prohibited by Article 86 if it involves, on the part of an undertaking holding a dominant position, certain abusive conduct such as the arbitrary refusal to supply spare parts to independent repairers, the fixing of prices for spare parts at an unfair level or a decision no longer to produce spare parts for a particular model even though many cars of that model are still in circulation, provided that such conduct is liable to affect trade between Member States".

(67) In the Magill judgment(29) (paragraphs 49, 50 and 54) cited above, the European Court of Justice declared that refusal to grant a licence, even if it is the act of an undertaking holding a dominant position, cannot in itself constitute abuse of a dominant position. However, the exercise of an exclusive right by a proprietor may, in exceptional circumstances, involve abusive conduct and the appellants' refusal to provide basic information by relying on national copyright provisions thus prevented the appearance of a new product, a comprehensive weekly guide to television programmes, which the appel-

lants did not offer and for which there was a potential consumer demand. Such refusal constitutes an abuse under heading b of the second paragraph of Article 86 of the Treaty. The Court therefore recognised that in exceptional circumstances the exercise of an exclusive right deriving from an intellectual copyright may be abusive even in the absence of abusive additional conduct when, inter alia, it prevents the appearance of a new product.
(68) In a subsequent case, Ladbroke, cited above (paragraph 131), the Court of First Instance stated that the refusal to supply the applicant could not fall within the prohibition laid down by Article 86 unless it concerned a product or service which was either essential for the exercise of the activity in question, in that there was no real or potential substitute, or was a new product whose introduction might be prevented, despite specific, constant and regular potential demand on the part of consumers. This judgment makes clear that a refusal to license may constitute an abuse not only when this refusal prevents the introduction of a new product but also when the product or service in question is essential for the exercise of the activity in question.
(69) In the Bronner judgment (paragraph 41) cited above, the Court said that therefore, even if that case-law on the exercise of the intellectual property right were applicable to the exercise of any property right whatever, it would still be necessary for the Magill judgement to be effectively relied upon in order to plead the existence of an abuse within the meaning of Article 86 of the Treaty in a situation such as that which forms the subject matter of the first question, not only that the refusal of the service comprised in home delivery be likely to eliminate all competition in the daily newspaper market on the part of the person requesting the service and that such refusal be incapable of being objectively justified, but also that the service in itself be indispensable to carrying on that person's business, inasmuch as there is no actual or potential substitute in existence for that home-delivery scheme. [...] Moreover, it does not appear that there are any technical, legal or even economic obstacles capable of making it impossible, or even unreasonably difficult, for any other publisher of daily newspapers to establish, alone or in cooperation with other publishers, its own nationwide home-delivery scheme and use it to distribute its own daily newspapers.
(70) Therefore the criteria for the establishment of abuse under Article 82 in cases relating to the exercise of a property right, as further clarified by the Court in Bronner, are whether:
- the refusal of access to the facility is likely to eliminate all competition in the relevant market,
- such refusal is not capable of being objectively justified, and
- the facility itself is indispensable to carrying on business, inasmuch as there is no actual or potential substitute in existence for that facility.
(71) In the present case and following the above reasoning, the Commission is required to assess whether the 1860-brick or compatible structure is indispensable to compete on the relevant market, that is to say whether there is a realistic possibility for undertakings wishing to offer regional sales data services in Germany to employ - instead of the 1860-brick or a compatible structure - another structure which would not infringe IMS' copyright.
(72) Clearly the answer to this question depends on whether there is a real possibility for customers of regional sales data of buying data formatted in another structure. To ascertain this, the Commission requested information from first 20, then a further 90 pharmaceutical companies. A total of 85 replies were received.

(73) According to IMS the Commission's initial market survey was inadequate and no conclusions should be drawn from it. In all, the 110 requests for information from the Commission have yielded 85 replies. The responding companies represent 56 % of total pharmaceutical sales in Germany. The companies which responded to the Commission's inquiry contained a representative survey both of pharmaceutical companies generally and customers of regional sales data services, including almost all of the largest companies and a sample of both small and medium-sized firms.
(74) In the present case, the Commission considers that the following facts show clearly that the legal tests set out above have been met.

[.....]

7.5. Conclusion on abuse under Article 82

(179) The Commission considers that this case meets the requirements for the establishment of abuse under Article 82 as developed in European Court of Justice and Court of First Instance jurisprudence, beginning with the Commercial Solvents and Volvo judgments and taken further in Magill, Ladbroke and Bronner.
(180) The Commission considers that there are "exceptional circumstances" in this case within the meaning of the phrase used by the European Court of Justice in Magill (paragraph 50) read in conjunction with the Ladbroke and Bronner cases. IMS has created, in collaboration with the pharmaceutical industry over a long period of time, a brick structure which has become the de facto industry standard for the presentation of regional data services and which the Frankfurt Court has found is its intellectual property right. IMS is now excluding all competition from the market for regional data services by refusing, without objective justification, to license this structure to competitors. As clarified in the Ladbroke judgment, there is no requirement for a refusal to supply to prevent the emergence of a new product in order to be abusive.
(181) It is clear that refusal of access to the 1860-brick structure is likely to eliminate all competition in the relevant market, since without it is not possible to compete on the relevant market. IMS' reasons for its refusal to licence are not capable of being objectively justified. Moreover, use of the 1860 structure is indispensable to carrying on business on the relevant market; there is no actual or potential substitute for it. These exceptional circumstances meet the test set out in Bronner for a refusal to supply to be considered an abuse of a dominant position.
(182) IMS makes a number of arguments attacking the legal analysis set out in the statement of objections. It says that there is no suggestion that IMS has engaged in any abusive conduct or has tried to use its control of intellectual property to monopolise downstream or related markets. IMS is entitled to refuse licences of its copyright to competitors for the market to which copyright relates (see the Volvo case). A refusal is only abusive if coupled with additional abusive behaviour, and there is none here.
(183) Furthermore, IMS does not consider that the 1860-brick structure is an essential facility, since there is no second related market on which competition is restricted.
(184) As regards the first of these two arguments, European Court of Justice and Court of First Instance case-law subsequent to the Volvo case makes clear that in exceptional circumstances the refusal to license an intellectual property right in itself can be considered to be an abuse under Article 82. As described above in recitals 75 to 174, such circumstances exist here. A dominant company has negotiated over a long

period with its customer industry so as to produce a structure on which the industry is now very highly dependent, to the extent that they consider it a de facto industry standard, and which a national court has now found is the dominant company's intellectual property. This dominant company now refuses to license this structure to competitors, so that no competing products based on this structure can be produced. On the second argument, the fact that the cases considered by the European Court of Justice and Court of First Instance to which IMS refers involved two markets does not preclude the possibility that a refusal to licence an intellectual property right can be contrary to Article 82. In the Magill case cited above, the basic information about television programmes was considered to be an indispensable input to allow an undertaking to compete in a downstream market (that for television-listings magazines). The circumstances are similar in this case, in that use of the 1860-brick structure is an indispensable input to allow undertakings to compete in the market for regional sales data services in Germany. As explained above in recitals 15 and 16, there is an important distinction between the product, which is regional sales data services, and the brick structure in which data used to create these services is formatted. In this case, in the specific and exceptional circumstances in which the 1860-brick structure was developed and copyright was asserted and found to subsist, the work in question for the technical, legal and economic constraints referred to above is incapable of being replicated by means of a non-infringing parallel creation.

(185) The finding here is that there is a prima facie case that use of the 1860-brick structure is indispensable to compete on the relevant market. The input which the pharmaceutical companies have made to the structure has contributed greatly to its status as a de facto industry standard and to their current dependence on this structure as a format for the receipt of regional sales data services. It is therefore the case that refusing access to this structure to competitors on the relevant market would exclude all competition from this market, and that therefore IMS' refusal to license the 1860-brick structure involves abusive conduct.

(186) The overall conclusion here is therefore that, on the evidence available at present, there is sufficient prima facie case of behaviour constituting abuse under Article 82 to order interim measures, if the other conditions for ordering such measures are fulfilled.

[.....]

[Footnotes not included]

Case cross-references:

▸ Case T-184/01 *IMS Health* [2001] ECR II-3193, suspension of decision 2002/65 ordered; Case C-418/01 P *IMS Health* [2002] ECR I-3401(order).

▸ Cases on essential facilities, in particular the cases C-241 & 242/91 P *RTE (Magill TV Guides)* [1995] ECR I-743 & C-7/97 *Bronner* [1998] ECR I-7791 (see II-F-4 and II-F-5).

6) Case C-418/01 *IMS Health* [2004] ECR I-5039

Almost six months before NDC had made its complaint to the Commission about IMS's behaviour, IMS had started proceedings before the national court in order to prohibit NDC from using its brick structure. The Landgericht Frankfurt am Main referred several questions on the compatibility of such a prohibition with Article 102 to the ECJ.

Relevance: obligatory licensing requires 'special circumstances'.

[.....]

Operative part of the judgment

[.....]

1. For the purposes of examining whether the refusal by an undertaking in a dominant position to grant a licence for a brick structure protected by copyright which it owns is abusive, the degree of participation by users in the development of that structure and the outlay, particularly in terms of cost, on the part of potential users in order to purchase studies on regional sales of pharmaceutical products presented on the basis of an alternative structure are factors which must be taken into consideration in order to determine whether the protected structure is indispensable to the marketing of studies of that kind.
2. The refusal by an undertaking which holds a dominant position and owns a copyright of a brick structure indispensable to the presentation of regional sales data on pharmaceutical products in a Member State to grant a licence to use that structure to another undertaking which also wishes to provide such data in the same Member State, constitutes an abuse of a dominant position within the meaning of Article 82 EC where the following conditions are fulfilled:
- the undertaking which requested the licence intends to offer, on the market for the supply of the data in question, new products or services not offered by the copyright owner and for which there is a potential consumer demand;
- the refusal is not justified by objective considerations;
- the refusal is such as to reserve to the copyright owner the market for the supply of data on sales of pharmaceutical products in the Member State concerned by eliminating all competition on that market.

[.....]

Case cross-references:

▸ Case C-320/91 *Corbeau* [1993] ECR I-2533 (IV-B-4).
▸ Case C-7/97 *Bronner* [1998] ECR I-7791 (II-F-5).
▸ Case T-201/04 *Microsoft v. Commission*, [2007] ECR II-3601.
▸ F. Vogelaar, 'The compulsory licence of intellectual property rights under the EC competition rules: an analysis of the exception to the general rule of ownership immunity from competition rules', *CompLRev.* 2009, Vol. 6 no. 1, pp. 117-137.
▸ B. Ong, 'Building brick barricades and other barriers to entry: abusing a dominant position by refusing to licence Intellectual property rights', (2005) 4 *ECLR*, 215.

7) *AstraZeneca*, Comm. Press Release 2005 (IP/05/737), non-confidential version of decision published on 19th July 2006 on DG Comp's website.

Relevance: Misusing rules and procedures when applying for patents constitutes an abuse of a dominant position.

IP/05/737, Brussels, 15th June 2005

Commission fines AstraZeneca € 60 million for misusing patent system to delay market entry of competing generic drugs.
The European Commission has fined Anglo-Swedish group AstraZeneca € 60 million for misusing the patent system and the procedures for marketing pharmaceuticals to block or delay market entry for generic competitors to its ulcer drug Losec. The Commission has decided that AstraZeneca's actions constitute serious abuses of its dominant market position in violation of EC and EEA competition rules.

Competition Commissioner Neelie Kroes commented: "I fully support the need for innovative products to enjoy strong intellectual property protection so that companies can recoup their R & D expenditure and be rewarded for their innovative efforts. However, it is not for a dominant company but for the legislator to decide which period of protection is adequate. Misleading regulators to gain longer protection acts as a disincentive to innovate and is a serious infringement of EU competition rules. Health care systems throughout Europe rely on generic drugs to keep costs down. Patients benefit from lower prices. By preventing generic competition AstraZeneca kept Losec prices artificially high. Moreover, competition from generic products after a patent has expired itself encourages innovation in pharmaceuticals."
From 1993 to 2000 AstraZeneca infringed EC and EEA competition rules by blocking or delaying market access for generic versions of Losec and preventing parallel imports of Losec. AstraZeneca did this by:
· giving misleading information to several national patent offices in the EEA resulting in AstraZeneca gaining extended patent protection for Losec through so-called supplementary protection certificates (SPCs). In this specific case, the patent offices essentially relied on information supplied by AZ and they were not obliged – as in normal patent assessments – to consider whether the products were innovative. AZ's misleading conduct amounted to an abuse in Belgium, Denmark, Germany, the Netherlands, Norway and the United Kingdom.
· misusing rules and procedures applied by the national medicines agencies which issue market authorisations for medicines by selectively deregistering the market authorisations for Losec capsules in Denmark, Norway and Sweden with the intent of blocking or delaying entry by generic firms and parallel traders. At the time, generic products could only be marketed and parallel importers only obtain import licenses if there was an existing reference market authorization for the original corresponding product (Losec). The purpose of a market authorization is the right to sell a medicine and not to exclude competitors. Unlike patents, SPCs and data exclusivity, market authorizations are not intended to reward innovation and the finding of an abuse cannot therefore affect incentives to innovate. Subsequent changes in the applicable EU legislation have made it impossible to repeat this specific conduct.

Losec pioneered a new generation of medicines to treat stomach ulcers and other acid-related diseases – so-called proton pump inhibitors. Losec initially received patent protection in Europe in 1979. During part of this period, Losec was the world's best-selling prescription medicine.
The Commission's decision does not prohibit AstraZeneca's dominant position on the proton pump inhibitor market but the company's abuse of that position. The fine takes into account that some features of the abuses can be considered as novel.

Case cross-references:

▸ Appeal pending before the GC, Case T-321/05, judgment to be expected in the summer of 2010.

F. Essential facilities

Cross-references for this part:

▸ B. Doherty, 'Just what are essential facilities?', (2001) 38 *CMLRev*, 397.

▸ F. Fine, 'NDC/IMS: A Logical Application of Essential Facilities Doctrine', (2002) 23 *ECLR*, 457.

▸ J. Temple Lang, 'Defining Legitimate Competition: Companies' Duties to Supply Competitors, and Access to Essential Facilities', (1994) *Fordham Corp. L. Inst.* (B. Hawk ed. 1995), 245.

▸ C. Stothers, 'Refusal to Supply as Abuse of a Dominant Position: Essential Facilities in the European Union', (2001) 22 *ECLR*, 256.

▸ C. Ritter, 'Refusal to deal and 'essential facilities': does intellectual property require special deference compared to tangible property?', (2005), 28 (3) *World Competition Law and Economics Review*, 299.

Cases 2-5 show the development of the case law on 'essential facilities' proper in four consecutive logical steps.

1) Case 311/84 *Telemarketing* [1985] ECR 3261

See above for facts of the case and relevant paragraphs (II-B-18, p. 113).

Relevance: (preliminary) development essential facilities doctrine (essential facilities not yet mentioned; paragraph 26 speaks of 'indispensable').

2) *Port of Rødby* Commission decision 94/119/EC [1994] OJ L 55/52

DSB, a public undertaking, was owner of the (public) port of Rødby and was the sole provider of ferry services between Rødby and Puttgarden (downstream integration). Stena was not allowed to either build a private commercial port or to use the existing port facilities. According to the Commission, this refusal amounted to an abuse of dominance.

Relevance: *first step*: definition of essential facilities (vertical integration: owner, who at the same time, is also the user of the facility has to be non-discriminatory towards other users).

[.....]

Abuse of dominant position

(12) [...] According to the case law of the Court, an abuse within the meaning of Article 86 is committed in cases where, without any objective necessity, an undertaking holding a dominant position on a particular market reserves to itself an ancillary activity which might be carried out by another undertaking as part of its activities on a neighbouring but separate market, with the possibility of eliminating all competition from such undertaking (Case 311/84 CBEM v. CLT and IPB [1985] ECR 3261, paragraph 27).
Thus an undertaking that owns or manages and uses itself an essential facility, i.e. A facility or infrastructure without which its competitors are unable to offer their services to customers, and refuses to grant them access to such facility is abusing its dominant position.
Consequently, an undertaking that owns or manages an essential port facility from which it provides a maritime transport service may not, without objective justification, refuse to grant a shipowner wishing to operate on the same maritime route access to that facility without infringing Article 86.
(13) According to the case-law of the Court (judgment of 13 December 1991 in Case C-18/88, paragraphs 20 and 21), Article 90 (1) prohibits Member States from placing, by law, regulation or administrative provision, public undertakings and undertakings to which they grant exclusive rights in a position in which those undertakings could not place themselves by their own conduct without infringing Article 86. The Court added that, where the extension of the dominant position of a public undertaking or an undertaking to which the State has granted exclusive rights resulted from a State measure, such a measure constituted an infringement of Article 90, read in conjunction with Article 86 of the Treaty. This principle was confirmed in the judgment of 17 November 1992 in Cases C-271, 281 and 289/90 (paragraph 36).
Thus, for the reasons given above, any firm in the same position as DSB which refused to grant another shipping operator access to the port it controlled would be abusing a dominant position. Where, as in the present case, a Member State has refused such access and has strengthened the effects of the refusal by also refusing to authorize the construction of a new port, it constitutes a State measure in breach of Article 90, read in conjunction with Article 86.

[.....]

3) *British Midland (Zaventem)* Commission decision 95/364/EC [1995] OJ L 216/8

See above for facts of the case (II-B-10, p. 115).

Relevance: *second step*: extension essential facilities doctrine (favouring of a third party, i.e., one of the users of the essential facility, by the owner of the essential facility who is not a user thereof may amount to an abuse).

[.....]

Article 86
The relevant market

(8) The relevant market is the market in services linked to access to airport infrastructures for which a fee is payable, i.e. the exploitation and maintenance of runways, taxiways and aprons, and approach guidance.
As the Court of Justice has held, the organization of port facilities for third parties at a single port may constitute a relevant market within the meaning of Article 86 (judgment of 10 December 1991 in Case C-179/90, Porto di Genova spa v. Siderurgica Gabrielli spa (1), paragraph 15). Likewise, the Court considered piloting services in the Port of Genoa to constitute the relevant market in its judgment of 17 May 1994 in Case C-18/93, Corsica Ferries v. Corpo dei Piloti del Porto di Genova (2).
The Court based its reasoning on the fact that, if an operator wishes to offer a transport service on a given maritime route, access to port installations situated at either end of that route is essential to the provision of the service.
This reasoning can easily be transposed to the air-transport sector and access to airports. In the case at issue, there is no genuine alternative offering the same advantages as Brussels Airport for short and medium-haul transport services to or from the Brussels catchment area.
(9) Moreover, short and medium-haul air services within the Community constitute a neighbouring but distinct market which is affected by the conduct of the undertaking active on the market in landing and take-off services.
As emerges from the explanations supplied in recital 5, Brussels Airport is, for short and medium-haul services within the Community operating from or to the Brussels catchment area, of limited substitutability with other available routes and faces only minor competition from them (see the judgment of 11 April 1989 in Case 66/86, Ahmed Saeed v. Zentrale zur Bekaempfung unlauteren Wettbewerbs (3)).

[.....]

Dominant position

(11) According to the case-law of the Court of Justice, an undertaking which has a legal monopoly to provide certain services holds a dominant position within the meaning of Article 86 of the Treaty (judgment of 3 October 1985 in Case 311/84 (5), 'Telemarketing'). Such is the case with the Airways Authority, a public enterprise which, by virtue of the exclusive right granted by Article 1 of the Royal Decree of 5 October 1970, holds a dominant position - in its capacity as airport authority - on the market in aircraft landing and take-off services, for which the fee in question is charged.

[.....]

Abuse of a dominant position

[.....]

(17) While most of the abuses committed by undertakings in a dominant position are designed to maximize their profits or strengthen their dominance, Article 86 also applies to cases in which an undertaking in a dominant position discriminates against its partners for reasons other than its own interest. This may involve, for example, giving preference to another undertaking from the same State or to an undertaking which is pursuing the same general policy. One example of an abuse committed by an undertaking in a dominant posi-

tion for reasons other than its own interest is afforded by the pilots in the Port of Genoa, who applied preferential tariffs approved by the State to maritime-transport undertakings operating between ports situated on the national territory (see Case C-18/93).
Thus, in the case at issue, unlike in the case of the systems of so-called loyalty rebates examined by the Court (judgment of 13 February 1979 in Case 85/76, Hoffmann-La Roche, v. Commission (1), and judgment of 9 November 1983 in Case 322/81, Michelin v. Commission (2)), the airways authority is not attempting to obtain the loyalty of its customers or to attract new ones, as has been demonstrated in recitals 13, 14 and 15, but rather the State, acting through its intermediary, is giving preferential treatment to a specific undertaking, i.e. The national airline Sabena.
(18) In this regard, the Belgian authorities have stated that the policy of landing fees as imposed by the Royal Decree in question even goes against the interests of the airways authority since the discounts reduce the revenues which the airways authority might obtain from the fees. The system was therefore introduced in order to benefit certain airlines since only Sabena, Sobelair, and, to a lesser extent, British Airways, are able to qualify for them, and this in breach of Article 86.

[.....]

4) Joined Cases C-241 & 242/91 P *RTE (Magill TV Guides)* [1995] ECR I-743

Irish televisions stations published their own weekly television guides containing an overview of their own programmes. Since newspapers were only allowed to publish comprehensive daily listings, Magill came up with the idea to publish a comprehensive weekly television guide. However, the BBC, ITP and RTE had claimed copyright protection for their listings. Reproduction was not allowed without a licence, and Magill had not been given one.

Relevance: *third step*: an IPR may, in exceptional circumstances, constitute an essential facility. The doctrine is extended, but not in general.

[.....]

(b) Existence of abuse

48 With regard to the issue of abuse, the arguments of the appellants and IPO wrongly presuppose that where the conduct of an undertaking in a dominant position consists of the exercise of a right classified by national law as "copyright", such conduct can never be reviewed in relation to Article 86 of the Treaty.

49 Admittedly, in the absence of Community standardization or harmonization of laws, determination of the conditions and procedures for granting protection of an intellectual property right is a matter for national rules. Further, the exclusive right of reproduction forms part of the author's rights, so that refusal to grant a licence, even if it is the act of an undertaking holding a dominant position, cannot in itself constitute abuse of a dominant position (judgment in Case 238/87 Volvo, cited above, paragraphs 7 and 8).

50 However, it is also clear from that judgment (paragraph 9) that the exercise of an exclusive right by the proprietor may, in exceptional circumstances, involve abusive conduct.

[.....]

54 The appellants' refusal to provide basic information by relying on national copyright provisions thus prevented the appearance of a new product, a comprehensive weekly guide to television programmes, which the appellants did not offer and for which there was a potential consumer demand. Such refusal constitutes an abuse under heading (b) of the second paragraph of Article 86 of the Treaty.
55 Second, there was no justification for such refusal either in the activity of television broadcasting or in that of publishing television magazines (RTE judgment, paragraph 73, and ITP judgment, paragraph 58).
56 Third, and finally, as the Court of First Instance also held, the appellants, by their conduct, reserved to themselves the secondary market of weekly television guides by excluding all competition on that market (see the judgment in Joined Cases 6/73 and 7/73 Commercial Solvents v Commission [1974] ECR 223, paragraph 25) since they denied access to the basic information which is the raw material indispensable for the compilation of such a guide.
57 In the light of all those circumstances, the Court of First Instance did not err in law in holding that the appellants' conduct was an abuse of a dominant position within the meaning of Article 86 of the Treaty.
58 It follows that the plea in law alleging misapplication by the Court of First Instance of the concept of abuse of a dominant position must be dismissed as unfounded. It is therefore unnecessary to examine the reasoning of the contested judgments in so far as it is based on Article 36 of the Treaty.

[.....]

Case cross-reference:

▸ J. Smith, 'Television Guides: The European Court Doesn't Know There's So Much in It', (1992) 13 *ECLR*, 135.

5) Case C-7/97 *Bronner* [1998] ECR I-7791

Bronner was publisher of Der Standard, an Austrian newspaper that was published in a limited edition and distributed mainly in Austria and to a much lesser degree in Munich, Germany. He wanted Mediaprint, which issued two daily newspapers, to include Der Standard in its (national) distribution system since he could not afford to set-up an efficient and competitive distribution network of his own. Mediaprint refused, after which it was accused of abusing its dominant power. Bronner claimed that he had no alternative to Mediaprint's home delivery scheme. Moreover, he also claimed that the Mediaprint distribution network constituted for him an essential facility.

Relevance: *fourth step*: development essential facilities doctrine by the ECJ (angle: relation between essential facility doctrine - no IPRs being involved - and successful private market performance). (Please note: summary of '*Magill*-criteria' in recital 40.)

[.....]

32 In examining whether an undertaking holds a dominant position within the meaning of Article 86 of the Treaty, it is of fundamental importance, as the Court has emphasised many times, to define the market in question and to define the substantial part of the Common Market in which the undertaking may be able to engage in abuses which hinder effective competition (Case C-242/95 GT-Link v DSB [1997] ECR I-4449, paragraph 36).

33 It is settled case-law that, for the purposes of applying Article 86 of the Treaty, the market for the product or service in question comprises all the products or services which in view of their characteristics are particularly suited to satisfy constant needs and are only to a limited extent interchangeable with other products or services (Case 31/80 L'Oréal v De Nieuwe AMCK [1980] ECR 3775, paragraph 25; Case C-62/86 AKZO v Commission [1991] ECR I-3359, paragraph 51).

[.....]

36 In that event, the national court would also have to find that Mediaprint holds a dominant position in a substantial part of the Common Market, since the case-law indicates that the territory of a Member State over which a dominant position extends is capable of constituting a substantial part of the Common Market (see, to that effect, Case 322/81 Michelin v Commission [1983] ECR 3461, paragraph 28; Case C-323/93 Centre d'Insémination de la Crespelle [1994] ECR I-5077, paragraph 17).

37 Finally, it would need to be determined whether the refusal by the owner of the only nationwide home-delivery scheme in the territory of a Member State, which uses that scheme to distribute its own daily newspapers, to allow the publisher of a rival daily newspaper access to it constitutes an abuse of a dominant position within the meaning of Article 86 of the Treaty, on the ground that such refusal deprives that competitor of a means of distribution judged essential for the sale of its newspaper.

38 Although in Commercial Solvents v Commission and CBEM, cited above, the Court of Justice held the refusal by an undertaking holding a dominant position in a given market to supply an undertaking with which it was in competition in a neighbouring market with raw materials (Commercial Solvents v Commission, paragraph 25) and services (CBEM, paragraph 26) respectively, which were indispensable to carrying on the rival's business, to constitute an abuse, it should be noted, first, that the Court did so to the extent that the conduct in question was likely to eliminate all competition on the part of that undertaking.

39 Secondly, in Magill, at paragraphs 49 and 50, the Court held that refusal by the owner of an intellectual property right to grant a licence, even if it is the act of an undertaking holding a dominant position, cannot in itself constitute abuse of a dominant position, but that the exercise of an exclusive right by the proprietor may, in exceptional circumstances, involve an abuse.

40 In Magill, the Court found such exceptional circumstances in the fact that the refusal in question concerned a product (information on the weekly schedules of certain television channels) the supply of which was indispensable for carrying on the business in question (the publishing of a general television guide), in that, without that information, the person wishing to produce such a guide would find it impossible to publish it and offer it for sale (paragraph 53), the fact that such refusal prevented the appearance of a new product for which there was a potential consumer demand

(paragraph 54), the fact that it was not justified by objective considerations (paragraph 55), and that it was likely to exclude all competition in the secondary market of television guides (paragraph 56).

41 Therefore, even if that case-law on the exercise of an intellectual property right were applicable to the exercise of any property right whatever, it would still be necessary, for the Magill judgment to be effectively relied upon in order to plead the existence of an abuse within the meaning of Article 86 of the Treaty in a situation such as that which forms the subject-matter of the first question, not only that the refusal of the service comprised in home delivery be likely to eliminate all competition in the daily newspaper market on the part of the person requesting the service and that such refusal be incapable of being objectively justified, but also that the service in itself be indispensable to carrying on that person's business, inasmuch as there is no actual or potential substitute in existence for that home-delivery scheme.

42 That is certainly not the case even if, as in the case which is the subject of the main proceedings, there is only one nationwide home-delivery scheme in the territory of a Member State and, moreover, the owner of that scheme holds a dominant position in the market for services constituted by that scheme or of which it forms part.

43 In the first place, it is undisputed that other methods of distributing daily newspapers, such as by post and through sale in shops and at kiosks, even though they may be less advantageous for the distribution of certain newspapers, exist and are used by the publishers of those daily newspapers.

44 Moreover, it does not appear that there are any technical, legal or even economic obstacles capable of making it impossible, or even unreasonably difficult, for any other publisher of daily newspapers to establish, alone or in cooperation with other publishers, its own nationwide home-delivery scheme and use it to distribute its own daily newspapers.

45 It should be emphasised in that respect that, in order to demonstrate that the creation of such a system is not a realistic potential alternative and that access to the existing system is therefore indispensable, it is not enough to argue that it is not economically viable by reason of the small circulation of the daily newspaper or newspapers to be distributed.

46 For such access to be capable of being regarded as indispensable, it would be necessary at the very least to establish, as the Advocate General has pointed out at point 68 of his Opinion, that it is not economically viable to create a second home-delivery scheme for the distribution of daily newspapers with a circulation comparable to that of the daily newspapers distributed by the existing scheme.

47 In the light of the foregoing considerations, the answer to the first question must be that the refusal by a press undertaking which holds a very large share of the daily newspaper market in a Member State and operates the only nationwide newspaper home-delivery scheme in that Member State to allow the publisher of a rival newspaper, which by reason of its small circulation is unable either alone or in cooperation with other publishers to set up and operate its own home-delivery scheme in economically reasonable conditions, to have access to that scheme for appropriate remuneration does not constitute abuse of a dominant position within the meaning of Article 86 of the Treaty.

The second question

48 In its second question, the national court asks whether the refusal by that undertaking, in the circumstances mentioned in the

first question, to allow the publisher of a rival daily newspaper to have access to its home-delivery scheme where the latter does not at the same time entrust to it the carrying out of other services, such as sale in kiosks and printing, constitutes an abuse of a dominant position within the meaning of Article 86 of the Treaty.
49 Given the reply to the first question, there is no need to answer the second.

[.....]

Case cross-references:

▸ *IMS Health* Commission decision 2002/165/EC [2002] OJ L 59/18; Case C-418/01 *IMS Health*[2004] ECR I-5039 (see II-E-5 and II-E-6).
▸ M.A. Bergman, 'The Bronner Case – A Turning Point for the Essential Facilities Doctrine?', (2000) 21 *ECLR*, 59.
▸ L. Hancher, 'Annotation Case C-7/97, Oscar Bronner', (1999) 36 *CMLRev*, 1289.
▸ In an environmental context, Case T-289/01 *Der Grüne Punkt- Duales System Deutschland GmbH v. Commission* [2007] ECR II-1691; T-151/01 *Der Grüne Punkt - Duales System Deutschland GmbH v. Commission*, [2007] ECR II-1607. Judgment upheld on appeal by the ECJ in Case C-385/07 P, [2009] ECR I-0000.

CHAPTER III

The 'Useful Effect' Doctrine

General Introductory Remarks

Over the years, this doctrine has been developed by the Court of Justice. In the pre-Lisbon era the doctrine was based on a combination of the Articles 3(1) sub g, 10 and 81-82 EC. For that reason, it was also referred to as the 'Trias-norm'. Now that the Treaty of Lisbon has come into effect, Article 3 has no longer an equivalent in either the TEU or the TFEU but has been replaced by the Protocol No. 27 on the Internal Market and Competition, attached to the Lisbon Treaty. The equivalent of Article 10 EC on what used to be known as 'Community Loyalty' may now be found in Article 4(3) TEU (and will be referred to as *Union Loyalty*) whereas obviously the Articles 81 and 82 are now the Articles 101 and 102 TFEU. In this manner, the *useful effect doctrine* will remain based on a combination of three different rules, and may for that reason also continue to be referred to as the *'Trias Norm.'*

General chapter cross-references:

- ▸ A.B. Hoffman, 'Anti-competitive State Legislation Condemned under Articles 5, 85 and 86 of the EEC Treaty: How Far should the Court go after Van Eycke?', (1990) 11 *ECLR*, 11.
- ▸ Lisbon Treaty, Protocol No. 27 on the Internal Market and Competition.
- ▸ Article 4(3) TEU.

A. Introduction to *'useful effect'* doctrine

1) Case 13/77 *INNO v. ATAB* [1977] ECR 2115

INNO, a company that runs several supermarkets in Belgium, sold cigarettes at a price that was lower than the one indicated on the tax label. This lower pricing practice infringed the (Belgian) Tobacco Excise Tax Code that specifically stated that the "the price stated on the tax label ... must be the compulsory selling price". Accordingly, the ATAB (the Association of Tobacco Retailers in Belgium) started proceedings. INNO was ordered to stop the infringement by both the Belgium Court of Commerce and the Court of Appeal. The Belgian Cour de Cassation, however, referred a question to the ECJ as to the compatibility of the Belgian rule, which in fact fixed a selling price determined by tobacco manufacturers or importers, with EU law.

Relevance: introduction to *'useful effect'* doctrine.

[.....]

The first question

[.....]

28 First, the single market system which the Treaty seeks to create excludes any national system of regulation hindering directly or indirectly, actually or potentially, trade within the Community.

29 Secondly, the general objective set out in Article 3 (f) is made specific in several Treaty provisions concerning the rules on competition, including Article 86, which states that any abuse by one or more undertakings of a dominant position shall be prohibited as incompatible with the common market in so far as it may affect trade between Member States.

30 The second paragraph of Article 5 of the Treaty provides that Member States shall abstain from any measure which could jeopardize the attainment of the objectives of the Treaty.

31 Accordingly, while it is true that Article 86 is directed at undertakings, nonetheless it is also true that the Treaty imposes a duty on Member States not to adopt or maintain in force any measure which could deprive that provision of its effectiveness.
32 Thus Article 90 provides that, in the case of public undertakings and undertakings to which Member States grant special or exclusive rights, Member States shall neither enact nor maintain in force any measure contrary inter alia to the rules provided for in Articles 85 to 94.
33 Likewise, Member States may not enact measures enabling private undertakings to escape from the constraints imposed by Articles 85 to 94 of the Treaty.
34 At all events, Article 86 prohibits any abuse by one or more undertakings of a dominant position, even if such abuse is encouraged by a national legislative provision.
35 In any case, a national measure which has the effect of facilitating the abuse of a dominant position capable of affecting trade between Member States will generally be incompatible with Articles 30 and 34, which prohibit quantitative restrictions on imports and exports and all measures having equivalent effect.
36 In assessing the compatibility with the Treaty of a system for fixing retail selling prices, a national court must take into account all the conditions for the application of the provisions of Community law which have been referred to.
37 In this connexion, the Hof van Cassatie has taken into consideration, first, the possibility that the fact that manufacturers and importers of tobacco products can oblige retailers in a Member State to adhere to the prices for sale to the consumer fixed by them could constitute a dominant position, and, secondly, that the measure regarded as possibly infringing Article 86 in conjunction with the second paragraph of Article 5 is a provision whereby on a sale to the consumer those prices must be adhered to.
38 In order to assess the compatibility of the introduction or the maintenance in force of such a measure with those provisions of Community law, the national court must also determine, taking into account the obstacles to trade in manufactured tobacco between states which may result from the nature of the fiscal arrangements in question, whether that measure as such is capable of affecting trade between Member States, for this condition has to be satisfied for the prohibitions laid down in Article 86 to be applicable.

[.....]

2) Case 267/86 *Van Eycke v. Aspa* [1988] ECR 4769

Aspa, a Belgian financial institution, had advertised a certain interest rate on savings deposits. Van Eycke, attracted by the advertisement, made a deposit. In Belgium, however, only yields from deposits that had an interest rate not exceeding the rate fixed by a Royal Decree qualified for fiscal benefits. Aspa's rates were above these rates and, as a consequence, it had to apply less favourable terms. Van Eycke claimed that the Decree was contrary to Article 101 and started proceedings. The national court asked the ECJ for a preliminary ruling on the compatibility with EU law of the Belgian provisions, which in fact confirmed an existing banking practice of low returns on saving accounts.

Relevance: national legislative or other public acts that might take away the *'useful effect'* of EU law. Interpretation of the notion of 'Union loyalty' in competition matters.

[.....]

First and second questions

[.....]

16 It must be pointed out (...) that Articles 85 and 86 of the Treaty per se are concerned only with the conduct of undertakings and not with national legislation. The Court has consistently held, however, that Articles 85 and 86 of the Treaty, in conjunction with Article 5, require the Member States not to introduce or maintain in force measures, even of a legislative nature, which may render ineffective the competition rules applicable to undertakings. Such would be the case, the Court has held, if a Member State were to require or favour the adoption of agreements, decisions or concerted practices contrary to Article 85 or to reinforce their effects, or to deprive its own legislation of its official character by delegating to private traders responsibility for taking decisions affecting the economic sphere.

17 According to the findings made in the order for reference, before the adoption of the legislation in question there were agreements between banks or concerted practices designed to restrict the yield on savings deposits. However, it is not apparent either from those findings or from the observations submitted to the Court that the legislation in question was intended to require or favour the adoption of new restrictive agreements or the implementation of new practices. In order to assess the true scope of that legislation in the light of the criteria laid down by the Court in its case-law it is therefore necessary merely to ascertain, first, whether it may be regarded as intended to reinforce the effects of pre-existing agreements and, secondly, whether there are circumstances capable of depriving the legislation of its official character.

18 With regard to the first point it is sufficient to note that, as the Court has consistently held, legislation may be regarded as intended to reinforce the effects of pre-existing agreements, decisions or concerted practices only if it incorporates either wholly or in part the terms of agreements concluded between undertakings and requires or encourages compliance on the part of those undertakings. Although the prospect of losing the entire benefit of the preferential tax treatment for savings deposits constitutes a significant inducement to comply with the legislation in question, it is not apparent from any of the findings made by the national court in its judgment that such legislation merely confirmed both the method of restricting the yield on deposits and the level of maximum rates adopted under pre-existing agreements, decisions or practices. However, it is for the national court to enquire further into that point if it considers that there may be doubts in that regard.

19 With regard to the second point, it is apparent from the legislation in question that the authorities reserved to themselves the power to fix the maximum rates of interest on savings deposits and did not delegate that responsibility to any private trader. That legislation thus has an official character which cannot be called in question by the mere fact, emphasized by the plaintiff in the main proceedings, that according to the preamble to the Royal Decree of 13 March 1986 the Decree was adopted following consultations with the representatives of associations of credit establishments.

[.....]

Case cross-references:

- Case 231/83 *Cullet v. Leclerc* [1985] ECR 305.
- Case 209/84 *Ministère Public v. Asjes* [1986] ECR 1425.
- Case 66/86 *Ahmed Saeed Flugreisen* [1989] ECR 805.

B. Examples that illustrate the operating of this doctrine in practice

Re-inforcing (pre-existing) private agreements that would run against competition law

Cross-references for this part:

- Case 123/83 *BNIC v. Clair* [1985] ECR 391.
- Case 311/85 *Flemish travel agents* [1988] 3801 (see VI-D-1).
- Case C-115-117/97 *Brentjens* [1999] ECR I-6025 (see I-J-3).

1) Case 136/86 *BNIC v. Aubert* [1987] ECR 4789

Wine-growers and wine-dealers organized in the Bureau National Interprofessionnel du Cognac (BNIC) had agreed to establish a marketing quota and a storage quota for pure alcohol per hectare. Non-compliance would result in the imposition of a fine. According to French law, such an inter-trade agreement could become generally binding by ministerial order, as was the case here. BNIC started proceedings for payment of the levy when Yves Aubert had exceeded the fixed quota. The French court, though, asked the ECJ two preliminary questions on the compatibility of the aforementioned system with EU law. The Court ruled that the agreement was indeed contrary to Article 101 (1).

Relevance: reinforcing (pre-existing) private agreements that would themselves fall within the prohibition of Article 101 (1).

[.....]

The compatibility with Article 5 of the EEC Treaty of the order making the agreement generally binding

22 The issue is whether and to what extent it is contrary to the obligations imposed on Member States by Article 5 of the EEC Treaty, read together with Articles 3 (f) and 85, for a measure adopted by the public authorities to make generally binding an agreement which is contrary to Article 85.

23 As the Court has consistently held, Articles 85 and 86 of the Treaty concern the conduct of undertakings and not legislative or regulatory measures adopted by the Member States, but it is nevertheless true that the Treaty imposes a duty on them not to adopt or maintain in force any measure which could deprive those provisions of their effectiveness (judgment of 16 November 1977 in Case 13/77 INNO v ATAB (1977) ECR 2115).

24 That is the case in particular when a Member State, by means of an order making them generally binding, reinforces the effects of agreements which are contrary to Article 85.

25 The answer to the national court's questions must therefore be that:

an inter-trade agreement entered into by two groups of traders in the framework and in accordance with the procedure of an organization such as BNIC which provides for the payment of a levy where a production quota for pure alcohol per hectare has been exceeded is contrary to article 85 (1) of the EEC Treaty;

a ministerial order which makes such an agreement generally binding is contrary to the obligations imposed on the Member States by Article 5 of the EEC Treaty read together with Article 3 (f) and 85 thereof.

[.....]

Imposing obligations that would lead to infringement

2) Case C-245/91 *Ohra* [1993] ECR I-5851

Ohra, a Dutch insurance company, had published advertisements in which it offered its (potential) clients various rebates and discounts. Under Dutch law, however, it was illegal for insurance companies to grant such financially quantifiable advantages (Article 16 of the Law on insurance agencies). Furthermore, infringement of this Article was penalized under criminal law. Before the national court, Ohra pleaded that the Dutch provisions were not compatible with the 'useful effect' rule. The District Court, which was to decide the dispute, turned to the ECJ for a preliminary ruling on the interpretation of said doctrine.

Relevance: illustration of the borderline between independent state policy and the imposition of obligations that lead to the formation of cartels.

[.....]

10 It must be noted at the outset that Article 85 of the Treaty, read in isolation, relates only to the conduct of undertakings and does not cover legislative measures or regulations adopted by Member States. The Court has also consistently held that Article 85, read in conjunction with Article 5 of the Treaty, requires the Member States not to introduce or maintain in force measures, even of a legislative or regulatory nature, which may render ineffective the competition rules applicable to undertakings. By virtue of the same case-law, such is the case where a Member State requires or favours the adoption of agreements, decisions or concerted practices contrary to Article 85 or reinforces their effects or deprives its own legislation of its official character by delegating to private traders responsibility for taking economic decisions affecting the economic sphere (see Case 267/86 Van Eycke v ASPA [1988] ECR 4769, paragraph 16).

11 It must first be observed in that regard that the Netherlands rules on insurance agencies neither require nor favour the conclusion of any unlawful agreement, decision or concerted practice by insurance intermediaries, since the prohibition which they lay down is self-sufficient.

12 It must then be determined whether the rules have the effect of reinforcing an anti-competitive agreement. In that regard, it is common ground that the rules at issue were not preceded by any agreement in the sectors to which they relate.

13 Finally, it must be observed that the rules themselves prohibit the grant of financial advantages to policyholders and beneficiaries of policies and do not delegate to private traders responsibility for taking decisions affecting the economic sphere.

14 It follows that rules like those at issue in the main proceedings do not fall within the categories of State rules which, according to the case-law of the Court of Justice, undermine the effectiveness of Article 3 (f), the second paragraph of Article 5 and Article 85 of the Treaty.
15 Accordingly, it must be stated in reply to the questions submitted by the national court that Article 3 (f), the second paragraph of Article 5 and Article 85 of the EEC Treaty do not, in the absence of any link with conduct on the part of undertakings of the kind referred to in Article 85 (1) of the Treaty, preclude State rules which prohibit insurance companies, whether or not they operate through brokers, and brokers themselves from granting financial advantages to policyholders or the beneficiaries of policies.

[.....]

Case cross-references:

▸ Case C-2/91 *Meng* [1993] ECR I-5751.
▸ Case C-198/01 *Consorzio Industrie Fiammiferi (CIF)* [2003] ECR I-8055 (see X-A-2).
▸ A. Bach, 'Annotation Case C-185/91, Reiff, Case C-2/91, Meng; Case C-245/91, Ohra', (1994) 31 *CMLRev*, 1357.

Delegation to deprive Member State legislation of its official public character

3) Case C-185/91 *Reiff* [1993] ECR I-5801

Under the German Law on the carriage of goods by road (GueKG), transport tariffs were fixed by various Tariff Boards; the members were representatives of the transport sector concerned appointed by the German authorities. The tariff became binding after approval of the Federal Minister of Transport. When a certain transport operation was invoiced lower than the established tariff, the Federal Office for Long-distance Carriage of Goods by Road (Bundesanstalt) was entitled, under certain circumstances, to claim the difference between the price actually paid and the tariff from the shipper. In this dispute, Reiff had paid a freight charge that was below the tariff. The Bundesanstalt had started proceedings. The Landgericht Koblenz, however, referred a preliminary question to the ECJ on the compatibility of the German provisions with Article 4 (3) TEU and 101 TFEU.

Relevance: no waiver of public policy right. Possibility for Member State to overrule tariff decisions taken by sector Board.

[.....]

11 It must be noted at the outset that it is not for the Court, in proceedings under Article 177 of the Treaty, to rule as to the compatibility of provisions of national law with those of Community law; however, the Court is competent to provide the national court with all information as to the interpretation of Community law which may help the national court to decide whether the provisions at issue are compatible with the Community rules.
12 It must also be observed that, as the Court held in Joined Cases 209/84 to 213/84 Ministère Public v Asjes [1986] ECR 1425, the competition rules of the Treaty, and in particular those of Articles 85 to 90, apply to the transport sector.

13 Accordingly, the question submitted by the Landgericht Koblenz must be construed as seeking essentially to determine whether Article 3(f), the second paragraph of Article 5 and Article 85 of the EEC Treaty preclude rules of a Member State which require the tariffs for long-distance road haulage to be fixed by Tariff Boards and made binding on all economic agents, after approval by the public authority, under conditions such as those laid down by the GueKG.
14 It must also be borne in mind that, in itself, Article 85 of the Treaty relates only to the conduct of undertakings and does not cover legislative measures or regulations adopted by Member States. The Court has consistently held, however, that Article 85, read in conjunction with Article 5 of the Treaty, requires the Member States not to introduce or maintain in force measures, even of a legislative nature, which may render ineffective the competition rules applicable to undertakings. By virtue of the same case-law, such is the case where a Member State requires or favours the adoption of agreements, decisions or concerted practices contrary to Article 85 or reinforces their effects or deprives its own legislation of its official character by delegating to private traders responsibility for taking economic decisions affecting the economic sphere (see Case 267/86 Van Eycke v ASPA [1988] ECR 4769, paragraph 16).
15 In order to provide a useful answer to the national court, it is therefore necessary to consider first whether legislation such as the GueKG is indicative of the existence of an agreement, decision or concerted practice within the meaning of Article 85 of the Treaty.
16 As regards the role of economic agents, the Court has held that the fact that the public authority appoints as members of a body responsible for fixing prices persons proposed by trade organizations which are directly concerned does not exclude the existence of an agreement, decision or concerted practice within the meaning of Article 85 of the Treaty if those persons have negotiated and concluded an agreement on prices as representatives of the organizations which proposed them (see Case 123/83 BNIC v Clair [1985] ECR 391).
17 The Tariff Boards provided for by the GueKG are made up of tariff experts from the relevant sectors of the road haulage industry who are not bound by orders or instructions from the undertakings or associations which proposed them to the Federal Minister of Transport for appointment. Those boards cannot therefore be regarded as meetings of representatives of undertakings in the industry concerned.
18 Moreover, the GueKG does not allow the Tariff Boards to fix the tariffs solely by reference to the interests of undertakings or associations of undertakings engaged in transport but requires them to take account of the interests of the agricultural sector and of medium-sized undertakings or regions which are economically weak or have inadequate transport facilities. Furthermore, the tariffs are fixed only after compulsory consultation of an advisory committee made up of representatives of the users of the services.
19 It follows that, under a system for the fixing of road haulage tariffs like that introduced by the GueKG, the members of the Tariff Boards, although chosen by the Federal Minister of Transport on a proposal from the trade organizations directly concerned, cannot be regarded as representatives of the latter, called on to negotiate and conclude an agreement on prices.
20 Secondly, it is necessary to decide whether the public authorities have delegated their powers regarding the fixing of tariffs to private economic agents.

21 The GueKG is intended to secure the best possible road haulage service and entrusts to the Federal Government the task of approximating the conditions of competition as between different means of transport and of ensuring an economically rational division of tasks between them. To that end, the GueKG expressly requires the Federal Minister of Transport to harmonize the services and the prices of the various means of transport in order to avoid unfair competition, in particular between road, rail and river transport.
22 In order to discharge that responsibility, the Federal Minister of Transport not only has the power to establish the Tariff Boards and advisory committees, and to decide on their composition and structure but may also personally attend their meetings or be represented at them or delegate that right to agents of the Bundesanstalt. Furthermore, if the tariffs decided on by a Tariff Board are inimical to the public interest, the Federal Minister of Transport may, by agreement with the Federal Minister for Economic Affairs, fix the tariffs himself in the stead of the Tariff Board.
23 It follows that under a system for the fixing of road haulage tariffs of the kind introduced by the GueKG, the public authorities have not delegated their powers regarding the fixing of tariffs to private economic agents.
24 It must therefore be stated in reply to the question submitted that Article 3(f), the second paragraph of Article 5 and Article 85 of the EEC Treaty do not preclude rules of a Member State which provide that tariffs for the long distance transport of goods by road are to be fixed by tariff boards and are to be made compulsory for all economic agents, after approval by the public authorities, if the members of those boards, although chosen by the public authorities on a proposal from the relevant trade sectors, are not representatives of the latter called on to negotiate and conclude an agreement on prices but are independent experts called on to fix the tariffs on the basis of considerations of public interest and if the public authorities do not abandon their prerogatives but in particular ensure that the boards fix the tariffs by reference to considerations of public interest and, if necessary, substitute their decision for that of the boards.

[.....]

Case cross-reference:

▸ A. Bach, 'Annotation Case C-185/91, Reiff, Case C-2/91 Meng, Case C-245/91 Ohra', (1994) 31 *CMLRev*, 1357.

4) Case C-35/99 *Arduino* [2002] ECR I-1529

This judgment concerned the binding tariff for fees and emoluments payable to members of the Italian Bar in civil and criminal proceedings. This tariff was fixed by the National Council of the Bar (CNF) and needed governmental approval.

Relevance: no waiver of State powers. Exceptional circumstances for deviation needed.

[.....]

The questions

32 By its questions, which it is appropriate to examine together, the national court seeks essentially to ascertain whether Article 5 of the EC Treaty (now Article 10 EC) and Article 85 of the Treaty preclude a Member State from adopting a law or regulation which approves, on the basis of a draft produced by a professional body of members of the Bar, a tariff fixing minimum and maximum fees for members of the profession, where that State measure forms part of a procedure such as that laid down in the Italian legislation.
33 As a preliminary point, the Court observes that, since that State measure extends to the whole of the territory of a Member State, it may affect trade between Member States within the meaning of Article 85(1) of the Treaty (see, to that effect, Commission v Italy, cited above, paragraph 48).
34 Although Article 85 of the Treaty is, in itself, concerned solely with the conduct of undertakings and not with laws or regulations emanating from Member States, that article, read in conjunction with Article 5 of the Treaty, none the less requires the Member States not to introduce or maintain in force measures, even of a legislative or regulatory nature, which may render ineffective the competition rules applicable to undertakings (Case 267/86 Van Eycke [1988] ECR 4769, paragraph 16; Case C-185/91 Reiff [1993] ECR I-5801, paragraph 14; Case C-153/93 Delta Schiffahrts- und Speditionsgesellschaft [1994] ECR I-2517, paragraph 14; Case C-96/94 Centro Servizi Spediporto [1995] ECR I-2883, paragraph 20; and Commission v Italy, cited above, paragraph 53; as to Article 86 of the EC Treaty (now Article 82 EC), see also Case 13/77 GB-Inno-BM [1977] ECR 2115, paragraph 31).
35 The Court has held that Articles 5 and 85 of the Treaty are infringed where a Member State requires or favours the adoption of agreements, decisions or concerted practices contrary to Article 85 or reinforces their effects, or where it divests its own rules of the character of legislation by delegating to private economic operators responsibility for taking decisions affecting the economic sphere (Van Eycke, paragraph 16; Reiff, paragraph 14; Delta Schiffahrts- und Speditionsgesellschaft, paragraph 14; Centro Servizi Spediporto, paragraph 21; and Commission v Italy, paragraph 54).
36 In that regard, the fact that a Member State requires a professional organisation to produce a draft tariff for services does not automatically divest the tariff finally adopted of the character of legislation.
37 That would be the case where the members of the professional organisation can be characterised as experts who are independent of the economic operators concerned and they are required, under the law, to set tariffs taking into account not only the interests of the undertakings or associations of undertakings in the sector which has appointed them but also the public interest and the interests of undertakings in other sectors or users of the services in question (see, to that effect, Reiff, paragraphs 17 to 19 and 24; Delta Schiffahrts- und Speditionsgesellschaft, paragraphs 16 to 18 and 23; Joined Cases C-140/94 to C-142/94 DIP and Others [1995] ECR I-3257, paragraphs 18 and 19; and Commission v Italy, paragraph 44).
38 In the main proceedings, it is clear from the description of the national legislation that the Italian State obliges the CNF, composed exclusively of members of the Bar elected by their fellow members, to present every two years a draft tariff for fees payable to members of the Bar including minimum and maximum limits. Although, under

Article 58 of the Royal Decree-Law, fees and emoluments must be fixed on the basis of the monetary value of disputes, the level of the court seised and, in criminal matters, the duration of the proceedings, the Royal Decree-Law does not lay down public-interest criteria, properly so-called, which the CNF must take into account.

39 In those circumstances, the national legislation at issue in the main proceedings does not contain either procedural arrangements or substantive requirements capable of ensuring, with reasonable probability, that, when producing the draft tariff, the CNF conducts itself like an arm of the State working in the public interest.

40 That said, it does not appear that the Italian State has waived its power to make decisions of last resort or to review implementation of the tariff. [...]

41 First, the CNF is responsible only for producing a draft tariff which, as such, is not compulsory. Without the Minister's approval, the draft tariff does not enter into force and the earlier approved tariff remains applicable. Accordingly, the Minister has the power to have the draft amended by the CNF. Furthermore, the Minister is assisted by two public bodies, the Consiglio di Stato and the CIP whose opinions he must obtain before the tariff can be approved.

42 Second, Article 60 of the Royal Decree-Law provides that fees are to be settled by the courts on the basis of the criteria referred to in Article 57 of that decree-law, having regard to the seriousness and number of the issues dealt with. Moreover, in certain exceptional circumstances and by duly reasoned decision, the court may depart from the maximum and minimum limits fixed pursuant to Article 58 of the Royal Decree-Law.

43 In those circumstances, the Italian State cannot be said to have delegated to private economic operators responsibility for taking decisions affecting the economic sphere, which would have the effect of depriving the provisions at issue in the main proceedings of the character of legislation. Nor, for the reasons set out in paragraphs 41 and 42 above, is the Italian State open to the criticism that it requires or encourages the adoption of agreements, decisions or concerted practices contrary to Article 85 of the Treaty or reinforces their effects.

44 The answer to the questions referred for a preliminary ruling must therefore be that Articles 5 and 85 of the Treaty do not preclude a Member State from adopting a law or regulation which approves, on the basis of a draft produced by a professional body of members of the Bar, a tariff fixing minimum and maximum fees for members of the profession, where that State measure forms part of a procedure such as that laid down in the Italian legislation.

[.....]

Case cross-reference:

- ▸ Case C-309/99 *Wouters* [2002] ECR I-1577 of the same date as the *Arduino* judgment.
- ▸ Joined Cases C-94/04 and C-202/04 *Federico Cipolla and Others* [2006] ECR I-11421.

CHAPTER IV

Public Undertakings and Undertakings Entrusted with the Operation of Services of Economic Interest

General chapter cross-references:

- ▸ Article 106 TFEU in conjunction with Article 102 TFEU.
- ▸ Protocol No. 26 concerning Services of General Interest.
- ▸ Commission Communication - Services of general interest in Europe, [2001] OJ C 17/4.
- ▸ V. Auricchio, 'Services of General Economic Interest and the Application of EC Competition Law', (2001) 24 *World Competition*, 65.
- ▸ G. Monti, 'Article 81 and public policy', (2002) 39 *CMLRev*, 1057.
- ▸ M. Ross,. 'Article 16 EC and services of general interest: from derogation to obligation?', (2000) 25 *ELR*, 22.

G. Davies, 'Article 86, the EC's economic approach to competition law and the general interest', (2009) 5 *European Competition Journal* 549-584.

A. Article 106 (1) TFEU is no stand-still clause

1) Case 155/73 *Sacchi* [1974] ECR 409

The Italian government had conferred on a public undertaking the exclusive right to operate (cable) television. Sacchi, who operated a private television-relay station, had failed to pay a required licence fee and had thereby infringed the above mentioned right. Criminal proceedings followed. The national court that was to decide the matter asked several questions to the ECJ, amongst others, on the relationship between Article 102 and 106 TFEU.

Relevance: existence of an exclusive right is not as such incompatible with EU competition rules.

[.....]

14 Article 90 (1) permits Member States inter alia to grant special or exclusive rights to undertakings.
Nothing in the Treaty prevents Member States, for considerations of public interest, of a non-economic nature, from removing radio and television transmissions, including cable transmissions, from the field of competition by conferring on one or more establishments an exclusive right to conduct them.
However, for the performance of their tasks these establishments remain subject to the prohibitions against discrimination and, to the extent that this performance comprises activities of an economic nature, fall under the provisions referred to in Article 90 relating to public undertakings and undertakings to which member states grant special or exclusive rights.
The interpretation of Articles 86 and 90 taken together leads to the conclusion that the fact that an undertaking to which a member state grants exclusive rights has a monopoly is not as such incompatible with Article 86.
It is therefore the same as regards an extension of exclusive rights following a new intervention by this state.
15 Moreover, if certain Member States treat undertakings entrusted with the operation of television, even as regards their commercial activities, in particular advertising, as undertakings entrusted with the operation of services of general economic interest, the same prohibitions apply, as regards their behaviour within the market, by reason of Article 90 (2), so long as it is not shown that the said prohibitions are incompatible with the performance of their tasks.
[.....]

2) Joined Cases C-115-117/97 *Brentjens* [1999] ECR I-6025

See above for facts of the case (I-J-3, p. 51).

Relevance: refinement of Sacchi (paragraphs 90-93), objective of Article 106 (2) (paragraphs 102-106), scope of exception (paragraphs 107-108), national court should check on abuse and Article 106 (2) (paragraphs 121-122).

[.....]

The fourth question

[.....]

90 It must be observed at the outset that the decision of the public authorities to make affiliation to a sectoral pension fund compulsory, as in this case, necessarily implies granting to that fund an exclusive right to collect and administer the contributions paid with a view to accruing pension rights. Such a fund must therefore be regarded as an undertaking to which exclusive rights have been granted by the public authorities, of the kind referred to in Article 90(1) of the Treaty.

91 Next, it should be noted that according to settled case-law an undertaking which has a legal monopoly in a substantial part of the common market may be regarded as occupying a dominant position within the meaning of Article 86 of the Treaty (see Case C-179/90 Merci Convenzionali Porto di Genova [1991] ECR I-5889, paragraph 14, and Case C-18/88 GB-Inno-BM [1991] ECR I-5941, paragraph 17).

92 A sectoral pension fund of the kind at issue in the main proceedings, which has an exclusive right to manage a supplementary pension scheme in an industrial sector in a Member State and, therefore, in a substantial part of the common market, may therefore be regarded as occupying a dominant position within the meaning of Article 86 of the Treaty.

93 It must not be forgotten, however, that merely creating a dominant position by granting exclusive rights within the meaning of Article 90(1) of the Treaty is not in itself incompatible with Article 86 of the Treaty. A Member State is in breach of the prohibitions contained in those two provisions only if the undertaking in question, merely by exercising the exclusive rights granted to it, is led to abuse its dominant position or when such rights are liable to create a situation in which that undertaking is led to commit such abuses (Höfner and Elser, cited above, paragraph 29; Case C-260/89 ERT [1991] ECR I-2925, paragraph 37; Merci Convenzionali Porto di Genova, cited above, paragraphs 16 and 17; Case C-323/93 Centre d'Insémination de la Crespelle [1994] ECR I-5077, paragraph 18; and Case C-163/96 Raso and Others [1998] ECR I-533, paragraph 27).

[.....]

102 It is important to bear in mind first of all that, under Article 90(2) of the Treaty, undertakings entrusted with the operation of services of general economic interest are subject to the rules on competition in so far as the application of such rules does not obstruct the performance, in law or in fact, of the particular tasks assigned to them.

103 In allowing, in certain circumstances, derogations from the general rules of the Treaty, Article 90(2) of the Treaty seeks to reconcile the Member States' interest in using certain undertakings, in particu-

lar in the public sector, as an instrument of economic or fiscal policy with the Community's interest in ensuring compliance with the rules on competition and preservation of the unity of the common market (Case C-202/88 France v Commission [1991] ECR I-1223, paragraph 12, and Case C-157/94 Commission v Netherlands [1997] ECR I-5699, paragraph 39).
104 In view of the interest of the Member States thus defined they cannot be precluded, when determining what services of general economic interest to entrust to certain undertakings, from taking account of objectives pertaining to their national policy or from endeavouring to attain them by means of obligations and constraints which they impose on such undertakings (Commission v Netherlands, cited above, paragraph 40).
105 The supplementary pension scheme at issue in the main proceedings fulfils an essential social function within the Netherlands pensions system by reason of the limited amount of the statutory pension, which is calculated on the basis of the minimum statutory wage.
106 Moreover, the importance of the social function attributed to supplementary pensions has recently been recognised by the Community legislature's adoption of Council Directive 98/49/EC of 29 June 1998 on safeguarding the supplementary pension rights of employed and self-employed persons moving within the Community (OJ 1998 L 209, p. 46).
107 Next, it is not necessary, in order for the conditions for the application of Article 90(2) of the Treaty to be fulfilled, that the financial balance or economic viability of the undertaking entrusted with the operation of a service of general economic interest should be threatened. It is sufficient that, in the absence of the rights at issue, it would not be possible for the undertaking to perform the particular tasks entrusted to it, defined by reference to the obligations and constraints to which it is subject (Commission v Netherlands, cited above, paragraph 52) or that maintenance of those rights is necessary to enable the holder of them to perform tasks of general economic interest which have been assigned to it under economically acceptable conditions (Case C-320/91 Corbeau [1993] ECR I-2533, paragraphs 14 to 16, and Commission v Netherlands, cited above, paragraph 53).
108 If the exclusive right of the fund to manage the supplementary pension scheme for all workers in a given sector were removed, undertakings with young employees in good health engaged in non-dangerous activities would seek more advantageous insurance terms from private insurers. The progressive departure of 'good' risks would leave the sectoral pension fund with responsibility for an increasing share of 'bad' risks, thereby increasing the cost of pensions for workers, particularly those in small and medium-sized undertakings with older employees engaged in dangerous activities, to which the fund could no longer offer pensions at an acceptable cost.

[.....]

121 It should be noted, however, that national courts adjudicating, as in this case, on an objection to a requirement to pay contributions must subject to review the decision of the fund refusing an exemption from affiliation, which enables them at least to verify that the fund has not used its power to grant an exemption in an arbitrary manner and that the principle of non-discrimination and the other conditions for the legality of that decision have been complied with.
122 Finally, as regards Brentjens' argument that an adequate level of pension for workers could be assured by laying down mini-

mum requirements to be met by pensions offered by insurance companies, it must be emphasised that, in view of the social function of supplementary pension schemes and the margin of appreciation enjoyed, according to settled case-law, by the Member States in organising their social security systems (Case 238/82 Duphar and Others [1984] ECR 523, paragraph 16; Poucet and Pistre, cited above, paragraph 6; and Case C-70/95 Sodemare and Others [1997] ECR I-3395, paragraph 27), it is incumbent on each Member State to consider whether, in view of the particular features of its national pension system, laying down minimum requirements would still enable it to ensure the level of pension which it seeks to guarantee in a sector by compulsory affiliation to a pension fund.

[.....]

3) Case T-289/03 *British United Provident Association Ltd (BUPA) and others v. Commission* [2008] ECR II-741

This case is concerned with the way in which a new health care scheme has been financed in the Irish Republic. The scheme aims at making health care available to all Irish citizens by making them choose between a private insurance or a tax-financed public health care scheme. Private health insurance companies carry an obligation for so-called open enrolment, i.e. they have to insure indiscriminately everyone applying to them for insurance. In this context, private health insurance companies have to contribute to a risk equalization scheme. BUPA filed a complaint with the Commission alleging that the scheme contained elements in breach of Article 107(1) TFEU. BUPA appealed the Commission decision rejecting that claim. Although the case is therefore essentially a dispute about state aid, issues of Article 106 TFEU played a role as well. In particular the question as to whether an undertaking could be entrusted with services of general economic interest or public service obligations by a general Member State measure or that an explicit official act would always be required. In this context, the GC was given the opportunity to rule on the nature of that article and give directions to the national courts to establish whether such an official act was indeed been issued.

Relevance: Where lies the power to define and control 'services of general economic interest' (SGEI)?

[.....]

2. Findings of the Court

[.....]

ii) The concept of an SGEI mission and the powers to define and control SGEIs

165 It must be made clear that in Community law and for the purposes of applying the EC Treaty competition rules, there is no clear and precise regulatory definition of the concept of an SGEI mission and no established legal concept definitively fixing the conditions that must be satisfied before a Member State can properly invoke the existence and protection of an SGEI mission,

either within the meaning of the first *Altmark* condition or within the meaning of Article 86(2) EC.

166 As regards competence to determine the nature and scope of an SGEI mission within the meaning of the Treaty, and also the degree of control that the Community institutions must exercise in that context, it follows from paragraph 22 of the Communication on SGEIs (see paragraph 12 above) and from the case-law of the Court of First Instance that Member States have a wide discretion to define what they regard as SGEIs and that the definition of such services by a Member State can be questioned by the Commission only in the event of manifest error (see Case T-17/02 *Fred Olsen* v *Commission* [2005] ECR II-2031, paragraph 216 and the case-law there cited).

167 That prerogative of the Member State concerning the definition of SGEIs is confirmed by the absence of any competence specially attributed to the Commission and by the absence of a precise and complete definition of the concept of SGEI in Community law. The determination of the nature and scope of an SGEI mission in specific spheres of action which either do not fall within the powers of the Community, within the meaning of the first paragraph of Article 5 EC, or are based on only limited or shared Community competence, within the meaning of the second paragraph of that article, remains, in principle, within the competence of the Member States. As the defendant and Ireland maintain, the health sector falls almost exclusively within the competence of the Member States. In that sector, the Community can engage, under Article 152(1) and (5) EC, only in action which is not legally binding, while fully respecting the responsibilities of the Member States for the organisation and provision of health services and medical care. It follows that the determination of SGEI obligations in this context also falls primarily within the competence of the Member States. That division of powers is also reflected, generally, in Article 16 EC, which provides that, given the place occupied by SGEIs in the shared values of the Union as well as their role in promoting social and territorial cohesion, the Community and the Member States, each within their respective powers and within the scope of application of the Treaty, are to take care that such services operate on the basis of principles and conditions which enable them to fulfill their missions.

168 In that regard, the applicants cannot validly rely on Case 41/83 *Italy* v *Commission*, paragraph 100 above (paragraph 30), to demonstrate the need for full and unrestricted control by the Community institutions of the existence of an SGEI mission in the health sector. In effect, that judgment shows that the Member State's power to take action under Article 86(2) EC and, accordingly, its power to define SGEIs is not unlimited and cannot be exercised arbitrarily for the sole purpose of removing a particular sector, such as telecommunications, from the application of the competition rules.

169 Consequently, the control which the Community institutions are authorised to exercise over the use of the discretion of the Member State in determining SGEIs is limited to ascertaining whether there is a manifest error of assessment. In the contested decision (recital 44), the Commission did in fact exercise that control by considering whether Ireland's assessment of the presence of an SGEI mission and of the characterisation of the PMI obligations as SGEI obligations was vitiated by a manifest error.

170 Accordingly, the complaint that the Commission unlawfully delegated to the Irish authorities the definition of the SGEIs in question and that it failed to exercise full and unrestricted control of the assessment made by those authorities with respect to a

strict and objective definition of the SGEIs in Community law cannot be upheld.

[.....]

Case cross-references:

▸ Case C-280/00 *Altmark* [2003] ECR I-7747.
▸ Case T-222/04 *Italy v. Commission* [2004] ECR II-1877.
▸ Case 172/80 *Züchner* [1981] ECR 2021 (see IV-C-1).
▸ W. Sauter, Case note on T-289/03 BUPA in *C.M.L.Rev.* (2009) 269-286.
▸ Johan W. van de Gronden, 'Financing Health Care in EU Law: Do the European State Aid Rules write out an effective prescription for integrating Competition Law with Health Care' in *CompLRev* 2009 Vol.6 no.1, pp. 5-29.

B. Abuse of dominance – Article 106 (1) *juncto* Article 102 TFEU

1) Case C-260/89 *ERT* [1991] ECR I-2925

The Greek government had given ERT, the state-owned radio and television undertaking, the exclusive right to broadcast. Despite the existence of this right, DEP and the mayor of Thessaloniki had set up another television station, which had commenced to relay television programmes. ERT, naturally, tried to protect its position and started proceedings. The national court referred several questions to the ECJ on the compatibility of the exclusive right with the Community's competition provisions.

Relevance: interface between Article 106 sections (1) and (2). Abuse of dominance by virtue of being an undertaking vested with exclusive or special rights.

[.....]

The television monopoly

10 In Case C-155/73 Sacchi [1974] ECR 409, paragraph 14, the Court held that nothing in the Treaty prevents Member States, for considerations of a non-economic nature relating to the public interest, from removing radio and television broadcasts from the field of competition by conferring on one or more establishments an exclusive right to carry them out.
11 Nevertheless, it follows from Article 90(1) and (2) of the Treaty that the manner in which the monopoly is organized or exercised may infringe the rules of the Treaty, in particular those relating to the free movement of goods, the freedom to provide services and the rules on competition.
12 The reply to the national court must therefore be that Community law does not prevent the granting of a television monopoly for considerations of a non-economic nature relating to the public interest. However, the manner in which such a monopoly is organized and exercised must not infringe the provisions of the Treaty on the free movement of goods and services or the rules on competition.

[.....]

The rules on competition

27 As a preliminary point, it should be observed that Article 3(f) of the Treaty states

only one objective for the Community which is given specific expression in several provisions of the Treaty relating to the rules on competition, including in particular Articles 85, 86 and 90.

28 The independent conduct of an undertaking must be considered with regard to the provisions of the Treaty applicable to undertakings, such as, in particular, Articles 85, 86 and 90(2).

29 As regards Article 85, it is sufficient to observe that it applies, according to its own terms, to agreements "between undertakings". There is nothing in the judgment making the reference to suggest the existence of any agreement between undertakings. There is therefore no need to interpret that provision.

30 Article 86 declares that any abuse of a dominant position within the common market or in any substantial part of it is prohibited as incompatible with the common market in so far as it may affect trade between Member States.

31 In that respect it should be borne in mind that an undertaking which has a statutory monopoly may be regarded as having a dominant position within the meaning of Article 86 of the Treaty (see the judgment in Case C-311/84 CBEM, COT IPB [1985] ECR 3261, paragraph 16) and that the territory of a Member State over which the monopoly extends may constitute a substantial part of the common market (see the judgment in Case C-322/81 Michelin v Commission [1983] ECR 3461, paragraph 28).

32 Although Article 86 of the Treaty does not prohibit monopolies as such, it nevertheless prohibits their abuse. For that purpose Article 86 lists a number of abusive practices by way of example.

33 In that regard it should be observed that, according to Article 90(2) of the Treaty, undertakings entrusted with the operation of services of general economic interest are subject to the rules on competition so long as it is not shown that the application of those rules is incompatible with the performance of their particular task (see in particular, the judgment in Sacchi, cited above, paragraph 15).

34 Accordingly it is for the national court to determine whether the practices of such an undertaking are compatible with Article 86 and to verify whether those practices, if they are contrary to that provision, may be justified by the needs of the particular task with which the undertaking may have been entrusted.

35 As regards State measures, and more specifically the grant of exclusive rights, it should be pointed out that while Articles 85 and 86 are directed exclusively to undertakings, the Treaty none the less requires the Member States not to adopt or maintain in force any measure which could deprive those provisions of their effectiveness (see the judgment in Case C-13/77 INNO v ATAB [1977] ECR 2115, paragraphs 31 and 32).

36 Article 90(1) thus provides that, in the case of undertakings to which Member States grant special or exclusive rights, Member States are neither to enact nor to maintain in force any measure contrary to the rules contained in the Treaty.

37 In that respect it should be observed that Article 90(1) of the Treaty prohibits the granting of an exclusive right to retransmit television broadcasts to an undertaking which has an exclusive right to transmit broadcasts, where those rights are liable to create a situation in which that undertaking is led to infringe Article 86 of the Treaty by virtue of a discriminatory broadcasting policy which favours its own programmes.

38 The reply to the national court must therefore be that Article 90(1) of the Treaty prohibits the granting of an exclusive right to transmit and an exclusive right to retransmit television broadcasts to a single undertak-

ing, where those rights are liable to create a situation in which that undertaking is led to infringe Article 86 by virtue of a discriminatory broadcasting policy which favours its own programmes, unless the application of Article 86 obstructs the performance of the particular tasks entrusted to it.

[.....]

2) Case C-41/90 *Höfner & Elser v. Macrotron* [1991] ECR I-1979

See above for facts of the case (I-B-1, p. 8).

Relevance: grant of exclusive right may result in breach of Article 102 TFEU.

[.....]

The interpretation of Articles 86 and 90 of the EEC Treaty

16 In its fourth question, the national court asks more specifically whether the monopoly of employment procurement in respect of business executives granted to a public employment agency constitutes an abuse of a dominant position within the meaning of Article 86, having regard to Article 90(2). In order to answer that question, it is necessary to examine that exclusive right also in the light of Article 90(1), which is concerned with the conditions that the Member States must observe when they grant special or exclusive rights. Moreover, the observations submitted to the Court relate to both Article 90(1) and Article 90(2) of the Treaty.

[.....]

24 It must be pointed out that a public employment agency which is entrusted, under the legislation of a Member State, with the operation of services of general economic interest, such as those envisaged in Article 3 of the AFG, remains subject to the competition rules pursuant to Article 90(2) of the Treaty unless and to the extent to which it is shown that their application is incompatible with the discharge of its duties (see judgment in Case 155/73 Sacchi [1974] ECR 409).

25 As regards the manner in which a public employment agency enjoying an exclusive right of employment procurement conducts itself in relation to executive recruitment undertaken by private recruitment consultancy companies, it must be stated that the application of Article 86 of the Treaty cannot obstruct the performance of the particular task assigned to that agency in so far as the latter is manifestly not in a position to satisfy demand in that area of the market and in fact allows its exclusive rights to be encroached on by those companies.

26 Whilst it is true that Article 86 concerns undertakings and may be applied within the limits laid down by Article 90(2) to public undertakings or undertakings vested with exclusive rights or specific rights, the fact nevertheless remains that the Treaty requires the Member States not to take or maintain in force measures which could destroy the effectiveness of that provision (see judgment in Case 13/77 Inno [1977] ECR 2115, paragraphs 31 and 32). Article 90(1) in fact provides that the Member States are not to enact or maintain in force, in the case of public undertakings and the undertakings to which they grant special or exclusive rights, any measure contrary to the rules contained in the Treaty,

in particular those provided for in Articles 85 to 94.

27 Consequently, any measure adopted by a Member State which maintains in force a statutory provision that creates a situation in which a public employment agency cannot avoid infringing Article 86 is incompatible with the rules of the Treaty.
28 It must be remembered, first, that an undertaking vested with a legal monopoly may be regarded as occupying a dominant position within the meaning of Article 86 of the Treaty (see judgment in Case 311/84 CBEM [1985] 3261) and that the territory of a Member State, to which that monopoly extends, may constitute a substantial part of the common market (judgment in Case 322/81 Michelin [1983] ECR 3461, paragraph 28).
29 Secondly, the simple fact of creating a dominant position of that kind by granting an exclusive right within the meaning of Article 90(1) is not as such incompatible with Article 86 of the Treaty (see Case 311/84 CBEM, above, paragraph 17). A Member State is in breach of the prohibition contained in those two provisions only if the undertaking in question, merely by exercising the exclusive right granted to it, cannot avoid abusing its dominant position.
30 Pursuant to Article 86(b), such an abuse may in particular consist in limiting the provision of a service, to the prejudice of those seeking to avail themselves of it.
31 A Member State creates a situation in which the provision of a service is limited when the undertaking to which it grants an exclusive right extending to executive recruitment activities is manifestly not in a position to satisfy the demand prevailing on the market for activities of that kind and when the effective pursuit of such activities by private companies is rendered impossible by the maintenance in force of a statutory provision under which such activities are prohibited and non-observance of that prohibition renders the contracts concerned void.
32 It must be observed, thirdly, that the responsibility imposed on a Member State by virtue of Articles 86 and 90(1) of the Treaty is engaged only if the abusive conduct on the part of the agency concerned is liable to affect trade between Member States. That does not mean that the abusive conduct in question must actually have affected such trade. It is sufficient to establish that that conduct is capable of having such an effect (see Case 322/81 Michelin, above, paragraph 104).
33 A potential effect of that kind on trade between Member States arises in particular where executive recruitment by private companies may extend to the nationals or to the territory of other Member States.
34 In view of the foregoing considerations, it must be stated in reply to the fourth question that a public employment agency engaged in employment procurement activities is subject to the prohibition contained in Article 86 of the Treaty, so long as the application of that provision does not obstruct the performance of the particular task assigned to it. A Member State which has conferred an exclusive right to carry on that activity upon the public employment agency is in breach of Article 90(1) of the Treaty where it creates a situation in which that agency cannot avoid infringing Article 86 of the Treaty. That is the case, in particular, where the following conditions are satisfied:
- the exclusive right extends to executive recruitment activities;
- the public employment agency is manifestly incapable of satisfying demand prevailing on the market for such activities;
- the actual pursuit of those activities by private recruitment consultants is rendered impossible by the maintenance in force of a statutory provision under which such activ-

ities are prohibited and non-observance of that prohibition renders the contracts concerned void;
- the activities in question may extend to the nationals or to the territory of other Member States.

[.....]

3) Case C-179/90 *Porto di Genova* [1991] ECR I-5889

See above for facts of the case (II-A-13, p. 100).

Relevance: a company is induced by national and municipal legislation to commit abuses within the meaning of Article 102. Also infringement of other Treaty provisions.

[.....]

The first question

8 By its first question the national court is essentially asking whether Article 90(1) of the Treaty, in conjunction with Articles 7, 30 and 86 thereof, precludes rules of a Member State which confer on an undertaking established in that State the exclusive right to organize dock work and require it, for the performance of such work, to have recourse to a dock-work company formed exclusively of nationals, and whether those Articles give rise to rights for individuals which the national courts must protect.
9 To answer this question, as it has been reformulated, it should be noted in limine that a dock-work undertaking enjoying the exclusive right to organize dock work for third parties, as well as a dock-work company having the exclusive right to perform dock work must be regarded as undertakings to which exclusive rights have been granted by the State within the meaning of Article 90(1) of the Treaty.
10 That Article provides that in the case of such undertakings Member States shall neither enact nor maintain in force any measure contrary to the rules contained in the Treaty, in particular those provided for in Article 7 and the Articles relating to competition.
11 As regards, in the first place, the nationality condition imposed on the workers of the dock-work company, it should be recalled, to begin with, that according to the case-law of the Court, the general prohibition of discrimination on grounds of nationality laid down in Article 7 of the Treaty applies independently only to situations governed by Community law in regard to which the Treaty lays down no specific prohibition of discrimination (see for example Case 305/87 Commission v Greece [1989] ECR 1461, paragraphs 12 and 13; Case C-10/90 Masgio v Bundesknappschaft [1991] ECR I-1119, paragraph 12).
12 As regards workers, that principle has been specifically applied by Article 48 of the Treaty.
13 In this respect it should be recalled that Article 48 of the Treaty precludes, first and foremost, rules of a Member State which reserve to nationals of that State the right to work in an undertaking of that State, such as the Port of Genoa company which is at issue before the national court. As the Court has already declared (see, for example, the judgment in Case 66/85 Lawrie-Blum v Land

Baden-Wuerttemberg [1986] ECR 2121, paragraph 17) the concept of "worker" within the meaning of Article 48 of the Treaty presupposes that for a certain period of time a person performs services for and under the direction of another person in return for which he receives remuneration. That description is not affected by the fact that the worker, whilst being linked to the undertaking by a relationship of employment, is linked to other workers by a relationship of association.

14 In the second place, as to the existence of exclusive rights, it should be stated first that with regard to the interpretation of Article 86 of the Treaty the Court has consistently held that an undertaking having a statutory monopoly over a substantial part of the common market may be regarded as having a dominant position within the meaning of Article 86 of the Treaty (see the judgments in Case C-41/90 Höfner and Elser v Macrotron [1991] ECR I-1979, paragraph 28; Case C-260/89 ERT v DEP [1991] ECR I-2925, paragraph 31).

15 As regards the definition of the market in question, it may be seen from the order for reference that it is that of the organization on behalf of third persons of dock work relating to ordinary freight in the Port of Genoa and the performance of such work. Regard being had in particular to the volume of traffic in that port and its importance in relation to maritime import and export operations as a whole in the Member State concerned, that market may be regarded as constituting a substantial part of the common market.

16 It should next be stated that the simple fact of creating a dominant position by granting exclusive rights within the meaning of Article 90(1) of the Treaty is not as such incompatible with Article 86.

17 However, the Court has had occasion to state, in this respect, that a Member State is in breach of the prohibitions contained in those two provisions if the undertaking in question, merely by exercising the exclusive rights granted to it, cannot avoid abusing its dominant position (see the judgment in Case C-41/90 Höfner, cited above, paragraph 29) or when such rights are liable to create a situation in which that undertaking is induced to commit such abuses (see the judgment in Case C-260/89 ERT, cited above, paragraph 37).

18 According to subparagraphs (a), (b) and (c) of the second paragraph of Article 86 of the Treaty, such abuse may in particular consist in imposing on the persons requiring the services in question unfair purchase prices or other unfair trading conditions, in limiting technical development, to the prejudice of consumers, or in the application of dissimilar conditions to equivalent transactions with other trading parties.

19 In that respect it appears from the circumstances described by the national court and discussed before the Court of Justice that the undertakings enjoying exclusive rights in accordance with the procedures laid down by the national rules in question are, as a result, induced either to demand payment for services which have not been requested, to charge disproportionate prices, to refuse to have recourse to modern technology, which involves an increase in the cost of the operations and a prolongation of the time required for their performance, or to grant price reductions to certain consumers and at the same time to offset such reductions by an increase in the charges to other consumers.

20 In these circumstances it must be held that a Member State creates a situation contrary to Article 86 of the Treaty where it adopts rules of such a kind as those at issue before the national court, which are capable of affecting trade between Member States as in the case of the main proceedings, regard

being had to the factors mentioned in paragraph 15 of this judgment relating to the importance of traffic in the Port of Genoa.
21 As regards the interpretation of Article 30 of the Treaty requested by the national court, it is sufficient to recall that a national measure which has the effect of facilitating the abuse of a dominant position capable of affecting trade between Member States will generally be incompatible with that Article, which prohibits quantitative restrictions on imports and all measures having equivalent effect (see the judgment in Case 13/77 GB-INNO-BM v ATAB [1977] ECR 2115, paragraph 35) in so far as such a measure has the effect of making more difficult and hence of impeding imports of goods from other Member States.
22 In the main proceedings it may be seen from the national court's findings that the unloading of the goods could have been effected at a lesser cost by the ship's crew, so that compulsory recourse to the services of the two undertakings enjoying exclusive rights involved extra expense and was therefore capable, by reason of its effect on the prices of the goods, of affecting imports.
23 It should be emphasized in the third place that even within the framework of Article 90, the provisions of Articles 30, 48 and 86 of the Treaty have direct effect and give rise for interested parties to rights which the national courts must protect (see in particular, as regards Article 86 of the Treaty, the judgment in Case 155/73 Sacchi [1974] ECR 409, paragraph 18).
24 The answer to the first question, as reformulated, should therefore be that:
Article 90(1) of the EEC Treaty, in conjunction with Articles 30, 48 and 86 of the Treaty, precludes rules of a Member State which confer on an undertaking established in that State the exclusive right to organize dock work and require it for that purpose to have recourse to a dock-work company formed exclusively of national workers;
Articles 30, 48 and 86 of the Treaty, in conjunction with Article 90, give rise to rights for individuals which the national courts must protect.

[.....]

4) Case C-320/91 *Corbeau* [1993] ECR I-2533

According to Belgium law, the Régie des Postes had the exclusive right to collect, carry and distribute mail. Paul Corbeau, however, provided a small-scale postal service in his hometown that interfered with this exclusive right. Contrary to the service offered by the Régie des Postes, Corbeau collected the letters and parcels from the address of the sender and delivered these on the same day within town. The Régie started (criminal) proceedings to end the infringement of its rights. The Tribunal Correctionnel de Liège, though, turned to the ECJ for a preliminary ruling on the compatibility of the Belgium law with the EU competition rules.

Relevance: an undertaking with exclusive rights may cross-subsidize loss making operations in the operation of providing services of general economic interest. 'Cherry picking' by undertakings wishing to compete cannot be allowed unless they offer a 'new' service to the market.

[.....]

7 With regard to the facts in the main proceedings, the questions referred to the Court must be understood as meaning that the national court is substantially concerned with the question whether Article 90 of the Treaty must be interpreted as meaning that it is contrary to that Article for the legislation of a Member State which confers on a body such as the Régie des Postes the exclusive right to collect, carry and distribute mail to prohibit an economic operator established in that State from offering, under threat of criminal penalties, certain specific services on that market.
8 To reply to that question, as thus reformulated, it should first be pointed out that a body such as the Régie des Postes, which has been granted exclusive rights as regards the collection, carriage and distribution of mail, must be regarded as an undertaking to which the Member State concerned has granted exclusive rights within the meaning of Article 90(1) of the Treaty.
9 Next it should be recalled that the Court has consistently held that an undertaking having a statutory monopoly over a substantial part of the common market may be regarded as having a dominant position within the meaning of Article 86 of the Treaty (see the judgments in Case C-179/90 Merci Convenzionali Porto di Genova [1991] ECR I-5889 at paragraph 14 and in Case C-18/88 RTT v GB-Inno-BM [1991] ECR I-5941 at paragraph 17).
10 However, Article 86 applies only to anti-competitive conduct engaged in by undertakings on their own initiative, not to measures adopted by States (see the RTT v GB-Inno-BM judgment, cited above, paragraph 20).
11 The Court has had occasion to state in this respect that although the mere fact that a Member State has created a dominant position by the grant of exclusive rights is not as such incompatible with Article 86, the Treaty none the less requires the Member States not to adopt or maintain in force any measure which might deprive those provisions of their effectiveness (see the judgment in Case C-260/89 ERT [1991] ECR I-2925, paragraph 35).
12 Thus Article 90(1) provides that in the case of public undertakings to which Member States grant special or exclusive rights, they are neither to enact nor to maintain in force any measure contrary to the rules contained in the Treaty with regard to competition.
13 That provision must be read in conjunction with Article 90(2) which provides that undertakings entrusted with the operation of services of general economic interest are to be subject to the rules on competition in so far as the application of such rules does not obstruct the performance, in law or in fact, of the particular tasks assigned to them.
14 That latter provision thus permits the Member States to confer on undertakings to which they entrust the operation of services of general economic interest, exclusive rights which may hinder the application of the rules of the Treaty on competition in so far as restrictions on competition, or even the exclusion of all competition, by other economic operators are necessary to ensure the performance of the particular tasks assigned to the undertakings possessed of the exclusive rights.
15 As regards the services at issue in the main proceedings, it cannot be disputed that the Régie des Postes is entrusted with a service of general economic interest consisting in the obligation to collect, carry and distribute mail on behalf of all users throughout the territory of the Member State concerned, at uniform tariffs and on similar quality conditions, irrespective of the specific

situations or the degree of economic profitability of each individual operation.
16 The question which falls to be considered is therefore the extent to which a restriction on competition or even the exclusion of all competition from other economic operators is necessary in order to allow the holder of the exclusive right to perform its task of general interest and in particular to have the benefit of economically acceptable conditions.
17 The starting point of such an examination must be the premise that the obligation on the part of the undertaking entrusted with that task to perform its services in conditions of economic equilibrium presupposes that it will be possible to offset less profitable sectors against the profitable sectors and hence justifies a restriction of competition from individual undertakings where the economically profitable sectors are concerned.
18 Indeed, to authorize individual undertakings to compete with the holder of the exclusive rights in the sectors of their choice corresponding to those rights would make it possible for them to concentrate on the economically profitable operations and to offer more advantageous tariffs than those adopted by the holders of the exclusive rights since, unlike the latter, they are not bound for economic reasons to offset losses in the unprofitable sectors against profits in the more profitable sectors.
19 However, the exclusion of competition is not justified as regards specific services dissociable from the service of general interest which meet special needs of economic operators and which call for certain additional services not offered by the traditional postal service, such as collection from the senders' address, greater speed or reliability of distribution or the possibility of changing the destination in the course of transit, in so far as such specific services, by their nature and the conditions in which they are offered, such as the geographical area in which they are provided, do not compromise the economic equilibrium of the service of general economic interest performed by the holder of the exclusive right.
20 It is for the national court to consider whether the services at issue in the dispute before it meet those criteria.
21 The answer to the questions referred to the Court by the Tribunal Correctionnel de Liège should therefore be that it is contrary to Article 90 of the EEC Treaty for legislation of a Member State which confers on a body such as the Régie des Postes the exclusive right to collect, carry and distribute mail, to prohibit, under threat of criminal penalties, an economic operator established in that State from offering certain specific services dissociable from the service of general interest which meet the special needs of economic operators and call for certain additional services not offered by the traditional postal service, in so far as those services do not compromise the economic equilibrium of the service of general economic interest performed by the holder of the exclusive right. It is for the national court to consider whether the services in question in the main proceedings meet those criteria.

[.....]

Case cross-reference:

▸ L. Hancher and J.-L. Buendia Sierra, 'Cross-subsidization and EC Law', (1998) 35 *CMLRev*, 901.

5) Case C-39/94 *SFEI* [1996] ECR I-3547

The Syndicat Français de l'Express International (SFEI) had complained that the French Post Office (La Poste) had given logistical and commercial assistance for an abnormally low return payment to its subsidiaries Société Française de Messagerie Internationale (SFMI) and Chronopost, for their delivery express activities. It was alleged that by doing so La Poste expanded its already existing dominance on the market for ordinary postal services onto the (international) market for express delivery services.

Relevance: does cross-subsidization of 'commercial' activities by an undertaking in the public sector constitute abuse? Definition of abuse as opposed to (il)legal state aid.

[.....]

The first question

54 By its first question the national court seeks in essence to ascertain whether the provision of logistical and commercial assistance by a public undertaking to its subsidiaries, which are governed by private law and carry on an activity open to free competition, without normal consideration in return is capable of constituting State aid within the meaning of Article 92 of the Treaty.
55 As a preliminary point it should be observed that the measures in question have never been notified to the Commission, since the French Government did not regard them as constituting State aids, and, furthermore, that although a complaint was made to it in 1990 the Commission is still unable, following the withdrawal of a first decision rejecting that complaint in 1992, to give a decision on how the logistical and commercial assistance afforded by the Post Office to SFMI and Chronopost is to be categorized.
56 Furthermore, the French Government and the Commission are at one in considering that the first question, as formulated, calls for an affirmative answer. They both also point out that the determination of what constitutes normal consideration calls for a detailed and complex economic analysis of the costs connected with the services in question and that the judgment making the reference does not contain sufficient information in that respect.
57 The view that the provision of logistical and commercial assistance by a public undertaking to its subsidiaries, which are governed by private law and carry on an activity open to free competition, without normal consideration in return is capable of constituting State aid within the meaning of Article 92 of the Treaty must be upheld.
58 The aim of Article 92 of the Treaty is to prevent trade between Member States from being affected by advantages granted by public authorities which, in various forms, distort or threaten to distort competition by favouring certain undertakings or certain products (see Case C-387/92 Banco Exterior de España v Ayuntamiento de Valencia [1994] ECR I-877, paragraph 12, and Case 173/73 Italy v Commission [1974] ECR 709, paragraph 26). The concept of aid thus encompasses not only positive benefits, such as subsidies, but also interventions which, in various forms, mitigate the charges which are normally included in the budget of an undertaking and which, without therefore being subsidies in the strict sense of the word, are of the same character and have the same effect (see Case C-387/92 Banco Exterior de España, cited above, paragraph 13).
59 It follows from the foregoing considerations that the supply of goods or services on

preferential terms is capable of constituting State aid (see Joined Cases 67/85, 68/85 and 70/85 Van der Kooy and Others v Commission [1988] ECR 219, paragraph 28, and Case C-56/93 Belgium v Commission [1996], not yet published in the European Court Reports, paragraph 10).
60 Accordingly, in order to determine whether a State measure constitutes aid, it is necessary to establish whether the recipient undertaking receives an economic advantage which it would not have obtained under normal market conditions.
61 In examining that question, it is for the national court to determine what is normal remuneration for the services in question. Such a determination presupposes an economic analysis taking into account all the factors which an undertaking acting under normal market conditions should have taken into consideration when fixing the remuneration for the services provided.

[.....]

Case cross-reference:
▸ Joined Cases C-83, 93 & 94/01 P *La Poste* [2003] ECR I-6993.
▸ Case C-280/00 *Altmark* [2003] ECR I-7747.

C. No implied granting of exclusive or special rights

1) Case 172/80 *Züchner* [1981] ECR 2021

The German Bayerische Vereinsbank had charged a 0,15% levy when it transferred DM 10,000 from the account of one of its holders to a payee in Italy. According to the account holder, this service charge was contrary to EU law since it was part of a (prohibited) concerted practice fixing prices and tariffs followed by most banks. The Vereinsbank then claimed that this alleged price fixing arrangement fell within the scope of the exception as mentioned in Article 106 (2). The national court, which was to decide the matter, asked the ECJ for a preliminary ruling on the compatibility of the uniform charge with Articles 101 and 102.

Relevance: reliance on the exception of Article 106 (2) can never be assumed to be 'implied' as an act of government is needed for undertakings to become vested with 'special' or 'exclusive' rights.

[.....]

7 Although the transfer of customers' funds from one Member State to another normally performed by banks is an operation which falls within the special task of banks, particularly in connexion with international movements of capital, that is not sufficient to make them undertakings within the meaning of Article 90 (2) of the Treaty unless it can be established that in performing such transfers the banks are operating a service of general economic interest with which they have been entrusted by a measure adopted by the public authorities.
8 As to Article 104 et seq. of the Treaty, those provisions in no way have the effect of exempting banks from the competition rules of the Treaty. They appear in Chapter 2 of Title II of the Treaty, which concerns "balance of payments", and are restricted to stipulating that there must be coordination between the Member States on economic policy, and to that end they provide for collab-

oration between the appropriate national administrative departments and the central banks of the Member States in order to attain the objectives of the Treaty.

9 In the light of all those considerations the objection raised by the defendant in the main proceedings must therefore be dismissed.

[.....]

2) Case C-393/92 *Almelo v. IJsselmij* [1994] ECR I-1477

By Royal Decree, IJsselmij (IJM, formerly known as IJC), a regional distributor of electric power, had been given a non-exclusive concession to distribute electricity in a certain area. It supplied both local distributors, such as the Municipality of Almelo, and end-users in rural areas. By means of an exclusive purchase clause contained in its general conditions, IJM prevented the import of electric power by the local distributors from amongst others Germany. Moreover, IJM charged them a so-called equalization supplement, i.e., IJM wanted compensation for the costs arising from the supply of energy to consumers in rural areas. These costs were, in comparison, higher than the costs incurred by local distributors when supplying users in urban areas. The local distributors lodged a complaint with the Commission concerning these practices and, at the same time, initiated arbitration proceedings. The arbitrators, however, rejected their claim after which the distributors appealed to the Court of Appeal of Arnhem. This national court turned to the ECJ for, inter alia, an interpretation of Article 106 in the light of the said exclusive purchase obligation.

Relevance: the granting of a non-exclusive public law licence suffices.

[.....]

Article 90(2) of the Treaty

46 Article 90(2) of the Treaty provides that undertakings entrusted with the operation of services of general economic interest may be exempted from the application of the competition rules contained in the Treaty in so far as it is necessary to impose restrictions on competition, or even to exclude all competition, from other economic operators in order to ensure the performance of the particular tasks assigned to them (see the judgment in Case C-320/91 Corbeau [1993] ECR I-2533, paragraph 14).

47 As regards the question whether an undertaking such as IJM has been entrusted with the operation of services of general interest, it should be borne in mind that it has been given the task, through the grant of a non-exclusive concession governed by public law, of ensuring the supply of electricity in part of the national territory.

[.....]

D. The exception under Article 106 (2) TFEU

Cross-references for this part:

- ▸ Case C-320/91 *Corbeau* [1993] ECR I-2533 (see IV-A-4).
- ▸ Joined Cases C-83, 93 & 94/01 P *La Poste* [2003] ECR I-6993.

1) Case C-393/92 *Almelo v. IJsselmij* [1994] ECR I-1477

See above for facts of the case (IV-C-2, p. 188).

Relevance: interpretation of the exception contained in Article 106 (2). Criteria concerning the application thereof formulated by ECJ for the benefit of the national court.

[.....]

48 Such an undertaking must ensure that throughout the territory in respect of which the concession is granted, all consumers, whether local distributors or end-users, receive uninterrupted supplies of electricity in sufficient quantities to meet demand at any given time, at uniform tariff rates and on terms which may not vary save in accordance with objective criteria applicable to all customers.

49 Restrictions on competition from other economic operators must be allowed in so far as they are necessary in order to enable the undertaking entrusted with such a task of general interest to perform it. In that regard, it is necessary to take into consideration the economic conditions in which the undertaking operates, in particular the costs which it has to bear and the legislation, particularly concerning the environment, to which it is subject.

50 It is for the national court to consider whether an exclusive purchasing clause prohibiting local distributors from importing electricity is necessary in order to enable the regional distributor to perform its task of general interest.

51 The answer to the second question submitted by the Gerechtshof te Arnhem must therefore be that:

(a) Article 85 of the Treaty precludes the application, by a regional electricity distributor, of an exclusive purchasing clause contained in the general conditions of sale which prohibits a local distributor from importing electricity for public supply purposes and which, having regard to its economic and legal context, affects trade between Member States;

(b) Article 86 of the Treaty precludes the application, by a regional electricity distributor where it belongs to a group of undertakings occupying a collective dominant position in a substantial part of the common market, of an exclusive purchasing clause contained in the general conditions of sale which prohibits a local distributor from importing electricity for public supply purposes and which, in view of its economic and legal context, affects trade between Member States;

(c) Article 90(2) of the Treaty is to be interpreted as meaning that the application by a regional electricity distributor of such an exclusive purchasing clause is not caught by the prohibitions contained in Articles 85 and 86 of the Treaty in so far as that restriction of competition is necessary in order to enable that undertaking to perform its task of general interest. It is for the national court to consider whether that condition is fulfilled.

[.....]

2) Case C-209/98 *Sydhavnens* [2000] ECR I-3743

Sydhavnens, which recycled environmentally non-hazardous building waste, had built a plant for the sorting and crushing of building waste near Copenhagen, for which the Municipality had given permission. Yet, it had refused to give Sydhavnens the concession it needed to process building waste produced within the boundaries of the said Municipality. That waste was exclusively handled by a limited number of undertakings. Copenhagen had concluded contracts with RSG, which had a processing centre in Grøften, and with two smaller companies. Sydhavnens, which did not agree with this policy, brought an action before the national court. The Østre Landsret, in turn, referred several questions to the ECJ.

Relevance: exclusive rights granted to undertakings performing services of general economic interest that are contrary to Article 102 can be justified by economic reasons, even in the case of non-hazardous waste.

[.....]

The rules on competition referred to in Articles 90 and 86 of the Treaty

52 Second, the national court asks essentially whether Article 90 of the Treaty, read in conjunction with Article 86 of the Treaty, precludes the establishment of a local system, such as the system at issue in the case in the main proceedings, under which a limited number of specially selected undertakings can process environmentally non-hazardous building waste destined for recovery and produced in the area concerned, thus ensuring a sufficiently large flow of such waste to those undertakings, and excludes other undertakings even though they are qualified to process the waste.

53 It should be pointed out, first, that pursuant to the rules at issue in the main proceedings, three undertakings were authorised to receive building waste produced within the boundaries of the Municipality of Copenhagen with a view to recovering it and that the other undertakings, including Sydhavnens Sten & Grus, are precluded from doing so. Apart from those three undertakings, no undertaking in Denmark can receive building waste produced in that municipality with a view to processing it.

54 It follows that those three undertakings must be regarded as undertakings to which the Member State concerned has granted an exclusive right within the meaning of Article 90(1) of the Treaty (see, in that regard, Case C-320/91 Corbeau [1993] ECR I-2533, paragraph 8, and Joined Cases C-147/97 and C-148/97 Deutsche Post [2000] ECR I-825, paragraph 37).

55 Second, it should be pointed out that, pursuant to Article 90(1) of the Treaty, in the case of the undertakings to which they grant special or exclusive rights, Member States are neither to enact nor to maintain in force any measure contrary to the rules contained in the Treaty, in particular to the rules on competition.

56 In considering whether rules such as those at issue in the case in the main proceedings are contrary to Article 90 of the Treaty, read in conjunction with Article 86 of the Treaty, it must be determined whether they give rise to a dominant position on the part of the undertaking to which the special or exclusive right is granted and whether they give rise to an abuse.

The existence of a dominant position

57 As regards the question of the existence of a dominant position, the Court has repeatedly emphasised that the definition of the relevant market is of fundamental importance, as is the delimitation of the substantial part of the common market in which the undertaking may be able to engage in abuses which hinder effective competition (see, for example, Case C-242/95 GT-Link [1997] ECR I-4449, paragraph 36).

[.....]

61 As regards the product or service in question, the national court will have, inter alia, to determine whether the processing of environmentally non-hazardous building waste is a distinct market from the processing of other types of waste.
62 As regards the geographical market, it will have to take into account the fact that an exclusive right was granted to three undertakings, including RGS, the operator of the Grøften centre, which is the main beneficiary. If producers of waste in the municipality wish to have their waste processed in Denmark they can only deal with one of those three undertakings. That could have the effect of restricting the market to the area over which the exclusive right extends.
63 However, in view of the importance of the Municipality of Copenhagen in greater Copenhagen, whose building waste represents approximately one third of the building waste produced in Denmark, the national court must determine whether the exclusive right might have the effect of restricting effective competition not only within the boundaries of the municipality but also in a wider area.
64 Next, once the limits of the area affected have been defined, it will be necessary to consider whether that area constitutes a substantial part of the common market having regard, in particular, to the volume of building waste produced and processed in the Municipality of Copenhagen and its importance in relation to building waste processing operations as a whole in Denmark (see, in that regard, Case C-179/90 Merci Convenzionali Porto di Genova [1991] ECR I-5889, paragraph 15, and GT-Link, cited above, paragraph 37).
65 Only if the national court considers that the undertakings concerned have a dominant position on a market thus defined will it be necessary to consider the question of possible abuse.

The existence of abuse

66 It must be borne in mind that merely creating a dominant position by the grant special or exclusive rights within the meaning of Article 90(1) of the Treaty is not in itself incompatible with Article 86 of the Treaty. A Member State is in breach of the prohibitions contained in those two provisions only if the undertaking in question, merely by exercising the exclusive rights granted to it, is led to abuse its dominant position or when such rights are liable to create a situation in which that undertaking is led to commit such abuses (see, for example, Joined Cases C-115/97 to C-117/97 Brentjens [1999] ECR I-6025, paragraph 93).
67 The Court has thus held that a Member State may, without infringing Article 86 of the Treaty, grant exclusive rights to certain undertakings provided they do not abuse their dominant position or are not led necessarily to commit an abuse (see Case C-266/96 Corsica Ferries France [1998] ECR I-3949, paragraph 41).
68 In that regard, it should be pointed out, first, that the grant of an exclusive right over part of the national territory for environmental purposes, such as establishing the capacity necessary for the recycling of building

waste, does not in itself constitute an abuse of a dominant position.
69 It must next be considered whether the exclusive right does not nevertheless lead to an abuse of a dominant position.

[.....]

74 (...) it must be pointed out that it follows from the combined effect of paragraphs 1 and 2 of Article 90 that paragraph 2 may be relied upon to justify the grant by a Member State, to an undertaking entrusted with the operation of services of general economic interest, of exclusive rights which are contrary to, in particular, Article 86 of the Treaty, to the extent to which performance of the particular task assigned to that undertaking can be assured only through the grant of such rights and provided that the development of trade is not affected to such an extent as would be contrary to the interests of the Community (see, as regards exclusive rights contrary to Article 37 of the EC Treaty (now, after amendment, Article 31 EC), Case C-154/94 Commission v France [1997] ECR I-5815, paragraph 49).
75 The management of particular waste may properly be considered to be capable of forming the subject of a service of general economic interest, particularly where the service is designed to deal with an environmental problem.
76 It is clear from the documents before the Court that the Municipality of Copenhagen, acting in accordance with national legislation, entrusted to three undertakings the task of processing building waste produced in that municipality and that those undertakings are required to receive that waste and process it so that it can be reused as far as possible. In those circumstances, it must be acknowledged that a task of general economic interest was entrusted to those undertakings.
77 Next, it is necessary to consider whether the exclusive right granted to the three undertakings is necessary for them to be able to perform the task of general economic interest which has been assigned to them under economically acceptable conditions (see Corbeau, cited above, paragraphs 14 and 16, and Brentjens, cited above, paragraph 107).
78 It is apparent from the evidence before the Court that when the Grøften centre was set up and an exclusive right was granted to a limited number of undertakings, the Municipality of Copenhagen was faced with what was regarded as a serious environmental problem, namely the burial of most building waste in the ground when it could have been recycled. Recycling was impossible owing to the lack of undertakings capable of processing the waste. In order to deal with the volumes of waste produced in the municipality and to ensure that it was recycled to a high standard, the municipality considered it necessary to set up a high-capacity centre; and, in order to ensure that this newly-established centre would be profitable, the municipality considered it necessary to ensure that the centre was guaranteed a significant flow of waste by granting it an exclusive processing right.
79 Admittedly, that exclusive right had the effect of excluding even qualified undertakings wishing to enter the market, such as Sydhavnens Sten & Grus. In the absence of undertakings capable of processing the waste at issue in the main proceedings, however, the Municipality of Copenhagen considered it necessary to set up a high-capacity centre. Furthermore, in order to ensure that undertakings would be interested in participating in the operation of a high-capacity centre, it was also considered necessary to grant an exclusive right, limited in time to the period over which the investments could foreseeably

be written off and in space to the land within the boundaries of the municipality.
80 A measure having a less restrictive effect on competition, such as rules which merely required undertakings to have their waste recycled, would not necessarily have ensured that most of the waste produced in the municipality would be recycled, precisely because there was not sufficient capacity to process that waste.
81 In those circumstances, it must be held that even if the grant of an exclusive right led to a restriction of competition in a substantial part of the common market, that grant could be regarded as necessary for the performance of a task serving the general economic interest.
82 Nor is there anything in the documents before the Court to suggest that the exclusive right granted in the present case is such that it will necessarily lead the undertakings in question to abuse their dominant position.
83 The answer to the second part of the first question must therefore be that Article 90 of the Treaty, read in conjunction with Article 86 of the Treaty, does not preclude the establishment of a local system, such as the system in issue in the main proceedings, under which, in order to resolve an environmental problem resulting from the absence of processing capacity for non-hazardous building waste destined for recovery, a limited number of specially selected undertakings may process such waste produced in the area concerned, thus making it possible to ensure a sufficiently large flow of such waste to those undertakings, which precludes other undertakings from processing that waste, even though they are qualified to do so.

[.....]

3) Case C-203/96 *Dusseldorp* [1998] ECR I-4075

According to the Netherlands' Long-term Plan for the Disposal of Dangerous Waste, export of oil filters was only permitted when the processing abroad was superior to the methods of disposal found in the Netherlands. The Plan also stated that AVR Chemie was to be responsible for 'waste management'. On the basis of this Long-term Plan, together with an EU Regulation dealing with the shipment of waste between Member States, the Netherlands Minister for Housing, Regional Development and the Environment had refused to authorise the export of two loads of oil filters and related waste by Dusseldorp. This waste was to be processed by Factron, a German undertaking. Dusseldorp objected and lodged a complaint, which was declared unfounded, after which it brought an action before the Council of State. The latter asked several preliminary questions on the compatibility of the Dutch provisions with EU law.

Relevance: when granting exclusive or special rights the Member State must adhere to the principle of proportionality.

[.....]

The fourth question

53 By its fourth question, the national court asks whether the exclusive rights conferred on AVR Chemie within the framework of the policy implemented in accordance with the Long-term Plan are compatible with the competition rules contained in Articles 90 and 86 of the Treaty. As the Advocate General points out at paragraph 97 of his Opinion, the exclusive rights referred to by the national court should be taken to include both the general exclusivity granted for incineration and any exclusivity resulting from the contested rule. The latter concerns the prohibition on exporting oil filters unless processing abroad is superior to that performed in the Netherlands.

[.....]

58 It is apparent from the documents before the Court that AVR Chemie was designated as the sole end-processor for the incineration of dangerous waste. That undertaking can therefore be regarded as having an exclusive right within the meaning of Article 90(1) of the Treaty.
59 That provision stipulates that Member States are neither to enact nor to maintain in force any measure contrary to the rules of the Treaty, in particular the competition rules.
60 The grant of exclusive rights for the incineration of dangerous waste on the territory of a Member State as a whole must be regarded as conferring on the undertaking concerned a dominant position in a substantial part of the common market (see, to that effect, Case C-260/89 ERT [1991] ECR I-2925, paragraph 31).
61 Although merely creating a dominant position is not, in itself, incompatible with Article 86 of the Treaty, a Member State breaches the prohibitions laid down by Article 90 in conjunction with Article 86 if it adopts any law, regulation or administrative provision which enables an undertaking on which it has conferred exclusive rights to abuse its dominant position (see, to that effect, Case C-18/88 GB-Inno-BM [1991] ECR I-5941, paragraph 20).
62 It is apparent from the documents before the Court that, on the basis of the Long-term Plan, the Netherlands Government prohibited the applicant in the main proceedings from exporting and, by doing so, in practice imposed an obligation on it to deliver its oil filters - waste for recovery - to the national undertaking which held the exclusive right to incinerate dangerous waste, even though the quality of processing available in another Member State was comparable to that performed by the national undertaking.
63 Such an obligation has the effect of favouring the national undertaking by enabling it to process waste intended for processing by a third undertaking. It therefore results in the restriction of outlets in a manner contrary to Article 90(1) in conjunction with Article 86 of the Treaty.
64 However, it is necessary to consider whether that obligation could be justified by a task of general economic interest within the meaning of Article 90(2) of the Treaty.
65 It follows from the case-law of the Court that that provision may be relied upon to justify a measure contrary to Article 86 of the Treaty adopted in favour of an undertaking to which the State has granted exclusive rights if that measure is necessary to enable the undertaking to perform the particular task assigned to it and if it does not affect the development of trade in a manner contrary to the interest of the Community (see, to that effect, Case C-320/91 Corbeau [1993] ECR I-2533, paragraph 14, and Case C-159/

94 Commission v France [1997] ECR I-5815, paragraph 49).
66 The Netherlands Government submits that the rules in question are intended to reduce the costs of the undertaking responsible for the incineration of dangerous waste and thus to enable it to be economically viable.
67 Even if the task conferred on that undertaking could constitute a task of general economic interest, however, it is for the Netherlands Government, as the Advocate General points out at paragraph 108 of his Opinion, to show to the satisfaction of the national court that that objective cannot be achieved equally well by other means. Article 90(2) of the Treaty can thus apply only if it is shown that, without the contested measure, the undertaking in question would be unable to carry out the task assigned to it.
68 In those circumstances, the answer to the fourth question must be that Article 90 of the Treaty, in conjunction with Article 86, precludes rules such as the Long-term Plan whereby a Member State requires undertakings to deliver their waste for recovery, such as oil filters, to a national undertaking on which it has conferred the exclusive right to incinerate dangerous waste unless the processing of their waste in another Member State is of a higher quality than that performed by that undertaking if, without any objective justification and without being necessary for the performance of a task in the general interest, those rules have the effect of favouring the national undertaking and increasing its dominant position.

[.....]

Case cross-references:

▸ Case C-232/93 *La Crespelle* [1994] ECR I-5077.
▸ Joined Cases T-528, 542, 543 & 546/93 *Métropole Télévision I* [1996] ECR II-649 (see IV-E-1).

4) Case C-475/99 *Ambulanz Glöckner* [2001] ECR I-8089

In Germany, a federal law governed private patient transport services. Public ambulance services, on the other hand, were governed by laws adopted at the level of the Länder. From 1989 onwards, the Land law also governed the private operators. In 1994, Ambulanz Glöckner, a private independent operator, requested renewal of its authorization to perform ambulance services in the Pirmasens area. In that area, two medical aid organisations, which provided both emergency and non-emergency transports, were entrusted with the public ambulance services. These organisations claimed that their own emergency transport facilities were not fully exploited and were operating at a loss. So, on the basis of paragraph 18 (3) of the Rettungsdienstgesetz (RettDG 1991), renewal of Ambulanz Glöckner's authorization was refused. The said paragraph read: 'authorisation shall be refused if it would be likely to have an adverse effect on the general interest in the operation of an effective public ambulance service'. Proceedings followed.

Relevance: should services of general economic interest be provided under economically acceptable conditions? And who decides and on which criteria? Cross-subsidization allowed?

[.....]

Justification under Article 90 (2) of the Treaty

55 [...] the medical aid organisations are incontestably entrusted with a task of general economic interest, consisting in the obligation to provide a permanent standby service of transporting sick or injured persons in emergencies throughout the territory concerned, at uniform rates and on similar quality conditions, without regard to the particular situations or to the degree of economic profitability of each individual operation.
56 However, Article 90(2) of the Treaty, read in conjunction with paragraph (1) of that provision, allows Member States to confer, on undertakings to which they entrust the operation of services of general economic interest, exclusive rights which may hinder the application of the rules of the Treaty on competition in so far as restrictions on competition, or even the exclusion of all competition, by other economic operators are necessary to ensure the performance of the particular tasks assigned to the undertakings holding the exclusive rights (Case C-320/91 Corbeau [1993] ECR I-2533, paragraph 14).
57 The question to be determined, therefore, is whether the restriction of competition is necessary to enable the holder of an exclusive right to perform its task of general interest in economically acceptable conditions. The Court has held that the starting point in making that determination must be the premiss that the obligation, on the part of the undertaking entrusted with such a task, to perform its services in conditions of economic equilibrium presupposes that it will be possible to offset less profitable sectors against the profitable sectors and hence justifies a restriction of competition from individual undertakings in economically profitable sectors (Corbeau, paragraphs 16 and 17).
58 In the case before the national court, [...] it appears that the system put in place by the RettDG 1991 is such as to enable the medical aid organisations to perform their task in economically acceptable conditions. In particular, the evidence placed before the Court shows that the revenue from non-emergency transport helps to cover the costs of providing the emergency transport service.
59 It is true that, in paragraph 19 of Corbeau, the Court held that the exclusion of competition is not justified in certain cases involving specific services, severable from the service of general interest in question, if those services do not compromise the economic equilibrium of the service of general economic interest performed by the holder of the exclusive rights.
60 However, that is not the case with the two services now under consideration, for two reasons in particular. First, unlike the situation in Corbeau, the two types of service in question, traditionally assumed by the medical aid organisations, are so closely linked that it is difficult to sever the non-emergency transport services from the task of general economic interest constituted by the provision of the public ambulance service, with which they also have characteristics in common.
61 Second, the extension of the medical aid organisations' exclusive rights to the non-emergency transport sector does indeed enable them to discharge their general-interest task of providing emergency transport in conditions of economic equilibrium. The possibility which would be open to private operators to concentrate, in the non-emergency sector, on more profitable journeys could affect the degree of economic

viability of the service provided by the medical aid organisations and, consequently, jeopardise the quality and reliability of that service.
62 However, as the Advocate General explains in point 188 of his Opinion, it is only if it were established that the medical aid organisations entrusted with the operation of the public ambulance service were manifestly unable to satisfy demand for emergency ambulance services and for patient transport at all times that the justification for extending their exclusive rights, based on the task of general interest, could not be accepted.
63 In this regard, Ambulanz Glöckner contends that Paragraph 18(3) of the RettDG 1991 does indeed promote the creation of a situation in which the medical aid organisations are not always able to satisfy all demand for patient transport services at acceptable prices (see, by analogy, Case C-41/90 Höfner and Elser [1991] ECR I-1979, paragraph 31, and Case C-55/96 Job Centre [1997] ECR I-7119, paragraph 35). On the other hand, the Landkreis and the ASB maintain that the public ambulance service is incontestably able to satisfy both demand for emergency transport and that for patient transport, even without private undertakings.
64 It is for national court to determine whether the medical aid organisations which occupy a dominant position on the markets in question are in fact able to satisfy demand and to fulfil not only their statutory obligation to provide the public emergency ambulance services in all situations and 24 hours a day but also to offer efficient patient transport services.
65 Consequently, a provision such as Paragraph 18(3) of the RettDG 1991 is justified under Article 90(2) of the Treaty provided that it does not bar the grant of an authorisation to independent operators where it is established that the medical aid organisations entrusted with the operation of the public ambulance service are manifestly unable to satisfy demand in the area of emergency transport and patient transport services.

[.....]

Cross-reference:

▸ Case C-115-117/97 *Brentjens* [1999] ECR I-6025 (see I-J-3, with case cross-references).

E. Interrelation Article 106 (2) and 101 (3) TFEU

1) Joined Cases T-528, 542, 543 & 546/93 *Métropole Télévision I* [1996] ECR II-649

Métropole Télévision (M6), and other private channels, sought to annul a Commission decision in which the Commission had exempted the (discriminatory) membership rules of the European Broadcast Union (EBU). EBU's members were mainly public undertakings while (new) commercial television channels, such as M6, had not been admitted. One of the arguments used by M6 was that the Commission had wrongly found that only members of the EBU fulfilled a "particular public mission". Moreover, it was claimed that the concept of "particular public mission" was not relevant under Article 101 (3).

Relevance: relationship between the exceptions provided for in Article 106 (2) and Article 101 (3). Notion of 'public mission'.

[.....]

The concept of particular public mission having regard to Article 85 (3)(a) of the Treaty

[.....]

Findings of the Court

114 In the context of the supervisory jurisdiction normally exercised by the Court, it considers that it should also consider ex abundanti cautela, given that it has just found an infringement of Article 85(3) of the Treaty warranting the annulment of the Decision whether or not the concept of particular public mission, as employed in the Decision, constitutes a relevant factor which may be taken into consideration for the purposes of the application of Article 85(3), particularly as regards the condition set out under (a). If it is not such a factor, the Court will have to conclude that the Commission committed a manifest error of law in taking account of such a factor which may have distorted its assessment of the indispensable nature of the restrictions of competition for which it granted exemption (see La Cinq v Commission, paragraph 63, and Joined Cases T-163/94 and T-165/94 NTN Corporation and Koyo Seiko v Council [1995] ECR II-1381, paragraphs 113 and 114).
115 From simply reading the Decision, it must be held that, contrary to the Commission's assertion, the concept of particular public mission which it utilized proves to be a fundamental component of the statement of reasons of the Decision. According to the statement of reasons (points 5, 11, 19, 20, 45, 60, 72 and 74), fulfilment of a particular public mission enables broadcasters to become active members of the EBU and the constraints associated with such a mission are such as to justify the EBU's having a special status with regard to the competition rules. The concept of particular public mission, as defined by the Commission, is therefore the principal factor in defining the circle of beneficiaries of the exemption at issue.
116 According to the Decision, the particular public mission is characterized in particular by the "obligation to provide varied programming including cultural, educational, scientific and minority programmes without any commercial appeal and to cover the entire national population irrespective of the costs" (point 5). The Decision therefore essentially takes over the elements of the particular mission of operating services of general economic interest provided for in Article 90(2) of the Treaty, as it has been interpreted by the Community Court, namely and in particular, operation "on behalf of all users throughout the territory of the Member State concerned (...) irrespective of the specific situations or the degree of economic profitability of each individual operation" (see Case C-320/91 Corbeau [1993] ECR I-2533, paragraph 15). In order to hold that the condition relating to Article 85(3)(a) of the Treaty was fulfilled, the Commission therefore took account of factors falling within the field of application of Article 90(2) of the Treaty.
117 However, inasmuch as, according to the Decision itself (point 78), Article 90(2) is not applicable, factors coming essentially within the ambit of that article cannot in this case constitute a criterion for the application of Article 85(3) in the absence of other justification.

[.....]

F. Article 106 (3) TFEU

1) Case C-202/88 *France v. Commission* [1991] ECR I-1223

In this dispute, France tried to annul several articles of Commission Directive 88/301/EEC. This Directive, which was concerned with competition in the markets in telecommunications terminal equipment, had been adopted on the basis of Article 106 (3). It, inter alia, ordered the Member States to withdraw the special or exclusive rights conferred on the undertakings, which were active on the said market. France, together with a number of other Member States, accused the Commission of misinterpreting Article 106 (3) as well as of having exceeded its powers. The ECJ partly ruled against the Commission.

Relevance: scope of 'competence' of the Commission to adopt Directives pursuant to Article 106 (3).

[.....]

II - Misuse of procedure

16 In its first plea in law the French Government claims that the Commission adopted the contested directive pursuant to Article 90(3) of the Treaty instead of initiating the procedure provided for in Article 169. In its view, Article 90(3) is intended to enable the Commission to inform the Member States, in cases where it is unclear how compliance with the Treaty is to be achieved, of the means which must be used in order to ensure such compliance. In contrast, recourse must be made to Article 169 where it is clear that a measure is wholly contrary to the Treaty and must be brought to an end forthwith.
17 It must be held in that regard that Article 90(3) of the Treaty empowers the Commission to specify in general terms the obligations arising under Article 90(1) by adopting directives. The Commission exercises that power where, without taking into consideration the particular situation existing in the various Member States, it defines in concrete terms the obligations imposed on them under the Treaty. In view of its very nature, such a power cannot be used to make a finding that a Member State has failed to fulfil a particular obligation under the Treaty.
18 However, it appears from the content of the directive at issue in this case that the Commission merely determined in general terms obligations which are binding on the Member States under the Treaty. The directive therefore cannot be interpreted as making specific findings that particular Member States failed to fulfil their obligations under the Treaty, with the result that the plea in law relied upon by the French Government must be rejected as unfounded.

III - Competence of the Commission

19 In its second plea in law the French Government, supported by the interveners, argues that by adopting a directive providing simply for the withdrawal of special and exclusive rights for the importation, marketing, connection, bringing into service and/or maintenance of telecommunications terminal equipment, the Commission exceeded the supervisory powers conferred upon it by Article 90(3) of the Treaty. In the French Government' s view, that provision presupposes the existence of special and exclusive rights. Accordingly, to take the view that the maintenance of those rights constitutes in

itself a measure within the meaning of Article 90 disregards the scope of that Article.
20 The Belgian and French Governments further consider that a policy on the restructuring of the telecommunications sector, as envisaged by the Directive, fell within the sole competence of the Council, acting under Article 100a. The Belgian and Italian Governments maintain in addition that the directive is contrary to Article 87 of the Treaty inasmuch as only the Council is empowered to lay down rules for the application of Articles 85 and 86 of the Treaty in specific sectors.
21 As far as the first argument is concerned, it must be held in the first place that the supervisory power conferred on the Commission includes the possibility of specifying, pursuant to Article 90(3), obligations arising under the Treaty. The extent of that power therefore depends on the scope of the rules with which compliance is to be ensured.
22 Next, it should be noted that even though that Article presupposes the existence of undertakings which have certain special or exclusive rights, it does not follow that all the special or exclusive rights are necessarily compatible with the Treaty. That depends on different rules, to which Article 90(1) refers.
23 As regards the allegation that the Commission has encroached on the powers conferred on the Council by Articles 87 and 100a of the Treaty, those provisions have to be compared with Article 90, taking into account their respective subject-matter and purpose.
24 Article 100a is concerned with the adoption of measures for the approximation of the provisions laid down by law, regulation or administrative action in Member States which have as their object the establishment and functioning of the internal market. Article 87 is concerned with the adoption of any appropriate regulations or directives to give effect to the principles set out in Articles 85 and 86, that is to say the competition rules applicable to all undertakings. As for Article 90, it is concerned with measures adopted by the Member States in relation to undertakings with which they have specific links referred to in the provisions of that Article. It is only with regard to such measures that Article 90 imposes on the Commission a duty of supervision which may, where necessary, be exercised through the adoption of directives and decisions addressed to the Member States.
25 It must therefore be held that the subject-matter of the power conferred on the Commission by Article 90(3) is different from, and more specific than, that of the powers conferred on the Council by either Article 100a or Article 87.
26 It should also be noted that, as the Court held in Joined Cases 188 to 190/80 (France, Italy and United Kingdom v Commission [1982] ECR 2545, at paragraph 14), the possibility that rules containing provisions which impinge upon the specific sphere of Article 90 might be laid down by the Council by virtue of its general power under other Articles of the Treaty does not preclude the exercise of the power which Article 90 confers on the Commission.
27 The plea in law alleging lack of powers on the part of the Commission must therefore be rejected.

[.....]

V. Application of the rules of the Treaty

[.....]

3. Legality of Article 7 of Directive 88/301 (termination of leasing or maintenance contracts)

53 Article 7 of the contested directive requires Member States to take the necessary steps to make it possible to terminate, with maxi-

mum notice of one year, leasing or maintenance contracts which concern terminal equipment subject to exclusive or special rights granted to certain undertakings at the time of the conclusion of the contracts.
54 Paragraph 18 in the preamble to the directive states that:
"The holders of special or exclusive rights in the terminal equipment in question have been able to impose on their customers long-term contracts preventing the introduction of free competition from having a practical effect within a reasonable period. Users must therefore be given the right to obtain a revision of the duration of their contracts".
55 In that regard, it should be noted that Article 90 of the Treaty confers powers on the Commission only in relation to State measures (see paragraph 24) and that anti-competitive conduct engaged in by undertakings on their own initiative can be called in question only by individual decisions adopted under Articles 85 and 86 of the Treaty.
56 It does not appear either from the provisions of the directive or from the preamble thereto that the holders of special or exclusive rights were compelled or encouraged by State regulations to conclude long-term contracts.
57 Article 90 cannot therefore be regarded as an appropriate basis for dealing with the obstacles to competition which are purportedly created by the long-term contracts referred to in the directive. It follows that Article 7 must be declared void.

[.....]

2) Case C-141/02 *Commission v. T-mobile Austria* [2005] ECR I-1283

Mobilkom was the first mobile operator on the Austrian market. The shares of this incumbent were partially owned by the Austrian State. It was a subsidiary of the previous state monopolist PTA and, as such, entrusted with a legal monopoly over the mobile telephony sector. Following the liberalization of the market, Max.mobil entered the market. This second mobile operator (now called T-mobile Austria) lodged a complaint with the Commission seeking a finding that Austria had infringed its obligations arising from the combined provisions of Art. 86 and 90(1) EC Treaty (now Art. 102 and 106(1) TFEU). The complaint related essentially to the lack of any distinction between the fee charged to Max.mobile and that charged to Mobilkom, to the fee payment advantages enjoyed by Mobilkom, and to the alleged breach of EU Law consisting in the legal recognition of competitive advantages granted to Mobilkom and in PTA supporting its subsidiary in establishing and operating the latter's GSM network.
The Commission communicated by letter its intention not to prosecute the Austrian State. Max.mobil was dissatisfied by this answer and sought the annulment of that letter.

Relevance : Limiting the power of individuals to complain under Article 106 (3) TFEU.

[.....]

66 Article 90(3) of the Treaty requires the Commission to ensure that the Member States comply with the obligations imposed on them, in regard to the undertakings covered by Article 90(1) of that Treaty, and expressly confers on it the power to take action for that purpose by way of directives and decisions. The Commission is empowered to determine that a given State measure is incompatible with the rules of the Treaty and to indicate what measures the State to which a decision is addressed must adopt in order to comply with its obligations under Community law (Bundesverband der Bilanzbuchhalter v Commission, paragraph 23).

[.....]

68 It follows from paragraph 24 of the judgment in Bundesverband der Bilanzbuchhalter v Commission that individuals may, in certain circumstances, be entitled to bring an action for annulment against a decision which the Commission addresses to a Member State on the basis of Article 90(3) of the Treaty if the conditions laid down in the fourth paragraph of Article 173 of the EC Treaty (now, following amendment, the fourth paragraph of Article 230 EC) are satisfied.
69 It follows, however, from the wording of Article 90(3) of the Treaty and from the scheme of that article as a whole that the Commission is not obliged to bring proceedings within the terms of those provisions, as individuals cannot require the Commission to take a position in a specific sense.
70 The fact that max.mobil has a direct and individual interest in annulment of the Commission's decision to refuse to act on its complaint is not such as to confer on it a right to challenge that decision. The letter by which the Commission informed max.mobil that it was not intending to bring proceedings against the Republic of Austria cannot be regarded as producing binding legal effects, with the result that it is not a challengeable measure that is capable of being the subject of an action for annulment.

[.....]

CHAPTER V

Horizontal Agreements

General chapter cross-references:

▸ F, Vogelaar, 'Modernisation of EC Competition Law, Economy and Horizontal Co-operation between undertakings', in Intereconomics, *Review of European Economic Policy*, Vol. 37 2002 no.1, pp. 19-27.

▸ R. Whish, 'Competition Law', Chapter 13 (Horizontal Agreements - Cartels), 6th edition (OUP 2008).

A. Price cartels

1) Case 48/69 *ICI v. Commission (Dyestuffs)* [1972] ECR 619

See above for facts of case (I-G-2, p. 35).

Relevance: example of the functioning of a price cartel.

[.....]

The increases of 1964, 1965 and 1967

83 The increases of 1964, 1965 and 1967 covered by the contested decision are interconnected.
84 The increase of 15 per cent in the prices of most aniline dyes in Germany on 1 January 1965 was in reality nothing more than the extension to another national market of the increase applied in January 1964 in Italy, the Netherlands, Belgium and Luxembourg.
85 The increase in the prices of certain dyes and pigments introduced on 1 January 1965 in all the Member States, except France, applied to all the products which had been excluded from the first increase.
86 the reason why the price increase of 8 per cent introduced in the autumn of 1967 was raised to 12 per cent for France was that there was a wish to make up for the increases of 1964 and 1965 in which that market had not taken part because of the price control system.
87 Therefore the three increases cannot be isolated one from another, even though they did not take place under identical conditions.
88 In 1964 all the undertakings in question announced their increases and immediately put them into effect, the initiative coming from Ciba-Italy which, on 7 January 1964, following instructions from Ciba-Switzerland, announced and immediately introduced an increase of 15 per cent. This initiative was followed by the other producers on the Italian market within two or three days.
89 On 9 January ICI Holland took the initiative in introducing the same increase in the Netherlands, whilst on the same day Bayer took the same initiative on the Belgo-Luxembourg market.
90 With minor differences, particularly between the price increases by the German undertakings on the one hand and the Swiss and United Kingdom undertakings on the other, these increases concerned the same range of products for the various producers and markets, namely, most aniline dyes other than pigments, food colourings and cosmetics.
91 As regards the increase of 1965 certain undertakings announced in advance price increases amounting, for the German market, to an increase of 15 per cent for products whose prices had already been similarly increased on the other markets, and to 10 per cent for products whose prices had not yet been increased. These announcements were

spread over the period between 14 October and 28 December 1964.

92 The first announcement was made by BASF, on 14 October 1964, followed by an announcement by Bayer on 30 October and by Castella on 5 November.

93 These increases were simultaneously applied on 1 January 1965 on all the markets except for the French market because of the price freeze in that state, and the Italian market where, as a result of the refusal by the principal Italian producer, ACNA, to increase its prices on the said market, the other producers also decided not to increase theirs.

94 ACNA also refrained from putting its prices up by 10 per cent on the German market.

95 Otherwise the increase was general, was simultaneously introduced by all the producers mentioned in the contested decision, and was applied without any differences concerning the range of products.

96 As regards the increase of 1967, during a meeting held at Basel on 19 August 1967, which was attended by all the producers mentioned in the contested decision except ACNA, the Geigy undertaking announced its intention to increase its selling prices by 8 per cent with effect from 16 October 1967.

97 On that same occasion the representatives of Bayer and Francolor stated that their undertakings were also considering an increase.

98 From mid-September all the undertakings mentioned in the contested decision announced a price increase of 8 per cent, raised to 12 per cent for France, to take effect on 16 October in all the countries except Italy, where ACNA again refused to increase its prices, although it was willing to follow the movement in prices on two other markets, albeit on dates other than 16 October.

99 Viewed as a whole, the three consecutive increases reveal progressive cooperation between the undertakings concerned.

100 In fact, after the experience of 1964, when the announcement of the increases and their application coincided, although with minor differences as regards the range of products affected, the increases of 1965 and 1967 indicate a different mode of operation. Here, the undertakings taking the initiative, BASF and Geigy respectively, announced their intentions of making an increase some time in advance, which allowed the undertakings to observe each other's reactions on the different markets, and to adapt themselves accordingly.

101 By means of these advance announcements the various undertakings eliminated all uncertainty between them as to their future conduct and, in doing so, also eliminated a large part of the risk usually inherent in any independent change of conduct on one or several markets.

102 This was all the more the case since these announcements, which led to the fixing of general and equal increases in prices for the markets in dyestuffs, rendered the market transparent as regard the percentage rates of increase.

103 Therefore, by the way in which they acted, the undertakings in question temporarily eliminated with respect to prices some of the preconditions for competition on the market which stood in the way of the achievement of parallel uniformity of conduct.

104 The fact that this conduct was not spontaneous is corroborated by an examination of other aspects of the market.

105 In fact, from the number of producers concerned it is not possible to say that the European market in dyestuffs is, in the strict sense, an oligopoly in which price competition could no longer play a substantial role.

106 These producers are sufficiently powerful and numerous to create a considerable

risk that in times of rising prices some of them might not follow the general movement but might instead try to increase their share of the market by behaving in an individual way.

107 Furthermore, the dividing-up of the Common Market into five national markets with different price levels and structures makes it improbable that a spontaneous and equal price increase would occur on all the national markets.

108 Although a general, spontaneous increase on each of the national markets is just conceivable, these increases might be expected to differ according to the particular characteristics of the different national markets.

109 Therefore, although parallel conduct in respect of prices may well have been an attractive and risk-free objective for the undertakings concerned, it is hardly conceivable that the same action could be taken spontaneously at the same time, on the same national markets and for the same range of products.

110 Nor is it any more plausible that the increases of January 1964, introduced on the Italian market and copied on the Netherlands and Belgo-Luxembourg markets which have little in common with each other either as regards the level of prices or the pattern of competition, could have been brought into effect within a period of two or three days without prior concertation.

111 As regards the increases of 1965 and 1967 concertation took place openly, since all the announcements of the intention to increase prices with effect from a certain date and for a certain range of products made it possible for producers to decide on their conduct regarding the special cases of France and Italy.

112 In proceeding in this way, the undertakings mutually eliminated in advance any uncertainties concerning their reciprocal behaviour on the different markets and thereby also eliminated a large part of the risk inherent in any independent change of conduct on those markets.

113 The general and uniform increase on those different markets can only be explained by a common intention on the part of those undertakings, first, to adjust the level of prices and the situation resulting from competition in the form of discounts, and secondly, to avoid the risk, which is inherent in any price increase, of changing the conditions of competition.

114 The fact that the price increases announced were not introduced in Italy and that ACNA only partially adopted the 1967 increase in other markets, far from undermining this conclusion, tends to confirm it.

115 The function of price competition is to keep prices down to the lowest possible level and to encourage the movement of goods between the Member States, thereby permitting the most efficient possible distribution of activities in the matter of productivity and the capacity of undertakings to adapt themselves to change.

116 Differences in rates encourage the pursuit of one of the basic objectives of the Treaty, namely the interpenetration of national markets and, as a result, direct access by consumers to the sources of production of the whole Community.

117 By reason of the limited elasticity of the market in dyestuffs, resulting from factors such as the lack of transparency with regard to prices, the interdependence of the different dyestuffs of each producer for the purpose of building up the range of products used by each consumer, the relatively low proportion of the cost of the final product of the user undertaking represented by the prices of these products, the fact that it is useful for users to have a local supplier and the influ-

ence of transport costs, the need to avoid any action which might artificially reduce the opportunities for interpenetration of the various national markets at the consumer level becomes particularly important on the market in the products in question.
118 Although every producer is free to change his prices, taking into account in so doing the present or foreseeable conduct of his competitors, nevertheless it is contrary to the rules on competition contained in the Treaty for a producer to cooperate with his competitors, in any way whatsoever, in order to determine a coordinated course of action relating to a price increase and to ensure its success by prior elimination of all uncertainty as to each other's conduct regarding the essential elements of that action, such as the amount, subject-matter, date and place of the increases.
119 In these circumstances and taking into account the nature of the market in the products in question, the conduct of the applicant, in conjunction with other undertakings against which proceedings have been taken, was designed to replace the risks of competition and the hazards of competitors' spontaneous reactions by cooperation constituting a concerted practice prohibited by Article 85 (1) of the Treaty.

[.....]

2) Joined Cases 40-48, 50, 54-56, 111 & 113-114/73 *European Sugar Industry* [1975] ECR 1663 (summary of judgment)

See above for facts of case (I-G-3, p. 36).

Relevance: example of the functioning of a price cartel.

Summary

1. There is no reason at all why the Commission should not make a single decision covering several infringements of Articles 85 or 86 of the EEC Treaty, even if some of the undertakings to which it is addressed are unconnected with some of these infringements, provided that the decision permits each addressee to obtain a clear picture of the complaints made against it.
2. Community institutions are under a duty to send an undertaking to which a decision is addressed a copy of that decision in the language of the Member State to which this undertaking belongs.
If this requirement is fulfilled, the fact that the Commission also sent an undertaking copies of the decision in other languages is not such as to call into question its validity.
3. For the purpose of determining the persons to whom a decision, which finds that there has been an infringement of Articles 85 or 86 of the Treaty, applies, only the operative part of this decision must be considered, provided that it is not open to more than one interpretation.
4. The concept of a 'concerted practice' refers to a form of coordination between undertakings, which, without having been taken to the stage where an agreement properly so-called has been concluded, knowingly substitutes for the risks of competition, practical cooperation between them which leads to conditions of competition which do not correspond to the normal conditions of the market, having regard to the nature of the products, the importance and number of the undertakings as well as the size and nature of the said market.

Such practical cooperation amounts to a concerted practice, particularly if it enables the persons concerned to consolidate established positions to the detriment of effective freedom of movement of the products in the Common Market and of the freedom of consumers to choose their suppliers.
These criteria of 'coordination' and 'cooperation' laid down by the case-law of the Court, which in no way require the working out of an actual plan, must be understood in the light of the concept inherent in the provisions of the Treaty relating to competition that each economic operator must determine independently the policy which he intends to adopt on the Common Market including the choice of the persons and undertakings to which he makes offers or sells.
Although it is correct to say that this requirement of independence does not deprive economic operators of the right to adapt themselves intelligently to the existing and anticipated conduct of their competitors, it does however strictly preclude any direct or indirect contact between such operators, the object or effect whereof is either to influence the conduct on the market of an actual or potential competitor or to disclose to such a competitor the course of conduct which they themselves have decided to adopt or contemplate adopting on the market.
If an economic operator accepts the complaints made to him by another operator in connexion with the competition to which the products manufactured by the former operator expose the latter, the conduct of the operators concerned amounts to a concerted practice.
The fact that a vendor aligns his price on the highest price charged by a competitor is not necessarily evidence of a concerted practice but may be explained by an attempt to obtain the maximum profit.

5. When Article 85 (1) not only prohibits agreements, decisions or practices having regard to their object but also to their actual effects in the field of competition, it implies that these effects must be considered in the context in which they take place, that is to say in their surrounding economic and legal circumstances within which they may, together with other factors, have a cumulative effect on competition.
In order to determine whether an agreement is caught by Article 85 (1) it cannot therefore be severed from this context; in particular, the existence of similar contracts may be taken into consideration to the extent to which these kinds of contracts are in general likely to restrict free trade.
6. (a) The fact that a trade representative contract, which imposes upon the representative a prohibition of competition, complies with the national law governing this contract or that this law even imposes a similar prohibition is not determinative when considering whether such a contract is not caught by Article 85 or 86.
(b) Nevertheless if an agent sells in the name and for the account of a producer or association of producers he may in principle be treated as an auxiliary organ forming an integral part of the latter's undertaking, who must carry out his principal's instructions and thus, like a commercial employee, forms an economic unit with this undertaking.
In these circumstances incompatibility with Article 85 or Article 86 is not simply due to the fact that the principal forbids such an auxiliary to trade without his consent in products which might compete with his own products.
(c) As purchases from a 'trade representative' are in fact direct purchases from his principal the fact that the latter forced wholesalers to apply to its representatives and not

to itself can neither be an abuse nor evidence thereof.

(d) Even if an agent is called a 'trade representative' under the terms of the agreement which he has entered into with his principal, he cannot be regarded as an auxiliary organ forming an integral part of his principal's undertaking:

1. If the said agreement confers upon the agent or allows him to perform duties which from an economic point of view are approximately the same as those carried out by an independent dealer, because they provide for the agent accepting the financial risks of the sales or the performance of contracts entered into with third parties,

or

2. If the agent is a large business house which at the same time as it distributes products for the account of the principal undertakes as an independent dealer a very considerable amount of business on the market for the product in question.

Therefore a clause prohibiting competition entered into between such an agent and his principal may be an agreement between undertakings which is prohibited under Article 85.

If such a clause is inserted at the insistence of an undertaking occupying a dominant position, it may in the circumstances referred to in 1 above be an abuse under Article 86.

(e) Clauses prohibiting competition imposed by an undertaking occupying a dominant position on trade representatives may constitute an abuse, if foreign competitors find that there are no independent operators who can market the product in question on a sufficiently large scale, and are in practice forced to apply to the said undertaking's trade representatives if they wish to sell this product in the latter's sales territory, or if the said undertaking enlarges the scope of the prohibition of competition to such an extent that it no longer corresponds to the nature of the legal and economic relationship in question.

7. For the purpose of determining whether a specific territory is large enough to amount to 'a substantial part of the Common Market' within the meaning of Article 86 of the Treaty the pattern and volume of the production and consumption of the said product as well as the habits and economic opportunities of vendors and purchasers must be considered.

Article 86 of the Treaty refers in each case to the position occupied by the undertaking concerned on the Common Market as the time when the latter acted in a way which is alleged to amount to an abuse.

In order to determine in the case of a complaint made against an undertaking under this Article whether a specific area is a substantial part of the Common Market it is therefore only necessary to compare the statistical data relating to this area with the corresponding data relating to the Common Market as it was when the facts giving rise to these proceedings existed; any subsequent enlargement of the Common Market cannot be taken into consideration.

8. If an economic operator adopts a system of loyalty rebates leading to the application of different net prices to two customers who bought the same amount from the said operator if one of them purchased from another producer as well, such a system amounts to 'applying dissimilar conditions to equivalent transactions with other trading parties' within the meaning of Article 86 (c).

9. If a producer adopts a system of loyalty rebates which gives producers having their places of business in other Member States no chance or restricts their opportunities of competing with goods sold by the said producer, such a system amounts to 'limiting markets to the prejudice of consumers' within the meaning of Article 86 (b).

10. There is no reason why the Commission and the Court should not accept as evidence of an undertaking's conduct correspondence exchanged between third parties, provided that the content thereof is credible to the extent to which it refers to the said conduct.
11. For the purpose of fixing the amount of the fine under Article 15 (2) of Regulation No 17 regard shall be had to the gravity and duration of the infringement, so that particular account has to be taken of the legislative background and economic context of the conduct to which exception is taken, the nature of the restrictions of competition as well as the number and size of the undertakings concerned.
12. If a producer, acting independently, may be justified in endeavouring to prevent the sugar, which he has sold at a relatively low price for denaturing, from being sold at too low a price on the market for human consumption, the objectives of Article 39 of the Treaty do not however in any way require that he pursues this aim by means of concerted practices.
Nevertheless, if he does so, the concerted practices cannot come within the scope of the second exception specified in the first sentence of Article 2 (1) of Regulation No 26.
13. There is nothing in Regulation No 1009/67 to justify the assertion that this price is also 'guaranteed' to producers for sugar which they supply to other producers other than the intervention agencies referred to in Article 9 of the said regulation.
14. It follows from the wording of Article 17 (1) of Regulation No 1009/67 that Community institutions are not required to introduce a system of export refunds and still less to fix the amount thereof in such a way that if sugar producers export they obtain this intervention price.

B. Market access/foreclosure

1) *Meldoc* Commission decision 86/596/EEC [1986] OJ 348/50

The Meldoc organization, a cartel that consisted of the five major producers of 'fresh' milk (MU, DOMO, Coberco, Campina and ML), was active on the Netherlands dairy market. Its aim was, amongst others, to take coordinated action against the threat presented by import from Belgium and Germany of 'fresh' milk, inter alia, to supermarkets in the southern part of the country. The participating dairy producers had agreed (in the 1978 Basic Agreement) to carry out a joint commercial policy (e.g. a joint price policy) and a joint production and distribution policy. Moreover, each company was to adhere to a certain (agreed) quota. Furthermore, the cartel members jointly funded the financial means to fight the above-mentioned imports.

Relevance: example of an arrangement that resulted in market access foreclosure.

[.....]

II. LEGAL ASSESSMENT

[.....]

B. Article 85 (1)

[.....]

Basic Agreement

(58) The agreement covering the cooperation of the five-member 'greater Meldoc group' in the field of liquid milk and dairy products, the Dairy Industry Basic Cooperation Agreement, was adopted by Meldoc's Policy Group on 19 December 1978 in its fourth draft and constitutes an agreement within the meaning of Article 85 (1). The Policy Group was composed of senior officers and executives of the five companies.

(59) The Basic Agreement contains a large number of provisions which restrict competition, especially in the fields of sales, prices, production, distribution and markets. The closeness of the cooperation is further demonstrated by the great number of meetings that took place within the Meldoc organization.

The documentary evidence gathered by the Commission, some of which has been discussed above (including the minutes of meetings of the Milk Steering Committee, the Policy Group and the various working parties) prove that regular consultations took place on all the abovementioned forms of cooperation.

(60) Full consultations were traditionally held about quoting to each other's customers. The meetings of the various working parties (long-life and fresh) were essentially devoted to coordination of sales and prices, thereby implementing the objective of a joint commercial policy.

Apart from the general impact of the quota arrangements on the members' freedom to decide reductions or increases in output, actual output restrictions concerned especially the long-life milk sector. The growing imports of long-life (plastic-bottled) milk from Belgium and later of UHT milk from Belgium and Germany led to agreements to increase production.

The quota arrangements shared out the market between the members in quantitative terms. The Basic Agreement also involved geographical market-sharing. The bulk of each member's sales was subject to quotas. The rise in the proportion of the Netherlands market supplied by the Meldoc organization (from 70,2 % in 1978 to 91,4 % in 1983) and the proportion of the market accounted for by Meldoc sales subject to quotas (from 65,2 % in 1978 to 78 % in 1983) show that the Meldoc cooperation excluded or restricted competition on a nation-wide scale. Competition was restricted not only because of the allocation of quotas but also because of the financial transfers between the parties if they fell short of or exceeded the agreed quotas and because of the consultation on quoting to each other's customers and agreements concerning production levels.

Actions against imports

61) In assessing the Meldoc partners' market behaviour it becomes clear that the Basic Agreement cannot be isolated from earlier and later documentary evidence. Even though the text of the Basic Agreement contains no references to imports or exports it does provide for the specific obligation of the parties to protect their sales volumes against third parties. The discussion paper, which served as a contribution to

the discussion on the Basic Agreement, had already recognized the 'increasing concentration of retailers' and the 'further penetration of our domestic market from abroad' as developments which would urge closer cooperation. The advantages of cooperation were, amongst other things, the ability to take joint action including mounting 'massed attacks on the remaining competition, joint infiltration over the borders'. As is shown by the facts the Meldoc partners protected their sales volumes against third parties by taking joint action to curb imports. One of the documents of a later date than the Basic Agreement also confirms that this agreement cannot be viewed separately from the later evidence such as the memorandum of 29 December 1982 which stated that the protection of the home market against 'further inroads by long-life milk from abroad' was among the original policy objectives of the cartel. This document was drawn up in relation to a discussion on joint actions by the Meldoc partners against imports of UHT milk.

Imports of long-life milk

(62) The Meldoc partners wanted to stop the competition from Belgian milk on the Netherlands market because of the pressure on their prices caused by lower-priced Belgian milk and because they feared an erosion of their shares of the fresh milk market. In order to achieve this aim, different joint actions were carried out. As is shown in paragraph 31 the Meldoc partners regularly exchanged information on quotations in connection with imported milk and in other contexts. This not only distorted competition between the members of the cartel, because information on prices and customers was shared and because they respected each other's positions, but also distorted competition between the Netherlands and foreign milk.

(63) The decision referred to in paragraph 26 to freeze Belgian sales of long-life milk in the Netherlands and to capture the anticipated growth in this segment is another example of a decision which distorted competition. The scheme of special UHT deliveries was also a Meldoc operation to distort competition within the Netherlands and eliminate competition from Germany and Belgium. The scheme involved selective low offers to the Netherlands customers concerned to make it worth their while not to import the cheaper UHT milk. The losses were shared between the members. The quotations given in paragraph 30 show that the Meldoc group thought their action a success.

Imports of fresh milk

(64) The multi-annual contracts which MU concluded with Ziko was clearly intended to prevent loss of business to German suppliers. This emerges most clearly from the second quotation in paragraph 36 stating that MU reacted to Ziko's intention of buying milk from Germany by offering an extra discount. In return for this extra discount Ziko was prepared to sign a multi-annual contract, which, as the first quotation in paragraph 36 shows, prevented Ziko outlets from purchasing from any other supplier than MU 'basic' range of fresh milk and dairy products for the duration of the contract, thus shutting out other, particularly German, suppliers. MU's contract with Ziko fitted into the general policy of the Meldoc group to keep imports of long-life and fresh milk out of the Netherlands market. The evidence presented in paragraphs 35 and 36 also proves that the Meldoc group regarded it as a matter of common interest that MU should secure the Ziko contract. Not only was the Ziko case discussed at several Meldoc meetings but the

cost of reimbursing Ziko for packaging it had ordered from the German supplier, which was part of the price MU paid to gain the contract, was shared between the partners. It is concluded that MU's contract with Ziko followed from the Basic Agreement which, amongst other things, aimed at protecting the Meldoc partners' share of the Netherlands market against inroads by foreign milk suppliers.

Action on the Belgian market

(65) Imports of Belgian milk and possible measures to prevent them from increasing or to recapture business the members had lost to Belgian suppliers were regular topics of discussion in Meldoc. Apart from the Meldoc members' action against Belgian imports of long-life milk and dairy products in the Netherlands, in 1983 they also undertook joint action on the Belgian market to induce Belgian suppliers to stop their deliveries of fresh milk to Netherlands customers. In 1983, Edah began importing Belgian fresh milk and several other customers followed Edah's example. To force the Belgian suppliers to stop these exports and avoid losing sales on the important fresh-milk market, the members of Meldoc decided to mount a 'dumping' operation on the Belgian market. Initial attempts to stop the imports by talking to the Belgian suppliers had failed. That the 'dumping' operation was explicitly directed against the Belgian imports is proved by several documents, including those mentioned in paragraphs 39 and 40. These documents also show that it was a joint action by the members of Meldoc. The margin of loss on the 'dumped' milk was considerable, as is shown by the figures given in paragraph 43, and this was openly admitted in the memorandum quoted in paragraph 44, which spoke of loss-making sales. The considerable scale of these sales is shown by the figures given in paragraph 45. The aggressiveness and covert nature of the operation emerge from the quotations given in paragraph 41. The aim was the 'maximum fall in prices' and, to avoid giving the impression that 'the Netherlands dairy industry is acting together', Volnij channelled its deliveries to Dial under one of Melkunie's brand names.

[.....]

Effect on trade between Member States

(70) It has been established by the Court of Justice that an agreement which covers the whole territory of a Member State 'has by its nature the effect of reinforcing the compartmentalizaton of markets on a national basis, thereby holding up the economic interpenetration which the Treaty is designed to bring about and protecting domestic production' (VCH judgment of 17 October 1972 in Case 8/72).

(71) In the defence to the Statement of Objections, the point is raised that the VCH judgment concerned a cartel between traders which is different from the present case which concerns a cartel between manufacturers. According to the defence, the principle laid down in the Court's judgment is based on the understanding that foreign suppliers depend normally on local distributors when they try to penetrate a foreign market. A situation in which most distributors are deprived of their freedom to take commercial decisions independently would almost inevitably have an impact on other parties (especially manufacturers) from abroad, since they would suffer from the lack of independence among distributors. The defence states that this reasoning cannot be applied to an agreement between manufacturers which has a

strictly national character, particularly when the manufacturers in question have no exclusive relationships with their buyers.
(72) The rationale of the VCH judgment, which concerned a cartel between traders, is equally applicable in this case. The present agreement which covers – practically – the whole of the territory of the Netherlands is indeed able to render the penetration of the Netherlands market more difficult than would have been the case otherwise. The size of the cartel, together with the obligation to defend sales against third parties and the intensive cooperation in terms of sales and prices, have an inherently adverse effect on the possibilities for foreign suppliers to penetrate the Netherlands market. These suppliers are confronted with a market which is divided between members of a cartel which ultimately covered more than 90 % of the relevant product market and who acted together to defend their sales volume. Furthermore, the cooperation in quoting prices has a distorting effect on the competition from any third supplier, including foreign suppliers.

[.....]

2) *FEG* Commission decision 2000/117/EC [2000] OJ L 39/1

FEG, a Dutch association active in the wholesale business for the electrotechnical fittings sector, was, together with NAVEG (association of suppliers/manufacturers of these products) and UNETO (association for the installation business for the sector concerned), accused of sealing off the Netherlands market from foreign distributors of electrotechnical fittings. A system of exclusive collective dealing agreements, combined with price agreements, made it nearly impossible for non-FEG members to expand their business to the Netherlands.

Relevance: example of a (gentlemen's) agreement (=concerted practice) that resulted in market access foreclosure.

[.....]

2. Restriction of competition

2.1. Collective exclusive dealing

(103) From the facts described in recitals 44 to 52, it is clear that in the period from 28 April 1986 to 25 February 1994 there was a collective exclusive dealing arrangement in operation on the Dutch market in electrotechnical fittings, which consisted in a gentleman's agreement. Under this arrangement NAVEG assured the FEG that it would advise its members to supply only to wholesalers who were members of the FEG. This collective exclusive dealing was not reciprocal since members of the FEG were under no obligation to buy only from NAVEG members.
(104) The FEG and its members, especially TU, sought to broaden the application of the collective exclusive dealing arrangement. Between 29 August 1989 and 2 September 1993 at any rate, individual suppliers who were not represented in NAVEG by agents or by importers or sole distributors were put under pressure not to supply non-members of the FEG. It is apparent from the facts set out in recitals 53 to 66 that FEG and its members

succeeded in this attempt, as a substantial number of suppliers acted in accordance with the collective exclusive dealing arrangement.
(105) The collective exclusive dealing arrangement as described in recitals 103 and 104 has as its object or effect the restriction of competition within the Common Market within the meaning of Article 81 (1). The arrangement restricts the freedom of suppliers to determine themselves which wholesalers they wish to supply. The result is that both the suppliers and the wholesalers who do not belong to the FEG are placed at a disadvantage.
(106) There are only a limited number of suppliers or suppliers' representatives to whom non-members of the FEG can address themselves. NAVEG members have an estimated share of the market in supply to the wholesale trade of about 20 %. The joint market share of the individual suppliers who also take part in the collective exclusive dealing arrangement is difficult to estimate; but, as will be seen from the table in the Annex, the suppliers whom the FEG and its members, TU in particular, put under pressure not to supply to non-FEG members were (almost) all major suppliers in their product group (see references to Draka Polva, Hager, Holec, Klöckner Moeller and ABB in recitals 53 to 66). The letter drafted by TU to be sent to Klöckner Moeller is also indicative: it points out that Klöckner Moeller is one of the first large suppliers of electro technical goods to supply to a non-member of the FEG. This suggests that a substantial number of suppliers are involved in the collective exclusive dealing arrangement.
(107) The refusals to supply make it very difficult for wholesalers who are not members of the FEG to assemble a range that is sufficiently broad and includes the products essential to every wholesaler in electrotechnical fittings, that is to say the products needed in order to put in an electric system. Given that the market in most individual categories of electrotechnical fittings is dominated by a limited number of manufacturers, it will be clear that refusal to supply by any of them will immediately lead to stock difficulties for non-members of the FEG.
(108) The FEG's strict admissions policy makes access to the market even more difficult for newcomers. Although the FEG is of the opinion that the admission criteria set by it are objective in character, and that the turnover criterion which it applies, at NLG 5 million (EUR 2,26 million) on the Dutch market, is extremely low, it is evident that various FEG members did not themselves at that time meet the turnover requirement. According to the FEG, the turnover criterion ensures that the firm has "proved itself" on the market. But precisely as a result of the collective exclusive dealing arrangement it is extremely difficult for newcomers to "prove themselves" on the market, and to achieve the turnover that would entitle them to FEG membership. Moreover, firms which have acquired a reputation as electro technical fittings wholesalers in another Member State have in fact already proved that they can operate as such. Up to 23 June 1994, however, only the turnover generated on the Dutch market was taken into account. This made it considerably more difficult for existing foreign wholesalers to extend their field of operations to the Dutch wholesale market.
(109) Furthermore, the turnover requirement was clearly not the only criterion applied by the FEG in turning down applications for membership. In practice, the "interest of the association" criterion is also cited as grounds for refusal. Even though it is stipulated that only "objective, fair and non-discriminatory norms" may be applied in this respect, this criterion offers the FEG board, which pursuant to Article 3 (3) of the Articles of

association has to decide unanimously on the admission of new members, such wide discretionary powers that it is not possible to verify whether members have not in practice been refused admission on non-objective grounds. In practice, it may be seen that applications for membership are submitted to the FEG members, which are able to block the membership of unwelcome competitors. In this way the effects of the collective exclusive dealing arrangement are strengthened.
(110) In view of the above, and in particular of the total turnover in electro technical fittings at wholesale level in the Netherlands (between EUR 0,68 and 0,91 billion in 1992 to 1994), the market share held by the FEG and its members (96 %), and the estimated market shares of the suppliers, agents and sole dealers taking part in the collective exclusive dealing arrangement (over 20 %), these restrictions of competition are appreciable.

2.2. Horizontal price agreements

(111) The collective exclusive dealing arrangement is supplemented by practices concerted between FEG members and between the FEG and its members, and by two FEG decisions that affect the prices and discounts offered by FEG members. All these decisions and concerted practices are aimed at establishing an artificial price stability serving mainly to ensure that the margins of the FEG members do not come under pressure. The intentions of the FEG and its members are clear. Reference can be made to various documents in which this intention is expressed:
- The Articles of association of the FEG: it is here stated that the object of the FEG is to protect the common interests of stockkeeping wholesalers of electrotechnical products, among other things by promoting "orderly market relations in the broadest sense of the term".
- The manual that the FEG issued to the FEG product committees: this manual states that "In order to obtain an accurate picture of what is taking place in the market [...] it is of crucial importance to be apprised of turnover and margins. Without knowledge of these, it is impracticable to do anything to influence the market".
- The minutes of the meeting of the FEG Wire and Cable product committee on 16 May 1990: "the objective of the product committee is to endeavour to keep the market calm and maintain prices".
- The FEG's Binding Decision on publications: the recitals to this decision state that "it is undesirable to cause, promote or permit a sharp drop in prices, market dislocation, loss of profits and unbridled internecine competition".
- The draft letter drafted by TU, which was to be sent to Klöckner Moeller and to be signed by 26 FEG members: "by now entering into a direct relationship with CEF, your products fall within the discount formula applied. The inevitable consequence will be that prices and, therefore, margins will come under increasing pressure".
(112) The FEG and its members sought to achieve the objectives referred to in recital 111 by applying several instruments largely at the same time, each of which was intended, and did in fact help, to influence FEG members' pricing strategy and to restrict price competition between them. The instruments were the Binding Decision on fixed prices, the Binding Decision on publications, the discussions between FEG members on prices and discounts and the sending of price recommendations by the FEG to its members.
(113) Under the Binding Decision on fixed prices, which was in force from 2 November 1984 to 23 November 1993, FEG members

were not to decide independently whether and to what extent they wished to pass on to their customers any increases in their suppliers' prices that took place after the date of the order. The margins by which the price was to be increased in such cases, and the times when the increases were to be carried out, were determined by the FEG. Failure to comply with the decision could lead to expulsion from the association and the imposition of fines. This is a decision by an association of undertakings in respect of prices to be charged. Such decisions restrict competition within the meaning of Article 81 (1) by their very nature. The parties contend that the decision was intended to prevent increases in suppliers' prices after the fitter had ordered the goods from the wholesaler from being entirely for the account and at the risk of the wholesale trade. It is not clear why in order to do this a decision had to be adopted requiring all FEG members to react in more or less the same way. The decision in any event deprived the individual FEG member of the possibility of refraining from passing on a particular price increase in order to secure a competitive advantage over its competitors.

(114) On the basis of another decision, the Binding Decision on publications, which was in force from 2 August 1978 to 23 November 1993, the FEG forbade its members to offer loss-leader or specially reduced prices in advertising and the like. Failure to comply with the decision could lead to expulsion. This too is a decision by an association of undertakings in respect of the prices to be applied. By its very nature the decision restricts competition within the meaning of Article 81 (1). It deprives FEG members of the possibility of winning customers from competitors by more attractive pricing. In general the decision forms part of the FEG policy aimed at reducing the danger that FEG members might find themselves in a price war with one another, which would put pressure on the level of prices and on wholesale margins. It will be seen from recitals 77 and 78 that this decision was in fact applied in practice.

(115) As has been explained in recitals 79 to 84, discussions regularly took place between FEG members regarding prices and discounts to be applied, at the regular FEG meetings, the FEG product committee meetings and the regional FEG meetings. In any event, the discussions took place in the period between 6 December 1989 and 30 November 1993. These meetings provided a forum in which the FEG members could discuss a wide range of subjects related to prices and discounts. Among the points discussed were the setting of rates of discount (see recital 83), compliance with FEG price guidelines (recital 87), complaints against other members who were not applying certain agreements in respect of prices and discounts (recital 82), and steps to introduce uniform rules for the discounts to be allowed (recital 81). These discussions in any event had the effect that it was quite clear to FEG members that they should avoid any intense price competition between themselves, in view of the negative impact that might have on the level of prices and on wholesalers' margins. The discussions therefore helped to influence the pricing of electrotechnical fittings on the Dutch wholesale market, and restricted competition within the meaning of Article 81 (1).

(116) Between 21 December 1988 and 24 April 1994, the FEG sent its members price lists showing net and gross prices - at least for the products referred to in recital 85. The parties contend that these were merely advisory. As has been seen in recital 87, pressure was brought to bear on the FEG members to comply with these guidelines, which casts doubt on their voluntary character. By send-

ing the price lists, the FEG sought to ensure that FEG members would react in a uniform fashion to increases or reductions in their suppliers' prices. This reduced the danger that price increases or reductions might be seized upon by individual FEG members in order to secure a competitive advantage over other FEG members by refraining from passing on an increase or reduction to their customers, or by passing it on only in part. Conduct of that sort would have disturbed the calm which the FEG wanted to see on the market, and might have stirred up price competition between FEG members.

(117) The joint application of the above instruments had the effect that in practice there was only limited price competition between FEG members. An example is provided by the price catalogues issued by the larger FEG wholesalers. Their catalogues were very similar. In many cases both the gross prices and the discounts shown in the price catalogues of FEG members TU, Bernard and Wolff were identical. The catalogues were published in the same month, and price changes were made at virtually the same time. The parties take the view that no importance should be attached to the similarity between these price catalogues, because in some cases the discounts actually applied were not the standard ones indicated in the price catalogues. But they have conceded that this was not the case with every transaction. In practice, higher discounts might be given, for example where the customer was buying larger quantities, or where there was a long-standing relationship with the particular customer. This means that two situations have to be distinguished. In some cases the gross prices and standard discounts shown in the price catalogues were applied as they stood, and in those cases the similarity between the price catalogues indicates a lack of price competition between the issuers of the catalogues. In other cases the standard discounts were departed from, and the standard discount operated as a minimum discount. In any event, there was no competition here between the issuers of the catalogues in respect of the size of the minimum discount.

(118) In practice the smaller wholesalers, who have not got the resources to draw up a catalogue of their own, use the catalogues issued by TU, Bernard or Wolff as a guideline for their own pricing, so that the observations made here regarding the lack of price competition apply not only to those three wholesalers but have a more general relevance too.

(119) The lack of price competition between FEG members is also apparent from the price level on the Dutch wholesale market. There is a variety of evidence that the level of prices for electrotechnical fittings is higher in the Netherlands than in the other Member States. In the TU report "Market Research on Electrotechnical Fittings", which dates from 1994, it is observed that parallel imports, especially from Belgium and Germany, seem to be on the increase. Commenting on a price comparison it carried out, the FEG Lighting product committee says that "Dutch prices are certainly not the lowest in Europe". Another illustration is provided by the brochure issued by Hokamo Import BV: it links the price level to the fact that the Dutch market is known to be a "protected market": "Hokamo Import BV is playing a pioneering role with respect to the pricing of electrical cable in the Netherlands. As well as supplying the traditional Ymvk and Ymvk-as cables, we dared to introduce the Nyy and Nycwy, German quality cables that are up to 40 % cheaper. And that was on a protected market. At European level this means that the Dutch fitter can compete better in terms of price and quality".

(120) Together, the practices described in recitals 113 to 116 enable the FEG and its members, in line with the FEG's efforts

described in recital 111, to concert the pricing of its members and to stabilise or increase the market prices of their products. The prices of electrotechnical fittings on the Dutch wholesale market are consequently held at an artificial level. According to the Commission's established practice and the case-law of the Court of Justice and of the Court of First Instance, agreements or concerted practices in respect of prices or discounts to be applied restrict competition within the meaning of Article 81 (1) by their very nature.

(121) In view of the total turnover in electrotechnical fittings in the Netherlands (between EUR 0,68 and EUR 0,91 billion in the period 1992 to 1994) and the market share held by the FEG and its members (96 %), these restrictions of competition are appreciable.

2.3. The relationship between the collective exclusive dealing arrangement and the horizontal price agreements

(122) There is a direct relation between the collective exclusive dealing arrangement and the price agreements within the FEG. As has been explained in recital 111, the price agreements are aimed at establishing an artificially stable price level with "healthy margins" for the wholesale trade. This can succeed only if the wholesalers observe a measure of price discipline. The FEG has therefore brought various forms of pressure to bear on its members to avoid any intense price competition. This meant that intense price competition was to be feared only from wholesalers outside the FEG. The collective exclusive dealing arrangement prevented deliveries to these potential "price cutters", thus reducing the danger that the artificial price level might come under pressure. In this way the collective exclusive dealing arrangement helped to underpin the price agreements.

3. Effect on trade between Member States

(123) As has been explained in recital 19, a large proportion of electrotechnical fittings sold on the Dutch market is imported from other Member States (30 to 52 %), primarily from Belgium and Germany. NAVEG members alone, for example, represent more than 400 mainly foreign manufacturers on the Dutch market. It is clear, therefore, that electrotechnical fittings by their nature lend themselves to international trading, certainly now that Europe-wide harmonisation has taken place (see recital 18).

3.1. Collective exclusive dealing arrangement

(124) The collective exclusive dealing arrangement restricts the access of foreign wholesalers in electrotechnical fittings, such as CEF, to the Dutch wholesale market. It also restricts the possibilities open to manufacturers from other Member States. Given the combined market share of the FEG members, the collective exclusive dealing arrangement means that such outsiders have difficulty in selling their goods on the Dutch market through distribution channels not approved by the FEG.

(125) There is therefore an effect on trade between Member States. In view of the total turnover in electrotechnical fittings (between EUR 0,68 and 0,91 billion in 1992 to 1994) and the FEG's market share (96 %), this effect is appreciable.

3.2. Horizontal price agreements

(126) The practices affecting prices may also influence trade between Member States. In this connection, reference is made to the fact

mentioned in recital 123 that a considerable proportion of the electrotechnical fittings on the Dutch market are imported from other Member States. In view of the total turnover in the electrotechnical fittings trade (between EUR 0,68 and 0,91 billion in 1992 to 1994) and the FEG's market share (96 %), this effect is appreciable.

Case cross-reference:

▸ Joined Cases T-5 & 6/00 *FEG v. Commission* [2003] ECR II-5761, decision confirmed by the GC both in substance and insofar as fines were imposed.

[.....]

C. Quota cartels/market sharing

1) *Julien v. Van Katwijk*, Comm., Bulletin 12-1970, Ch. 1, section 4

Relevance: example of an agreement that was banned because it would lead to limited market access and market sharing.

Market-sharing agreement banned

4. On 29 October 1970 the Commission adopted, pursuant to Article 85 (1) of the EEC Treaty, a decision banning an agreement between the Belgian company SA Tuberies Louis Julien and the Dutch company Van Katwijk's Industrieën NV, under which the former had undertaken to limit the volume of its exports to the Netherlands and the latter to make no further sales whatsoever in Belgium.
The agreement covered cardboard tubes used mainly in the textile industry; SA Tuberies Louis Julien and Van Katwijk's Industrieën NV are the train makers and exporters of cardboard tubes in their home countries, so that the agreement was a typical market-sharing arrangement appreciably restraining trade between two Member States and therefore falling under the ban of Treaty Article 85 (1). Furthermore, the agreement did not fulfill any of the conditions laid down by Article 85 (3) for exemption from the ban, since it contributed neither to improving production or distribution of goods nor to promoting technical or economic progress.
The two companies had notified their agreement to the Commission in good time and were furthermore bound; under orders issued by a Dutch Court, to comply fully with all the obligations contained in the agreement pending a Commission decision. The possibility of fining the two companies was therefore not envisaged.

2) *Heating Pipes*, Comm. Press Release (IP/98/917), full decision published in [1999] OJ L 24/1

Relevance: example of a cartel that did not only engage in market sharing, bid-rigging and price agreements but that also aggressively tried to eliminate a major competitor who had refused to join the cartel. (Note: even after the Commission had initiated its investigations, the illegal practices continued).

IP/98/917, Brussels, 21st October 1998

Commission imposes heavy fines for price fixing and bid-rigging in district heating pipe cartel

The European Commission has fined ten companies a total of ECU 92.21 million for running a secret market-sharing, price-fixing and bid-rigging cartel in pipes used for District Heating systems and for attempting to eliminate a competitor. ABB was fined ECU 70,000,000, Løgstør ECU 8,900,000, Henss/Isoplus ECU 4,950,000, Tarco ECU 3,000,000, Pan-Isovit ECU 1,500,000, Dansk Rør ECU 1,475,000, Brugg ECU 925,000, KWH ECU 700,000, Sigma ECU 400,000 and Ke-Kelit ECU 360,000. The cartel began in Denmark in late 1990 and soon extended to Germany and other markets. From 1994 onwards the whole European market (worth around ECU 400 million) was cartellised. In Germany and Denmark, the two largest markets, the producers operated a particularly sophisticated system of bid-rigging: a ",favourite" was nominated to win each contract and the other cartel members put in higher offers. A particular aggravating factor was that the cartel was continued for nine months after the Commission had discovered the evidence in surprise investigations in June 1995.

District Heating systems are common in Northern and Eastern Europe but examples are found even in Greece and Portugal. Instead of each building being individually heated, whole localities are served via a system of underground pipes carrying hot water into each house from a central heat generation source (often a power station; excess energy is used to heat the water).
The cartel concerns the pipes, which consist of an inner steel carrier pipe for the hot water, an outer plastic casing pipe and foam insulation between. The customers for district heating pipes are mainly public and local government authorities. Contracts are awarded on the basis of competitive tendering and the larger projects are subject to European Union (EU) Public Procurement rules; these were deliberately flouted by the cartel. Moreover, the cartel allocated national market quotas to its members and fixed prices in the pipes market.
The Commission also found that the cartel systematically tried to force out of business the only competitor not in the "ring", Powerpipe of Sweden. Powerpipe informed the Commission in January 1995 of a cartel which it claimed was also taking reprisals against it because it refused to join. These retaliatory measures had intensified since it entered the German market in 1994.
After Powerpipe had won a major project in Germany which was so large the cartel had allocated it to a consortium of ABB, Henss/Isoplus and Pan-Isovit, the other producers had organised a collective boycott and had prevented Powerpipe getting supplies.
In setting the fines, the Commission applied Article 15 of Regulation 17/62 and its Guidelines, under which the Commission must weigh the deliberate nature, gravity and duration of an infringement. The Guidelines authorise the Commission to set the 'starting point' for fines for very serious infringements at ECU 20 million. The Guidelines also allow for a distinction to be made in fines to reflect a considerable disparity between the sizes of the undertakings committing infringements of the same type. Fines would have been substantially higher had not most of the producers admitted the violation, thus benefiting from the Commission's policy on reduction of fines. The "Leniency Notice" issued on 18 July 1996 provides for a 10 to 50% reduction where companies provide substantial information to the

Commission after the latter started an investigation and where after receiving a Statement of Objections, a company does not substantially contest the facts on which the Commission bases its allegations. If the main message is again that cartels will not be tolerated, the Commission also wishes to signal very clearly to industry that timely co-operation pays.
Competition Commissioner Karel Van Miert commented: "Major industrial groups taking part in secret cartels cannot expect fines to be limited to 10 per cent of their turnover in the particular business; this would be a mere pinprick. Fines have got to be felt. In this particular instance, it is difficult to imagine a worse cartel. The main producers tried to bankrupt the only competitor who was willing to take them on. They deliberately flouted the EU Public Procurement rules. Bid-rigging is no better than fraud. They continued the violation for nine months after the Commission investigators had caught them red-handed. This violation calls for condign fines."
The fine imposed on ABB reflects the fact that one of its most senior officers in Zurich master-minded and directed the cartel. The cartel was not therefore the unauthorised and atypical action of a minor subsidiary but a deliberate act decided at the top level. On the occasion of this decision, Commissioner Van Miert emphasised again the Commission's absolute determination to fight cartels as well as other distortions of competition. However, the Commission is pleased to note ABB's assurances that it would take all measures called for by this decision, including those ensuing from personal responsibilities within the company. ABB's position is underscored by the recent resignation of the company's former Executive Vice-President who effectively co-ordinated the cartel.

Background information

1. District Heating Pipe Producers
The main production centre for District Heating steel pipes is Denmark, three of the producers in fact being based in one town, Fredericia (Jutland).
ABB is the largest producer with 40% of the European market (EU market in 1995 = ECU 400 million). It is the acknowledged leader in almost every national market. Besides its Fredericia plant (ABB IC Møller), it has production units in Germany (ABB Isolrohr, Fulda); Finland, Sweden and Poland.
Other main producers in the cartel almost from the start were Løgstør, Tarco and Dansk Rør (Starpipe) of Denmark; Henss/Isoplus of Germany and Austria, and Pan-Isovit, also of Germany but now taken over by Løgstør. KWH (Finland); Brugg (Germany); Sigma (Italy) and Ke-Kelit (Austria) joined the arrangements later in 1994-95. Løgstør is the No 2 producer but with a total turnover of ECU 127 million in 1997 it is only a fraction of the size of the ABB combine (Total Sales in 1997: ECU 27,600 million).
Contracts for the supply of pipes are almost all awarded on the basis of competitive tendering procedures. Since 1994, large projects (those worth over ECU 400,000) are subject to EU Public Procurement Rules.

2. Procedure
The Commission carried out surprise investigations in June 1995 at all the major producers and obtained a large volume of evidence: unusually for a cartel case, incriminating cartel documents were found at almost every firm visited.
It might have been expected that this success would have put an immediate stop to the cartel but as later enquiries revealed, the members had decided to take the risk of carrying on. It was only 9 months later, after

the Commission sent detailed information requests, that the cartel fell apart and several members approached the Commission's Directorate-General for Competition (DG IV) offering to co-operate with its enquiries. Most of the firms in the cartel did not contest the allegations at a two-day oral hearing held in Brussels in November 1997, in which most of the producers claimed the benefit of the Commission's "Leniency Notice".

The cartel

1. The earlier phases
The investigations uncovered a highly formalised structure of collaboration beginning in late
1990 among the four Danish producers. This covered exports as well as the local market and soon extended to other markets and brought in the two German producers Henss/Isoplus and Pan-Isovit. The Managing Directors of the six producers met regularly in secret meetings, often held just after legitimate trade association meetings. (They called themselves "the Popes".)
The cartel was in its earlier days particularly well organised in Denmark where bid-rigging was the norm. There was even a "compensation system" to correct departures from quota if a producer which was not the named "favourite" won the bid. (According to one producer, such compensation was at one time paid in cash and disguised in the company accounts.)

2. Later stages
The cartel was reformed in mid-1994 to cover the whole of the EU, as well as the non-EU Baltic States and several Eastern European markets. A uniform scheme was devised with quotas not only on an overall European level but also for each national market. On the European level, the quotas fixed in November 1994 were:ABB 37%, Løgstør 20%, Tarco 10%, Pan-Isovit10%, Isoplus 10%, Starpipe 6% and others 7%. Later Brugg was given 2% and KWH 4%. A so-called "EU price list" was devised as a model to be used to bring prices up by 30%-35% over two years.
If any producer undercut the allocated "favourite", it would be called to account and pressurized to withdraw its bid or increase the price to let the favourite win: Henss/Isoplus was particularly prominent as the "enforcer" of the cartel in Germany.

3. Actions against Powerpipe
Powerpipe had been the object of concerted actions by the cartel since 1992 but these intensified when it entered the German market and won a contract (Neubrandenburg). Powerpipe was offered a place in the cartel provided it withdraw its offer and when it refused it was again subjected to threats to get out of the market or risk a price war.
After Powerpipe outbid the cartel and won the Leipzig-Lippendorf project in March 1995 the reaction of the cartel was immediate: the German Contact Group met in Düsseldorf on 24 March and decided on a collective boycott. Tarco's note of the meeting records:
"Powerpipe has been awarded the Leipzig-Lippendorf contract. No producer to supply at all to L-L, IKR, Mannesmann-Seiffert, VEAG;*... None of our sub-contractors may work for Powerpipe; if they do, further co-operation will be stopped; We shall try to prevent Powerpipe from obtaining supplies of for example) plastic."
* [NOTE: these were the contractors for the L-L project.]

4. Continuation of the cartel after the investigations
Only a few days after the Commission's investigations in late June 1995 the Managing Directors met and decided to continue,

but with extra security measures to conceal the cartel: e.g. their meetings were all to be held outside the EU, mainly in Zurich (which is where ABB's Headquarters are located); the Danish participants would travel not by scheduled airline but in Løgstør's private airplane.
As late as October 1995 ABB faxed KWH with tables showing the adjusted market quotas of each producer for 1995. The following revealing annotation is made: "Pekka: to be destroyed completely... EU case looks bad. Be careful for Christ's sake." Even as the companies were realizing that the "game was up" and some approached the Commission, meetings were still held to discuss how the cartel could continue "by other means".
After signalling their wish to co-operate, several companies (Løgstør, Tarco, KWH) provided cartel documents to the Commission which had escaped the surprise investigations in June 1995. ABB having also expressed its wish to co-operate supplied a full historical account of the cartel's activities to the Commission. The fine imposed on ABB reflects the fact that the violation represented corporate policy at the highest level; one of its most senior officers in Zurich master-minded and directed the cartel.

Case cross-reference:

▸ Joined Cases C-189/02 P, 202/02 P, 205/02 P to 208/02 P and 213/02 P [2005] I-5425. Ruling of the GC upheld.

3) *The Vitamin Cartel*, Comm. Press Release (IP/01/1625), full decision published in [2003] OJ L 6/1

Relevance: example of fines imposed by the Commission. Leniency for one player.

IP/01/1625, Brussels, 21 November 2001

Commission imposes fines on vitamin cartels

The European Commission today fined eight companies a total of € 855.22 million for participating in eight distinct secret market-sharing and price-fixing cartels affecting vitamin products. Each cartel had a specific number of participants and duration, although all operated between September 1989 and February 1999. Because Swiss-based company Hoffman-La Roche was an instigator and participated in all the cartels it was given the highest cumulative fine of € 462 million. "This is the most damaging series of cartels the Commission has ever investigated due to the sheer range of vitamins covered which are found in a multitude of products from cereals, biscuits and drinks to animal feed, pharmaceuticals and cosmetics" said Competition Commissioner Mario Monti. "The companies' collusive behaviour enabled them to charge higher prices than if the full forces of competition had been at play, damaging consumers and allowing the companies to pocket illicit profits. It is particularly unacceptable that this illegal behaviour concerned substances which are vital elements for nutrition and essential for normal growth and maintenance of life".

Following the opening of an investigation in May 1999, the European Commission has found that 13 European and non-European companies participated in cartels aimed at eliminating competition in the vitamin A, E, B1, B2, B5, B6, C, D3, Biotin (H), Folic Acid

(M), Beta Carotene and carotinoids markets. A striking feature of this complex of infringements was the central role played by Hoffmann-La Roche and BASF, the two main vitamin producers, in virtually each and every cartel, whilst other players were involved in only a limited number of vitamin products. Fines were imposed on the following eight companies as follows:

F. Hoffmann-La Roche AG (Switzerland) : € 462 million
BASF AG (Germany) : € 296.16 million
Aventis SA (France) : € 5.04 million
Solvay Pharmaceuticals BV (Netherlands) : € 9.10 million
Merck KgaA (Germany) : € 9.24 million
Daiichi Pharmaceutical Co Ltd (Japan) : € 23.4 million
Eisai Co Ltd (Japan) : € 13.23 million
Takeda Chemical Industries Ltd (Japan) : € 37.05 million

The five remaining companies, Lonza AG (Germany), Kongo Chemical Co Ltd (Japan), Sumitomo Chemical Co Ltd (Japan), Sumika Fine Chemicals Ltd (Japan) and Tanabe Saiyaku Co Ltd (Japan) were not fined because the cartels in which they were involved Vitamin H or Folic Acid -- ended five years or more before the Commission opened its investigation. Under EU law, prescription applies under these circumstances. Prescription also applied to cartels in vitamins B1 and B6.

The Cartels

The participants in each of the cartels fixed prices for the different vitamin products, allocated sales quotas, agreed on and implemented price increases and issued price announcements in accordance with their agreements. They also set up a machinery to monitor and enforce their agreements and participated in regular meetings to implement their plans.

The modus operandi of the different cartels was essentially the same if not identical ("target" and "minimum" prices; maintenance of the status quo in market shares and compensation arrangements), in particular it included:

the establishment of formal structure and hierarchy of different levels of management, often with overlapping membership at the most senior levels to ensure the functioning of the cartels;

the exchange of sales values, volumes of sales and pricing information on a quarterly or monthly basis at regular meetings;

in the case of the largest cartels, the preparation, agreement and implementation and monitoring of an annual "budget" followed by the adjustment of actual sales achieved so as to comply with the quotas allocated;

The cartel arrangements generally followed this scheme, pioneered in vitamins A and E, with certain variants in other products. Hoffmann-La Roche acted as the agent and representative of the European producers in the meetings and negotiations held in Japan and the Far East.

The simultaneous existence of the collusive arrangements in the various vitamins was not a spontaneous or haphazard development, but was conceived and directed by the same persons at the most senior levels of the undertakings concerned.

The Players

The prime mover and main beneficiary of these schemes was Hoffmann-La Roche, the largest vitamin producer in the world, with some 50% of the overall market. The cartel arrangements covered its full range of vitamin products. The involvement of some of its most senior executives tends to confirm that the arrangements were part of a strategic plan conceived at the highest levels to control the world market in vitamins by illegal means.

BASF, the next largest vitamin producer worldwide, assumed a paramount role in following Hoffmann-La Roche's lead. Both major European producers effectively formed a common front in conceiving and implementing the arrangements with the Japanese producers concerned. Together, for example, they recruited Eisai to their "Club" in vitamin E.

Takeda, as one of the main world producers of bulk vitamins, was fully involved in the cartel arrangements for vitamins B1, B2, B6, C and Folic Acid. Takeda's involvement in the arrangements in each of these vitamin products was instrumental to Hoffmann-La Roche's designs to secure the illegal coordination of the vitamin markets it was active in, including those in the range of vitamin products it shared with Takeda.

The other vitamin producers were all active members of the cartel arrangements in the respective vitamin product markets in which they operated.

The Products

The cartels concerned bulk synthetic substances which belong to the following groups of vitamins and closely related products: A, E, B1, B2, B5, B6, C, D3, Biotin (H), Folic Acid (M), Beta Carotene and carotinoids.

Vitamins are vital elements for human and animal nutrition. They are essential for normal growth, development and maintenance of life. There are some 15 major vitamins, each has specific metabolic functions and is therefore not interchangeable with the others. In addition, the various group of vitamins when combined have a complementary synergistic effect.

Vitamins are added to both compound animal feeds and human food products. Vitamins for pharmaceutical purposes are marketed to the public as diet supplements in tablet or capsule form. In the cosmetics industry, vitamins are added to skin- and health-care products.

The Commission estimates that the European Economic Area (EEA) market for the products covered in the decision was worth around € 800 million 1998. This includes vitamin E, which in 1998 was worth approximately € 250 million in the EEA and vitamin A, which represented some € 150 million. Strikingly, European revenues in vitamin C slumped from € 250 million in the last year the cartel arrangements were in place (1995) to less than half, € 120 million, three years later (1998).

Destination of the fines

Fines imposed by the Commission as a result of infringements of EU competition law are accounted into the general budget of the European Union once they have become definitive. The overall EU budget is predefined and therefore any unscheduled revenues is be deducted from the contributions made by Member States to the EU budget, ultimately to the benefit of the European tax payer.

Calculation of the fines

Given the continuity and similarity of method, the Commission has considered it appropriate to treat in one and the same procedure the complex of agreements covering the different vitamins. The Commission therefore covers several infringements in a single decision.

When setting fines, the Commission takes into account the gravity of the infringement, its duration, any aggravating or mitigating circumstances as well as the cooperation of a company. It also takes account of a company's market share in the product market concerned and its overall size. The upper limit of any fine is established at 10% of a company's total annual turnover. Companies have three months in which to pay any fine imposed.

The Commission considers that each cartel in this case represents a very serious infringement of EU competition law. Furthermore, most of the cartel participants committed infringements of long duration, i.e. more than five years (see table below).

The Commission considers that Hoffmann-La Roche and BASF were joint leaders and instigators of the collusive arrangements affecting the common range of vitamin products they produced and therefore their role in the different cartels is an aggravating factor. The combination of the market power that the leading participants held in each of the individual vitamin markets increased their overall ability to implement and maintain the anti-competitive agreements.

Aventis (formerly Rhône-Poulenc) was granted full immunity in regard to its participation in the cartels in vitamins A and E because it was the first company to co-operate with the Commission and provided decisive evidence in the case of these two products. This is the first time that the Commission has granted a 100% reduction of a fine under the terms of the Leniency Notice. A fine was, however, imposed on Aventis for its passive participation in the vitamin D3 infringement, on which it provided no information to the Commission.

"The fact that the Commission has granted, for the first time, a total exemption of fines to a company illustrates its willingness to grant companies that actively co-operate at the earliest stage a unique opportunity to get off the hook. Those companies that do not seize this chance must be aware of the responsibilities they will face", Mr Monti said.

Both Hoffmann La Roche and BASF also co-operated with the Commission at an early stage of the investigation providing crucial information on all of the vitamins cartels they have been involved in. The Commission granted a 50 percent reduction of the fines to each company.

All other companies on which fines have been imposed have co-operated with the Commission during the course of its investigation and their corresponding fines have been reduced in accordance with the level of their co-operation.

In 1999 the main players of the cartels covered in the Commission's decision pleaded guilty to similar anti-competitive conduct in the US and paid heavy fines, including $500 million for Hoffmann La Roche, $225 million for BASF and $72 million for Takeda.

[.....]

Case cross-references:

▸ Joined Cases 40-48, 50, 54-56, 111 & 113-114/73 *European Sugar Industry* [1975] ECR 1663 (see I-G-3).

▸ *Meldoc* Commission decision 86/596/EEC [1986] OJ L 348/50 (see V-B-1).

D. Leniency/mitigating circumstances

Cross-reference for this part:

▸ Notice on immunity from fines and reduction of fines in cartel cases, [2006] OJ C 298/17 (the 'Leniency' Notice).

▸ D. Jarret Arp and C.R.A. Swaak, 'Tempting offer: Immunity from Fines for Cartel Conduct under the European Commission's New Leniency Notice', (2003) 24 *ECLR*, 9.

1) *Citric Acid*, Comm. Press Release (IP/01/1743), full decision published in [2002] OJ L 239/18

Relevance: application Leniency Notice.

IP/01/1743, Brussels, 05 December 2001

Commission fines five companies in citric acid cartel

The European Commission today fined Hoffmann-La Roche AG, Archer Daniels Midland Co (ADM), Jungbunzlauer AG, Haarmann & Reimer Corp and Cerestar Bioproducts B.V. a total of € 135.22 million for participating in a price-fixing and market-sharing cartel in citric acid, the world's most widespread acidulent and preservative used mainly in non-alcoholic beverages and in preserved food such as jams, gelatine-based deserts and tinned fruit. "As with the vitamins case, the behaviour of ADM, Hoffmann-La Roche and others shows a disregard for their customers and, ultimately, the consumers which paid more for the products concerned than if the companies had engaged in healthy price competition," said Competition Commissioner Mario Monti. "The fact that some of the companies have only recently been sanctioned for similar conduct, ADM and Jungbunzlauer in the Sodium Gluconate case; Roche in the Vitamins case, illustrates how widespread these secret practices are, or at least used to be. I am confident that the message is now being clearly received. Companies must by now be fully aware of the risks they are taking should they be tempted to collude."

After a careful investigation which started in 1997, the European Commission has found that US companies Archer Daniels Midland (ADM) and Haarmann & Reimer (H&R), the latter ultimately owned by Bayer AG, Dutch company Cerestar Bioproducts B.V., Hoffmann-La Roche and Jungbunzlauer (JBL), both Swiss, participated in a worldwide cartel between 1991 and 1995, through which they fixed the price and shared out the market for citric acid.

Citric acid is one of the most widely used additives in the food and beverage industry both as an acidulent and preservative. It is found in non-alcoholic beverages as well as in jams, gelatine-based deserts and tinned vegetables and fruit. Citric acid is also used in household detergent products especially as a substitute for phosphates considered harmful for the environment. Citric acid also enters in the composition of dissolving tablets in the pharmaceuticals industry and is used in the cosmetics industry.

During the infringement period, the annual market was worth around €320 million in the European Economic Area the 15 EU member states plus Norway, Iceland and Liechtenstein.

The cartel started on 6 March 1991 at the Hotel Plaza in Basle (Switzerland), as stated by the companies in documents submitted to the Commission. There, and following on previous informal contacts, the founding members ADM, H&R, Roche and JBL agreed on the main features of their plan to eliminate competition between them. Cerestar joined the group in May 1992, shortly after it entered the citric acid market. The cartel continued until May 1995 and pursued four main objectives:
Allocation of specific sales quotas for each member and adherence to these quotas;
Fixing 'target' and 'floor prices' for citric acid;
Exchanging specific customer information, and
Eliminating price discounts.
A limited exception was made to the last objective in relation to the five major consumers of citric acid world-wide, since it was considered unrealistic by the cartel members to expect them to pay the price published on the public price lists. It was, however, agreed that a discount of no more than 3% would be offered to these larger consumers.
The companies held regular and frequent meetings, which were the hallmark of the cartel's organisation. After 1993 and in order to resolve certain grievances and market "difficulties" additional, more technically oriented, meetings were organised that become known as 'Sherpa' meetings in contrast to the more high-level and strategic 'Masters' meetings.
A sophisticated monitoring system was established, whereby each company would report its monthly sales figures to a previously agreed member, who would then ensure the distribution of the confidential information to all the others. In order to ensure that each player would stick to the quotas assigned, a compensation scheme was created, obliging any member that over-sold its allocated quota to provide compensation to the others.
A further striking feature of the cartel was the concerted action taken by the companies against Chinese manufacturers, who had increased their exports to the European market as a result of the significant rise in prices for citric acid during the time the cartel operated. The cartel participants tried to regain some of the customers lost to the Chinese suppliers through a concerted and carefully targeted price war. The list of the clients lost and targeted by the cartel for "recovery" came to be known as the 'Serbia List' and was regularly monitored during the 'Sherpa' meetings.
The companies' conduct was a very serious infringement of the competition rules, as set out in Article 81 of the European Union Treaty and Article 53 of the EEA-Agreement.
The following is a list of the individual fines (in million Euro):
F. Hoffmann-La Roche AG: 63.5
Archer Daniels Midland Company Inc: 39.69
Jungbunzlauer AG (JBL): 17.64
Haarmann & Reimer Corp.: 14.22
Cerestar Bioproducts B.V.: 0.17
Competition Commissioner Mario Monti again said: "This Decision sets out and punishes inadmissible and illegal behaviour by apparent competitors to raise prices and deceive consumers in a product essential for the food industry and illustrates how a few companies can be determined in their attempt to bypass competition, an essential pillar of a market economy."

Background

The Commission started to investigate the case in 1997, when it became aware that some of the addressees of the present decision had been charged by the US authorities with participating in an international conspiracy. The parties to the cartel pleaded guilty and paid fines in the US and/or in Canada.

Calculation of the fines

To calculate fines in cartel behaviour the Commission takes account of the gravity of the infringement, its duration and the existence of any aggravating or mitigating circumstances. It also takes account of a companies' share of the market concerned and its overall size to ensure that the punishment is proportional and has a deterrence effect. The calculation of the fines is, therefore, not made solely with reference to a company's turnover, although the fine can never go beyond 10 percent of a company's total annual turnover, as set out in Regulation 17/62.

The citric acid cartel was a very serious violation of EU competition law, but was of a medium duration (between one and five years).

Because they acted as co-leaders of the cartel, an aggravating factor, the basic fines on ADM and Roche were increased by 35 percent. This figure is below the level applied for a leadership role in previous cartel cases, which is usually 50%, but takes account of the fact that, whilst these two companies clearly had an outstanding role in the infringement, other members of the cartel also carried out activities usually associated with a leadership role (like chairing meetings or centralising data distribution).

Application of the Leniency notice

Part of the evidence on the cartel was provided to the Commission by the companies involved, under EU rules providing for full or partial immunity from fines for companies that co-operate with the Commission in cartel cases. See Leniency Notice on http://europa.eu.int/comm/competition/antitrust/legislation/96c207_en.html.

Cerestar Bioproducts was the first undertaking to provide the Commission with decisive information. But because its application for Leniency was not entirely spontaneous, and since it approached the Commission only after it was fully aware that the citric acid cartel was object of an on-going investigation by the Commission, it was granted a 90 percent reduction of the fine rather than full immunity.

All the other participants co-operated in one way or another with the Commission and were granted appropriate reductions.

ADM provided detailed information, which together with that obtained from Cerestar Bioproducts was used to draft requests for information that largely contributed to trigger the admission by H&R, Roche and JBL of their participation in the citric acid cartel. ADM was able to provide the Commission with documents contemporaneous to the infringement, including inter alia hand-written notes taken during cartel meetings and price instructions related to the decisions taken by the cartel. On these grounds, ADM was granted a 50 percent reduction.

JBL and H&R confirmed the vast majority of the meetings, the identity of the participants, as well as the facts in question. JBL also submitted to the Commission a number of tables created contemporaneously to the time of the infringement, indicating the quotas that were allocated to each of the cartel participants. Nevertheless, a large part of the information submitted by both companies was provided in reply to detailed requests for information and therefore fell within the ambit of an undertaking's duty to fully reply to these requests as set out in Article 11 of Regulation 17. The Commission granted these two companies a reduction of 40% and 30 percent of their respective fines.

Roche confirmed its participation in the cartel and the purpose of the meetings related to it prior to the receipt of the Commission's Statement of Objections, which was sent on March 28, 2000. The Commission therefore granted Hoffmann-La Roche a 20 percent reduction of its fine.

[.....]

Case cross-reference:

▸ The Vitamin Cartel, Press Release (IP/01/1625), full decision published in [2003] OJ L 6/1 (see V-C-3).

2) Case T-224/00 *Archer Daniels Midland* [2003] ECR II-2597

The US-based Archer Daniels Midland Company (ADM Company) and its European subsidiary, Archer Daniels Midland Ingredients (ADM Ingredients), had been fined 47,300,000 euro for their participation in a cartel that had fixed the prices of lysine, an additive used in animal feedstuffs. The fine itself was calculated on the basis of the Commission's Guidelines on the method of setting fines and the Leniency Notice. ADM appealed this decision, claiming inter alia that the CFI should reduce the fine since there were mitigating circumstances.

Relevance: mitigating circumstances can vary from case to case; adoption of a so-called compliance programme does not automatically lead to a reduction of the fine.

[.....]

VI - Mitigating circumstances
Arguments of the parties

[......]

2. ADM's adoption of a code of conduct
257 The applicants contend that, when calculating the fine, the Commission ought to have taken account of the fact that ADM had set up a rigorous and ongoing programme for compliance with the competition rules incorporating, in particular, the adoption of a code of conduct addressed to all company employees and the establishment of a special department.

[.....]

Findings of the Court

[.....]

2. ADM's adoption of a code of conduct
280 It should be borne in mind that, whilst it is important that an undertaking should take steps to prevent fresh infringements of Community competition law from being committed in the future by members of its staff, that does not alter the fact that an infringement has been committed. Thus, the mere fact that in certain of its previous decisions the Commission took the implementation of a compliance programme into consideration as a mitigating factor does not mean that it is obliged to act in the same manner in any given case (Case T-7/89 Hercules Chemicals v Commission, cited above, paragraph 357, and Mo och Domsjö v Commission, cited above, paragraphs 417 and 419), especially where the infringement in question is, as in the present case, a clear infringement of Article 81(1)(a) and (b) EC.

281 The Commission is therefore not required to take a circumstance such as that into account as a mitigating factor, provided that it adheres to the principle of equality of treatment, which requires that it should not assess the matter differently for any undertaking addressed by the same decision. That, however, was not the case here.

[.....]

3) Joined Cases T-236/01, T-239/01, T-244/01 to T-246/01, T-251/01 and T-252/01 *Graphite electrodes cartel* [2004] ECR II-1181

See above for facts of the case (I-D-4-p. 21).

Relevance: Admitting to cartel responsibility (self-incrimination) where the right to remain silent prevailed is a factor of relevance for the application of Leniency, also in case such admission was not made voluntarily.

[.....]

401 Next, the essential reason why the Commission granted SGL a reduction of only 30% is set out in recital 174 of the Decision: according to the Commission, an undertaking deserves a reduction in its fine only if its cooperation is 'voluntary' and is outside the exercise of 'any investigatory power': the Commission considered that 'a substantial part of the information provided [by SGL] in fact constitute[d] SGL's reply to the Commission's formal request for information [and that] SGL's statement [would] be regarded as a voluntary contribution within the meaning of the Leniency Notice only where the information provided went beyond that requested under Article 11'. Furthermore, SGL sent its statement of 8 June 1999 only after it had received a reminder in which the Commission reserved the right to adopt a formal decision under Article 11(5) (recital 173 of the Decision). Relying on the judgment of the Court of Justice in Case 374/87 Orkem v Commission [1989] ECR 3283, paragraphs 27, 28 and 32 to 35, the Commission therefore did not make recompense for the information which it considered that SGL was required to provide in any event in reply to a request for information or to a decision ordering, under threat of penalties, communication of the information requested.
402 In that context, it is appropriate to observe that the absolute right to silence on which SGL relies in support of its contention that it was not required to respond to any request for information, cannot be recognised. To acknowledge the existence of such a right would be to go beyond what is necessary in order to preserve the rights of defence of undertakings, and would constitute an unjustified hindrance to the Commission's performance of its duty to ensure that the rules on competition within the common market are observed. A right to silence can be recognised only to the extent that the undertaking concerned would be compelled to provide answers which might involve an admission on its part of the existence of an infringement which it is incumbent upon the Commission to prove (Case T 112/98 Mannesmannröhren-Werke v Commission [2001] ECR II-729, paragraphs 66 and 67).
403 In order to ensure the effectiveness of Article 11 of Regulation No 17, the Commission is therefore entitled to compel the under-

takings to provide all necessary information concerning such facts as may be known to them and to disclose to the Commission, if necessary, such documents relating thereto as are in their possession, even if the latter may be used to establish the existence of anti-competitive conduct (see Mannesmannröhren-Werke v Commission, cited at paragraph 402 above, paragraph 65, and the case-law cited there).

404 This power of the Commission to obtain information, enshrined in Orkem v Commission and Mannesmannröhren-Werke v Commission, cited at paragraphs 401 and 402 above respectively, does not fall foul of either Article 6(1) and (2) of the ECHR (Mannesmannröhren-Werke v Commission, cited above, paragraph 75) or the case-law of the European Court of Human Rights.

[.....]

406 In any event, the mere fact of being obliged to answer purely factual questions put by the Commission and to comply with its requests for the production of documents already in existence cannot constitute a breach of the principle of respect for the rights of defence or impair the right to fair legal process, which offer, in the specific field of competition law, protection equivalent to that guaranteed by Article 6 of the Convention. There is nothing to prevent the addressee of a request for information from showing, whether later during the administrative procedure or in proceedings before the Community Courts, when exercising his rights of defence, that the facts set out in his replies or the documents produced by him have a different meaning from that ascribed to them by the Commission (Mannesmannröhren-Werke v Commission, cited at paragraph 402 above, paragraphs 77 and 78).

407 As regards, next, the extent to which SGL was required to reply, in accordance with the case-law referred to above, to the request for information of 31 March 1999, it must be observed that, in addition to the purely factual questions and the requests to produce documents already in existence, the Commission requested SGL to describe the object of and what occurred at a number of meetings in which SGL participated and also the results/conclusions of those meetings, when it was clear that the Commission suspected that the object of the meetings was to restrict competition. It follows that a request of that nature was of such a kind as to require SGL to admit its participation in an infringement of the Community competition rules.

408 The same applies to the requests for the protocols of those meetings, the working documents and the preparatory documents concerning them, the handwritten notes relating to them, the notes and the conclusions pertaining to the meetings, the planning and discussion documents and also the implementing projects concerning the price increases put into effect between 1992 and 1998.

409 As SGL was not required to answer questions of that type in the request for information of 31 March 1999, the fact that it none the less provided information on those points must be regarded as voluntary collaboration on the part of the undertaking apt to justify a reduction in the fine under the Leniency Notice.

410 That conclusion cannot be affected by the Commission's argument that the information in question was not provided voluntarily but in reply to a request for information. point D, paragraph 2, first indent, of the Leniency Notice does not require a voluntary act taken solely on the initiative of the undertaking concerned, but merely requires information which contributes to establishing the existence of the infringement. Even point C, moreover, which relates to a more substantial reduction in the fine than that referred to

in point D, makes it possible to reward cooperation provided 'after the Commission has undertaken an investigation ordered by decision on the premises of the parties to the cartel'. Accordingly, the fact that a request for information was sent to SGL under Article 11(1) of Regulation No 17 cannot minimise the cooperation provided by that undertaking under point D, paragraph 2, first indent, of the Leniency Notice, especially not as a request for information is a less coercive measure than an investigation ordered by decision.

Case cross-reference:

▸ Case T-112/98 *Mannesmannröhren-Werke v. Commission* [2001] ECR II-729 (see IX-B-2).

[.....]

4) Case C-328/05 P *SGL Carbon AG v. Commission* [2007] ECR I-3921

In this case, SGL Carbon AG seeks to set aside the parts of the judgment of the GC whereby the GC dismissed its action against Commission Decision. The SGL Carbon unsuccessfully claims a reduction of fine and interests. SGL Carbon alleged that the fine was disproportionate, that the interest rates fixed by the Commission were illegal and the Commission failed to take SGL Carbon's cooperation with the Commission into account.

Relevance: the Commission's discretion in calculating the fines, the power of the Commission to fix interest rates higher than the applicable market rate offered to the average borrower

[.....]

81 As observed at paragraph 43 of this judgment, the Commission has a wide discretion as regards the method of calculating fines and it may, in that regard, take account of numerous factors, including the cooperation provided by the undertakings concerned during the investigation conducted by its departments. In that context, the Commission is required to make complex assessments of fact, such as those relating to the cooperation provided by the individual undertakings concerned.

82 As regards the present case, it must be observed that, at paragraphs 358 to 362 of the judgment under appeal, the Court of First Instance based its assessments in that regard, in reliance on the Leniency Notice, on the consideration that a single undertaking, namely the first one to provide evidence concerning the existence of a cartel, may receive a substantial reduction in the fine, to the exclusion of other undertakings which, at a subsequent stage in the administrative procedure, produce particular evidence relating to the same cartel.

83 With respect to the cooperation which an undertaking provides to the Commission, it is settled case-law that such a contribution may justify a reduction in the fine under the Leniency Notice only if it actually allows the Commission to achieve its task of establishing the existence of an infringement and putting an end to it (see, to that effect, Case C-297/98 P *SCA Holding* v *Commission* [2000] ECR I-10101, paragraph 36, and *Dansk*

Rørindustri and Others v. *Commission*, paragraph 399).

[...]

87 As regards SGL Carbon's argument concerning the taking into consideration of its cooperation with the Commission, independently of the fact that the appellant was characterised as ringleader of the cartel, it must be noted that the Court of First Instance was correct to hold, at paragraph 368 of the judgment under appeal, that the Commission was not required to reward such cooperation by a substantial reduction in the fine, since that cooperation had not effectively facilitated the establishment of the existence of that cartel and enabled the Commission to put an end to it.
88 As regards, finally, SGL Carbon's claim that the cooperation provided by it was undervalued by comparison with that of the other members of the cartel, it should be noted, as the Court of First Instance rightly pointed out at paragraph 371 of the judgment under appeal, that the Commission enjoys a wide discretion in assessing the quality and usefulness of the cooperation provided by an undertaking, in particular by reference to the contributions made by other undertakings

[...]

100 As regards the argument that the Court of First Instance failed to take account of SGL Carbon's financial capacity, it must be observed that, according to settled case-law which rightly provides inspiration for paragraph 333 of the judgment under appeal, the Commission is not required, when determining the amount of the fine, to take into account the financial situation of an undertaking, since recognition of such an obligation would be tantamount to giving unjustified competitive advantages to undertakings least well adapted to the market conditions (see Joined Cases 96/82 to 102/82, 104/82, 105/82, 108/82 and 110/82 *IAZ International Belgium and Others* v *Commission* [1983] ECR 3369, paragraphs 54 and 55, and *SGL Carbon* v *Commission*, paragraphs 105 and 106).

[...]

109 It must be borne in mind that the Court of First Instance, in response to the plea raised before it, referred at paragraph 411 of the judgment under appeal to the consistent case-law according to which the Commission's powers under Article 15(2) of Regulation No 17 include the power to set the date by which the fines are payable and on which interest begins to accrue, and also the rate of that interest and the detailed arrangements for implementing its decision.
110 If the Commission did not have such a power, undertakings might be able to take advantage of late payments, thereby weakening the effect of penalties (*SGL Carbon* v *Commission*, paragraph 114).
111 Accordingly, the Court of First Instance was right to hold that the Commission was entitled to adopt a point of reference higher than the applicable market rate offered to the average borrower, to an extent necessary to discourage dilatory behaviour in relation to payment of the fine (*SGL Carbon* v *Commission*, paragraph 115).

[.....]

E. Exchange of market data

Cross-reference for this part:

▸ Case C-238/05 *Asnef-Equifax v. Ausbanc* [2006] ECR I-11125 (*see I-P-3*).

1) *UK Tractors* Commission decision 92/157/EEC [1992] OJ L 68/19

Eight members of the Agricultural Engineers Association (AEA), a private undertaking, had concluded an information exchange agreement (referred to as the Exchange in the decision). The undertakings concerned were either importers or manufactures (or both) of agricultural tractors. The exchanged information specified the volume of retail sales and market shares of the parties to the agreement. The AEA administered the Exchange, assisted by the computer bureau SIL (Systematic International Group of Companies).

Relevance: a private undertaking may, under certain rather strict conditions, organise an exchange of statistical data with its competitors.

[.....]

II. LEGAL ASSESSMENT

[.....]

Data identifying sales of individual competitors

(35) For the assessment of that part of the Exchange which identifies the sales of the individual members, the Commission takes account of:
- the market structure, i.e.:
1) high concentration: four firms with approximately 80 % of the market, seven firms with 87 to 88 % of the market, a still higher degree of concentration for smaller geographic areas or product breakdowns, the members are also major suppliers in the other Community markets, and the gap and dispersion of the market shares of the non-members who together hold only about 12 % of the market,
2) high barriers to entry: the need for an extensive distribution and service network, the low volume and stagnant / declining market, the advantage of brand loyalty for established suppliers and the effects of the information Exchange, and
3) the absence of significant imports from outside the Community for agricultural tractors above 30 hp;
- the nature of the information exchanged: i.e. the exact quantities of the retail sales and the exact market shares which are trade secrets between genuine competitors in a highly concentrated market,
- the detail of the information exchanged: i.e. detailed product breakdowns, small geographic breakdowns and time periods below one year, i.e. daily, monthly and quarterly market sensitive information on competitors, and,
- the fact that the members meet regularly within the AEA Committee which gives them a forum for contacts.

(36) The Exchange leads to restrictions of competition for two reasons:

(a) Prevention of hidden competition in a highly concentrated market

(37) The Exchange restricts competition because it creates a degree of market trans-

parency between the suppliers in a highly concentrated market which is likely to destroy what hidden competition there remains between the suppliers in that market on account of the risk and ease of exposure of independent competitive action. In this highly concentrated market, 'hidden competition' is essentially that element of uncertainty and secrecy between the main suppliers regarding market conditions without which none of them has the necessary scope of action to compete efficiently.
Uncertainly and secrecy between suppliers is a vital element of competition in this kind of market. Indeed active competition in these market conditions becomes possible only if each competitor can keep its actions secret or even succeeds in misleading its rivals.
This reasoning, however, in no way undermines the positive competitive benefits of transparency in a competitive market characterized by many buyers and sellers. Where there is a low degree of concentration, market transparency can increase competition in so far as consumers benefit from choices made in full knowledge of what is on offer. It is emphasized that the United Kingdom tractor market is neither a low concentration market nor is the transparency in question in any way directed towards, or of benefit to, consumers.
On the contrary, the high market transparency between suppliers on the United Kingdom tractor market which is created by the Exchange takes the surprise effect out of a competitor's action thus resulting in a shorter space of time for reactions with the effect that temporary advantages are greatly reduced. Because all competitive actions can immediately be noticed by an increase in sales, the consequences are that in the case of a price reduction or any other marketing incentives by one company the other can react immediately, thus eliminating any advantage of the initiator. This effect of neutralizing and thus stabilizing the market positions of the oligopolists is in this case likely to occur because there are no external competitive pressures on the members of the Exchange except parallel imports which are however also monitored as has been explained above.

(38) The United Kingdom tractor market is clearly a highly concentrated market where competition is already weakened by the fact that:
- four firms dominate the market with a combined market share of approximately 80 %,
- these four firms have created an information exchange with four, now three, other well-known suppliers capable of challenging their market position with the effect that the conditions of a narrow oligopoly have been artificially created between the eight, now seven, best established competitors on this market by giving them information on any change in volumes and market shares at manufacturer and dealer level,
- these eight, now seven, suppliers are active in all other Community markets and know the pattern of trade and products supplied on the United Kingdom market for a long period of time; in particular, there is no difficulty knowing the prices charged by each member because in this industry there are list prices and a simple telephone enquiry will readily reveal the general level of discounts applied by each manufacturer's dealer network; this information is also available from customers who inform the dealers of competitors' prices in a given territory,
- the market is protected from competition from outside the United Kingdom by the fact that there are high barriers to entry and that there are only insignificant imports from outside the Community.

(39) In addition, demand is very dispersed. There are numerous buyers, the majority of whom do not have the possibility of purchas-

ing tractors in other Member States (transport difficulties, import formalities, registration, service, trade-ins, etc.). Thus, demand transferability in this market is very low which weakens the competitive pressure from the demand side on the limited number of suppliers established within the United Kingdom and therefore reinforces their economic strength on that market.

(40) On the United Kingdom tractor market, therefore, the only difficult, but very important, market data to obtain is the exact volume of sales of each manufacturer / dealer so as to be able to notice instantly changes in sales volumes and market shares of each member of the oligopoly and of each dealer at the level of dealer territories. This market knowledge allows each member and dealer to react immediately and thus to neutralize whatever initiative any one of the members / dealers of the oligopoly would take to increase its sales (see recital (37)). However, the result in practice is that few such initiatives will be taken precisely because every supplier knows very well that the position of each of the others is and that, thanks to the transparency created by the system, any initiative on his part can be detected at once by the others.

(41) The very detailed product and geographic market information on retail sales (see recitals (17) to (23)) gives each manufacturer and dealer fully reliable market knowledge (100 % coverage and 100 % accuracy) which is accessible on an instant or very short time basis (daily, monthly or quarterly). It allows them:

- to establish with accuracy the market positions and performances of their rivals and to follow constantly any changes of these market positions,
- to see at once whether there has been any increase in the retail sales of a rival, to see the territory in which such an increase takes place, to detect the models which contribute such an increase and finally to follow whether and to what extent any price or other marketing strategies of rivals are successful,
- to limit price competition as far as possible by allowing suppliers and dealers to react to any price-cutting or other market strategies selectively by limiting their response to the absolute minimum degree necessary in terms of product and territory and by being sure to hit the right target,
- to react more quickly if the market positions start changing.

(42) The Exchange further helps the established firms and dealers with considerable market shares (i.e. the four biggest firms holding approximately 80 % of the United Kingdom market) to defend their market positions more efficiently than they could do without the detailed information on retail sales of their rivals and any changes thereof. By their wider market coverage and sales volume, these firms and dealers already have the advantage of better market knowledge which is further strengthened by the fact that they can react more effectively to any increase in sales by the smaller competitors on the market. This is confirmed by the fact that, during their participation in the Exchange, the main four suppliers have essentially maintained their combined market share vis-à-vis the other members of the Exchange on the United Kingdom market.

(43) In the absence of the Exchange, firms would have to compete in a market with some measure of uncertainty as to the exact place, degree and means of attack by rivals. This uncertainty is a normal competitive risk bringing about stronger competition because reaction and reduction of prices cannot be limited to the absolute minimum degree necessary to defend an established position. Uncertainty would lead the firms to compete more strongly than if they knew exactly how much of a response was necessary to meet competition. They would have to exceed a

minimum response, for instance by offering more favourable discounts to move their stock or by offering discounts for more products and in more territories. The Exchange reduces uncertainty by revealing the actions and reactions of all participating competitors who represent 87 to 88 % of the United Kingdom market. There is thus a prevention of hidden competition which results necessarily from the Exchange.

(b) Increase of barriers to entry for non-members

(44) The Exchange not only lessens competition between members of the Exchange and between their dealers, it also restricts competition between members and non members of the Exchange even if the Exchange in principle admits any manufacturer or importer to the information Exchange.
(45) If a supplier chooses not to become a member of the Exchange, he is disadvantaged by the fact that he does not have available the detailed and accurate market information about other suppliers which is available to members of the Exchange. Detailed knowledge of the sales pattern for tractors on the United Kingdom market improves the members' ability to defend their positions vis-à-vis non-members.
(46) If a supplier chooses to become a member of the Exchange, he must reveal his exact retail sales by product and by every small geographic territory with the result that the Exchange then permits the established suppliers with considerable market shares and extensive dealer networks to become aware of the existence of new entry and to instantly detect the market penetration by any such new member. This market information on any new member will permit the established suppliers to defend their acquired positions by placing selective actions designed to contain the new member.
(47) As a result, for a small supplier it is neither advantageous to become a member of the Exchange nor to stay outside the Exchange. In both cases the Exchange advantages the big suppliers who already belong to it. The presence of the smaller suppliers in the Exchange shows indeed that these suppliers have not been able to contest the position of the four biggest suppliers, i.e. Ford, Case, Massey-Ferguson and John Deere, and that market expansion is only possible through acquisition - such as the recent acquisition of Ford by Fiat. The presence of the four smaller suppliers can therefore only be explained by the fact that the UK Exchange is part of a network of similar Exchanges in other Community countries and that the eight suppliers participate in various exchanges on a reciprocal basis. These other exchanges are presently under investigation.
(48) In consequence, the Exchange permits its members to effectively prevent new entry and to contain the expansion of other suppliers on the United Kingdom market who are not members of the Exchange. This constitutes a serious restriction on the development of new competition in a highly concentrated market which is already characterized by high barriers to entry with the result that the members of the Exchange can jointly maximize profits to the detriment of farmers. This restriction affects in particular the smaller suppliers from other Community countries who will not be able to penetrate the United Kingdom market if they wanted to sell or increase their sales on that market.

(c) Main arguments put forward by the parties

(49) The parties have submitted that the Exchange is based on registration data made available to the industry by the United King-

dom Department of Transport and that these data do not constitute trade secrets. This argument cannot be accepted.
First, the Exchange does not deal in mere estimates, but in wholly accurate information on the quantities sold and the market shares of each participating member and of its dealers. Such information is normally considered to be a trade secret which confers legitimate competitive advantages and is, for that reason, not to be revealed or shared with competitors (see Court of Justice, Case 236/81, Celanese Chemical Company Inc. v. Council and Commission, Case T-30/89, Hilti v. Commission, Seventh Report on Competition Policy, Chapter I, paragraph 2, points 5-8; Commission Decisions 87/1/EEC, 77/592/EEC and 79/90/EEC). Unlike prices or other trading conditions which can be found out by telephone enquiries or customer feedback, exact quantities sold and market shares are the most difficult market information to be obtained and the only accurate indicator of the trade pattern in a market and changes thereof.
Secondly, the parties have themselves described information identifying the exact quantities sold and market shares of individual competitors as sensitive and confidential which can only be shared on a mutual and reciprocal basis and with the express agreement of the firms whose figures are being revealed (see recital (22)).
Thirdly, even if the registration data of the United Kingdom Department of Transport were accessible to each manufacturer on an individual basis, they could not be exploited to the same extent as they are through the Exchange. The Exchange provides detailed product, geographic and periodic break downs in respect of the retail sales and the market shares of all members which allows manufacturers instantly and constantly to follow the evolution of each member's market position.
In addition, the members have all agreed to organize their respective dealer territories on the basis of the five digit postcode areas which is a prerequisite for any comparison of the full and detailed information on the individual members and their dealers. Furthermore, for tractors sold but not registered, the dealers have undertaken to return the completed V55 forms to the manufacturer who sends them to SIL for processing. Thus, even if the registrations were accessible on an individual basis, they are not exploitable without the Exchange's agreement.
Lastly, the fact that a Government department makes available to the industry registration data identifying the sales of individual competitors in a given market as opposed to aggregate data not identifying individual companies does not prevent the application of Article 85 to the conduct of the undertakings in question. On the contrary, it only means that the public authority may, in certain circumstances, also be laying itself open to the allegations of an infringement, in this case of Article 5, for it follows from the combined provisions of Article 85, Article 3 (f) and the second paragraph of Article 5 that provisions of national law or national administrative practices may not adversely affect the application in full of the Community competition rules (see the judgment of the Court of Justice in Case 45/85, Verband der Sachversicherer v. Commission [1987] ECR, p. 405).
(50) The parties have further submitted that the information relates only to past transactions as opposed to future planned actions. Therefore, in their view the exchanged information is historical information which has no impact on competition in the market concerned. This argument cannot be accepted either.
In a market where demand is stable or declining as is the case for the agricultural tractor market in the United Kingdom, forecasts

of competitors' future actions can largely be determined on the basis of past transactions. All the restrictive effects of the Exchange described above depend on the observation of competitors' actions and performance in the past. The more accurate and the more recent the information on quantities sold and on market shares, the more impact this information has on future behaviour of the firms in the market (see the judgment of the Court of Justice in Case 172/80, Zuechner v. Bayerische Vereinsbank AG [1981] ECR, p. 2021 (10)).

However, the Commission accepts that from a certain point in time, market information relating to past transactions becomes truly historic and no longer has any real impact on future behaviour. In the present case, the Commission considers that an annual exchange of one-year-old sales figures of individual competitors at the United Kingdom, MAFF region and land use level and with a breakdown by model can be accepted as commercial data with no appreciable distorting effect on competition between the manufacturers or between the dealers operating on the United Kingdom market.

(51) The parties have also submitted that the Commission has no proof of actual restrictions of competition resulting from the Exchange and that on the contrary an analysis of the past performance of companies on the United Kingdom market shows changes in market shares which are not reconcilable with the anticompetitive effects of the Exchange alleged by the Commission in the Statement of Objections. This argument cannot be accepted either.

The nature of the information exchanged and the detail of that information is such that it creates a degree of transparency in a highly concentrated market shielded from outside competition (high entry barriers, virtually no extra-Community imports) which necessarily leads to a reduction of competition between the competitors operating on that market.

In addition, account must be taken not only of the immediate visible effects on an agreement but also of its potential effects and of the fact that an agreement can create a structure likely to be used for anticompetitive purposes.

Article 85 (1) must be interpreted as including potential anticompetitive effects because the objective of that provision is the maintenance of an effective competitive structure within the meaning of Article 3 (f). This objective is particularly material in a highly concentrated market where an information exchange creates a structure of transparency which prevents hidden competition and increases barriers to entry for non-members.

As to the changes in the market shares, it first needs to be pointed out that the overall United Kingdom market shares for the participants in the Exchange have remained relatively stable during the existence of the Exchange. However, fluctuations in market shares have taken place at national and local levels. These variations in themselves do not exclude a lessening of competition on the United Kingdom tractor market as a result of the Exchange. In order to be restrictive of competition, the Exchange does not need to create an absolute stability of market shares or exclude even fierce competition in certain areas. In the present case, the anticompetitive effect of the Exchange lies in the fact that, for the reasons explained above, it can be said with sufficient certainty that the market shares and market positions of the members would have been different in the absence of the Exchange and are likely to be different in the future if the Exchange does not continue. However, to provide proof of actual differences is impossible in practice. In this case, it is the economic context, the structure of the market and the nature of the information exchanged which all lead to the conclusion

that a lessening of competition as a result of the Exchange is inevitable.
(52) Finally, the parties submit that the heterogeneous nature of the products concerned creates strong non-price competition (quality competition) in the tractor market as each manufacturer tries to differentiate its products from those of its competitors in order to gain the consumers' preference.
This argument neglects the fact that for farmers, the purchase of a tractor represents a very high financial investment. Therefore, in the farmer's final choice, the price of the tractor remains an important element, in particular since all tractors of the members of the Exchange, however differentiated they may be, fulfil the same functions and are compatible with all other agricultural machines to be attached to a tractor. Reliability and brand loyalty are therefore not the only elements taken into account by a farmer. Price competition still plays an important role in this market. This means that there is scope for the manufacturers and dealers to lessen the intensity of competition between them by avoiding price fights which would erode their margins. By increasing the transparency in a highly concentrated market and by strengthening the cohesion between the major suppliers in that market through regular and secret contacts, it is possible to maintain a general high price level in the market concerned in spite of price differences between the various products offered on the market.

Data on dealer sales of own company

(53) The Exchange also reveals to each individual manufacturer detailed information about the retail sales of its own dealers. This in itself is not objectionable provided that such information does not permit the identification of sales of competitors and provided that such information does not permit interference with the retail activity of dealers or parallel importers.
(54) As to the possibility of identifying sales of individual competitors, this risk exists where, in respect of geographic areas, product breakdowns or time periods, the number of industry sales amounts to less than 10 tractor units sold for any such specific breakdown by territory, product or time period. In such cases, a comparison between the industry sales and own company sales can facilitate, either directly or by deduction, identification of the exact sales made by individual competitors or dealers of competitors.
(55) As to the possibility of interfering with the retail activity of dealers or parallel importers, the Exchange entails the following potential anticompetitive effects:
- the dealer import and dealer export analyses show for each dealer territory the exact number of sales made to customers within that territory both by the local dealer and by other dealers of the same network. These analyses further show in which dealer territories outside his own a dealer makes sales. The Exchange thus reveals the exact destination of each specific tractor and reveals the export activities of each dealer into the territories of other dealers in the United Kingdom. This monitoring of dealers' sales outside their allocated territory allows manufacturers to exercise pressure on dealers engaging in any perceived excessive export activity. It is the very nature of such reports to give rise to misuse which in most cases cannot be controlled a posteriori (a manufacturer could, for instance, reduce supplies to a dealer who sells too many tractors in other dealers' territories). The import/export analyses are thus highly likely to reduce intrabrand competition with the result that dealers can maintain higher profit margins for both themselves and the manufacturers,
- until September 1988, the members of the Exchange also received from SIL a copy of

each V55 registration form which enabled manufacturers to identify parallel imported tractors and to trace the origin of these tractors (see recitals (27) to (30)). The documents referred to in recital (30) show that the information made available to each member has been used to stop parallel imports of tractors from other Community countries into the United Kingdom. The Exchange was thus a facilitating mechanism for interference with parallel imports which brought about competitive pressure on the United Kingdom dealerships.

(56) As regards the restriction of parallel imports, the present decision only addresses the Exchange in so far as it constitutes a facilitating mechanism for interference with parallel imports. The use made by certain members of the Exchange actually to stop parallel imports through this mechanism will be dealt with in separate proceedings.

Effect on trade between Member States

(57) An exchange of information identifying in great detail the exact retail sales volume and the market shares of 88 % of the suppliers of a national market, which includes all major importers from other Community countries, which prevents hidden competition in a highly concentrated market and which increases the barriers to entry for non-members, is liable to substantially affect trade between Member States because the lessening of competition resulting from this exchange necessarily influences the volume of imports to the United Kingdom.

The pattern of trade between the United Kingdom and the rest of the Common Market will be different from what it would be in the absence of this information exchange. In addition, the Exchange has been and could in future be used to hinder parallel imports to the United Kingdom.

(58) The appreciable effect on trade between Member States is all the more likely to exist as the information exchange is not one between two or three market participants but a quasi industry-wide exchange arrangement covering nearly nine-tenths of a national market which itself is a substantial market within the Community. In the same way, the information system facilitates interference with parallel trade not just for one or two undertakings but for virtually all suppliers of the United Kingdom market. Finally, the possibility of interference with the retail activity of the dealers within the United Kingdom by misusing the dealer import/export analyses reduces intrabrand competition on the United Kingdom market which is a substantial part of the Common Market. All these effects are likely to lead to the result that the prices charged in the United Kingdom for agricultural tractors can be maintained at a supracompetitive level while tractor imports by non-members to the United Kingdom market are rendered more difficult as a result of the increased market knowledge in the hands of the major United Kingdom suppliers.

[.....]

Case cross-reference:

▸ T-35/92 *John Deere Ltd v. Commission* [1994] ECR II-957, appeal dismissed; C-7/95 P *John Deere Ltd v. Commission* [1998] ECR I-3111, appeal dismissed.

2) Case C-49/92 *Commission v. Anic* [1999] ECR I-4125

See above for facts of the case and relevant paragraphs (I-F-2, p. 28).

Relevance: Presumption of anti-competitive behaviour in case of an organized exchange of sensitive information amongst competitors.

F. Export cartel

1) *Floral* Commission decision 80/182/EEC [1980] OJ L 39/51

In 1986 CDF, COFAZ and GESA, French manufacturers of nitrogen compound fertilizers, set up Floral (previously known as Alfa), which was to increase their exports to Germany. The fourth shareholder was Mr Schiffer, a German fertilizer dealer, who was appointed as managing director. Eleven years later, he became the sole shareholder of Floral. So, in practice, the three fertilizer producers had the same commercial agent in Germany and, albeit in disguise, shared the market.

Relevance: example of a prohibited export cartel.

[.....]

1. Agreements and concerted practices between undertakings

The cooperation between the relevant companies, expressed in the joint formation and management of Floral (formerly Alfa), is based on an agreement, or at least a concerted practice, consisting in exportation by the three French manufacturers to Germany via the distribution undertaking formed and controlled by them jointly. Before the joint subsidiary was formed there were talks between Auby (now COFAZ) and Mr Schiffer in the course of which it was agreed that it would be worth bringing in other manufacturers so as to set the cooperation on a broader footing. The equal participation of the three French manufacturers in Floral (Alfa) presupposes an understanding between them which need not necessarily be evidenced in writing.

The business activities of the companies concerned within the joint distribution undertaking also presupposes a standing agreement. While the French manufacturers may not have explicitly undertaken to channel all their exports to Germany exclusively through Floral (Alfa), they nevertheless did so until 1974/75, and since then they have channelled the bulk of their exports (with the exception of only small quantities supplied to only one other customer) through their joint venture. Not until the Commission opened investigations did they increase their individual exports to Germany. Even in the absence of any explicit exclusive rights clause, the three manufacturers as parent companies can hardly be expected to compete with their joint subsidiary. Inevitably, if they make any exports to Germany otherwise than through Floral, they will take account of the sales policy jointly determined with the other companies through Floral and align their sales activities on the common policy practised there.

The fact that the quantities sold by the three manufacturers through Floral do not correspond exactly to their shareholdings is immaterial for the purposes of Article 85 (1). Because the profits of the joint distribution subsidiary are distributed in proportion to their holdings they are obliged, even if no quotas are set, to coordinate their activities in the compound fertilizer export business.

2. Restriction of competition within the Common Market

The cooperation between the undertakings concerned restricts competition between them as regards exports of compound fertilizers to Germany.

In the absence of the joint distribution subsidiary they could offer compound fertilizers for sale in Germany in competition with each other. They have adequate output available for sale and have plant that is quite capable of supplying for export to Germany. In 1968 Auby planned exports via Firma Schiffer although its plant was not so close to the German border as, for instance, CdF's plant. Following the closure of its Carling plant in 1975 and before taking up production at Ottmarsheim, CdF exported substantial quantities from more distant plants. Carriage costs in France are at least one-third lower than in Germany; carriage over greater distances within France would thus cause only a slight increase in total carriage costs. There are favourably located plants, such as the CdF Ottmarsheim plant and the GESA plant at Riemst, Belgium, from which supplies can also be made by inland waterway, enabling northern Germany, which is excluded from Firma Schiffer's allotted sales territory, to be supplied. Certainly Floral's customers may attach particular importance to receiving supplies by road. But this is not to say that French manufacturers are incapable of making such deliveries by road or waterway outside Floral's regular clientele, whether or not situated in Floral's area of operations.

If the three French manufacturers unanimously refrain from so doing, this can only be attributed to their collective undertakings through Floral as their jointly-controlled sales subsidiary. If, as they argue, supplies by road account for a segment of the market that has been neglected by the German manufacturers, the fact that they make no supplies by inland waterway, where the French manufacturers would be in direct competition with the German manufacturers, can only be explained by a concerted decision of the French manufacturers to work through their joint subsidiary Floral in such a way as to refrain from competing directly with it and with their German competitors, so that there should be no interference by the German manufacturers with the joint subsidiary's sales policy.

The coordination of exports to Germany by the three French manufacturers is evidenced by the fact that German customers are confronted with uniform terms of supply: products of the French manufacturers are offered for sale by Floral or Firma Schiffer at identical prices and on identical terms. This is a result of the fact that in the case of bulk goods the products offered for sale are absolutely interchangeable, while packed goods all uniformly bear the additional Floral trademark.

In the face of this standardized supply German customers have virtually no opportunity of obtaining their requirements direct from the three manufacturers. On 6 July 1977 COFAZ refused to meet an order from a Cologne wholesaler on the grounds that the company already had a sales outlet and did not at that time wish to expand its sales, since its plants were at such a distance. This

refusal is merely the logical consequence of the three French manufacturers' cooperation through Floral: so long as they are the controlling members of their joint sales subsidiary Floral, they cannot be expected to supply German customers outside Floral, and there is no doubt that, if they did, their prices and terms would not be more advantageous than those offered by Floral.
The three French manufacturers have not only channelled and standardized their supplies to Germany but also imposed geographical limits on them by requiring Firma Schiffer, via Floral, to sell their fertilizers only in a specified territory. This territory is not even predetermined by carriage costs, since for one thing it includes places that are further away from the French plants than what the companies concerned allegedly regard as the maximum tolerable distance of 310 km; and secondly, this calculation takes account neither of the lower cost for the part of the journey accomplished within France (which varies according to the production plant concerned) nor of the lower cost of waterway transport; and thirdly, if carriage costs were prohibitive above a certain distance, there would be no need to delimit expressly the sales territory.
The competitive intentions of the three French manufacturers are thus geographically confined by means of action concerted in advance without their being any real economic constraints militating in favour of this. Moreover, this geographically restricted supply, standardized by means of the jointly determined sales policy, is aligned on German domestic market prices. Finally, for the purposes of carriage the manufacturers do not use the particularly cheap mode of inland waterways but prefer road transport. The three French manufacturers have thus conceived their competitive intentions on the German market in agreement with each other and in such a way as to create only the minimum of conflict with the German manufacturers. This, combined with their agreement in practice to refrain from competing with each other outside Floral, is the nub of the anti-competitive effect of the cooperation between them.

[.....]

2) *ANSAC* Commission decision 91/301/EEC [1991] OJ L 152/54

ANSAC, the American Natural Soda Ash Corporation, had notified several arrangements concerning the sale of soda-ash into the EC to the Commission. ANSAC organised all exports for its members; moreover, it could autonomously decide what to ship, to whom and at what price.

Relevance: US export cartel into the EC cannot be 'saved' for non-objective environmental reasons. Extraterritoriality doctrine. Joint sales office. Market sharing.

[.....]

II. LEGAL ASSESSMENT
A. Article 85 (1)

(19) The Ansac membership agreement is an agreement between undertakings of the kind envisaged in Article 85 (1). Any decisions or resolutions made by Ansac's Board of Directors under the agreement are decisions of an association of undertakings within the meaning of that Article.
The agreement has as its object and likely effect a restriction of competition within

the common market with respect to prices and quantities. The agreement obliges the members to sell soda-ash for export exclusively through Ansac and prevents them from selling individually, with the exception of sales or deliveries to associated companies. The overall size of the United States producers, their low production costs (compensating largely for higher transport costs) and the fact that some of them have sold regularly on an individual basis show however that they could compete effectively among themselves and with the European producers. Their past sales activities show that they have, on their own initiative, been capable of overcoming storage and transport problems and assuring regular supplies to their customers. They are therefore capable of acting independently within the common market.
(20) The object and effect of the Ansac arrangements is that customers are confronted with a single supplier of natural soda-ash applying uniform prices and conditions. Ansac's members are entitled to a fair share of the sales allocated to them. The fact that one member - General Chemical - has been allocated an additional tonnage equivalent to its current annual deliveries to the United Kingdom demonstrates that Ansac is bound to respect the contractual rights of its members and to assure coordination between them. The Commission therefore does not accept the argument that Ansac enjoys an autonomous structure and organization such as to exclude any anticompetitive cooperation. The fact that Ansac is set up as a separate corporation in order to function as a single selling agent for all United States producers, rather than to coordinate the activities of its members, is not relevant to an assessment under Article 85 (1). Ansac as a joint sales organization must therefore be seen as the vehicle for eliminating competition between its members.
(21) Moreover, the Commission does not accept the argument that the restrictions are needed to allow a strong and credible new entrant to open up the structure of the market in the EEC:
1. It does not follow from the limited success of attempts to enter the market by General Chemical and TG Soda Ash that Ansac's proposals fall outside the scope of Article 85 (1) as being the only way to achieve increased competition. The Commission found in Floral that the parties in that case had failed to demonstrate the need for their collaborative arrangements. In Woodpulp the Commission found that the members of the Pulp, Paper and Paperboard Export Association (KEA) - like Ansac a Webb-Pomerene association - had refrained from pursuing independent pricing policies in the EEC, thereby restricting competition between themselves. Ansac's proposed role in the present case is more active than that of the KEA in Woodpulp.
2. Ansac has stated that it expects to gain only a very limited share of the market - 200 000 tonnes, an amount which, although important to the competitive structure of the market as a second source of supply, could easily be supplied by one or two of its members.
(22) If Ansac enters the EEC soda-ash market on the terms set out in the notification there will be only one new operator on the market. Trade within the Community will necessarily be conducted on different terms from those which would prevail if all or any of Ansac's members were to enter the market individually. The notified arrangements are thus liable to affect trade between Member States.

B. Article 85 (3)

(23) The notified arrangements will not contribute to improving production or promoting technical progress. The Commis-

sion does not dispute the environmental arguments in favour of the use of natural, rather than synthetic, soda-ash. Those arguments have no bearing, however, on the marketing of the product, with which alone Ansac's proposals are concerned. Ansac's environmental argument in any case presupposes that it is the only vehicle by which natural soda-ash could reach the Community, i.e. that if Ansac were not granted an exemption, no individual United States producers or producers would market the product in the EEC. As shown in recital (25), the Commission does not accept that this would be the case. Further, as Ansac's own documents show, its current marketing plans are limited to supplying only a very small percentage (around 5 %) of total demand.

(24) Ansac has also failed to demonstrate that its proposals will lead to an improvement in the distribution of soda-ash or promote economic progress in the common market. To be exempted under Article 85 (3) restrictions should bring about an objective improvement over the situation which would have existed in their absence.

(25) The Commission does not accept Ansac's contention that its entry would enhance competition and lead to the improvement of the present rigidly oligopolistic market structure. If Ansac were granted an exemption under Article 85 (3) there would be no possibility of competition between its member companies, which would be obliged to grant it exclusive sales rights in the EEC for all natural soda-ash produced by them. Ansac would thus control, and be able to restrict, the amount of United States natural soda-ash produced for, imported into and sold within the Community; and would also determine the price at which it was sold. United States producers acting independently, however, would compete amongst themselves and improve competition in the EEC soda-ash market generally. They are all large undertakings with sufficient trading experience and resources to provide their customers with a reliable source of supply. The ending of the anti-dumping review without the imposition of protective measures means that they are now free to enter the EEC market.

(26) Furthermore, the concentration of all supplies of natural soda-ash imported from the United States in the hands of a single sales agency would facilitate the opportunity for collusion with the existing suppliers. Even if there is no express collusion on pricing, Ansac's current intention is to limit its sales in the Community to a level of around 200 000 tonnes and effectively to accept the role of a permanent secondary supplier. Ansac would at this level of business be in the market as a price follower, as indeed was clear from the presentation during the oral hearing of the economics expert called by Ansac.

(27) The Ansac agreement also forecloses an important element of competition which would otherwise be available. A number of major EEC glass producers have expressed an interest in buying soda-ash directly from producers in the United States, a plan which would be impossible under Ansac's membership agreement which specifically prohibits such direct sales for export by its members.

(28) The notified arrangements cannot be said to be indispensable or to offer consumers advantages which could not have been achieved by less restrictive means. The Commission does not accept the argument that the only means by which the rigidity of the EEC market can be reduced is by permitting the United States producers to combine as Ansac. Collusive pricing or marketing arrangements between the EEC producers do not by themselves keep out competition: if they set prices above the market level, competitors outside the arrangements should in theory be able to enter more easily by underpricing the collusive price. The prin-

cipal obstacles to the entry of American natural-ash into the EEC were the anti-dumping measures which have now been removed and the exclusionary rebate systems operated by Solvay and ICI which are the subject of a prohibition in decisions of 19 December 1990.

(29) The only advantages which Ansac's entry might offer consumers flow from the economies of scale achievable by shipping and storing soda-ash in much larger quantities than would be possible for any of Ansac's members acting individually.

However Ansac itself does not intend those economies of scale to be passed on to the consumer in the form of lower prices. Its own forecasts (produced during the oral hearing) show that it intends to charge slightly higher prices in the EEC than it believes would be achieved by the individual United States producers. For Ansac, the main benefit flowing from any cost savings in the form of joint shipping or storage facilities would be the possibility in any future anti-dumping proceedings of showing a higher notional ex-mine price than would be the case for individual producers. Such considerations are not however relevant under Article 85 (3).

(30) In any case, joint-selling arrangements go far beyond what might be necessary to achieve economies of scale that could be passed on to the consumer. The Commission has indicated to Ansac on numerous occasions, both before and during the present proceedings, that it would be prepared, in accordance with the provisions of its notice concerning agreements, decisions and concerted practices in the field of cooperation between enterprises (1), to give favourable consideration to arrangements limited to joint storage and transport facilities. While claiming that cost savings are its main rationale, Ansac and its members have not been prepared to limit cooperation to such measures.

[.....]

[Footnotes in the original text of the case have not been included]

G. State Action Defence

1) Joined Cases C-359 & 379/95 P *Ladbroke Racing* [1997] ECR I-6265

The General Court had annulled a Commission decision in which the latter had rejected a complaint lodged by Ladbroke Racing against the French Republic, ten racing companies and the PMU, which managed the rights of several companies to organize off-course totalizor betting on horse racing. The complaints ranged from abuse of dominant position by racing companies to infringement of the 'useful effect' doctrine by the French government. The Commission, however, appealed the ruling. The ECJ set aside the judgment and referred the case back to the GC.

Relevance: reliance on public policy or national legislation may suffice to bring an undertakings' coordinated market behaviour outside the prohibition of Article 101 (1).

[.....]

33 Articles 85 and 86 of the Treaty apply only to anti-competitive conduct engaged in by undertakings on their own initiative (see to that effect, as regards Article 86 of the Treaty, Case 41/83 Italy v Commission [1985] ECR 873, paragraphs 18 to 20; Case C-202/88 France v Commission - the so-called 'telecommunications terminals' judgment - [1991] ECR I-1223, paragraph 55; and Case C-18/88 GB-Inno-BM [1991] ECR I-5941, paragraph 20). If anti-competitive conduct is required of undertakings by national legislation or if the latter creates a legal framework which itself eliminates any possibility of competitive activity on their part, Articles 85 and 86 do not apply. In such a situation, the restriction of competition is not attributable, as those provisions implicitly require, to the autonomous conduct of the undertakings (see also Joined Cases 40/73 to 48/73, 50/73, 54/73 to 56/73, 111/73, 113/73 and 114/73 Suiker Unie and Others v Commission [1975] ECR 1663, paragraphs 36 to 72, and more particularly paragraphs 65, 66, 71 and 72).
34 Articles 85 and 86 may apply, however, if it is found that the national legislation does not preclude undertakings from engaging in autonomous conduct which prevents, restricts or distorts competition (Joined Cases 209/78 to 215/78 and 218/78 Van Landewyck and Others v Commission [1980] ECR 3125; Joined Cases 240/82 to 242/82, 261/82, 262/82, 268/82 and 269/82 Stichting Sigarettenindustrie and Others v Commission [1985] ECR 3831; and Case C-219/95 P Ferriere Nord v Commission [1997] ECR I-0000).

[.....]

Case cross-references:

- ▸ Case C-2/91 *Meng* [1993] ECR I-5751.
- ▸ Case C-245/91 *Ohra* [1993] ECR I-5851 (see III-B-2).
- ▸ Case C-137/00 *Milk Marque* [2003] ECR I-7975 (see X-A-1).
- ▸ Case C-198/01 *Consorzio Industrie Fiammiferi (CIF)* [2003] ECR I-8055 (see X-A-2).
- ▸ *Zinc Producer Group (ZPG)* Commission decision 84/405/EEC [1984] OJ L 220/27.
- ▸ *Aluminium imports from Eastern Europe* Commission decision 85/206/EEC [1985] OJ L 92/1.
- ▸ V. Korah, 'The Ladbroke Saga', (1998) 19 *ECLR*, 169.

H. Crisis and re-structuration cartels

1) Reduction of structural overcapacity, XIIth Report on Competition Policy (1982), points 38-41

Relevance: crisis cartels may qualify for the exception of Article 101 (3), provided that certain conditions are fulfilled.

§ 8 - The competition rules and measures to reduce structural overcapacity

38. As the economic recession persists, problems of overcapacity are appearing in increasingly acute form in individual firms and entire industries. The associated employment problems are particularly worrying at a time of high unemployment in all the Member States. In such circumstances, the Commission must offer guidance as to how far it considers the solutions sought by firms as compatible with Article 85 of the EEC Treaty.

Structural overcapacity exists where over a prolonged period all the undertakings concerned have been experiencing a significant reduction in their rates of capacity utilization, a drop in output accompanied by substantial operating losses and where the information available does not indicate that any lasting improvement can be expected in this situation in the medium-term.
In a predominantly free market economy such as the Community's, it is up to each undertaking to assess for itself whether and at which point such overcapacity becomes economically unsustainable and to take the necessary measures to reduce it. However, within a given crisis-struck industry, economic circumstances do not necessarily guarantee a reduction of the least profitable surplus capacity. Undertakings which have failed to make the necessary adjustments may have their losses offset within their groups, to the detriment of healthy undertakings and there may be additional distortion from external subsidies.
39. Against this background, and in order to combat the structural problems of individual sectors, the Commission may be able to condone agreements in restraint of competition which relate to a sector as a whole, provided they are aimed solely at achieving a coordinated reduction of overcapacity and do not otherwise restrict free decision-making by the firms involved. The necessary structural reorganization must not be achieved by unsuitable means such as price-fixing or quota agreements, nor should it be hampered by State aids which lead to artificial preservation of surplus capacity.
The Commission will be able however to authorize sectoral agreements where it is satisfied that the other conditions of Article 85 (3) of the EEC Treaty are met, notably in the following circumstances:
(i) production can be considered to be improved if the reduction in capacity are likely in the long run to increase profitability and restore competitiveness, and if the coordination of closures helps to mitigate, spread and stagger their impact on employment. for this purpose, the agreement must contain a detailed and binding programme of closures for each production centre, which ensures, on the one hand, that overcapacity is irreversibly dismantled and, on the other, that while the plan is in operation no new capacity is created, except for replacement capacities provided for in the reorganization programme;
(ii) consumers can be considered to enjoy a fair share of the benefits resulting from the agreement if, at the end of the agreement, they can rely on a competitive and economically healthy structure of supply in the Community, without having been deprived during its operation, despite the effects of the capacity cutbacks, of their freedom of choice or the benefit of continued competition between the participating firms;
(iii) the restrictions of competition which the agreement involves can be considered to be indispensable to the objective of the planned restructuration, if the agreement is concerned solely with reducing surplus capacity and is limited from the outset to the period necessary for the technical implementation of the envisaged programme of cutbacks. The creation of a system for exchanging information to check that promised reductions of capacity are being implemented is admissible provided that it does not in any way help to coordinate policy on the utilization of remaining capacity or to align conditions of sale;
(iv) the parties to the agreement will not be afforded the possibility of eliminating competition eventually for the following reasons: first, since the orderly reduc-

tion of excess capacity is only one element, albeit an important one, of the competitive strategy of the participating undertakings, they will not have surrendered all freedom of action in the marketplace, so that a degree of internal competition will be maintained. Secondly, the presence in the market of firms not party to the agreement and the fact that the Community is open to imports from third countries will usually provide a source of external competition. Finally, as the agreement is from the outset to run for a limited period only, the certainty of a return to completely unfettered competition in the near future will prompt the undertakings concerned to take account, in the decisions they make even during the course of the agreement, of the fact that in due course they will again become full competitors.
40. As an alternative to such sectoral agreements, the Commission can also envisage agreements between a small number of firms providing for reciprocal specialization which would enable them to close excess capacity.
41. Whatever type of solution is chosen, the Commission will always have to satisfy itself that after the reorganization programme is completed there will still be a sufficient number of Community manufacturers left to maintain effective competition in the Community. This condition is necessary to ensure that the economy as a whole, and users and consumers in particular, will also benefit from the positive results of the arrangements.
Reorganization operations should also be such as to stabilize and secure the employment situation within the sector concerned.

Case cross-references:
▸ *BPCL/ICI* Commision decision 84/387/EEC [1984] OJ L 212/1.
▸ *Stichting Baksteen* Commission decision 94/296/EC [1994] OJ L 131/15.
▸ F.O.W. Vogelaar, 'The Impact of the Economic Recession on EEC Competition Policy. Part two: Crisis and Export Cartels', (1985) *Swiss Review of International Competition Law*, 35.

I. Co-operation and environment

Cross-references for this part:
▸ Commission Guidelines on horizontal co-operation agreements, [2001] OJ C 3/2, paragraphs 179-198.
▸ *CECED* Commission decision 2000/476/EC [2000] OJ L 187/47 (see I-P-2).
▸ *ANSAC* Commission decision 91/301/EEC [1991] OJ L 152/54 (see V-F-2).
▸ F.O.W. Vogelaar, 'Towards an Improved Integration of EC Environmental Policy and EC Competition Policy: an Interim Report', (1994) *Fordham Corporate L. Inst* (B. Hawk, ed. 1995), 529.
▸ H. Vedder, *Competition Law and Environmental Protection in Europe: towards sustainability?*, Europa Law Publishing, Groningen 2003.
▸ S. Kingston, *The Role of Environmental Protection in EC Competition Law and Policy*, Ph.D Leyden 2009.

1) *VOTOB*, XXIInd Report on Competition Policy (1992), points 177-186

Relevance: the Commission can be over-strict with regard to (parts of) agreements that have environmental protection as their object.

Competition policy towards enterprises, main decisions and measures taken by the Commission

Agreements relating to charges connected with environmental protection

VOTOB

177. Although the Commission welcomes voluntary initiatives to improve the environmental conditions in a given sector, it has to ensure that undertakings competing in that sector do not resort to agreements which go beyond what is necessary to achieve that goal, to the detriment of competition.

178. This is the position maintained by the European Commission since commencing proceedings against a Dutch association of companies in the chemicals storage business.

179. The association, Vereniging van Onafhankelijke Tankopslag Bedrijven (VOTOB), groups six undertakings offering tank storage facilities (land tanks) in Amsterdam, Dordrecht and Rotterdam. They are independent operators, offering storage services for third parties only. They decided to increase prices charged by VOTOB members to their customers by a uniform, fixed amount as from 1 April 1990. This uniform 'environmental charge' (to be applied for an undetermined period) was to cover, albeit in part only, the costs of investment required to reduce vapour emissions from members' storage tanks. VOTOB took this decision after concluding a covenant with the Dutch Government to improve environmental standards. However, this covenant made no mention of a uniform, fixed price increase, nor was there any obligation on VOTOB by the Dutch Government to adopt one.

180. The Commission objected to this charge as being incompatible with Article 85 for three reasons. Firstly, it is fixed. All members are to apply it regardless of their own considerations. Secondly, it is uniform. Though varying from product to product, the increase is identical for all VOTOB members. Thirdly, it is invoiced to customers as a separate item, suggesting it is a 'charge' imposed by the government.

181. When a price or an element of it is fixed, competition on that price element is excluded. By fixing the charge and thus a source of recovery members have less incentive to make investments as cheaply and efficiently as possible. This has a knock-on effect on the market for undertakings providing reconstruction and improvement services. There will be less incentive for members to contract with those undertakings which can achieve the best results for the least expenditure or effort.

182. Uniform adoption of the charge ignores differences in each individual member's circumstances. The covenant with the Dutch Government stipulates an agenda for vapour emission reduction that spans the period 1990 to 2000. The first phase is to end in 1994. Some members are already very close to the 1994 objectives, while others are not. Furthermore, members employ different techniques to reduce emissions, and do not expend investment costs simultaneously. The charge ignores this. In addition, all VOTOB members retain the proceeds of the charge individually.

183. The Commission maintains that had there been no horizontal fixing of this particular cost element, individual members could have calculated the cost of necessary investment, decided whether to meet it from their own profit or to pass it on to their customers, and, if they decided to pass it on to their customers, determined by how much to increase their prices. This would have been done by the companies independently, having regard to prevailing market conditions and according to their own competitive position.

184. Prior to the Commission's proceeding to a decision, VOTOB agreed to renounce

its separate charging system as from 1 January 1993, taking account of the fact that contracts with customers are negotiated on a calendar-year basis, and to stop invoicing in this manner as from 1 July 1992 for new contracts. The uniformly fixed charge will no longer be applied as from 1 January 1993.

185. The case makes clear that the Commission is not opposed to the possible passing on to customers of 'polluter pays' investment costs, since this makes them more aware of environmental problems and their implications. However, customers should not be barred from challenging price increases and shopping around for the smallest increase. A system whereby members invoiced a total price, stating that it included the additional environmental investment cost, would be acceptable to the Commission. Customers reluctant to accept a higher price would, while becoming environmentally aware, remain in a position to negotiate conditions.

186. The Commission agreed to suspend proceedings and review the situation in the light of VOTOB's undertakings.

CHAPTER VI

Vertical Agreements

General chapter cross-references:

► Regulation 330/2010 on the application of Article 101(3) of the Treaty on the Functioning of the European Union to categories of vertical agreements and concerted practices, [2010] OJ L 102/1.

► Guidelines on Vertical Restraints, [2010] OJ C 130/1.

► S. Bishop and D. Ridyard, 'Vertical Restraint Guidelines: Effect-Based or Per se Policy?', (2002) 23 *ECLR*, 35.

► S.C. Salop, 'Analysis of Foreclosure in the EC Guidelines on Vertical restraints', (2000) *Fordham Corp. L. Inst.* (B. Hawk, ed. 2001), 177.

► R. Whish, 'Regulation 2790/99: The Commission's "new style" block exemption for vertical agreements', (2000) 37 *CMLRev*, 887.

► A. Reindl, 'Resale Price Maintenance and Article 81: developing a more sensible analytical approach' 2009 Fordham Corp.L.Inst. 567-592 (B. Hawk ed. 2010).

A. Export bans

1) Joined Cases 56 & 58/64 *Consten & Grundig* [1966, English special edition] ECR 299

See above for facts of the case (I-E-1, p. 23).

Relevance: example of an export ban. (Note: See also paragraphs of *Consten & Grundig* on object and effect.

[.....]

The complaints concerning the applicability of Article 85 (1) to sole distributorship contracts

The applicants submit that the prohibition in Article 85 (1) applies only to so-called horizontal agreements. The Italian government submits furthermore that sole distributorship contracts do not constitute 'agreements between undertakings' within the meaning of that provision, since the parties are not on a footing of equality. With regard to these contracts, freedom of competition may only be protected by virtue of Article 86 of the Treaty.

Neither the wording of Article 85 nor that of Article 86 gives any ground for holding that distinct areas of application are to be assigned to each of the two Articles according to the level in the economy at which the contracting parties operate. Article 85 refers in a general way to all agreements which distort competition within the Common Market and does not lay down any distinction between those agreements based on whether they are made between competitors operating at the same level in the economic process or between non-competing persons operating at different levels. In principle, no distinction can be made where the Treaty does not make any distinction.

Furthermore, the possible application of Article 85 to a sole distributorship contract cannot be excluded merely because the grantor and the concessionnaire are not competitors inter se and not on a footing of equality. Competition may be distorted within the meaning of Article 85 (1) not only by agreements which limit it as between the parties, but also by agreements which prevent or restrict the competition which might take place between one of them and third parties. For this purpose, it is irrelevant whether the parties to the agreement are or are not on a footing of equality as regards their position and function in the economy. This applies all the more, since, by such an agreement, the parties might seek, by preventing or limiting the competition of third parties in respect of the products, to create or guarantee for their benefit an unjustified advantage at the expense of the consumer or user, contrary to the general aims of Article 85.

It is thus possible that, without involving an abuse of a dominant position, an agreement between economic operators at different levels may affect trade between Member States and at the same time have as its object or effect the prevention, restriction or distortion of competition, thus falling under the prohibition of Article 85 (1).

In addition, it is pointless to compare on the one hand the situation, to which Article 85 applies, of a producer bound by a sole distributorship agreement to the distributor of his products with on the other hand that of a producer who includes within his undertaking the distribution of his own products by some means, for example, by commercial representatives, to which Article 85 does not apply. These situations are distinct in law and, moreover, need to be assessed differently, since two marketing organizations, one of which is integrated into the manufacturer's undertaking whilst the other is not, may not necessarily have the same efficiency. The wording of Article 85 causes the prohibition to apply, provided that the other conditions are met, to an agreement between several undertakings. Thus it does not apply where a sole undertaking integrates its own distribution network into its business organization. It does not thereby follow, however, that the contractual situation based on an agreement between a manufacturing and a distributing undertaking is rendered legally acceptable by a simple process of economic analogy – which is in any case incomplete and in contradiction with the said Article. Furthermore, although in the first case the Treaty intended in Article 85 to leave untouched the internal organization of an undertaking and to render it liable to be called in question, by means of Article 86, only in cases where it reaches such a degree of seriousness as to amount to an abuse of a dominant position, the same reservation could not apply when the impediments to competition result from agreement between two different undertakings which then as a general rule simply require to be prohibited.

Finally, an agreement between producer and distributor which might tend to restore the national divisions in trade between Member States might be such as to frustrate the most fundamental objections of the Community. The Treaty, whose preamble and content aim at abolishing the barriers between states, and which in several provisions gives evidence of a stern attitude with regard to their reappearance, could not allow undertakings to reconstruct such barriers. Article 85 (1) is designed to pursue this aim, even in the case of agreements between undertakings placed at different levels in the economic process.

The submissions set out above are consequently unfounded.

[.....]

2) *Volkswagen* Commission decision 98/273/EC [1998] OJ L 124/60

Volkswagen AG, parent company of the Volkswagen group, had a 98,99% holding in Audi and a 100% holding in Autogerma, which was Volkswagen's and Audi's (joint) importer for Italy. These three companies, together with their Italian dealers, had concluded agreements in which they conspired to create an export ban. As a result, end-consumers in Member States other than Italy were practically unable to order motor vehicles from Italian dealers.

Relevance: example of how an export ban works.

[.....]

LEGAL ASSESSMENT

[.....]

A. Article 85 (1)

[.....]

II. The agreement

1. The export ban/restriction
(111) An examination of the agreements and concerted practices entered into by Volkswagen, Audi and Autogerma and described in Chapter 1, Section C demonstrates that within the framework provided by the exclusive and selective distribution network they and their Italian dealers have agreed a policy for partitioning the market. That market-partitioning policy takes the form of an export ban/restriction imposed on Italian dealers.
(112) The export ban/restriction derives from a system of measures consisting of preventive measures, monitoring measures and penalties. In the course of its investigations the Commission has found documents which list these various measures. The main evidence is provided by the documents specified in Chapter 1, Section C.I (see footnotes 14 to 18 and the Maßnahmenprogramm (Programme of measures) dated 10 February 1995 and referred to in footnote 123).
(113) The specific measures include the warnings and instructions to dealers described in Chapter 1, Section C.II.1 (see the documents referred to in footnotes 14 and 61 to 70).
(114) Surveillance of dealers through monitoring of incoming orders, monitoring of sales (including an obligation on authorised dealers to refrain from selling vehicles to non-Italian customers without Autogerma's prior consent), monitoring of vehicle registrations and monitoring by means of 'audits' are described in Chapter 1, Section C.I (see the documents referred to in footnotes 40 to 48 and 143). The cooperation between the manufacturers and the importer in the surveillance of the sales activities of the Italian dealers is apparent from Chapter 1, Section C.I (see the documents referred to in footnotes 19 to 31).
(115) Examples of penalties applied to Italian authorised dealers, such as cautions, warnings and termination of dealership contracts, are indicated in Chapter 1, Section C.II.6; reference may be made in particular to the documents listed in footnotes 71 and 120 to 127, and the document Export aus Italien (Exports from Italy) dated 13 June 1994 and referred to in footnote 62.
The clause to the effect that bonuses are in principle payable only for dealers' sales within their contract territories, which has

been contained in Italian dealers' contracts since 1987 at least, is described in Chapter 1, Section C.II.3 (see the documents referred to in note 94). The clause was tightened up when the dealership contract was amended, with effect from 1 January 1995 (see the document referred to in note 98), to make payment of the bonus in principle conditional on the qualifying vehicles also being registered in the dealer's contract territory as is also described in Chapter 1, Section C.II.3. That bonuses were in fact withheld at least since 1993 is explained in Chapter 1, Section C.II.3 (see the documents referred to in footnotes 18, 95 and 96). The introduction of a split margin, beginning with the VW Polo and Audi A4 models, is shown by the documents referred to in footnotes 78 to 81, 84 and 85 relating to Volkswagen's marketing (Chapter 1, Section C.III.1. and Chapter 1, Section C.II.2.) and the documents referred to in footnotes 82, 87, 88 and 89 relating to Audi's marketing (Chapter 1, Section C.II.2).

(116) The export ban/restriction incorporates a prohibition of cross-deliveries, that is deliveries within the distribution network. Italian authorised dealers are prohibited from supplying to VW and Audi authorised dealers in other Member States. This is evident from Autogerma's information to Audi regarding German authorized dealers 'bothering' their Italian counterparts, and its request to Audi to prevail upon German authorised dealers to refrain from cross-purchases. Evidence is listed especially in footnotes 112 and 113 (Chapter 1, Section C.II.5) and footnotes 14 and 116 (Chapter 1, Section C.II.5). In addition, Autogerma itself refused requests from non-Italian authorised dealers on the ground that it had insufficient stocks, rather than on the ground that as the importer it did not sell direct (see the document referred to in note 117, Chapter 1, Section C.II.6).

(117) The export ban/restriction has also been underpinned by the restriction of supply to the Italian market (see 'Maßnahmenprogramm' of 10 February 1995, note 123). The documents found by the Commission in its investigations show that VW, since November 1993 (see the document referred to in footnote 106, Maßnahmen zur Begrenzung von Re-Exporten aus Italien (Measures to restrict re-exports from Italy), Chapter 1, Section C.II.4) and Audi, since at least December 1993 (see the memo Gespräch am 14.12.93 in Wolfsburg, Marken Audi und VW: Preisplanung Italien/EG-Preisharmonisierung (Discussion held on 14 December 1993 in Wolfsburg concerning Audi and VW vehicles: planning of prices for Italy/harmonisation of EC prices) referred to in note 106), have been compelling Italian authorised dealers to comply with the prohibition/restriction on exports by restricting deliveries to the Italian market.

(118) In its letter to Audi Export aus Italien dated 13 June 1994, Autogerma confirmed the existence of that restriction on deliveries (see footnote 62, with translation):
'... Obwohl die Lieferzeiten für den Audi 80 von bis zu 8 Monaten deutlich reduziert werden konnten, werden die Händler noch immer kontingentiert. Ein Händler, der eine übergroße Anzahl an Audi 80 bestellt, bekommt diese nicht geliefert...'.

(119) Volkswagen stated in a discussion with Audi on 22 March 1995 (see the minutes of this discussion, dated 27 March 1995, referred to in footnote 107) that the supply of VW vehicles had been adapted to demand in Italy. Dealers received only the number of vehicles necessary to enable them to supply customers in their contract territory. And in an internal memo, Stand Maßnahmen gegen Graumarkt, 25.11.1994 (The state of measures against the grey market at 25 November 1994), Audi indicated with

regard to the new Audi A4 (see the document referred to in footnote 82, with translation): '... Belieferung wird so gesteuert, daß nur die italienische Nachfrage befriedigt wird...'.

(120) Among the measures taken in connection with the export ban/restriction is the imposition of the rule that dealers should make the conclusion of sales contracts with final consumers conditional on such consumers giving a written undertaking (see Chapter 1, Section C.II.7 and the documents referred to in footnotes 127 and 128).

2. *Agreement*

(121) The export ban/restriction forms part of the contractual relations which Autogerma maintains with dealers in the selective distribution network in Italy for the VW and Audi makes. The export ban/restriction was agreed with the dealers partly by means of circulars and partly by word of mouth, and the dealers consented to this agreement.

(122) Autogerma sent dealers two circulars implementing Volkswagen's instructions regarding new arrangements for margins. It had already established the legal basis for this action with effect from 1 January 1994; an agreement (convenzione) appended to the dealership contract discontinued the application of the previous margins scheme for new models, without, however, determining new arrangements for such margins (see Chapter 1, Section C.II.2, in particular Chapter 1, Section C.II.2©). Autogerma subsequently provided the following details of a new margins scheme, by circulars dated 20 October and 2 November 1994 (see Chapter 1, Section C.II.2 and the documents referred to in footnote 85). In the circular of 20 October 1994, Autogerma set out the structure of the new scheme, giving the example of the new VW Polo, which was arriving on the market [...]

(123) By the circular of 2 November 1994 (see footnote 85) dealers were informed that the new margins scheme, as set out in the circular of 20 October 1994 would apply with immediate effect and until at least 30 April 1995. Both circulars form part of the contractual relations between Autogerma and the dealers, since the purpose of the circulars was to flesh out the provisions of the dealership contract laid down in the 'convenzione' appended to the contract, which excluded the new models from the previous margins scheme. In its circular of 2 November 1994, Autogerma states that the new arrangements for margins are to apply forthwith. Since 2 November 1994, the new margins scheme has formed a part of the contractual relations between Autogerma and the authorised dealers. This interpretation is substantiated by the rulings of the Court of Justice of the European Communities in Ford-Werke and BMW v. ALD (150).

(124) Autogerma acted on Audi's instructions regarding the margins scheme, bringing it into effect not later than November 1994; the scheme was embodied in the Italian dealership contracts by means of an additional agreement (see Autogerma's letter to Audi dated 10 November 1994 Splitmargensystem – Audi A 4 (split margins scheme – Audi A 4) in footnote 87, Chapter 1, Section C.II.2© (2), and the document referred to in footnote 93).

(125) Furthermore, Autogerma has since 1987 been specifying in dealership contracts concluded with Italian dealers that bonuses would be paid in principle only on sales to customers in the contract territory (whether final consumers, intermediaries, other authorised dealers or independent dealers not being members of the distribution network). 'Convenzione B' covering the bonus arrangements was framed in more stringent terms with effect from 1 January 1995: the bonus

was now payable only on vehicles which were registered in the dealer's contract territory. This is established by the document referred to in note 98.
(126) Authorised dealers have also given an express undertaking to the importer that they will refrain from making sales outside their contract territory, in particular abroad (see Chapter 1, Section D.II). This is shown by the documents referred to in footnote 142.
(127) The following conduct on the part of the authorised dealers likewise shows that they have consented to the export ban/restriction:
- on the basis of the export ban/restriction, authorised dealers have required subdealers to refrain from foreign sales. As evidence of this the Commission would point to the letter of 6 March 1995 from the VW/Audi dealer, Eurocar SpA, to its subdealers, Fantini, Mansutti, Torresan, Ciesse Car, Tonero, Fantini and Autogris, in which it is stated that Autogerma absolutely prohibits foreign sales of vehicles and tolerates a volume of sales outside a dealer's contract territory only up to 15 % of total sales [...]
- authorised dealers have dismissed employees who have concluded foreign sales. This is shown by the memo Oggetto: Colloquio con Sig. Beikricher.-BZ, (Subject: Conversation with Mr Beikircher of Bolzano/Bozen) dated 21 October 1994, referred to in footnote 143,
- authorised dealers have requested Autogerma for permission before they conclude sales contracts with final consumers abroad (see Chapter 1, Section D.II). Reference may be made to Brenner Garage's letter to Autogerma of 19 December 1994 and Dorigoni's letter of 22 June 1995, referred to in footnote 143,
- authorised dealers have refused sales to final consumers resident outside Italy, and to other VW/Audi dealers, on the grounds that they no longer sell abroad (see Chapter 1, Section D.III). This can be seen from the letters from the dealer Dorigoni referred to in footnotes 145 and 146,
- authorised dealers have suggested to final consumers and to other dealers in the distribution network that they would be wiser not to purchase, as delivery times can be longer than a year (see Chapter 1, Section D.III). This can be seen from the letters from Auto Brenner referred to in footnote 147,
- authorised dealers have requested the written undertakings from final consumers. This is established by the sales contracts indicated in footnote 128,
- authorised dealers have acquiesced in the withholding of bonuses on all sales outside their contract territory. Autogerma's chairman was able to claim the sole right to authorise bonuses without anticipating trouble from dealers. This is shown by the internal memo Non riconoscimento/trattenuta del Maggior Sconto per vendite fuori zona (compreso esportazioni parallele) (Non-payment/withholding of the extra bonus for out-of-area sales (including parallel exports)) of 28 June 1994 (see footnote 97).

3. Conclusion

(128) The measures adopted by Volkswagen, Audi and Autogerma to prevent or obstruct parallel exports do not constitute unilateral conduct that falls outside the scope of the prohibition contained in Article 85 (1) : they form part of the contractual relations which the manufacturers maintain, through Autogerma, with the dealers in their selective distribution network, since they were adopted by mutual agreement for the practical application of the dealership contract. The Court of Justice has already held in Case 107/82 AEG v. Commission (151), that admission of a distributor to a selective distribution system is based on acceptance, tacit or express, of the policy pursued by the manufacturer.

The restrictive deliveries policy applied by Volkswagen and Audi, viewed in its economic and legal context, likewise produces its effects within the framework of the distribution agreements concluded with the authorised dealers. It alters the contractual relations between Volkswagen, Audi, Autogerma and the dealers. Orders placed by dealers are no longer met by the manufactures. [...]
(129) It is irrelevant whether or not the dealers have complied with the prohibition/restriction on exports as a result of pressure brought to bear by the manufacturers. In its Decision 82/367/EEC in Hasselblad, the Commission has stated that for a concerted practice to exist it is sufficient 'for... an undertaking knowingly and of its own accord to adjust its behaviour in line with the wishes of another undertaking. The motive or the knowledge that the act is unlawful is irrelevant'.

[.....]

[Footnotes not included]

Case cross-references:

▸ Eco System/Peugeot Commission decision 92/154/EEC [1992] OJ l 66/1.
▸ Case T-62/98 *Volkswagen v. Commission* [2000] ECR II-2707, Commission decision partly annulled; Case C-338/00 P *Volkswagen v. Commission* [2003] ECR I-9189, ruling GC confirmed.
▸ Case T-450/05 *Peugeot Automobiles SA and Peugeot Nederland NV v. Commission* [2009] ECR II-2533.

3) *Nintendo*, Comm. Press Release (IP/02/1584), full decision published in [2003] OJ L 255/33

Relevance: export ban so as to maintain high price differences in the EU; active collaboration between manufacturer and its distributors.

IP/02/1584, Brussels, 30 October 2002

Commission fines Nintendo and seven of its European distributors for colluding to prevent trade in low priced products

The European Commission has imposed a total fine of €167.8 million on Japanese video games maker Nintendo and seven of its official distributors in Europe for colluding to prevent exports to high-priced from low-priced countries. The fine on Nintendo alone was calculated at €149 million to reflect its size in the market concerned, the fact that it was the driving force behind the illicit behaviour and also because it continued with the infringement even after it knew the investigation was going on. Prices for play consoles and games differed widely from one European Union country to another during the period investigated by the Commission, with the United Kingdom up to 65 percent cheaper than Germany and the Netherlands. "Every year, millions of European families spend large amounts of money on video games. They have the right to buy the games and consoles at the lowest price the market can possibly offer and we will not tolerate collusive behaviour intended to keep prices artificially high," European Competition Commissioner Mario Monti said.

The decision concerns Nintendo and seven distributors of Nintendo products, namely John Menzies plc (Nintendo's distributor for the United Kingdom), Concentra - Produtos para crianças S.A. (Portugal), Linea GIG. S.p.A. (Italy), Bergsala AB (Sweden), the

Greek unit of Japan's Itochu Corp, Nortec A.E. (Greece), and the Belgian unit of Germany's CD-Contact Data GmbH.
The Commission has collected evidence showing that Nintendo and its distributors colluded to maintain artificially high price differences in the EU between January 1991 and 1998. According to the arrangements, each distributor was under the obligation to prevent parallel trade from its territory, i.e. exports from one country to another via unofficial distribution channels. Under the leadership of Nintendo, the companies intensively collaborated to find the source of any parallel trade. Traders that allowed parallel exports to occur were punished by being given smaller shipments or by being boycotted altogether.

UK by far the cheapest country

The investigation showed that during the seven-year period price differences in the European Economic Area (EEA) - EU plus Norway, Iceland and Liechtenstein - were frequent and significant. The UK usually had the lowest prices by far, which understandably tempted traders into re-exporting cheap goods to high-price countries.
The most striking price differences were observed in early 1996, when certain Nintendo products were up to 65% cheaper in the UK when compared with the Netherlands and Germany. They were also more affordable than in Spain (up to 67% more expensive than the UK), Italy (54%) and Sweden (39%). The difference narrowed but remained significant in 1997, when the UK price for all N64 game consoles and game cartridges was 33% lower (in October) than everywhere else in the EEA.
A Memo written by John Menzies for Nintendo on 11 April 1996 which was voluntarily submitted to the Commission outlined the strategy and steps to maintain the huge price differences: "I fully understand the difficulty that this differential pricing creates for other mainland European countries where the market can clearly stand a much higher price than that which the market can stand here in the UK. [...] I am sure that we can, by working closely together, better control the situation on grey imports and find a much better way of isolating our products and our prices to within the shores of the UK, thus reducing the impact that this differential pricing has upon mainland Europe".
Subsequently, John Menzies took action as a letter obtained via a formal request for information to Nintendo explained: "I can tell you that a significant amount of activity has been undertaken by THE (John Menzies's subsidiary called THE Games Ltd) since January/February this year [1996] with a view to stopping the grey exporting of products from the UK into the continental European market. Our major activities in this regard have been to either shut off supplies completely or to really control/restrict the supply of product into the UK market place, to certain questionable retailers."
It should be noted that, before this happened, John Menzies itself had been boycotted by Nintendo to force it to collaborate better with the infringement.
As a result of the illicit behaviour of Nintendo and its official distributors, families on continental Europe had to put up with high prices. To measure the harm caused to consumers it is sufficient to note that Nintendo sold five million game consoles and 12 million games in Europe in 1997 alone.

Article 81 of the EU treaty specifically prohibits agreements and concerted practices "which may affect trade between Member States and which may have as their object or effect the prevention, restriction or distortion

of competition within the (EU's) common market".
Restrictions of parallel trade represent a very serious infringement of Article 81 as confirmed by the European Courts as early as 1966 in the landmark Grundig-Consten case(1) and, more recently, in the 1998 Volkswagen decision(2).
The seriousness of the infringement and the harm caused to end-consumers led the Commission to impose a total fine of €167.843 million, i.e. the fifth largest ever imposed for any anti-trust infringement. It is also by far the largest fine ever imposed for a so-called vertical infringement i.e., in this case, between a producer and its distributors as opposed to a horizontal cartel between manufacturers of the same product. The fine on Nintendo is also the fourth largest ever imposed on an individual firm for a single infringement.

Individual fines
Following is a breakdown of the fines per company (all figures expressed in million EUR):
Nintendo Corporation and Nintendo of Europe GmbH (jointly liable): 149.128
John Menzies plc: 8.64
Concentra - Produtos para crianças S.A.: 0.825
Linea GIG. S.p.A.: 1.5
Bergsala AB: 1.25
Itochu Corporation: 4.5
Nortec A.E.: 1.0
CD-Contact Data GmbH: 1.0
The amounts reflect the real impact of the offending conduct of each firm on competition as well as their different size to ensure a sufficient deterrent effect. Nintendo, John Menzies and Itochu are much bigger than the others.
Nintendo was the instigator and the leader of the infringement and carried on with the illicit behaviour even after the Commission had started its investigation as did John Menzies. This constitutes an aggravating circumstance. The latter also tried to mislead the Commission with regard to the real scope of the infringement in mid-1997. These aggravating factors were duly balanced with the fact that, after December 1997, John Menzies and Nintendo co-operated with the Commission. Similarly, in setting the final fine on Nintendo, the Commission also took into consideration its decision to offer substantial financial compensation to third parties, which suffered material harm. Nintendo and John Menzies were, nevertheless, granted large reductions, which stresses the importance the Commission attaches to co-operation by companies that have infringed EC competition law even if this was not through participation in a 'classic' horizontal cartel(3).
The small fine on Concentra reflects its passive role in the illicit agreement.

Background information
Nintendo produces game consoles and games compatible with those consoles. The products concerned by this decision are the 'static' NES and SNES consoles, the N64 game console that superseded them and the 'handheld' Game Boy.
In some Member States, Nintendo acts as the official importer and distributes its products to wholesalers and retailers itself. This is the case in Germany, the Netherlands, France, and Spain. At the beginning of the investigation period, Nintendo also distributed its products itself in Belgium, the UK and Ireland, but later appointed independent official importers for these countries. The Games Ltd, part of John Menzies, became Nintendo's official distributor for the UK and Ireland in 1995. CD-Contact Data GmbH became Nintendo's official importer for

Belgium in 1997. In Portugal, Italy and the Scandinavian countries the official importers are or were Concentra, Linea GIG Spa and Bergsala AB. In Greece, Nintendo products were distributed by Itochu Hellas EPE, a subsidiary of Itochu, until 1997. At that point, the distribution was taken over by Nortec EA. After the investigation period, Nintendo reorganised its distribution system. The Commission's investigation started in 1995 but gained momentum when, in December 1997, John Menzies and, subsequently, Nintendo begun to co-operate with the Commission. On 25 April 2000, the Commission issued a Statement of Objections. (See also IP/00/419 of 28/04/2000). All the companies replied in writing but did not request an oral hearing. They were also given the right to access the Commission's file.

[Footnotes in the original text of the case have not been included]

B. Selective distribution

Cross-reference for this part:

▸ Guidelines on Vertical Restraints, [2010] OJ C 130/1, paragraphs 174-188.

1) *Omega*, Comm., Bulletin 12-1970, Ch. 1, section 3

Relevance: example of a 'quantitative' selective distribution system.

The Commission approves a "selective distribution" system

3. Many makers of branded Articles use the "selective distribution" system, only authorizing the retail sale of their products by "approved retailers" or "official distributors" who satisfy certain conditions, to the exclusion of other retailers of their type of goods. There are various reasons for this policy, amongst them a desire to provide customers with an efficient after-sales service (for products involving a high degree of technology), to ensure unvarying quality (for perishable goods) and to promote the reputation of their brand (for luxury Articles).

This system can raise problems with regard to the competition rules of the Treaty of Rome when it is used regularly at Common Market level by enterprises holding an important position in their segment of the economy. The Commission has already held, in a decision adopted at the end of June last, that the Treaty provisions on agreements were not infringed by the refusal of the Community companies of the Kodak group to allow their products to be distributed by wholesalers and retailers who fail to satisfy the required professional qualifications and lack appropriate material facilities.

The Commission has further clarified its position on the matter in its recent decision on the agreements underlying the organization of sales of Omega watches in the Common Market. The characteristic feature of Omega's selective distribution system is, in fact, that this firm spontaneously limits the number of points of sale for its watches, not only by requiring that its official distributors should satisfy objective conditions as to professional qualifications and selling facilities but also by fixing a maximum number of retailers per town or suburb, on the basis of the local population and its presumed

degree of affluence. The result is that a substantial proportion of clockmaker-jewellers cannot sell Omega watches because they are not recognized as official distributors, even though they satisfy the aforementioned objective conditions.
The Commission considered that this limitation of the number of retailers, which is an appreciable restraint on competition at distribution level can be authorized in this particular case since, while allowing wide availability of Omega watches - which for material reasons can only be produced in relatively limited numbers - it is vitally necessary to ensure that authorize distributors have a large enough turnover to enable them to make a genuine effort to promote sales and serve customers (maintenance and repairs). In addition, official Omega distributors can henceforth obtain their supplies from any of the firm's five exclusive importers in the EEC, and are at liberty to export to other Common Market countries by selling to other official Omega distributors or to private customers, at prices which they fix at their discretion. There is therefore adequate competition between retailers which should furthermore, ensure downward alignment of the prices quoted for Omega watches in the Member States.

2) Case 26/76 *Metro v. Commission (Saba I)* [1977] ECR 1875

See above for facts of the case and for the paragraphs 42 to 50 (I-P-1, p. 67).

Relevance: example of a selective distribution system; refusal to accept a new dealer; relation with Article 102; criteria for Article 101 (3) to apply.

[.....]

II - the application of Article 85

19 The applicant maintains that Article 2 of the contested decision is vitiated by misuse of powers inasmuch as the Commission has failed to recognize 'what is protected under Article 85 (namely) freedom of competition for the benefit of the consumer, not the coincident interests of a manufacturer and a given group of traders who wish to secure selling prices which are considered to be satisfactory by the latter'.
Furthermore, if it were to be considered that an exemption from the prohibition might be granted in respect of the distribution system in dispute pursuant to Article 85 (3), the applicant maintains that the Commission has misapplied that provision by granting an exemption in respect of restrictions on competition which are not indispensable to the attainment of the objectives of improving production or distribution or promoting technical or economic progress and which lead to the elimination of competition from self-service wholesale traders.

A - misuse of powers

20 The requirement contained in Articles 3 and 85 of the EEC Treaty that competition shall not be distorted implies the existence on the market of workable competition, that is to say the degree of competition necessary to ensure the observance of the basic requirements and the attainment of the objectives of the Treaty, in particular the creation of a single market achieving conditions similar to those of a domestic market.

In accordance with this requirement the nature and intensiveness of competition may vary to an extent dictated by the products or services in question and the economic structure of the relevant market sectors.
In the sector covering the production of high quality and technically advanced consumer durables, where a relatively small number of large- and medium-scale producers offer a varied range of items which, or so consumers may consider, are readily interchangeable, the structure of the market does not preclude the existence of a variety of channels of distribution adapted to the peculiar characteristics of the various producers and to the requirements of the various categories of consumers.
On this view the Commission was justified in recognizing that selective distribution systems constituted, together with others, an aspect of competition which accords with Article 85 (1), provided that resellers are chosen on the basis of objective criteria of a qualitative nature relating to the technical qualifications of the reseller and his staff and the suitability of his trading premises and that such conditions are laid down uniformly for all potential resellers and are not applied in a discriminatory fashion.
21 It is true that in such systems of distribution price competition is not generally emphasized either as an exclusive or indeed as a principal factor.
This is particularly so when, as in the present case, access to the distribution network is subject to conditions exceeding the requirements of an appropriate distribution of the products.
However, although price competition is so important that it can never be eliminated it does not constitute the only effective form of competition or that to which absolute priority must in all circumstances be accorded.
The powers conferred upon the Commission under Article 85 (3) show that the requirements for the maintenance of workable competition may be reconciled with the safeguarding of objectives of a different nature and that to this end certain restrictions on competition are permissible, provided that they are essential to the attainment of those objectives and that they do not result in the elimination of competition for a substantial part of the Common Market.
For specialist wholesalers and retailers the desire to maintain a certain price level, which corresponds to the desire to preserve, in the interests of consumers, the possibility of the continued existence of this channel of distribution in conjunction with new methods of distribution based on a different type of competition policy, forms one of the objectives which may be pursued without necessarily falling under the prohibition contained in Article 85 (1), and, if it does fall there under, either wholly or in part, coming within the framework of Article 85 (3).
This argument is strengthened if, in addition, such conditions promote improved competition inasmuch as it relates to factors other than prices.
22 Although the figures submitted by both sides concerning the existence of price competition amongst SABA distributors ultimately indicate that the price structure is somewhat rigid, they do not, especially in view of the existence at the same time of competition between products of the same brand (intra-brand competition) and the existence of effective competition between different brands, permit the conclusion that competition has been restricted or eliminated on the market in electronic equipment for leisure purposes.
Nevertheless, the Commission must ensure that this structural rigidity is not reinforced, as might happen if there were an increase in

the number of selective distribution networks for marketing the same product.
Since the Commission granted the desired exemption only for a period expiring on 21 July 1980 it retains the possibility of reconsidering within a reasonable time the consequences of this aspect of its decision.
In those circumstances the submission based on the existence of a misuse of powers must be rejected.

[.....]

24 Before commencing consideration of those complaints it should be observed that, according to the Commission, whilst the provisions of the selective distribution system referred to in Article 2 of the contested decision have as a whole been granted an exemption pursuant to Article 85 (3), it does not, however, follow that every element of that system is incompatible with the prohibition contained in Article 85 (1). On the contrary, both the statement of reasons for the contested decision and the further information provided in the course of the oral procedure make it clear that only certain of those elements constitute restrictions on competition for which the grant of an exemption was necessary.
The defendant maintains that the following do not constitute restrictions on competition: (a) those conditions for appointment as a distributor which relate to the technical qualifications of distributors, to the specialist knowledge of sales staff, to participation by SABA wholesalers in the creation of the distribution network and service system and the suitability of trading premises (paragraph 28 of the decision), and (b) the prohibition on supplies to so-called 'institutional' consumers (paragraph 34 of the decision).
On the other hand, the following elements are said to fall within the prohibition of Article 85 (1) but to qualify for an exemption: the obligation imposed upon distributors to check whether the resellers to whom they deliver supplies have been appointed by SABA, and the obligation to keep a register containing the serial numbers of Articles sold and the names of purchasers (paragraphs 11 (b) and (c) and 29 of the decision), together with the obligations imposed under the cooperation agreement (paragraph 29 of the decision).

[.....]

3) *Givenchy* Commision decision 92/428/EEC [1992] OJ L 236/11

In the following decision, the Commission looked into the standard-form authorized retailer contract as notified by Givenchy. The latter was active on the market of luxury perfumery products. Retailers were selected by Givenchy (or its exclusive agents) on the basis of qualitative criteria such as the shop-front and interior design of the outlet in question (which should "reflect the prestige of Givenchy") and the presence of a trained sales staff. In order to be admitted, however, the retailers also had to comply with obligations that could not be classified as having a 'qualitative nature'. The Commission exempted those obligations on the basis of Article 101 (3). One of the requirements concerned the carrying of competing brands.

Relevance: example of 'qualitative' selective distribution; obligation for a distributor to carry a 'sufficient number of competing brands'.

[.....]

II. Legal Assessment
A. Article 85 (1)

(4) As the Court of Justice has pointed out (Case 107/82, AEG v. Commission [1983] ECR 3151, paragraph 33), agreements constituting a selective distribution system necessarily affect competition in the common market. However, it has always been recognized that certain products which are not ordinary products or services have properties such that they cannot properly be supplied to the public without the intervention of specialized distributors. A system of selective distribution may thus constitute an element of competition which is in conformity with Article 85 (1), if it is established that the properties of the products in question necessitate the establishment of such a system in order to preserve their quality and ensure their proper use (Case 31/80, L'Oréal v. De Nieuwe AMCK [1980] ECR 3775, paragraph 16) and provided that resellers are chosen on the basis of objective criteria of a qualitative nature relating to the technical qualifications of the reseller and his staff and the suitability of his trading premises and that such conditions are laid down uniformly for all potential resellers and are not applied in a discriminatory fashion (Case 26/76, Metro v. Commission [1977] ECR 1875, paragraph 20).
(5) In this instance, the standard-form contract underlying the network for the selective distribution of Givenchy products is not covered by Article 85 (1) in so far as it is limited to establishing, for access to distribution, qualitative criteria of a technical and professional nature laid down in a uniform manner for all potential resellers and in so far as such criteria are not applied in a discriminatory manner.

[.....]

(6) However, the selective distribution contracts must be assessed from another angle where they contain authorization requirements and criteria that go beyond the limits indicated above. They are then caught by Article 85 (1), although they may, where appropriate, be exempted under Article 85 (3) (Case 99/79, Lancôme v. Etos [1980] ECR 2511). The contracts notified do contain such specific obligations.

[.....]

(c) The authorized retail outlet must, within eighteen months of the date on which the distribution is concluded, carry a sufficient number of competing brands to reflect the image and reputation of Givenchy products. Although the sole purpose of this clause, whether seen in isolation or in the framework of the Givenchy standard-form selective distribution contract, is to maintain a distribution system based on the sale of Givenchy products alongside other competing luxury brands without restructing the freedom of choice of retailers in this respect, it could nevertheless have the effect of restricting the ability of authorized retailers to gain access to the selective distribution network as a result of the possible overlapping of the contractual obligations imposed by competing manufacturers, notably as regards the minimum annual purchases figure.

[.....]

B. Article 85 (3)

[.....]

2) Improving production and distribution

[.....]

The requirement that authorized retailers carry, in their outlet, a sufficient number of competing brands to reflect the image and reputation of Givenchy products is intended to maintain a distribution system based on the sale of Givenchy products alongside other competing luxury brands, which ensures that retailers are able to run a specialized business that is capable of offering consumers a wide range of competing products and thereby attract customers. This also helps to ensure the enhanced presentation of the contract goods whilst stimulating inter-brand competition.
The requirements on the holding of stocks have the effect of extending the range of Givenchy products available through authorized retailers, so that consumers can always find, at each retail outlet, the main products in each of the ranges marketed by Givenchy and rely on the products which they desire being rapidly available.

[.....]

3) Benefits to consumers

[.....]

In addition, since the Givenchy distribution system is based on the products being sold alongside other prestige brands, and authorized retailers are no longer restricted in the choice of competing brands to be sold in their outlets, consumers can always decide not to buy the Givenchy brand if the level of its prices are considered no longer to correspond to the quality of its products. The clause requiring competing brands to be sold in the retail outlet gives customers the opportunity to compare a range of competing products when making a purchase.

[.....]

4) Indispensable nature of the restriction of competition

[.....]

The clause requiring retailers to carry a sufficient number of competing brands is necessary in order to attract and retain the loyalty of consumers who expect to find, in each retail outlet, a specialized commercial environment allowing them to choose from a range of competing brands. It should also be stressed that, following amendments made by Givenchy at the request of the Commission, authorized retailers are no longer restricted in choice to the list drawn up by the manufacturer of the brands likely to constitute such an environment. Retailers are now free to choose from competing brands, which, forming part of the same market for luxury cosmetic products, are usually distributed through networks of authorized retailers. As regards the requirement that a sufficient number of brands be carried in the retail outlet, it seems that the minimum number of four brands imposed until now by Givenchy is not unduly high, given the degree of specialization that is currently a usual feature of the distribution of luxury cosmetic products in the Community.

[.....]

5) Elimination of competition

The contracts on which the Givenchy selective distribution system is based do not afford the undertakings concerned the possibility of eliminating competition in respect of a substantial part of the products in question. Since, on the one hand, the contracts do not contain any no-competition clauses and since, on the other, the Community market comprises a large number of undertakings manufacturing or marketing luxury cosmetic products, authorized Givenchy retailers are able to take advantage of inter-brand competition.

[.....]

Case cross-reference:

▸ T-87/92 *BVBA Kruidvat v. Commission* [1996] ECR II-1931, appeal dismissed; C-70/97 P *BVBA Kruidvat v. Commission* [1998] ECR I-7183, appeal dismissed.

C. Franchising

Cross-reference for this part:

▸ Guidelines on Vertical Restraints, [2010] OJ C 130/1, paragraphs 188-191.

1) Case 161/84 *Pronuptia* [1986] ECR 353

See above for facts of the case and relevant paragraphs (I-J-4, p. 52).

Relevance: franchise agreements can be assessed under Article 101, although many seemingly 'restrictive' clauses fall outside the prohibition.

D. Agency contracts

Cross-references for this part:

▸ Guidelines on Vertical Restraints, [2010] OJ C 130/1, paragraphs 12-21.

▸ *Pittsburgh Corning Europe* Commission decision 72/403/CEE [1972] 272/35 (not available in English).

▸ Cases on economic unit doctrine (see I-D).

1) Case 311/85 *Flemish Travel Agents* [1987] ECR 3801

According to a Belgian legislative Decree, travel agents (intermediaries for tour operators) should observe the prices and fares agreed upon or required by law. Moreover, it was prohibited to share commissions or to offer rebates to their customers (consumers!). The Association of Flemish Travel Agencies (the "Vereniging" in the judgment) claimed that the Social Service of the Local and Regional Public Services (the "Sociale Dienst"), which, inter alia, functioned as a travel agent for employees of the above-mentioned Social Service, did not adhere to this Decree.

Relevance: agency contracts can be assessed under Article 101 in so far as these contracts restrict (horizontal) competition between agents.

[.....]

Question a

9 Although the first question refers expressly only to Article 85 (1) of the Treaty, it must be understood, as the Belgian and French governments and the Commission have suggested, as seeking to ascertain whether legislative provisions or regulations of a Member State requiring travel agents to observe the prices and tariffs for travel set by tour operators, prohibiting them from sharing commissions paid in respect of the sale of such travel with their customers or granting rebates to their customers and regarding such acts as contrary to fair commercial practice are incompatible with the obligations of the Member States pursuant to Article 5, in conjunction with Articles 3 (f) and 85, of the EEC Treaty.
10 As the Court has consistently held (see, most recently, the judgment of 30 April 1986 in Joined Cases 209 to 213/84 Ministère public v Asjes [1986] ECR 1425), while it is true that Articles 85 and 86 of the Treaty concern the conduct of undertakings and not laws or regulations of the Member States, the Treaty nevertheless imposes a duty on Member States not to adopt or maintain in force any measure which could deprive those provisions of their effectiveness. The Court has held that that would be the case, in particular, if a Member State were to require or favour the adoption of agreements, decisions or concerted practices contrary to Article 85 or to reinforce their effects.
11 In order to reply in a useful manner to the national Court it is necessary first of all to determine whether the documents before the Court disclose the existence of agreements, decisions or concerted practices of that kind in the area of activities concerned by the question referred, and then to determine whether provisions such as the Belgian provisions at issue are intended to reinforce the effects of such agreements, decisions or concerted practices, or have that effect.
12 The documents before the Court show that the Belgian provisions form part of a structure involving agreements at various levels intended to oblige travel agents to observe the prices of tours fixed by tour operators.
13 First of all, according to information provided by the Commission, which was not disputed, in 1963 the Belgische Beroepsvereniging voor Reisbureaus (Union of Belgian Travel Agents, hereinafter referred to as the "BBR") adopted a code of conduct binding on its members. Article 22 of that code, the content of which was incorporated in Article 22 of the Royal Decree of 30 June 1966, at issue in the main proceedings, treated the sharing of commissions with customers and the granting to them of prohibited rebates or rebates contrary to commercial usage as unfair competition.
14 Secondly, again according to the information provided by the Commission, in 1975 a framework agreement was concluded within the BBR regarding cooperation between the council of travel agents and the group of charter flight operators belonging to the BBR. Article 8 (b) of that agreement provides that an agent may not transfer part of his commission to a third party in any form and must observe the price and conditions of sale laid down by the organizer.
15 With regard to contractual relations between tour operators and travel agents, the standard-form contract attached to the observations of the Belgian government provides under point 1 of the general conditions of cooperation that a tour operator "may refuse to sell [tours] to agents who refuse to comply with the rules of commercial practice and act contrary to the spirit of the legislation". That wording allows tour operators to rescind

their contracts with travel agents who do not observe the rules of commercial practice applicable to them, including those prohibiting the sharing of commissions and the granting of rebates.

16 The existence of a system of agreements intended to prevent such practices is confirmed, moreover, by the very wording of Article 22 of the Royal Decree of 30 June 1966, at issue in the main proceedings. Article 22 (2) (d), concerning the obligations of a travel agent "with regard to suppliers", states that the agent must "observe the agreed prohibition on the sharing of commissions with clients".

17 It must therefore be concluded, on the basis of the documents before the Court, that with regard to the activities of travel agents there is a system of agreements both between travel agents themselves and between agents and tour operators intended to oblige agents to observe the prices for travel set by tour operators, and having that effect. Such agreements have the object and effect of restricting competition between travel agents. That is to say, they prevent travel agents from competing on prices by deciding, on their own initiative, to pass on to their customers some portion of the commission which they receive.

18 Furthermore, such agreements may affect trade between Member States in several respects. First of all, travel agents operating in one Member State may sell travel organized by tour operators established in other Member States. Secondly, these agents may sell travel to customers residing in other Member States. Thirdly, the travel in question is often to other Member States.

19 The Belgian government denied that Article 85 (1) can apply to the relationship between a tour operator and a travel agent, arguing that the relationship is one of principal and agent. A travel agent must therefore be regarded as an auxiliary organ of the tour operator. In support of its argument the Belgian government emphasized that a travel agent does not enter into contracts with clients in his own name but in the name and on behalf of the tour operator organizing the travel in question.

20 However, a travel agent of the kind referred to by the national Court must be regarded as an independent agent who provides services on an entirely independent basis. He sells travel organized by a large number of different tour operators and a tour operator sells travel through a very large number of agents. Contrary to the Belgian government's submissions, a travel agent cannot be treated as an auxiliary organ forming an integral part of a tour operator's undertaking.

21 It follows from those considerations that agreements such as those at issue in the main proceedings are incompatible with Article 85 (1) of the Treaty.

22 It remains to be determined whether provisions such as those at issue before the national Court, viewed in this context, are of such a nature as to reinforce the effects of the agreements between travel agents and tour operators.

23 First of all, by transforming an originally contractual prohibition into a legislative provision a provision such as Article 22 of the Royal Decree of 1966 reinforces the effect of the agreements in question between the parties, inasmuch as the rule acquires a permanent character and can no longer be rescinded by the parties. Secondly, by treating the failure to observe agreed prices and tariffs or the prohibition on the sharing of commissions with clients as contrary to fair commercial practice it allows travel agents who comply with the agreed rules of commercial practice to bring proceedings for a restraining order against travel agents who

are not party to the agreement and do not comply with those rules. Thirdly, with regard both to parties to the agreements and to third parties the possible withdrawal of the licence to operate as a travel agent in the event of failure to observe the agreed rules of commercial practice constitutes a highly effective sanction.

24 The answer to question a referred by the national Court must therefore be that legislative provisions or regulations of a Member State requiring travel agents to observe the prices and tariffs for travel set by tour operators, prohibiting them from sharing the commission paid in respect of the sale of such travel with their clients or granting rebates to their clients and regarding such acts as contrary to fair commercial practice are incompatible with the obligations of the Member States pursuant to Article 5, in conjunction with Articles 3 (f) and 85, of the EEC Treaty, where the object or effect of such national provisions is to reinforce the effects of agreements, decisions or concerted practices which are contrary to Article 85.

[.....]

Case cross-reference:

▸ Cases on useful effect doctrine (see chapter III).

E. Conspiratorial pressure on dealers (implied market sharing)

1) Case 107/82 *AEG-Telefunken* [1983] 3151 (summary of judgment)

This dispute concerned the selective distribution system as operated by AEG-Telefunken. Distributors were selected by reference to objective quality criteria. In practice, however, the company discriminated against some distributors, such as discount stores. These types of distributors were not admitted to AEG-Telefunken's distributions network. More generally, it appeared that only distributors that adhered to an 'advisory' resale price (price maintenance) were accepted. The question was whether these refusals should be classified as part of a concerted practice (tacit understanding) between AEG-Telefunken and its existing distributors or as a unilateral marketing policy of the former undertaking.

Relevance: example of pressure on or by dealers resulting in the limiting of the number and 'type' of distributors.

Summary

1. Where, in the course of a proceeding for establishing whether there has been an infringement of Community competition rules, the Commission takes the view that a document cannot be communicated in its entirety to the undertaking concerned for reasons of confidentiality and the protection of trade secrecy, it must abstain from using that document as evidence. An undertaking cannot allow to be used against it a document part of which has not been communicated to it and it is not for the Commission to judge whether a document or a part thereof is or is not of use for the defence of the undertaking concerned.

2. Where documents mentioned in a decision under Article 85 of the Treaty were not mentioned in the statement of objections, the undertaking concerned is entitled to take the

view that they are of no importance for the purposes of the case.
By not informing the undertaking that such documents are to be used in the decision, the Commission prevents it from putting forward at the appropriate time its view of the probative value of the documents. It follows that such documents cannot be regarded as admissible evidence even if the undertaking is acquainted with them inasmuch as they originate in its own offices.
3. An infringement of the rights of the defence affecting only certain special aspects of a proceeding for establishing whether there has been an infringement of Community competition rules cannot imply that the procedure as a whole is irregular. The exclusion of certain documents used by the Commission in infringement of the rights of the defence is of no significance except to the extent to which the Commission's objections can be proved only by reference to those documents.
4. Although selective distribution systems necessarily influence competition in the Common Market, legitimate requirements, such as the maintenance of a specialist trade capable of providing specific services as regards high-quality and high-technology products, justify a reduction of price competition in favour of competition relating to factors other than price. Systems of selective distribution, in so far as they aim at the attainment of a legitimate goal capable of improving competition in relation to factors other than price, therefore constitute an element of competition which is in conformity with Article 85 (1) of the Treaty.
The limitations inherent in a selective distribution system are however acceptable only on condition that their aim is in fact an improvement in competition in the sense above mentioned. Otherwise they would have no justification inasmuch as their sole effect would be to reduce price competition.
5. Selective distribution systems constitute one of a number of aspects of competition in conformity with Article 85 (1) of the Treaty provided that resellers are chosen on the basis of objective criteria of a qualitative nature relating to the technical qualifications of the reseller and his staff and the suitability of his trading premises and that such conditions are laid down uniformly for all potential resellers and are not applied in a discriminatory fashion.
The operation of a selective distribution system based on criteria other than those mentioned above constitutes an infringement of Article 85 (1). The position is the same where a system which is in principle in conformity with Community law is applied in practice in a manner incompatible therewith.
6. A refusal by a manufacturer to approve distributors who satisfy the qualitative criteria of his system of selective distribution does not constitute, on the part of the undertaking, unilateral conduct exempt as such from the prohibition contained in Article 85 (1) of the Treaty. On the contrary, such an attitude forms part of the contractual relations between the undertaking and resellers, since the admission of a distributor is based on the acceptance, tacit or express, by the contracting parties of the policy pursued by the undertaking, which requires inter alia the exclusion from the network of distributors who are qualified for admission but are not prepared to adhere to that policy.
7. A restriction of price competition, which is inherent in any selective distribution system, is lawful only to the extent to which the maintenance of a certain level of prices is strictly justified by the requirements of a system within which competition must continue to perform the function assigned to it by the Treaty, since the object of such a

system is solely the improvement of competition in so far as it relates to factors other than prices and not the guarantee of a high profit margin for approved resellers.
A manufacturer operating a system of selective distribution is therefore not justified in taking the view that the acceptance of a commitment to charge prices making possible a sufficiently high profit margin constitutes a lawful condition for admission to a selective distribution system. By the very fact that he is authorized not to admit to and not to keep in his distribution network traders who were not, or are no longer, in a position to provide services typical of the specialist trade, he has at his disposal all the means necessary to enable him to ensure the effective application of the system. In such circumstances the existence of a price commitment constitutes a condition which is manifestly foreign to the requirements of a selective distribution system and thus also affects freedom of competition.
8. The fact that a subsidiary has separate legal personality is not sufficient to exclude the possibility of imputing its conduct to the parent company, in particular where the subsidiary, although having separate legal personality, does not decide independently upon its own conduct on the market but carries out, in all material respects, the instructions given to it by the parent company.
9. An undertaking possessing roughly 5 % of the market concerned is an undertaking of sufficient importance for its behaviour to be, in principle, capable of affecting trade between Member States.
10. The mere fact that at a certain time traders applying for admission to a selective distribution network or who have already been admitted are not engaging in intra-Community trade cannot suffice to exclude the possibility that restrictions on their freedom of action imposed by the manufacturer may impede intra-Community trade, since the situation may change from one year to another in terms of alterations in the conditions or composition of the market both in the Common Market as a whole and in the individual national markets.
11. A distribution policy motivated by a desire both to guarantee a high profit margin for approved resellers and to impede, so far as at all possible, the admission of new forms of trade, which are regarded a priori as being incapable of satisfying the specialist trade conditions, exhibits characteristics which cannot be reconciled with a correct application of a selective distribution system.
12. An undertaking on which a fine has been imposed under Article 15 of Regulation No 17 is required to pay default interest up to the date of actual payment of the fine.

2) *John Deere*, XIVth Report on Competition Policy (1984), point 67

Relevance: example of pressure on dealers to restrict parallel trade.

67. A prohibition decision was also taken in another case involving market segregation, this time in the agricultural machinery sector. I The agricultural machinery manufacturer Deere and Company, trading in the EEC through several branches and subsidiaries, together with three of its independent distributors in the Common Market, were found to have infringed Article 85 (1) by imposing, accepting and practising bans on the export of its products by dealers or by

the distributors themselves to other Member States within the Common Market. Fluctuations in the prices for agricultural machinery have given rise to parallel trading between various Member States. Deere, however, attempted to prevent such trading, either by explicit export bans, going back to 1967, or otherwise. In view of the gravity and duration of this infringement, but taking into account certain mitigating factors, for example the state of the market and the fact that, although late in the proceeding, Deere introduced a compliance programme, the Commission imposed a fine of 2 million ECU on Deere.

The three distributors (NV Cofabel in Belgium, NV Nagel of the Netherlands and DOMI of Denmark) and indeed other Deere dealers who have accepted contracts containing export bans, have also broken the competition rules by doing so. However, the contractual export bans in this case are contained in pre-printed standard contracts; clearly the dealers had not taken the initiative to have the bans included in their contracts and have in many cases ignored them. The Commission has felt it appropriate, therefore, not to impose a fine on dealers in this case.

F. Unilateral behaviour

1) Case T-41/96 *Bayer AG v. Commission (Adalat)* [2002] ECR II-3383

Bayer, active on the chemical and pharmaceutical market, produced and sold medical preparations under the trade name Adalat (or Adalate) through its subsidiaries. The price of Adalat, however, was determined by national health authorities, which meant that prices varied considerably throughout the Community. In Spain and France, prices were on average 40% lower than in the United Kingdom, which resulted in an influx of Adalat from these countries. Due to this parallel import, Bayer UK sustained losses. In response, Bayer adjusted its delivery policy. It no longer satisfied the disproportional demand for Adalat from Spanish and French wholesalers; only orders that reflected the 'normal' demand for a certain delivery area were fulfilled. According to the Commission, this policy was in fact an agreement between Bayer and the wholesalers (which co-operated out of fear for sanctions, viz. reduced deliveries), while Bayer maintained that it was a unilateral line of conduct that would fall outside the prohibition of Article 101 (1).

Relevance: refinement of AEG-Telefunken and John Deere. What constitutes a unilateral action? What qualifies as an agreement?

[.....]

B. The concept of an agreement within the meaning of Article 85 (1) of the Treaty

66 The case-law shows that, where a decision on the part of a manufacturer constitutes unilateral conduct of the undertaking, that decision escapes the prohibition in Article 85 (1) of the Treaty (Case 107/82 AEG v Commission [1983] ECR 3151, paragraph 38; Joined Cases 25/84 and 26/84 Ford and Ford Europe v Commission [1985] ECR 2725, paragraph 21; Case T-43/92 Dunlop Slazenger v Commission [1994] ECR II-441, paragraph 56).

67 It is also clear from the case-law in that in order for there to be an agreement within the meaning of Article 85 (1) of the Treaty it is sufficient that the undertakings in question should have expressed their joint intention to conduct themselves on the market in a specific way (Case 41/69 ACF Chemiefarma v Commission [1970] ECR 661, paragraph 112; Joined Cases 209/78 to 215/78 and 218/78 Van Landewyck and Others v Commission [1980] ECR 3125, paragraph 86; Case T-7/89 Hercules Chemicals v Commission [1991] ECR II-1711, paragraph 256).

68 As regards the form in which that common intention is expressed, it is sufficient for a stipulation to be the expression of the parties' intention to behave on the market in accordance with its terms (see, in particular, ACF Chemiefarma, paragraph 112, and Van Landewyck, paragraph 86), without its having to constitute a valid and binding contract under national law (Sandoz, paragraph 13).

69 It follows that the concept of an agreement within the meaning of Article 85 (1) of the Treaty, as interpreted by the case-law, centres around the existence of a concurrence of wills between at least two parties, the form in which it is manifested being unimportant so long as it constitutes the faithful expression of the parties' intention.

70 In certain circumstances, measures adopted or imposed in an apparently unilateral manner by a manufacturer in the context of his continuing relations with his distributors have been regarded as constituting an agreement within the meaning of Article 85 (1) of the Treaty (Joined Cases 32/78, 36/78 to 82/78 BMW Belgium and Others v Commission [1979] ECR 2435, paragraphs 28 to 30; AEG, paragraph 38; Ford and Ford Europe, paragraph 21; Case 75/84 Metro v Commission (Metro II [1986] ECR 3021, paragraphs 72 and 73; Sandoz, paragraphs 7 to 12; Case C-70/93 BMW v ALD [1995] ECR I-3439, paragraphs 16 and 17).

71 That case-law shows that a distinction should be drawn between cases in which an undertaking has adopted a genuinely unilateral measure, and thus without the express or implied participation of another undertaking, and those in which the unilateral character of the measure is merely apparent. Whilst the former do not fall within Article 85 (1) of the Treaty, the latter must be regarded as revealing an agreement between undertakings and may therefore fall within the scope of that Article. That is the case, in particular, with practices and measures in restraint of competition which, though apparently adopted unilaterally by the manufacturer in the context of its contractual relations with its dealers, nevertheless receive at least the tacit acquiescence of those dealers.

72 It is also clear from that case-law that the Commission cannot hold that apparently unilateral conduct on the part of a manufacturer, adopted in the context of the contractual relations which he maintains with his dealers, in reality forms the basis of an agreement between undertakings within the meaning of Article 85 (1) of the Treaty if it does not establish the existence of an acquiescence by the other partners, express or implied, in the attitude adopted by the manufacturer (BMW Belgium, paragraphs 28 to 30; AEG, paragraph 38; Ford and Ford Europe, paragraph 21; Metro II, paragraphs 72 and 73; Sandoz, paragraphs 7 to 12; BMW v ALD, paragraphs 16 and 17).

[.....]

Case cross-references:

- Joined Cases C-2 & 3/01 P *Commission v. Bayer AG (Adalat)* [2004] ECR I-23, ruling of the GC upheld.
- Case T-168/01, *GlaxoSmithKline v. Commission*, [2006] ECR II-2969 (*see I-G-6*).

CHAPTER VII

Introduction to Concentration Control and Structural Joint Ventures

General chapter cross-references:

▸ Regulation 139/2004 of 20 January 2004 on the control of concentrations between undertakings (the EC Merger Regulation), [2004] OJ L 14/1.

▸ Guidelines on the assessment of horizontal mergers under the Council Regulation on the control of concentrations between undertakings, [2004] C 31/5.

▸ Guidelines on the assessment of non-horizontal mergers under the Council Regulation on the control of concentrations between undertakings, [2007] OJ C 265/7.

▸ Commission Consolidated Jurisdictional Notice under Council Regulation (EC) No. 139/2004 on the control of concentrations between undertakings, [2007] OJ C 95/1.

▸ Best Practices on the Subject of EC Merger Control Proceedings (http://europa.eu.int/comm/competition/mergers/legislation/regulation/best_practices.pdf).

▸ C. Bright and M. Persson, 'Article 22 of the EC Merger Regulation: An Opportunity Not to be Missed?', (2003) 24 *ECLR*, 490.

▸ D. Domínguez Pérez and R. Burnley, 'The Article 9 Referral Back Procedure: A Solution to the Jurisdictional Dilemma of the European Merger Regulation?', (2003) 24 *ECLR*, 364.

▸ K. Kiljanski, 'Pass-on in Merger Efficiency Defence', (2003) 26 *World Competition*, 651.

▸ C. Luescher, 'Efficiency Considerations in European Merger Control – Just Another Battle Ground for the European Commission, Economics and Competition Lawyers?', (2004) 25 *ECLR*, 72.

▸ G. Robert and C. Hudson, 'Past Co-ordination and the Commission Notice on the Appraisal of Horizontal Mergers', (2004) 25 *ECLR*, 163.

▸ I. Kokkouris, 'The concept of market definition and the SSNIP test in the merger appraisal', (2005) 4 *ECLR*, 209.

▸ A-L. Hinds, 'The New EC Merger Regulation-The More Things Change the More They Stay the Same', *European Business Law Review*, 2006, Volume 17, Issue 6,

▸ C. Esteva Mosso, 'Non-Horizontal Mergers – a European perspective', 2007 Fordham Corp.L.Inst. 43-75 (B. Hawk ed. 2008).

▸ M.T. Brouwer, 'Horizontal mergers and efficiencies; theory and anti trust practice', *European Journal of Law and Economics*, Volume 26, Number 1, 2008, pp. 11-26.

▸ R. di Brozolo, Arbitration in EC Merger Control: Old Wine in a New Bottle, *European Business Law Review*, Volume 19, Issue 1, 2008.

▸ J. Galloway, 'Convergence in International Merger Control', *CompLRev.* 2008, Vol. 5(2) pp. 179-192.

A. The situation before 1989

1) Case 6/72 *Continental Can* [1973] ECR 215

See above for facts of the case and relevant paragraphs (II-A-6, p. 92).

Relevance: before 1989, Article 102 did apply to external growth achieved by a take-over (concentration), although *ex post* only.

Case cross-references:

▸ Case T-51/89 *Tetra Pak I* [1990] ECR II-309 (see II-D-1).

▸ *Gillette (Wilkinson Sword)* Commission decision 93/252/EEC [1993] OJ 116/21 (sse II-D-2).

B. Borderline between concentration and co-operation

1) *Renault/Volvo*, XXth Report on Competition Policy (1990), point 147

Relevance: difference in nature between an acquisition (partial concentration) and a joint venture (form of cooperation where cooperating undertakings remain independent vis-à-vis each other). One agreement; same parties concerned.

147. The Commission adopted its first decision under Regulation No 4064/89 on the control of concentrations between undertakings in the Renault/Volvo case. The case involved exchanges of shares and the setting-up of joint committees with decision making powers, one for cars and the other for industrial vehicles.

The Commission decided that the transaction concerning cars had not reached the stage of a concentration within the meaning of Article 3 of the Regulation. It based its decision on the fact that the share swaps were limited to 25%, and that the parties could act independently in the event of disagreement within the joint committee for cars. As a result, the parties were not continuously subject to a single economic management in respect of their car activities.

As regards trucks, however, the parties exchanged 45% of their shares and decided permanently to merge their R&D, production and other truck, coach and bus operations. Their alliance in this sector created lasting and irreversible joint control in this sector. The Commission therefore considered that this operation constituted a concentration within the meaning of Article 3 of the merger control Regulation. As concerns this part of the operation, the Commission considered the merger compatible with the Common Market as the combined market shares held by Renault and Volvo in the Community barely exceeded 25%. Although the firms undoubtedly held larger shares of certain national markets in the Community, the existing and potential competition from several other major producers in a strong financial position and present on all the national markets would prevent Renault/Volvo alone from significantly determining prices and other conditions of competition on the national markets for industrial vehicles. As a result, the Commission considered that the alliance between Renault and Volvo would not create or strengthen a dominant position liable significantly to impede effective competition in the Common Market or in a substantial part of it.

As regards the part of the operation concerning cars which was not regarded as constituting a concentration, the Commission informed the parties by letter that there were no grounds for further action under Articles 85 or 86.

C. Co-operative full-function joint ventures

Cross-reference for this part:

▸ L.G. Radicati di Brozolo and M. Gustafsson, 'Full-function Joint Ventures Under the Merger Regulation: The Need for Clarification', (2003) 24 *ECLR*, 574.

1) *Telia/Telenor/Schibsted*, Case No IV/JV.1, [1999] OJ C 220/28

Telia and Telenor, respectively a Swedish and a Norwegian telecommunications operator, and Schibsted, a Norwegian group involved in media and Internet related activities, had notified the intended creation of joint venture called NewCoI. Other undertakings concerned were Nextel, a subsidiary of Telenor, InfoMedia, part of Telia, and Scandinavia On-Line (SOL), which was jointly owned by Telenor and Schibsted. The joint ventures' activities were to entail A) the provision of Internet gateway services and B) the production (design) of web sites. The Commission declared the concentration to be compatible with the Internal Market.

Relevance: explanation of article 2 (4) of Regulation 4064/89. First JV to be assessed under this rule (new since March 1998).

[.....]

III. Concentration

Full function entity

8. The parties will contribute to NewCoI most of the assets and activities of InfoMedia and SOL. Both companies currently operate as independent business entities.

9. NewCoI will have its own organisation and will initially have around [Deleted: business secret] staff which will enable it to perform all its functions independently. After a start-up period NewCoI is expected to finance its activities through own resources or financing. The sales which NewCoI will make to its parent companies are estimated by the parties to be less than 10% of its total sales. The joint venture will acquire certain services from the parents, for example [Deleted: business secret] However, these will be acquired on an arm's length basis and will also be available from other suppliers.

10. The shareholders' agreement is valid until [Deleted: business secret] and subsequently subject to automatic renewal for [Deleted: business secret] year periods. Telia and Schibsted are prohibited from transferring their shares in NewCoI until [Deleted: business secret]. Nextel may transfer its shares from [Deleted: business secret]. NewCoI will accordingly perform on a long-lasting basis all the functions of an autonomous economic entity.

[.....]

VII. Competitive assessment

[.....]

B. Co-ordination of Competitive Behaviour

28. Pursuant to Article 2 (4) Merger Regulation, a joint venture having as its object or effect the co-ordination of the competitive behaviour of (at least two of) its parent

companies has to be appraised in accordance with the criteria of Article 85 (1) and 85 (3) EC-Treaty. In order to establish a restriction of competition in the sense of Article 85 (1) EC-Treaty, it is necessary that the co-ordination of the parent companies' competitive behaviour is likely and appreciable and that it results from the creation of the joint venture, be it as its object or its effect.

1. Definition of candidate markets for co-ordination

29. Candidate markets for co-ordination are those on which the joint venture and at least two parent companies are active, or closely related neighbouring markets where at least two parent companies remain active.

a) Relevant product markets (services and access markets)

30. The joint venture will be active in the provision of various services linked to the use of Internet, which are described above (Section V). As far as these markets are concerned, at least two of the parent companies are active on the market for web site production. However, beside these joint venture markets, another market could be identified on which at least two of the parent companies are active. This market, which concerns the provision of dial-up access to the Internet, constitutes a market which is closely related to that of the joint venture, in the sense of Article 2(4) of the Merger Regulation.

(1) Advertising over the Internet

31. Concerning the market for the provision of advertising over the Internet, it can be stated that only Schibsted Multimedia AS remains active on it after the creation of the joint venture. Therefore, this market can not be considered as a candidate market for co-ordination.

(2) Paid for content provision

32. Concerning the market for the provision of subscriber content over the Internet, none of the three parent companies will remain active on the same product market as the joint venture following the operation. Telenor Nextel AS and Schibsted Multimedia AS were, prior to the creation of the joint venture, active on it through their jointly owned subsidiary Scandinavia OnLine AB. This subsidiary being entirely transferred to the joint venture as Telenor Nextel's and Schibsted's joint contribution to it, these two parent companies are not active on this market as a result of the creation of the joint venture. Telia has contributed its activities on this market to the joint venture. Schibsted provides content through the on-line version of the newspaper it owns (Aftonbladet), but this service is offered for free and therefore is on the Internet advertising market. Therefore, this market cannot be considered as a candidate market for co-ordination.

(3) Web site production and related services

33. According to the indications submitted by the parties in the notification, two of the parent companies remain active on the market for the production of web sites. These companies are Telia, through its subsidiary Telia Promotor AB, and Telenor Nextel, through Bonnier Telenor Företagsinfo AB. InfoMedia, which also provides these services, will be contributed to the joint venture. The production of web sites therefore constitutes a candidate market for co-ordination between the parent companies of the joint venture.

(4) Dial up Internet access

34. Generally speaking, dial up Internet access provided by Internet Service Providers (ISPs) who charge subscriptions to customers constitutes a discrete market, according to the market definitions as set out above.

35. All three parent companies are active on different markets from the above mentioned

joint venture markets. Both Telia and Telenor (through Telenordia which has entered into a joint venture with BT and TeleDanmark) provide a full range of telecommunication services, whereas Schibsted is active in the field of multimedia services.

36. Telia and Telenordia (Algonet) provide dial up Internet access to users. Access to the Internet is a necessary prerequisite for the use of any Internet service. The dial up Internet access market must therefore be considered as a market upstream to the joint venture's markets. This upstream market is to be considered as closely related to the joint venture's markets and therefore constitutes a candidate market for co-ordination in the sense of Article 2(4) of the Merger Regulation.

Given that the creation of the joint venture does not raise concerns under Article 2 of the Merger Regulation, all of the above market definitions can be left open.

b) Relevant geographical market

37. For web site production, as it is likely to be generally done in Swedish, the relevant geographic market is at least as wide as Sweden or Sweden plus the Swedish language communities in other Nordic countries. However, there is no technical barrier to these services being provided outside Sweden and the Nordic countries. The Internet services of the joint venture will be offered in Swedish language for private and business users in Sweden. Although access to Internet content in Sweden is available from outside Sweden, this does not widen the market definition as the content offered is aimed specifically at consumers in Sweden. Therefore, the relevant geographical market for dial up Internet access is Sweden.

2. Assessment under Article 2(4)

38. The parties submitted that co-ordination of the competitive behaviour between the parent companies is not the object of the creation of the joint venture. In the absence of clear indications to prove that such an object is pursued, an intended co-ordination of the parent companies' behaviour can not be established.

39. However, it might be the effect of the operation to give way to co-ordination of competitive behaviour. This question has to be examined separately for the web site production market and for the dial up Internet access market.

Web site production and related services

40. On the web site production market, which is one of the joint venture markets, two parent companies will remain active. According to the parties' indications, the combined market share of the parent companies does not exceed [Business secret: less than 5%] % on this market and the joint venture will have a market share of [Business secret: less than 5%] %. This total market share of [Business secret: less than 10%] % on the Swedish market, which is the narrowest and most unfavourable to the parties, in any event would not allow the conclusion that any restriction of competition is appreciable..

41. Therefore, in the light of the above, even if the parent companies were to co-ordinate their activities on the web site production market this co-ordination could not lead to an appreciable restriction of competition and it is therefore not necessary to establish a causal link between the creation of the joint venture and the behaviour of the parent companies outside the joint venture on this closely related market.

Dial up Internet access

42. The dial up Internet access market is characterised by high growth [According to information obtained during the Commission's investigation, the growth rate in

Sweden in the next three years will be around 30%] and relatively low barriers to entry. The costs of starting a small ISP providing a dial up service are low and small companies can and do provide dial up Internet access. According to information supplied by the parties, there are around 100 such ISPs in Sweden. Entry is also possible from both local start-up ISPs and global ISPs entering the Swedish market. In addition, as the market is very price sensitive, in particular given the low switching costs, this would prevent higher prices through co-ordination from being sustained. Any increase in prices would result in the parties quickly losing market share to rival companies as new subscribers opted for lower price offerings.

43. Telia is present on this market. Telenor, through Telenordia (33%, the other parent companies are BT and TeleDanmark), is also present. Telia and Telenordia hold substantial market shares [Telia has a [25-40%] market share and Telenordia has [10-25%] of the market defined above. The largest service provider offering dial up Internet access in Sweden is Tele2 (a telecommunications company which is a member of the Kinnevik Group, a leading Nordic media company), which has a [40-50%] market share. However, on the basis of other information received, it appears that if the market share of Telenordia were to be attributed to Telenor, their total market share would be [35-65%]. Figures in square brackets are business secrets. This data is on the basis of information obtained from the notifying parties and other third parties during the investigation. Other third party estimates have put the leading three companies market shares as being lower than these figures (Tele2: 36%; Telia: 25%; Telenordia (Algonet): 13%)]. However, market shares are of limited significance on this growing market. In any case, the combined market share of Telia and Telenordia has fallen by between 15% and 20% of the total market over the last nine months.

44. Given the characteristics identified above, the market structure is not conducive to co-ordination of competitive behaviour.

45. The relative size of the markets for Internet advertising, content and web site production (the markets of the joint venture) compared with that of dial up Internet access is relevant to the likelihood of co-ordination. The dial up Internet access market is substantially larger than the other markets mentioned above [According to information obtained by the Commission during its investigation, the proportion of revenues derived from access is 93% in Sweden compared with 7% from all other Internet revenue sources] and therefore given the relative sizes of the markets concerned, the likelihood of co-ordination is reduced further.

46. Therefore, in the light of the above and on the basis that the narrowest market definition has been chosen, there is no likelihood that the parent companies would co-ordinate on the dial up Internet access market and it is therefore not necessary to establish a causal link between the creation of the joint venture and the behaviour of the parent companies outside the joint venture on this related market.

[.....]

2) *ENEL/FT/DT,* Case No IV/JV.2, [1999] OJ C 178/15

ENEL, France Telecom (FT) and Deutsche Telekom (DT) had notified the establishment of a joint venture, namely Wind. FT and DT were telecommunications operators; ENEL was an Italian provider of electricity. The joint venture was to provide telecommunications services on the Italian market. The Commission decided that this concentration was compatible with the Internal Market. One of the issues raised in its decision concerned the issue of (possible) coordination of competitive behaviour.

Relevance: notion of 'coordination' in cases in which there already was (or could have been) coordination between the parent companies (coordination is not the result of the creation of the joint venture as such).

[.....]

B Co-ordination of competitive behaviour

29. Pursuant to Article 2 (4) of the Merger Regulation, to the extent that the creation of a joint venture has as its object or effect the co-ordination of the competitive behaviour of undertakings that remain independent, such co-ordination shall be appraised in accordance with the criteria of Article 85 (1) and (3) of the EC Treaty. In order to establish a restriction of competition in the sense of Article 85 (1) of the EC Treaty, it is necessary that the co-ordination of the parent companies' competitive behaviour is likely and appreciable and that it results from the creation of the joint venture, be it as its object or its effect.

1. Definition of candidate markets for co-ordination

30. According to Article 2 (4) (2) of the Merger Regulation, the Commission shall, when making the said appraisal, take into account in particular whether two or more parent companies retain to a significant extent activities in the same market as the joint venture or in a market which is downstream or upstream from that of the joint venture or in a neighbouring market closely related to this market. Only the relationship between FT and DT needs to be considered in this context. After having leased its telecommunications network to Wind for a period of at least [Deleted. Business secret.] years, ENEL cannot be regarded as a competitor on any of the markets to be considered in the following.

(a) Fixed line telephony

31. In so far as domestic and international voice and data telecommunications services are concerned, neither ENEL nor FT or DT are active on the Italian markets. In view of the substantial investments in Wind which the parties have already made or will have to make, it is unlikely that they would enter these markets on their own in the future. This is reflected by their agreement not to compete with each other on these markets.

32. FT and DT are active on the markets for domestic and international voice and data telecommunications services in France and Germany respectively. In view of their geographical proximity and their importance to Italy (Germany and France are the two most important countries for Italy in terms of bilateral traffic; in 1997 for example, bilateral traffic between Italy and Germany alone amounted to around [Deleted. Business secret] minutes) these markets may be considered as closely related markets which fall to be assessed under Article 2 (4).

Both DT and FT hold a strong (if not dominant) position in these markets in its respective country. FT has so not so far expanded its operations to Germany to any important degree since it sold its shares in Info AG in the context of the Atlas/GlobalOne transaction. Neither has DT entered the French markets to any noticeable degree. FT and DT could be considered as (at least) potential competitors on the French and German markets. However, in view of the assessment below it is not necessary to decide this question.

33. In so far as advanced international services are concerned, FT and DT will remain active in Italy through GlobalOne. This market therefore has to be considered under Article 2 (4).

(b) Mobile telephony

34. In so far as mobile telephony services are concerned, FT and DT will be - depending on the definition of the relevant geographical market chosen - either actual competitors of Wind or at least active in a neighbouring market closely related to the Italian market. It is therefore necessary to assess whether there is any co-ordination between FT and DT in this regard.

2. Assessment under Article 2 (4)

35. There are no clear indications which would allow the conclusion that the creation of Wind has the object of co-ordinating the competitive behaviour of FT and DT on any of the markets to be considered here.

36. The following considerations appear to be relevant when examining whether the creation of Wind will have the effect of co-ordinating the competitive behaviour of FT and DT.

Fixed line telephony

37. As mentioned above, DT and FT have already so far (at least since the Atlas/GlobalOne transaction) not competed strongly with each other in their respective home countries despite the possibilities to do so which the liberalisation of the telecommunications sector has created. The two companies have, through their joint venture Atlas, entered into a joint venture with Sprint Corporation (GlobalOne) for the purpose of providing advanced telecommunications services which has already been mentioned. The lack of competition on their respective home markets in the past therefore appears to stem from a deliberate choice on the part of these companies. It is not possible to claim with the requisite degree of certainty that such lack of competition (if it were to continue in the future) would be the result of the creation of Wind.

38. The fact that both FT and DT will in the future be able to route (if they so wish) their traffic with Italy through the network of Wind may give the two companies certain advantages over their competitors. However, there is no indication that this would result in a co-ordination of the competitive behaviour of these two companies.

39. Neither is there a causal link between the creation of Wind and any co-ordination of the competitive behaviour of FT and DT in so far as advanced international services are concerned. Any such co-ordination would be the result of the creation of Atlas/GlobalOne which was approved of by the Commission in 1996 (see Cases No. IV/35.337 and 35.617).

Mobile telephony

40. In so far as mobile telephony is concerned, the possibility that the creation of Wind will entail a risk of co-ordination between DT and FT appears remote, given that the market shares of the two companies are rather modest (virtually nil on the Italian market and less than 15 % on the EC market).

41. It follows that in the present case there is no likelihood that the creation of the joint

venture company would lead to a co-ordination of the competitive behaviour of the parent companies on the market of the joint venture or on other closely related markets and it is therefore not necessary to establish a causal link between the creation of the joint venture and the behaviour of the parent companies outside the joint venture on the mobile market(s).

[.....]

3) *ENW/EASTERN*, Case No IV/M.1315, [1998] OJ C 344/7

The Dutch Noord West Energie (ENW), a large energy distribution company, and the British Eastern Group (Eastern), an electricity and natural gas group, had notified the creation of a joint venture, Compass. This joint venture, however, did not fall in the scope of the Merger Regulation (Article 3) since it could not be classified as an autonomous economic entity.

Relevance: notion of 'full-function' and some of its requirements.

[.....]

II. Community dimension

6. The combined aggregate world-wide turnover of the undertakings concerned exceeds ECU 5 000 million. The aggregate Community wide turnover of each party exceeds ECU 250 million. They do not achieve more than two-thirds of their turnover in one and the same Member State. The operation has therefore a Community dimension.

III. Concentration

7. The transaction, involving the establishment of Compass, is not a concentration within the meaning of article 3(1) (b) of the Merger Regulation since Compass will not be a full function joint venture. The joint venture does not have access to sufficient resources including finance, staff, and assets in order to conduct on a lasting basis its business activities. In particular, Compass will have limited financial autonomy. [Deleted, business secret]

8. [Deleted, business secret]

9. Another element suggesting that the joint venture will lack autonomy from the parents is that its staff (initially 3 people and over the next 5 years approximately 7-10 people) will be mainly seconded from the parents. In addition, pursuant to the shareholders' agreement, the parties will provide or secure the provision of a number of services to the joint venture, such as marketing, tendering, information technology, metering and financial support. In connection with the last point, the parties have expressely agreed that if parental support is requested by trading counterparties those counterparties may seek the parents' guarantees to support Compass's payment obligations.

IV. Conclusion

10. For the above reasons, the Commission has concluded that the notified operation does not constitute a concentration within the meaning of Article 3(2) of Council Regulation (EEC) No 4064/89 and consequently does not fall within the scope of that Regu-

lation. This decision is adopted in application of Article 6(1) (a) of Council Regulation 4064/89.
11. The Commission will treat the notification pursuant to Article 5 of Commission Regulation No 447/98 as an application within the meaning of Article 2 or a notification under Article 4 of Council Regulation 17 as requested by the parties in their notification.

[.....]

D. Minority participation

Cross-references for this part:

▸ R.A. Struijlaart, 'Minority Share Acquisitions Below the Control Threshold of the EC Merger Control Regulation: An Economic and Legal Analysis', (2002) 25 *World Competition*, 173.
▸ F. Russo, 'Abuse of protected position? Minority shareholdings and restriction of markets' competitiveness in the European Union', (2006) 29 (4) *World Competition Law and Economics Review*, 607.

1) Joined Cases 142 & 156/84 *BAT & Reynolds v. Commission* [1987] ECR 4487 (summary of judgment)

Rembrandt, an investment company active on the tobacco market and owner of Rothmans Holding, which in its turn had a substantial holding in Rothmans International, had agreed to give cigarettes manufacturer Philip Morris a direct shareholding in Rothmans International. The latter's holding was intended to be 30.8%, representing 24.9% of the votes. In comparison, Rembrandt had the same amount of shares, but it had 43.6% of the votes. Initially the two companies had wanted Philip Morris to have half the shares of Rothmans Holding, but the Commission found that this agreement infringed both Articles 101 and 102. It did not raise objections to the new (amended) agreement, which also provided for some degree of monitoring by the Commission. Still, BAT and Reynolds, which were also active on the cigarettes market, did not concur with the Commission's opinion and challenged the Commission's findings before the ECJ.

Relevance: example of the application of Article 101 (1) in case of minority participation by an undertaking in one of its competitors.

Summary

[.....]

2. Where the acquisition of shares in a competing company is the subject-matter of agreements entered into by companies which remain independent after the entry into force of the agreements, the issue must first be examined from the point of view of Article 85 of the Treaty.
Although the acquisition by one company of an equity interest in a competitor does not in itself constitute conduct restricting competition, such an acquisition may nevertheless serve as an instrument for influencing the commercial conduct of the companies in question so as to restrict or distort competition on the market on which they carry on business.
That would be true in particular where, by the acquisition of a shareholding or through

subsidiary clauses in the agreement, the investing company obtains legal or de facto control of the commercial conduct of the other company or where the agreement provides for commercial cooperation between the companies or creates a structure likely to be used for such cooperation, or where the agreement gives the investing company the possibility of reinforcing its position at a later stage and taking effective control of the other company.

Every agreement must be assessed in its economic context and in particular in the light of the situation on the relevant market. Where the companies concerned are multinational corporations which carry on business on a worldwide scale, their relationships outside the Community cannot be ignored, and it is necessary in particular to consider the possibility that the agreement in question may be part of a policy of global cooperation between them. The Commission must exercise particular vigilance in the case of a stagnant and oligopolistic market, such as that for cigarettes.

3. Although as a general rule the Court undertakes a comprehensive review of the question whether or not the conditions for the application of Article 85 (1) of the Treaty are met, its review of the Commission's appraisals of complex economic matters is necessarily limited to verifying whether the relevant rules on procedure and on the statement of reasons have been complied with, whether the facts have been accurately stated and whether there has been any manifest error of appraisal or a misuse of powers.

4. The acquisition by one company of a shareholding in a competing company can constitute an abuse of a dominant position within the meaning of Article 86 of the Treaty only where that shareholding results in effective control of the other company or at least in some influence on its commercial policy.

5. Where the Commission rejects an application pursuant to Article 3 of Regulation No 17/62, it need only state the reasons for which it did not consider it possible to hold that an infringement of the rules on competition had occurred, and it is not obliged to explain any differences in relation to the statement of objections, since that is a preparatory document containing assessments which are purely provisional in nature and are intended to define the scope of the administrative proceedings with regard to the companies against which they are brought, or to discuss all the matters of fact and of law which may have been dealt with during the administrative proceedings.

[.....]

E. Extraterritorial application and aspects of public international law

1) *Boeing/McDonnell Douglas*, Case M.877 [1997] OJ L 336/16

Boeing, a US corporation, notified to the Commission of the intended acquisition of another US corporation, namely McDonnell Douglas Corporation (MDC). The former was active in two fields: commercial aircrafts and defence and space; the latter in four: military aircraft; missiles space and electronic systems; commercial aircraft; and financial services. After the acquisition, only two competitors, Boeing and Airbus, would remain on the market for large commercial jet aircrafts. This notified concentration raised serious doubts as to its compatibility with the Internal Market, and the Commission accordingly initiated proceedings (see Article 6 sub 1 C of the Merger Regulation).

Relevance: a concentration between two non-EU corporations may fall within the ambit of the Merger Regulation.

[.....]

III. The concentration

(6) The operation constitutes a concentration within the meaning of Article 3 of the Merger Regulation since Boeing acquires within the meaning of Article 3 (1) (b) of the Regulation control of the whole of MDC.

IV. The Community dimension

(7) Boeing and MDC have a combined aggregate worldwide turnover in excess of ECU 5 billion (Boeing ECU 17 billion, MDC ECU 11 billion). Each of them has a Community-wide turnover in excess of ECU 250 million (Boeing [...] (4), MDC [...]), but they do not both achieve more than two thirds of their aggregate Community-wide turnover within one and the same Member State. The notified operation therefore has a Community dimension.

V. The impact of the operation within the European Economic Area

(8) Not only does the operation have a Community dimension within the legal sense of the Merger Regulation (Section IV above), it also has an important economic impact on the large commercial jet aircraft market within the EEA, as will be shown below in Section VII 'Competitive assessment'.
(9) The relevant market for the purposes of assessing the operation is the world market for large commercial jet aircraft. The EEA is an integral and important part of this world market, and its competitive structure is very similar. According to Boeing's 1997 Current Market Outlook, European airlines will account for about 30 % of cumulated forecast world demand over the next ten years. The average market shares of Boeing and MDC in the EEA over the last 10 years have been 54 % and 12 % respectively (in the world 61 % and 12 % respectively). As far as the existing fleet in service in the EEA is concerned, Boeing has a share of about 58 %, MDC about 20 %, and Airbus about 21 % (5) (corresponding world figures are 60 %, 24 %, and 14 %).
(10) It is therefore evident that the operation is of great significance in the EEA as it is in the world market of which the EEA is an important part.

[.....]

VIII. Conclusion

(113) For the reasons outlined above, the Commission has reached the conclusion that the proposed concentration would lead to the strengthening of a dominant position through which effective competition would be significantly impeded in the Common Market within the meaning of Article 2 (3) of the Merger Regulation.

[.....]

Case cross-reference:

▸ A.F. Bavasso, 'Boeing/McDonnell Douglas: Did the Commission Fly too High?', (1998) 19 *ECLR*, 243.

2) Case T-102/96 *Gencor v. Commission* [1999] ECR II-753

Substantively, this dispute concerned the concentration as notified by Gencor, a South African company, and Lonrho, a company incorporated under English law. The undertakings, which had both developed activities in the platinum group metal sector (PGM), were to acquire joint control of the South African Implats, a company in which Gencor already had a holding of 46,5%. Implats was to be given sole control over Eastplats and Westplats (also known as Lonrho Platinum Division, LPD), an undertaking incorporated under South African law in which Lonrho had a 73% holding. The Commission, however, found the concentration incompatible with the Internal Market, even after Gencor and Lonrho had offered commitments. Its main concern was that the acquisition might lead to duopolistic dominance and, consequently, to an output reduction and an inflation of prices of platinum.

Relevance: extraterritorial application of EU competition law in the field of concentration control to an acquisition with a relatively small presence on the Internal Market. Aspects of public international law explained.

[.....]

1. Assessment of the territorial scope of the Regulation

78 The Regulation, in accordance with Article 1 thereof, applies to all concentrations with a Community dimension, that is to say to all concentrations between undertakings which do not each achieve more than two-thirds of their aggregate Community-wide turnover within one and the same Member State, where the combined aggregate worldwide turnover of those undertakings is more than ECU 5 000 million and the aggregate Community-wide turnover of at least two of them is more than ECU 250 million.
79 Article 1 does not require that, in order for a concentration to be regarded as having a Community dimension, the undertakings in question must be established in the Community or that the production activities covered by the concentration must be carried out within Community territory.
80 With regard to the criterion of turnover, it must be stated that, as set out in paragraph 13 of the contested decision, the concentration at issue has a Community dimension within the meaning of Article 1 (2) of the Regulation. The undertakings concerned have an aggregate worldwide turnover of more than ECU 10 000 million, above the ECU 5 000 million threshold laid down by the Regulation. Gencor and Lonrho each had a Community-wide turnover of more than ECU 250 million in the latest financial year. Finally, they do not each achieve more than two-thirds of their aggregate Community-wide turnover within one and the same Member State.
81 The applicant's arguments to the effect that the legal bases for the Regulation and the wording of its preamble and substantive provisions preclude its application to the concentration at issue cannot be accepted.
82 The legal bases for the Regulation, namely Articles 87 and 235 of the Treaty, and more particularly the provisions to which they are intended to give effect, that is to say Articles 3 (g) and 85 and 86 of the Treaty, as well as the first to fifth, ninth and eleventh recitals in the preamble to the Regulation, merely point to the need to ensure that competition is not distorted in the Common Market, in

particular by concentrations which result in the creation or strengthening of a dominant position. They in no way exclude from the Regulation's field of application concentrations which, while relating to mining and/or production activities outside the Community, have the effect of creating or strengthening a dominant position as a result of which effective competition in the Common Market is significantly impeded.

83 In particular, the applicant's view cannot be founded on the closing words of the 11th recital in the preamble to the Regulation.

84 That recital states that 'a concentration with a Community dimension exists... where the concentrations are effected by undertakings which do not have their principal fields of activities in the Community but which have substantial operations there'.

85 By that reference, in general terms, to the concept of substantial operations, the Regulation does not, for the purpose of defining its territorial scope, ascribe greater importance to production operations than to sales operations. On the contrary, by setting quantitative thresholds in Article 1 which are based on the worldwide and Community turnover of the undertakings concerned, it rather ascribes greater importance to sales operations within the Common Market as a factor linking the concentration to the Community. It is common ground that Gencor and Lonrho each carry out significant sales in the Community (valued in excess of ECU 250 million).

86 Nor is it borne out by either the 30th recital in the preamble to the Regulation or Article 24 thereof that the criterion based on the location of production activities is well founded. Far from laying down a criterion for defining the territorial scope of the Regulation, Article 24 merely regulates the procedures to be followed in order to deal with situations in which non-member countries do not grant Community undertakings treatment comparable to that accorded by the Community to undertakings from those non-member countries in relation to the control of concentrations.

87 The applicant cannot, by reference to the judgment in Wood pulp, rely on the criterion as to the implementation of an agreement to support its interpretation of the territorial scope of the Regulation. Far from supporting the applicant's view, that criterion for assessing the link between an agreement and Community territory in fact precludes it. According to Wood pulp, the criterion as to the implementation of an agreement is satisfied by mere sale within the Community, irrespective of the location of the sources of supply and the production plant. It is not disputed that Gencor and Lonrho carried out sales in the Community before the concentration and would have continued to do so thereafter.

88 Accordingly, the Commission did not err in its assessment of the territorial scope of the Regulation by applying it in this case to a proposed concentration notified by undertakings whose registered offices and mining and production operations are outside the Community.

2. Compatibility of the contested decision with public international law

89 Following the concentration agreement, the previously existing competitive relationship between Implats and LPD, in particular so far as concerns their sales in the Community, would have come to an end. That would have altered the competitive structure within the Common Market since, instead of three South African PGM suppliers, there would have remained only two. The implementation of the proposed concentration would have led to the merger not only of the parties' PGM

mining and production operations in South Africa but also of their marketing operations throughout the world, particularly in the Community where Implats and LPD achieved significant sales.

90 Application of the Regulation is justified under public international law when it is foreseeable that a proposed concentration will have an immediate and substantial effect in the Community.

91 In that regard, the concentration would, according to the contested decision, have led to the creation of a dominant duopoly on the part of Amplats and Implats/LPD in the platinum and rhodium markets, as a result of which effective competition would have been significantly impeded in the Common Market within the meaning of Article 2 (3) of the Regulation.

92 It is therefore necessary to verify whether the three criteria of immediate, substantial and foreseeable effect are satisfied in this case.

93 With regard, specifically, to the criterion of immediate effect, the words 'medium term' used in paragraphs 206 and 210 of the contested decision in relation to the creation of a dominant duopoly position are, contrary to the applicant's assertion, entirely unambiguous. They clearly refer to the time when it is envisaged that Russian stocks will be exhausted, enabling a dominant duopoly on the part of Amplats and Implats/LPD to be created on the world platinum and rhodium markets and, by the same token, in the Community as a substantial part of those world markets.

94 That dominant position would not be dependent, as the applicant asserts, on the future conduct of the undertaking arising from the concentration and of Amplats but would result, in particular, from the very characteristics of the market and the alteration of its structure. In referring to the future conduct of the parties to the duopoly, the applicant fails to distinguish between abuses of dominant position which those parties might commit in the near or more distant future, which might or might not be controlled by means of Articles 85 and/or 86 of the Treaty, and the alteration to the structure of the undertakings and of the market to which the concentration would give rise. It is true that the concentration would not necessarily lead to abuses immediately, since that depends on decisions which the parties to the duopoly may or may not take in the future. However, the concentration would have had the direct and immediate effect of creating the conditions in which abuses were not only possible but economically rational, given that the concentration would have significantly impeded effective competition in the market by giving rise to a lasting alteration to the structure of the markets concerned.

95 Accordingly, the concentration would have had an immediate effect in the Community.

96 So far as concerns the criterion of substantial effect, it should be noted that, as held in paragraph 297 below, the Commission established to the requisite legal standard that the concentration would have created a lasting dominant duopoly position in the world platinum and rhodium markets.

97 The applicant cannot maintain that the concentration would not have a substantial effect in the Community in view of the low sales and small market share of the parties to the concentration in the EEA. While the level of sales in western Europe (20% of world demand) and the Community market share of the entity arising from the concentration ((...) % in respect of platinum) were already sufficient grounds for the Community to have jurisdiction in respect of the concentration, the potential impact of the concentration proved even higher than those figures suggested. Given that the concentration

would have had the effect of creating a dominant duopoly position in the world platinum and rhodium markets, it is clear that the sales in the Community potentially affected by the concentration would have included not only those of the Implats/LPD undertaking but also those of Amplats (approximately 35% to 50%), which would have represented a more than substantial proportion of platinum and rhodium sales in western Europe and a much higher combined market share held by Implats/LPD and Amplats (approximately (...) % to 65%).

98 Finally, it is not possible to accept the applicant's argument that the creation of the dominant position referred to by the Commission in the contested decision is not of greater concern to the Community than to any other competent body and is even of less concern to it than to others. The fact that, in a world market, other parts of the world are affected by the concentration cannot prevent the Community from exercising its control over a concentration which substantially affects competition within the Common Market by creating a dominant position.

99 The arguments by which the applicant denies that the concentration would have a substantial effect in the Community must therefore be rejected. 100 As for the criterion of foreseeable effect, it follows from all of the foregoing that it was in fact foreseeable that the effect of creating a dominant duopoly position in a world market would also be to impede competition significantly in the Community, an integral part of that market.

101 It follows that the application of the Regulation to the proposed concentration was consistent with public international law.

102 It is necessary to examine next whether the Community violated a principle of non-interference or the principle of proportionality in exercising that jurisdiction.

103 The applicant's argument that, by virtue of a principle of non-interference, the Commission should have refrained from prohibiting the concentration in order to avoid a conflict of jurisdiction with the South African authorities must be rejected, without it being necessary to consider whether such a rule exists in international law. Suffice it to note that there was no conflict between the course of action required by the South African Government and that required by the Community given that, in their letter of 22 August 1995, the South African competition authorities simply concluded that the concentration agreement did not give rise to any competition policy concerns, without requiring that such an agreement be entered into (see, to that effect, Wood pulp, paragraph 20).

104 In its letter of 19 April 1996 the South African Government, far from calling into question the Community's jurisdiction to rule on the concentration at issue, first simply expressed a general preference, having regard to the strategic importance of mineral exploitation in South Africa, for intervention in specific cases of collusion when they arose and did not specifically comment on the industrial or other merits of the concentration proposed by Gencor and Lonrho. It then merely expressed the view that the proposed concentration might not impede competition, having regard to the economic power of Amplats, the existence of other sources of supply of PGMs and the opportunities for other producers to enter the South African market through the grant of new mining concessions.

105 Finally, neither the applicant nor, indeed, the South African Government in its letter of 19 April 1996 have shown, beyond making mere statements of principle, in what way the proposed concentration would affect the vital

economic and/or commercial interests of the Republic of South Africa.

106 As regards the argument that the Community cannot claim to have jurisdiction in respect of a concentration on the basis of future and hypothetical behaviour, namely parallel conduct on the part of the undertakings operating in the relevant market where that conduct might or might not fall within the competence of the Community under the Treaty, it must be stated, as pointed out above in connection with the question whether the concentration has an immediate effect, that, while the elimination of the risk of future abuses may be a legitimate concern of any competent competition authority, the main objective in exercising control over concentrations at Community level is to ensure that the restructuring of undertakings does not result in the creation of positions of economic power which may significantly impede effective competition in the Common Market. Community jurisdiction is therefore founded, first and foremost, on the need to avoid the establishment of market structures which may create or strengthen a dominant position, and not on the need to control directly possible abuses of a dominant position.

107 Consequently, it is unnecessary to rule on the question whether the letter of 22 August 1995 from the South African Competition Board constituted a definitive position on the concentration, on whether or not the South African Government was an authority responsible for competition matters and, finally, on the scope of South African competition law. There is accordingly no need to grant the application for measures of organisation of procedure or of inquiry made by the applicant in its letter of 3 December 1996.

108 In those circumstances, the contested decision is not inconsistent with either the Regulation or the rules of public international law relied on by the applicant.

109 For the same reasons, the objection, based on Article 184 of the Treaty, that the Regulation is unlawful because it confers upon the Commission competence in respect of the concentration between Gencor and Lonrho must be rejected.

110 As regards the reasoning in the contested decision justifying Community jurisdiction to apply the Regulation to the concentration, it must be held that the explanations contained in paragraphs 4, 13 to 18, 204 to 206, 210 and 213 of the contested decision satisfy the obligations incumbent on the Commission under Article 190 of the Treaty to give reasons for its decisions so as to enable the Community judicature to exercise its power of review, the parties to defend their rights and any interested party to ascertain the conditions in which the Commission applied the Treaty and its implementing legislation.

111 Accordingly, both pleas of annulment which have been examined must be rejected, without it being necessary to grant the application for measures of organisation of procedure or of inquiry made by the applicant in its letter of 3 December 1996.

[.....]

Case cross-references:

- ▸ E.M. Fox, 'Merger Regulation and Its Territorial Reach: Gencor Ltd v. Commission', (1999) 20 *ECLR*, 334.
- ▸ Y. van Gerven and L. Hoet, 'Gencor: Some Notes on Transnational Competition Law Issues', (2001) 28 *LIEI*, 195.

F. Failing company defence

Cross-references for this part:

▸ V. Bacccaro, 'Failing Firm Defence and Lack of Causality: Doctrine and Practice in Europe of Two Closely Related Concepts', (2004) 25 *ECLR*, 11.

▸ G. Monti and E. Rousseva, 'Failing firms in the Framework of the EC Merger Control Regulation', (1999) 24 *ELR*, 38.

1) *Kali und Salz*, Case M.308 [1994] OJ L 186/38

Kali und Salz (K + S) and Treuhand had agreed to form and jointly control the concentrative joint venture MdK (Mitteldeutsche Kali), thus reuniting over an estimated 80% of the relevant market. MdK, which originated from the former German Democratic Republic (GDR), was currently owned by Treuhand (sole shareholder), a public law organization that was to restructure and, in the end, privatise the GDR's former state enterprises. The joint venture itself would operate in the market for potash (mineral fertilizer) and rock salt.

Relevance: example of a failing company defence.

[.....]

D. Rescue merger

(70) The parties have argued that, without the merger, MdK would soon be forced out of the market and that the market shares then becoming available would essentially go to K + S. The requirements for the application of the 'failing company defence', according to which the creation or reinforcement of a dominant position has to be accepted under merger law in such circumstances, would then be satisfied.

(71) In this context, the Commission considers that this line of argument can be taken into account pursuant to Article 2 (2) of the merger Regulation, as far as the causality of a concentration for the creation or strengthening of a dominant position is concerned. A merger which should normally be considered to lead to the creation or reinforcement of a dominant position on the part of the acquiring firm can be regarded as not causing such a position on the market if, even in the event of the merger's being prohibited, the acquirer would inevitably achieve or reinforce a dominant position. Accordingly, a merger generally is not the cause of the deterioration of the competitive structure if it is clear that:
- the acquired undertaking would in the near future be forced out of the market if not taken over by another undertaking,
- the acquiring undertaking would take over the market share of the acquired undertaking if it were forced out of the market,
- there is no less anticompetitive alternative purchase.

In a situation where, as in this case, a merger leads to a de facto monopoly on the market, it is particularly important that the three conditions should be met.

(72) The lack of causality means that it is the disappearance of the failing company, which would be unavoidable even in the event of the concentration's being prohibited, and not the concentration itself, which creates or strengthens the dominant position. In

those circumstances, the legal consequences provided in Article 2 (3) do not apply. Such a situation occurs, however, only in exceptional cases. Normally, there would be a presumption that a concentration which results in the creation or strengthening of a dominant position is the cause of this deterioration of the competitive structure. Consequently, the burden of proof for a missing link of causality lies with the merging undertakings.

1. MdK's withdrawal from the market

(73) The parties have submitted that MdK is in an extremely critical economic situation. Although capacity has been cut by one-third since 1990, utilization of the firm's potash capacity is currently only around 50 %. In MdK's first financial year from 1 July 1990 to 31 December 1991 losses reached [...] of the turnover. In 1992, this percentage increased to [...]. However, the result in that year was influenced negatively by special measures, for example, reserves for mining-subsidence damage and the complete deduction for depreciation of mines closed down and mines that have to be closed down. But even after the restructuring completed by 1 January 1993 losses in the first half year of 1993 amount to [...] of the turnover. On 31 July 1993 the operating costs already exceeded sales revenue by [...]. If interest is taken into consideration, this figure amounts to [...].
(74) Those immense losses are on the one hand due to the fact that most of the plants are too old and have accordingly high production costs. Furthermore, there is a high rate of employment and a lack of storage capacity. The losses are also due to a considerable decrease in sales. In 1992, sales were 28 % below the 1991 forecasts and in 1993, they are expected to be 46 % down on the forecasts. While overseas sales in 1992 were 8 % up on the forecasts, they will be 18 % down on them in 1993, and while sales in western Europe in 1993 will also be a comparatively slight 10 % down on the forecasts, sales in eastern Europe have slumped dramatically. Eastern European sales in 1992 were 76 % down on the forecast and will be 88 % down in 1993.
(75) MdK's current economic situation is accordingly mainly a result of the firm's operating structure and a crisis in sales attributable primarily to the collapse of markets in eastern Europe. In addition, MdK's sales on the German market have fallen quite substantially, since, following German unification, supplies to the old Laender have come to a virtual halt. Furthermore, MdK does not dispose of an efficient distribution system.
(76) In the actual economic situation, MdK would not seem to be able to survive. The undertaking could not continue to operate without the Treuhandanstalt which has covered the losses until now. A long-term covering of losses by the Treuhandanstalt using State aids for an undertaking that is not competitive cannot be expected. Furthermore it would not be compatible with the State aid rules of Articles 92 and 93 of the EC Treaty, and in particular the Commission decisions adopted in 1991 and 1992 pursuant to those Articles and relating to the measures taken by the Treuhandanstalt. It is also likely that MdK on a stand-alone basis would continue to make losses, even if it were given the same amount of financial aid for restructuring by the Treuhand that was made available for the proposed concentration. Without an acquisition by a private industrial partner with the necessary management expertise and in the absence of synergies, a rescue of MdK would appear to be impossible in the long term. In this case, it is at least to be expected that the costs of restructuring would be higher than the aid provided

for the merger. The explanation of the Treuhandanstalt as to why it will close down MdK completely if it could not be sold to a private undertaking therefore seems to be convincing and is relevant as far as the lack of causality is concerned. An administration charged with privatization cannot be expected to rescue with extraordinary high aids one of its own undertakings that cannot be expected to survive and to hold it in the long term as a State-owned company.

(77) The Commission therefore is of the opinion that there is sufficient proof that MdK will withdraw from the market if it is not taken over by a private undertaking. Even if this does not happen immediately, for social, regional and general political reasons, a closure of MdK is to be expected in the near future with a sufficient degree of probability. In view of the special conditions of the case which concerns the privatization of a State-owned enterprise which cannot be considered as competitive by normal standards, the Commission is of the opinion that the first condition of the lack of causality as mentioned above has to be considered to be fulfilled.

2. Accrual of MdK's market share to K + S

(78) As convincingly argued by the parties and in accordance with the facts known to the Commission, it is reasonable to suppose that MdK's share of the German potash market would accrue to K + S if MdK had to withdraw from the market. As explained above, the German potash market is sealed off against competitors from other countries because of a number of structural factors. Since, as the parties have submitted, K + S could increase its potash production without any further expenditure and become the sole supplier of the German market, MdK's market share would in such circumstances go to K + S. The same conclusion has been reached in respect of the special market for magnesium products where basically only K + S and MdK are active.

(79) As far as MdK's market position in the Community outside Germany is concerned, it is not sufficiently clear that, if MdK were no longer on the market, the competitive situation would essentially be identical to the situation that would exist if the proposed merger took place. The parties argue that the similarity of the products of MdK and K + S and the similarity of the commercial relations with at least one German supplier indicate that former MdK clients will buy from K + S. This argument does not take into consideration the fact that the major part of Kali exports made by MdK to the Community outside Germany concerns Kali 60 and not the magnesium-containing specialty products exclusively offered by German producers. In the light of the above, the Commission considers that the conditions for the lack of causality as described in paragraph 71 are not fulfilled with regard to the deterioration of the competitive structure in the Community market outside Germany.

3. Alternative purchasers

(80) In the opinion of the Commission, it is established with sufficient certainty that a purchase of all or a substantial part of MdK by companies other than K + S can be discounted. The existing offer of the Peine Group to take over the Bischofferode mine cannot in this context be considered as a possible alternative, because it does not relate to a substantial part of MdK.

(a) Alternative acquisition of all or a substantial part of MdK

(81) As the parties have demonstrated, as part of the privatization of MdK 48 firms worldwide were approached by Goldman Sachs International Limited, which was responsible for inviting tenders. Of these 48 firms, 19 expressed an interest and received a confidentiality declaration with a summary of the purchase options. This declaration was signed by the 19 firms who then received the offering memorandum. The parties have submitted that, subsequently, intensive talks were held with only three interested parties, namely K + S, Potash Corporation of Saskatchewan (PCS) and EMC. The negotiations with PSC and EMC did not, however, get beyond the initial stage.
(82) According to the detailed records of the privatization process passed on by the Treuhandanstalt, the Commission has come to the conclusion that Goldman Sachs made a great effort to interest as many firms as possible in purchasing MdK. Even those firms which clearly hesitated to express an interest were sent repeated reminders. On top of the offering memorandum, firms which expressed a corresponding interest were given detailed information on MdK. It also appears from the documents that Goldman Sachs and the Treuhandanstalt, despite a basic preference for the privatization of the whole of MdK emphasized the flexibility of the Treuhand and followed up every reasonable possibility, even if it only concerned a substantial part of MdK. Despite this, Goldman Sachs did not succeed in obtaining a firm offer from any firm other than K + S. Lastly, the firms which at the beginning of the privatization process showed a certain interest in MdK distanced themselves from further negotiations.
(83) Despite the intensive aforementioned efforts to interest other firms in an acquisition of MdK, the proof of the non-existence of an alterantive purchaser cannot be supported only by the procedure followed by the Treuhandanstalt and Goldman Sachs.
In the context of the examination of a possible lack of causality, it had to be taken into account that the financial support for the K + S/MdK merger was not fully known to the other potential purchasers during the privatization process, because the financial aid given by the Treuhandanstalt was the result of the negotiations with K + S. To be sure, the Treuhandanstalt and Goldman Sachs indicated to all interested potential buyers that the Treuhandanstalt was prepared to provide substantial financial aid going beyond the legal mandatory investment aid. However, no potential buyer could have foreseen the financial magnitude of the aid which was finally agreed. The financial amount agreed in the final stages of negotiation was only communicated to EMC which, at that stage, was the only remaining interested party.
(84) As a result of the above, during the merger proceedings the Commission has therefore approached in particular EMC and PCS as well as other undertakings contacted by Goldman Sachs, which could be assumed to be interested in acquiring all or a substantial part of MdK. All these undertakings gave a clear negative answer to the question whether they would be interested, in the event that the proposed merger could not be implemented, in acquiring all or a substantial part of MdK now that they had been made aware of the financial support promised by the Treuhandanstalt. In the course of the merger proceedings an undertaking with worldwide mining activities, which as a result of a recent reorganization is now also active in the potash sector and which had not previously been contacted by Goldman Sachs, stated to the Commission that it could be interested in acquiring MdK, if it could be guaranteed financial aid comparable to that made available by the Treuhandanstalt for

the joint venture. However, following a first examination of its intention to acquire MdK, even this undertaking stated to the Commission that it no longer intended to pursue the possible acquisition of MdK.

(85) Under these circumstances, the Commission is of the opinion that there is sufficient evidence to suggest that an acquisition of all or a substantial part of MdK by any undertaking other than K + S can be ruled out. In view of the results of the first privatization procedure and the Commission's findings in the course of the merger proceedings, the possibility that, in the event of a further call for offers, there might be a serious alternative buyer with a viable business plan appears to be practically excluded. In this respect, it must also be noted that no other undertaking could achieve the same synergies as K + S would be able to realize as purchaser of MdK, because of its geographical location and product range. In these circumstances, it would be unreasonable to prohibit the merger with the prospect of a later possible call for offers after considerable delay following a new but equally unsuccessful privatization procedure. The extremely small possibility that a new interested buyer might appear would be unreasonably disproportionate to the possible damage that would result from the continuing losses of MdK and the persisting uncertainty about the future of the company during the new procedure for receiving offers.

(b) Bischofferode potash mine

(86) Under the business plan agreed K + S and the Treuhandanstalt for the proposed joint venture, the Bischofferode mine, one of MdK's four currently operating potash mines, is to be closed by the end of 1993. After final agreement had been reached between the Treuhand and K + S on the merger, but before the Federal Minister for Finance had given his final authorization, the firm Peine made an offer to the Treuhand to take over the Bischofferode mine. On the basis of a report by the auditing company C& L Treuarbeit, the Treuhandanstalt turned down the offer. Irrespective of whether this appears to be objectively justified, Peine's offer cannot be regarded as an alternative acquisition in the context of a lack of causality.

(87) Bearing in mind the causality considerations outlined above, a merger leading to the creation or reinforcement of a dominant position must take place in such a way as to cause the least possible damage to competition. This means that any alternative partial disposal of the target company which will reduce the deterioration of the competitive structure must as a rule be carried out if the rest of the merger is to be accepted under merger law.

(88) The particular characteristic of this case, however, is that the offer of the Peine group involves that part of MdK which is not included in the activites to be transferred to the joint venture. Peine's proposal is also based on the assumption that the Treuhandanstalt will provide substantial financial support. The implementation of this offer would therefore involve an additional privatization as well as claims for additional State aids, and would not be a partial acquisition of those MdK activities which are to be transferred to K + S and for which the necessary financial resources have been set aside.

(89) Considering a possible lack of causality, the fact that it would be theoretically possible to accept the offer of the firm Peine in the place of the proposed merger between K + S and MdK could not be held against the Treuhandanstalt. According to the Commission, in the context of a lack of causality the Treuhandanstalt must examine an alternative

acquisition proposal, even if it is not in all respects identical with the proposed merger. An alternative proposal would therefore have to be considered, even if, compared to the concentration plan, it involved different or even smaller mines of MdK. However, this will only be required if the proposal involves at least a substantial part of MdK.
(90) According to the Commission, a line must be drawn if there is a gross discrepancy between the scope of the privatization proposals. A comparison of the two existing proposals, that is, either to implement the merger plan or to accept Peine's offer, reveals such a discrepancy. While the merger plan concerns 3 000 jobs in total, after the necessary restructuring has taken place, Peine's offer relates to a part of MdK, which, following necessary restructuring, would involve 536 jobs. This amounts to about 18 % of the jobs involved in the merger proposal. If the turnover figures are considered, Peine's proposal is also clearly below 20 % of the K + S/MdK proposal. If, therefore, Peine's proposal were carried out, it would not lead to a comparable alternative acquisition, but to a completely different and much more limited privatization.

[.....]

Case cross-references:

▸ Joined Cases C-68/94 & C-30/95 *SCPA & EMC v. Commission* [1998] ECR I-1375, the Court partially annulled decision 94/449.

▸ S.B. Bishop, 'Power and Responsibility: The ECJ's Kali-Salz Judgment', (1999) 20 *ECLR*, 37.

▸ J. Venit, 'Two steps forward and no steps back: Economic analysis and oligopolistic dominance after Kali & Salz', (1998) 35 *CMLRev*, 1101.

G. Portfolio power/conglomerate mergers

Cross-references for this part:

▸ S. Baker and D. Ridyard, 'Portfolio Power: A Rum Deal?', (1999) 20 *ECLR*, 181.

▸ OECD Roundtable on Portfolio effects, oecd.org/dataoecd/39/3/1818237.pdf, p.239 on definition of 'conglomerate mergers'.

▸ R. Burnley, 'Who's afraid of conglomerate mergers? A comparison of the US and EC approaches', (2005) 28 (1) *World Competition Law and Economics Review*, 43.

1) *Coca Cola/Carlsberg*, Comm. Press Release IP/97/787, Case M.833; full decision published in [1998] OJ L 145/41

Relevance: divesture commitments to counteract portfolio power.

IP/97/787, Brussels, 11th September 1997

The Commission approves bottling joint venture between the Coca-Cola Company and Carlsberg A/S

The European Commission has decided to declare the joint venture Coca-Cola Nordic Beverages (CCNB) between The Coca-Cola Company (TCCC) and Carlsberg A/S (Carlsberg) compatible with the Common Market, subject to full compliance by the parties with commitments submitted to the Commission.
The Commission has found that the proposed joint venture would lead to a strengthening of a dominant position in the Danish market for carbonated soft drinks

(CSDs). Subsequently, TCCC and Carlsberg have offered certain commitments to resolve the competition problems identified by the Commission. These include:
- the sale of all Carlsberg's shares in Jyske Bryg Holding A/S, which holds directly and indirectly 62% of the shares and 49% of the votes in Bryggerigruppen A/S, the current bottler of PepsiCo brands and the second largest CSD producer in Denmark, and
- the sale of all Carlsberg's shares in Dansk Coladrik A/S, which produces Jolly Cola, the third largest cola brand in Denmark.
These divestiture commitments are considered adequate to resolve the competition concerns raised by the operation. In particular, Carlsberg's divestiture of its shares in Jyske Bryg will allow Bryggerigruppen to become an independent second force in the Danish CSD market, since this divestiture would break the link between the two largest CSD producers in Denmark - Carlsberg and Bryggerigruppen.

The Commission will strictly monitor compliance with these commitments and take whatever appropriate measures foreseen by the Merger Regulation in the event of non-compliance.
The transaction involves the creation of CCNB, which will be jointly controlled by TCCC and Carlsberg. CCNB will hold interests in national bottlers which will produce, distribute and sell mainly TCCC's brands. CCNB will acquire Carlsberg's wholly owned CSD bottling subsidiary, Dadeko A/S, in Denmark and TCCC's bottling entity, Coca-Cola Drycker Sverige (CCDS), in Sweden. Later the parties intend to extend the activities of CCNB to the other Nordic countries, as well as St. Petersburg and the Baltic states.
TCCC is the largest producer of CSDs in the world with its main brands being Coca-Cola, Coca-Cola Light, Fanta and Sprite. Carlsberg is a significant international brewing company, which has a major soft drinks business in Denmark, where it is the bottler of its own brands (including Tuborg), as well as the TCCC brands. In Sweden, Carlsberg holds 50% of the third largest Swedish brewer, Falcon.
The Commission examined the likely effects of the proposed operation in the CSD market at both the brand owner and bottling (production, distribution and sale) levels in Denmark and Sweden, respectively.
In Denmark: At present TCCC has a market share of 40-45% and Carlsberg 5-10% at the brand level, and Carlsberg has a market share of 60-65% at the bottling level (of which Dadeko accounts for 40-45%). The largest competitor at the brand level is PepsiCo with a market share of 5-10%. At the bottling level, PepsiCo's bottler is Bryggerigruppen, which with a market share of approximately 15-20%, is Carlsberg's largest competitor. With respect to Bryggerigruppen's market position, the Commission found that Carlsberg controls Jyske Bryg, which has the possibility to exercise substantial influence over Bryggerigruppen. Based on the investigation, the Commission has concluded that TCCC is dominant at the brand level and Dadeko is dominant at the bottling level.
The establishment of CCNB would strengthen the dominant position of TCCC at the brand level and of Dadeko at the bottling level. The Commission determined that this strengthening would arise from the vertical integration of TCCC into bottling activities, Carlsberg's licensing of certain soft-drink brands to TCCC, the elimination of Carlsberg as an actual and potential competitor to TCCC and the foreclosure of the Carlsberg and Tuborg distribution systems for third party CSD brands.
Sweden: There are indications that TCCC is dominant in the Swedish market. However, TCCC has recently cancelled its CSD bottling

agreement with the largest Swedish brewer, Pripps, and established its own bottling operation, CCDS. This has led to significant capacity being freed within Pripps' production and distribution operations. Therefore, in the Swedish market the concentrative elements of the operation will not lead to a strengthening of the present positions of either TCCC or CCDS.
Undertakings: To resolve the competition concerns, the parties have submitted a package of undertakings, including the two divestiture commitments mentioned above. In particular, the divestiture of Carlsberg's shares in Jyske Bryg will enable Bryggerigruppen to become an independent second force in the Danish market by removing Carlsberg's influence over this company, its largest competitor in the Danish market. The Commission considers Bryggerigruppen to have the necessary resources to become a viable alternative in the Danish CSD market since, among other things, it has a sufficiently broad range of products in its portfolio, it holds the licence for the PepsiCo brands, and it has an extensive nationwide distribution system. This divestiture will thus compensate for the foreclosure of the Carlsberg and Tuborg distribution systems, as well as the elimination of Carlsberg as an actual and potential competitor to TCCC. Furthermore, the divestiture of Dansk Coladrik will enable Dansk Coladrik to compete with Carlsberg and TCCC in the CSD market.
In addition to the two main divestiture commitments, the package of undertakings also includes the following commitments: Carlsberg will retain the brand management of the brands it licenses to TCCC; Carlsberg will be allowed to compete in CSDs within the CCNB territory; and TCCC will not purchase certain Falcon brands in Sweden. The Commission has taken note of these additional undertakings.

Background:

CCNB will become the ninth so-called "anchor bottler" in the TCCC bottling system. TCCC has identified "anchor bottlers" as those bottling companies in which TCCC holds a minority stake and which are strongly committed to the strategic goals of TCCC. They tend to be large, geographically diverse and have strong financial and management resources.
CSDs encompass colas and other flavoured CSDs. In analysing the markets for CSDs at both the brand and bottling levels, the Commission took into consideration that there are only three major CSD brand owners in the world, specifically, TCCC, PepsiCo and Cadbury Schweppes. These companies supply the brand names and the concentrate, from which CSDs are produced, to bottlers who produce, market, distribute, and sell the finished products.

Falcon can continue to bottle soft drinks in Sweden

As a result of a separate analysis under Art.85 of the Treaty - the Commission has also approved agreements relating to the bottling of soft drinks in Sweden.
These agreements concern only the Swedish market and relate in particular to the setting up of a joint physical distribution company between CCDS and Falcon, the transfer of some non-alcoholic beverage brands from Falcon to TCCC, and an exclusive sales arrangement between CCDS and Falcon for the resale of CCDS products in certain HORECA outlets. The Commission's Directorate-General for Competition has expressed concern with some of the aspects of these arrangements. The parties came forward with proposed modifications, which address the main concerns expressed.

The principal concern was that Falcon could effectively have been closed off as a bottler of its own and third parties' soft drink products in Sweden. The parties have however agreed to give an undertaking whereby Falcon will be allowed to continue to compete in the field of soft drinks, both as a brand owner and as a bottler of its own and third parties' products.

2) Case T-5/02 *Tetra Laval v. Commission* [2002] ECR II-4381

Tetra Laval SA had acquired, through a public bid, approximately 95% of the shares and 95% of the voting rights in Sidel. Tetra Laval was fully owned by Tetra Laval BV (called 'Tetra' or 'the applicant' in the judgment), which was part of the Tetra Laval Group. Moreover, Tetra comprised Tetra Pak, the manufacturer of carton packages. Sidel, on the other hand, designed and produced packaging equipment and systems, such as the SBM machine (stretch blow moulding machines) for the production of PET (polyethylene terephthalite) plastic bottles. The merger was notified to the Commission, which declared it incompatible with the Internal Market on the basis of Article 8 (3) of Merger Regulation.

Relevance: what is a 'conglomerate merger'? What may be the downside thereof for the market?

[.....]

C - The plea based on the lack of foreseeable conglomerate effect

1. Preliminary observations

142 It is common ground between the parties that the modified merger is conglomerate in type, that is, a merger of undertakings which, essentially, do not have a pre-existing competitive relationship, either as direct competitors or as suppliers and customers. Mergers of this type do not give rise to true horizontal overlaps between the activities of the parties to the merger or to a vertical relationship between the parties in the strict sense of the term. Thus it cannot be presumed as a general rule that such mergers produce anti-competitive effects. However, they may have anti-competitive effects in certain cases.

143 In the contested decision, the Commission essentially considers that the modified merger will have foreseeable anti-competitive conglomerate effects in three ways. First, the merger would enable the merged entity to use its dominant position on the global carton packaging market as a 'lever' in order to achieve a dominant position on the PET packaging equipment markets. Second, the merger would reinforce the current dominant position of Tetra on the markets for aseptic carton packaging equipment and aseptic cartons, because it would eliminate the competitive constraint, represented by Sidel, coming from the neighbouring PET markets. Third, the merger would generally strengthen the overall position of the merged entity on the market for packaging of sensitive products.

144 At the hearing, the Commission stressed the intrinsically prospective nature of its analysis, in which it must assess the future effects of a merger transaction notified to it.

It stressed that, in a case involving a merger with a conglomerate effect, just as in a case involving a classical horizontal merger, the concern of the Commission is to prevent future anti-competitive conduct which would be likely to follow from the transaction, and that its analysis must be conducted having regard to the existing means and capacities of the parties to the notified transaction. The mere fact that with a conglomerate-type merger, unlike other types of merger, the probability of such conduct does not result directly from the combination in a single market of the market shares which will be held in future by the merged entity does not mean that a different approach must be adopted.

[.....]

146. It should be observed, first, that the Regulation, particularly at Article 2(2) and (3), does not draw any distinction between, on the one hand, merger transactions having horizontal and vertical effects and, on the other hand, those having a conglomerate effect. It follows that, without distinction between those types of transactions, a merger can be prohibited only if the two conditions laid down in Article 2(3) are met (see paragraph 120 above). Consequently, a merger having a conglomerate effect must, like any other merger (see paragraph 120 above), be authorised by the Commission if it is not established that it creates or strengthens a dominant position in the common market or in a substantial part of it and that, as a result, effective competition will be significantly impeded.

[.....]

Case cross-references:

- ▸ Case T-310/01 *Schneider* [2002] ECR II-4071.
- ▸ Case C-12/03 P *Commission v. Tetra Laval* [2005] ECR I-987, appeal dismissed.
- ▸ J. Temple Lang, 'Two important Merger Regulation judgments: the implications of Schneider – Legrand and Tetra Laval-Sidel', (2003) 28 *ELR*, 259.
- ▸ *GE/Honeywell* Commission Decision 2004/134/EC [2004] OJ L 48/1.
- ▸ M.836 *Gillette/Duracell.*
- ▸ *SEB/Moulinex* Commission decision 2005/408/EC [2005] OJ L 138/18.
- ▸ *Guinness/Grand Metropolitan* Commission decision 98/602/EC [1998] OJ L 288/24.
- ▸ *Coca Cola/Amalgamated Beverages* Commission decision 97/540/EC [1997] OJ L 218/15.

H. Collective dominance

Cross-references for this part:

- ▸ Commission Guidelines on the assessment of horizontal mergers, [2004] OJ C 31/5, paragraphs 24-57.
- ▸ J. Temple Lang, 'Oligopolies and Joint Dominance in Community Antitrust Law', (2001) *Fordham Corp. L. Inst.* (B. Hawk, ed. 2002), 269.
- ▸ R. Whish, 'Collective dominance', in: D. O'Keefe, M. Andenas, *Liber Amicorum for Lord Slynn*, Volume 1 (Kluwer, 2000).
- ▸ J. Ysewyn and C. Caffarra, 'Two's Company, Three's A Crowd: The Future of Collective Dominance after the Kali & Salz Judgment', (1998) 19 *ECLR*, 468.

1) Case T-102/96 *Gencor v. Commission* [1999] ECR II-753

See above for facts of the case *(VII-E-2, p. 292)**.*

Relevance: analysis of collective dominance.

[.....]

D - The Commission's categorisation of the collective dominant position

1. The market share criterion

Arguments of the parties

195 The applicant observes that the parties' shares of the world platinum market on which the Commission relied are respectively (...)% (for Implats) and (...)% (for LPD), representing a combined market share of (...)%. In the Community market, those shares amounted respectively to (...)% (LPD), (...)% (Implats) and (...)% (combined share). However, in other merger control cases in which collective dominance was found, such as those giving rise to the Nestlé-Perrier Decision and to Commission Decision 94/449/EC of 14 December 1993 relating to a proceeding pursuant to Council Regulation (EEC) No 4064/89 (Case No IV/M.308 - Kali + Salz/MdK/Treuhand) (OJ 1994 L 186, p. 38; the 'Kali und Salz Decision'), the combined market shares were substantially higher than in the present case, yet the Commission allowed those concentrations to proceed.

196 In the Nestlé-Perrier case, Nestlé and BSN had a combined market share of 82% of the market at issue, namely the French mineral water market (paragraph 119 of that decision). The concentration was cleared subject to compliance with certain conditions.

197 In the Kali und Salz case, the market share of Kali und Salz increased from 17% to 25% of the Community market excluding Germany and resulted in a de facto monopoly consisting in a 98% share of the German market which was considered to be a relevant geographical market in its own right. Again, the concentration was conditionally cleared by the Commission.

198 The Commission maintains that the comparison made by the applicant between the market shares of the parties to the concentration and the aggregate market share of all the members of the oligopoly in the Nestlé-Perrier case (82%) is incorrect, as is the comparison drawn with the Kali und Salz case.

Findings of the Court

199 The prohibition enacted in Article 2(3) of the Regulation reflects the general objective assigned by Article 3(g) of the Treaty, namely the establishment of a system ensuring that competition in the common market is not distorted (first and seventh recitals in the preamble to the Regulation). The prohibition relates to concentrations which create or strengthen a dominant position as a result of which effective competition would be significantly impeded in the common market or in a substantial part of it.

200 The dominant position referred to is concerned with a situation where one or more undertakings wield economic power which would enable them to prevent effective competition from being maintained in the relevant market by giving them the opportu-

nity to act to a considerable extent independently of their competitors, their customers and, ultimately, of consumers.

201 The existence of a dominant position may derive from several factors which, taken separately, are not necessarily decisive. Among those factors, the existence of very large market shares is highly important. Nevertheless, a substantial market share as evidence of the existence of a dominant position is not a constant factor. Its importance varies from market to market according to the structure of those markets, especially so far as production, supply and demand are concerned (Hoffmann-La Roche, cited above, paragraphs 39 and 40).

202 In addition, the relationship between the market shares of the undertakings involved in the concentration and their competitors, especially those of the next largest, is relevant evidence of the existence of a dominant position. That factor enables the competitive strength of the competitors of the undertaking in question to be assessed (Hoffmann-La Roche, paragraph 48).

203 Accordingly, the fact that the Commission has relied in other concentration cases on higher or lower market shares in support of its assessment as to whether a collective dominant position might be created or strengthened cannot bind it in its assessment of other cases concerning, in particular, markets in which the structure of supply and demand and the conditions of competition are different.

204 Thus, since there is no reliable evidence that the mineral water market and/or the potash market examined in the Nestlé-Perrier case and the Kali und Salz case, on the one hand, and the platinum and rhodium market under consideration in this case, on the other, have fundamentally similar characteristics, the applicant cannot rely on any differences in the market shares held by the members of the oligopoly which were taken into account by the Commission in one or other of those two cases in order to call into question the market-share threshold adopted as indicative of a collective dominant position in this case.

205 Furthermore, although the importance of the market shares may vary from one market to another, the view may legitimately be taken that very large market shares are in themselves, save in exceptional circumstances, evidence of the existence of a dominant position (Case C-62/86 Akzo v Commission [1991] ECR I-3359, paragraph 60). An undertaking which has a very large market share and holds it for some time, by means of the volume of production and the scale of the supply which it stands for - without those having much smaller market shares being able rapidly to meet the demand from those who would like to break away from the undertaking which has the largest market share - is in a position of strength which makes it an unavoidable trading partner and which, already because of this, secures for it, at the very least during relatively long periods, that freedom of action which is the special feature of a dominant position (Hoffmann-La Roche, paragraph 41).

206 It is true that, in the context of an oligopoly, the fact that the parties to the oligopoly hold large market shares does not necessarily have the same significance, compared to the analysis of an individual dominant position, with regard to the opportunities for those parties, as a group, to act to a considerable extent independently of their competitors, their customers and, ultimately, of consumers. Nevertheless, particularly in the case of a duopoly, a large market share is, in the absence of evidence to the contrary, likewise a strong indication of the existence of a collective dominant position.

207 In the instant case, as the Commission stated in the contested decision (paragraphs 81 and 181), Implats/LPD and Amplats would,

following the concentration, each have had a market share of about 30% to 35%, that is to say a combined market share of approximately 60% to 70%, in the world PGM market and approximately 89% of the world PGM reserves. Russia had a 22% market share and about 10% of world reserves, the North American producers held a 5% market share and 1% of world reserves, and the recycling undertakings had a 6% market share. It was probable that, after Russia had disposed of its stocks, that is to say in all likelihood in the two years following the contested decision, Implats/LPD and Amplats would each have had a market share of about 40%, that is to say a combined market share of 80%, which would have constituted a very large market share.

208 Thus, having regard to the allocation of market share between the parties to the concentration and to the gap in market share which would open up following that concentration between, on the one hand, the entity arising from the merger and Amplats and, on the other, the remaining platinum producers, the Commission was entitled to conclude that the proposed concentration was liable to result in the creation of a dominant position for the South African undertakings.

[.....]

(e) Structural links

[.....]

Findings of the Court

[.....]

276 Furthermore, there is no reason whatsoever in legal or economic terms to exclude from the notion of economic links the relationship of interdependence existing between the parties to a tight oligopoly within which, in a market with the appropriate characteristics, in particular in terms of market concentration, transparency and product homogeneity, those parties are in a position to anticipate one another's behaviour and are therefore strongly encouraged to align their conduct in the market, in particular in such a way as to maximise their joint profits by restricting production with a view to increasing prices. In such a context, each trader is aware that highly competitive action on its part designed to increase its market share (for example a price cut) would provoke identical action by the others, so that it would derive no benefit from its initiative. All the traders would thus be affected by the reduction in price levels.

277 That conclusion is all the more pertinent with regard to the control of concentrations, whose objective is to prevent anti-competitive market structures from arising or being strengthened. Those structures may result from the existence of economic links in the strict sense argued by the applicant or from market structures of an oligopolistic kind where each undertaking may become aware of common interests and, in particular, cause prices to increase without having to enter into an agreement or resort to a concerted practice.

[.....]

Case cross-references:

► C. Caffarra and K.-U. Kühn, 'Joint Dominance: The CFI Judgment on Gencor/Lonhro', (1999) 20 *ECLR*, 355.

► V. Korah, 'Gencor v. Commission: Collective Dominance', (1999) 20 *ECLR*, 337.

2) Case T-342/99 *Airtours v. Commission* [2002] ECR II-2585

Airtours, a British tour operator, had notified its intention to become the sole shareholder of First Choice, another UK tour operator. This acquisition would bring an end to the competitive relation between the two operators. The Commission did not approve the proposed concentration, since it would lead to a collective dominant position in the UK short-haul foreign package holiday market between the new combination and a third tour operator, who stayed out of the transaction and was to remain independent.

Relevance: a concentration that creates a collective dominant position may not be compatible with the Internal Market. Interpretation of notion of 'collective dominance.' Heavy burden on Commission to 'reason' its decision.

[.....]

The second plea alleging infringement of Article 2 of Regulation No 4064/89, breach of the principle of legal certainty and infringement of Article 253 EC inasmuch as the Commission applied an incorrect definition of collective dominance in its appraisal of the present case

49 The applicant complains that the Commission, for the purposes of the Decision, applied a new and incorrect definition of 'collective dominance', which is set out generally at paragraphs 51 to 56 of the Decision, departing from its previous decisions, from Community case-law and from sound economic principles, and also infringing Article 2 of Regulation No 4064/89. The Commission thereby also acted in breach of the principle of legal certainty and Article 253 EC, inasmuch as the Decision is vitiated by a defective statement of reasons.
50 The Commission denies that it adopted a new approach and maintains that it applied the test for collective dominance already used by it in previous cases and approved by the Court of First Instance in its judgment in Case T-102/96 Gencor v Commission [1999] ECR II-753.
51 It is appropriate to point out that the abovementioned paragraphs of the Decision (51 to 56) are in Part VA of the Decision, in which the Commission sets out, purely by way of introduction and summary, the reasons which led it to conclude that the concentration would give rise to the creation of a dominant position and in which it replies generally to observations made by the applicant during the administrative procedure concerning certain of the characteristics of a collective dominant position.
52 In the introduction to its legal analysis of the concentration, the Commission merely sketches the broad outlines of its findings on the effects of the merger, which are subsequently explained and developed in detail at paragraphs 57 to 180 of the Decision.
53 Since the Decision is a measure applying Article 2 of Regulation No 4064/89 to a specific concentration, the Court must, in its review of the legality of the Decision, confine itself to the position adopted by the Commission in relation to the transaction as notified, that is to say, it must examine the way in which the law has been applied to the facts and adjudicate on the merits of the Commission's findings concerning the effects of the concentration on competition. In this case, the specific findings relating to the impact of the transaction on competition, which led the Commission to conclude that the concentration should be prohibited, are stated and

developed in paragraphs 57 to 180 of the Decision and are challenged by the applicant in its third plea.

54 It is therefore necessary to consider, first, the merits of the arguments raised by the applicant in its third plea and, at the same time, to take into account its arguments concerning the Commission's general findings at paragraphs 51 to 56 of the Decision.

The third plea alleging (i) infringement of Article 2 of Regulation No 4064/89 in that the Commission found that the concentration would create a collective dominant position, and (ii) infringement of Article 253 EC

55 By this plea, the applicant seeks to show that the Commission made an error of assessment in deciding that the proposed merger should be prohibited. It claims that the Decision does not prove to the requisite legal standard that the outcome of the transaction would be the creation of a collective dominant position of such a kind as significantly to impede competition in the relevant market. In prohibiting the merger, the Commission thus infringed Article 2 of Regulation No 4064/89.

A - General considerations

56 Under Article 2 (2) of Regulation No 4064/89, a concentration which does not create or strengthen a dominant position as a result of which effective competition would be significantly impeded in the Common Market or in a substantial part of it is to be declared compatible with the Common Market.

57 Under Article 2 (3) of the Regulation, a concentration which creates or strengthens a dominant position as a result of which effective competition would be significantly impeded in the Common Market or in a substantial part of it is to be declared incompatible with the Common Market.

58 Where, for the purposes of applying Regulation No 4064/89, the Commission examines a possible collective dominant position, it must ascertain whether the concentration would have the direct and immediate effect of creating or strengthening a position of that kind, which is such as significantly and lastingly to impede competition in the relevant market (see, to that effect, Gencor v Commission, paragraph 94). If there is no substantial alteration to competition as it stands, the merger must be approved (see, to that effect, Case T-2/93 Air France v Commission [1994] ECR II-323, paragraphs 78 and 79, and Gencor v Commission, paragraph 170, 180 and 193).

59 It is apparent from the case law that 'in the case of an alleged collective dominant position, the Commission is... obliged to assess, using a prospective analysis of the reference market, whether the concentration which has been referred to it leads to a situation in which effective competition in the relevant market is significantly impeded by the undertakings involved in the concentration and one or more other undertakings which together, in particular because of factors giving rise to a connection between them, are able to adopt a common policy on the market and act to a considerable extent independently of their competitors, their customers, and also of consumers' (Kali & Salz, cited above, paragraph 221, and Gencor v Commission, paragraph 163).

60 The Court of First Instance has held that: 'There is no reason whatsoever in legal or economic terms to exclude from the notion of economic links the relationship of interdependence existing between the parties to a tight oligopoly within which, in a market with the appropriate characteristics, in particular in terms of market concentration, transparency and product homogeneity,

those parties are in a position to anticipate one another's behaviour and are therefore strongly encouraged to align their conduct in the market, in particular in such a way as to maximise their joint profits by restricting production with a view to increasing prices. In such a context, each trader is aware that highly competitive action on its part designed to increase its market share (for example a price cut) would provoke identical action by the others, so that it would derive no benefit from its initiative. All the traders would thus be affected by the reduction in price levels.' (Gencor v Commission, paragraph 276).

61 A collective dominant position significantly impeding effective competition in the Common Market or a substantial part of it may thus arise as the result of a concentration where, in view of the actual characteristics of the relevant market and of the alteration in its structure that the transaction would entail, the latter would make each member of the dominant oligopoly, as it becomes aware of common interests, consider it possible, economically rational, and hence preferable, to adopt on a lasting basis a common policy on the market with the aim of selling at above competitive prices, without having to enter into an agreement or resort to a concerted practice within the meaning of Article 81 EC (see, to that effect, Gencor v Commission, paragraph 277) and without any actual or potential competitors, let alone customers or consumers, being able to react effectively.

62 As the applicant has argued and as the Commission has accepted in its pleadings, three conditions are necessary for a finding of collective dominance as defined:

- first, each member of the dominant oligopoly must have the ability to know how the other members are behaving in order to monitor whether or not they are adopting the common policy. As the Commission specifically acknowledges, it is not enough for each member of the dominant oligopoly to be aware that interdependent market conduct is profitable for all of them but each member must also have a means of knowing whether the other operators are adopting the same strategy and whether they are maintaining it. There must, therefore, be sufficient market transparency for all members of the dominant oligopoly to be aware, sufficiently precisely and quickly, of the way in which the other members' market conduct is evolving;

- second, the situation of tacit coordination must be sustainable over time, that is to say, there must be an incentive not to depart from the common policy on the market. As the Commission observes, it is only if all the members of the dominant oligopoly maintain the parallel conduct that all can benefit. The notion of retaliation in respect of conduct deviating from the common policy is thus inherent in this condition. In this instance, the parties concur that, for a situation of collective dominance to be viable, there must be adequate deterrents to ensure that there is a long-term incentive in not departing from the common policy, which means that each member of the dominant oligopoly must be aware that highly competitive action on its part designed to increase its market share would provoke identical action by the others, so that it would derive no benefit from its initiative (see, to that effect, Gencor v Commission, paragraph 276);

- third, to prove the existence of a collective dominant position to the requisite legal standard, the Commission must also establish that the foreseeable reaction of current and future competitors, as well as of consumers, would not jeopardise the results expected from the common policy.

63 The prospective analysis which the Commission has to carry out in its review of concentrations involving collective dominance calls for close examination in particular of the circumstances which, in each indi-

vidual case, are relevant for assessing the effects of the concentration on competition in the reference market (Kali & Salz, paragraph 222). As the Commission itself has emphasised, at paragraph 104 of its decision of 20 May 1998 Price Waterhouse/Coopers & Lybrand (Case IV/M.1016) (OJ 1999 L 50, p. 27), it is also apparent from the judgment in Kali and Salz that, where the Commission takes the view that a merger should be prohibited because it will create a situation of collective dominance, it is incumbent upon it to produce convincing evidence thereof. The evidence must concern, in particular, factors playing a significant role in the assessment of whether a situation of collective dominance exists, such as, for example, the lack of effective competition between the operators alleged to be members of the dominant oligopoly and the weakness of any competitive pressure that might be exerted by other operators.

64 Furthermore, the basic provisions of Regulation No 4064/89, in particular Article 2 thereof, confer on the Commission a certain discretion, especially with respect to assessments of an economic nature, and, consequently, when the exercise of that discretion, which is essential for defining the rules on concentrations, is under review, the Community judicature must take account of the discretionary margin implicit in the provisions of an economic nature which form part of the rules on concentrations (Kali & Salz, paragraphs 223 and 224, and Gencor v Commission, paragraphs 164 and 165).

65 Therefore, it is in the light of the foregoing considerations that it is necessary to examine the merits of the grounds relied on by the applicant to show that the Commission made an error of assessment in finding that the conditions for, or characteristics of, collective dominance would exist were the transaction to be approved.

B - The Decision

66 The Decision identifies two types of players on the relevant market (see paragraphs 72 and 75), the large tour operators on the one hand, and the secondary or small tour operators on the other:

- the major tour operators are characterised by their relatively large size - each of them having a market share exceeding 10% (according to the Commission's data, Thomson accounts for 27% of sales, Airtours for 21%, Thomas Cook for 20% and First Choice for 11%, that is, overall for 79% of sales. On Airtours' figures, Thomson accounts for 30.7% of sales, Thomas Cook for 20.4%, Airtours for 19.4% and First Choice for 15%, that is, overall for 85.5% of sales). A further characteristic is that they are all integrated both upstream (operation of charter airlines) and downstream (travel agencies);
- the secondary operators are smaller, none of them having a market share in excess of 5%, and in general they do not own either their own charter airlines or their own travel agencies. Apart from Cosmos (which, since it is linked to Monarch, one of the major charter airlines in the United Kingdom, is exceptional among secondary operators where there is no vertical integration), Manos and Kosmar, which are the fifth, sixth and seventh tour operators accounting respectively for 2.9%, 1.7% and 1.7% of sales, there are several hundred competing small tour operators, none of them accounting for more than 1% of sales.

67 It is apparent from the Decision (see the summary of the Commission's appraisal at paragraphs 168 to 172 of the Decision) that the Commission formed the view that the proposed merger would create a dominant position in the United Kingdom market for short-haul foreign package holidays, the effect of which would be to impede competition significantly in the Common Market for

the purposes of Article 2 (3) of Regulation No 4064/89, and that it would do so for the following reasons:
- the proposed merger would remove competition between the three large players remaining after the concentration (combined Airtours/First Choice, Thomson and Thomas Cook). Because of the structural features of the market and the way that it operates, which is dependent on capacity decisions, and because of the high degree of market concentration (the three remaining large tour operators would have about 80% of the market if the operation took place) (Decision, paragraph 169), they would no longer have an incentive to compete with each other;
- the operation would increase the degree of transparency and interdependence which already exists, with the result that the three remaining large tour operators would have every interest in adopting parallel conduct so far as the decision as to how many package holidays to put onto the market is concerned, reducing capacity below what is required as a result of market trends (Decision, paragraph 170);
- an examination of past competition bears out this conclusion, since it demonstrates that the relevant market already had a tendency towards collective dominance (Decision, paragraphs 128 to 138);
- deterrents or scope for retaliation exist, which are connected with the fact that if one of the three remaining large tour operators decided not to restrict capacity, there would be a risk that the two others would do the same, which would result in oversupply and serious financial consequences for each of the operators (Decision, paragraph 170);
- the smaller operators or new entrants, that is to say current and future competitors, would be further marginalized as a result of the operation, since they would lose First Choice both as a supplier of airline seats and as a potential distribution channel. In any event, those operators would not have the ability to offset any reductions in capacity brought about by the three remaining large tour operators (Decision, paragraph 171).
68 So far as the effects of the merger on effective competition are concerned, the Commission found that the effect of restricting overall capacity put onto the market would be to tighten the market and bring about an increase in the prices and profits of the members of the dominant oligopoly (see, in particular, paragraph 56 and the final part of paragraph 168 of the Decision).

C - The Commission's alleged errors of assessment

69 The applicant argues that, contrary to the Commission's contention, the factors put forward by the Commission in the Decision to characterise the situation as one of collective dominance were not present at the time of the notification and would not occur were the merger to proceed.
70 More specifically, the applicant claims, first, that, given the characteristics of the relevant market, the Commission has not proved conclusively that, were the merger to proceed, the three remaining large tour operators would have an incentive to cease competing with each other.
71 Second, it argues that, even supposing that such an incentive did exist, the absence of any deterrents or adequate means of retaliation would prevent the emergence of the alleged dominant oligopoly.
72 Third, and in any event, smaller operators and new entrants, namely current and future competitors, would challenge any capacity restrictions brought into effect and consumers would react as a result, so that the three remaining major operators would not be able, as a result of the concentration, to act together to any appreciable extent independently of other competitors and consumers.

73 Fourth, the applicant claims that the Commission incorrectly assessed the impact of the merger on competition in the relevant market.

[.....]

(d) Conclusion

277 In view of the foregoing observations, the Court concludes that the Commission's assessment of the foreseeable reaction of smaller tour operators, potential competitors, consumers and hotel-owners was incorrect and that it underestimated their reaction as a countervailing force capable of counteracting the creation of a collective dominant position.

5. *The assessment of the impact of the transaction on competition*

278 The Commission sets out its findings on the effect of the transaction at paragraphs 139 to 147 of the Decision.

279 First (paragraph 139), it argues that the transaction would result in increased concentration, since the combined market share of the three leading tour operators would increase substantially: 83% on the Commission's calculations (85% according to Nielsen), compared with around 70% before the merger (for Airtours, Thomson and Thomas Cook). In addition, the share of the fourth operator (Cosmos) would be less than 5%, whereas the operator currently in fourth position (First Choice) has a market share of 11%. However, it is apparent from paragraphs 139 to 147 of the Decision that the Commission did not regard the fact that the combined market share was high (above 80%) as sufficient to establish that there was a collective dominant position.

280 Second, the Commission maintains (paragraphs 140 and 141 of the Decision) that as a result of the merger First Choice would be lost as a supplier/distributor for secondary operators, which would further marginalize the smaller independent and non-integrated tour operators. However, it is appropriate to point out that when consideration is given to whether a collective dominant position might be created, the assessment of the foreseeable impact of the operation on other competitors in the market must ascertain whether those competitors would be in a position to challenge the stability of the alleged dominant oligopoly. The Court has found that the Commission did not prove that they would be incapable of doing so.

281 Third, the Commission contends (Decision, paragraphs 142 to 147) that the merger would increase transparency and the degree of interdependence between the large tour operators. At paragraph 143 of the Decision, it concludes that the fact that the merger would reduce the number of competitive relationships that are possible among the major operators by half, from six to three, would increase significantly the interdependence of the members of the oligopoly, which would be a further incentive to them to restrict capacity because it would be much more clear to them that competing for market share would mean depressed profits for each of them. The further marginalisation of secondary operators would increase the likelihood of that happening. At paragraph 144, the Commission points out that the reduction in the number of competitive and cooperative bilateral relationships would thus increase the transparency of the market, since it would become much easier for one of the major suppliers to detect efforts to destabilise the market involving, for example, attempts to capture market share. That greater transparency would increase the risk that competitive offensives would create oversupply, which would depress profits and consequently be counter-productive.

282 Consequently, the Commission reached the conclusion (Decision, paragraph 147) that the market structure to which the operation

would give rise would make it rational for the oligopolists to restrict supply.
283 However, it is appropriate to bear in mind, as regards the level of market transparency foreseeable after the merger, that the Court has found that the Commission was wrong to conclude that the degree of market transparency was sufficient to allow each of the major tour operators to be aware of the conduct of the others, to detect any deviations from the common policy and to see retaliatory measures for what they are. The Commission has failed to establish that the situation would be any different if there was a move from four major tour operators to three. Although there would certainly be some increase in market transparency after the reduction in the number of competitive bilateral relationships between the major tour operators from six to three, it is nevertheless the case that each of the three remaining major tour operators would continue to find it difficult to anticipate the intentions of the other two in sufficient time and to see any deviations from the common policy for what they are.
284 As regards the finding that the operation would significantly increase the interdependence of the major tour operators, it should be noted that the Commission has been inconsistent: it has argued, on the one hand, that in the relevant market it is necessary to become vertically integrated in order to be genuinely competitive and, on the other, that the fact that each of the integrated tour operators sells seats on charter flights to the others in the upstream market and sells the others' package holidays in the downstream market has an anti-competitive effect inasmuch as it increases their interdependence. In the absence of any evidence to the contrary, there must be a presumption, given the logic of the way the market operates, that vertical integration makes the large tour operators more independent from each other and thus reduces their interdependence.
285 Similarly, the Commission has not explained why what it regards as commercial links (purchase of airline seats from the others and sale of its own products in agencies owned by the others) must be explained solely in terms of strong economic links between the major operators (Decision, paragraph 142) and cannot simply be explained on the ground that it is profitable to maintain those links in a competitive situation, given that the major tour operators are economic units, firmly entrenched in several markets within the industry and that it is in their interest to be profitable and to maximise their revenues in those markets as a whole.
286 The Decision is not specific about the strong economic links between the major operators or the way in which they increase the interdependence of the integrated tour operators. At paragraph 57 of the Decision, the Commission states that 'the extent and nature of the vertical integration of the major suppliers, the extensive commercial and other links between them' are among the characteristics which distinguish the conditions of competition in the relevant product market. Then, at paragraph 71, the Decision is a little more specific about the nature of the links in question. It points out that there are a number of commercial links between the integrated companies, deriving in part from their vertical integration, downstream through the use of each other's travel agency chains and upstream because they share airline capacity to some extent, both through direct purchase from each other and from swaps and consolidation arrangements whereby they maximise the use of their respective fleets. At paragraphs 102 to 113, the Commission sets out a number of considerations under the heading 'Transparency, interdependency and commercial links'. Those paragraphs are devoted to an exposé of the

Commission's view of the degree of market transparency. The Commission, in that regard, states that vertical integration and the commercial links between the main suppliers help them to obtain precise and up to date estimates of their market share and those of their competitors. However, those paragraphs explain neither the reasons for the tour operators' interdependence nor what effect is produced by the commercial links arising from vertical integration and the way the market operates in that regard (apart from the fact that there is increased transparency).

287 Next, at paragraph 142, in its assessment of the impact of the merger, the Commission states that there is already a certain degree of mutual dependency between the tour operators, owing to the impact on market conditions of the overall level of capacity put on to the market for a season. The Commission adds that 'this creates strong economic links between the major operators'. However, the kind of economic links to which that passage refers is not specified and the Decision does not explain what the strong economic links are. In any event, the Decision does not seem to be referring in that passage to the commercial links stemming from vertical integration (namely, the fact that each of the large tour operators purchases airline seats from the others and sells the other operators' holidays).

288 It is clear from the foregoing that the Commission did not examine to what extent in the pre-concentration situation the commercial links stemming from vertical integration and from the way the market operates increase the interdependence of the integrated tour operators, other than to point out that they increase the degree of market transparency.

289 As the Commission has not provided evidence to the contrary, there must be a presumption that in the conditions obtaining in the relevant market prior to the concentration the fact that each integrated tour operator buys airlines seats from, and sells its products to, companies owned by a competitor no more constitutes evidence of interdependence than it does of independence. It seems to be merely an aspect of the way the economy operates, where business prevails and the integrated tour operators must attempt to capitalise on capacity and business opportunities in an industry with very high fixed costs and low profit margins. As the Decision points out, the integrated tour operators are present in three markets and, therefore, in three different businesses: short-haul charter flights, short-haul package holiday operation and holiday sales in travel agencies. First Choice even carries on a fourth business, that of seat broking (see paragraph 1 of the Decision). The economic logic underlying a group of undertakings demands that each of the undertakings making up the group strives to be as successful as possible.

290 In that regard, it is appropriate to observe that in its assessment of the impact of the transaction, the Commission does not appear to have considered the effect of the economic logic of the group, namely maximising income by maximising overall profits for the group as a whole. The Decision does acknowledge (paragraph 59) that tour operators' margins are fairly low, of the order of 7% in recent years, and that, by contrast, vertically integrated operators will normally also receive income from their airline and travel agency activities, areas in which (particularly so far as airlines are concerned) the margins may be higher. It also acknowledges that for that reason 'gross margins on the total operations of the integrated operators may be larger than those on their tour operating activities alone'.

291 Since that economic logic tends to favour achievement of the greatest synergies possible, the profitability of the various activities of the group (charter airlines, tour operating

and travel agencies) will be correspondingly higher where the benefits of vertical integration are fully exploited.

292 Finally, even if the synergies to which the merger is expected to lead did not exceed 1% of the overall costs of the combined entity (Decision, paragraph 146), there is no evidence that Airtours decided to finance the cost (usually higher in the case of a hostile takeover bid) of the shares in First Choice by relying on that large investment being made profitable by the benefits derived from a sustainable collective dominant position.

293 In view of the foregoing considerations and without a more detailed assessment of the implications of the increased market transparency and interdependence of the major tour operators to which the transaction is likely to give rise, the Court finds that the Commission has failed to prove that the result of the transaction would be to alter the structure of the relevant market in such a way that the leading operators would no longer act as they have in the past and that a collective dominant position would be created.

D - General conclusion

294 In the light of all of the foregoing, the Court concludes that the Decision, far from basing its prospective analysis on cogent evidence, is vitiated by a series of errors of assessment as to factors fundamental to any assessment of whether a collective dominant position might be created. It follows that the Commission prohibited the transaction without having proved to the requisite legal standard that the concentration would give rise to a collective dominant position of the three major tour operators, of such a kind as significantly to impede effective competition in the relevant market.

295 In those circumstances, the third plea must be declared to be well founded and, therefore, the Decision must be annulled, without it being necessary to examine the other complaints and pleas put forward by the applicant

[.....].

Case cross-references:

▸ *Kali und Salz* Commission decision 94/449/EC [1994] OJ L 186/38 (see VII-F-1).

▸ M.190-*Nestlé/Perrier.*

▸ M.1016-*Price Waterhouse/Coopers & Lybrand.*

▸ M.1044-*KPMG/Ernst & Young.*

▸ E.A. Raffaelli, 'European Union Competition Policy subsequent to the Airtours Case', (2002) *Fordham Corp. L. Inst.* (B. Hawk, ed. 2003), 129.

▸ I. Kokkoris, 'Assessment of Mergers Inducing Coordinated Effects in the Presence of Explicit Collusion', *World Competition* 31 no. 4 (2008): 499-522.

▸ Case C-413/06 P *Bertelsmann and Sony Corporation of America v. Impala* [2008] ECR I-4951 (*see IX-F-7*).

I. Vertical integration/gatekeeper issue

1) *MCI-Worldcom/Sprint*, Comm. Press Release (IP/00/668), Case M.1741; full decision published in [2003] OJ L 300/1

Relevance: setting limits to vertical integration. Merger shown to be one bridge too far after earlier concentration of MCI and Worldcom in 1998. Parallel investigation by EU and US competition authorities. Application of EU-US 1991 Agreement on anti-trust cooperation.

IP/00/668, Brussels, 28 June 2000

Commission prohibits merger between MCI WorldCom and Sprint

The European Commission has decided to prohibit the merger between US telecommunications firms MCI WorldCom Inc and Sprint Corp as it would have resulted in the creation of a dominant position in the market for top-level universal Internet connectivity. In the course of the review, the companies proposed to divest Sprint's Internet business but this was insufficient to resolve the competition concerns resulting from the merger.

MCI WorldCom is the world's leading provider of Internet connectivity, with Sprint one of its main competitors. An in-depth investigation by the Commission showed that the merger would, through the combination of the merging parties' extensive networks and large customer base, have led to the creation of such a powerful force that both competitors and customers would have been dependent on the new company to obtain universal Internet connectivity.

This would have allowed the merged company to behave independently of both its competitors and customers and, therefore, to dictate conditions and prices in the market to the detriment of consumers around the world and particularly in the 15 European Union states.

The companies informed the Commission yesterday of their intention to withdraw their notification of the deal. But the Commission felt compelled to take a formal decision as its review had come to an end and as it can only accept a withdrawal if the deal is no longer legally binding. This is not the case, as the companies have not formally cancelled their merger agreement.

Following the Commission's objections, the companies offered on 8 June 2000, the last day for the submission of undertakings according to the strict EU merger review timetable -- to divest Sprint's Internet business from Sprint's other activities. However, the Commission's investigation showed that this proposal was insufficient as it would not re-establish, with enough certainty as to its effect, immediate and effective competition in the market for top-level Internet connectivity. In any case, the companies withdrew this undertaking yesterday.

When assessing the feasibility of the proposed divestiture, the Commission also took into account issues raised by Cable & Wireless after its purchase of Internet MCI which was divested from MCI's other activities to gain clearance of the WorldCom/MCI merger in 1998.

'It was vital for the Commission that the divested business became a strong, viable competitor to prevent the merged WorldCom/Sprint from dominating Internet backbone. The companies' offer failed to guarantee this because Sprint's Internet business is completely intertwined with its traditional telecoms activities," European Competition Commissioner Mario Monti said.

The Commission also studied the impact of the merger in the market for the provision of global telecommunications services to multinational companies where together with British Telecommunications's Concert alliance with AT&T the merged entity would appear to control the majority of the market.

The Commission could not, however, show the absence of competitive constraints from actual competitors in this market and that customers would not be able to countervail against any parallel behaviour by the two leading players. Therefore, the Commission concluded that a collective dominant position could not be established between the merged entity and the Concert alliance.

During the course of its investigation, the Commission also received a number of critical comments from US and EU based operators that the merger would lead to the creation of a joint dominant position in the international voice telephony market with AT&T on the US retail and wholesale long distance market. The Commission's investigation showed that if there was any risk for competition in this market it would be a consequence of the exercise of market power on upstream domestic US markets and that these effects in the EU would not be immediate or foreseeable enough to grant jurisdiction over this issue to the European Commission. The Commission therefore decided to draw the US authorities attention to these possible effects and to request them to take them into account in their investigation.
Pursuant to the EU-US agreement of 1991 on antitrust co-operation, the European Commission has examined the merger in parallel with the US Department of Justice. The two authorities have conducted independent and separate investigations but the Commission and the US Department of Justice have enjoyed a good working relationship. This co-operation will continue in future cases, especially if and when the two authorities identify common competition concerns that might require a jointly pursued remedial action.
This is the 13th time the Commission has blocked a merger since 1990, when it was given the mandate to review all mergers and acquisitions involving companies with combined global sales in excess of five billion euros and European Union sales of at least 250 million euros for each of them, irrespective of their nationality. But a similar number of deals have been withdrawn in the face of European antitrust opposition.

Case cross-references:

- M.1069-*Worldcom/MCI (II)*.
- M. Monti, 'European Competition Policy for the 21st Century'. (2000) *Fordham Corp. L. Inst.* (B. Hawk, ed. 2001), 257.

J. Commitments offered and remedies acceptable

Cross-references for this part:

- Commission Notice on restrictions directly related and necessary to concentrations, [2005] OJ C 56/24
- G. Drauz, 'Remedies under the Merger Regulation', (1996) *Fordham Corp. L. Inst.* (B. Hawk, ed. 1997), 219.

1) *Boeing/McDonnell Douglas*, Case M.877 [1997] OJ L 336/16

See above for facts of case (VII-E-1, p. 290).

Relevance: extensive example of a variety of commitments offered.

[.....]

IX. Remedies

A. Undertakings submitted by Boeing

(114) With a view to removing the competition concerns, Boeing has given the Commission the following undertakings:

(115) Boeing proposal on leveraging of DAC installed base
1. Boeing undertakes to provide the following structural remedy: for a period of 10 years Boeing will maintain DAC in a separate legal entity and will supply to the Commission a report certified by an independent auditor which describes the business performance and results on a commercial line of business basis for the continued DAC business activities. The report will also be made available to the public. On these conditions, Boeing will have the right to manage fully the separate legal entity and make all business decisions it deems appropriate. The above period may be reduced in agreement with the Commission should Boeing not maintain two or more of the DAC aeroplane programmes.
2. Boeing commits to providing customer support for DAC aircraft at the same high quality level provided for Boeing aircraft. This includes all of Boeing's traditional services available from time to time for Boeing aircraft (which currently include the global network of field representatives, 24-hour technical service hotline, all aspects of spares support, including next-day shipment, responsive AOG support and world-class maintenance and flight training). Boeing also will apply the same Boeing guidelines and procedures for spare parts availability and pricing, and ensure appropriate levels of engineering support.
3. Boeing agrees it will not withhold or threaten to withhold support for DAC aircraft (including spare parts) or penalize or threaten to penalize an operator with respect to support for its DAC aircraft (for example, by raising prices or increasing delivery times for spare parts) because the operator proposes to purchase another manufacturer's aircraft. Boeing undertakes to continue to make publicly available the information (including pricing) currently available in the DAC spare parts catalogue.
4. Boeing will not use its privileged access to the existing fleet in service of DAC aircraft in order to leverage its opportunities for persuading current DAC operators to purchase Boeing aircraft. In particular, Boeing will not provide spare parts and product support on more favourable terms to some DAC operators rather than others, in order to persuade them to purchase Boeing aircraft.

(116) Boeing proposal on exclusive agreements
Boeing will not enter into any additional exclusive agreements until 1 August 2007 except for those campaigns in which another manufacturer has offered to enter into an exclusive agreement.
Boeing will not enforce its exclusivity rights under the agreements with American, Delta and Continental announced on 21 November 1996, 20 March 1997 and 10 June 1997, respectively.
An exclusive agreement for the purposes of this undertaking means a contractual commitment by a customer not to purchase or lease any other aircraft manufacturer's commercial jet aircraft or within a specific range of maximum take-off gross weight capability or to purchase a fixed percentage of aircraft from one manufacturer.

(117) Boeing proposal on patents
Boeing will, upon request by a commercial aircraft manufacturer, license on a non-exclusive, reasonable royalty-bearing basis,

any 'government-funded patent' which could be used in the manufacture or sale of commercial jet aircraft. Boeing will also licence the know-how related to such a patent which is necessary for the full, effective and rapid exploitation of the patent.
'Government-funded patent' means any patent which claims an invention conceived or first actually reduced to practice by Boeing in the performance of one or more of its contracts with the US Government, and which Boeing legally may so license.
Boeing also will license on a non-exclusive, reasonable royalty-bearing basis any blocking patent, including the related know-how as defined in the first paragraph, to another aircraft manufacturer which agrees to similar terms for cross-licensing of its blocking patents.
If Boeing and the other commercial aircraft manufacturer cannot agree on the royalty or whether the patent is a 'government-funded patent' which could be used in the manufacture or sale of commercial jet aircraft or whether the patent is blocking, such disagreement shall be submitted to independent arbitration under terms and procedures to be mutually agreed between Boeing and the other manufacturer.
For a period of 10 years, or until such earlier time as the Commission agreed that similar information is provided pursuant to governmental bilateral agreements or a significant change has occurred in the competitive environment including market share and product line, Boeing will supply to the Commission an annual report of its current un-expired patents which claim an invention conceived or first actually reduced to practice by Boeing in the performance of one or more of its contracts with the US Government.

(118) Boeing proposal on transparency of R&D projects
In order to provide increased transparency regarding US Government aeronautics R&D projects in which Boeing participates, Boeing will supply to the Commission an annual report for 10 years, or until such earlier time as the Commission has agreed that similar information is provided pursuant to governmental bilateral agreements or a significant change has occurred in the competitive environment including market share and product line, which contains the following information for non-classified aeronautics R&D projects (that is projects which are not classified under US Government national security laws and regulations) :
- name of project,
- description of project adequate to enable an understanding of the nature of the R&D being performed,
- authority contracting the project,
- description of Boeing's participation in the project,
- value of Boeing's contract,
- description of application of that year's results which have been incorporated or which Boeing intends to incorporate in large commercial aircraft. In subsequent reports, Boeing will advise the Commission of results from R&D projects identified in prior reports which have been incorporated or which Boeing intends to incorporate in large commercial aircraft. Upon request of the Commission with respect to a particular R&D project identified in a prior report, Boeing will identify whether it is studying the feasibility of application of the results for incorporation into large commercial aircraft,
- description of patents obtained by Boeing that year for an invention conceived or first actually reduced to practice by Boeing in the performance of its contract.
Upon request of the Commission, Boeing will provide another version of the report which complies with all applicable US laws and regulations with regard to disclosure of information which the Commission may provide to other aircraft manufacturers.

(119) Boeing proposal on suppliers
In order to meet the Commission's concerns that Boeing could leverage its supply relationships to discriminate against other manufacturers of large commercial aircraft, Boeing makes the following commitments.
1. Boeing will not exert or attempt to exert undue or improper influence on its suppliers, directly or indirectly, by promising an increase in supplies or subcontracted R&D activities, threatening to decrease supplies or subcontracted R&D activities, or leveraging in any other way its own supply relationships, in order that these suppliers should:
- refuse to take up or seek out supply relationships with other manufacturers of large commercial aircraft,
- refuse to increase their supply relationships with other manufacturers of large commercial aircraft,
- refuse to enter into subcontracts with other manufacturers on research or development for large commercial aircraft,
- refuse to enter into risk-sharing partnerships with other manufacturers of large commercial aircraft,
- delay R&D activities for or supplies to other manufacturers of large commercial aircraft,
- grant preferential treatment to Boeing in terms of lead times for supplies or priority for R&D activities subcontracted by Boeing without a reasonable business justification.
2. Boeing retains its right to select its suppliers, enforce its contracts with respect to price, quality scheduling and delivery and to protect its proprietary information.

B. Assessment

(120) There are two areas of competition problems:
- the additional competitive potential of MDC in commercial aircraft (horizontal effects),
- the large increase in Boeing's defence and space business (overall effects).

(121) Although DAC, which operates the commercial business of MDC, is no longer a real force in the market, the concentration would nonetheless lead to a strengthening of Boeing's dominant position in large commercial aircraft. As a consequence of the undertakings submitted by Boeing:
- Boeing's enhanced capability to enter into exclusive agreements will become irrelevant in the foreseeable future given that Boeing is not allowed to enter into future exclusive agreements for a period of 10 years. Furthermore, the abandonment of the exclusivity rights in the three existing exclusive agreements will remove the foreclosure of the market resulting from the exclusivity,
- the competitive advantages of Boeing's access to DAC's fleet in service are further reduced by Boeing's commitments not to leverage the product support for the DAC fleet with respect to the purchase of new aircraft,
- the risk that Boeing, by continuing the production lines of DAC, may use DAC aircraft as 'discount' aircraft is reduced if DAC is operated as a separate legal entity with annual public reporting obligations certified by an independent auditor.
(122) As regards, the strengthening of Boeing's dominant position resulting from its large increase in the defence and space business, the undertakings submitted by Boeing have the following consequences:
- the commitment on patents gives other aircraft manufacturers access to intellectual property gained by publicly funded R&D and also with respect to blocking patents, meets the general concern about Boeing's increased patents portfolio,
- the commitment on transparency contributes to more discipline in publicly funded R&D and makes the spill-over from defence and space R&D to the civil sector more transparent,

- the commitments on supply relationships reduce the risk that Boeing may abuse its increased bargaining power in order to impede competitors through inter alia exclusive contracts with suppliers.
(123) The Commission has taken into consideration two specific aspects of the present case. Firstly, post-concentration there will be only two operators on the market for large commercial aircraft, Boeing and Airbus. In the absence of any interest on the part of Airbus to acquire DAC, but also in the absence of any interest of other companies to enter this market through an acquisition of DAC, it is highly unlikely that a buyer could be found for DAC. A commitment on a divestiture would not therefore have resolved the competition problems resulting from the horizontal effects. Secondly, the spill-over effects from the defence and space business on the commercial aircraft business are by their very nature difficult to quantify or even fully identify. They are difficult to address fully in the context of the present procedure under the Merger Regulation.
Moreover, within the framework of the Agreement between the European Communities and the Government of the United States of America regarding the application of their competition laws, the Commission has also taken into consideration the important interests of the United States of which the Commission was informed by the US Department of Defence and Department of Justice, on behalf of the US Government (see paragraph 12).
The package of undertakings submitted by Boeing contains a combination of structural and behavioural elements. In the specific circumstances explained above, relating in particular to the manifest absence of any possible buyer for DAC, the Commission accepts this combination of undertakings, which should be treated as a whole, and considers that, on balance, they adequately address the competition problems identified in the present decision and removes the concerns about a strengthening of Boeing's dominant position in the market for large commercial aircraft. To ensure full compliance by Boeing with its commitments, in application of Article 8 (2), second subparagraph, the Commission shall monitor this compliance. In particular, Boeing shall allow the Commission, or any expert appointed by the Commission, access to internal data relevant to the implementation of this monitoring, and, whenever requested by the Commission, be prepared to discuss its compliance with the commitments.

[.....]

Case cross-references:
- ▸ M.1069-*Worldcom/MCI (II)*.
- ▸ M.1845-*AOL/Time-Warner*.
- ▸ M.2050-*Vivendi/Canal+/Seagram*.
- ▸ M.2305-*Vodaphone Airtouch/Mannesmann*.

2) Case C-12/03 *Commission v. Tetra Laval* [2005] ECR I-987

See above for facts of the case (VII-G-2, p. 305).

Relevance: Commission's obligation to take into consideration all commitments offered. It is immaterial whether these are of a behavioural or of a structural nature.

[.....]

85 With respect to consideration of the behavioural commitments offered by Tetra, the Court of First Instance was right to hold, in paragraph 161 of the judgment under appeal, that the fact that Tetra had, in the present case, offered commitments relating to its future conduct was a factor which the Commission had to take into account when assessing the likelihood that the merged entity would act in such a way as to make it possible to create a dominant position on one or more of the relevant markets for PET equipment.

86 In that regard, the Court points to the considerations set out by the Court of First Instance in paragraphs 318 and 319 of the judgment in Gencor. Contrary to what the Commission claims, it is not apparent from that judgment that the Court of First Instance ruled out consideration of behavioural commitments. On the contrary, in paragraph 318, the Court of First Instance laid down the principle that the commitments offered by the undertakings concerned must enable the Commission to conclude that the concentration at issue will not create or strengthen a dominant position within the meaning of Article 2(2) and (3) of the Regulation. Then, in paragraph 319, it inferred from that principle that the categorisation of a proposed commitment as behavioural or structural is immaterial and that the possibility cannot automatically be ruled out that commitments which are prima facie behavioural, for instance a commitment not to use a trade mark for a certain period or to make part of the production capacity of the entity arising from the concentration available to third-party competitors or, more generally, to grant access to essential facilities on non-discriminatory terms, may also be capable of preventing the emergence or strengthening of a dominant position.

[.....]

CHAPTER VIII

Joint Ventures, Forms of Horizontal Co-Operation and Article 101 TFEU

General chapter cross-references:

- ▸ Regulation 2658/2000 on the application of Article 81(3) of the EC Treaty to categories of specialisation agreements, [2000] OJ L 304/3.
- ▸ Regulation 2659/2000 on the application of Article 81(3) of the EC Treaty to categories of research and development agreements, [2000] OJ L 304/7.
- ▸ Guidelines on the applicability of Article 81 to horizontal co-operation agreements, [2001] OJ C 3/2.
- ▸ Regulation 772/2004 on the application of Art. 81(3) of the Treaty to categories of technology transfer agreements, [2004] OJ L 123/11.
- ▸ C. Ritter, 'New Regulation Transfer Technology', (2004) 31-3 *LIEI*.
- ▸ F.O.W. Vogelaar, 'Modernisation of EC Competition Law, Economy and Horizontal Cooperation between Undertakings', (2002) 37-1 *Intereconomics*, 19.

A. Partners are (potential) competitors

1) *Mitchell Cotts/Sofiltra* Commission decision 87/100/EEC [1987] OJ L 41/31

M.C. Engineering, a UK company, and Sofiltra, a French undertaking, had acquired joint control in Mitchell Cotts Air Filtration. Both M.C. Engineering and Mitchell Cotts Air Filtration had previously been wholly controlled by the (British) Mitchell Group. The joint venture was to produce and market high-efficiency air filters using micro-fine glass fibre for the nuclear, chemical and computer markets. The commercial know-how was provided by Mitchell Cotts Environmental Controls, the technological know-how by Sofiltra, which had exclusively licensed the joint venture to produce the said air filter in the United Kingdom.

Relevance: are the parent companies to the JV actual or potential competitors, or maybe only partly? No foreclosure of competitors and no creation of a network of competing JVs.

[.....]

II. Legal assessment

A. Article 85 (1)

(18) Since Sofiltra's consent is required for the adoption of important decisions relating to the conduct of the Joint Venture's business, Sofiltra is not merely a minority shareholder. Day-to-day management decisions in the Joint Venture are the responsibility of the Board of Directors on which M. C. Engineering holds a majority (see paragraph 8). Nevertheless, Sofiltra's influence will be brought to bear on the Joint Venture's conduct, since it is the key provider of technology, an important shareholder, and participates on an equal footing with M. C. Engineering in the Shareholders' Committee, whose prior approval is required for certain important decisions (see paragraph 7). Sofiltra must therefore be considered a full partner in the Joint Venture, sharing control with M. C. Engineering. As a result, the Joint Venture Agreement has to be considered under Article 85 (1).

(19) Since competitive conditions are broadly similar for the products concerned throughout the Common Market, the EEC as a whole

is the relevant geographical market in which the parties' positions should be assessed. The question arises whether the participating undertakings are competitors within the relevant geographical and product markets. The relevant product market for the assessment of competitive relations between the parent undertakings prior to the conclusion of the agreements in question is that for the manufacture and sale of the complete finished product including the key component, pleated glass fibre paper.
As regards manufacture, M. C. Engineering was not an actual or potential competitor of Sofiltra since M. C. Engineering lacked the requisite know-how and research and development facilities for the production of pleated glass fibre paper, the crucial component in the finished product and the subject of the technology transfer in this case. The mere availability of purchases or licences from other sources does not alter this analysis: M. C. Engineering had an evident economic and commercial interest in developing its own technology in this field and has not been able to do so, resorting first to purchases from Sofiltra and later to a joint venture coupled with a know-how licence. Therefore, M. C. Engineering and Sofiltra were neither actual nor potential competitors for the manufacture of the complete finished product incorporating the essential technical component which is also the major cost component. Furthermore, due to the number of other undertakings competing in this market and the relatively small market shares of the parties to the Joint Venture in the relevant geographical market, the creation of the Joint Venture does not pose any risk in terms of the foreclosure of similar possibilities to other competitors. Since the parties are not competitors and there is no loss of competition involved and no foreclosure risk, and the agreement does not involve the creation of a network of competing joint ventures, the agreement to undertake joint manufacturing does not in itself fall within the terms of Article 85 (1).
(20) On the other hand, as regards sales and distribution of the final product, Sofiltra and the Joint Venture are competitors and, as a result, territorial restrictions between them fail to be analysed as a separate matter under Article 85 (1) since, even if the agreement to undertake joint manufacturing between non-competitors does not fall under Article 85 (1), the agreements and their specific provisions must be examined in order to determine whether competition is restricted in any other way.

[.....]

(23) However, the exclusive licence granted to the Joint Venture to manufacture air filters in the United Kingdom means that Sofiltra will not itself manufacture in that territory or appoint other licensees there. This cannot, without some time limitation, be considered strictly necessary for the creation and proper operation of the Joint Venture. It is not inconceivable that Sofiltra could decide after such a period, and especially when the Joint Venture has reached full capacity, to establish its own production unit rather than extend that of the Joint Venture. Such a course of action would not, in these circumstances, undermine the existence of the Joint Venture. Similarly, if the Joint Venture is unable to meet an order, Sofiltra should normally be free to do so and this would not undermine the operation of the Joint Venture. The exclusive right granted to the Joint Venture to sell the licensed products in the United Kingdom, Ireland and seven non-EEC countries prohibits Sofiltra and possible future licensees, save in certain exceptional cases, from actively selling air filters in those territories. For its part, the

Joint Venture is prohibited from actively selling in territories reserved for the Licensor. This mutual ban on active sales, although it allows for passive sales by licensor and licensee in each other's territory, must be considered to fall within Article 85 (1) since such a restriction results in the sharing of markets between Sofiltra and the Joint Venture which have become competitors and are offering competing products. As it is highly unlikely that there will be intermediate trade in the product, a ban on active sales constitutes a particularly perceptible restriction as there is no alternative source of supply.

[.....]

2) *KSB/Goulds/Lowara/ITT* Commission decision 91/38/EEC [1991] OJ L 19/25

KSB, a German undertaking, was the world largest pump manufacturer. Goulds, a US-based undertaking, ranked third. These two undertakings, together with Lowara and ITT, had set up Quattro, a joint venture that was to develop and produce the wet end of a single-stage, single-flow radial centrifugal pump. These wet ends (also called units or components) were made of chrome nickel stainless steel. Traditionally, though, pump components were made of grey cast iron.

Relevance: parent companies are competitors.

[.....]

II. Legal assessment

A. Article 85 (1)

[.....]

Restrictions of competition

(16) The four undertakings are actual competitors. They are all manufacturers of conventional pumps having the same fields of application as the new stainless steel pumps. They are represented in the Community for these products either directly or through subsidiaries.
Contrary to their submissions, they must also be considered to be potential competitors in respect of the chrome nickel steel components of the new pumps. In view of their size, it must be assumed that each group of undertakings would have been in a financial position to develop the components alone. From the day on which the agreement on the setting up of a joint venture was concluded, 5 November 1985, Lowara was a wholly-owned subsidiary of Goulds. Nor can the position of the parties as potential competitors be contested on the basis of the argument that because Lowara alone was in possession of the basic technology, only Lowara was capable of developing the wet end components of chrome nickel steel pumps. Such basic technology was indisputably available to other pump manufacturers (for example, Grundfos, Hilge and Ebara), and, therefore, it is at least conceivable that each of the groups could have acquired the basic technology by means of a licence from manufacturers other than Lowara.
Nor, lastly, can the existence of potential competition between the parties be ruled out on the basis of the argument that none

of them would, on its own, have decided to develop the product because none, on its own, would have been able to use the volume of units necessary for cost-effective series production. Here too, other methods, such as the licensing or production for third parties, could have been used to recover the development costs over the long term. Taking account of the overall circumstances of the case, the profitability arguments put forward are not so convincing as to provide any objective evidence of the existence or non-existence of possible competition.

(17) By concluding their agreement, the undertakings have opted for cooperation on the research, development and use of wet end components for chrome nickel steel pumps, rather than proceeding independently in competition with one another. This involves a restriction of their freedom of action. Even if the other components of the pumps differ, so that the user has the choice of a number of brands, the fact remains that the new components would represent the key aspect of a user's decision to buy the new pumps.

In view of the advantages of chrome nickel steel pumps set out in recital 3 and the parties' claim that there is fierce competition on the market for water pumps, particular importance attaches precisely to competition in new products.

[.....]

There is only limited competition between the parties themselves. According to the information provided by the parties, Goulds and ITT do not have any significant share of the market for water pumps in the Community or in its regions. Lowara is hardly a serious competitor for KSB (other than in Italy) on those markets on which KSB has a strong position, because Lowara's position in such markets is too weak compared with KSB's. It must therefore be assumed that the new pumps will be supplied on these markets mainly by KSB.

[.....]

Case cross-reference:

▸ *British Interactive Broadcasting/Open* Commission decision 1999/781/EC [1999] OJ L 312/1.

B. Prohibition Article 101 (1) EC

1) *WANO Schwarzpulver*, VIIIth Report on Competition Policy (1978), point 134

Relevance: joint venture in a duopolistic market. Rare example of Commission formally prohibiting a JV under Article 101 (1).

Imperial Chemical Industries-Wasagchemie (WANO Schwarzpulver)

134. The Commission adopted its first prohibition Decision under Article 85 of the Rome Treaty in respect of agreements for the creation of a joint venture company. The agreements, which had been notified to the Commission, were entered into by Wasagchemie GmbH and some of its group companies (WASAG) with subsidiary companies of Imperial Chemical Industries Ltd (ICI). The joint company was to operate in the Federal Republic of Germany and to be controlled equally by the WASAG and ICI groups for the manufacture and sale of black powder.

Black powder is a low-power explosive. Its main uses are in the manufacture of fireworks, other pyrotechnical devices, safety fuse and for blasting. Small quantities are used for military purposes. In most of its applications other explosives cannot be used. ICI, which no longer has its own production facilities for black powder, has a near-100% share of the sales of black powder in the United Kingdom. WASAG, through a controlled company, produces black powder and has around 50% of the sales in the Federal Republic of Germany. Each of the parties has, outside the sphere of the agreements, its separate interests in explosives other than black powder, and in safety fuse, an important down-stream product of black powder. Pursuant to the agreements and the parties' participation in the joint venture, neither party (each being a natural competitor of the other in black powder and safety fuse) could, without approval of the other, have made independent decisions within the joint venture field and neither party would have competed with the other or with the joint venture in relation to black powder. In respect of safety fuse, which was not to be a joint venture product, the parties would through their control of the joint venture have knowingly created for themselves opportunities and strong inducements for cooperation in the alignment of prices and the sharing of markets.

135. It would have been the additional effect of the agreements, particularly in the light of ICI's near-100% share in the UK black powder market and in the light also of its control of distribution and transport facilities for explosives in the UK, that the UK black powder market would for the foreseeable future have been blocked to other producers, for example, producers in France and Italy with considerable over-capacities. Pursuant to the joint-venture arrangements, ICI would have purchased black powder for substantially the entire UK demand only from the production of the joint venture and ICI would not have been free to procure black powder for resale on the best terms from time to time available also from other sources.

The Commission could not accept as a ground for exemption that in this case a pooling of technology and resources would have enabled manufacturers on a scale to bring about new developments in an industry in which manufacturing methods had remained essentially the same for centuries. The Commission also found that security of supplies of black powder for the UK could not be regarded as a sufficient benefit for the purposes of an exemption in circumstances of considerably under-used production capacities in the black powder industry as a whole. Moreover, the overriding reason why the Commission was not able to grant an exemption in this case was because competition for the supply of black powder to the UK would for all practical purposes have been ruled out if ICI had participated in the joint venture.

136. The effectiveness of the agreements between the parties had been expressed to be subject to the approval by the Commission and the joint venture had not been formally established, although the parties had already taken some steps to implement their intended association, in that ICI had purchased all or substantially all of its requirements of black powder from the works to be assigned to the proposed joint company. Following receipt of the Commission's objections, the parties informed the Commission that they proposed no longer to implement the agreements for the creation of the joint venture. The Commission nevertheless regards it of importance to have adopted this Decision, to establish clearly, also for the benefit of other producers and of customers of black powder, that the agreements in ques-

tion infringed Article 85 (1) and could not be exempted under Article 85 (3).
The Commission had also warned the parties that implementation on their part of the joint venture agreements could in this case have additionally amounted to an abuse of ICI's dominant position in the UK black powder market.

C. Joint bidding venture

1) *Plessey/GEC-Siemens*, XIXth Report on Competition Policy (1989), point 66

Relevance: is joint bidding by actual or potential competitors in conformity with Article 101? Example of a rejection of a complaint by decision.

Plessey/GEC-Siemens

66. On 1 September, the Commission formally rejected the complaints from Plessey plc, the British electronics manufacturer, that the proposed joint take-over by GEC-Siemens infringed the EEC competition rules. The complaint concerned the agreement between GEC and Siemens to purchase Plessey, combined with plans for the future joint and/or separate management of certain assets.

The Commission considered that certain elements of the agreement micht constitute appreciable restrictions of competition within the meaning of Article 85 (1) of the EEC Treaty, particularly concerning telecommunications and integrated circuits. However, in the light of the particular circumstances of the case, it considered that an individual Article 81 (3) exemption could be envisaged regarding these aspects of the agreement. With regard to these sectors, it was expected that the transaction would produce advantages in the form of economic and technical progress thanks to the pooling of research and development resources in the markets where there was a sharp and steady rise in R&D costs. Moreover, a number of international competitors that were more powerful than the companies in question existed on the markets.

In relation to the other areas covered by the complaint, i.e. traffic control systems and defence equipment, the Commission found no appreciable restriction of competition in the context of Article 85 (1).
The Commission adopted the decision as a matter of urgency following the renewed bid by GEC-Siemens on 17 August 1989, so that Plessey could exercise its right of appeal. On 16 April, the Commission had already announced the initiation of formal proceedings with a view to approval of the transaction.

D. No economic unit between parent and joint venture

1) *Philips/Thompson/Sagem*, XXIIIth Report on Competition Policy (1993), point 215

Relevance: is the transaction a concentration or rather a form of co-operation? Nature of joint venture in case of potentially alternating majorities.

Philips-Thomson-Sagem

215. The Commission cleared the creation of a joint venture company called Flat Panel Display BV (FPD) under Article 85 of the EC Treaty. The parents of the joint venture are Philips Electronics N.V., Thomson Consumer Electronics S.A. and Sagem.
FPD will be active in the development, design, manufacture and sale of active matrix liquid crystal displays (AM-LCD). AM-LCDs are used inter alia for direct view TV modules, consumer and professional projection displays and datagraphic modules. AM-LCDs belong to a family of technologies currently referred to as liquid crystal displays (LCD), which, in turn, are one of the alternative technologies, under various degrees of development, generally known as flat screen technologies.
FPD will be the first European company capable of producing very large series of screens. It was expected that FPD would start mass-production in 1993. It will have its own process and product development departments, facilities and personnel. Its production will be made available to third parties worldwide.
The share capital of FPD will be held by Philips (80%), Thomson (10%) and Sagem, (10%). However, in spite of its majority, Philips alone will not be in a position to adopt a number of strategic decisions without the support of at least one of the other shareholders. In addition, the parties envisage other companies joining as new shareholders in FPD.
The agreement establishing FPD was originally notified under the provisions of the Merger Control Regulation on 8 December 1992. However, by formal decision issued on 18 January 1993, the Commission decided that FPD did not constitute a concentration within the meaning of Article 3 of the Merger Control Regulation. Subsequently, and at the request of the parties, the notification was converted into a notification within the meaning of Article 4 of Council Regulation No 17.
The Commission, therefore, assessed the proposed joint venture from the point of view of the application of Article 85 of the EC Treaty and came to the conclusion that the notified cooperative joint venture fell under the scope of Article 85 (l).
This conclusion was mainly supported by the fact that the parent companies, given their remaining activities within the AM-LCD field, in the LCD field in general and in respect of other types of flat screens, as well as in respect of cathode ray tubes (where Thomson and Philips are very important players on a worldwide basis), have to be considered as being potential and even actual competitors either among themselves or in respect of the joint venture.
However, the Commission considered that the conditions for the granting of an individual exemption to FPD were fulfilled in the present case.

In particular, the Commission ascertained that the joint venture is going to be a means for the parent companies to develop and sustain mass-production in Europe of new high technology products in a field where competition from foreign suppliers (mainly Japan) is strong, where production and marketing within a tight time schedule on an economically viable scale is essential and where the technical and industrial framework is uncertain.
In addition, screens manufactured by FPD will be sold to sophisticated buyers (i.e. consumer electronics manufacturers, car manufacturers and telecommunications equipment manufacturers) to be integrated either in existing families of products or in completely new ones that will enlarge the range of products offered to consumers. This aspect is also important because such purchasers can represent an effective counterweight to the joint venture.
Finally, the Commission was convinced that the joint venture is not a means for the parent companies to eliminate competition either in respect of displays in general or AM-LCDs in particular. In respect of the latter, it can be said that a new technology will be put into production in the EC. More importantly, this is a sector in which the market is worldwide. Consequently, the important position acquired by the joint venture in the Community must be seen in a global context. In this instance, it is apparent that the new entity will not have a dominant position on the market.
For the reasons mentioned above and given the urgency of the case, which is part of a wider programme supported by the Commission under the Esprit III programme, the case was closed by means of a comfort letter sent to the parties.
This important case was one of the first in which the new internal rules for the assessment of cooperative joint ventures of a structural nature were applied.

E. Joint production

1) *Exxon/Shell and four other cases*, XXIVth Competition Report (1994) points 163-171

Relevance: joint production between competitors. Effects under Article 101 explained.

3 - R&D, production and sales joint ventures limited to specific products

163. The Commission exempted by formal decision five joint ventures between important competitors in oligopolistic markets which almost all related to the development and production of new products in specific markets: Exxon/Shell (low density polyethylene), Pasteur Mérieux/Merck (human vaccines), Philips/Osram (leadglass for lamps), Fujitsu/AMD (semiconductors) and Asahi/St Gobain (automotive safety glass). These cases show that the Commission is prepared to consider favourably certain joint ventures (full-function and non-full-function joint ventures), even when they do not fulfil the conditions set out in block exemption regulations and involve competitors with market shares exceeding the thresholds laid down in these regulations, because of their overall economic advantages.
164. Apart from Pasteur Mérieux/Merck, which was a joint venture for joint devel-

opment and sales (production remained with the parents), all other cases essentially involved R&D and/or production joint ventures, which maintain a separate distribution of the final product by the parents (non-full-function joint ventures). Three cases (Philips/Osram, Asahi/St Gobain and Fujitsu/AMD) related to an input product mainly sold to the parents for incorporation in a final product to be produced and sold separately by the parents (input joint ventures). Two other cases (Exxon/Shell and Pasteur Mérieux/Merck) concerned a final product (final-product joint ventures).

165. Under Article 85(1) of the Treaty, the Commission examined both restrictions of competition between the parties resulting from the creation and operation of the joint venture (which depends on whether or not the parties are actual or potential competitors in the field of activities of the joint venture) and restrictions of competition affecting third parties (territorial restrictions, foreclosure effect, etc.).

As regards restrictions of competition between the parties, the Commission examines both the direct elimination of competition resulting from the pooling of development and/or production and the risk of spill-over effects (indirect effects) on the separate sales activity by the parents for the final product or on other closely related markets (upstream, downstream or neighbouring markets).

In the cases involving input joint ventures decided by the Commission, the spill-over effects on the final product market depended principally on two factors: the importance of the jointly produced input in the cost of the final product (ratio common cost/total final cost) and the market position of the parents. The higher the common cost and the combined market share of the parents in the final product market, the greater the risk of spill-over effects is likely to be. In the case of final product joint ventures, the commonality of costs and the proximity of the parents' cooperation to the final product market are such that appreciable spill-over effects are very likely to occur (for instance by alignment of sales prices), in particular where the parties have important market shares or operate in an oligopolistic market.

166. The Commission also identified a certain number of ancillary restrictions in the context of the examined joint ventures. Ancillary restrictions are restrictions only imposed on the parties or the joint venture (not on third parties) which are objectively necessary for the successful functioning of the joint venture and thus by their very nature inherent in the operation concerned (e.g. non-compete obligation of the parents towards their joint venture). Such ancillary restrictions are not assessed separately under Article 85(1) of the Treaty if the joint venture itself does not infringe Article 85(1) or is exempted under Article 85(3). While ancillary restrictions are normally only accepted for a limited period of time, in the context of joint ventures they are usually allowed for the whole duration of the joint venture.

167. Under Article 85(3), the Commission ensured in particular that the restrictions of competition were indispensable for the attainment of the benefits resulting from the cooperation (this indispensability needs to be distinguished from the question of whether or not the parties are actual or potential competitors for the application of Article 85(1)) and that there remained sufficient external competition to guarantee the maintenance of an effective competitive structure on the markets concerned. In the case of cooperation between competitors, even if such cooperation is limited in scope (non-full-function joint ventures for specific products), the Commission cannot rely exclu-

sively on the internal competition between the parties for the maintenance of effective competition under Article 85(3).

168. In three cases (Exxon/Shell, Pasteur Mérieux/Merck and Asahi/St Gobain), the Commission made its exemption subject to conditions or substantial changes in the operation in order either to reduce the restrictions of competition to what was indispensable for file achievement of the benefits found to exist under Article 85(3) or to guarantee the maintenance of effective competition on the market concerned (for details, see hereafter).

169. In Exxon/Shell, the fourth and the fifth largest producers on the EC market for LDPE/LLDPE (low-density polyethylene/linear low-density polyethylene) formed a joint venture for the production of a considerable part of their overall requirements of LLDPE designed for distribution on the market by the parent companies without further processing (final-product joint venture with separate distribution). The parents also continue themselves to produce LDPE, which is in the same product market as LLDPE. LLDPE is a new product providing a high degree of flexibility in production and reducing health and environmental risks (production based on the Unipol technology). This production joint venture created the second largest production capacity in Europe. The market concerned is characterized by an oligopolistic structure, a considerable degree of price transparency and a certain stability of production capacities and market shares.

170. Since Exxon and Shell were competitors on the relevant market and capable of setting up LLDPE production facilities in the EC independently (independent facilities having half the capacity of the joint venture would have been of a technically and economically feasible size), the Commission concluded that the production joint venture had the effect of restricting competition within the meaning of Article 85(I) of the Treaty in the following respects:

- the parents will necessarily coordinate their investment plans and give up the possibility of enlarging their polyethylene businesses by individual action;
- the parents will inevitably be led to coordinate their production within the joint venture (allocation of production output between the parties),
- joint production followed by separate distribution without further processing generally leads to coordination of the parents' future competitive behaviour at the distribution level, in particular in relation to prices (spill-over effect); and
- the high joint investment, the joint production and the flow of information between the parents allowed by the joint venture are further likely to have an indirect effect on the polyethylene production plans of the Exxon and Shell groups as a whole, hence on activities outside the joint venture (spill-over effect).

In evaluating these restrictions of competition, the Commission did not focus on particular provisions in the agreements, but on the inherent effects resulting trim, tile creation and operation of the joint venture, underlining the central role of the independent decision-making of companies, which must not be subject to reciprocal influence resulting from structural cooperation within a joint venture.

171. In spite of the oligopolistic market structure and the abovementioned restrictive effects of the Exxon/Shell production joint venture, the Commission exempted the cooperation for a period of 10 years for the following reasons. This joint venture was the first LLDPE plant in the EC utilizing the Unipol

technology for the production of a new product (LLDPE); it created new production capacity and output on the market; the parties' combined capacity and market share only marginally exceeded the 20% market share threshold of the group exemption regulations on R&D and specialization (market share threshold applicable to production joint ventures not involving joint selling); the size of the remaining competitors guaranteed that effective competition was not eliminated. In addition, the parties accepted to make certain changes to their agreements which guaranteed each party a greater scope for separate investments inside the joint venture in order to adapt the output of the joint venture to the respective needs of each parent and a right to take over, without the approval of the other party, unused capacity normally reserved for the other party.

F. Network of joint ventures with one parent in common

1) *Optical Fibres*, XVIth Competition Report (1986) point 67

Relevance: similar JVs between one US partner and two European undertakings. Competitive dangers related to JVs that form part of a network. Rapid introduction of new technology for the benefit of the European industry.

Joint exploitation of complementary technology
Optical fibres

67. The Commission has granted an exemption under Article 85(3) in respect of two sets of agreements involving the US corporation, Corning Glass Works. Under the agreements Corning has set up joint ventures in the United Kingdom with BICC plc and in Germany with Siemens AG for the production and sale of optical fibres.
Corning Corporation is one of the major producers and distributors of optical fibres in the world and its joint ventures in the European Community account for almost 50% of productive capacity in the Community. BICC plc and Siemens AG are leading cable makers in the United Kingdom and Germany respectively.
Optical fibres are high-technology carriers of information. The main use of optical fibres is in the field of telephone communications, where they art tending to replace the more traditional copper wire or coaxial cables.
The Commission found that the individual joint venture agreements notified to it did not as such restrict competition between Corning and its partners They did not contain obligations which went beyond what would be admitted in licensing agreements between non-competitors.
However, the Commission found that there was a distortion of competition in the relationship between the joint ventures, and the existence of other similar joint ventures in which Corning participated actively. The joint ventures had substantially the same activity, namely the production and marketing of optical fibres. They were therefore direct competitors. The agreements taken together with other agreements which do not form part of the decision created a network of inter-related joint ventures in an oligopolistic market in which Corning as owner and supplier of the relevant technology held an influential position.
This network of joint ventures distorted competition between the individual joint ventures and was, therefore, likely to lead to

market sharing between them. This brought the agreement within the scope of Article 85(1). However, following amendments to the agreements the Commission found that they fulfilled the conditions for exemption under Article 85(3). They enabled several European companies to manufacture a high-technology product with significant advantages over traditional cables in the Community, thereby promoting technical progress and benefiting consumers. The agreements were essential to achieve these objectives. Corning's participation in the joint venture made possible the rapid transfer of fast moving technology. There was no possibility of eliminating competition. Although competition between the joint ventures was distorted, they were not able to eliminate competition entirely since there were several other producers of optical fibres in the Common Market, and producers in the Common Market were subject to global competition. Optical fibres, in spite of their advantages over other forms of cable, did not supplant the latter and in effect remained in competition with them. The exemption was granted for a period of 15 years in order to enable the parties to enforce the agreements and to obtain a satisfactory return on their capital.

G. Re-entry potential after termination of joint venture

1) *De Laval-Stork* Commission decision 77/543/EEC [1977] OJ L 215/11

De Laval Turbine, part of the US-based De Laval Group, manufacturer of compressors, turbines and pumps, and KMS (manufacturer of machines), subsidiary of the Dutch VMF and in control of Stork, had set up De Laval-Stork. The two parent companies were and remained competitors; the joint venture agreement (JVA) itself was subject to a termination clause. The Commission found that the joint venture agreement infringed Article 101 (1), especially since both De Laval Turbine and KMS were (part of) large multinationals, which potentially reinforced the negative effects on competition. Exemption could only be granted under certain conditions.

Relevance: conditions for competition to be restored between the JV partners after termination of the joint venture.

[.....]

IV. Conditions and obligations

Under Article 8 (1) of Regulation No 17, conditions and obligations may be attached to a declaration of exemption, in which respect the following considerations are relevant.
15. Exemption in this case should be subject to the two following conditions by reason of the fact that certain clauses of the JVA do not satisfy the tests of Article 85 (3).

(1) If for any reason the joint venture cannot meet an order from a customer, the exclusive nature of the patents and know-how licences granted to it by the parent companies shall not prevent such companies from dealing directly with such customer or from granting non-exclusive licences to third parties to deal with that customer.
(2) The licences to be granted under clause 8 (4) of the basic agreement shall afford the parties the opportunity:

- to continue to have the benefit after the expiration of the period of three years following the dissolution of the joint venture of the patent and know-how rights licensed to the joint venture to the extent that the exercise of those rights is indispensable for the exploitation of patents and know-how jointly acquired through the joint venture,
- to export the products manufactured under these patent and know-how licences to all Common Market and non-member countries.
The royalties payable under the licences granted by the parties in accordance with this provision shall not exceed the lowest amount of royalty payable under any licence granted by the parties to third parties in respect of the same patents or know-how.
The effect of this latter condition must not be to make it impossible for the parties, on the expiration of the three-year period provided for in respect of the licences in question, to prevent the use of the designs for the purpose of reproducing the form and presentation of the relevant products. They must remain free to use the know-how embodied in these designs, although they may be prohibited after that three-year period from making exact copies of the form and presentation of the designs such that each other's products are not recognizably differentiated.
16. Article 8 (2) of Regulation No 17 requires the Commission to ensure that the requirements of Article 85 (3) continue to be satisfied. To this end the undertakings to which this decision is addressed must be required to inform the Commission of any change or addition to the agreements and to make a report to the Commission every two years on the activities of the joint venture so that the actual effects of their agreement can be determined.
The Commission must also be in a position to verify whether competition within the Common Market is restricted by any other practices of the companies concerned. Such restrictions might arise as the result of financial holdings or new links in these sectors, whether direct or indirect, between any company in one group and any company in the other group (the parties themselves included) or between any such company and another company where any of these companies is directly or indirectly engaged in either the turbine or the compressor industry within the Common Market. Such might be the case if one of the parties or any company belonging to its group develops new business in these industries independently. In such a situation the Commission must be enabled to verify whether the competitive capacity of the parties has been altered.
A company belonging to a party's group is, for these purposes, a company in which such party or any other company in either the De Laval Turbine Incorporated Group or the Verenigde Machinefabrieken NV group, directly or indirectly, controls at least half the voting rights, or has the right to appoint half the members of the board of directors or in any other way is able to control the affairs of such company.
For the reasons stated above, therefore, obligations must be imposed to ensure that the parties inform the Commission without delay of such relationships or new activities.
The opportunities for the parties to compete on the dissolution of the joint venture must not be prejudiced by any agreement or practice entered into or operated by the parties in order to retain or employ those employees of the dissolved subsidiary who are required by either party in order to continue in business. If they do terminate the joint venture the parties must be required to inform the Commission of any agreements or practices in that connection so that the Commission can ensure that competition is not thereby restricted.

[.....]

CHAPTER IX

Enforcement and Procedure: Capita

General chapter cross-references:

- ▸ Regulation 1/2003, [2003] OJ L 1/1.
- ▸ Commission Notice on cooperation within the Network of Competition Authorities, [2004] OJ C 101/43.
- ▸ Commission Notice on the co-operation between the Commission and the Courts of the EU Member States in the application of Articles 81 and 82 EC, [2004] OJ C 101/54.
- ▸ Regulation 773/2004 relating to the conduct of proceedings by the Commission pursuant to Articles 81 and 82 of the EC Treaty, [2004] OJ L 123/18.
- ▸ C. Baudenbacher, 'Judicialization of European Competition Policy?', (2002) *Fordham Corp. L. Inst.* (B. Hawk, ed. 2003), 353.
- ▸ J. Bornkamm, 'Judicial Control and Review of Antitrust Administrative Authorities', (2002) *Fordham Corp. L. Inst.* (B. Hawk, ed. 2003), 369.
- ▸ J. Coyet, C. Fellenius-Omnell and C. Landström, 'Modernizing EC Competition Law: Will a system of Parallel Appplication of EC and National Competition Laws ensure Convergence?', (2002) *Fordham Corp. L. Inst.* (B. Hawk, ed. 2003), 97.
- ▸ A. Erlandsson, 'The Defendant's Right of Access to the Commission's File in Competition Cases', (1998) 25 *LIEI*, 139.
- ▸ E. Paulis, 'Checks and Balances in the EU Antitrust Enforcement System', (2002) *Fordham Corp. L. Inst.* (B. Hawk, ed. 2003), 381.
- ▸ P.J. Slot, 'A view from the mountain: 40 years of developments in EC competition law', (2004) 41 *CMLRev*, 443.
- ▸ J. Venit, 'Brave new world: The modernization and decentralization of enforcement under Articles 81 and 82 of the EC treaty', (2003) 40 *CMLRev*, 537.
- ▸ R. Wesseling. 'The Modernization of EC Anti-Trust Law', Hart Publishing (2000).
- ▸ W.P.J. Wils, 'The Modernisation of the Enforcement of Articles 81 and 82: A legal and Economic Analysis of the Commission's Proposal for a New Council Regulation Replacing Regulation No. 17', (2000) *Fordham Corp. L. Inst.* (B. Hawk, ed. 2001), 313.
- ▸ W.P.J. Wils, *Optimal enforcement of EC competition laws: a study in law and economics*, Kluwer Law International (2003).
- ▸ E. Paulis, E. De Smijter, 'Enhanced enforcement of the EC Competition rules since 1 May 2004 by the Commission and the NCA's', in *Antitrust reform in Europe: a year in practice*, (2005) 1.
- ▸ Notice on the rules for access to the Commission file in cases pursuant to Articles 81 and 82 of the EC Treaty, Articles 53, 54 and 57 of the EEA Agreement and Council Regulation (EC) No 139/2004, [2005] OJ C 325/7.
- ▸ Commission Notice on the conduct of settlement procedures in view of the adoption of Decisions pursuant to Article 7 and Article 23 of Council Regulation (EC) No 1/2003 in cartel cases, [2008] OJ C 167/1
- ▸ W. Wils, 'The Use of Settlements in Public Antitrust Enforcement: Objectives and Principles', *World Competition* 31 no. 3 (2008): 335-352.
- ▸ Katalin J. Cseres, Maarten Pieter Schinkel, Floris O.W. Vogelaar (eds.), *Criminalization of Competition Law Enforcement: economic and legal implications for the EU Member States*, Edward Elgar Publishing Limited, 2006.
- ▸ P. Whelan, A Principled Argument for Personal Criminal Sanctions as Punishment under EC Cartel Law, *The Competition Law Review*, Volume 4 Issue 1, 2007, pp. 7-40.

A. Legal privilege

1) Case 155/79 *AM & S* [1982] ECR 1575

AM & S, producer and distributor of zinc metals, had been under scrutiny by the Commission for participating in a cartel. Commission officials had, when exercising their investigatory powers, visited the undertaking's premises and requested copies of several documents, but AM & S had refused to produce those documents that it considered to be covered by 'legal privilege'.

Relevance: notion of 'legal privilege'. Role of outside counsel in competition matters.

[.....]

(B) Applicability of the protection of confidentiality in Community law

18 However, the above rules do not exclude the possibility of recognizing, subject to certain conditions, that certain business records are of a confidential nature. Community law, which derives from not only the economic but also the legal interpenetration of the Member States, must take into account the principles and concepts common to the laws of those states concerning the observance of confidentiality, in particular, as regards certain communications between lawyer and client. That confidentiality serves the requirements, the importance of which is recognized in all of the Member States, that any person must be able, without constraint, to consult a lawyer whose profession entails the giving of independent legal advice to all those in need of it.
19 As far as the protection of written communications between lawyer and client is concerned, it is apparent from the legal systems of the Member States that, although the principle of such protection is generally recognized, its scope and the criteria for applying it vary, as has, indeed, been conceded both by the applicant and by the parties who have intervened in support of its conclusions.
20 Whilst in some of the Member States the protection against disclosure afforded to written communications between lawyer and client is based principally on a recognition of the very nature of the legal profession, inasmuch as it contributes towards the maintenance of the rule of law, in other Member States the same protection is justified by the more specific requirement (which, moreover, is also recognized in the first-mentioned states) that the rights of the defence must be respected.
21 Apart from these differences, however, there are to be found in the national laws of the Member States common criteria inasmuch as those laws protect, in similar circumstances, the confidentiality of written communications between lawyer and client provided that, on the one hand, such communications are made for the purposes and in the interests of the client's rights of defence and, on the other hand, they emanate from independent lawyers, that is to say, lawyers who are not bound to the client by a relationship of employment.
22 Viewed in that context Regulation No 17 must be interpreted as protecting, in its turn, the confidentiality of written communications between lawyer and client subject to those two conditions, and thus incorporat-

ing such elements of that protection as are common to the laws of the Member States.
23 As far as the first of those two conditions is concerned, in Regulation No 17 itself, in particular in the eleventh recital in its preamble and in the provisions contained in Article 19, care is taken to ensure that the rights of the defence may be exercised to the full, and the protection of the confidentiality of written communications between lawyer and client is an essential corollary to those rights. In those circumstances, such protection must, if it is to be effective, be recognized as covering all written communications exchanged after the initiation of the administrative procedure under Regulation No 17 which may lead to a decision on the application of Articles 85 and 86 of the Treaty or to a decision imposing a pecuniary sanction on the undertaking. It must also be possible to extend it to earlier written communications which have a relationship to the subject-matter of that procedure.
24 As regards the second condition, it should be stated that the requirement as to the position and status as an independent lawyer, which must be fulfilled by the legal adviser from whom the written communications which may be protected emanate, is based on a conception of the lawyer's role as collaborating in the administration of justice by the courts and as being required to provide, in full independence, and in the overriding interests of that cause, such legal assistance as the client needs. The counterpart of that protection lies in the rules of professional ethics and discipline which are laid down and enforced in the general interest by institutions endowed with the requisite powers for that purpose. Such a conception reflects the legal traditions common to the Member States and is also to be found in legal order of the Community, as is demonstrated by Article 17 of the Protocols on the Statutes of the Court of Justice of the EEC and the EAEC, and also by Article 20 of the Protocol on the Statute of the Court of Justice of the ECSC.
25 Having regard to the principles of the Treaty concerning freedom of establishment and the freedom to provide services the protection thus afforded by Community law, in particular in the context of Regulation No 17, to written communications between lawyer and client must apply without distinction to any lawyer entitled to practice his profession in one of the Member States, regardless of the Member State in which the client lives.
26 Such protection may not be extended beyond those limits, which are determined by the scope of the common rules on the exercise of the legal profession as laid down in Council Directive 77/249/EEC of 22 March 1977 (OJ l 78, p. 17), which is based in its turn on the mutual recognition by all the Member States of the national legal concepts of each of them on this subject.
27 In view of all these factors it must therefore be concluded that although Regulation No 17, and in particular Article 14 thereof, interpreted in the light of its wording, structure and aims, and having regard to the laws of the Member States, empowers the Commission to require, in the course of an investigation within the meaning of that Article, production of the business documents the disclosure of which it considers necessary, including written communications between lawyer and client, for proceedings in respect of any infringements of Articles 85 and 86 of the Treaty, that power is, however, subject to a restriction imposed by the need to protect confidentiality, on the conditions defined above, and provided that the communications in question are exchanged between an independent lawyer, that is to say one who is not bound to his client by a relationship of employment, and his client.
28 Finally, it should be remarked that the principle of confidentiality does not prevent

a lawyer's client from disclosing the written communications between them if he considers that it is in his interests to do so.

(C) the procedures relating to the application of the principle of confidentiality

29 If an undertaking which is the subject of an investigation under Article 14 of Regulation No 17 refuses, on the ground that it is entitled to protection of the confidentiality of information, to produce, among the business records demanded by the Commission, written communications between itself and its lawyer, it must nevertheless provide the Commission's authorized agents with relevant material of such a nature as to demonstrate that the communications fulfil the conditions for being granted legal protection as defined above, although it is not bound to reveal the contents of the communications in question.

30 Where the Commission is not satisfied that such evidence has been supplied, the appraisal of those conditions is not a matter which may be left to an arbitrator or to a national authority. Since this is a matter involving an appraisal and a decision which affect the conditions under which the Commission may act in a field as vital to the functioning of the Common Market as that of compliance with the rules on competition, the solution of disputes as to the application of the protection of the confidentiality of written communications between lawyer and client may be sought only at Community level.

31 In that case it is for the Commission to order, pursuant to Article 14 (3) of Regulation No 17, production of the communications in question and, if necessary, to impose on the undertaking fines or periodic penalty payments under that regulation as a penalty for the undertaking's refusal either to supply such additional evidence as the Commission considers necessary or to produce the communications in question whose confidentiality, in the Commission's view, is not protected in law.

32 The fact that by virtue of Article 185 of the EEC Treaty any action brought by the undertaking concerned against such decisions does not have suspensory effect provides an answer to the Commission's concern as to the effect of the time taken by the procedure before the Court on the efficacy of the supervision which the Commission is called upon to exercise in regard to compliance with the Treaty rules on competition, whilst on the other hand the interests of the undertaking concerned are safeguarded by the possibility which exists under Articles 185 and 186 of the Treaty, as well as under Article 83 of the rules of procedure of the Court, of obtaining an order suspending the application of the decision which has been taken, or any other interim measure.

[.....]

2) Case T-30/89 *Hilti v. Commission (Hilti II)* [1990] ECR I-163, order

In this dispute, Hilti claimed confidential treatment for certain documents that were prepared by its in-house counsel so as to prevent their disclosure to the interveners in the main proceedings before the ECJ.

Relevance: legal privilege also available to in-house counsel, though limited only to cases of internal documents reporting the content of 'privileged' advice obtained in a meeting with independent outside counsel.

[.....]

Order

[.....]

13 The Court of Justice has held (judgment of 18 May 1982 in Case 155/79 AM & S v Commission ((1982)) ECR 1575) that Regulation No 17 of the Council of 6 February 1962, the first regulation implementing Articles 85 and 86 of the Treaty (Official Journal, English Special Edition 1959-62, p. 87) must be interpreted as protecting the confidentiality of written communications between lawyer and client provided that, on the one hand, such communications are made for the purposes and in the interests of the client's right of defence and, on the other hand, they emanate from independent lawyers, that is to say, lawyers who are not bound to the client by a relationship of employment. In the same judgment the Court of Justice held that that protection must, in the administrative procedure before the Commission, be recognized as covering all written communications exchanged after the initiation of the administrative procedure which may lead to a decision on the application of Articles 85 and 86 of the Treaty or to a decision imposing a pecuniary sanction on the undertaking. The Court of Justice further held that that protection must be extended to earlier written communications which have a relationship to the subject-matter of that procedure.
14 In this case the letter in point is one sent to the applicant by an independent lawyer, after the initiation of the administrative procedure before the Commission, for the purposes and in the interests of the applicant's right of defence. Since it thus falls within the criteria laid down by the Court of Justice in the judgment cited above, that letter must accordingly be regarded as confidential within the meaning of Article 93(4) of the Rules of Procedure. It follows that the applicant's request must be allowed.
15 The second category of documents for which confidential treatment is requested is composed of two documents, excerpts from which have been incorporated in the defence. According to the applicant, those documents report on legal advice which was received by it and which itself was covered by legal professional privilege. The applicant submits that a report of such advice is by its very nature confidential and should not be disclosed to the interveners.
16 An examination of the aforesaid documents shows that they are, essentially, notes internal to the undertaking reporting the content of advice received from independent, and thus external, legal advisers.
17 Such legal advice would be covered by the principle of the protection of confidentiality laid down by the Court of Justice if it had been received from independent legal advisers by way of written communication.
18 In this case it appears that that legal advice was reported on in internal notes distributed within the undertaking so that it might be the subject of consideration by managerial staff. In such a case, and although the aforesaid legal advice was not received by way of correspondence, it must be held that the principle of the protection of written communications between lawyer and client may not be frustrated on the sole ground that the content of those communications and of that legal advice was reported in documents internal to the undertaking. Thus the principle of the protection of written communications between lawyer and client must, in view of its purpose, be regarded as extending also to the internal notes which are confined to reporting the text or the content of those communications. It follows that the request for confidential treatment made by the applicant must be allowed in so far as it refers to those documents.

Case cross-reference:
▸ C-53/92 *Hilti AG v. Commission* [1994] ECR I-667, appeal dismissed.

3) Joined Cases T-125/03 and T-253/03 *AKZO Nobel Chemicals and Akcros Chemicals v. Commission* [2007] ECR II-3523

The Commission adopted a decision ordering an investigation aimed at seeking evidence of possible anti-competitive practices. In the course of the operations, the Commission officials took copies of a considerable number of documents. The applicants, AKZO and Akcros informed the Commission that five documents were covered by 'legal professional privilege'.
Originally, the President of the GC, in his 'order' [2003] ECR II-4771, seemed willing to extend the category of lawyers relying on the 'legal privilege' to in-house counsel (provided they are members of their national Bar). However, in the case on the merits, the full Chamber of the GC did not uphold the President's order and reverted to the traditional AM&S-doctrine (see IX-A-1)

Relevance: Should in-house lawyers who are members of their national Bar Associations benefit from the rules on protection of *'Legal Privilege'* in the same manner as outside counsel?

[...]

166 As regards, first of all, the applicants' principal argument, it must be pointed out that in its judgment in *AM & S*, the Court of Justice expressly held that the protection accorded to LPP under Community law, in the application of Regulation No 17, only applies to the extent that the lawyer is independent, that is to say, not bound to his client by a relationship of employment (paragraphs 21, 22 and 27 of the judgment). The requirement as to the position and status as an independent lawyer, which must be met by the legal adviser from whom the written communications which may be protected emanate, is based on a concept of the lawyer's role as collaborating in the administration of justice by the courts and as being required to provide, in full independence, and in the overriding interests of the administration of justice, such legal assistance as the client needs (*AM & S*, paragraph 24).

167 It follows that the Court expressly excluded communications with in-house lawyers, that is, legal advisers bound to their clients by a relationship of employment, from protection under LPP. [...]

168 The Court therefore concludes that, contrary to what the applicants and certain interveners submit, the Court in its judgment in *AM & S* defined the concept of independent lawyer in negative terms in that it stipulated that such a lawyer should not be bound to his client by a relationship of employment (see paragraph 166 above), rather than positively, on the basis of membership of a Bar or Law Society or being subject to professional discipline and ethics. The Court thus laid down the test of legal advice provided 'in full independence' (*AM & S*, paragraph 24), which it identifies as that provided by a lawyer who, structurally, hierarchically and functionally, is a third party in relation to the undertaking receiving that advice.

[...]

170 [...] the Court would point out, first, that an examination of the laws of the Member States shows that, even though it is the case, as the applicants and certain interveners submit, that specific recognition of the role of in-house lawyers and the protection of communications with such lawyers under LPP is relatively more common today than when the judgment in *AM & S* was handed down, it is not possible, nevertheless, to identify tendencies which are uniform or have clear majority support in that regard in the laws of the Member States.

[...]

173 [...] , communications between in-house lawyers and outside lawyers are in principle protected under LPP, provided that they are made for the purpose of the undertaking's exercise of the rights of defence. It is therefore clear that the personal scope of that protection, as laid down in *AM & S*, is not a real obstacle preventing undertakings from seeking the legal advice they need and does not prevent their in-house lawyers from taking part in self-assessment exercises or strategy definition. Finally, it must be pointed out that the modernisation of competition law does not necessarily mean that the respective roles of outside lawyers and in-house lawyers have changed substantially in this respect since the judgment in *AM & S*. In any event, since Community competition law is aimed at undertakings, it would not be permissible, in principle, for purely internal communications within a particular undertaking to fall outside the Commission's investigatory powers, with the exception, as has been stated above, of notes which do no more than report the text or the content of communications with outside lawyers containing legal advice, and of preparatory documents drawn up exclusively in order to seek legal advice from an outside lawyer in exercise of the rights of defence.

174 [...] , it is settled case-law that the principle of equal treatment is infringed only where comparable situations are treated differently or different situations are treated in the same way, unless such difference in treatment is objectively justified (Case C-174/89 *Hoche* [1990] ECR I-2681, paragraph 25; Case T-311/94 *BPB de Eendracht* v *Commission* [1998] ECR II-1129, paragraph 309, and Case T-304/02 *Hoek Loos* v *Commission* [2006] ECR II-1887, paragraph 96). It must be pointed out, however, that in-house lawyers and outside lawyers are clearly in very different situations, owing, in particular, to the functional, structural and hierarchical integration of in-house lawyers within the companies that employ them. Accordingly, no infringement of the principle of equal treatment arises from the fact of treating such professionals differently in respect of protection under LPP.

[...]

Case cross-reference:

▸ AKZO appealed the judgment of the GC, Case C-550/07. In her opinion of 29 April 2010, Advocate General Kokott advises that the appeal should be dismissed. She takes the view that in-house counsel inherently lack sufficient independence from their employers. Judgment of the ECJ in this case is to be expected in the autumn of 2010.

B. Fact-finding

Cross-reference for this part:

- K.P.E. Lasok, 'The Privilege against Self-incrimination in Competition cases', (1990) 11 *ECLR*, 90.
- W.P.J. Wils, 'Self-incrimination in EC Antitrust Enforcement: A Legal and Economic Analysis', (2003) 26 *World Competition*, 567.

1) Joined Cases 97-99/87 *DOW* [1989] ECR 3165 (summary of judgment)

This dispute concerned the scope of Article 14 of Regulation No 17/62. Dow Ibérica claimed that the Commission had infringed several rights, among others the fundamental right to the inviolability of the home and respect for private life, when it conducted an investigation at its premises.

Relevance: due fairness to be observed during investigations.

Summary

1. Respect for the rights of the defence constitutes a fundamental principle and must therefore be ensured not only in administrative procedures which may lead to the imposition of penalties but also during preliminary inquiry procedures such as investigations under Article 14 of Regulation No 17, which may be decisive in providing evidence of the unlawful nature of conduct engaged in by undertakings for which they may be liable.
2. Although the existence of a fundamental right to the inviolability of the home must be recognized in the Community legal order as a principle common to the laws of the Member States in regard to the private dwellings of natural persons, the same is not true in regard to undertakings, because there are not inconsiderable divergences between the legal systems of the Member States in regard to the nature and degree of protection afforded to business premises against intervention by the public authorities. No other inference is to be drawn from Article 8 of the European Convention on Human Rights.
None the less, in all the legal systems of the Member States, any intervention by the public authorities in the sphere of private activities of any person, whether natural or legal, must have a legal basis and be justified on the grounds laid down by law, and, consequently, those systems provide, albeit in different forms, protection against arbitrary or disproportionate intervention. The need for such protection must be recognized as a general principle of Community law.
3. Both the purpose of Regulation No 17 and the list of powers conferred on the Commission's officials by Article 14 thereof show that the scope of investigations may be very wide. In that regard, the right to enter any premises, land and means of transport of undertakings is of particular importance inasmuch as it is intended to permit the Commission to obtain evidence of infringements of the competition rules in the places in which such evidence is normally to be found, that is to say, on the business premises of undertakings.
That right of access would serve no useful purpose if the Commission's officials could do no more than ask for documents or files which they could identify precisely in advance. On the contrary, such a right implies the power to search for various items

of information which are not already known or fully identified. Without such a power, it would be impossible for the Commission to obtain the information necessary to carry out the investigation if the undertakings concerned refused to cooperate or adopted an obstructive attitude.
However, the exercise of the wide powers of investigation conferred on the Commission is subject to conditions serving to ensure respect for the rights of undertakings. In that regard, the Commission's obligation to specify the subject-matter and purpose of the investigation is a fundamental requirement not merely in order to show that the investigation to be carried out on the premises of the undertakings concerned is justified but also to enable those undertakings to assess the scope of their duty to cooperate while at the same time safeguarding the rights of the defence.
4. Where investigations are carried out with the cooperation of the undertakings concerned by virtue of an obligation arising under a decision ordering an investigation, the Commission's officials have, inter alia, the power to have shown to them the documents they request, to enter such premises as they choose, and to have shown to them the contents of any piece of furniture which they indicate. On the other hand, they may not obtain access to premises or furniture by force or oblige the staff of the undertaking to give them such access, or carry out searches without the permission of the management of the undertaking, which may, however, be implied, in particular by the provision of assistance to the Commission's officials.
On the other hand, if the undertakings concerned oppose the Commission's investigation, its officials may, on the basis of Article 14 (6) of Regulation No 17 and without the cooperation of the undertakings, search for any information necessary for the investigation with the assistance of the national authorities, which are required to afford them the assistance necessary for the performance of their duties. Although such assistance is required only if the undertaking expresses its opposition, it may also be requested as a precautionary measure, in order to overcome any opposition on the part of the undertaking.
5. It follows from Article 14 (6) of Regulation No 17 that it is for each Member State to determine the conditions under which the national authorities will afford assistance to the Commission's officials. In that regard, the Member States are required to ensure that the Commission's action is effective, while respecting the general principles of Community law. Within those limits, the appropriate procedural rules designed to ensure respect for undertakings' rights are those laid down by national law.
The Commission is required to respect the relevant procedural rules laid down by national law and must make sure that the competent body under national law has all that it needs to exercise its own supervisory powers.
That body, whether judicial or otherwise, cannot in this respect substitute its own assessment of the need for the investigations ordered for that of the Commission, the lawfulness of whose assessments of fact and law is subject only to review by the Court of Justice. On the other hand, it is within the powers of the national body, after satisfying itself that the decision ordering the investigation is authentic, to consider whether the measures of constraint envisaged are arbitrary or excessive having regard to the subject-matter of the investigation and to ensure that the rules of national law are complied with in the application of those measures.
6. The validity of a decision cannot be affected by acts subsequent to its adoption, with the result that any irregularities

committed in the implementation of the decision are irrelevant in assessing the validity thereof.
7. The validity of measures adopted by the institutions can only be judged in the light of Community law and, therefore, reference either to infringements of fundamental rights as formulated in the Constitution of a Member State or to the principles of a national constitutional structure cannot affect the validity of a Community measure or its effect in the territory of that State.
8. Article 14(3) of Regulation No 17 lays down the essential constituents of the statement of the reasons upon which a decision is based. The Commission's obligation to specify the subject-matter and purpose of the investigation constitutes a fundamental guarantee of the rights of the defence of the undertakings concerned. It follows that the scope of the obligation to state the reasons on which decisions ordering investigations are based cannot be restricted on the basis of considerations concerning the effectiveness of the investigation. Although the Commission is not required to communicate to the addressee of a decision ordering an investigation all the information at its disposal concerning the presumed infringements, such as the precise definition of the relevant market or the period when the infringements were supposedly committed, or to make a precise legal analysis of those infringements, it must none the less clearly indicate the presumed facts which it intends to investigate.
9. The decision empowering the Member of the Commission with responsibility for competition to adopt a decision under Article 14 (3) of Regulation No 17 on behalf of and under the responsibility of the Commission does not infringe the principle of collegiate responsibility enshrined in Article 17 of the Merger Treaty.
10. Since no derogation from Regulation No 17 is provided for in the Act concerning the conditions of accession of the Kingdom of Spain, that regulation is applicable in the new Member States as from the time of accession by virtue of the general rule laid down in Article 2 (2) of the said Act. Consequently, undertakings established in Spain could be the subject of investigations with effect from 1 January 1986.
The subject-matter of investigations carried out by the Commission after that date into undertakings established in Spain may be limited only by the scope of the Community competition rules. No such rule limits the Commission' s powers of investigation merely to conduct after accession.

2) Case T-112/98 *Mannesmannröhren-Werke* [2001] ECR II-729

The Commission had requested information from Mannesmannröhren, a producer of pipes that was under investigation for alleged anti-competitive behaviour. Mannesmannröhren refused to answer questions which concerned the so-called 1962 agreement and several meetings with other pipe producers (Special Circle and Europe-Japan Club meetings). Following this refusal, the Commission adopted a decision in which Mannesmannröhren was ordered to reply within 30 days. Mannesmannröhren tried to have this decision annulled.

Relevance: right to remain silent during investigations. Issue of self-incrimination. Relevance of European Convention on Human Rights (ECHR) in investigatory operations.

[.....]

Findings of the Court

59 It must be emphasised at the outset that the Court of First Instance has no jurisdiction to apply the Convention when reviewing an investigation under competition law, inasmuch as the Convention as such is not part of Community law (Case T-374/94 Mayr-Melnhof v Commission [1998] ECR II-1751, paragraph 311).
60 However, it is settled case-law that fundamental rights form an integral part of the general principles of Community law whose observance is ensured by the Community judicature (see, in particular, Opinion 2/94 the Court of Justice of 28 March 1996 [1996] ECR I-1759, paragraph 33, and the judgment in Kremzow, cited above, paragraph 14). For that purpose, the Court of Justice and the Court of First Instance draw inspiration from the constitutional traditions common to the Member States and from the guidelines supplied by international treaties for the protection of human rights on which the Member States have collaborated and to which they are signatories. The Convention has special significance in that respect (Case 222/84 Johnston [1986] ECR 1651, paragraph 18, and Kremzow, cited above, paragraph 14). Furthermore, paragraph 2 of Article F of the Treaty on European Union (now Article 6(2) EU) provides that the Union shall respect fundamental rights, as guaranteed by the [Convention] and as they result from the constitutional traditions common to the Member States, as general principles of Community law.
61 Next, it must be borne in mind that the purpose of the powers conferred on the Commission by Regulation No 17 is to enable that institution to fulfil its duty under the Treaty to ensure that the rules on competition within the common market are observed.
62 During the preliminary-investigation procedure, Regulation No 17 does not give an undertaking that is subjected to an investigative measure any right to avoid the application of that measure on the ground that the results thereof might provide evidence of an infringement by it of the competition rules. On the contrary, it places the undertaking under a duty of active cooperation, which means that it must be prepared to make available to the Commission any information relating to the subject-matter of the investigation (Orkem, paragraph 27, and Société Générale, paragraph 72).
63 In the absence of any right to silence expressly provided for in Regulation No 17, it is necessary to consider whether certain limitations on the Commission's powers of investigation during a preliminary investigation are, however, implied by the need to safeguard the rights of defence (Orkem, paragraph 32).
64 In this respect, it is necessary to prevent the rights of defence from being irremediably impaired during preliminary-investigation procedures which may be decisive in providing evidence of the unlawful nature of conduct engaged in by undertakings (Orkem, paragraph 33, and Société Générale, paragraph 73).
65 However, it is settled case-law that, in order to ensure the effectiveness of Article 11(2) and (5) of Regulation No 17, the Commission is entitled to compel an undertaking to provide all necessary information concerning such facts as may be known to it and to disclose to the Commission, if necessary, such documents relating thereto as are in its possession, even if the latter may be used to establish, against it or another undertaking, the existence of anti-competitive conduct (Orkem, paragraph 34, and Case 27/88 Solvay v Commission [1989]

ECR 3355, summary publication, and Société Générale, paragraph 74).
66 To acknowledge the existence of an absolute right to silence, as claimed by the applicant, would go beyond what is necessary in order to preserve the rights of defence of undertakings, and would constitute an unjustified hindrance to the Commission's performance of its duty under Article 89 of the EC Treaty (now, after amendment, Article 85 EC) to ensure that the rules on competition within the common market are observed.
67 It follows that an undertaking in receipt of a request for information pursuant to Article 11(5) of Regulation No 17 can be recognised as having a right to silence only to the extent that it would be compelled to provide answers which might involve an admission on its part of the existence of an infringement which it is incumbent upon the Commission to prove (Orkem, paragraph 35).
68 Those are the limits within which the arguments raised by the applicant must be assessed.
69 It is appropriate in this case to review first of all the legality of questions 1.6, 1.7 and 2.3, which are almost identical, and then that of question 1.8.
70 In their first three indents, questions 1.6, 1.7 and 2.3 contain requests for purely factual information and the production of documents already in existence. Comparable questions were not held to be unlawful by the Court of Justice in its judgment in Orkem. The applicant was therefore under an obligation to provide answers in response to those requests.
71 By contrast, the last indent of each of those three questions does not concern exclusively factual information. In the last indent, the Commission calls upon the applicant, in identical terms, to describe in particular the purpose of the meetings it attended and the decisions adopted during them, even though it is clear that the Commission suspected that their purpose was to arrive at agreements, in respect of selling prices, of a nature such as to prevent or restrict competition. It follows that requests of this kind are such that they may compel the applicant to admit its participation in an unlawful agreement contrary to the Community rules on competition.
72 On this point, it must be observed that the Commission expressly indicated in the last indent of the three questions at issue that the applicant was to provide it with the information in question only in the event that it was unable to find the relevant documents requested in the preceding indent. The applicant was therefore required to reply to the last indent of the questions only in so far as it was unable to produce the documents requested. Nevertheless, because of the order and content of the first three indents of the questions, it cannot be excluded that the applicant would have been obliged to reply to the last indent.
73 Consequently, it must be held that the last indent of each of questions 1.6, 1.7 and 2.3 infringes the applicant's rights of defence.
74 As far as question 1.8 is concerned, it should be observed that the Commission is requiring the applicant to comment, first, on the relationship between, on the one hand, the four OCTG and linepipe agreements concluded in 1962 and notified to the Bundeskartellamt and, on the other hand, the Europe-Japan Club and Special Circle, and, second, on the decisions adopted within the Europe-Japan Club and the Special Circle, that is to say, decisions which the Commission regards as possibly constituting infringements of the rules laid down by the Treaty. Answering this question would require the applicant to give its assessment of the nature of those decisions. It must be held that, in accordance with the judgment in Orkem, question 1.8 also constitutes an

infringement of the applicant's rights of defence.

75 As regards the arguments to the effect that Article 6(1) and (2) of the Convention enables a person in receipt of a request for information to refrain from answering the questions asked, even if they are purely factual in nature, and to refuse to produce documents to the Commission, suffice it to repeat that the applicant cannot directly invoke the Convention before the Community courts.

76 As regards the potential impact of the Charter, to which the applicant refers (see paragraph 15 above), upon the assessment of this case, it must be borne in mind that that Charter was proclaimed by the European Parliament, the Council and the Commission on 7 December 2000. It can therefore be of no consequence for the purposes of review of the contested measure, which was adopted prior to that date. That being so, there is no reason to accede to the applicant's request for the oral procedure to be re-opened.

77 However, it must be emphasised that Community law does recognise as fundamental principles both the rights of defence and the right to fair legal process (see Baustahlgewebe v Commission, cited above, paragraph 21, and Case C-7/98 Krombach [2000] ECR I-1935, paragraph 26). It is in application of those principles, which offer, in the specific field of competition law, at issue in the present case, protection equivalent to that guaranteed by Article 6 of the Convention, that the Court of Justice and the Court of First Instance have consistently held that the recipient of requests sent by the Commission pursuant to Article 11(5) of Regulation No 17 is entitled to confine himself to answering questions of a purely factual nature and to producing only the pre-existing documents and materials sought and, moreover, is so entitled as from the very first stage of an investigation initiated by the Commission.

78 The mere fact of being obliged to answer purely factual questions put by the Commission and to comply with its requests for the production of documents already in existence cannot constitute a breach of the principle of respect for the rights of defence or impair the right to fair legal process. There is nothing to prevent the addressee of such questions or requests from showing, whether later during the administrative procedure or in proceedings before the Community courts, when exercising his rights of defence, that the facts set out in his replies or the documents produced by him have a different meaning from that ascribed to them by the Commission.

[.....]

Case cross-references:

- ▸ Case 374/87 *Orkem* [1989] ECR 3283.
- ▸ P.R. Willis, 'You have the right to remain silent..., or do you? The privilege against self-incrimination following Mannesmannröhren-Werke and other recent decisions', (2001) 22 *ECLR*, 313.

C. Complaints

Cross-reference for this part:
▸ Notice on the handling of complaints by the Commission under Articles 101 and 102 of the EC Treaty, [2004] OJ C 101/65.

1) Case C-234/89 *Delimitis* [1991] ECR I-935

See above for facts of the case (I-H-2, p. 44).

Relevance: Commission's responsibility for the general orientation of competition law.

[.....]

44 [...] it should be stressed, first of all, that the Commission is responsible for the implementation and orientation of Community competition policy.

[.....]

2) Case 210/81 *Demo-Studio Schmidt v. Commission* [1983] ECR 3045

Revox, distributor of audiovisual products, had operated a selective distribution system for so-called "B Series" Revox products. The German Oswald Schmidt, owner of Demo-Studio Schmidt, had not been appointed as a reseller because, according to Revox, he did not satisfy the qualitative criteria of the said distribution system. Foremost, his opening hours did not reflect normal business hours since his shop was only open in the afternoon and on Saturday morning. Schmidt filed a complaint with the Commission, claiming that Revox's refusal to appoint him infringed Community Law. The Commission, however, decided that Revox did not infringe either Article 101 or Article 102. Schmidt turned to the ECJ for a declaration of nullity of the said decision.

Relevance: complainant cannot force the Commission to take a decision against the parties complained at.

[.....]

Admissibility

10 According to the wording of Article 3 of Regulation No. 17, which concerns the termination of infringements:
" (1) Where the Commission, upon application or upon its own initiative, finds that there is infringement of Article 85 or 86 of the Treaty, it may by decision require the undertakings or associations of undertakings concerned to bring such infringement to an end.
(2) Those entitled to make application are:
... (b) natural or legal persons who claim a legitimate interest".

11 Although the formal complaint lodged by the applicant on 7 June 1980 sought an order that Revox should supply him immediately, it must be interpreted - as indeed it was interpreted by the Commission during the phase prior to these proceedings and as is apparent

from an analysis of the pleadings submitted to the court - as a request for the Commission to establish an infringement of the provisions of Articles 85 and 86 of the Treaty, in accordance with article 3 (1) and (2) (b) of Regulation No. 17 and, by decision, to require Revox to bring the infringement to an end.

12 The Commission does not dispute the fact that its decision on the applicant's complaint does constitute a measure which the Court may be called upon to declare void, since a "notice" or "communication" of that kind is definitive.

13 However, the Commission states that it leaves it to the Court to assess to what extent the applicant really has an interest in taking legal proceedings, regard being had in particular to the fact that, in the commission's opinion, the powers vested in it by Article 85 do not include the power to compel a company to approve a dealer as a specialized distributor or to supply him with products.

14 As the Court held in its judgment of 25 October 1977 in Case 26/76 (Metro v Commission (1977) ECR 1875) "it is in the interests of the satisfactory administration of justice and of the proper application of Articles 85 and 86 that natural or legal persons who are entitled, pursuant to Article 3 (2) (b) of Regulation No. 17, to request the Commission to find an infringement of Articles 85 and 86 should be able, if their request is not complied with either wholly or in part, to institute proceedings in order to protect their legitimate interests".

15 The Court considers that the refusal to grant Mr Schmidt a dealership for Revox products, which was regarded by him as constituting an infringement of Articles 85 and 86 of the Treaty, was capable of affecting his legitimate interests. Moreover, as the Court held in its judgment of 6 March 1974 (Joined Cases 6 and 7/73 Istituto Chemioterapico Italiano SpA (1974) ECR 223) and in its order of 17 January 1980 (Case 792/79 R Camera Care Limited v Commission (1980) ECR 119), where the Commission has found an attitude on the part of a producer which constitutes an infringement of Articles 85 and 86, it has the power to order the undertaking in question to take any measures necessary to bring the infringement to an end.

16 The application must therefore be regarded as admissible.

[.....]

Case cross-reference:

▸ Joined Cases 142 & 156/84 *BAT & Reynolds v. Commission* [1987] ECR 4487 (see VII-D-1).

3) Case T-24/90 *Automec II* [1992] ECR II-2223 (summary of judgment)

Automec had complained to the Commission about the behaviour of certain undertakings. The Commission, however, made clear that it did not envisage taking any action on the basis of Automec's complaints.

Relevance: does the Commission have to deal with all complaints that it receives? Notion of 'Union interest'. Wide discretionary powers for the Commission. Application of the administrative law 'principle of opportunity'.

Summary

1. Among the civil-law consequences which an infringement of the prohibition laid down in Article 85(1) of the Treaty may have, only one is expressly provided for in Article 85(2), namely the nullity of the agreement. The other consequences attaching to an infringement of Article 85 of the Treaty, such as the obligation to make good the damage caused to a third party or a possible obligation to enter into a contract are to be determined under national law. It is therefore the national courts which, where appropriate, may, in accordance with the rules of national law, order one trader to enter into a contract with another.

So far as the Commission is concerned, since freedom of contract must remain the rule, it cannot in principle be considered to have - among the powers to issue orders which it has for the purpose of bringing to an end infringements of Article 85(1) of the Treaty - the power to order an undertaking to enter into contractual relations, since in general it has appropriate means at its disposal for requiring an undertaking to terminate an infringement.

In particular, there cannot be held to be any justification for such a restriction on freedom of contract where there are several ways of bringing an infringement to an end. This is true of infringements of Article 85(1) of the Treaty arising from the application of a distribution system. Such infringements can also be eliminated by the abandonment or amendment of the distribution system. Consequently, the Commission undoubtedly has the power to find that an infringement exists and to order the undertakings concerned to bring it to an end, but it is not for the Commission to impose upon them its own choice from among all the various potential courses of action which are in conformity with the Treaty.

2. Where a complaint has been submitted to the Commission under Article 3 of Regulation No 17, it is not bound either to give a decision on the existence of the alleged infringement unless the subject-matter of the complaint falls within its exclusive purview, as in the case of the withdrawal of an exemption granted under Article 85(3) of the Treaty, or to conduct an investigation. Since the Commission has been entrusted with an extensive and general supervisory and regulatory task in the field of competition, it is consistent with its obligations under Community law for it to apply different degrees of priority to the cases submitted to it.

However, on the one hand, the procedural safeguards provided for in Article 3 of Regulation No 17 and Article 6 of Regulation No 99/63 oblige it to examine carefully the factual and legal particulars brought to its notice by the complainant in order to assess whether they disclose conduct of such a kind as to distort competition in the Common Market and affect trade between Member States and, on the other, every decision closing the file relating to a complaint must state reasons, so that the Community judicature is able to carry out a review of its legality.

3. The Commission is entitled to refer to the Community interest in order to determine the degree of priority to be applied to a case brought to its notice. In assessing the Community interest, it should take account of the facts of the case in question, and in particular of the legal and factual considerations which have been adduced. In particular, it should balance the significance of the alleged infringement as regards the functioning of the Common Market, the probability of establishing the existence of the infringement and the scope of the investiga-

tion required in order to fulfil, under the best possible conditions, its task of ensuring that Articles 85 and 86 of the Treaty are complied with.
4. Where the Commission gives as its reason for closing, without taking action, the file on a complaint from an undertaking alleging infringement of the Community competition rules the fact that the complainant can assert his rights before the national courts, the Community Court called on to review the legality of the decision closing the file should check whether the extent of the protection which national courts can provide in respect of the complainant' s rights under provisions of the Treaty was properly assessed by the Commission.

Case cross-references:

▸ V. Korah, 'Restrictions on Conduct and Enforceability: Automec v Commmision II, (1994) 15 *ECLR*, 175.

▸ F. Stroud, 'Automec II Revisited: BEUC v. Commission of the European Communities', (1994) 15 *ECLR*, 272.

4) Case T-7/92 *Asia Motors* [1993] ECR II-669 (summary of judgment)

Also, in this case the Commission, following a complaint, did not handle the case in a manner that fully satisfied the complainant.

Relevance: degree of diligence required when the Commission handles complaints.

Summary

1. The statement of reasons of a decision adversely affecting a person must be such as to enable the person concerned to ascertain the matters justifying the measure adopted so that he can if necessary defend his rights and verify whether or not the decision is well founded and to enable the Community judicature to exercise its power of review.
The Commission is not obliged to adopt a position, in stating the reasons for the decisions which it is required to take in order to apply the competition rules, on all the arguments relied on before it by the parties concerned. It is sufficient if it sets out the facts and legal considerations having decisive importance in the context of the decision.
2. Judicial review of Commission measures involving an appraisal of complex economic matters must be limited to verifying whether the relevant rules on procedure and on the statement of reasons have been complied with, whether the facts have been accurately stated and whether there has been any manifest error of appraisal or a misuse of powers. Where the Commission has a power of appraisal in connection with the performance of its duties, respect for the rights guaranteed by the Community legal order in administrative procedures assumes fundamental importance. Those guarantees include, in particular, the duty of the Commission to examine carefully and impartially all the relevant aspects of the individual case.
3. In the context of investigating applications submitted to the Commission pursuant to Article 3 of Regulation No 17, although the Commission cannot be compelled to conduct an investigation, the procedural safeguards provided for by Article 6 of Regulation No 99/63 oblige it nevertheless to examine carefully the factual and legal particulars brought to its notice by the complainant in order to decide whether they disclose conduct of such a kind as to distort competition in the

Common Market and affect trade between the Member States.
Likewise, once it decides to proceed with an investigation, the Commission must, in the absence of a duly substantiated statement of reasons, conduct it with the requisite care, seriousness and diligence so as to be able to assess with full knowledge of the case the factual and legal particulars submitted for its appraisal by the complainants.
4. The fact that anti-competitive conduct was fostered or encouraged by the authorities of a Member State has in itself no bearing on the applicability of Article 85 of the Treaty.

5) Case T-114/92 *Bemim* [1995] ECR II-147 (summary of judgment)

The Bureau Européen des Médias de l'Industrie Musicale (BEMIM) lodged a complaint against the Société des Auteurs, Compositeurs et Editeurs de Musique (SACEM). The former represented discothèque operators; the latter was a copyright management society. SACEM was amongst other things accused of charging excessive royalties (infringement of Article 102). The complaint was rejected because, according to the Commission, there was no Union interest involved while, at the same time, several French courts were also looking into the matter. BEMIM appealed.

Relevance: refinement of *Automec II*. Circumstances in which the Commission can reject a complaint for lack of Union interest.

Summary

1. Natural or legal persons who are entitled to submit an application under Article 3(2)(b) of Regulation No 17 calling on the Commission to ascertain an infringement of Articles 85 and 86 of the Treaty may, if their request is not complied with either wholly or in part, institute proceedings in order to protect their legitimate interests. Thus, an association of undertakings must be regarded as having a sufficient interest in bringing proceedings before the Court against the Commission decision rejecting its application, provided that it had a legitimate interest in submitting that application.
An association of undertakings has a legitimate interest in lodging a complaint even if it is not directly concerned, as an undertaking operating in the relevant market, by the conduct complained of, provided however that, first, it is entitled to represent the interests of its members and, secondly, the conduct complained of is liable adversely to affect those interests.
2. The statement of reasons on which a decision adversely affecting a person is based must, first, be such as to enable the person concerned to ascertain the matters justifying the measure adopted so that, if necessary, he can defend his rights and verify whether the decision is well founded and, secondly, enable the Community judicature to exercise its power of review. However, the Commission is not obliged, in stating the reasons for the decisions which it takes to ensure the application of the competition rules, to adopt a position on all the arguments relied on by the persons concerned in support of their application for a finding of an infringement of those rules; it need only set out the facts and legal considerations which are of decisive importance in the context of the decision.

A statement of the reasons for a Commission decision rejecting a complaint comprising three allegations, which deals with two of those allegations but does not disclose why the complaint was rejected in respect of the third allegation, does not meet the requirements of Article 190 of the Treaty.
3. Articles 85(1) and 86 of the Treaty produce direct effects in relations between individuals and create direct rights for individuals which the national courts must safeguard. In view of that division of powers between the Commission and the national courts and of the resulting protection available to individuals before the national courts, it must be concluded that Article 3 of Regulation No 17 does not confer upon a person who lodges an application under that article the right to obtain from the Commission a decision, within the meaning of Article 189 of the EC Treaty, regarding the existence or otherwise of an infringement of the abovementioned provisions of the Treaty, even if the Commission has become persuaded that such an infringement has occurred. The position would be different only if the complaint fell within the exclusive purview of the Commission, as in the case of the withdrawal of an exemption granted under Article 85(3) of the Treaty.
4. Where the Commission rejects, on the ground of lack of a Community interest, an application for a finding of an infringement under Article 3 of Regulation No 17, the review of legality which the Community judicature must undertake focuses on whether or not the contested decision is based on materially incorrect facts or is vitiated by an error of law, a manifest error of appraisal or misuse of powers
5. The Commission is entitled to reject a complaint where it finds, either before commencing an investigation or after taking investigative measures, that the case does not display sufficient Community interest to justify further investigation of it. In order to assess that interest, the Commission must take account of the circumstances of the case and in particular the matters of fact and law to which its attention is drawn. It must, in particular, balance the significance of the alleged infringement as regards the functioning of the Common Market, the probability of its being able to establish the existence of the infringement and the extent of the investigative measures required for it to perform, under the best possible conditions, its task of making sure that Articles 85 and 86 of the Treaty are complied with. The fact that a national court or national competition authority is already dealing with a case concerning the compatibility of an agreement or practice with Article 85 or 86 of the Treaty is a factor which the Commission may take into account in evaluating the extent to which a case displays a Community interest.
In particular, where the effects of the infringements alleged in a complaint are essentially confined to the territory of one Member State and where proceedings in respect of those infringements have been brought before the courts and competent administrative authorities of that Member State by the complainant, the Commission is entitled to reject the complaint through lack of a Community interest, provided however that the rights of the complainant can be adequately safeguarded by the national courts, which presupposes that the latter are in a position to gather the factual information necessary in order to determine whether the practices at issue constitute an infringement of the abovementioned provisions of the Treaty.

[.....]

D. Statute of limitation

1) Case T-213/00 *CMA CGM* [2003] ECR II-913

One of the issues raised in the following judgment concerned Regulation No 2988/74 regarding limitation periods in proceedings and the enforcement of sanctions under the rules of the EU that related to transport and competition. The Commission had fined several shipping companies for breach of Article 101, but according to these companies the Commission's powers had been time-barred under the above Regulation. They argued that some of the requests for information on turnover figures could not be seen as indispensable 'for the purpose of the preliminary investigation or proceedings in respect of an infringement' within the meaning of the Regulation. The Commission, on the other hand, maintained that the five-year limitation period had been validly interrupted.

Relevance: how to interrupt a 'statute of limitation'?

[.....]

5. The plea in law concerning the limitation period

[.....]

Findings of the Court

[.....]

487 Thus, it follows from the foregoing considerations that in order validly to interrupt the five-year limitation period laid down by Article 1(1)(b) of Regulation No 2988/74 a request for information must be necessary for the preliminary investigation or proceedings.

488 Although a request for information may interrupt the limitation period for fines where its purpose is to enable the Commission to comply with its obligations in fixing the fine, therefore, the Commission cannot, for instance, make requests for information the sole purpose of which is to prolong the limitation period artificially so as to preserve the power to impose a fine (see, to that effect, Austria v Commission, cited at paragraph 43 above, paragraphs 45 to 67). Requests for information solely for that purpose cannot be necessary for infringement proceedings. Furthermore, if the Commission were able to interrupt the limitation period by sending requests for information not necessary for the proceedings it would be able systematically to prolong the limitation period up to the 10-year maximum laid down by Article 2(3) of Regulation No 2988/74, thereby subverting the five-year limitation period laid down by Article 1(1) of that regulation and converting it into a 10-year one.

[.....]

490 It must be accepted that a request for information seeking turnover figures for undertakings which are the subject of a proceeding applying the Community competition rules is a necessary step in the infringement proceedings, since it enables the Commission to check that the fines it intends to impose on those undertakings do not exceed the maximum amount permitted by the regulations cited above for infringements of the Community competition rules.

[.....]

Case cross-references:
▸ Article 25 of Regulation 1/2003, [2003] OJ L 1/1.
▸ Case C-236/03 P *Commission v. CMA CGM & others*. Order of 28 October 2004, unpublished.

2) Case T-120/04 *Peróxidos Orgánicos SA v. Commission* [2006] ECR II-4441

Peróxidos Orgánicos is an undertaking which took part in the cartel on the market for organic peroxides. The cartel was founded in 1971, aimed at preserving the market shares of the participating companies and coordinating price increases. Peróxidos Orgánicos filed an appeal against the decision of the Commission. One of the pleas concerned the interpretation of the rules on the statute of limitation.

Relevance: The burden of proof in relation to the duration of an infringement

[.....]

– Apportionment of the burden of proof between the applicant and the Commission

50 As regards the issue of the date on which the applicant's participation in the infringement ceased, as a preliminary point it is appropriate to recall the settled case-law that it is for the party or the authority alleging an infringement of the competition rules to prove its existence by establishing, to the requisite legal standard, the facts constituting an infringement, and it is for the undertaking invoking the benefit of a defence against a finding of an infringement to demonstrate that the conditions for applying such defence are satisfied, so that the authority will then have to resort to other evidence (see, to that effect, Case C-185/95 P Baustahlgewebe v Commission [1998] ECR I-8417, paragraph 58, and Joined Cases C-204/00 P, C-205/00 P, C-211/00 P, C-213/00 P, C-217/00 P and C-219/00 P Aalborg Portland and Others v Commission [2004] ECR I-123, paragraph 78).
51 In addition, the duration of the infringement is an intrinsic element of an infringement under Article 81(1) EC, the burden of proof of which is borne principally by the Commission. In this respect, according to the case-law, if there is no evidence directly establishing the duration of an infringement, the Commission should adduce at least evidence of facts sufficiently proximate in time for it to be reasonable to accept that that infringement continued uninterruptedly between two specific dates (Case T-43/92 *Dunlop Slazenger* v *Commission* [1994] ECR II-441, paragraph 79).
52 In the present case, the general principle that the Commission is required to prove every constituent element of the infringement, including its duration, that is likely to have an effect on its definitive findings as to the gravity of that infringement, is not called into question by the fact that the applicant raised a defence of limitation, the burden of proof of which is in principle borne by the applicant. Not only does that defence not relate to the finding of an infringement, but it is clear that reliance on such a plea necessarily requires that the duration of the infringement and the date on which it came to an end be established. Those circumstances cannot alone provide justification for transferring the burden in this regard to the applicant. The duration of the infringement, which requires that the date on which it ended be known, is one of the essential elements of the infringement, which must be proved by the Commission, irrespective of the fact that the disputing of those elements also forms part of the defence of

limitation (see paragraph 21 above). That conclusion is also justified in light of the fact that the non-limitation of a Commission proceeding under the regulation on limitation is the application of an objective legal criterion, pursuant to the principle of legal certainty (see, to that effect, *Sumitomo Chemical and Sumika Fine Chemicals* v *Commission*, paragraph 15 above, paragraphs 80 to 82), confirmed by the second recital in the preamble to that regulation, and, thus, is a condition for the validity of any decision imposing a penalty. The Commission is required to comply with this condition even if the undertaking concerned has raised no defence in this regard.

53 That apportionment of the burden of proof is likely to vary, however, inasmuch as the evidence on which a party relies may be of such a kind as to require the other party to provide an explanation or justification, failing which it is permissible to conclude that the burden of proof has been discharged (see, to that effect, *Aalborg Portland and Others* v *Commission*, paragraph 50 above, paragraph 79).

54 It is in the light of these principles that it should be ascertained whether the Commission correctly established the facts on which it based its assessment that the applicant's participation in the Spanish sub-arrangement ended in 1999. More specifically, given that the limitation period was interrupted on 20 March 2002, which the applicant accepts, it suffices to establish whether the Commission proved, to the requisite legal standard, that that participation lasted at least until 20 March 1997.

[....]

E. Sanctions

Cross-references for this part:

▸ Commission Guidelines on the method of setting fines imposed pursuant to Article 23 (2)(a) of Regulation No 1/2003, [2006] OJ C 210/2.

▸ Commission Notice on immunity from fines and reduction of fines in cartel cases, [2006] OJ C 298/17.

▸ Case 48/69 *ICI v. Commission (Dyestuffs)* [1972] ECR 619.

▸ Case 176/03 *Commission and EP v. Council* [2005] ECR I-7879.

▸ P. Whelan, 'A Principled Argument for Personal Criminal Sanctions as Punishment under EC Cartel Law', *CompLRev*, 2007 Vol. 4 Issue 1, pp. 7-40.

▸ M.P. Schinkel, 'Effective Cartel Enforcement in Europe', *World Competition* 30 no. 4 (2007): 539-572

▸ I. Forrester, 'Remedies and Sanctions for Unilateral conduct in Competition Cases', Fordham Corp.L.Inst. 559-571 (B. Hawk ed. 2008).

▸ W. Wils, 'The Increased Level of EU Antitrust Fines, Judicial review and the ECHR', World Competition 33 no. 1 (2010): 5-29

1) Joined Cases T-236/01, T-239/01, T-244/01 to T-246/01, T-251/01 and T-252/01 *Graphite electrodes cartel* [2004] ECR II-1181

See above for facts of the case (I-D-4, p. 21).

Relevance: Possibility to impose fines on a subsidiary company rather than on its parent company. The undertakings' realistic ability to pay the fine. Who picks up the fine in case of inheriting an infringement by later acquisition of control?

[.....]

See above for relevant paragraphs related to the 'economic unit' issue (I-D-4).

[.....]

f) The maximum limit of the fines and the ability to pay of certain applicants within the meaning of point 5 of the Guidelines

[.....]

369 The difficult situation in the graphite electrodes sector does not constitute a 'specific' economic context within the meaning of point 5(b) of the Guidelines. As stated above, cartels come into being, in particular, at a time when a sector is experiencing difficulties. If that circumstance did not justify the grant of an attenuating circumstance (see paragraph 345 above), it cannot justify a reduction in the fine in the present context either.
370 The same applies to the precarious financial situation of SGL, UCAR and C/G. According to settled case-law, the Commission is not required when determining the amount of the fine to take account of an undertaking's financial losses since recognition of such an obligation would have the effect of conferring an unfair competitive advantage on the undertakings least well adapted to the conditions of the market (LR AF 1998 v Commission, cited at paragraph 38 above, paragraph 308; HFB and Others v Commission, cited at paragraph 280 above, paragraph 596; and FETTCSA, cited at paragraph 47 above, paragraph 351, and the case-law cited there). The fact that the Commission has found in previous decisions that it was appropriate to take account of the financial difficulties of a given undertaking does not mean that it is obliged to do so in subsequent decisions as well (FETTCSA, paragraphs 353 and 354).
371 That line of decisions is not called in question by point 5(b) of the Guidelines, which states that an undertaking's real ability to pay must be taken into consideration. That ability applies only in a 'specific social context' consisting of the consequences which payment of the fine would have, in particular, by leading to an increase in unemployment or deterioration in the economic sectors upstream and downstream of the undertaking concerned. In that regard, the applicants have adduced no evidence capable of determining the 'specific social context'.

372 Furthermore, the fact that a measure taken by a Community authority leads to the insolvency or liquidation of a given undertaking is not prohibited as such by Community law (see, to that effect, Case 52/84 Commission v Belgium [1986] ECR 89, paragraph 14, and Case C-499/99 Commission v Spain [2002] ECR I-6031, paragraph 38). Although the liquidation of an undertaking in its existing legal form may adversely affect the financial interests of the owners, investors or shareholders, it does not mean that the personal, tangible and intangible elements represented by the undertaking would also lose their value.

[.....]

2) Case T-62/02 *Union Pigments v. Commission* [2006] OJ C 36/29

Following investigations carried out on its own initiative, the Commission discovered that the six companies controlling the world zinc production had become parties in a cartel. In the administrative procedure, two of those companies (including Union Pigments) informed the Commission of their intention to cooperate fully in accordance with "the Leniency Notice."
Following the imposition of fines by the Commission, Union Pigments filed an application to the GC alleging an erroneous assessment of the facts and a miscalculation of the amount of the fine whilst also alleging breach of general principles of administrative law.

Relevance: In EU competition law procedures, the principle applies that penalties must be commensurate with the offence.

[.....]

118 As is clear from the case-law, where an infringement has been committed by several undertakings, the relative gravity of the participation of each of them must be examined (see, to that effect, Suiker Unie and Others v Commission, cited in paragraph 35 above, paragraph 623, and Commission v Anic Partecipazioni, cited in paragraph 39 above, paragraph 150) in order to determine whether there are any aggravating or attenuating circumstances relating to them.

119 That conclusion follows logically from the principle that penalties must fit the offence, so that an undertaking may be penalised only for acts imputed to it individually, a principle applying in any administrative procedure that may lead to the imposition of sanctions under Community competition law (see, as regards fines, Joined Cases T 45/98 and T-47/98 Krupp Thyssen Stainless and Acciai speciali Terni v Commission [2001] ECR II-3757, paragraph 63).

3) Case C-338/00 P *Volkswagen v. Commission* [2003] ECR I-9189

See above for facts of the case (VI-A-2, p. 258).

Relevance: Should the Commission refrain from revealing details of a fine to the press before the actual sanction decision has been taken by the Commission?

[.....]

163 It must first be pointed out that, after finding in paragraphs 280 to 282 of the judgment under appeal that, by disclosing to the press, with a high degree of accuracy, an essential element of the contested decision before its adoption, namely the amount of the fine envisaged, the Commission adversely affected the dignity of the undertaking charged and acted contrary to the interests of proper Community administration, the Court of First Instance rejected annulment of that decision, as requested by the appellant, on the basis of the reasons set out in paragraph 283 of the judgment under appeal, which is worded as follows:

It is settled case-law that an irregularity of the type found above may lead to annulment of the decision in question if it is established that the content of that decision would have differed if that irregularity had not occurred (... Suiker Unie and Others v Commission [cited above], paragraph 91; Dunlop Slazenger v Commission, cited above, paragraph 29). However, in the present case the applicant has not adduced such proof. There are no grounds for supposing that if the information at issue had not been disclosed the Advisory Committee or the College of Commissioners would have altered the proposed amount of the fine or the content of the decision.

[.....]

165 Finally, it must be added that, contrary to what the appellant claims, the criterion upheld in the two judgments mentioned in paragraph 283 of the judgment under appeal, namely that an irregularity resulting from premature disclosure of an element of the decision may result in its annulment only if it is established that, had it not been for that irregularity, that decision would have differed in content, does not have the effect that irregularities of this kind remain practically unpunished. Quite apart from the possibility of securing annulment of the decision in question in the event that the irregularity committed affected the content of the decision, the person concerned is entitled to seek to establish the liability of the institution involved for any harm which he claims to have suffered by reason of that irregularity.

[.....]

4) Case C-97/08 P *AKZO Nobel NV and three subsidiaries v. Commission* [2009] ECR I-0000

On 9 December 2004, the Commission adopted a decision in Case No. C.37.553 (OJ 2005, L 190/22). In Article 1 thereof, it found that a number of undertakings, including the appellants, had infringed Article 81(1) EC and Article 53 of the EEA Agreement by participating in a series of agreements and concerted practices concerning price fixing, market sharing and concerted actions against competitors in the choline choloride sector in the EEA. All participants to the cartel lost their appeal before the GC (Case T-112/05). AKZO Nobel and its three subsidiaries involved in the choline chloride market appealed the GC's judgment before the ECJ.

Relevance: imputation to the parent group holding company of an infringement of the competition rules by a subsidiary – justification for doing so.

[.....]

Findings of the Court

54 It must be observed, as a preliminary point, that Community competition law refers to the activities of undertakings (Joined Cases C-204/00 P, C-205/00 P, C-211/00 P, C-213/00 P, C-217/00 P and C-219/00 P *Aalborg Portland and Others* v *Commission* [2004] ECR I-123, paragraph 59), and that the concept of an undertaking covers any entity engaged in an economic activity,

regardless of its legal status and the way in which it is financed (see, in particular, *Dansk Rørindustri and Others* v *Commission*, paragraph 112; Case C-222/04 *Cassa di Risparmio di Firenze and Others* [2006] ECR I-289, paragraph 107; and Case C-205/03 P *FENIN* v *Commission*, [2006] ECR I-6295, paragraph 25).

55 The Court has also stated that the concept of an undertaking, in the same context, must be understood as designating an economic unit even if in law that economic unit consists of several persons, natural or legal (Case C-217/05 *Confederación Española de Empresarios de Estaciones de Servicio* [2006] ECR I-11987, paragraph 40).

56 When such an economic entity infringes the competition rules, it falls, according to the principle of personal responsibility, to that entity to answer for that infringement (see, to that effect, Case C-49/92 P *Commission* v *Anic Partecipazioni* [1999] ECR I-4125, paragraph 145; Case C-279/98 P *Cascades* v *Commission* [2000] ECR I-9693, paragraph 78; and Case C-280/06 *ETI and Others* [2007] ECR I-10893, paragraph 39).

57 The infringement of Community competition law must be imputed unequivocally to a legal person on whom fines may be imposed and the statement of objections must be addressed to that person (see, to that effect, *Aalborg Portland and Others* v *Commission*, paragraph 60, and Joined Cases C-322/07 P, C-327/07 P and C-338/07 P *August Koehler and Others* v *Commission* [2009] ECR I-0000, paragraph 38). It is also necessary that the statement of objections indicate in which capacity a legal person is called on to answer the allegations.

58 It is clear from settled case-law that the conduct of a subsidiary may be imputed to the parent company in particular where, although having a separate legal personality, that subsidiary does not decide independently upon its own conduct on the market, but carries out, in all material respects, the instructions given to it by the parent company (see, to that effect, *Imperial Chemical Industries* v *Commission*, paragraphs 132 and 133; *Geigy* v *Commission*, paragraph 44; Case 6/72 *Europemballage and Continental Can* v *Commission* [1973] ECR 215, paragraph 15; and *Stora*, paragraph 26), having regard in particular to the economic, organisational and legal links between those two legal entities (see, by analogy, *Dansk Rørindustri and Others* v *Commission*, paragraph 117, and *ETI and Others*, paragraph 49).

59 That is the case because, in such a situation, the parent company and its subsidiary form a single economic unit and therefore form a single undertaking for the purposes of the case-law mentioned in paragraphs 54 and 55 of this judgment. Thus, the fact that a parent company and its subsidiary constitute a single undertaking within the meaning of Article 81 EC enables the Commission to address a decision imposing fines to the parent company, without having to establish the personal involvement of the latter in the infringement.

60 In the specific case where a parent company has a 100% shareholding in a subsidiary which has infringed the Community competition rules, first, the parent company can exercise a decisive influence over the conduct of the subsidiary (see, to that effect, *Imperial Chemical Industries* v *Commission*, paragraphs 136 and 137) and, second, there is a rebuttable presumption that the parent company does in fact exercise a decisive influence over the conduct of its subsidiary (see, to that effect, *AEG-Telefunken* v *Commission*, paragraph 50, and *Stora*, paragraph 29).

61 In those circumstances, it is sufficient for the Commission to prove that the subsidiary is wholly owned by the parent company

in order to presume that the parent exercises a decisive influence over the commercial policy of the subsidiary. The Commission will be able to regard the parent company as jointly and severally liable for the payment of the fine imposed on its subsidiary, unless the parent company, which has the burden of rebutting that presumption, adduces sufficient evidence to show that its subsidiary acts independently on the market (see, to that effect, *Stora*, paragraph 29).
62 As the Court of First Instance rightly held in paragraph 61 of the judgment under appeal, while it is true that at paragraphs 28 and 29 of *Stora* the Court of Justice referred, not only to the fact that the parent company owned 100% of the capital of the subsidiary, but also to other circumstances, such as the fact that it was not disputed that the parent company exercised influence over the commercial policy of its subsidiary or that both companies were jointly represented during the administrative procedure, the fact remains that those circumstances were mentioned by the Court of Justice for the sole purpose of identifying all the elements on which the Court of First Instance had based its reasoning and not to make the application of the presumption mentioned in paragraph 60 of this judgment subject to the production of additional indicia relating to the actual exercise of influence by the parent company.
63 It is clear from all those considerations that the Court of First Instance did not commit any error of law in holding that where a parent company has a 100% shareholding in its subsidiary there is a rebuttable presumption that that parent company exercises a decisive influence over the conduct of its subsidiary.
64 Accordingly, since the Commission is not required, as regards the imputability of the infringement, to submit, at the stage of the statement of objections, evidence other than proof relating to the shareholding of the parent company in its subsidiaries, the appellants' argument relating to the infringement of the rights of defence cannot be accepted.
65 As regards the criticism of paragraph 62 of the judgment under appeal, it is sufficient to observe that there is nothing in that paragraph which suggests that the Court of First Instance limited the possibility of rebutting the presumption mentioned in paragraph 60 of this judgment solely to cases where instructions have been issued by the parent company. On the contrary, it is clear from paragraphs 60 and 65 of the judgment under appeal that the Court of First Instance adopted a relatively open position in that respect, holding, in particular, that it is for the parent company to put before the Court any evidence relating to the organisational, economic and legal links between its subsidiary and itself which are apt to demonstrate that they do not constitute a single economic entity.

[.....]

Case cross-reference:

▸ K. Hofstetter and M. Ludescher, 'Fines against Parent Companies in EU Antitrust Law: Setting Incentives for 'Best Practice Compliance', *World Competition* 33 no. 1 (2010): 55-76.

5) Joined Cases T-101/05 and T-111/05 *BASF and UCB v. Commission* [2007] ECR II-4949

Also BASF and UCB participated in the choline chloride cartel (see IX-E-4). The appellants found themselves being fined more severely because over the years they had shown to be repeat infringers of the competition rules. The appeal was inter alia directed at the 50% increase in fine.

Relevance: Discretion of the Commission to increase fines in case of repeat infringements

[.....]

64 The Court rejects at the outset BASF's argument that a case of repeated infringement can be recognised only where the infringements relate to the same product market. It is sufficient that the Commission is dealing with infringements falling under the same provision of the EC Treaty.
65 Next, it should be observed that Article 15(2) of Regulation No 17 and Article 23(2) of Regulation No 1/2003 are the relevant legal bases on which the Commission may impose fines on undertakings and associations of undertakings for infringements of Articles 81 EC and 82 EC. Under those provisions, in order to determine the amount of the fine, the duration and gravity of the infringement must be taken into consideration. The gravity of the infringement is determined by reference to numerous factors, for which the Commission has a margin of discretion. The fact that aggravating circumstances are taken into account in setting the fine is consistent with the Commission's task of ensuring compliance with the competition rules (Case C-3/06 *Groupe Danone* v *Commission* [2007] ECR I-1331, paragraphs 24 and 25).
66 Furthermore, the analysis of the gravity of the infringement must take any repeated infringement into account (Joined Cases C-204/00 P, C-205/00 P, C-211/00 P, C-213/00 P, C-217/00 P and C-219/00 P *Aalborg Portland and Others* v *Commission* [2004] ECR I-123, paragraph 91, and *Groupe Danone* v *Commission*, paragraph 65 above, paragraph 26), and such repeated infringement may justify a significant increase in the basic amount of the fine (Case T-203/01 *Michelin* v *Commission* [2003] ECR II-4071, paragraph 293). In the light of that case-law, the Court rejects BASF's assertions, first, that its previous infringements have no influence on the gravity of the infringement in question and, second, that there is no clear legal basis for the application of an increase for repeated infringement.
67 As regards the objection that a time-limit must be placed on the possibility to take any repeated infringement into account, the Court finds that the fact that Regulation No 17, Regulation No 1/2003 and the Guidelines lay down no maximum period for making a finding of repeated infringement does not breach the principle of legal certainty. The finding and the appraisal of the specific features of a repeated infringement come within the Commission's discretion in relation to the choice of factors to be taken into consideration for the purpose of determining the amount of fines. In that connection, the Commission cannot be bound by any limitation period for such a finding. In that regard, it must be borne in mind that repeated infringement is an important factor which the Commission is required to appraise, since taking repeated infringement into account is intended to

provide undertakings which have shown a propensity to breach the competition rules with an incentive to change their conduct. The Commission may therefore, in each case, take into consideration the indicia which tend to confirm such a propensity, including, for example, the time which has elapsed between the infringements at issue (*Groupe Danone* v *Commission*, paragraph 65 above, paragraphs 37 to 39).

68 In the present case, the decisions on which the Commission based its assessment of repeated infringement (see paragraph 18 above) show that BASF infringed the competition rules between 1964 and 1967 (fixing the rate of price increases and the conditions under which those increases were applied in the dyestuffs sector) and between August 1980 and May 1984 (fixing 'target' prices and 'target' quotas and planning concerted initiatives to raise prices and to monitor their implementation).

69 It is held that the latter of those two infringements can in itself justify the application of an increase of 50% to the basic amount of the fine imposed on BASF (see, to that effect, *Michelin* v *Commission*, paragraph 66 above, paragraph 293).

70 In any event, the Court points out that the exercise of its unlimited jurisdiction may justify the production and taking into consideration of additional information which did not have to be referred to as such under the obligation to state reasons laid down in Article 253 EC (Case C-248/98 P *KNPO BT* v *Commission* [2000] ECR I-9641, paragraph 40).

71 In that context, account must be taken of the fact that BASF was also the object of Commission Decision 86/398/EEC of 23 April 1986 relating to a proceeding pursuant to Article [81 EC] (IV/31.149 – Polypropylene) (OJ 1986 L 230, p. 1). Following the judgment of the Court of First Instance of 17 December 1991 in Case T-4/89 *BASF* v *Commission* [1991] ECR II-1523, BASF was fined ECU 2.125 million for participating in agreements and concerted practices in order to define its business policy, fixing target prices and agreeing on measures for that purpose, increasing prices and sharing the market between the end of 1978 or the beginning of 1979 until November 1983. When questioned at the hearing, the Commission was unable to explain why that decision had been omitted, although it is mentioned at paragraph 29 of the statement of objections.

72 In the light of that factor, it must be held that between 1964 and 1993 BASF was in flagrant breach of the competition rules for approximately 13 years. It follows that the increase of the basic amount by 50% is appropriate.

[.....]

6) Case C-429/07 *Inspecteur der Belastingen v. X BV* [2009] ECR I-0000

In 2005 the Commission imposed fines on the participants of the Plasterboard cartel (Case No. COMP/E-1/37.152, OJ 2005 L166/8). One of the participants in this cartel, the German undertaking Knauf Gips, passed on part of its fine to subsidiaries within the group of which it is the parent company, in particular also to its Netherlands subsidiary which then deducted the amount which had been passed on from its corporate tax. This deduction was rejected by the Netherlands Tax Authorities on purely national fiscal grounds, no argument of Union law playing a role in this rejection. The subsidiary appealed this rejection and saw the rejection quashed before the District Court of Haar-

lem, once again on purely national legal and fiscal grounds. On appeal before the Court of Appeal in Amsterdam, the Commission of its own initiative intervened as amicus curiae and argued the non-deductibility of cartel fines imposed by it on Union law grounds. The Court of Appeal then referred the case to the Court in Luxembourg asking whether the Commission could on its own initiative act as amicus curiae on the basis of Article 15(3) of Regulation 1/2003.

Relevance: The Commission acting in its role as *amicus curiae* – (indirect) deductibility under national tax laws of fines imposed by the Commission.

[....]

20 In order to ensure the coherent application of the competition rules in the Member States, a cooperation mechanism between the Commission, the national competition authorities and the courts of the Member States was set up in Chapter IV of Regulation No 1/2003.
21 That cooperation is part of the general principle of sincere cooperation, referred to in Article 10 EC, which governs the relationships between the Member States and the Community institutions. As the Court has held, the duty of sincere cooperation imposed on the Community institutions is of particular importance where that cooperation involves the judicial authorities of a Member State who are responsible for ensuring that Community law is applied and respected in the national legal system (see order in Case C-2/88 IMM *Zwartveld and Others* [1990] ECR I-3365, paragraph 18).

[.....]

30 Consequently, a literal interpretation of the first subparagraph of Article 15(3) of Regulation No 1/2003 leads to the conclusion that the option for the Commission, acting on its own initiative, to submit written observations to courts of the Member States is subject to the sole condition that the coherent application of Articles 81 EC or 82 EC so requires. That condition may be fulfilled even if the proceedings concerned do not pertain to issues relating to the application of Article 81 or Article 82 of the Treaty.
31 That interpretation is not called in question by the fourth sentence of recital 21 in the preamble to Regulation No 1/2003, according to which the Commission and the competition authorities of the Member States should be able to submit written or oral observations to courts called upon to apply Articles 81 EC or 82 EC. That recital refers merely to a typical situation but does not exclude other situations in which the Commission may intervene. Moreover, whilst a recital in the preamble to a regulation may cast light on the interpretation to be given to a legal rule, it cannot in itself constitute such a rule (Case 215/88 *Casa Fleischhandels* [1989] ECR 2789, paragraph 31, and Case C-136/04 *Deutsches Milch-Kontor* [2005] ECR I-10095, paragraph 32 and case-law cited).
32 Moreover, contrary to what X BV and the Netherlands Government submit, the interpretation of the first subparagraph of Article 15(3) of Regulation No 1/2003 given in paragraph 30 of this judgment is not contradicted by points 31 to 35 of the Commission Notice on the cooperation between the Commission and the courts of the EU Member States in the application of Articles 81 and 82 EC, which state that the Commission may submit observations on issues relating to the application of Articles 81 EC or 82 EC. The general

concept of 'issues relating to the application of Articles 81 ... EC or 82 [EC]' adopted by that notice includes the possibility for the Commission to submit written observations to national courts where the coherent application of Articles 81 EC or 82 EC so requires. In any event, the content of a Commission notice cannot prevail over the provisions of a regulation.

33 Community law has established a comprehensive system for monitoring cartels and abuses of dominant positions which sets out a principle of prohibition, contained in Articles 81 EC and 82 EC, and sanctions for its infringement, on the basis of Article 83 EC. Those articles must be understood as forming part of a comprehensive set of provisions designed to prohibit and punish anti-competitive practices.

34 It is apparent from Article 83(2)(a) EC that the fines and periodic penalty payments which may be imposed on undertakings in connection with the application of Community competition law are designed to 'ensure compliance with the prohibitions laid down in Article 81(1) [EC] and in Article 82 [EC]'. The purpose of Article 83 EC is therefore inter alia to ensure the effective supervision of cartels and abuses of dominant positions.

35 The Commission's power to impose fines on undertakings which intentionally or negligently commit an infringement of Articles 81(1) EC or 82 EC is one of the means conferred on the Commission in order to enable it to carry out the task of supervision entrusted to it by Community law (see, to that effect, Joined Cases 100/80 to 103/80 *Musique Diffusion française and Others* v *Commission* [1983] ECR 1825, paragraph 105, and Case C-76/06 P *Britannia Alloys & Chemicals* v *Commission* [2007] ECR I-4405, paragraph 22).

36 To dissociate the principle of prohibition of anti-competitive practices from the penalties provided for where that principle has not been observed would therefore deprive of any effectiveness the action taken by the authorities responsible for monitoring compliance with that prohibition and punishing such practices. Thus, the provisions of Articles 81 EC and 82 EC would be ineffective if they were not accompanied by enforcement measures provided for in Article 83(2)(a) EC. As the Advocate General stated at point 38 of his Opinion, there is an intrinsic link between the fines and the application of Articles 81 and 82 EC.

37 The effectiveness of the penalties imposed by the national or Community competition authorities on the basis of Article 83(2)(a) EC is therefore a condition for the coherent application of Articles 81 EC and 82 EC.

38 In proceedings relating to the penalties in respect of anti-competitive practices provided for in Article 83(2)(a) EC, the decision that the court seized must give is capable of impairing the effectiveness of those penalties and therefore might compromise the coherent application of Articles 81 EC or 82 EC.

39 In the circumstances of the action in the main proceedings, it is quite clear that the outcome of the dispute relating to the tax deductibility of part of a fine imposed by the Commission is capable of impairing the effectiveness of the penalty imposed by the Community competition authority. The effectiveness of the Commission's decision by which it imposed a fine on a company might be significantly reduced if the company concerned, or at least a company linked to that company, were allowed to deduct fully or in part the amount of that fine from the amount of its taxable profits, since such a possibility would have the effect of offsetting the burden of that fine with a reduction of the tax burden.

40 It follows from all of the foregoing that the third sentence of the first subparagraph

of Article 15(3) of Regulation No 1/2003 must be interpreted as meaning that it permits the Commission to submit on its own initiative written observations to a national court of a Member State in proceedings relating to the deductibility from taxable profits of the amount of a fine or a part thereof imposed by the Commission for infringement of Articles 81 EC or 82 EC.

[.....]

F. Scope of judicial review in administrative law enforcement

Cross-reference for this part:

▸ N. Parr, 'Observations on Burden and Standard of Proof and Judicial review in EC and UK Merger Control', 2008 Fordham Corp.L.Inst. 155-182 (B. Hawk ed. 2009).

1) Case C-12/03 P *Commission v. Tetra Laval* [2005] ECR I-987

See above for facts of the case (VII-G-2, p. 305).

Relevance: Role of the Judiciary in reviewing decisions of Competition Authorities.

[...]

39. Whilst the Court recognises that the Commission has a margin of discretion with regard to economic matters, that does not mean that the Community Courts must refrain from reviewing the Commission's interpretation of information of an economic nature. Not only must the Community Courts, inter alia, establish whether the evidence relied on is factually accurate, reliable and consistent but also whether that evidence contains all the information which must be taken into account in order to assess a complex situation and whether it is capable of substantiating the conclusions drawn from it. Such a review is all the more necessary in the case of a prospective analysis required when examining a planned merger with conglomerate effect.

40. Thus, the Court of First Instance was right to find, in paragraph 155 of the judgment under appeal, in reliance on, in particular, the judgment in *Kali & Salz*, that the Commission's analysis of a merger producing a conglomerate effect is subject to requirements similar to those defined by the Court with regard to the creation of a situation of collective dominance and that it calls for a close examination of the circumstances which are relevant for an assessment of that effect on the conditions of competition on the reference market.

41. Although the Court of First Instance stated, in paragraph 155, that proof of anticompetitive conglomerate effects of a merger of the kind notified calls for a precise examination, supported by convincing evidence, of the circumstances which allegedly produce those effects, it by no means added a condition relating to the requisite standard of proof but merely drew attention to the essential function of evidence, which is to establish convincingly the merits of an argument or, as in the present case, of a decision on a merger.

42. A prospective analysis of the kind necessary in merger control must be carried out with great care since it does not entail the

examination of past events – for which often many items of evidence are available which make it possible to understand the causes – or of current events, but rather a prediction of events which are more or less likely to occur in future if a decision prohibiting the planned concentration or laying down the conditions for it is not adopted.

43. Thus, the prospective analysis consists of an examination of how a concentration might alter the factors determining the state of competition on a given market in order to establish whether it would give rise to a serious impediment to effective competition. Such an analysis makes it necessary to envisage various chains of cause and effect with a view to ascertaining which of them are the most likely.

44. The analysis of a 'conglomerate-type' concentration is a prospective analysis in which, first, the consideration of a lengthy period of time in the future and, secondly, the leveraging necessary to give rise to a significant impediment to effective competition mean that the chains of cause and effect are dimly discernible, uncertain and difficult to establish. That being so, the quality of the evidence produced by the Commission in order to establish that it is necessary to adopt a decision declaring the concentration incompatible with the common market is particularly important, since that evidence must support the Commission's conclusion that, if such a decision were not adopted, the economic development envisaged by it would be plausible.

45. It follows from those various factors that the Court of First Instance did not err in law when it set out the tests to be applied in the exercise of its power of judicial review or when it specified the quality of the evidence which the Commission is required to produce in order to demonstrate that the requirements of Article 2(3) of the Regulation are satisfied.

46. With respect to the particular case of judicial review exercised by the Court of First Instance in the judgment under appeal, it is not apparent from the example given by the Commission, which relates to the growth in the use of PET packaging for sensitive products, that the Court of First Instance exceeded the limits applicable to the review of an administrative decision by the Community Courts. Contrary to what the Commission claims, paragraph 211 of the judgment under appeal merely restates more concisely, in the form of a finding by the Court of First Instance, the admission made by the Commission at the hearing, which is summarised in paragraph 210 of the judgment, that its forecast in the contested decision with regard to the increase in the use of PET for packaging UHT milk was exaggerated. In paragraph 212 of the judgment under appeal, the Court of First Instance gave the reasons for its finding that the evidence produced by the Commission was unfounded by stating that, of the three independent reports cited by the Commission, only the PCI report contained information on the use of PET for milk packaging. It went on, in that paragraph, to show that the evidence produced by the Commission was unconvincing by pointing out that the increase forecast in the PCI report was of little significance and that the Commission's forecast was inconsistent with the undisputed figures on the use of HDPE contained in the other reports. In paragraph 213 of the judgment under appeal, the Court of First Instance merely stated that the Commission's analysis was incomplete, which made it impossible to confirm its forecasts, given the differences between those forecasts and the forecasts made in the other reports.

47. Amongst the other examples given by it, the Commission challenges the Court of First Instance's finding, in paragraph 289 of the judgment under appeal, that 'fresh milk is not a product for which the marketing advantages offered by PET have any particular importance' and its conclusions as to the cost of PET in comparison to that of carton, which are set out in paragraphs 288 and 328 of the judgment under appeal. It should be noted that these are findings of fact, which are not subject to review by the Court in appeal proceedings. It is therefore unnecessary to give a ruling on the merits of those findings by the Court of First Instance and it need be stated only that the Court of First Instance was able to base those findings on various items in the contested decision.

48. It follows from these examples that the Court of First Instance carried out its review in the manner required of it, as set out in paragraph 39 of this judgment. It explained and set out the reasons why the Commission's conclusions seemed to it to be inaccurate in that they were based on insufficient, incomplete, insignificant and inconsistent evidence.

49. In doing so, the Court of First Instance observed the criteria to be applied in exercising the Community Courts' power of judicial review and, accordingly, complied with Article 230 EC.

[.....]

Case cross-references:

▸ J.H. Johnson, 'Economic evidence in criminal cartel cases', (2006) Nera Economic Consulting, Antitrust Insights, January/February.

▸ B.Vesterdorf, 'Standard of proof in merger cases: reflections in the light of recent case law of the community courts', (2005) 1 (1) *ECJ*, 3.

▸M. Bay and J. Ruiz Calzado, 'Tetra Laval II, the coming of age of judicial review of merger decisions', (2005) 28 (4) *World Competition*, 433.

2) Joined Cases C-204/00 P, C-205/00 P, C- 211/00 P, C-213/00 P, C-217/00 P and C-219/00 P *Aalborg Portland v. Commission* [2004] ECR I-123

Following an investigation carried out on its own initiative, the Commission found the existence of a concerted practice amongst several cement producers (mainly through their association of undertakings) organising the exchange of sensitive market information (particularly about price) and sharing of the market.

Relevance: How far should the judicial review of the Commission's economic analysis go?

[.....]

279 As regards the exchanges of price information, Aalborg, Buzzi Unicem and Cementir are essentially reproducing the same arguments as they had already raised in vain before the Court of First Instance. Examination by the Community judicature of the complex economic assessments made by the Commission must necessarily be confined to verifying whether the rules on procedure and on the statement of reasons have been complied with, whether the facts have been accurately stated and whether there has been any manifest error of appraisal or misuse of powers (see, inter alia, Case 42/84 Remia and Others v Commission [1985] ECR 2545, paragraph 34, and BAT and Reynolds v Commission, paragraph 62).

[.....]

3) Joined Cases C-68/94 and 30/95 *Société commerciale des potasses et de l'azote and Entreprise minière et chimique v. Commission (Kali und Salz)* [1998] ECR I-1375

Applying the 'failing company defence' theory, the Commission declared compatible with the common market a merger between Kali und Salz AG and Mitteldeutsche Kali AG (both active on the potash, rock salt and waste disposal sectors) under the condition that the two merging firms would comply with certain commitments as previously offered to the Commission in the notification proceedings. It should be noted that the recitals refer to Article 2 of Reg. 4064/89, but the same principle would be applicable to Article 2 of the new Merger Regulation 139/2004.

Relevance: The scope of the Commission's discretion in its economic assessment of concentrations should be a factor to be taken into consideration by the Court on appeal.

[.....]

223 In this respect, however, the basic provisions of the Regulation, in particular Article 2 thereof, confer on the Commission a certain discretion, especially with respect to assessments of an economic nature.
224 Consequently, review by the Community judicature of the exercise of that discretion, which is essential for defining the rules on concentrations, must take account of the discretionary margin implicit in the provisions of an economic nature which form part of the rules on concentrations.

[.....]

4) Case T-114/02 *BaByliss v. Commission* [2003] ECR II-1279

The Commission declared compatible with the common market – subject to conditions - the merger between SEB and Moulinex, two French companies which are active worldwide in the development, production and marketing of small electrical household appliances. BaByliss, a competitor of the two merging firms, lodged an application to seek the annulment of the Commission's decision.

Relevance: Which legal standard would be required for the Commission carrying out its economic analysis?

[.....]

363 It follows that the Commission has not established to the requisite legal standard the correctness of its theory of the range effect, which it has used to justify the absence of serious doubts in countries not covered by the commitments.

[.....]

5) Case T-210/01 *General Electric v. Commission* [2005] ECR II-5575

The Commission declared incompatible with the Internal Market the notified merger between General Electric (GE) – a undertaking active on several markets and dominant in the production of engines for large aircrafts – and Honeywell, an undertaking active on several vertical though related markets.
The combination of the activities of these two companies would have resulted in the creation or strengthening of dominant positions on a number of markets. The Commission found in particular that GE's existing dominant position on the worldwide market for large commercial jet aircraft engines would be strengthened on account of the 'vertical' effects of the merger. These were likely to result from the integration of GE's activity as a manufacturer of those engines with Honeywell's activities as a manufacturer of starters for those engines. The Commission also concluded that dominant positions would be created on the various world markets for avionics products and non-avionics products. On these markets and as a result of these conglomerate effects, Honeywell enjoyed strong positions prior to the merger already.

Relevance: Criticism expressed (by the Court) in the assessment of the consistency (with previous cases) of the economic analysis which was carried out by the Commission in its decision.

[.....]

462 [.....] in the absence of a detailed economic analysis applying the Cournot effect theory to the particular circumstances of the present case, it cannot be concluded from the Commission's brief mention of that theory in the contested decision that the merged entity would have been likely to engage in mixed bundling after the merger. The Commission could produce convincing evidence within the meaning of the judgment in Tetra Laval v Commission, paragraph 58 above, by relying on the Cournot effect only if it demonstrated its applicability to this specific case. Accordingly, by merely describing the economic conditions which would in its view exist on the market after the merger, the Commission did not succeed in demonstrating, with a sufficient degree of probability, that the merged entity would have engaged in mixed bundling after the merger.

[.....]

6) Case T-328/03 *O2 Germany GmbH & Co. OHG v. Commission* [2006] ECR II-1231

O2 GmbH & Co. (a former subsidiary of BT), found a willing ear with the GC for its arguments that the Commission had done a poor investigative job. They argued successfully that without proper investigation the Commission had qualified certain aspects of a cooperation agreement between O2 and its competitor T-Mobile to be a restriction of competition. The GC severely criticized the evidence brought forward by the Commission accusing this institution of having gone no further than issuing a petitio principii and broad and general statements only.

Relevance: the economic assessment conducted by the Commission in the light of Article 101(1) TFEU must include the impact of the agreement on existing and potential competition as well as the competition situation in the absence of the agreement.

[.....]

Findings of the Court:

[.....]

66 In order to assess whether an agreement is compatible with the common market in the light of the prohibition laid down in Article 81(1) EC, it is necessary to examine the economic and legal context in which the agreement was concluded (Case 22/71 *Béguelin Import* [1971] ECR 949, paragraph 13), its object, its effects, and whether it affects intra-Community trade taking into account in particular the economic context in which the undertakings operate, the products or services covered by the agreement, and the structure of the market concerned and the actual conditions in which it functions (Case C-399/93 *Oude Luttikhuis and Others* [1995] ECR I-4515, paragraph 10).
67 That method of analysis is of general application and is not confined to a category of agreements (see, as regards different types of agreements, Case 56/65 *Société minière et technique* [1966] ECR 235, at 249-250; Case C-250/92 *DLG* [1994] ECR I-5641, paragraph 31; Case T-35/92 *John Deere* v *Commission* [1994] ECR II-957, paragraphs 51 and 52; and Joined Cases T-374/94, T-375/94, T-384/94 and T-388/94 *European Night Services and Others* v *Commission* [1998] ECR II-3141, paragraphs 136 and 137).
68 Moreover, in a case such as this, where it is accepted that the agreement does not have as its object a restriction of competition, the effects of the agreement should be considered and for it to be caught by the prohibition it is necessary to find that those factors are present which show that competition has in fact been prevented or restricted or distorted to an appreciable extent. The competition in question must be understood within the actual context in which it would occur in the absence of the agreement in dispute; the interference with competition may in particular be doubted if the agreement seems really necessary for the penetration of a new area by an undertaking (*Société minière et technique* at 249-250).
69 Such a method of analysis, as regards in particular the taking into account of the competition situation that would exist in the absence of the agreement, does not amount to carrying out an assessment of the pro- and anti-competitive effects of the agreement and thus to applying a rule of reason, which the Community judicature has not deemed to have its place under Article 81(1) EC (Case C-235/92 P *Montecatini* v *Commission* [1999] ECR I-4539, paragraph 133; *M6 and Others* v *Commission*, paragraphs 72 to 77; and Case T-65/98 *Van den Bergh Foods* v *Commission* [2002] ECR II-4653, paragraphs 106 and 107).
70 In this respect, to submit, as the applicant does, that the Commission failed to carry out a full analysis by not examining what the competitive situation would have been in the absence of the agreement does not mean that an assessment of the positive and negative effects of the agreement from the point of view of competition must be carried out at the stage of Article 81(1) EC. Contrary to the defendant's interpretation of the applicant's arguments, the applicant relies only on the method of analysis required by settled case-law.
71 The examination required in the light of Article 81(1) EC consists essentially in taking account of the impact of the agreement on existing and potential competition (see, to that effect, Case C-234/89 *Delimitis* [1991]

ECR I-935, paragraph 21) and the competition situation in the absence of the agreement (*Société minière et technique* at 249-250), those two factors being intrinsically linked.
72 The examination of competition in the absence of an agreement appears to be particularly necessary as regards markets undergoing liberalisation or emerging markets, as in the case of the 3G mobile communications market here at issue, where effective competition may be problematic owing, for example, to the presence of a dominant operator, the concentrated nature of the market structure or the existence of significant barriers to entry – factors referred to, in the present case, in the Decision.
73 In order to take account of the two parts which this plea actually contains, it is therefore necessary to examine, first, whether the Commission did in fact consider what the competition situation would have been in the absence of the agreement and, second, whether the conclusions which it drew from its examination of the impact of the agreement on competition are sufficiently substantiated.

[...]

114 It is therefore apparent from the examination carried out under Article 81(3) EC and Article 53(3) of the EEA Agreement that, in the light of the specific characteristics of the relevant emerging market, O2's competitive situation on the 3G market would probably not have been secure without the agreement, and it might even have been jeopardised. Those assessments confirm that the Commission's presuppositions in its examination under Article 81(1) EC and Article 53(1) of the EEA Agreement have not been established.
115 The argument relied on by the defendant at the hearing that there is a significant difference between not being able to penetrate a market and being able to do so with difficulty cannot, in any event, invalidate the above considerations since, in the Decision, the Commission specifically failed to analyse objectively the competition situation in the absence of the agreement under Article 81(1) EC and Article 53(1) of the EEA Agreement.
116 It follows from the foregoing that the Decision, in so far as it concerns the application of Article 81(1) EC and Article 53(1) of the EEA Agreement, suffers from insufficient analysis, first, in that it contains no objective discussion of what the competition situation would have been in the absence of the agreement, which distorts the assessment of the actual and potential effects of the agreement on competition and, second, in that it does not demonstrate, in concrete terms, in the context of the relevant emerging market, that the provisions of the agreement on roaming have restrictive effects on competition, but is confined, in this respect, to a *petitio principii* and to broad and general statements.

[....]

7) Case C-413/06 P *Bertelsmann and Sony Corporation of America v. Impala* [2008] ECR I-4951

Bertelsmann AG and Sony Corporation of America brought the present appeal in respect of the GC judgment (Case T-464/04 Impala v Commission [2006] ECR II-2289) in which that Court annulled the Commission's decision. Impala (third party, the other player on the market) opposed the Commission's decision declaring the concentration of Bertels-

mann and Sony compatible with the internal market, raising the argument that the merger would strengthen a collective dominant position in the recorded market.

Relevance: role of the statement of objections in the proceedings, standard of proof

[...]

48 [...] , it cannot therefore be inferred from the Regulation that there is a general presumption that a notified concentration is compatible with, or incompatible with, the common market.

[...]

51 However, it cannot be deduced from that that the Commission must, particularly where it pursues a theory of collective dominance, comply with a higher standard of proof in relation to decisions prohibiting concentrations than in relation to decisions approving them. That case-law merely reflects the essential function of evidence, which is to establish convincingly the merits of an argument or, as in the case of the control of concentrations, to support the conclusions underpinning the Commission's decisions (see, to that effect, *Commission* v *Tetra Laval*, paragraphs 41 and 44). Furthermore, the fact that an issue of collective dominance does, or does not, arise, cannot of itself have an impact on the standard of proof which applies. In that regard, the inherent complexity of a theory of competitive harm put forward in relation to a notified concentration is a factor which must be taken into account when assessing the plausibility of the various consequences such a concentration may have, in order to identify those which are most likely to arise, but such complexity does not, of itself, have an impact on the standard of proof which is required.

[...]

63 It follows, by analogy with the case-law on Articles 81 EC and 82 EC, that the statement of objections is a procedural and preparatory document which, in order to ensure that the rights of the defence may be exercised effectively, delimits the scope of the administrative procedure initiated by the Commission, thereby preventing the latter from relying on other objections in its decision terminating the procedure in question (see, in particular, the order in Joined Cases 142/84 and 156/84 *British American Tobacco and Reynolds Industries* v *Commission* [1986] ECR 1899, paragraphs 13 and 14). It is therefore inherent in the nature of the statement of objections that it is provisional and subject to amendments to be made by the Commission in its further assessment on the basis of the observations submitted to it by the parties and subsequent findings of fact (see, to that effect, *SGL Carbon* v *Commission*, paragraph 62). The Commission must take into account the factors emerging from the whole of the administrative procedure, in order either to abandon such objections as have been shown to be unfounded or to amend and supplement its arguments, both in fact and in law, in support of the objections which it maintains. Thus, the statement of objections does not prevent the Commission from altering its standpoint in favour of the undertakings concerned (see the order in *British American Tobacco and Reynolds Industries* v *Commission*, paragraph 13).

[...]

69 [...] It follows that notwithstanding the preparatory and provisional nature of the statement of objections and despite the fact

that the Commission is not obliged to explain any differences by comparison with the statement of objections, the Court of First Instance is not necessarily precluded from using the statement of objections in order to interpret a decision of the Commission, particularly as regards the examination of its factual basis.

[...]

92 [...] Having regard to the requirements of the rights of the defence, the arguments of the notifying parties submitted in reply to the statement of objections cannot be subject to more demanding standards as to their probative value and their cogency than those imposed in relation to the arguments of competitors, customers and other third parties questioned by the Commission in the course of the administrative procedure or in the light of information provided by the notifying undertakings at a previous stage of the Commission's investigation

[...]

Case cross-reference:

▸ B. van Rompuy, 'Implications for the Standard of Proof in Merger Proceedings (Bertelsmann and Sony Corp. v Impala, C-413/06)', Vol.29 [2008] *E.C.L.R.* 608-612.

8) Case C-440/07 P *Schneider Electric SA v. Commission* [2009] ECR I-0000

Schneider Electric SA and Legrand SA are French companies engaged in the production and sale of products and systems in the electrical distribution sector. Schneider planned to acquire control of Legrand by means of a public offer. The Commission decided that the concentration was incompatible with the internal market. The GC annulled the incompatibility decision on the grounds of manifest errors of analysis and errors in the assessment of the impact of the transaction on the national sectoral markets (Schneider I). The GC also annulled the divestiture decision on the grounds that it was a measure giving effect to the annulled incompatibility decision (Schneider II). Based on these judgments Schneider brought a successful action for damages in Case T-351/03. The GC awarded vast sums of money to Schneider for the alleged serious breach of Union law by the Commission. However, in the present case, the ECJ annulled that judgment

Relevance: non-contractual liability of the Union pursuant to Article 340 TFEU (ex Article 288 EC). Causal link required between Schneider's financially disadvantageous sale of Legrand to Wendel-KKR and the Commission's serious breach of EU law. *Res judicata*. Sharing of competences between the ECJ and the GC.

[.....]

[*On res judicata and the sharing of competences between the ECJ and the GC*]

102 The principle of res judicata extends to the matters of fact and law actually or necessarily settled by a judicial decision (Joined Cases C-238/99 P, C-244/99 P, C-245/99 P, C-247/99 P, C-250/99 P to C-252/99 P and C-254/99 P Limburgse Vinyl Maatschappij and Others v Commission [2002] ECR I-8375, paragraph 44 and the case-law cited).

103 Moreover, it is clear from Article 225 EC and the first paragraph of Article 58 of the Statute of the Court of Justice that the

Court of First Instance has exclusive jurisdiction, first, to find the facts, except where the substantive inaccuracy of its findings is apparent from the documents submitted to it and, second, to assess those facts. The Court of Justice thus has no jurisdiction to establish the facts or, in principle, to examine the evidence which the Court of First Instance accepted in support of those facts. Provided that the evidence has been properly obtained and the general principles of law and the rules of procedure in relation to the burden of proof and the taking of evidence have been observed, it is for the Court of First Instance alone to assess the value which should be attached to the evidence produced to it. Save where the clear sense of the evidence has been distorted, that appraisal does not therefore constitute a point of law which is subject as such to review by the Court of Justice (see, inter alia, Case C-413/06 P Bertelsmann and Sony Corporation of America v Impala [2008] ECR I-0000, paragraph 29).

104 In other words, the finding of facts and the appraisal of evidence by the Court of First Instance constitute points of law subject to review by the Court of Justice on appeal where the substantive inaccuracy of the findings of the Court of First Instance is apparent from the documents submitted to it or the clear sense of the evidence has been distorted (see, to that effect, Case C-119/97 P Ufex and Others v Commission [1999] ECR I-1341, paragraph 66).

[.....]

[*For the Community to incur non-contractual liability, there should be a causal link between Schneider's financially disadvantageous sale of Legrand to Wendel KKR and a serious breach of Union law committed by the Commission*]

197 In paragraph 303 of the judgment under appeal, the Court of First Instance states that it must consider whether the unlawfulness of the negative decision resulted in a reduction in the figure at which Schneider's shareholding in Legrand was valued in the sale and purchase agreement.

198 In paragraphs 315 and 316 of the judgment under appeal, it concludes that:

– the breach of the rights of the defence vitiating the negative decision must be regarded as being sufficiently directly linked to the deferral to 10 December 2002, in the sale and purchase agreement, of the final date for completion of the Legrand sale, because that deferral was essential to enable Schneider properly to exercise the right available to all companies in its position to obtain a lawful decision as to the compatibility with the common market of a duly notified concentration and, possibly, to be heard in a procedure offering it the requisite safeguards;

– consequently, the serious breach of Community law found by the Court of First Instance is to be regarded as displaying a sufficiently direct causal link with the damage suffered by Schneider as a result of the reduction in the Legrand transfer price associated with the deferral of completion of the transfer.

199 In order to arrive at that conclusion, the Court of First Instance, in paragraphs 304 to 312 of the judgment under appeal relies essentially on the following elements:

– the commencement of negotiations for the transfer of Legrand and conclusion of the sale and purchase agreement on 26 July 2002 both derived directly from the negative decision, which, although unlawful, produced full legal effects until its annulment by the *Schneider I* judgment on 22 October 2002;

– as a result of that decision, Schneider was obliged to commence and conclude negotiations for the transfer, even before delivery of

the judgment on its application for the annulment of that decision;
– Schneider was compelled, because of the existence of the negative decision, to fix a price for the transfer in the sale and purchase agreement concluded on 26 July 2002 and to make certain that it would be able to suspend effective completion of the transfer until 10 December 2002;
– that date fell sufficiently beyond the foreseeable date of delivery of the *Schneider I* judgment to enable Schneider both to obtain confirmation, in the event of dismissal of its application for annulment, of the lawfulness of the negative decision or, in the contrary case of annulment, to ensure that it would still be possible to secure re-examination of the transaction by the Commission on the basis of a new proposal for corrective measures, with a view to a final decision giving a lawful ruling as to the compatibility of the transaction with the common market;
– that obligation to defer effective completion of the sale necessarily prompted Schneider to offer to sell to the purchaser at a lower price than it would have obtained in the event of a firm sale accomplished in the absence of a negative decision tainted by illegality;
– deferral of effective completion of the sale until 10 December 2002 meant that the purchaser had to be paid for accepting the risk of depreciation of the assets in Legrand, if only because of the possibility of an adverse variation in the prices of industrial stocks during the period between signature of the sale and purchase agreement and the final date agreed between the parties for the sale to take effect.

[.....]

203 It is apparent from the documents before the Court that Schneider's decision was based essentially on its fear that, on resumption of the in-depth investigation, it would not obtain, even following a proposal for corrective measures, a decision upholding the compatibility of the concentration, although:
– the risk of a decision of incompatibility with the common market is inherent in every merger control procedure, either initially or, following the annulment of an initial incompatibility decision, where the administrative procedure is resumed;
– an incompatibility decision remains in any event subject to review by the Community judicature.
204 The normal legal consequence of annulment of the negative decision and the divestiture decision would, however, have been that Schneider participated in the resumed in-depth investigation until its conclusion, at which point, there would have been two possible outcomes, as the Commission has in substance argued in its appeal:
– either a decision finding the concentration to be compatible would have been adopted, in which case Schneider would not have been required to transfer Legrand and would thus not have been subject to the price reduction claimed;
– or a further incompatibility decision and divestiture decision would have been adopted, in which case the transfer would have been the legal consequence of the incompatibility found and would thus not have been the cause of damage to be compensated, since such a transfer is among the risks normally assumed by an undertaking which exercises the option provided for in Article 7(3) of the Regulation to implement a concentration through a public bid before the Commission has given a decision on the transaction concerned.
205 It is therefore apparent that the Court of First Instance did not draw its findings to their full conclusion and made an error

in the legal characterisation of the facts, since the direct cause of the damage claimed was Schneider's decision, which it was not obliged to take under the sale procedure entered into in the circumstances referred to above, to allow the transfer of Legrand to take effect on 10 December 2002.

206 That conclusion is not called in question by the fact that, in making that choice, Schneider was at risk of having to pay a penalty of EUR 180 million. That risk derived from the sale agreement which Schneider had entered into in the circumstances outlined above.

[.....]

CHAPTER X

The Role of Other Players in the Enforcement Process

General chapter cross-references:

▸ G. Tesauro, 'International Competition Network First Annual Conference, Naples, 28 September 2002, Opening speech', (2003) 26, *World Competition*, 227.

▸ Katalin J. Cseres, Maarten Pieter Schinkel and Floris O.W. Vogelaar (eds.), *Criminalization of competition law enforcement*, published by Edward Elgar Publishing Limited (2006).

▸ S. Brammer, *Co-operation between National Competition Agencies in the Enforcement of EC Competition Law*, Hart Publishing, 2009.

▸ See for the leeway of Member States to regulate competition autonomously, further or differently from EU law: F. Vogelaar, 'Interface: EC and Dutch Competition Law – In which fields or areas would the Netherlands still have autonomous regulating powers?' and K.J. Cseres, 'The interface between EC Competition Law and the Competition Laws of the New member States: Implementation or Innovation?' in D. Obradovic and N. Lavranos (*eds.*), *Interface between EU Law and National Law*, Europa Law Publishing Groningen, 2007.

A. Role of NCA's

Cross-references for this part:

▸ Articles 5, 11-14 and 29 of Regulation 1/2003, [2003] OJ L 1/1.

▸ Notice on cooperation within the Network of Competition Authorities, [2004] OJ C 101/43.

▸ J. Temple Lang, 'The implications of the Commission's leniency policy for national competition authorities', (2003) 28 *ELR*, 430.

1) Case C-137/00 *Milk Marque* [2003] ECR I-7975

According to Regulation No 26, the production or trade in milk was subject to the Community's competition regime. The same Regulation, however, also provided for exceptions to this rule. The target price for milk was fixed at Community level on the basis of a Regulation creating a common organisation for milk and milk products. Milk Marque was a British farmers' cooperative society engaged in the collection, distribution and supply of milk that had a powerful position on the market for raw cow's milk. According to the UK Competition Commission, Milk Marque had been engaged in activities such as charging high prices that were contrary to both the Fair Trade Act (FTA), the Competition Act (CA) and the public interest. It proposed to divide the cooperative society into a number of independent (and accordingly competing) quota-holding bodies. Moreover, it also recommended the adoption of interim measures. The Secretary of State accepted the proposed interim measures but not the recommended division. Instead, he wanted to adjust the body's sales procedures. Milk Marque, though, announced a proposal to divide itself into three cooperatives. The Secretary of State then decided not to pursue the interim measures. Still, Milk Marque, together with the National Farmer's Union (NFU), decided to start proceedings. It was claimed that both the UK Competition Commission's recommendation and the Secretary of State's decisions were contrary to EU Law. The High Court decided to turn to the ECJ for a preliminary ruling on the jurisdiction to intervene in the common organisation of the market in milk.

Relevance: relation between EU agricultural policy and the EU competition rules. Scope of jurisdiction in such matters for national authorities.

[.....]

Whether the Member States are competent to take steps under their national competition law in the sector governed by the common organisation of the market in milk and milk products

Findings of the Court

[.....]

63 Admittedly, in a sector covered by a common organisation of the market, a fortiori where that organisation is based on a common price system, the Member States are under an obligation to refrain from taking any measures which might undermine or create exceptions to it (see, inter alia, Case 111/76 Van den Hazel [1977] ECR 901, paragraph 13, Pigs Marketing Board, cited above, paragraph 56, and Case C-462/01 Hammarsten [2003] ECR I-781, paragraph 28). In particular, Member States can no longer take action, through national provisions taken unilaterally, affecting the machinery of price formation at the production and marketing stages established under the common organisation (see, inter alia, Toffoli and Others, cited above, paragraph 12).

64 However, having regard to the fact that, as is clear from paragraphs 57 to 60 of this judgment, the maintenance of effective competition is one of the objectives of the common organisation of the market in milk and milk products, it must be observed that any measure adopted by the authorities of a Member State in application of national competition law cannot be regarded, by its very nature, as undermining or creating exceptions to the functioning of the common organisation of the market. Moreover, national measures which seek to eliminate a distortion of competition which is the result of abuse of the powerful position enjoyed by an agricultural cooperative on the national market cannot a priori be regarded as measures affecting the machinery of price formation established under the common organisation at Community level, within the meaning of the case-law cited at paragraph 63 of this judgment.

65 Next, if Articles 32 to 38 EC and Regulations Nos 26 and 804/68 were interpreted as meaning that, in the sector governed by the common organisation of the market in milk and milk products, the competence of the authorities of the Member States to act in application of their national competition law is wholly excluded, there would be no means, in that sector, of eliminating distortions of competition where there is no Community dimension.

66 Finally, given that the scope of the Community competition rules is not the same as the scope of national competition rules, the mere fact that in Article 36 EC and Regulation No 26 the Community legislature has endeavoured to reconcile the objectives of the common agricultural policy with Community competition policy does not necessarily mean that any application of national competition law conflicts with Article 36 EC and Regulation No 26.

67 Having regard to those considerations, it must be concluded that Articles 32 to 38 EC and Regulations Nos 26 and 804/68 must be interpreted as meaning that, in the sector governed by the common organisation of the market in milk and milk products, the national authorities in principle retain jurisdiction to apply their national competition law to a milk producers' cooperative in a powerful position on the national market.

[.....]

The limits of the Member States' jurisdiction to act under national competition law in the sector governed by the common organisation of the market in milk and milk products

Findings of the Court

80 It must first of all be observed that, as is clear from the case-law cited at paragraph 63 of this judgment, where there is a regulation establishing the common organisation of the market in a given sector the Member States are under an obligation to refrain from taking any measures which might undermine or create exceptions to it.
81 Secondly, it is also clear from settled case-law that, even in regard to the competition rules of the Treaty, Article 36 EC gives precedence to the objectives of the common agricultural policy over those in relation to competition policy (see to that effect Case 139/79 Maizena v Council [1980] ECR 3393, paragraph 23, and Germany v Council, cited above, paragraph 61).
82 With regard to measures such as those at issue in the main proceedings, it is common ground that they do not undermine an express provision of the rules establishing the common organisation of the market in milk and milk products.
83 The question then arises as to whether such measures, in the light of the means employed to implement them, produce effects which are likely to impede the functioning of the mechanisms provided for by the common organisation concerned (see to that effect Joined Cases 36/80 and 71/80 Irish Creamery Milk Suppliers Association and Others [1981] ECR 735, paragraph 19).
84 As is clear from the documents before the Court, the purpose of the national measures at issue in the main proceedings is to reduce the market power of Milk Marque and its ability to increase the price of milk charged by member producers beyond levels judged to be competitive, and to do so in the interests of both producers and consumers.
85 As the Court has already held, the essential aim of the machinery of the common organisation of the market in milk and milk products is to achieve price levels at the production and wholesale stages which take into account both the interests of Community production as a whole in the relevant sector and those of consumers and which guarantee market supplies without encouraging overproduction (see Irish Creamery Milk Suppliers Association and Others, cited above, paragraph 20).
86 In consequence, the objectives of that common organisation cannot be compromised by national measures such as those at issue in the main proceedings since they do not as such affect the fixing of prices but rather seek to safeguard the proper working of the machinery for setting prices in order to achieve price levels which serve the interests of both producers and consumers.
87 With regard, in particular, to the question whether national measures such as those at issue in the main proceedings infringe the relevant Community legislation because the milk price of Milk Marque producers was lower than the target price laid down by Regulation No 1190/97 before the national authorities took action, it must be observed that that fact alone is not sufficient to render those measures unlawful under Community law.
88 First of all, this sort of price guideline is a political objective at Community level and is not a guarantee to all producers in every Member State that they will earn an income corresponding to the target price.
89 Secondly, given that, as is clear from paragraphs 57 to 60 of this judgment, the maintenance of effective competition is one of the objectives of the common organisation of

the market in milk and milk products, Article 3(1) of Regulation No 804/68 cannot be interpreted as meaning that producers of milk have the right to seek to earn an income corresponding to the target price by any means, including those that may constitute abuses or be anti-competitive.

90 The arguments advanced by Milk Marque and the NFU, however, seem to imply that the Competition Commission in its report and the Secretary of State in the subsequent decisions adopted by him failed to have regard to the fact that one of the objectives of the common agricultural policy is to ensure a fair standard of living for the agricultural community, in particular, by increasing the individual earnings of persons engaged in agriculture, and gave too much weight to the objective of ensuring that supplies reach consumers at reasonable prices.

91 In that connection, it must be observed that, in pursuing the various aims laid down in Article 33 EC, the Community institutions have a permanent duty to reconcile the individual aims. Although that duty to reconcile any contradictions means that no single aim may be pursued in isolation in such a way as to make the achievement of the others impossible, the Community institutions may allow one of them temporary priority in order to satisfy the demands of the economic or other conditions in light of which their decisions are made (see, to that effect, in particular, Vandemoortele v Commission, cited above, paragraph 20).

92 Whilst it is true that that case-law has been developed in relation to acts by the Community institutions in the area of the common organisation of the agricultural markets, the fact remains that it may be applied by analogy to acts of the national authorities in the exercise of their jurisdiction in the area of national competition policy. Given that, as is clear from paragraphs 80 and 81 of this judgment, in the course of those acts, the national authorities are under an obligation to respect the objectives of the common agricultural policy as set out in Article 33 EC, they must also ensure that any contradictions between those objectives are reconciled.

93 In this case, in order to reply to the question whether the Competition Commission's report and the decisions of the Secretary of State reconciled, in an acceptable manner, the various objectives laid down in Article 33 EC or whether in fact they had the effect of favouring the objective of ensuring reasonable prices in supplies to consumers to the point of rendering the realisation of the other objectives impossible, a thorough investigation is required in particular into the situation in the milk market in the United Kingdom during the relevant period and into the effects on that market of the application of the measures at issue. Since such an investigation necessarily involves the finding of facts in the main proceedings, it is for the national court to undertake it.

94 Having regard to all of those considerations, the reply to the first question must be that Articles 32 to 38 EC and Regulations Nos 26 and 804/68 must be interpreted as meaning that, in the sector governed by the common organisation of the market in milk and milk products, the national authorities in principle retain jurisdiction to apply national competition law to a milk producers' cooperative in a powerful position on the national market.

Where the national competition authorities act in the sector governed by the common organisation of the market in milk and milk products, they are under an obligation to refrain from adopting any measure which might undermine or create exceptions to that common organisation.

Measures taken by national competition authorities in the sector governed by the common organisation of the market in milk and milk products may not, in particular, produce effects which are such as to impede the working of the machinery provided for by that common organisation. However, the mere fact that the prices charged by a dairy cooperative were already lower than the target price for milk before those authorities intervened is not sufficient to render the measures taken by them in relation to that cooperative in application of national competition law unlawful under Community law. Furthermore, such measures may not compromise the objectives of the common agricultural policy as set out in Article 33(1) EC. The national competition authorities are under an obligation to ensure that any contradictions between the various objectives laid down in Article 33 EC are reconciled where necessary, without giving any one of them so much weight as to render the achievement of the others impossible.

[.....]

Case cross-reference:

▸ Case on state action defence: Joined Cases C-359 & 379/95 P *Ladbroke Racing* [1997] ECR I-6265 (see V-G-1).

2) Case C-198/01 *Consorzio Industrie Fiammiferi (CIF)* [2003] ECR I-8055

The CIF, the Italian consortium of domestic match manufacturers, and the national law establishing and governing this body had been under the scrutiny of the national competition authority (the Authority). The CIF had been established by Royal Decree in 1923. It had enjoyed a commercial and fiscal monopoly that ended in 1994. Membership had been both compulsory (until 1994) and restricted (until 1983). According to an agreement which formed an integral part of the Decree, the Italian State undertook to prohibit the distribution of matches that had been produced by non-CIF members while the CIF, on the other hand, ensured that its members paid the excise duty on matches. Two other Decrees approved further agreements concluded between the CIF and the Italian Government. The Authority, however, declared the national legislation at issue to be contrary to Articles 4 (3) TEU and 101 (1) TFEU since it required the CIF to engage in anti-competitive conduct. The CIF started proceedings; it stated that the Authority was not competent to declare provisions of national law invalid or inapplicable. The court turned to the ECJ for a preliminary ruling.

Relevance: obligation for NCA to set aside and disapply national rules that run contrary to the Articles 4 (3) TEU and 101 TFEU in conjunction with the Protocol no. 27.

[.....]

45 [...] it is appropriate to point out, first, that, although Articles 81 EC and 82 EC are, in themselves, concerned solely with the conduct of undertakings and not with laws or regulations emanating from Member States, those articles, read in conjunction with Article 10 EC, which lays down a duty to cooperate, none the less require the Member States not to introduce or maintain in force measures, even of a legislative or regulatory nature, which may render ineffective the competition rules applicable to undertakings (see Case 13/77 GB-Inno-BM [1977] ECR 2115, paragraph 31; Case 267/86 Van Eycke

[1988] ECR 4769, paragraph 16; Case C-185/91 Reiff [1993] ECR I-5801, paragraph 14; Case C-153/93 Delta Schiffahrts- und Speditionsgesellschaft [1994] ECR I-2517, paragraph 14; Case C-96/94 Centro Servizi Spediporto [1995] ECR I-2883, paragraph 20; and Case C-35/99 Arduino [2002] ECR I-1529, paragraph 34).
46 The Court has held in particular that Articles 10 EC and 81 EC are infringed where a Member State requires or favours the adoption of agreements, decisions or concerted practices contrary to Article 81 EC or reinforces their effects, or where it divests its own rules of the character of legislation by delegating to private economic operators responsibility for taking decisions affecting the economic sphere (see Van Eycke, paragraph 16; Reiff, paragraph 14; Delta Schiffahrts- und Speditionsgesellschaft, paragraph 14; Centro Servizi Spediporto, paragraph 21; and Arduino, paragraph 35).
47 Moreover, since the Treaty of Maastricht entered into force, the EC Treaty has expressly provided that in the context of their economic policy the activities of the Member States must observe the principle of an open market economy with free competition (see Articles 3a(1) and 102a of the EC Treaty (now Article 4(1) EC and Article 98 EC)).
48 It is appropriate to bear in mind, second, that in accordance with settled case-law the primacy of Community law requires any provision of national law which contravenes a Community rule to be disapplied, regardless of whether it was adopted before or after that rule.
49 The duty to disapply national legislation which contravenes Community law applies not only to national courts but also to all organs of the State, including administrative authorities (see, to that effect, Case 103/88 Fratelli Costanzo [1989] ECR 1839, paragraph 31), which entails, if the circumstances so require, the obligation to take all appropriate measures to enable Community law to be fully applied (see Case 48/71 Commission v Italy [1972] ECR 527, paragraph 7).
50 Since a national competition authority such as the Authority is responsible for ensuring, inter alia, that Article 81 EC is observed and that provision, in conjunction with Article 10 EC, imposes a duty on Member States to refrain from introducing measures contrary to the Community competition rules, those rules would be rendered less effective if, in the course of an investigation under Article 81 EC into the conduct of undertakings, the authority were not able to declare a national measure contrary to the combined provisions of Articles 10 EC and 81 EC and if, consequently, it failed to disapply it.
51 In that regard, it is of little significance that, where undertakings are required by national legislation to engage in anti-competitive conduct, they cannot also be held accountable for infringement of Articles 81 EC and 82 EC (see, to that effect, Commission and France v Ladbroke Racing, paragraph 33). Member States' obligations under Articles 3(1)(g) EC, 10 EC, 81 EC and 82 EC, which are distinct from those to which undertakings are subject under Articles 81 EC and 82 EC, none the less continue to exist and therefore the national competition authority remains duty-bound to disapply the national measure at issue.
52 As regards, by contrast, the penalties which may be imposed on the undertakings concerned, it is appropriate to draw a two-fold distinction by reference to whether or not the national legislation precludes undertakings from engaging in autonomous conduct which might prevent, restrict or distort competition and, if it does, by reference to whether the facts at issue pre-dated or post-dated the national competition authority's decision to disapply the relevant national legislation.
53 First, if a national law precludes undertakings from engaging in autonomous conduct which prevents, restricts or distorts compe-

tition, it must be found that, if the general Community-law principle of legal certainty is not to be violated, the duty of national competition authorities to disapply such an anti-competitive law cannot expose the undertakings concerned to any penalties, either criminal or administrative, in respect of past conduct where the conduct was required by the law concerned.

54 The decision to disapply the law concerned does not alter the fact that the law set the framework for the undertakings' past conduct. The law thus continues to constitute, for the period prior to the decision to disapply it, a justification which shields the undertakings concerned from all the consequences of an infringement of Articles 81 EC and 82 EC and does so vis-à-vis both public authorities and other economic operators.

55 As regards penalising the future conduct of undertakings which, prior to that time, were required by a national law to engage in anti-competitive conduct, it should be pointed out that, once the national competition authority's decision finding an infringement of Article 81 EC and disapplying such an anti-competitive national law becomes definitive in their regard, the decision becomes binding on the undertakings concerned. From that time onwards the undertakings can no longer claim that they are obliged by that law to act in breach of the Community competition rules. Their future conduct is therefore liable to be penalised.

56 Second, if a national law merely encourages, or makes it easier for undertakings to engage in autonomous anti-competitive conduct, those undertakings remain subject to Articles 81 EC and 82 EC and may incur penalties, including in respect of conduct prior to the decision to disapply that national law.

57 It must none the less be made clear that, although such a situation cannot lead to acceptance of practices which are likely further to exacerbate the adverse effects on competition, it nevertheless means that when the level of the penalty is set the conduct of the undertakings concerned may be assessed in the light of the national legal framework, which is a mitigating factor (see, to that effect, Joined Cases 40/73 to 48/73, 50/73, 54/73 to 56/73, 111/73, 113/73 and 114/73 Suiker Unie and Others v Commission [1975] ECR 1663, paragraph 620).

58 In light of the foregoing considerations, the answer to be given to the first question referred for a preliminary ruling is that, where undertakings engage in conduct contrary to Article 81(1) EC and where that conduct is required or facilitated by national legislation which legitimises or reinforces the effects of the conduct, specifically with regard to price-fixing or market-sharing arrangements, a national competition authority, one of whose responsibilities is to ensure that Article 81 EC is observed:

- has a duty to disapply the national legislation;
- may not impose penalties in respect of past conduct on the undertakings concerned when the conduct was required by the national legislation;
- may impose penalties on the undertakings concerned in respect of conduct subsequent to the decision to disapply the national legislation, once the decision has become definitive in their regard;
- may impose penalties on the undertakings concerned in respect of past conduct where the conduct was merely facilitated or encouraged by the national legislation, whilst taking due account of the specific features of the legislative framework in which the undertakings acted.

[.....]

Case cross-references:

- Case 103/88 *Fratelli Costanzo* [1989] ECR 1839.
- Case C-344/98 *Masterfoods v. HB Ice Cream* [2000] ECR I-11369 (see X-B-2).
- Case C-453/99 *Courage* [2001] ECR I-6297 (see X-B-3).
- Cases on useful effect doctrine (see chapter III).
- J. Temple Lang, 'National Measures restricting competition, and national authorities under Article 10 EC', (2004) 29 *ELR*, 407.

B. Role of national courts

Cross-references for this part:

- Articles 6, 15 and 16 of Regulation 1/2003 [2003] OJ L 1/1.
- Notice on the co-operation between the Commission and the Courts of the EU Member States in the application of Articles 81 and 82 EC, [2004] OJ C 101/54.
- C.D. Ehlermann (ed.), *European competition law annual 2001: Effective private enforcement of EC antitrust Law*, Hart Publishing (2003).
- W. van Gerven, 'Substantive Remedies for the Private Enforcement of EC Antitrust Cases before National Courts', 2001 EU Competition Law and Policy Workshop/Proceedings, www.iue.it.
- M. Gustafsson, 'Some Legal Implications Facing the Realisation of the Commission White paper on Modernisation of the EC Antitrust Procedure and the Role of National Courts in a Post-White Paper Era', (2000) 27 *LIEI*, 159.
- W.P.J. Wils, *Optimal enforcement of EC competition laws: a study in law and economics*, Kluwer Law International (2003).
- B. Vesterdorf, 'Judicial review in EC Competition Law: reflection on the role of the community courts in the EC system of competition law enforcement', (2005) 2 *Competition Policy International*, 3.
- N. Green, 'Application of EC Competition Rules by national courts', in *Antitrust reform in Europe: a year in practice*, (2005) 1.
- Green Paper – Damages action for breach of the EC antitrust rules, COM(2005) 672, published in December 2005 on the DG Competition website.

1) Case C-234/89 *Delimitis* [1991] ECR I-935

See above for facts of the case (I-H-2, p. 44).

Relevance: role of the national courts in the enforcement of the Articles 101 and 102. Co-operation between national courts and the Commission.

[.....]

The jurisdiction of the national court to apply Article 85 to an agreement not enjoying the protection of an exemption regulation

[.....]

45 [...] the Commission does not have exclusive competence to apply Articles 85 (1) and 86. It shares that competence with the national courts. As the Court stated in its judgment in Case 127/73 (BRT v SABAM [1974] ECR 51), Articles 85 (1) and 86 produce direct effect in relations between individuals and create rights directly in respect of the

individuals concerned which the national courts must safeguard.
46 The same is true of the provisions of the exemption regulation (judgment in Case 63/75, Fonderies Roubaix [1976] ECR 111). The direct applicability of those provisions may not, however, lead the national courts to modify the scope of the exemption regulations by extending their sphere of application to agreements not covered by them. Any such extension, whatever its scope, would affect the manner in which the Commission exercises its legislative competence.
47 It now falls to examine the consequences of that division of competence as regards the specific application of the Community competition rules by national courts. Account should here be taken of the risk of national courts taking decisions which conflict with those taken or envisaged by the Commission in the implementation of Articles 85(1) and 86, and also of Article 85(3). Such conflicting decisions would be contrary to the general principle of legal certainty and must, therefore, be avoided when national courts give decisions on agreements or practices which may subsequently be the subject of a decision by the Commission.

[.....]

50 If the conditions for the application of Article 85(1) are clearly not satisfied and there is, consequently, scarcely any risk of the Commission taking a different decision, the national court may continue the proceedings and rule on the agreement in issue. It may do the same if the agreement's incompatibility with Article 85(1) is beyond doubt and, regard being had to the exemption regulations and the Commission's previous decisions, the agreement may on no account be the subject of an exemption decision under Article 85(3).

[.....]

52 If the national court finds that the contract in issue satisfies those formal requirements and if it considers in the light of the Commission's rules and decision-making practices, that that agreement may be the subject of an exemption decision, the national court may decide to stay the proceedings or to adopt interim measures pursuant to its national rules of procedure. A stay of proceedings or the adoption of interim measures should also be envisaged where there is a risk of conflicting decisions in the context of the application of Articles 85(1) and 86.
53 It should be noted in this context that it is always open to a national court, within the limits of the applicable national procedural rules and subject to Article 214 of the Treaty, to seek information from the Commission on the state of any procedure which the Commission may have set in motion and as to the likelihood of its giving an official ruling on the agreement in issue pursuant to Regulation No 17. Under the same conditions, the national court may contact the Commission where the concrete application of Article 85(1) or of Article 86 raises particular difficulties, in order to obtain the economic and legal information which that institution can supply to it. Under Article 5 of the Treaty, the Commission is bound by a duty of sincere cooperation with the judicial authorities of the Member State, who are responsible for ensuring that Community law is applied and respected in the national legal system (Order of 13 July 1990 in Case C-2/88, Zwartveld [1990] ECR I-3365, paragraph 18).
54 Finally, the national court may in any event, stay the proceedings and make a reference to the Court for a preliminary ruling under Article 177 of the Treaty.

[.....]

2) Case C-344/98 *Masterfoods v. HB Ice Cream* [2000] ECR I-11369

HB Ice cream, controlled by the Unilever group and presumed dominant on the Irish market, not only manufactured ice creams but also supplied freezer cabinets. Yet, ice cream retailers were only allowed to use the said cabinets for HB products. Still, when Masterfoods, subsidiary of the American Mars Inc., expanded its business to Ireland, several retailers began to store Masterfoods products alongside HB ice creams in their freezers. HB strongly objected to this practice and took measures against its retailers. Masterfoods started proceedings before the national court arguing that EU competition rules were infringed as HB abused its dominant position to keep Masterfoods off the market. It lost and appealed the judgment of the Irish court of first instance. At the same time, Masterfoods lodged a complaint with the Commission, which found that the exclusivity clause did indeed infringe EU Law. HB appealed this decision before the GC. The question now was whether the Irish court of appeal should rule in accordance with the Commission's decision (and consequently, against the national judgment in the first instance) or whether it should stay the proceedings and await the outcome of the appeal before the GC.

Relevance: role of national courts so as to preserve uniform interpretation of EU competition law in relation to their tasks under national procedural law.

[.....]

Findings of the Court

45 First of all, the principles governing the division of powers between the Commission and the national courts in the application of the Community competition rules should be borne in mind.

46 The Commission, entrusted by Article 89(1) of the EC Treaty (now, after amendment, Article 85(1) EC) with the task of ensuring application of the principles laid down in Articles 85 and 86 of the Treaty, is responsible for defining and implementing the orientation of Community competition policy. It is for the Commission to adopt, subject to review by the Court of First Instance and the Court of Justice, individual decisions in accordance with the procedural rules in force and to adopt exemption regulations. In order effectively to perform that task, which necessarily entails complex economic assessments, it is entitled to give differing degrees of priority to the complaints brought before it (Delimitis, paragraph 44, and Case C-119/97 P Ufex and Others v Commission [1999] ECR I-1341, paragraph 88).

47 The Commission has exclusive competence to adopt decisions in implementation of Article 85(3) of the Treaty, pursuant to Article 9(1) of Regulation No 17 (Delimitis, paragraph 44). However, it shares competence to apply Articles 85(1) and 86 of the Treaty with the national courts ((Delimitis, paragraph 45). The latter provisions produce direct effects in relations between individuals and create direct rights in respect of the individuals concerned which national courts must safeguard (BRT I, paragraph 16). The national courts thus continue to have jurisdiction to apply the provisions of Articles 85(1) and 86 of the Treaty even after the Commission has initiated a procedure in application of Articles 2, 3 or 6 of Regulation No 17 (BRT I, paragraphs 17 to 20).

48 Despite that division of powers, and in order to fulfil the role assigned to it by the Treaty, the Commission cannot be bound by a decision given by a national court in application of Articles 85(1) and 86 of the Treaty. The Commission is therefore entitled to adopt at any time individual decisions under Articles 85 and 86 of the Treaty, even where an agreement or practice has already been the subject of a decision by a national court and the decision contemplated by the Commission conflicts with that national court's decision.
49 It is also clear from the case-law of the Court that the Member States' duty under Article 5 of the EC Treaty to take all appropriate measures, whether general or particular, to ensure fulfilment of the obligations arising from Community law and to abstain from any measure which could jeopardise the attainment of the objectives of the Treaty is binding on all the authorities of Member States including, for matters within their jurisdiction, the Courts (see, to that effect, Case C-2/97 IP v Borsana [1998] ECR I-8597, paragraph 26).
50 Under the fourth paragraph of Article 189 of the Treaty, a decision adopted by the Commission implementing Articles 85(1), 85(3) or 86 of the Treaty is to be binding in its entirety upon those to whom it is addressed.
51 The Court has held, in paragraph 47 of Delimitis, that in order not to breach the general principle of legal certainty, national courts must, when ruling on agreements or practices which may subsequently be the subject of a decision by the Commission, avoid giving decisions which would conflict with a decision contemplated by the Commission in the implementation of Articles 85(1) and 86 and Article 85(3) of the Treaty.
52 It is even more important that when national courts rule on agreements or practices which are already the subject of a Commission decision they cannot take decisions running counter to that of the Commission, even if the latter's decision conflicts with a decision given by a national court of first instance.
53 In that connection, the fact that the President of the Court of First Instance suspended the application of Decision 98/531 until the Court of First Instance has given judgment terminating the proceedings before it is irrelevant. Acts of the Community institutions are in principle presumed to be lawful until such time as they are annulled or withdrawn (Case C-137/92 P Commission v BASF and Others [1994] ECR I-2555, paragraph 48). The decision of the judge hearing an application to order the suspension of the operation of the contested act, pursuant to Article 185 of the Treaty, has only provisional effect. It must not prejudge the points of law or fact in issue or neutralise in advance the effects of the decision subsequently to be given in the main action (order in Case C-149/95 P(R) Commission v Atlantic Container Line and Others [1995] ECR I-2165, paragraph 22).
54 Moreover, if a national court has doubts as to the validity or interpretation of an act of a Community institution it may, or must, in accordance with the second and third paragraphs of Article 177 of the Treaty, refer a question to the Court of Justice for a preliminary ruling.
55 If, as here in the main proceedings, the addressee of a Commission decision has, within the period prescribed in the fifth paragraph of Article 173 of the Treaty, brought an action for annulment of that decision pursuant to that Article, it is for the national court to decide whether to stay proceedings until a definitive decision has been given in the action for annulment or in order to refer a question to the Court for a preliminary ruling.

56 It should be borne in mind in that connection that application of the Community competition rules is based on an obligation of sincere cooperation between the national courts, on the one hand, and the Commission and the Community Courts, on the other, in the context of which each acts on the basis of the role assigned to it by the Treaty.
57 When the outcome of the dispute before the national court depends on the validity of the Commission decision, it follows from the obligation of sincere cooperation that the national court should, in order to avoid reaching a decision that runs counter to that of the Commission, stay its proceedings pending final judgment in the action for annulment by the Community Courts, unless it considers that, in the circumstances of the case, a reference to the Court of Justice for a preliminary ruling on the validity of the Commission decision is warranted.
58 If a national court stays proceedings, it is incumbent on it to examine whether it is necessary to order interim measures in order to safeguard the interests of the parties pending final judgment.
59 In this case it appears from the order for reference that the maintenance in force of the permanent injunction granted by the High Court restraining Masterfoods from inducing retailers to store its products in freezers belonging to HB depends on the validity of Decision 98/531. It therefore follows from the obligation of sincere cooperation that the national court should stay proceedings pending final judgment in the action for annulment by the Community Courts unless it considers that, in the circumstances of the case, a reference to the Court of Justice for a preliminary ruling on the validity of the Commission decision is warranted.
60 The answer to Question 1 must therefore be that, where a national court is ruling on an agreement or practice the compatibility of which with Articles 85(1) and 86 of the Treaty is already the subject of a Commission decision, it cannot take a decision running counter to that of the Commission, even if the latter's decision conflicts with a decision given by a national court of first instance. If the addressee of the Commission decision has, within the period prescribed in the fifth paragraph of Article 173 of the Treaty, brought an action for annulment of that decision, it is for the national court to decide whether to stay proceedings pending final judgment in that action for annulment or in order to refer a question to the Court for a preliminary ruling.

[.....]

Case cross-references:

- L. Kjølbye, 'Annotation Case C-344/98 Masterfoods v. HB Ice Cream, (2002) 39 *CMLRev*, 175.
- S. Preece. 'Masterfoods Ltd. V. HB Ice Cream Ltd', (2001) 22 *ECLR*, 281.

3) Case C-453/99 *Courage* [2001] ECR I-6297

Inntrepreneur Estates Ltd (IEL) administrated the leased pubs of both Courage and Grand Metropolitan in the United Kingdom. The standard form of lease agreement contained an exclusive purchase obligation; tenants were obliged to order their beer exclusively from Courage. Crehan, one of the IEL tenants, failed to pay for supplied beer. Courage started proceedings, but Crehan claimed that the exclusive purchase obligation infringed Article 101 and that Courage charged higher (beer) prices for IEL tenants than for non-IEL tenants. Moreover, he counter-claimed for damages. Under English law, however, a party to an agreement that was held to be illegal from the outset cannot claim damages from the other party. The question was whether this national rule of law would be compatible with EU law.

Relevance: role of national courts. Supremacy of EU law over national law. Should the national court under circumstances set aside national laws that are conflicting with EU law, also in the field of competition?

[.....]

The questions

17 By its first, second and third questions, which should be considered together, the referring Court is asking essentially whether a party to a contract liable to restrict or distort competition within the meaning of Article 85 of the Treaty can rely on the breach of that provision before a national court to obtain relief from the other contracting party. In particular, it asks whether that party can obtain compensation for loss which he alleges to result from his being subject to a contractual clause contrary to Article 85 and whether, therefore, Community law precludes a rule of national law which denies a person the right to rely on his own illegal actions to obtain damages.

18 If Community law precludes a national rule of that sort, the national court wishes to know, by its fourth question, what factors must be taken into consideration in assessing the merits of such a claim for damages.

19 It should be borne in mind, first of all, that the Treaty has created its own legal order, which is integrated into the legal systems of the Member States and which their Courts are bound to apply. The subjects of that legal order are not only the Member States but also their nationals. Just as it imposes burdens on individuals, Community law is also intended to give rise to rights which become part of their legal assets. Those rights arise not only where they are expressly granted by the Treaty but also by virtue of obligations which the Treaty imposes in a clearly defined manner both on individuals and on the Member States and the Community institutions (see the judgments in Case 26/62 Van Gend en Loos [1963] ECR 1, Case 6/64 Costa [1964] ECR 585 and Joined Cases C-6/90 and C-9/90 Francovich and Others [1991] ECR I-5357, paragraph 31).

20 Secondly, according to Article 3(g) of the EC Treaty (now, after amendment, Article 3(1)(g) EC), Article 85 of the Treaty constitutes a fundamental provision which is essential for the accomplishment of the tasks entrusted to the Community and, in particular, for the functioning of the internal market (judgment in Case C-126/97 Eco Swiss [1999] ECR I-3055, paragraph 36).

21 Indeed, the importance of such a provision led the framers of the Treaty to provide expressly, in Article 85(2) of the Treaty, that any agreements or decisions prohibited pursuant to that Article are to be automatically void (judgment in Eco Swiss, cited above, paragraph 36).

22 That principle of automatic nullity can be relied on by anyone, and the Courts are bound by it once the conditions for the application of Article 85(1) are met and so long as the agreement concerned does not justify the grant of an exemption under Article 85(3) of the Treaty (on the latter point, see inter alia Case 10/69 Portelange [1969] ECR 309, paragraph 10). Since the nullity referred to in

Article 85(2) is absolute, an agreement which is null and void by virtue of this provision has no effect as between the contracting parties and cannot be set up against third parties (see the judgment in Case 22/71 Béguelin [1971] ECR 949, paragraph 29). Moreover, it is capable of having a bearing on all the effects, either past or future, of the agreement or decision concerned (see the judgment in Case 48/72 Brasserie de Haecht II [1973] ECR 77, paragraph 26).

23 Thirdly, it should be borne in mind that the Court has held that Article 85(1) of the Treaty and Article 86 of the EC Treaty (now Article 82 EC) produce direct effects in relations between individuals and create rights for the individuals concerned which the national courts must safeguard (judgments in Case 127/73 BRT and SABAM [1974] ECR 51, paragraph 16, (BRT I) and Case C-282/95 P Guérin Automobiles v Commission [1997] ECR I-1503, paragraph 39).

24 It follows from the foregoing considerations that any individual can rely on a breach of Article 85(1) of the Treaty before a national court even where he is a party to a contract that is liable to restrict or distort competition within the meaning of that provision.

25 As regards the possibility of seeking compensation for loss caused by a contract or by conduct liable to restrict or distort competition, it should be remembered from the outset that, in accordance with settled case-law, the national courts whose task it is to apply the provisions of Community law in areas within their jurisdiction must ensure that those rules take full effect and must protect the rights which they confer on individuals (see inter alia the judgments in Case 106/77 Simmenthal [1978] ECR 629, paragraph 16, and in Case C-213/89 Factortame [1990] ECR I-2433, paragraph 19).

26 The full effectiveness of Article 85 of the Treaty and, in particular, the practical effect of the prohibition laid down in Article 85(1) would be put at risk if it were not open to any individual to claim damages for loss caused to him by a contract or by conduct liable to restrict or distort competition.

27 Indeed, the existence of such a right strengthens the working of the Community competition rules and discourages agreements or practices, which are frequently covert, which are liable to restrict or distort competition. From that point of view, actions for damages before the national courts can make a significant contribution to the maintenance of effective competition in the Community.

28 There should not therefore be any absolute bar to such an action being brought by a party to a contract which would be held to violate the competition rules.

29 However, in the absence of Community rules governing the matter, it is for the domestic legal system of each Member State to designate the Courts and tribunals having jurisdiction and to lay down the detailed procedural rules governing actions for safeguarding rights which individuals derive directly from Community law, provided that such rules are not less favourable than those governing similar domestic actions (principle of equivalence) and that they do not render practically impossible or excessively difficult the exercise of rights conferred by Community law (principle of effectiveness) (see Case C-261/95 Palmisani [1997] ECR I-4025, paragraph 27).

30 In that regard, the Court has held that Community law does not prevent national courts from taking steps to ensure that the protection of the rights guaranteed by Community law does not entail the unjust enrichment of those who enjoy them (see, in particular, Case 238/78 Ireks-Arkady v Council and Commission [1979] ECR 2955, paragraph 14, Case 68/79 Just [1980] ECR 501,

paragraph 26, and Joined Cases C-441/98 and C-442/98 Michaïlidis [2000] ECR I-7145, paragraph 31).

31 Similarly, provided that the principles of equivalence and effectiveness are respected (see Palmisani, cited above, paragraph 27), Community law does not preclude national law from denying a party who is found to bear significant responsibility for the distortion of competition the right to obtain damages from the other contracting party. Under a principle which is recognized in most of the legal systems of the Member States and which the Court has applied in the past (see Case 39/72 Commission v Italy [1973] ECR 101, paragraph 10), a litigant should not profit from his own unlawful conduct, where this is proven.

32 In that regard, the matters to be taken into account by the competent national court include the economic and legal context in which the parties find themselves and, as the United Kingdom Government rightly points out, the respective bargaining power and conduct of the two parties to the contract.

33 In particular, it is for the national court to ascertain whether the party who claims to have suffered loss through concluding a contract that is liable to restrict or distort competition found himself in a markedly weaker position than the other party, such as seriously to compromise or even eliminate his freedom to negotiate the terms of the contract and his capacity to avoid the loss or reduce its extent, in particular by availing himself in good time of all the legal remedies available to him.

34 Referring to the judgments in Case 23/67 Brasserie de Haecht [1967] ECR 127 and Case C-234/89 Delimitis [1991] ECR I-935, paragraphs 14 to 26, the Commission and the United Kingdom Government also rightly point out that a contract might prove to be contrary to Article 85(1) of the Treaty for the sole reason that it is part of a network of similar contracts which have a cumulative effect on competition. In such a case, the party contracting with the person controlling the network cannot bear significant responsibility for the breach of Article 85, particularly where in practice the terms of the contract were imposed on him by the party controlling the network.

35 Contrary to the submission of Courage, making a distinction as to the extent of the parties' liability does not conflict with the case-law of the Court to the effect that it does not matter, for the purposes of the application of Article 85 of the Treaty, whether the parties to an agreement are on an equal footing as regards their economic position and function (see inter alia Joined Cases 56/64 and 58/64 Consten and Grundig v Commission [1966] ECR 382). That case-law concerns the conditions for application of Article 85 of the Treaty while the questions put before the Court in the present case concern certain consequences in civil law of a breach of that provision.

36 Having regard to all the foregoing considerations, the questions referred are to be answered as follows:

- a party to a contract liable to restrict or distort competition within the meaning of Article 85 of the Treaty can rely on the breach of that Article to obtain relief from the other contracting party;
- Article 85 of the Treaty precludes a rule of national law under which a party to a contract liable to restrict or distort competition within the meaning of that provision is barred from claiming damages for loss caused by performance of that contract on the sole ground that the claimant is a party to that contract;
- Community law does not preclude a rule of national law barring a party to a contract liable to restrict or distort competition from relying on his own unlawful actions to obtain damages where it is established that that party bears significant responsibility for the distortion of competition.

[.....]

Case cross-references:

▸ A.P. Komninos, 'New prospects for private enforcement of EC Competition law: Courage v. Crehan and the Community right to damages', (2002) 39 *CMLRev*, 447.

▸ N. Reich, 'The Courage doctrine: encouraging or discouraging compensation for antitrust injuries?', (2005) 42 (1) *CMLRev.*, 35.

▸ Case C-295/04 *Manfredi* (See X-B-4).

4) Joined Cases C-295/04 and 298/04 *Manfredi* [2006] ECR I-6619

With its decision of 28 July 2000, the Italian Competition Authority (the Autorità Garante) declared that the insurance companies offering a (compulsory) civil liability motor car insurance on the Italian market had been involved in an agreement to exchange information aimed at fixing prices between 1994 and 1999. The Italian Competition Authority found that the prices were raised on average by 20% compared to a competitive level. Therefore, the damage suffered by consumers was on average 20% of their insurance premium. Consumers then started to reclaim their damages in the lower Courts (Giudici di Pace). However, the Italian Competition Act provides for an application to an upper Court (Corte di Appello) in case of damages suffered as a result of a breach of Italian competition law. Such application would bring formalities and higher costs. One of the Giudici di Pace asked the ECJ whether the agreement concerned could possibly constitute an infringement of Article 101 also and, if so, what would be the consequences thereof for private damages claims.

Relevance: framework for private enforcement in the absence of EU harmonization rules. Nature of the claimable damages.

Operative part of the judgment:

[...]

1 An agreement or concerted practice, such as that at issue in the main proceedings, between insurance companies, consisting of a mutual exchange of information that makes possible an increase in premiums for compulsory civil liability insurance relating to accidents caused by motor vehicles, vessels and mopeds, not justified by market conditions, which infringes national rules on the protection of competition, may also constitute an infringement of Article 81 EC if, in the light of the characteristics of the national market at issue, there is a sufficient degree of probability that the agreement or concerted practice at issue may have an influence, direct or indirect, actual or potential, on the sale of those insurance policies in the relevant Member State by operators established in other Member States and that that influence is not insignificant.

2 Article 81 EC must be interpreted as meaning that any individual can rely on the invalidity of an agreement or practice prohibited under that article and, where there is a causal relationship between the latter and the harm suffered, claim compensation for that harm. In the absence of Community rules governing the matter, it is for the domestic legal system of each Member State to prescribe the detailed rules governing the exercise of that right, including those on the application of

the concept of 'causal relationship', provided that the principles of equivalence and effectiveness are observed.
3 In the absence of Community rules governing the matter, it is for the domestic legal system of each Member State to designate the courts and tribunals having jurisdiction to hear actions for damages based on an infringement of the Community competition rules and to prescribe the detailed procedural rules governing those actions, provided that the provisions concerned are not less favourable than those governing actions for damages based on an infringement of national competition rules and that those national provisions do not render practically impossible or excessively difficult the exercise of the right to seek compensation for the harm caused by an agreement or practice prohibited under Article 81 EC.
4 In the absence of Community rules governing the matter, it is for the domestic legal system of each Member State to prescribe the limitation period for seeking compensation for harm caused by an agreement or practice prohibited under Article 81 EC, provided that the principles of equivalence and effectiveness are observed.
In that regard, it is for the national court to determine whether a national rule which provides that the limitation period for seeking compensation for harm caused by an agreement or practice prohibited under Article 81 EC begins to run from the day on which that prohibited agreement or practice was adopted, particularly where it also imposes a short limitation period that cannot be suspended, renders it practically impossible or excessively difficult to exercise the right to seek compensation for the harm suffered.
5 In the absence of Community rules governing that field, it is for the domestic legal system of each Member State to set the criteria for determining the extent of the damages for harm caused by an agreement or practice prohibited under Article 81 EC, provided that the principles of equivalence and effectiveness are observed.
Therefore, first, in accordance with the principle of equivalence, if it is possible to award particular damages, such as exemplary or punitive damages, in domestic actions similar to actions founded on the Community competition rules, it must also be possible to award such damages in actions founded on Community rules. However, Community law does not prevent national courts from taking steps to ensure that the protection of the rights guaranteed by Community law does not entail the unjust enrichment of those who enjoy them.
Secondly, it follows from the principle of effectiveness and the right of individuals to seek compensation for loss caused by a contract or by conduct liable to restrict or distort competition that injured persons must be able to seek compensation not only for actual loss (damnum emergens) but also for loss of profit (lucrum cessans) plus interest.

Case cross-references:

- ▸ Green Paper Damage Actions for breach of EC Antitrust Rules, presented by the Commission on December 19, 2005 - COM (2005) 672 final.
- ▸ Ashurst report, Study on the conditions of Claims for damages in cases of infringement of EC competition rules, 2004, available on the DG Comp website.
- ▸ White paper on damages action for breach of the EC antitrust rules, COM (2008) 165 final, 2 April 2008.
- ▸ T. Eilmansberger, 'The Green Paper on Damages Actions for Breach of the EC Antitrust Rules and Beyond: Reflections on the Utility and Feasibility of Stimulating Private Enforcement Through Legislative Action', *CMLRev.* 44, 2007, pp. 431-478.
- ▸ J. Peysner, 'Costs and Financing in Private Third Party Competition Damages Actions', *CompLRev.*, Vol. 3 Issue 1, 2006, pp. 97-115.

► A.P. Komninos, 'Public and Private Antitrust Enforcement in Europe: Complement? Overlap?', *CompLRev.*, Vol. 3 Issue 1, 2006, pp. 5-26.

C. Role of arbitrators in applying EU competition rules

Cross-references for this part:

► A.P. Komninos. 'Arbitration and the Modernisation of Europan Competition Law Enforcement', (2001) 24 *World Competition*, 211.

► P.J. Slot, 'The Enforcement of EC Competiton Law in Arbitral Proceedings', 1996-1 *LIEI*, 101.

► H. van Houtte, 'The Application by Arbitrators of Articles 81 and 82 and Their Relationship with the European Commission', *European Business Law Review*, Volume 19, Issue 1, 2008 p. 63.

► R. Nazzini, 'A Principled Approach to Arbitration of Competition Law Disputes: Competition Law Authorities as Amici Curiae and the Status of Their Decision in Arbitral Proceedings', *European Business Law Review*, Volume 19, Issue 1, 2008, p. 89.

► See also for the scope of any possible *ex officio* application of EU Law by court/arbitrators, Joined Cases C-222/05 through C-225/05 *J. van der Weerd and others v. Minister van Landbouw, Natuur en Voedselkwaliteit* [2007] ECR I-4233 and Case C-455/06 *Heemskerk and Schaap v. Productschap Vee en Vlees* [2008] ECR I-8763.

1) Case C-126/97 *Eco Swiss v. Benetton* [1999] ECR I-3055

A national court in the Netherlands was seized with an appeal for annulment of an arbitral award that was issued in arbitration proceedings in accordance with the procedural rules of the Netherlands Arbitration Institute (NAI). One of the parties chose to rely on an argument of EU competition law in those appeal proceedings for the first time, not having brought up this argument before in the arbitration procedure.

Relevance: is EU competition law of 'public policy' and should also a national court to which an application is made for annulment of an arbitration award apply EU competition rules, even if it were 'ex officio' or, as in the present case, contrary to the general procedural rules prevailing in the arbitration?

[.....]

The second question

31 By its second question, which is best examined first, the referring court is asking essentially whether a national court to which application is made for annulment of an arbitration award must grant such an application where, in its view, that award is in fact contrary to Article 85 of the Treaty although, under domestic procedural rules, it may grant such an application only on a limited number of grounds, one of them being inconsistency with public policy, which, according to the applicable national law, is not generally to be invoked on the sole ground that, because of the terms or the enforcement of an arbitration award, effect will not be given to a prohibition laid down by domestic competition law.

32 It is to be noted, first of all, that, where questions of Community law are raised in an arbitration resorted to by agreement, the ordinary courts may have to examine those questions, in particular during review of the arbitration award, which may be more or less extensive depending on the circumstances

and which they are obliged to carry out in the event of an appeal, for setting aside, for leave to enforce an award or upon any other form of action or review available under the relevant national legislation (Nordsee, cited above, paragraph 14).

33 In paragraph 15 of the judgment in Nordsee, the Court went on to explain that it is for those national courts and tribunals to ascertain whether it is necessary for them to make a reference to the Court under Article 177 of the Treaty in order to obtain an interpretation or assessment of the validity of provisions of Community law which they may need to apply when reviewing an arbitration award.

34 In this regard, the Court had held, in paragraphs 10 to 12 of that judgment, that an arbitration tribunal constituted pursuant to an agreement between the parties is not a `court or tribunal of a Member State' within the meaning of Article 177 of the Treaty since the parties are under no obligation, in law or in fact, to refer their disputes to arbitration and the public authorities of the Member State concerned are not involved in the decision to opt for arbitration nor required to intervene of their own accord in the proceedings before the arbitrator.

35 Next, it is in the interest of efficient arbitration proceedings that review of arbitration awards should be limited in scope and that annulment of or refusal to recognise an award should be possible only in exceptional circumstances.

36 However, according to Article 3(g) of the EC Treaty (now, after amendment, Article 3(1)(g) EC), Article 85 of the Treaty constitutes a fundamental provision which is essential for the accomplishment of the tasks entrusted to the Community and, in particular, for the functioning of the internal market. The importance of such a provision led the framers of the Treaty to provide expressly, in Article 85(2) of the Treaty, that any agreements or decisions prohibited pursuant to that article are to be automatically void.

37 It follows that where its domestic rules of procedure require a national court to grant an application for annulment of an arbitration award where such an application is founded on failure to observe national rules of public policy, it must also grant such an application where it is founded on failure to comply with the prohibition laid down in Article 85(1) of the Treaty.

38 That conclusion is not affected by the fact that the New York Convention of 10 June 1958 on the Recognition and Enforcement of Foreign Arbitral Awards, which has been ratified by all the Member States, provides that recognition and enforcement of an arbitration award may be refused only on certain specific grounds, namely where the award does not fall within the terms of the submission to arbitration or goes beyond its scope, where the award is not binding on the parties or where recognition or enforcement of the award would be contrary to the public policy of the country where such recognition and enforcement are sought (Article V(1)(c) and (e) and II(b) of the New York Convention).

39 For the reasons stated in paragraph 36 above, the provisions of Article 85 of the Treaty may be regarded as a matter of public policy within the meaning of the New York Convention.

40 Lastly, it should be recalled that, as explained in paragraph 34 above, arbitrators, unlike national courts and tribunals, are not in a position to request this Court to give a preliminary ruling on questions of interpretation of Community law. However, it is manifestly in the interest of the Community legal order that, in order to forestall differences of interpretation, every Community provision should be given a uniform interpretation, irrespective of the circumstances in

which it is to be applied (Case C-88/91 Federconsorzi [1992] ECR I-4035, paragraph 7).
It follows that, in the circumstances of the present case, unlike Van Schijndel and Van Veen, Community law requires that questions concerning the interpretation of the prohibition laid down in Article 85(1) of the Treaty should be open to examination by national courts when asked to determine the validity of an arbitration award and that it should be possible for those questions to be referred, if necessary, to the Court of Justice for a preliminary ruling.
41 The answer to be given to the second question must therefore be that a national court to which application is made for annulment of an arbitration award must grant that application if it considers that the award in question is in fact contrary to Article 85 of the Treaty, where its domestic rules of procedure require it to grant an application for annulment founded on failure to observe national rules of public policy.

[.....]

Case cross-references:
- ▸ Joined Case C-430 & 431/94 *Van Schijndel* [1995] ECR I-470.
- ▸ M. Furse and L. Dárcy, 'Eco Swiss China Time Ltd v. Benetton: E.C. Competition Law and Arbitration', (1999) 20 *ECLR*, 392.
- ▸ A. Komninos, 'Annotation Case C-126/97, ECO Swiss China Time Ltd. V. Benetton International Nv', (2000) 37 *CMLRev*, 459.

D. Principle of dual enforcement/*Ne Bis in Idem*

Cross-references for this part:
- ▸ Articles 3, 5 and 11 of Regulation 1/2003, [2003] OJ L 1/1.
- ▸ Notice on cooperation within the Network of Competition Authorities, [2004] OJ C 101/43.
- ▸ Joined Cases C-238, 244, 245, 247, 250-52 & 254/99 *PVC II* [2002] ECR I-8375.
- ▸ W.P.J Wils, 'The Principle of *Ne Bis in Idem* in EC Antitrust Enforcement: A Legal and Economic Analysis', (2003) 26 *World Competition*, 131.

1) Case 14/68 *Walt Wilhelm* [1969] ECR 1

This dispute was concerned with the issue of 'parallel proceedings'. Several German undertakings had agreed to uniform increases in the price of aniline. This agreement infringed the German law against the restraints of competition and, accordingly, the undertakings were fined by the Bundeskartellamt (Federal Cartel Bureau). The price increases, however, had also been investigated by the Commission, which claimed that the agreement amounted to a concerted practice. Question was whether the Commission's proceedings affected the German national authorities' competence to act.

Relevance: principle of 'dual' enforcement. Ne bis in idem. Uniform application of EU law. Risk of concurrent though complementary sanctions.

[.....]

I - the first and third questions

In the first question the national court asks whether, when a procedure has already been initiated by the Commission under Article 14 of Regulation No 17 of 6 February 1962, it is compatible with the Treaty for the national authorities to apply to the same facts the prohibitions laid down by the national law on cartels. This request is elaborated in particular in the third question, relating to the risk of a different legal assessment of the same facts and to the possibility of distortions of competition in the Common Market to the detriment of those subject to the said national law. In this respect reference is made to Article 9 of Regulation No 17, to Articles 85, 3 (f) and 5 of the EEC Treaty and to the general principles of Community law.
3 Article 9 (3) of Regulation No 17 is concerned with the competence of the authorities of the Member States only in so far as they are authorized to apply Articles 85 (1) and 86 of the Treaty directly when the Commission has taken no action of its own. This provision does not apply where the said authorities are acting in pursuance not of the said Articles but only of their internal law. Community and national law on cartels consider cartels from different points of view. Whereas Articles 85 regards them in the light of obstacles which may result for trade between Member States, each body of national legislation proceeds on the basis of the considerations peculiar to it and considers cartels only in that context. It is true that as the economic phenomena and legal situations under consideration may in individual cases be interdependent, the distinction between Community and national aspects could not serve in all cases as the decisive criterion for the delimitation of jurisdiction. However, it implies that one and the same agreement may, in principle, be the object of two sets of parallel proceedings, one before the Community authorities under Article 85 of the EEC Treaty, the other before the national authorities under national law.
4 Moreover this interpretation is confirmed by the provision in Article 87 (2)(e), which authorizes the Council to determine the relationship between national laws and the Community rules on competition; it follows that in principle the national cartel authorities may take proceedings also with regard to situations likely to be the subject of a decision by the Commission. However, if the ultimate general aim of the Treaty is to be respected, this parallel application of the national system can only be allowed in so far as it does not prejudice the uniform application throughout the Common Market of the Community rules on cartels and of the full effect of the measures adopted in implementation of those rules.
Any other solution would be incompatible with the objectives of the Treaty and the character of its rules on competition. Article 85 of the EEC Treaty applies to all the undertakings in the Community whose conduct it governs either by prohibitions or by means of exemptions, granted - subject to conditions which it specifies - in favour of agreements which contribute to improving the production or distribution of goods or to promoting technical or economic progress. While the Treaty's primary object is to eliminate by this means the obstacles to the free movement of goods within the Common Market and to confirm and safeguard the unity of that market, it also permits the Community authorities to carry out certain positive, though indirect, action with a view to promoting a harmonious development of economic activities within the whole Community, in accordance with Article 2 of

the Treaty. Article 87(2)(e), in conferring on a Community institution the power to determine the relationship between national laws and the Community rules on competition, confirm the supremacy of Community law.

6 The EEC Treaty has established its own system of law, integrated into the legal systems of the Member States, and which must be applied by their Courts. It would be contrary to the nature of such a system to allow Member States to introduce or to retain measures capable of prejudicing the practical effectiveness of the Treaty. The binding force of the Treaty and of measures taken in application of it must not differ from one state to another as a result of internal measures, lest the functioning of the Community system should be impeded and the achievement of the aims of the Treaty placed in peril. Consequently, conflicts between the rules of the Community and national rules in the matter of the law on cartels must be resolved by applying the principle that Community law takes precedence.

7 It follows from the foregoing that should it prove that a decision of a national authority regarding an agreement would be incompatible with a decision adopted by the Commission at the culmination of the procedure initiated by it, the national authority is required to take proper account of the effects of the latter decision.

8 Where, during national proceedings, it appears possible that the decision to be taken by the Commission at the culmination of a procedure still in progress concerning the same agreement may conflict with the effects of the decision of the national authorities, it is for the latter to take the appropriate measures.

9 Consequently, and so long as a regulation adopted pursuant to Article 87 (2)(e) of the Treaty has not provided otherwise, national authorities may take action against an agreement in accordance with their national law, even when an examination of the agreement from the point of view of its compatibility with Community law is pending before the Commission, subject however to the condition that the application of national law may not prejudice the full and uniform application of Community law or the effects of measures taken or to be taken to implement it.

II - the second question

10 In the second question the Kammergericht asks whether "the risk of its resulting in a double sanction imposed by the Commission of the European Communities and by the national authority with jurisdiction in cartel matters..." renders impossible the acceptance for one set of facts of two parallel procedures, the one Community and the other national.

11 The possibility of concurrent sanctions need not mean that the possibility of two parallel proceedings pursuing different ends is unacceptable. Without prejudice to the conditions and limits indicated in the answer to the first question, the acceptability of a dual procedure of this kind follows in fact from the special system of the sharing of jurisdiction between the Community and the Member States with regard to cartels. If, however, the possibility of two procedures being conducted separately were to lead to the imposition of consecutive sanctions, a general requirement of natural justice, such as that expressed at the end of the second paragraph of Article 90 of the ECSC Treaty, demands that any previous punitive decision must be taken into account in determining any sanction which is to be imposed. In any case, so long as no regulation has been issued under Article 87 (2)(e), no means of avoiding such a possibility is to be found in the ge

neral principles of Community law; this leaves intact the reply given to the first question.

Case cross-reference:
▸ *Walt Wilhelm* was confirmed implicitly in Joined Cases C-295/04 and 298/04 *Manfredi*, in the operative part of the judgment nos. 2-5 (see *X-B-4*).

[.....]

2) Joined Cases T-236/01, T-239/01, T-244/01 to T-246/01, T-251/01 and T-252/01 *Graphite electrodes cartel* [2004] ECR II-1181

See above for facts of the case (I-D-4, p. 21).

Relevance: Does the principle of *Ne Bis in Idem* apply in case of parallel enforcement within and outside the EU? Deterring effect of fines.

[.....]

132 [.....] , the Court of Justice has held that the possibility of concurrent sanctions, one a Community sanction, the other a national one, resulting from two sets of parallel proceedings, each pursuing distinct ends, is acceptable because of the special system of sharing jurisdiction between the Community and the Member States with regard to cartels. However, a general requirement of natural justice demands that, in determining the amount of a fine, the Commission must take account of any penalties that have already been borne by the undertaking in question in respect of the same conduct where these were imposed for infringement of the law relating to cartels of a Member State and where, consequently, the infringement was committed within the Community (Wilhelm and Others, cited at paragraph 121 above, paragraph 11; Boehringer v Commission, cited at paragraph 120 above, paragraph 3; Case T-141/89 Tréfileurope v Commission [1995] ECR II-791, paragraph 191; and Sotralentz v Commission, cited at paragraph 121 above, paragraph 29).

[.....]

134 In those circumstances, the principle ne bis in idem cannot, a fortiori, apply in the present case because the procedures conducted and penalties imposed by the Commission on the one hand and the United States and Canadian authorities on the other clearly did not pursue the same ends. The aim of the first was to preserve undistorted competition within the European Union or the EEA, whereas the aim of the second was to protect the United States or the Canadian market (see, to that effect, Case 44/69 Buchler v Commission [1970] ECR 733, paragraphs 52 and 53). The application of the principle ne bis in idem is subject not only to the infringements and the persons sanctioned being the same, but also to the unity of the legal right being protected (Opinion of Advocate General Ruiz-Jarabo in Case C-213/00 P Italcementi v Commission [2004] ECR I-0000, point 89).
135 That conclusion is supported by the scope of the principle that a second penalty may not be imposed for the same offence, as laid down in Article 4 of Protocol No 7 to the ECHR. It is clear from the wording of Article 4 that the intended effect of the principle is solely to prevent the courts of any given State from trying or punishing an offence for which the person concerned has already been

acquitted or convicted in that same State. On the other hand, the principle ne bis in idem does not preclude a person from being tried or punished more than once in two or more different States for the same conduct. Consequently, the judgment in Fischer v Austria cited by SGL has no relevance to the present case, since it was delivered in application of Article 4 of Protocol No 7 and concerned two convictions in the same country.
136 It is also important to emphasise that the applicants have relied on no convention or rule of public international law that prevents the authorities or courts of different States from trying and convicting the same person on the basis of the same facts. Such a prohibition could arise today only through very close international cooperation leading to the adoption of common rules such as those contained in the abovementioned Convention implementing the Schengen Agreement. The applicants have not pointed to any binding agreement between the Community and non-member countries such as the United States or Canada that lays down such a prohibition.

[.....]

143 In any event, even if it should be inferred a contrario from the judgment in Boehringer v Commission that the Commission is in fact required to set off any penalty imposed by the authorities of a non-member country where the facts alleged against the undertaking in question by the Commission are the same as those alleged by the first authorities, it must be emphasised that, notwithstanding that the judgment delivered against SGL in the United States states that the purpose of the graphite electrodes cartel was to limit production and increase the prices of those products 'in the United States and elsewhere', it has in no way been shown that the penalty imposed in the United States related to applications of the cartel or its effects other than in the United States (see, to that effect, Boehringer v Commission, paragraph 6) and in the EEA in particular, an extension which, moreover, would have clearly encroached on the territorial jurisdiction of the Commission. That observation applies equally to the judgment handed down in Canada.
144 As regards the deterrent effect of the fines already imposed, according to the case-law, the Commission's power to impose fines on undertakings which, intentionally or negligently, infringe the provisions of Article 81(1) EC or Article 82 EC is one of the means conferred on the Commission to enable it to carry out the task of supervision entrusted to it by Community law. That task certainly includes the duty to investigate and punish individual infringements, but it also encompasses the duty to pursue a general policy designed to apply, in competition matters, the principles laid down by the Treaty and to guide the conduct of undertakings in the light of those principles (Joined Cases 100/80 to 103/80 Musique diffusion française and Others v Commission [1983] ECR 1825, paragraph 105).

145 It follows that the Commission has power to decide the level of fines so as to reinforce their deterrent effect where infringements of a given type, although established as being unlawful at the outset of Community competition policy, are still relatively frequent on account of the profit that certain of the undertakings concerned are able to derive from them (Musique diffusion française v Commission, cited above, paragraph 108).

[....]

147 Furthermore, as is clear from the case-law cited above, the objective of deterrence which the Commission is entitled to pursue

when setting fines is intended to ensure that undertakings comply with the competition rules laid down in the Treaty when conducting their activities within the Community or the EEA. Consequently, the deterrent effect of a fine imposed for infringement of the Community competition rules cannot be assessed by reference solely to the particular situation of the undertaking sanctioned or by reference to whether it has complied with the competition rules in non-member States outside the EEA.

148 It was therefore permissible for the Commission to impose on SGL a fine of a sufficiently deterrent level within the limits laid down in Article 15(2) of Regulation No 17, without being required to take account of the sanctions imposed in the United States and Canada for the purpose of determining those limits.

[.....]

Case cross-references:

- ▸ Case C-328/05 *SGL Carbon AG v. Commission* [2007] ECR I-3921.
- ▸ Case C-289/04 *Showa Denko v. Commission* [2006] ECR I-5859.
- ▸ Case C-308/04 *SGL Carbon v. Commission* [2006] ECR I-5977.

ANNEX I

Table of Cases, Decisions and other Materials (in numerical order)

The Court (ECJ)

The General Court (GC)

Commission decisions and press releases

Annual Reports on Competition Policy and EC Bulletins

ANNEX II

Table of Cases, Decisions and other Materials (in alphabetical order)

The Court (ECJ)

The General Court

Commission decisions and press releases

Annual Reports on Competition Policy and EC Bulletins

ANNEX III

Secondary Legislation and Commission Notices

Council Regulations and Decisions

- Regulation 19/65 on application of Art. 85(3) to certain categories of agreements and concerted practices, OJ English special edition: Series I Chapter 1965-1966 p. 35
- Regulation 2821/71 on application of Article 85 (3) of the Treaty to categories of agreements, decisions and concerted practices, OJ English special edition: Series I Chapter 1971 (III) p. 1032
- Decision 95/145/EC, ECSC, conclusion of the Agreement between EC and USA regarding the application of their competition laws, [1995] OJ L 95/45
- Regulation 1215/99 amending and extending the scope of Regulation 19/65, [1999] OJ L 148/1
- Regulation 1/2003 implementing Articles 81 and 82 EC, [2003] OJ L 1/1
- Regulation 139/2004 on the control of concentrations between undertakings (EC Merger Regulation), [2004] OJ L 24/1

Commission Regulations and Decisions

- Regulation 2658/2000 on the application of Article 81(3) of the EC Treaty to categories of specialisation agreements, [2000] OJ L 304/3
- Regulation 2659/2000 on the application of Article 81(3) of the EC Treaty to categories of research and development agreements, [2000] OJ L 304/7
- Commission Decision on terms of reference of hearing officers in certain competition proceedings, [2001] OJ L 162/21
- Regulation 1400/2002 on the application of Art. 81(3) to categories of vertical agreements and concerted practices in the motor vehicle distribution and servicing agreements, [2002] OJ L 203/30
- Regulation 772/2004 on the application of Art. 81(3) of the Treaty to categories of technology transfer agreements, [2004] OJ L 123/11
- Regulation 773/2004 relating to the conduct of proceedings by the Commission pursuant to Articles 81 and 82 of the EC Treaty, [2004] OJ L 123/18
- Commission Decision on the Application of Art. 86(2), [2005] OJ L 312/67
- Commission Decision on the Application of Art. 86(2), [2005] OJ L 312/67
- Commission Regulation (EC) No 622/2008 amending Regulation (EC) No 773/2004 as regards the conduct of settlement procedures in cartel cases, OJ 2008 L 171/3
- Regulation 330/2010 on the application of Article 101(3) of the Treaty on the Functioning of the EU to categories of vertical agreements and concerted practices, [2010] OJ L 102/1

Commission Notices and Guidelines

- Notice on subcontracting agreements, [1979] OJ C 1/2
- Notice on the definition of the relevant market, [1997] OJ C 372/3
- Notice on the competition rules in the telecommunications sector, [1998] OJ C 71/4
- Guidelines on the applicability of Article 81 to horizontal cooperation agreements, [2001] OJ C 3/2
- Communication – Services of general interest in Europe [2001] OJ C 17/4
- Notice on 'agreements of minor importance', [2001] OJ C 368/13 (the *'de minimis'* Notice)
- Guidelines on market analysis and the assessment of significant market power under the Community regulatory framework for electronic communications networks and services, [2002] OJ C 156/6
- Guidelines on the assessment of horizontal mergers under the Council Regulation on the control of concentration between undertakings, [2004] OJ C 31/5
- Guidelines on the application of Article 81 of the Treaty to technology transfer agreements, [2004] OJ C 101/2
- Notice on restrictions directly related and necessary to concentrations ('ancillary restraints'), [2005] OJ C 56/24
- Notice on the rules for access to the Commission file in cases pursuant to Articles 81 and 82 of the EC Treaty, Articles 53, 54 and 57 of the EEA Agreement and Council Regulation (EC) No 139/2004, [2005] OJ C 325/7
- Notice on the method of setting of fines imposed pursuant to Article 23(2)(a) of Regulation No 1/2003, [2006] OJ C 210/2
- Notice on the immunity from fines and reductions of fines in cartel cases, [2006] OJ C 298/17 (the 'Leniency' Notice)
- Consolidated Jurisdictional Notice under Council Regulation (EC) No 139/2004 on the control of concentration between undertakings, [2007] OJ C 95/1
- Guidelines on the assessment of non-horizontal mergers under the Council Regulation on the control of concentrations between undertakings, [2007] OJ C 265/7
- Notice on the conduct of settlement procedures in view of the adoption of Decisions pursuant to Article 7 and Article 23 of Council Regulation (EC) No 1/2003 in cartel cases, [2008] OJ C 167/1
- Notice on remedies acceptable under Council Regulation (EC) No 139/2004 and under Commission Regulation (EC) No 802/2004, [2008] OJ C267/1
- Guidance on the Commission's enforcement priorities in applying Article 82 of the EC Treaty to abusive exclusionary conduct by dominant undertakings [2009] OJ C 45/2
- Guidelines on Vertical Restraints, [2010] OJ C 130/1

The Commission's 'Modernization Package' of May 1st, 2004

Guidelines on the Substance of the Articles 101 and 102 TFEU

- Guidelines on the effect on trade concept contained in Articles 81 and 82 of the Treaty, [2004] OJ C 101/81
- Guidelines on the application of Article 81(3) of the Treaty, [2004] OJ C 101/97

Notices for market parties / undertakings involved

- Notice on the handling of complaints by the Commission under Articles 81 and 82 of the EC Treaty, [2004] OJ C 101/65
- Notice on informal guidance relating to novel questions concerning Articles 81 and 82 of the EC Treaty that arise in individual cases (guidance letters), [2004] OJ C 101/78

Notices on the Cooperation Network

- Notice on cooperation within the Network of Competition Authorities, [2004] OJ C 101/43
- Notice on the cooperation between the Commission and the Courts of the EU Member States in the application of Articles 81 and 82 EC, [2004] OJ C 101/54.

Green Papers, Reports, Discussion Papers and Draft Regulations and Notices subject to further discussion

- Green Paper – Damages actions for breach of the EC antitrust rules, COM(2005)672, December 2005.
- White paper on damages action for breach of the EC antitrust rules, COM (2008) 165 final, 2 April 2008
- Commission Staff Working Paper on Damages Action for Breach of the EC antitrust rules, SEC(2008) 404, published on the DG COMP website
- White Paper on services of general interest, launched by the Commission on 12 May 2004, COM(2004) 374 final.
- Draft Commission Regulation on the application of Article 101(3) of the Treaty on the Functioning of the European Union to categories of specialisation agreements, published in May 2010 on the DG COMP website
- Draft Commission Regulation on the application of Article 101(3) of the Treaty on the Functioning of the European Union to categories of research and development agreements, published in May 2010 on the DG COMP website
- Draft Guidelines on the applicability of Article 101 of the Treaty on the Functioning of the European Union to horizontal co-operation agreements, SEC(2010) 528/2, published in May 2010 on the DG COMP website
- The Future Competition Law framework applicable to the motor vehicle sector, 22 July 2009, COM (2009) 338 final
- Communication from the Commission to the European Parliament and the Council - Report on the functioning of Regulation 1/2003, COM (2009) 206 final

- Commission staff working paper accompanying the Communication from the Commission to the European Parliament and Council - Report on the functioning of Regulation 1/2003, SEC (2009) 574 final

Please note that documents and materials relating to the sectors of maritime and air transport have not been listed.

ANNEX IV

List of Selected Leading Legal Periodicals, and Websites Dealing with Competition Issues and List of NCA's within the Network

Legal periodicals

Commission's Annual Reports on Competition Policy (as from 1971)
Common Market Law Reports, CMLR
Common Market Law Review, CMLRev.
The Competition Law Review, CompLRev.
Europäische Zeitschrift für Wirtschaftsrecht, EuZW
European Competition Journal
European Competition Law Review, ECLR
European Law Review, ELR
Fordham Corporate Law Institute – International Antitrust Law & Policy (yearbooks)
Intereconomics, Review of European Economic Policy
International Review of Competition Law / Revue Internationale de la Concurrence
Legal Issues of Economic Integration, LIEI
Markt & Mededinging, M&M
Nederlands Tijdschrift voor Europees Recht, NTER
Oxford Journal of Competition Law and Economics
OECD Journal of Competition Law and Policy
Sociaal-Economische Wetgeving, SEW
Wirtschaft und Wettbewerb, WuW
World Competition
World Competition Law and Economics Review

EU websites

Commission's Competition website:
http://ec.europa.eu/dgs/competition/index_en.htm
Curia – the Court of Justice of the European Communities:
http://curia.europa.eu/
EUR-LEX – the portal to European Union Law:
http://eur-lex.europa.eu/en/index.htm

NCA's of Member States

For the websites of the various NCA's, the reader is hereby advised to use the hyperlink that can be found on DG Comp's web site's thematic page under the heading 'national authorities'

National Authorities within the Network of Competition Authorities

AUSTRIA
Bundeswettbewerbsbehörde
BELGIUM
Belgian Federal Minister of Economy, Energy, Foreign Trade and Science Policy
Corps des rapporteurs. Conseil de la Concurrence

BULGARIA
- Commission for the Protection of Competition
- State Aid Department of the Ministry of Finance

CYPRUS
- Commission for the Protection of Competition

CZECH REPUBLIC
- The Office for the Protection of Competition

DENMARK
- Danish Competition Authority

ESTONIA
- Estonian Competition Board

FINLAND
- Finnish Competition Authority

FRANCE
- Conseil de la Concurrence
- Ministry of Economy

GERMANY
- Federal Cartel Office, BKartA

GREECE
- Hellenic Competition Commission

HUNGARY
- Office of Economic Competition

IRELAND
- The Competition Authority

ITALY
- Banca D'Italia
- Italian Competition Authority, Autorità Garante

LATVIA
- Competition Council

LITHUANIA
- Competition Council

LUXEMBOURG
- Ministry of Economics

MALTA
- Ministry of Finance and Economic Affairs

NETHERLANDS
- The Netherlands Competition Authority, NMa
- The Netherlands Health Authority, NZa
- The Independent Post and Telecom Authority, OPTA

POLAND
- Office for Competition and Consumer Protection

PORTUGAL
- National Competition Authority

ROMANIA
- Competition Council of Romania
- Competition Office of Romania

SLOVAK REPUBLIC
Antimonopoly Office of the Slovak Republic
SLOVENIA
Competition Protection Office
SPAIN
Ministry of Economic Affairs and Finance – DG for Economic Policy and Protection of Competition
The Competition Defence Service, SDC
The Competition Defence Tribunal, TDC
SWEDEN
Swedish Competition Authority
UK
Office of Fair Trading, OFT
The Competition Commission
Office of Communications, Ofcom
Gas and Electricity Markets Authority, Ofgem
Northern Ireland Authority for Energy Regulation, Ofreg NI
Office of Water Services, Ofwat
Office of Rail Regulation, ORR
The Civil Aviation Authority, CAA